A Historical Study of
Women in Jamaica, 1655–1844

make a timeline
of Atlantic slavery

LUCILLE MATHURIN MAIR

P. 12
Henry Morgan
marries

A Historical Study of Women in Jamaica 1655–1844

Lucille Mathurin Mair

Edited and with an introduction by

Hilary McD. Beckles
and
Verene A. Shepherd

natalist

University of the West Indies Press
Jamaica • Barbados • Trinidad and Tobago

Centre for Gender and Development Studies
University of the West Indies, Jamaica

University of the West Indies Press
7A Gibraltar Hall Road   Mona
Kingston 7   Jamaica
www.uwipress.com

10 09 08 07 06   5 4 3 2 1

CATALOGUING IN PUBLICATION DATA

Mathurin Mair, Lucille.
A historical study of women in Jamaica, 1655–1844 / Lucille Mathurin Mair;
edited and introduced by Hilary McD. Beckles and Verene A. Shepherd.

p. cm.

Based on the author's PhD thesis.

Includes bibliographical references.

ISBN-10: 976-640-178-0
ISBN-13: 978-976-640-178-8

1.Women – Jamaica – History. 2. Women slaves – Jamaica – History.
3. Slave labour – Jamaica. 4. Jamaica – History. I. Beckles, Hilary, McD.,
1955–. II. Shepherd, Verene A. III. Title.

HQ1517.M28 2006   301.41

Cover illustration: *Eight Women in the Canefield*. Reproduced by courtesy
of the National Library of Jamaica.

Book and cover design by Robert Harris. (E-mail: roberth@cwjamaica.com)
Set in AdobeGaramond 11/14.5 x 24

Printed in the United States of America.

Contents

List of Tables / *vii*

Editors' Introduction / *ix*
Hilary McD. Beckles and *Verene A. Shepherd*

Author's Preface / *xxxi*

Part *1*   The Female Arrivants, *1655–1770*

CHAPTER 1   The Arrivals of White Women / *3*

CHAPTER 2   The Arrivals of Black Women / *41*

CHAPTER 3   The Growth of the Mulatto Group / *79*

Part *2*   Creole Slave Society, *1770–1834*

CHAPTER 4   The White Woman in Jamaican Slave Society / *101*

CHAPTER 5   The White Woman: Legal Status, Family,
             Philanthropy and Gender Constraints / *149*

CHAPTER 6   The Black Woman: Demographic Profile,
             Occupation and Violent Abuse / *190*

CHAPTER 7   The Black Woman: Agency, Identity and Voice / *234*

CHAPTER 8   The Mulatto Woman in Jamaican Slave Society / *268*

Part 3   *Postscript, 1834–1844*

CHAPTER 9   The Beginnings of a Free Society, 1834–1844 / *297*

AFTERWORD   Recollections into a Journey of a Rebel Past / *318*

APPENDIX   Population: St James Parish / *329*

Notes / *332*

Author's Bibliography / *434*

Editors' Selected Bibliography / *448*

Index / *475*

About the Author / *494*

List of Tables

1.1   Population and Acreage of Jamaica, Barbados and the Leeward Islands in the 1670s / 23

1.2   Jamaica's White Population, 1655–1722 / 25

1.3   Movement of Indentured Servants into Jamaica, 1671–1774 / 28

1.4   The Growth of Jamaica's Sugar Economy, 1703–1768 / 33

4.1   The White Population in Select Parishes, 1812, 1825–1829 / 106

4.2   White Inhabitants in Clarendon, 1788 / 107

4.3   Parish of Portland: Population Returns (White), 1812–1822 / 107

4.4   Women and Property-Holding, St James, 1774 / 131

4.5   Women and the Kingston Vestry, 1823 / 141

4.6   Whites and Coloured Children at Wolmer's School, 1814–1825 / 147

6.1   Maroon Population, 1770–1830 / 191

6.2   The Enslaved Population, 1817–1829 / 197

6.3   Percentages of Male/Female Field Workers on Seven Jamaican Estates, 1773–1834 / 200

6.4   Percentage of Male/Female Field Workers on William Beckford's Estates in Jamaica, 1780 / 202

6.5   Miscellaneous Occupations of Enslaved Women / 204

6.6   Incidence of Illness among Enslaved Females on William Beckford's Clarendon Estates, 1780 / 211

6.7   Female Ill-Health: Beckford Estates 1780–1781 / 213

6.8   Physical Condition of "Professional" Enslaved Females, 1780 and 1781 / 215

6.9   Births and Deaths on William Beckford's Estates, 1780 / 219

7.1   Sex Distribution of Runaways, 1 May 1779–1 April 1780 / 245

8.1   Persons of Colour in Eight Parishes, 1812 and 1829 / 275

8.2   Portland: Free-Coloured Population, 1812–1822 / 275

8.3   Schools in Kingston, 1832 / 291

Introduction

HILARY McD. BECKLES AND VERENE A. SHEPHERD

The activities and experiences of women in Jamaica have never been ignored entirely in the historical records. Gender-differentiated data have always existed in plantation records, statistical data sources, inventories, newspapers, colonial correspondence, court records, and the texts, diaries and journals generated by both male and female writers such as Thomas Thistlewood, Maria Nugent, Matthew Gregory "Monk" Lewis and Cynric Williams.[1] What is undeniable is that for a long time, the information on women remained unexplored, buried in these sources and repositories. Furthermore, before the 1970s, there was no single work dedicated to the history of Jamaican women, no definable field of "Women's History" and no attempt by scholars to utilize gender analysis in historical writing. Indeed, some even ignored the data on women contained in the contemporary sources; and the teaching and writing of history not only remained an essentially male preserve, but its contents lacked any awareness of the transformative potential of gender analysis.

Fortunately, by the 1970s, these deficiencies in the historiography and in the field of history had been addressed. The impetus for the initial adoption of gender as a mode of intellectual enquiry in Caribbean history and the continued focus on it in research and teaching are linked to parallel processes of post-colonial and feminist thinking that emerged regionally and internationally and permeated many scholarly fields, particularly in the 1960s and 1970s.[2] The discipline of history was not immune to such developments. History, after all, is a participant in the production of knowledge about sexual difference and records changes in the social organization of the sexes.

Therefore, as Joan Scott observes, "history's representations of the past help construct gender for the present".[3]

It was Lucille Mathurin Mair (*née* Walrond) who, influenced by some of these processes, started the self-conscious project of writing women into Caribbean history. She demonstrated the usefulness and revolutionizing potential of the methodology of "Women's History", in the process "rescuing the female ghosts of slavery from an improper burial", to use Jenny Sharpe's formulation.[4] We do not have to speculate about her motivation, objectives and challenges. In a 1990 semi-autobiographical speech, she recounted:

> In the early 1960s, I started to seek out the women of Jamaica's past during the period of slavery, women of all classes and of all colours, black, brown, white. . . . I was motivated mainly by intellectual inquisitiveness, the usual ambition of the doctoral candidate to investigate virgin territory, which it was at that time. There was almost nothing to guide such a search. There was, in fact, nothing in modern historical scholarship about the women who came before me. But this was not surprising, for historiography, which has for centuries been a male academic preserve, has been stunningly devoid of a consciousness of women as significant beings.[5]

Just over thirty years after its submission and her triumph over the research challenges identified above, Mathurin Mair's thesis is finally making its transition from PhD dissertation to published book. Unfortunately, debilitating ill health has prevented her from undertaking the task herself; and so the transformation process has fallen to us. Fortunately, she left signposts along the way in the form of conversations with the editors and with her daughter, Gail, over the many years of good health. Naturally, we utilized those signposts.

Of course, arranging the dissertation into book form was a labour of love, both of us having been influenced by the ideological direction of Mathurin Mair's work on women and gender as well as inspired by her exemplary life of agency and activism. Multiple ways were explored to identify and explain the enduring features of the epic journey of this text, from dissertation to monograph. None was more compelling than the approach that situates the unrelenting determination of Caribbean women to raise and respect their own voice within the anti-colonial discourse. Long overdue, its arrival comes at a critical moment in the women's movement that has highlighted the need to foreground social justice as a democratic imperative. In effect, it is relevant to go forward with a revised restatement of earlier demands and to account for the many objectives still not fully met.

For these and related reasons, it is undoubtedly a timely treat. As the principal comprehensive statement that sets out the first "woman's" grand historic stand against the elite, colonial Caribbean historiography, its publication is also a celebration of a major successful contribution made against the male tide. Critically, the consensus that surrounds its recognition as a seminal intervention serves as an appropriate reassurance to those who followed, that the most formidable reactionary currents invariably shine and signify what they shatter or shame.

It requires no introduction, but is entirely deserving of one. The first challenge, though, is to know and decide where to begin to tell a tale of a journey that has so completely transformed the thinking of so many. Perhaps we should start at the point where the decision to take up arms was made in order to facilitate the discursive, literary consolidation of the movement.

Over a period of several years, many requests were made to facilitate Lucille Mathurin Mair with the revision and publication of the text. It was no easy task to thaw her insistence that this work of a graduate's mind was at best a modest contribution, not worthy of persistent fussing about its publication from colleagues and friends. She took comfort in knowing that it offered young travellers a little support along the way. She steadfastly refused to entertain any serious discussion about the iconic status it had acquired. Then it came, the graceful surrender.

Thereafter, it was a commitment to engage a most extraordinary situation. There is no other such circumstance anywhere in academe that we know of, and it is worth recounting. In October 1974, Lucille Mathurin Mair submitted, and later defended successfully, a doctoral dissertation in history at the University of the West Indies, Mona, in Jamaica. In it, she posed new questions and rejected old answers with respect to the experiences of women – free and enslaved, black, brown and white – in the slave system of Jamaica and in the first decade of freedom. Over a period of three decades, it became the most sought-after unpublished work among students and scholars of Caribbean history and culture. We are not aware of any other dissertation, anywhere within the libraries of the University of the West Indies, more persistently pursued. Such is the consequence of the search for truth and belief in the burden of proof.

In some publishing circles, it would be considered a statement of folly to describe an unpublished work as a classic. But what if the criteria, save for one, are met? What if that which is not satisfied is hardly relevant, and can be set aside, or thrown out, without formal objection? And what if the text is consulted more often by a larger number of students and faculty than published texts that are embraced and celebrated by the criteria? There is arguably no sound reason to make such speculative comparisons. Suffice it to say that had Eric Williams not published his Oxford dissertation, which appeared in 1944 under the title *Capitalism and Slavery*,[6] similar reasons would have been invented in order to support the heresy.

The thirst for Williams's text would have escalated out of hand during the heat of the 1950s anti-colonial struggle that centred the discussion about the metropolitan exploitation of colonial resources. Then, it would have only been a matter of time before the political economic dialogue would have demanded an articulation of the relevant sociological issues. But Williams did publish, and his Caribbean colleagues did explore with a variety of sociological methods and techniques the social structures and ideological legacies of the plantation world.

The early 1970s remained a challenging time for young historians prepared to break free of the colonial academic scaffold. There was still a lack of formal enthusiasm, and certainly no professional percentage, for research that historicized, and inevitably politicized, persistent race and class divisions in Caribbean culture and society. Senior historians within the academy proceeded cautiously. They were still reeling from the aggression of the neo-colonial state, and its elite supporters, occasioned by Walter Rodney's earlier dropping of the revolutionary gauntlet. Lucille Mathurin Mair entered the discussion as a graduate student within this context and understood clearly where she wished to position herself.

Gender was not on the agenda. The academic culture seemed assured that there was no urgency to research issues surrounding the experiences of women in any way other than the most general. The manner in which their history influenced popular perceptions and institutional determinations with respect to their ascribed second-class citizenship was understood but not discerned as a crisis of post-colonial nationalism. Few scholars were willing to argue that this posture was a formidable part of the eruptive male intellectual leadership; and fewer still offered generalizations about the role

[handwritten annotation: the focus was on revising colonial mentality even if the revision perpetuated male domination]

of historiography within the reproduction of the patriarchal machinery of domination and exploitation. The few were female, and Lucille Mathurin Mair was one of them.

Determined to promote gender from the status of "any other business", she recognized the extent to which she was professionally exposed and intellectually vulnerable. It was "a male academic preserve", she recalls, reflecting on the battlefield where the colonialist canon had free reign and limitless range to fashion and define Caribbean historical writing. There was no emerging methodology that fostered focus on the "woman" as historical subject; neither was there mounting pressure from below, within conceptual and theoretical frameworks, to engage in the formalization of thinking about gender and its application to the study of the "woman" as political agent. The simple reason was that women's experiences were not considered shaped by a distinctive consciousness, the stuff from which historical identities are made. Without the availability of such a "research tool", Mathurin Mair recalls, she felt naked and nervous within the historians' fraternity at Mona.

The Mathurin Mair proposal was read and received as confrontational and rupturing. But she was serene within her enclosure. She was going to examine the ways in which women lived the world that was created by *[handwritten annotation: a gender approach]* Jamaican enslavers and to set out in specific terms their relationships to male authority within the colonial enterprise. It bore no epistemic relation, other than dialectical, to anything that had gone before. There was no programme to write a "woman's history". "Feminist history" was beyond the imagination, and references to gender as social construct were rare, even within the context of discussions about the planter-merchant elite that administered the plantation complex as entrepreneurs and politicians. In her words, she had to

> probe deeply into the conventional sources of Caribbean history to find those missing women, to attempt new interpretations, and imaginatively to bring new insights to the task of opening up the slaves' private world, where black women lived in cultural antithesis to the white plantation. The historical, sociological, and creative writings of Orlando Patterson and . . . Kamau Brathwaite in the 1960s and early 1970s indicated how and where one might find that Afro-Caribbean world. As Brathwaite expressed it, "history becomes anthropology and sociology, psychology and literature and archaeology, and whatever else is needed to make the fragments

whole".[7] In the 1960s, however, we were a long distance away from refining multi-disciplinary scholarship.[8]

The best that could be done, it was assumed by many around her, was to win the concession that there were indeed women of prominence in the history and to record the evidence of their distinction as subtext, neatly adding a layer to the interpretative scaffold that held up the patriarchal orientation of historical writing. But Mathurin Mair's intentions were far more rebellious. The challenges she faced were deciding how to function within the professional elasticity of the academic environment and working with what was institutionally feasible.

She was fond of the expression that the most serious decision one can make is taking the first step out the door in the morning, simply because one really has no idea what the journey has up its sleeve. She considered her project a first step in the morning. Having opened the door she was not prepared to follow the well-known markers along the old road. She crossed over to the other side, turned her face in the opposite direction and journeyed off in search of the woman lost to Caribbean history, the woman, she knew intuitively, who was not hidden from history or lost in it. Rather, she was hidden by history. The objective of the quest, therefore, was considered an act of restoration rather than of discovery.

The woman was there, in history, "voicing" her own voyage and forging possible futures. The chroniclers of colonialism who documented the social and financial accounts of the slave system heard these voices and took copious notes. Some recorders were secretaries of governance bodies such as representative assemblies and legislative councils; others were clergymen, plantation bookkeepers and managers, and travellers of empire. They produced over time an extensive archival monument that enabled detailed research into the everyday lives of women. Yet, it remained true when Mathurin Mair started that the early modern historians of Caribbean slavery heard little and saw less. They had succeeded in effectively locking away the woman in ways not anticipated by the record makers. The time had come for new eyes.

The archives would absorb her. No known source could be left untapped. The legal and (re)productive relations of slavery were conceived and designed in gendered terms. The system of status formation reproduced itself along the female line. The enslaved woman, for example, more so than the enslaved man, had to be accounted for as the critical legal party to human property reproduction. Only the offspring of an enslaved female was born legally enslaved. Males, both free and enslaved, could father free-born children. The status of the child at birth was therefore attached to the legal identity of the mother. The white woman could not give birth to an enslaved child, even when the father was enslaved.

The result was that women's lives were etched in the documents of the slave system in more detailed and comprehensive ways. Mothers and motherhood concerned plantation managers and bookkeepers whose remit it was to sustain property values. The documentation of fatherhood was less important in this regard and was generally ignored. Less visible, then, was the black male. Mathurin Mair illustrates the expression of this condition within the archival data. If the woman, then, was lost to history, the explanation could not be empirically rooted. Rather, it would be more reasonable to examine gender strategies in action as ideological instruments of patriarchy.

It was not a simple task. She soon discovered the necessity to "decode" the extensive archival evidence. First, there was the question of dealing with the interpretative world views of male record makers. While they saw women as vital subjects, often the focus of their text, dominant social and economic imperatives suggest approaches to recording that sometimes concealed as much as they revealed. Second, in the interest of survival, the women often understated, denied and imposed narrow limits upon the scope of their own mentalities. For many, self-censure was the norm, a circumstance that served to suppress the details of realities that, if not understood, easily led to flawed comprehension and weak analysis. Finally, it was important to keep in mind that the colonial programme was a part of the wider imperial male project in which legally free and enslaved women were assigned important but subordinate roles.

The diversity of experiences among different productive categories of women fostered a splintering of social consciousness across the social structure. This reality of everyday life assured that any notion of a conceptually coherent womanhood would be seriously problematic. As the book demonstrates, Mathurin Mair structured the narrative of her text to allow for the broadly equal empirical treatment of "black", "white" and "brown" women as categories found at all levels of the free–enslaved polarity. What emerged was a powerful statement that has served to shape subsequent understand-ings of these relations. In Jamaican slave society, she concluded, the white woman consumed, the coloured woman served and the black woman laboured. It is a powerful typology (even if the occupational reality was more complex) that continues to reveal more than it conceals. As a statement that identified ethnic diversity as determinant, it might have been designed to provide, or provoke, a critical context for a politics of "womanhood" and "feminism". But that aside, it is important to note that the use of over-whelming evidence sends the signal that she was confronted with a need to meet the highest possible threshold of proof. On account of being required to carry a greater burden, Mathurin Mair set out with a clear intention to travel the extra mile. The result was a text that stood the test of time on account of its empirical soundness and narrative richness.

A considerable amount of research data were gathered, organized and discussed over the nine chapters, with the result being the history of Jamaica through gendered lens. The sources for the chapter contents were not all found in the usual places along the well-worn paths. Mathurin Mair delved into the less familiar records of estates, family papers and the private correspondence of individuals who witnessed and participated in the crime of slavery. Only the creative use of these data that document daily life on the grounds of the fields, in the mills and in the mansions could enable a convincing exposure of women as agents of history. The sophistication of her research proficiency was achieved on account of her developed intuitive sense that allowed for maximum value extraction from each document and her knowledge of where research trails would lead. The blending of the finest historian's sense and sensibility with a capacity for research stamina enabled her to document an approach to writing that weaves powerful and at times colourful descriptions of how women, endured, succumbed and triumphed.

Chapters 1 to 3 pluralize the history of women's migration to Jamaica, explain the rationale for their arrival (or "arrivals" as she prefers), contextual-ize their socio-economic roles in seventeenth- and eighteenth-century Jamaican society, outline their interrelationships and their gender relations, their negotiation of family life and the disease environments, and their rep-resentation and misrepresentation in colonial writings. Of course, the author understood clearly that "the dichotomy between the concept and the reality of women's character and condition remained to be seen by all who had eyes to see".[9] These chapters explore the gender ideologies of Africa and Europe that influenced women's roles and their (mis)representations and, in the case of the black female arrivants, study their African ethnic origins, the demographics of the trade in captives, the new work environment in Jamaica and the beginnings of the guerilla warfare that became a constant feature of slave systems. In the case of the mulatto group, we get additional insights into their emergence and growth and their status in a slave system, which in the early years was organized along a black–white continuum. Above all, these chapters expose us to the inner lives and experiences of those women whose names and stories have come to light.

Chapters 4 to 8 focus on the period of plantation construction and mature capitalism and the creation of a racist creole society. In this period, 1770–1834, women of all ethnic groups and classes, distributed all over the island and occupied in a diverse range of rural and urban occupations, saw their minority status consolidated. She stressed the class differences among white women, manifested in their varied social lifestyles, although all classes were subjected to the same threats: misrepresentation in colonial writings, a disease environment that affected their demographic experience, black guerilla warfare that targeted both male and female enslavers and subordination on the basis of gender (reflected in inheritance laws and custom, legal status and lack of participation in the public sphere of politics). Those white women with resources became absentees as soon as they could. The lack of a humanitarian movement among white women in Jamaica and the preoccupation of the primarily urban-based mulatto women with their own strategies for upward social mobility stood in stark contrast to the activism of enslaved black women, the backbone of the economic life of the island, who, despite attempts to create a non-plantation socio-economic life, were faced with the constant threats of violence, disease and death. Yet, as Mair developed with great clarity, interethnic relationships facilitated a ranking system that sought to assign a subordinate social status to black women: the salt of the earth.

The politics of these experiences required careful scrutiny, especially as there was a tendency endemic to the historiography to explain social stability and instability in terms of gender roles and functions. What does it mean, for example, to say that the white woman consumed? For sure, it implied that she was unable or unwilling to participate in the galloping anti-slavery agenda in any formal and significant way, as was the norm in the slave systems of the United States. Mathurin Mair found that there was no Caribbean counterpart to the US female anti-slavery campaigner who worked tirelessly for abolition. While she did not suggest that the white woman was co-sponsor of the slavery project, she indicated that, within the white community, shared pro-slavery cultural values were hegemonic and ensured her silence with preferential treatment.

Not surprisingly, then, it was the norm in Jamaica, as Mathurin Mair showed, for elite white women, supported by their male counterparts, to question the "womanness" of black women and to suggest that female they may be, but feminine they were not. The denial of the feminine identity of black women was accompanied by description of them as devoid of grace and gentility. The attribution of masculine traits to the black woman also served to indicate the depth of the divide over which women gazed at each other. That the enslaved black woman was virtually alone among women in waging anti-slavery wars confirmed the usefulness of Mathurin Mair's typology.

Nanny of the Maroons was forcefully brought to the fore as a heroic figure left shadowy for reasons of the revolution she led. But there were also the less prominent life stories of thousands of nannies who nurtured and raised white children to be slaveholders in the image of their parents. Then there were hundreds of "brown" women in white residences, the objects of deep desire, whose task it was to ensure the social comfort of men of means who saw such relations as rights of property. Dangerous waters for sure, and Mathurin Mair had good reasons to be nervous about embarking on the venture alone.

In her broad-sweep postscript, she explored the first decade of freedom after the hard-won emancipation, opining that "the black woman presented free Jamaica with the great challenge of lifting her oppression and releasing her considerable creativity and resourcefulness for the better ordering of the whole society"; that "the challenge is yet to be met".[10] But she lived through the years when every effort was made by black women to meet this challenge – in some cases, with her help.

The graduate student period was an intellectually testing and a socially tense experience. There was only one distinguished female scholar within the Department of History: Elsa Goveia, her supervisor. Goveia was a powerful mind, not to be engaged in ways other than the profound. Yet, there was no greater humanist scholar and collegial being. Her well-known concern for the well-being of intellectually curious students provided an enormous comfort zone for the young Mathurin Mair. The philosophical complexity of her discursive style and her unwavering commitment to academic excellence, graduate training and the development of Caribbean historiography served as benchmarks and standards to emulate and to transcend. Mathurin Mair acknowledged that Elsa Goveia "inspired and supported" her along the way; and that the professor was as much a teacher as a friend.

But Elsa Goveia was no feminist as defined in modern terms. She was critical of the colonial traditions, and in nuanced ways she suggested that patriarchy across class and race lines manifested its ugly head in multiple ways, including the right to interpret and narrate the past. From this perspective, she would have seen her rebel student as a comrade for the future, an investment in the advancement of the discipline. Mathurin Mair herself admitted to having "no feminist motivation, or at least none that" she recognized when she started on the journey (although she became feminist later on). There is precious little evidence from Goveia's work to suggest that she ever considered gender a theoretically sound or useful tool of historical investigation or that there was ever such a thing as "women's history". Yet, she would have been curious to view the open fields on the other side of the street, while urging her apprentice not to lose sight of the anterior logic that determined the relations of power within the slave system.

The evidence to support this opinion is everywhere within Mathurin Mair's text. The judicious blend of radical forays and cautious analysis is a trademark not easily missed. Goveia's considerable influence is also displayed in the structure of the text, including its underlying assumption that the slave system did not rely entirely for its reproduction upon the brutal use of violent power, but also engaged the use of culture, gender and ethnicity. Racial domination was not its primary focus, even though it appeared that way in social relations. Enslavers' primary desire to sustain profit and class prestige would ultimately lead to the reform and abandonment of the slave system, a consideration that highlights, in Mathurin Mair's view, their preference for appropriation over other forms of exploitation.

In order to break new ground, then, Mathurin Mair had to break, at least conceptually, from the Goveia mould; this she did. It required from her the deployment of mature interpersonal skills. These were to serve her well in the years ahead as a diplomat and international civil servant. Among these were an extraordinary grasp of the nuances of negotiation, bridge-building and, critically, a willingness to be intellectually assertive with grace.

It is, then, the first literary monument that marks the small step into "women's history" and provides the framework for the giant leap into gender history. Recent histories of women in slave systems assume the existence of multiple and contesting mentalities among them and confirm Mathurin Mair's interpretation of the fragmentation that haunts the desire for a basis on which to construct a broad common front to the female experience. The journey from "women's history" through "feminist history" and on to "gender history" is well on its way, considered complete in some quarters. For sure, it was a turbulent movement, and the younger scholars so often encouraged by Mathurin Mair have done a great deal to ensure that her first step out the door has irreversibly transformed and advanced the discussion.

The active community of feminist and gender scholars is now making veritable strides, and in this regard Caribbean historical scholarship is alive and well. It is no longer possible to sustain, in reading or listening circles, an argument that the experiences of women in the slavery period, or any era, requires special permission or a courageous mind to find expression in the form of the scholarly monograph. The maleness of the colonial canon Mathurin Mair confronted and survived has subsequently been shot through by two generations of scholars, male and female, who drew strength from her stand and movement. Indeed, following her example, Caribbean historians, cognizant of the benefits of a gendered approach to historical investigation, have increasingly paid attention to the assumptions, practices, rhetoric and methodologies of the discipline of history to realize its full potential to construct gender for the present.

In transforming this work from thesis to book, we tried to ensure that editorial changes were kept to a minimum and that, as far as possible, the work retained its original format. The title, for example, has remained unchanged, even though, under normal circumstances, a PhD thesis title would change at the book stage. But as neither editors nor advisors had a clear indication from Mathurin Mair about an alternative title, we decided to keep her original title. We also retained the content of what in a thesis appears as "Abstract", making only minor editorial amendments; but for the purposes of the book version, "Abstract" is simply retitled "Preface". Mathurin Mair did not write an introduction to her thesis, and so we decided to add one, although our introduction departs from the style she would have chosen and is more in the style of editors' comments and reflections. In addition, we tidied up the table of contents, ensuring that there was consistency in its structure and style. For example, Mathurin Mair divided the work into three parts, titled some parts but not others; so we added section titles where there were none. Also, instead of retaining "The White Woman – Part 1", "The White Woman – Part 2", "The Black Woman – Part 1" and "The Black Woman – Part 2", as chapters 4 to 7 respectively were structured, we took the editorial decision, supported by the University of the West Indies Press, to use the contents of those chapters to provide clues for the substitution of subheadings for "parts". So, for example, chapter 5, "The White Woman – Part 2", has now become "The White Woman: Legal Status, Family, Philanthropy and Gender Constraints".

In the thesis version, Mathurin Mair used I, II, III, and so on, to break up the text at what she considered appropriate thematic breaks. We retained these breaks, but opted for subtitles that reflect the contents of each section. We toyed with the idea of adding other breaks, but eventually decided against it. We also streamlined the paragraphing, edited and streamlined the tables and appendix, added a list of tables, and sourced an illustration for the cover. In keeping with University of the West Indies Press style, we converted footnotes to endnotes and used consecutive numbering for the notes instead of the 1, 2, 3 style on each page used in the original.

We retained Mathurin Mair's original bibliography, editing it to conform to the Press's requirements and filling in the occasional gaps in publication details. But we also compiled and included an additional bibliography of works done since 1974; for while Mathurin Mair's thesis was state of the art in 1974, the field has expanded since then. We chose to demonstrate how the field of women's history has been enlarged since the 1970s and how many other scholars have followed in Mathurin Mair's footsteps to produce articles, books, research papers and theses on gender issues. Since Mathurin Mair did not stop writing in 1974, we also included her own publications in the bibliography. Finally, we included a somewhat autobiographical piece as an afterword to allow readers access into the author's mind and follow her on her journey from graduate student in 1974 to mature scholar and feminist activist in the 1980s and 1990s. This afterword can also serve as a conclusion, a section missing in the original.

Of course, these amendments and editorial decisions might not find favour with some readers, who would have preferred to have the work published intact; but we do not consider that such very minor changes will detract from the iconic status of the work. Readers should also be comforted by the knowledge that we added little new text to the chapters, the subheadings and tidier links to quotations being the most substantial changes.

The additional bibliography that we have compiled provides a vivid indication of the strides that have been made in the writing of Caribbean women's history since the 1970s. Clearly, the subject of slavery has continued to dominate historical writing on the British Caribbean in the post-colonial period. The post-1970s works cover the sociology and economics of slavery, illustrating the dynamic relations between modes of production and social life. The superstructures of slave systems have fascinated scholars perhaps to a greater degree than their economic substructures; as such, the debates on race and colour relations, health and mortality, religion, recreational culture, women, family organization and kinship patterns, as well as the endemic problems of social reproduction are represented in a number of works.

A considerable part of the historiography of slavery is focused on enslaved women. Those familiar with the detailed nature and wide coverage of Mathurin Mair's thesis might well ask: what did she leave unexplored for future scholars? While a perusal of these works show that many scholars have revisited the very themes explored by Mathurin Mair, it is also obvious that they have added new content and interpretations and have broadened the geographic focus to include the history of women in other Caribbean territories. Comparative analyses have also sharpened our understanding of Caribbean women's experiences. Whatever the geographic focus, the researchers agree with Mathurin Mair that women did not live the way men did and that slavery as an economic system as well as a social system of oppression had a differential impact on them. Comparative work done by Arlene Gautier and Bernard Moitt for the French Caribbean, and Digna Castañeda and Félix Matos Rodríguez for the Spanish Caribbean, indicate that the experiences of women varied sharply between particular colonies, but less so across imperial lines.[II]

They support the conclusion already made by Mathurin Mair that there

thesis

was also a sharp differentiation in the lives of women of different ethnic, class and colour groups, and that little solidarity existed across these lines, particularly because some white and freed blacks/coloureds were enslavers. As Bridget Brereton and others show, white women, active contributors to the development of a pro-slavery ideology in the Caribbean, were assigned special roles within the slave system, which in turn determined their experiences as free persons within the gender order.[12] European racism dictated that the progeny of these women could not be enslaved, because while white women could reproduce the slavery ideology in order to protect the myth of white supremacy, their bodies were not allowed to reproduce enslaved people, an act reserved for black women. Great efforts were made in places like Barbados, for example, through poor relief efforts, to prevent these women from relying on black men. Black women, both free and enslaved, field-hand and domestic, also experienced society in fundamentally different ways, though categories were not always clear and edges invariably blurred. An interesting angle introduced by Brereton is that women who wrote about slave society displayed no gender solidarity, with women writers like A.C. Carmichael and Maria Nugent just as likely to be racist and sexist as were the male writers like Charles Leslie, Edward Long and Cynric Williams.[13]

The quantitative study of the trade in African captives is an obvious growth area that has created an explosion of scholarship in the demographic history of slavery, the most recent being the CD-ROM produced by David Eltis and some of his colleagues.[14] In particular, there is continued concern over fertility, mortality and population growth and decline. Enslavers in the Caribbean were caught in the web of a major dilemma. As rational entrepreneurs, they sought to maximize profits by reducing the cost of productive inputs. Expenditures on those enslaved were suppressed to subsistence levels. At the same time, however, the protection of property rights in chattel was a top priority that required careful policy formulation and implementation. The effective social maintenance of the enslaved, then, meant that the daily management of subsistence and health care could not be left to chance. Those enslaved had to be properly nourished and medically assisted if they were to be productive workers. At the same time, the impact of class and race prejudice upon economic thinking often led to subsistence levels being located below what was required to maintain general health and population growth.

tension between the economic need to ensure high production by taking good care of the slaves and the racist tendency to treat them badly

It was the late 1970s and 1980s that saw the emergence of an impressive array of demographic bio-histories, which have widened the empirical base of knowledge on the internal demographic characteristics of Caribbean slave populations. Much of this was generated in response to the need to explain the differential demographic experiences of those enslaved in the Caribbean and North America; for while the enslaved population in the United States grew by natural means, with the exception of Barbados, the Bahamas and the Dutch Antilles, that of the Caribbean was not self-sustaining. Caribbean historians have been less concerned with the Tannenbaum-Freyre thesis, which focuses on treatment as an explanation for demographic features of the enslaved population.[15] They have been more focused on poor health and nutrition, as well as colour, sex ratio, work regime, age, gender, lactation practices and child-spacing, medical treatment, planter attitudes (pro- versus anti-natalist), origin (creole versus African born), family structure and the anti-natalist strategies of women. Works by B.W. Higman, Kenneth and Virginia Kiple, Meredith John and Richard Sheridan demonstrate that these factors contributed to the general inability of Caribbean enslaved populations, in particular those engaged in the sugar culture, to reproduce themselves naturally until the closing years of the slavery system.[16] Scholars have also shown that the pro-natalist policies of the post-1807 ameliorative period were doomed to fail as long as the majority of enslaved women laboured in the field. Women's productive capacity was not to be sacrificed for reproduction; thus there was a clear incompatibility between production and reproduction.

While the demographic historians are mostly agreed on the differential roles of diet, other material conditions and the work environment on the fertility and mortality experiences, scepticism still abounds over the feminist claim of "gynaecological resistance". Nevertheless, such claims, already made in the contemporary works of Monk Lewis[17] and others, and used effectively by Mathurin Mair, have been repeated by recent scholars.

Attention continues to be paid to the cultural life of the enslaved, their ability to recreate and maintain family within the restrictions of chattel enslavement, their relationship with owners, and their contribution through interracial sex to what Kamau Brathwaite has described as "Creole society".[18] The ways in which the subalterns or enslaved Africans pursued the right to be autonomous economic agents, as part of the legitimate use of their

independence ✓
resistance

"leisure" times, continue to be major concerns for historians and anthropologists, receiving new attention from Mary Turner and others.[19] Marketing symbolized a spirit of independence and was central to the process of non-violent protest and resistance which characterized day-to-day anti-slavery behaviour. The right to possession, and open engagement in the market as autonomous buyers and sellers, was aggressively demanded. Forms of collective bargaining, usually associated with industrial wage workers, emerged among the enslaved, as Bolland, Turner and others demonstrate;[20] and some owners acquiesced to the enslaved's demand rather than always relying on the coercive power of the whip.

family

Research into enslaved people's family has also expanded since the 1970s, with differences in perspectives and interpretations emerging between structuralists, who claim that totalistic systems like slavery constrain cultural expression, including family formation, and class theorists, who believe that slavery allowed the enslaved some autonomy in constructing kinship and other forms of culture. Their conclusions have been reinforced by more recent researchers like Barbara Bush and Marietta Morrissey, who, like Mathurin Mair, stress the multidimensionality of the family types among the enslaved and discount early perceptions of the inability of the enslaved to sustain lasting unions.[21]

Urban slaves

Slavery has been most closely associated with agricultural labour in the Caribbean. But beyond the farms and plantations, there were those who functioned in urban regimes. The urban dimension of slavery has received greater attention than given by Mathurin Mair as reflected in the published works of Higman, Lorna Simmonds, Pedro Welch and others.[22] They show that enslaved people in the urban areas were in the minority in all British Caribbean colonies. The enslaved urban population in the Caribbean was predominantly female, indicating that most were domestics. Urban enslaved people also worked as skilled labourers, sellers, transport and wharf workers, fishermen and general labourers. Women had a narrower range of occupations than men, working as, in addition to domestic servants, washerwomen, seamstresses and sellers. Interestingly, the majority of urban enslavers also tended to be female. The importance of non-sugar economic activities and social contexts for slave life are topics explored by several scholars.

The matter of slaveholding has been revisited, with scholars like Sheena Boa, Trevor Burnard and Kathleen Butler stressing that slaveholding was not

an exclusively white, male project, though it was overwhelmingly so.[23]
Women – freed black, free coloured, whites – were slaveholders and managers; and they were not necessarily more benevolent managers than men.
Free-coloured women were described as harsh enslavers and they were
among the first to lose their labourers in 1838. The narrative of Mary Prince,
which surfaced after Mathurin Mair wrote her thesis, demonstrates unam-
biguously the cruelty of white women who were slaveholders or managers.[24]
Butler's path-breaking research also indicates that while, on the whole,
women tended to own smaller properties than men, there were some very
large female landowners in the Caribbean and these acreages were not necessarily inherited from rich husbands, as women acquired and managed properties in their own right.[25]

Two other issues have attracted the energies of historians who write about
the slavery period, namely slavery and capitalist globalization, and resistance
and emancipation processes. The former has not thrown up much gender-
differentiated data, except that renewed emphasis has been placed on
women's contribution to capital generation for the economic development
of Britain. The role of women – inside and outside of the Caribbean – in the
process that led to legislative emancipation has received greater attention.
Mathurin Mair already incorporated women's resistant behaviour into the
discourse of anti-slavery. But others have expanded the discussion, incorpo-
rating the role of women in armed revolts other than Maroon Wars, and
assessing the role of "reproductive resistance" in slave resistance studies. An
emerging trend is the attempt to identify texts written and/or narrated by the
enslaved that would provide more accurate versions of resistance and socio-
economic life. Moreover, there has been the broadening of the discussion of
resistance to include those enslaved on non-sugar properties like livestock
farms.[26] The focus on women and resistance continues to be based on the
belief that the ideology of anti-slavery was not gender-free. While the struggles of the slavery period were inherently collective in that they were conceived in the consciousness of the communities inhabited by the enslaved,
the gender relations of slavery determined actions in many ways. The system
of slavery sought to degrade women and womanhood in ways which forced
aspects of their resistance to assume specific forms. The use of rape as a brutal form of control and punishment, for example, targeted women more
than men, as far as we know. Certainly those who have studied the

Thistlewood journals cannot help but be confronted by the violence of this enslaver towards women.

Maternity and fertility were also placed at the core of strategies for plantation survival, and so women's resistance to these policies (as Bush and Barry Gaspar and others, like Mathurin Mair, have shown) meant that their opposition to slavery was probably more broadly based.[27] While black women were in the forefront of the anti-slavery struggle in the Caribbean, benevolent white women were the campaigners in England. Claire Midgeley's 1992 work makes it clear that more credit should be given to white women who joined the anti-slavery campaign in Britain.[28] Resistance was not confined to sugar estates. Urban slaves and those enslaved on non-sugar properties also used various strategies to undermine slavery. Interestingly, Jamaican sugar planters, conscious of the potential of the enslaved on livestock farms to foment rebellions, tried to insulate their own bondspeople from contact with them – an impossibility given the symbiotic relations between pens and plantations.

While the greater focus has been on women's experiences, a few recent studies have taken on board the issue of male marginalization and the ways in which black men had their masculinity negated under slavery as a way of keeping white males dominant. The matter of patriarchy in the white community has also been addressed, with scholars like Burnard demonstrating the way it functioned in white society to marginalize white women who were seldom named as executors in their spouses' wills.[29]

Emancipation gave rise to new issues for documentation. Mathurin Mair had addressed the post-slavery period only in overview, and she stopped her analysis in 1844. Scholars have taken the analysis of post-slavery developments much further. The florescence of social history over the past few decades has been amenable to an exploration of the implications of "freedom" for the black majority, men and women. While there are no post-slavery narratives comparable to those for the slave era, several accounts have surfaced which allow a glimpse into the motivation and behaviour of the working population both before and just after full emancipation. Revisionist historians Woodville Marshall and Swithin Wilmot managed to mine sources that facilitate a recovery of workers' voices and experiences and have framed the discourse on apprenticeship and anti-apprenticeship within the articulated hopes and expectations of the freed men and women.[30] Although both writers conclude that the anticipated "revolution" did not materialize, their overwhelming concern is with the black strategists who possessed their own aspirations toward a new way of life and acted – whether through wage bargaining, absenteeism, or political struggle – to secure their goals.

The (post-apprenticeship period) – which represented something of a watershed in Caribbean history – has been subjected to even greater academic scrutiny. Indeed, an explosion of historical research has further expanded and pluralized the post-slavery historiography, particularly as it pertains to blacks' response to emancipation. Colonialist concerns with "free society" have been largely espoused by a continuing white male stream of nineteenth-century history-writers or British sojourners who shared the values and concerns of the planter class. Ironically, they were inclined to blame post-slavery misfortunes on the alleged "inefficiency" of the newly de-feminized work force.

The nineteenth-century works concerned with the immediate socio-economic impact of emancipation expressed sympathy for a planter class ruined by the actions and new mobility of the emancipated. Nancy Prince Gardner was the most significant female writer, although her concerns were not specifically with freed women.[31] The impact of emancipation on new forms of bonded labour are issues explored in the post-slavery historiography.

Women's experiences of emancipation, the apprenticeship process and indentureship have been a part of the modern post-slavery historiography. Thomas Holt, Diana Paton and Wilmot have been among those who have shown the ways in which apprenticed women, the most oppressed of the oppressed, brought the system into such disrepute – showcasing, for example, the conditions on the treadmills in the prisons – that apprenticeship, conceived in an unreflectively masculine gender, was doomed to fail.[32] Apprenticed women's conditions, indeed, gave much ammunition to the anti-slavery and anti-apprenticeship forces.

The lack of focus on gender differences in the early works on migration, a topic touched on only slightly by Mathurin Mair, has now largely been corrected, with scholars like Patricia Mohammed, Rhoda Reddock and others detailing the experiences of female immigrants.[33] The increasing body of literature on immigrant women has gone a long way in dispelling notions of familial patriarchy. While not dismissing the accounts of women suffering spousal abuse, studies are now becoming available that reveal that few were confined to a strictly domestic life. Research on the passage from India raises further questions about the alleged "social benefits" of emigration. The reworking of post-emancipation adjustments through a gendered lens, following the Mathurin Mair tradition, has also revealed that family and community goals were important. An essay by Brereton on the underexplored phenomenon of the post-emancipation withdrawal of female labour from estates alludes to women's involvement in "different kinds of family strategies" such as domestic food production and marketing, as well as child rearing.[34] Jean Besson's fieldwork on the minuscule hereditary plots of "family land" cultivated by women similarly identifies the phenomenon as both a way of strengthening family ties as well as a mechanism of resistance to the plantation.[35] The increasing body of literature on freed women reflects the influence of sociological theories on the sexual division of labour and has gone far to replace notions of familial patriarchy with the view that Caribbean women outside the upper and middle strata constructed their own way of life.

In the process, researchers have uncovered women's contribution to decolonization (including the labour protests and the independence movements) and asserted a distinct historical approach that treats colonial outcomes in a decidedly anti-colonial manner. Since Lord Olivier's 1933 indictment of Governor Eyre in the suppression controversy and Geoffrey Dutton's 1969 attempt to vindicate his Australian hero, attention has shifted towards the grass-roots participants.[36] Gad Heuman, Clinton Hutton and Wilmot highlight the striking role played by women; for example, during the actual confrontation at Morant Bay in 1865.[37] Since the late 1980s, the representation of decolonization as a male enterprise has been challenged with works both on women and trade unionism and on gender and representational politics. The obvious radical reorientation of the literature – a reflection, no doubt, of the increased interest in popular agency – is prominently reflected in the attitude of revisionist writers towards the key individuals involved in the various political crises.

The history of Caribbean women continues to attract the attention of modern scholars on both sides of the Atlantic, and the historiography is now not only vast but, on the whole, empirically rich, intellectually gripping and, frequently, conceptually contentious. The perspectives have not been unified. The growing body of work has been informed by increasing professionalism and reorientation in scholarly approaches. But two distinct trends are still observable in the writings on the colonial Caribbean: and one imperial/colonialist the other distinctly revisionist and located firmly in the creole/black nationalist genre. It is within this revisionist genre that Caribbean women's history is located.

Several people must be acknowledged for their role in ensuring that this work would no longer reside only on the shelves of the West Indies Collection in the Main Library at Mona but will make its transition to the world of published books. First of all, we express our gratitude to Lucille Mathurin Mair's daughter, Ambassador Gail Mathurin and to the Centre for Gender and Development Studies for determination to see the work published and for the confidence that they showed in us in entrusting us with this important project. The Centre for Gender and Development Studies also provided us with the financial resources necessary to prepare the work for publication. We thank Delroy Lawrence for his fast and efficient word-processing services and Dalea Bean for acting as our research assistant on the project we and recognize the assistance of the librarians at the National Library of Jamaica and the Main Library of the University of the West Indies, Mona, with sourcing the cover illustration. We also thank the reviewers for their helpful comments and extend thanks to Professor Selwyn Cudjoe and Calaloux Publications for permission to reproduce Mair's "Recollections" as an afterword.

Finally, we regret that in her present state of ill health, Lucille Mathurin Mair will be unaware of the publication of her seminal work; but we hope that her children, Adrian, David and Gail, will be pleased with the final product.

Author's Preface

The virtual destruction of the indigenous Jamaican people under Spanish occupation made it possible, by the seventeenth century, for English invaders and developers to mould the island's demographic contours in accordance with their economic needs. The population that emerged between 1655 and 1770 was characterized by striking racial and gender imbalances, which were not unrelated. The same forces compelling massive importation of enslaved African labour controlled other priorities and influenced which women were required, in what numbers and for what purposes. This applied to white as well as to black women.

The dominant Creole values of a society "whose business was business" continued, during the classic slavery period of 1770 to 1834, to determine the condition and interrelationships of women. Racism and colonialism combined with sexism to shape their life patterns. Women's acceptance of prevailing norms confirms the orthodox view of women as the silent, second sex, serving as a conservative, if not reactionary, social element. The conspicuous absenteeism of white elitist women is examined in this light, as well as the mulatto woman's adoption of the role of surrogate white. Counter-evidence, however, also suggests women's capacity for criticism, modification – rejection even – of these norms, in ways often peculiarly available to them, as women. In particular, black women, who suffered the acutest forms of multiple oppression, made strong assertions of their womanhood from the vantage point of a deep-rooted African communal base.

Emancipation did little at first to alter the status and interrelationships of Jamaica's women, who constituted one of the society's most vital elements, hitherto neglected by masculine historiography.

Mona 1974

Part One

THE FEMALE ARRIVANTS,
1655–1770

1   *The Arrivals of White Women*

Fifteenth- and sixteenth-century transatlantic adventures of exploration, conquest and settlement were primarily European male enterprises. The New World plantations which they produced all experienced, in their first stages, a shortage of women. Indigenous women were not easily accessible to the newcomers, whose attempts to claim them as hostages, workers and mates added to the many sources of conflict between them and native men. The American Indian peoples were, in any event, physically very vulnerable to the multiple demands of colonization. In Jamaica, they disappeared after approximately a century's contact with the Spaniards. If profitable exploitation of mainland and islands by Europeans was to proceed, a population had virtually to be remade. In the words of Professor Gabriel Debien, historian of the French West Indies, "no real colonization is possible before the establishment of hearth and home, and the birth of a Creole race".[1] The immigration of women from other continents, therefore, became a prerequisite for the development of the American plantations.

By the time of the English seizure of Jamaica in 1655, a pattern had been established that these women came from Europe and Africa. Different motives promoted the arrival of black African and white European women. Whereas the functions designed by the new societies for black women were from the beginning quite precise, that is, to provide labour, those for white women were more varied and equivocal.

3

Multiplicity of roles for European females characterized early colonization. The male pioneer was explorer/soldier, frontiersman/farmer, simultaneously, consecutively. The female was accordingly versatile. Often only a thin line, if any, divided the camp follower from the settler woman who helped her menfolk to tame the wilderness, establish a home, rear a family and so increase settler labour power. The process by which camp and garrison became homestead and colony, and women's part in this process, depended on the new community's concepts of its economic aims, its social responsibilities and its religious ethos, if it had one; and these were not always clearly articulated at foundation. The question of whether the particular colonizing undertaking saw itself as permanent settlement or as transient exploitation, whether it saw the new land as home or as business place would crucially influence the kind of social arrangements which evolved, the structure of the family and women's presence and purpose in that structure. Until a clear ethos of settlement could be identified, women's position tended to be fluid.[2]

The earliest discussion on English women in Jamaica speculated about that position. Some wives of officers and privates accompanied the British expedition of May 1655 to Jamaica.[3] The military leader General Robert Venables apparently paid such conspicuous attention to his wife Elizabeth as to create comment and criticism. She allegedly distracted him from his official business and was held partly responsible for the low morale of the army, the military fiasco at Santo Domingo in April 1655 and the General's later abandonment of his men in Jamaica.[4] She was, in the words of one contemporary, "not unjustly blamed, both for his sluggish and listless proceedings, as also for his unlicensed and immature return, furthered if not procured by her too opportune inculcations".[5] Her influence proved "a sad consequence to the English nation" and established conclusively that "soldiers' wives were more properly seated in their husbands' kitchen than his Tent".[6]

Venables suffered official censure as well. Accused of cowardice and incompetence, he spent six weeks in the tower of London,[7] during which time he composed his defence. In it, he justified the presence of his wife, as well as that of other white women with the troops. He had, he stated, informed the protector in advance that he intended taking to the West Indies with him his bride of a few months [his second wife]. Had objections been raised then, he might have left her behind or not gone at all himself. Other officers, he pointed out, had later taken their wives "without hindrance or blame".[8]

There was also the custom of the time which, in the absence of military hospitals and orderlies, welcomed soldiers' wives and widows as nurses at the front,[9] a custom justified by the experience of the Civil Wars: "for soldiers' wives whoever have observed in Ireland know the necessity of having that sex with an army to attend upon and help the sick and wounded, which men are unfit for".[10] This policy had been approved at a Council of War in Bridgetown, Barbados, on 18 March 1655, when Venables and his fellow officers met to consider the needs of the army. They resolved that "soldiers' wives [who offer to carry their own provisions] may be transported to take care of sick and wounded men".[11] In fact, Venables felt that if they had had more women with them they might have been spared some of the terrible mortality which devastated them throughout the whole campaign.[12] ✓

Venables also claimed that he understood the chief purposes of the expedition to be to promote the gospel in Catholic America and to establish a plantation "where women would be necessary"; and if he had not become seriously ill, they would have remained and settled in Jamaica.[13]

This apologia for women, with its implications of uncertain female status, echoes the complex of rationalizations advanced at various times by various persons for the whole uncertain Western Design itself. Cromwell had devised it as a challenge to Spanish Catholic power in the Western Hemisphere. A multi-purpose exercise, deviously conceived and deviously implemented, it never made clear whether its destination was Puerto Rico or Hispaniola, Cuba or the Spanish Main, whether its motivation was conquest or conversion, planting or plunder.[14]

Venables may well have been sincere in seeing it as a missionary-cum-planting undertaking and likely to be permanent. Mrs Venables loyally defended her husband's pious intentions, which she felt had been frustrated by sycophants and villains. In her autobiography, she deplored the shabby treatment he received from the powers that be:

> [N]othing of their promises performed. They pretended the honour of God and the propagating of the Gospel. But alas! Their intention was self honour and riches . . . and so the design prospered accordingly to their hypocrisy. Though the heart of Mr Venables I dare say was right, that the glory of God was his aim, yet the success was very ill for the work of God was not likely to be done by the Devil's instruments.[15]

For others, it seemed initially and essentially "a piratical venture" offering tempting prospects of quick and easy booty.[16] Aimed eventually at Santo Domingo, it missed its target and ended up on the next best island without supplies. "Jamaica might never have become a colony at all, if Cromwell had provided [the expedition] with enough food to support it in its career of rapine."[17]

Colonization by default brought with it questionable colonizing personnel, in the shape of the twenty-five hundred army rejects who comprised the English expeditionary force in 1655. En route, they collected an additional four thousand-odd recruits from St Christopher, Barbados, Nevis and Montserrat who, although presumably seasoned West Indians, proved to be equally unpromising settler material. They were mainly bankrupt small farmers and fugitive servants, the casualties of the Lesser Antilles' sugar revolution of the mid-seventeenth century. According to the expedition's commissioners, they generated "disorder and confusion"; they were remarkable only in retreat, and when dust of the fighting settled, they were as unwilling and inept with the hoe as with the musket.[18] It took later waves of migration to redeem the Eastern Caribbean's reputation as the nursery of colonizers.

Jamaica in 1655 provided this motley army of conquerors and would-be founding fathers with few guidelines for development. The Spanish occupiers who succeeded Columbus had destroyed Arawak [Taino][19] civilization and replaced it with little else. Observers had frequently commented on the island's great natural potential, but noted also its relative social and economic stagnation. Some growth of the population and economy may have started, however, at about the mid-seventeenth century. The appearance of a new church and a hospital in St Jago de la Vega [Spanish Town], increased payment of tithes, importation of Indians and Africans seemed to indicate this.[20]

It is probable, however, that there were no more than about twenty-five hundred persons in the island when the English arrived,[21] and the majority of these had gone into hiding in the mountains surrounding the southern plains.[22] The Spaniards were particularly protective of their women, and they declared "they would rather die in the bush than to see their daughters and wives in the power of heretics".[23]

In spite of precautions taken for their safety, Spanish women fell into the hands of the English. Juan Jimenez and his wife were among their first captives.[24] The invaders learnt too "from certain fugitive Negroes that there were many rich women" in the southern savannas.[25] There was, for example, the wealthy lady of Liguanea, who was probably the widow of Governor Caballero, who had been prominent in colonial factions and had been murdered in 1650.[26] She was reported to own "a sugar work and abundance of cattle in the savannas, nearly 40,000".[27] At least one of these wealthy ladies, possibly "the richest of the country", Doña Juana de Fuentes, became an early victim of the English troops.[28] With her were caught Doña Catalina Tello, sister of the Spanish colonial accountant, "other persons" and some slave women. A ransom was extracted for her release, with the connivance of her nephew Don Inigo de Fuentes.[29] Some ranchers' wives were caught and held during the military campaign on the Pedro Plains in July to August 1655.[30] Between February and March 1656, three women were taken prisoner by a raiding party sent to catch wild horses in the region of the "Mountains of the Manatinas", west of the Clarendon plains.[31]

Don Christoval de Ysassi, the last Spanish governor of Jamaica, wrote to his brother, Don Blas Ysassi, lieutenant governor of Cuba, that "on St Joseph's day 19 March 1656 the enemy came by way of St Jago and captured there the wife of Lope de Verdecia and her unmarried sister and the wife of Sebastian Dias".[32]

These female prisoners were probably assimilated by the invaders. The majority of their compatriots were evacuated to Cuba, with women receiving priority, even to the extent of embarrassing the military operations.[33] By 1658, "all ye women and children were gone for Cuba and only ye men and slaves remained".[34]

The last Spanish stand ended in defeat in 1660, with only a few of the fighting men left behind and the flight to Cuba of all but a few of the survivors.[35]

Elements of Iberian continuity in the island's development were assured, however, by a small conclave of Portuguese Jews who, at the beginning of the seventeenth century, numbered about seventy-five or less.[36] They surrendered early to the English[37] and, although never totally absorbed into early Anglo-Jamaica, they remained nevertheless a significant minority.[38]

The most important legacy of the Spanish period, which exercised a strong and sustained influence on Jamaica's development, was the ceaseless activity of the African guerillas. They were partners of the whites in the first phase of the Spanish resistance movement. They however became an independent force, and after the final surrender of Ysassi to the English in 1660, their continued harassment of would-be settlers effectively obstructed the opening up of the hinterland for nearly a century. The black freedom fighters became a major obstacle to the expansion of white society.[39]

An initial phase of warfare and social disorganization characterized nearly all American colonization. Caribbean islands, moreover, were helpless pawns in the European imperialist struggles for transatlantic trade and territory, and Jamaica's re-peopling took place against a background of wars and rumours of wars. This was aggravated by its unique status as the first overseas colony acquired by English conquest.[40] Unlike earlier proprietary plantations of the New World, it was also the first State colonizing experiment.[41] Having no official precedent, it was peculiarly vulnerable to the political manipulations of governments. It was possible for the island to fall an easy victim to the diplomatic double-dealing of both Protectorate and Restoration with regard to Spain's Caribbean empire. It was possible for much of the island's energies to be engaged for years, with secret governmental blessing, in semi-piratical assaults on Spanish ships and ports. Jamaicans became prime exponents of the cynical rationalizations of these illicit adventures.[42]

The Modyford family, which made its large fortune from pillaging both land and sea, soon dominated the crucial early period of the island's growth. Its most powerful member was buried in the church at St Jago de la Vega, and his epitaph reads:

> Here lyes not
> onely the deceased body of the Honoble
> Sir Thomas Modyford Barronett but even
> the Soule and Life of all Jamaica who first
> made what it now is[43]

The policy which helped to make Jamaica what it became, was succinctly expressed in a petition of 28 September 1670 to the Council of State for plantations from Modyford, then lieutenant governor, and his Jamaican caucus, which simultaneously recommended privateering and planting: privateers, they claimed, were necessary to protect planters.[44] In an era of hazardous settlement, this was a persuasive argument, which could dispense with the fact that the freebooting life, equally hazardous, could also be immensely profitable, elevating the trappings of boomtown Port Royal into the pinnacle of achievement. It indicated the kind of thinking which, in the absence of an alternative *raison d'être,* helped to prepare seventeenth-century Jamaica for the triumph of economic expediency and eased its progress from the condition of "a rough commonwealth" to that of "a most productive factory".

Class Groupings, the Geography of Early Settlement, Health and Security Fears

White women entered the uncertain social climate of early English Jamaica in trickles. An army muster of November 1655 estimated that there were 2,194 healthy men, 2,316 sick men (most of whom subsequently died) and 173 women and children.[45] Although their numbers were small, outlines of their class groupings can be distinguished.

The first colonial "women of quality" were the wives of the commissioned officers, the island's first governing class, of whom Elizabeth Venables was an example [although she did not stick it out]. In October 1655, the new Commissioner Robert Sedgwicke arrived from England with fresh troops under the command of Colonel Humphreys, whose wife accompanied him.[46] On 19 December 1655, the Council of State ordered the Committee of Jamaica "to report on the most convenient way of transporting those wives desirous to go to their husbands in Jamaica".[47] In July 1656, Mary Hope, the wife of Major Richard Hope, who was then stationed in Jamaica, appealed to the Council for help with her transportation difficulties. She had been accepted as a passenger on the *Grantham* bound for the West Indies and her belongings had been placed on board; but the commissioners of the admiralty, without warning, countermanded the order and left her stranded "ready to perish through want, if not relieved". The Council gave the necessary approval for her to have a free passage.[48] On 10 December 1657, the Council voted an allowance of £6 10s. per head to fourteen wives of officers (as well as privates) to be transported.[49] Elizabeth, the wife of Lieutenant Colonel Henry Archibould, major in the Liguanea Regiment, was granted

£20 in the following year to enable her and her family to join her husband.[50] These women, representatives of a scarce group, were nevertheless significant. Their social pre-eminence was only partly due to English upper-class origins. Lieutenant General Edward D'Oyley, writing to Nicholas, secretary of the Council of State, on 11 September 1660, claimed that the men under his command comprised "mostly gentlemen of good family".[51] D'Oyley himself may have been well connected: his wife in fact had a family link with Nicholas. But as a recanting parliamentarian, he was anxious to ingratiate himself with the Restoration by projecting an image of excessive loyalty and gentility.[52]

The antecedents of the first English settlers are not always clear: the tendency has been to exalt the obscure. The biographers of the influential planting family of the Prices comment: "The idea that their progenitors had been nobodies was anathema to the eighteenth century plantocracy. Though their forbears had obviously been less wealthy than themselves, they had come to Jamaica, it was maintained, not to make, but to regain their fortunes."[53]

There is not much evidence that those early arrivals had ever had fortunes behind them. Colonel Fortescue wrote to Thurloe on 21 July 1655: "I wish your army were as honest as poor. I am confident there is not an officer in the army hath above 40 shillings, hundreds not five shillings in their purse."[54] This was primarily due to their arrears of pay, notorious at the time as one of the least efficient aspects of Cromwell's military administration and a source of bitter discontent on both sides of the Atlantic: towards the close of the Protectorate 1659, £110,000 was owing to the soldiers serving in Jamaica.[55] The regiments received twelve days' pay in all during the first six months of 1655;[56] their families at home, entitled to receive a quarter of this, suffered acutely as a result. In many cases, officers had spent their all in outfitting themselves for the expedition and left their wives "miserably poor and indebted, with many children without either clothes, food or hope to continue in any habitation".[57] The series of petitions which went to the Council of State from the distressed families of officers, the financial arrangements for their travel referred to above, do not indicate backgrounds of affluence.[58]

The fact was that foreign service was unattractive, particularly to those known unhealthy spots like the West Indies. It was, therefore, relatively easy for men drawn from the ranks to get commissioned with troops going overseas. Of twelve officers whom General Monck sent to Jamaica with four reg-iments of Scottish Infantry, six had been promoted from the ranks of pri-vates.[59] Furthermore, it was cavalry rather than infantry which recruited gentlemen of birth, and of the seven thousand-odd men who constituted the Jamaican force, there were 121 horses with twenty-two cavalry officers.[60] The social composition of the army of occupation ensured that the *petit bour-geoisie,* at best, dominated the first creole ruling class.

Regardless of where the newcomers started in the home countries, what mattered once they crossed the Atlantic was high army ranking. The com-missioned man and his family slid into the social vacuum of the infant colony, instant "somebodies". The first civil governor was Colonel D'Oyley, whose first counsellors, appointed on 1 August 1660 "to consult and advise about the defence and security of this island and the English interest therein", were all officers of the army, including both Hope and Archibould.[61] Long after the disbandment of the army in 1662 and its replacement by a militia, Jamaica's civil establishment continued to be headed by military hierarchy.

Land holdings were soon allied to regional status to consolidate this overnight elite.[62] Officers received the most handsome grants, a minimum usually of 500 acres.[63] A survey of 1670 shows that 209,020½ acres had by then been patented; only three women were listed as substantial landown-ers.[64] Priscilla Willoughby stood out as the largest female planter in her own right. Having "transported herself together with her servants", she was granted 600 acres of land at Seven Plantations in Clarendon on 13 November 1664.[65] The Widow Allwincle held 600 acres in Clarendon,[66] and Elizabeth Reid held 927 in St John's. Her husband, Captain George Reid, owned 1,408 acres.[67] Forty-seven persons had properties over 1,000 acres each; twenty of these were listed as colonels, majors and captains. Hope and Archibould between them, with the connivance of governors at the time, collected over 4,000 acres of prize lands in St Andrew.[68] Of the nine largest landowners in the parish of St John's in 1680, six were officers, the other three were widows.[69]

Landowning and army rank, twin pillars of high status, were further linked and strengthened by marriage and intermarriage. Governing classes have always used marriage as a means of retaining their exclusive position. Jamaica's embryonic elite of the seventeenth century, needing to create its dynasties, embarked early on strategic domestic alliances, which were designed to speed the concentration in the fewest possible hands of landed holdings and of officers in the island's elected Assembly, its nominated Council, its judiciary, its civil and military establishments.

The matrimonial arrangements of the daughters of General Edward Morgan, deputy governor in 1664, illustrate this. Johanna Wilhelmina married the influential and propertied Henry Archibould of Constant Spring, after the death of his first wife Elizabeth.[70] Anna Petronella married Lieutenant Colonel Robert Byndloss, major in command of Fort Charles in the 1660s, proprietor of over 2,000 acres in the parishes of St Catherine and Clarendon, chief justice and member of the Council in the 1680s.[71] The third Morgan sister married a cousin, the celebrated Henry Morgan, later deputy governor of Jamaica.[72] It was characteristic of such colonial unions that each proliferated other unions, which in turn generated further assets of public as well as of personal significance. So that, for example, Polnitz Byndloss, the son of Robert and Anna Petronella, married into the politically eminent family of Matthew Gregory, Speaker of the House of Assembly, and this led to further matrimonial links with the Beckfords, one of Jamaica's oldest clans and eventually its wealthiest,[73] thus demonstrating the process by which a new creole oligarchy could, by its judicious matrimonial policies, consolidate its claims to power.

Security considerations determined the geography of settlement. Major-General Fortescue, Vice-Admiral Goodson, Major Sedgwick and Daniel Serle were instructed by the Council of State in 1655 to

> take care that those, as well soldiers as others, who shall become planters, may have their land set forth next adjoining to such harbours and landing places, and be likewise engaged to make some defencible fortifications thereupon, especially in such harbours or landing places, as are within 15 miles or less of St Jago: which you shall endeavour to be well peopled, and also to be fortified at the state's charge, if you cannot get it done upon the account of particular plantations.[74]

Population and power were therefore concentrated on the fertile plains of the southern coast, which offered maximum safety, as well as maximum returns on agricultural effort. In 1670, Jamaica had roughly fifteen thousand inhabitants, of whom over eight thousand (representing about five hundred or more settled families) were to be found in the parishes of St Andrew, St

Catherine, Clarendon, and the towns of Port Royal and Spanish Town. The rest of the island had in all a possible three hundred other families: the parish of St Thomas with fifty-nine families (590 persons), St David with eighty families (960 persons), St John's with eighty-three families (996 persons), all on the outskirts of the highest-density areas; while St George, St Mary, St Ann, St James and St Elizabeth together, containing about 1,500 persons, were virtual hinterland.[75]

Social and economic activity focused on Port Royal and Spanish Town. John Taylor, writing in the 1680s, described the former as "a formidable city", with "at least 600 well built houses and as many more built with timber . . . [where] Merchants and gentry live to the Heights of Splendour, in full ease and plenty".[76] As the centre of the island's legal and illegal trade, it projected something of the image of an opulent bourgeoisie. The Reverend Francis Crow, who numbered among his congregation "the better sort of merchants and mechanics", commented in 1687 that "tis the most proud and prodigal place that ever I beheld, especially it is so to the women among us. For a cooper's wife shall go forth in the best flowered silk and richest silver and gold lace that England can afford, with a couple of Negroes at her tail."[77]

Spanish Town, the seat of government and the heart of planting country, had more genteel pretensions. In 1672, it contained "several fair and well built houses and the inhabitants lived in great pleasure where they have their Havana, in which the better sort recreate themselves every evening in their coaches, or on horseback as the Gentry do here in Hide [*sic*] Park".[78]

The two towns expressed not only the pseudo-metropolitanism of colonial life, but the dualism of the creole society on the make, the privateer-planter syndrome, reflecting in a way the capitalist-seigniorial conflict-alliance of western Europe, mirrored in many early New World plantations, seeking resolution in Jamaica too.[79] By the beginning of the eighteenth century, the mercantile demands of the metropolitan, in powerful coalition with the interests of the local plantocracy, were pushing the economy into the direction of a massive agro-industrial operation, transforming the coastal valleys into sugar belts geared towards the overriding goal of production for a market overseas. In the ten years between the mid-1670s and mid-1680s, Jamaica multiplied its sugar tonnage five times over.[80] As the business of the island became exclusively business, its lifestyle jelled: money without a sophisticated haute and bourgeoisie, land without seigniorial lords and dames, a rural factory with a self-made gentry.

One dark side of the coin was the record of disease and death on those low-lying plains where the sugar cane thrived. Unfortunately, no quantitative vital statistics exist for this period, nothing comparable to, for example, the Barbados census of 1680. In a valuable analysis of its findings, Richard Dunn observes "the stunted family development of Bridgetown, mainly the result of the appallingly high mortality rate".[81] "Englishmen", he suggests, "were certainly not transferring to the tropics the strong family structure, they established in Bristol (New England) and everywhere else in mainland America." The average white family in Bridgetown in 1680 contained 3.74 persons, in contrast to the Bristol average of 5.97 in 1689.[82] No similar family analysis in depth is possible for Jamaica; however, a census for the parish of St John's in 1680 provides a small but suggestive sample. It had then forty-eight plantations containing forty-three white males, thirty-seven white females and seventy-two white children, a total of 152, or approximately 3.17 white family members per household (excluding servants and slaves); nine births and ten deaths had taken place in 1678.[83] It should be remembered that Barbados, in spite of its "appalling" death rate, was still a healthier spot for whites than Jamaica.[84] It was a settled colony, whose population was relatively more immunized to the new disease environment of the Western Hemisphere than Jamaicans were. The incidence of Caribbean mortality applied with peculiar force in the humid, mosquito infested swamps of St Catherine, St Andrew and Clarendon, where Jamaica's first families huddled.

In September 1661 Catherine Lyttleton the wife of Sir Charles Lyttleton, deputy governor, wrote to a family friend, Lord Hatton, a few months before she died in Spanish Town on 26 January 1662. The earliest extant letter from a woman in Jamaica, it marks the beginning of a long history of white female correspondence obsessed with the fear of tropical sickness and dying. She was very depressed by her own weak condition, as well as that of her husband, who was suffering "with the disease of the country which is a griping of the guts". But her baby, "a pretty little boy", did give her some comfort.[85] Hers is the oldest existing epitaph of an English settler in the Cathedral of Spanish Town; her infant outlived her by five days.[86]

Deborah Corker, the daughter of Dr John Burnell and the wife of Thomas Corker, Esq., died in 1727, at the age of twenty, "in childbed of her first child, having [been] married 4 years, 8 months, 5 days"; she was buried in St John's Church at Guanaboa Vale.[87] So too were the eight children of Colonel Charles Price and his wife Sarah, who died between the years 1716 and 1727 at ages ranging from fourteen years to three weeks.[88] The citation on Mary Oburne's headstone confirmed the continuing toll of death during childbirth:

> In Vertuous and Grateful Rememberance of
> Mrs Mary Oburne
> the wife of William Oburne of this
> Parish Merchant
> She Surrendered Human Life Under the
> Agonies and extreme Pangs in travel with Her
> First Child named Frances December the 21st
> Anno Dom: 1724 in the Twentieth Year of her
> Age[89]

Fevers and fluxes, tragedies of early marriage, childbirth and infancy, were all enemies of hearth and home, earning for Jamaica its reputation as "the grave rather than the granary" of early white settlement.

Overwhelming incentives would be needed to urge gentlewomen to migrate to what must have seemed a most hostile environment. Rowland Powell, island secretary and factor of the Royal African Company, obviously understood this, as his efforts to entice his mistress Mary Weekes to join him in Port Royal indicate. In his letter of 5 May 1680, he warned her against her friends' attempts to dissuade her. In addition to his deep devotion, he promised her a luxury cruise (a cabin on board ship as large as a "Bedchamber on shoare") and a life of domestic ease (twelve slaves and a well-trained daughter to keep house). The fact that his wife and sister had recently miscarried he attributed to the doctor's bunglings, and not "to the condition of the country where all is pleasant".[90] It is not clear if Mrs Weekes did undertake "this generous adventure".

However seductive the individual prospect, there were other risks to life and well-being which mitigated against extensive white immigration. There was the constant fear of foreign invasion and buccaneer harassment. In the raid on the south coast by the French governor of Hispaniola, du Casse, in 1694, a minister's widow, Mrs Barrow, had her "lone house at St Elizabeth" attacked by one party of Frenchmen led by Grubbin, "chief of these rogues".

All her possessions, including her slaves, were taken. She was tortured and together with "her maiden daughter", Miss Rachel Barrow of about fourteen years old, was carried off to Petit Goave, the privateer stronghold on the west coast of Hispaniola;[91] and there were other worse atrocities.[92] In times of such disturbances, white women suffered further hazards on the home front, for while their men took on the foreign enemy, they were left unprotected and exposed "to the insults of the Negroes".[93]

The main internal danger was identified by Sedgwicke early in 1656. "Concerning the state of the enemy on shore here," he wrote,

> the Spaniard is not considerable, but of the Blacks there are many, who like to prove as thorns and pricks in our sides, living in the mountains and woods, a kind of life both natural, and I believe acceptable to them, and are enemies to us, looking upon us as a bloody people, giving no quarter. I am sure they give none to us but destroy our men: there scarce a week passeth without one or two claim by them, and as we grow secure they grow bold and bloody: be assured they must either be destroyed or brought in upon some terms or other, or else there will be a great discouragement to the settling of a people here.[94]

In 1677, a letter from Mr Nevil to the Earl of Carlisle sounded another note of warning against the threat of runaway, rebellious blacks, "a taste of the latter of which mischief they had the last year when many families were murdered by some few slaves that went out of the whole Island Alarmed and disturbed with fears and apprehension of the rest".[95]

John Wilson wrote about the property sales of his family in the 1690s: "My grandfather and Father sold by their Attorneys diverse parcels of land at Port Royal and other places: but ye estate in St George's parish, being a remote part of ye island and overrun by ye wild Negroes, was not at that time capable of being sold: by reason no whites would go to settle there."[96]

White settlers in the seventeenth and early eighteenth centuries had to accept as a fact of life the unremitting campaign of terrorism mounted by the black guerillas, who were relatively few in number but were regularly reinforced by runaway Africans from settled estates. With their superior knowledge of the trackless mountains and from their inaccessible strongholds in St Thomas-in-the-East, Trelawny and St Elizabeth, they could effectively ambush, hit-and-run, swoop on unprotected properties and hold the whites to ransom.

Their female victims were numerous enough to cause alarm. The Spanish Town Cathedral contains "the bodys of Edmon Ducke Esq. and Martha his wife, she being most barbarously / murthered by some of their own Negroes / Slaves departed this life the 28th day / of April 1678".[97] The estate of the Widow Grey at Guanaboa in St Catherine was the scene of a black uprising in 1685. It spilled over into the parishes of St Ann and St Mary, leaving a trail of death and destruction. A small family of rum retailers in St Ann, including a man, a woman and two children, were among the casualties, as was a widow in St Mary "living in a house remote from all others".[98] Captain Herring's wife and some of his children were killed in a slave rebellion which took place on his Clarendon plantation during his absence in 1696.[99] Mrs Mary Guthrie lost her husband Colonel Guthrie in the first Maroon War of the 1730s. Had he survived, he would have received "a genteel maintenance"; the Jamaica Assembly agreed that his widow should receive it instead.[100]

The Maroon bogey was partly laid to rest by the truce of 1739, although white Jamaica's fear of black revolt never disappeared. But as a result of the economy's thrust and its hunger for African labour, by the 1740s the black presence, now ten times that of the white,[101] had become a pervasive, intimate and inextricable part of the white domestic scene. As Jamaica's complexion darkened and simultaneously varied, the white woman's always tenuous footing in the island became increasingly insecure; this was particularly true of the upper class, in which social prejudices reinforced feelings of racial exclusiveness.

Women of that group remained a small, troubled minority. An estimate of the number of whites in 1730 showed "2,171 masters and mistresses",[102] indicating a very small feminine elite. They came to embody the phenomenon of absenteeism in its most extreme form. By the 1770s, the greatest scarcity of white women was to be found among the families of the largest estate owners.[103] Increasing wealth from sugar profits offered them the facilities for travel. As woman and as mother, the rigours of the climate and their children's education could give unanswerable cause for frequent and prolonged trips home.

Mary Jervis, the sister of John Jervis, First Viscount and Earl St Vincent, married William Ricketts, of a prominent creole planting family, in England in 1757.[104] Shortly after their marriage, they went to Jamaica to live at her husband's estate at Midgham in Westmoreland. Her letters to her family in

England revealed her contempt for Jamaica, "this dull, illiterate part of the world".[105] The "evils" which she encountered there included her husband's sudden and dangerous illness with "an inflammatory fever",[106] from which he luckily recovered. Those "talky wretches, the negroes" disturbed her greatly: she swore she would never have any with her in England.[107] Island life became for her increasingly "a lingering death", and she begged her brother's help "to deliver her from this vile place".[108] Jervis was sympathetic to his sister's state of "exile",[109] especially as her health declined when she found that she seldom "escaped fever for a day".[110] Her plans to depart materialized in 1759. Her husband accompanied her to England, but returned shortly afterwards to attend his estates. He remained in Jamaica for the next thirty-odd years, except for one or two brief visits to his wife and sons in England. Mrs Ricketts never revisited Jamaica,[111] and when she did look back it was with distaste and fear. In a letter of 6 October 1764, which was to be opened by her husband after her death, she wrote: "I make it my last and most earnest request that our child may never go to a country I cannot think of without the utmost horror, nothing but the most settled aversion."[112] Her experience, like that of Elizabeth Venables, was that of many ladies of quality, who came, who saw, who fled.

MATERIAL INCENTIVES FOR EMIGRATION AND SETTLEMENT

Early plans for settlement and population growth did not overtly push the cause of the large landed proprietor. It was tacitly assumed that the concerns of the upper class were power and wealth to be shared among a select minority. It was the middle and lower classes who peopled the earth, and it was their cause which was consciously promoted, in the interest of providing stable family units, manpower sufficient for the economy's purposes and an adequate defence force. Hardworking and prolific farming men and women were expected to meet these requirements. The chief expressed intention was therefore to encourage the twenty-, thirty- or fifty-acre farmer. This class of person was to be found among the soldiers of the original occupation troops, seasoned settlers from older American colonies and civilian emigrants from the British Isles.

The rank and file of Cromwell's army were recruited by impressment.

Many were married, and privates, like their officers, were encouraged to take their wives to the Caribbean with them.[113] Those who remained behind in England suffered even greater financial hardships than officers' wives, through the irregular payments of family allowances.[114] This may have been a factor prompting some women to join their husbands in Jamaica, women like Mary Ramsey, for example, who petitioned the Council on 11 January 1656 to receive the arrears of her husband's pay due to her, as well as passages for herself and family to join him.[115] Mary Ryder, Paulina Pindar, Anne Cadaway, Alice Leverett and several others were among those on record who, "desirous of being transported to that island at the expense of the state", went to join their husbands serving in Jamaica.[116]

Some of the troops' wives, probably the majority, went with the recruits from Barbados and the Leeward Islands, who outnumbered the regiments from Britain.[117] There were some unsavoury women among them, although it is not clear whether these were wives or merely camp followers.[118] Not many settled down to establish farming families. The first attempt at planting was an obstacle rather than an incentive to privates to become agricultural settlers. Organized on a quasi-military basis, each regiment was responsible for its food production, the ranks being field workers required to till land patented by officers. Agricultural work was so repugnant to the men that only reluctant and inefficient cultivation resulted.[119] Policy discussions in the 1660s centred round land offers, so that soldiers could "forthwith become planters". The proposal was to give 50 acres to each soldier and thirty to his wife.[120] This was later modified to 30 acres to each.[121]

But the mortality of the early arrivals, which was said to be 140 weekly in the first months of 1665,[122] did not permit many soldiers to survive as settlers. In 1660, it was estimated that 2,200 of the original contingent of 7,000 remained.[123] This was a great deterrent to the women. Sedgwicke, in January 1656 wrote: "Many women that came down to their husbands, finding them dead, have sold themselves for servants to be gone upon other plantations rather than abide with us, although we have offered them . . . encouragements to remain here."[124]

Army numbers in any event were small. Once the first phase of occupation was past, Jamaica's military establishment in 1659 was fixed at 1,500 men,[125] and the high sex ratio, which prevailed, ruled out the forces as a major permanent reservoir for peopling the colony. In 1661, the white population was estimated at 2,458 men, 454 women and 44 children.[126] In 1662, the first recorded census of the island showed 2,600 men, 645 women and 408 children.[127]

Cromwell's abortive Irish immigration scheme was an ambitious, if tasteless attempt to adjust the prevailing sexual imbalance overnight and ensure a natural increase of population. His proposal for collecting one thousand young girls for breeding purposes was conveyed to Secretary Thurloe on 11 September 1655, as follows:

> [C]oncerning the younge women, although we must use force in taking them up, yet it beinge so much for their own good and likely to be of soe great advantage to the publique, it is not in the least doubted, that you may have such number of them as you shall thinke fitt to make use uppon this account.[128]

Lord Broghill, who was assessing the possibilities of Scottish immigration, echoed Cromwell's views. "For women and maids," he wrote, "I believe you may get many more out of Ireland than heer, which I thought not impertinent to mind you of."[129] The project was expanded to include boys, and the Council of State on 3 October 1655 approved an expenditure "not exceeding twenty shillings each for 1,000 Irish girls and the like number of youths of 14 years or under".[130] Possibly because of Anglo-Irish political difficulties and also because of practical transportation problems, the proposal was never implemented;[131] it provided, however, inexhaustible material for those convinced that even a Puritan commonwealth was not incapable of the villainy of white slave traffic.[132]

Broghill had also implied that a fruitful source for female colonists would be "such women, as wil adventure to seek husbands ther".[133] The Earl of Marlborough's proposals of 1660 further illustrated officialdom's view of female emigration: women should be sent over as planters' wives, "Newgate and Bridgewell to be spared as much as may be and poor maids instead, with which few parishes are unburdened, sent over".[134] Little evidence, however, appeared of poor maids or husband hunters rushing off to the new Eden. A handsome dowry in such a context seemed a luxury one could dispense with; so that Marlborough conceded, as an added attraction to female immigrants, that "the custom of the planter is to give, not require anything with his wife".[135] Cary Helyar, the owner of Bybrook estate noted that in 1672 he wed one Pricilla, "though 2 cows and 1 horse was all she brought with her".[136]

Women were also eligible for the land grants offered in the Royal Proclamation of 10 September 1662 designed to encourage settlement. It promised "thirtie acres of improveable land . . . to every such person, male or female, being twelve years old or upwards".[137] These grants, which allotted freeholds on payment of an annual quit rent of 1d. to 2d. per acre, were also tied to service in the militia and therefore mitigated against single women.[138] A mere handful exploited the land grant facilities to attempt independent enterprise. Of the 390 patentees registered between 1662 and 1664, nine were women;[139] and only three, Priscilla Willoughby with her large Clarendon holdings,[140] Elizabeth Tounes with 182 acres in St Andrew[141] and Susanna Baker with 150 acres in St Catherine,[142] appeared to be planting women. The others owned house plots and small allotments in St Catherine and Port Royal. All of these women undertook "to be ready to serve in any insurrection."[143] The 1670 survey of Jamaican landowners lists twenty-one women, of whom eight were widows;[144] and in 1680, St John's census contained five women, all widows.[145]

Women, on the whole, migrated in family groups and came in greatest numbers from the New World itself. Cromwell's hope, in fact, was that Jamaica's open hinterland would also appeal to those Europeans who had already survived the transatlantic crossing but whose land hunger or wanderlust had not yet been satisfied in the Americas. He looked to Puritan New England for frontiersmen and women of solid virtues, sending his agent Daniel Gookin to lure them from "that desert and barren wilderness" to "a land of plenty".[146] His first offer was 20 acres to each person who settled in Jamaica.[147] The response was cool. New Englanders were put off by what they had heard of the great mortality, the profanity of the soldiers and the constant danger of "skulking Negroes and Spaniards".[148] About three hundred persons initially showed interest, mainly "heads of familyes, goodly, honest and industrious people",[149] but there is no firm evidence that they reached Jamaica, and it is most likely that, with the rest of their countrymen, they preferred the "known wilderness to the unknown".

Jamaica was sensitive about its shortcomings and would have silenced detractors if it could. Marye Boyfield, a Bermudan and a prospective emigrant, testified that her countryman William Philips had told her at chapel that Jamaica "was not a place he could sit downe in hemselfe, neither would he wish any ffriend of his, or any tending to him".[150] He claimed that he had visited the island recently and "non but the scumme of the Indias was there".[151] For this kind of talk, guaranteed to frustrate the protector's development plans for Jamaica, Philip was imprisoned "3 daies in Irons".[152]

Bermudan families of poor to middling circumstances did in fact respond to Jamaica's need for people. Some two hundred sailed in 1655, among them fifty-four male heads of families, twenty-three of whom had their wives and children with them, several having four and more children each. Only two childless couples migrated, and two women unaccompanied by husbands: "Alice How and 2 children" and "Frances Condall, her 6 sons and daughters".[153]

The largest numbers of family units initially came from the Eastern Caribbean. The Leeward Islands and Barbados were experiencing that phase, characteristic of much of tropical colonization in the New World, when limited cash crop farming was giving way to extensive export monoculture. Inherent in that first stage of subsistence production was the concept of the white family and household as important sources of labour and goods, home being virtually granary and workshop. The menial role of the colonist as subtenant and as indentured servant was recognized. Although this process in the Caribbean never developed to the same extent as it did on the North American mainland, particularly in New England, it had clearly affected the shape and size of the population and the family in the earlier West Indian settlement: their ratio of children to the adults, for example, was significant.[154]

The Lesser Antilles sugar revolution of the mid-seventeenth century, spearheaded by the big planters and relying increasingly on black imported manpower, gravely dislocated the situation of early colonial families in relation to land, capital and labour; and it made many domestic groups ready for the outward trek. Table 1.1 illustrates the comparative population patterns of the islands most concerned and highlights the magnetic pull of Jamaica's virgin acreage virtually going a-begging.

In response to Cromwell's offer of free land, Luke Stokes, the governor of Nevis, pointed out that the majority of the men there were ready to migrate "with their wives, children and servants".[155] Most of them were poor, "several of the rich not willing to stir",[156] and in the hope of better prospects, Stokes and his wife, their three sons, and some 1,600 of their countrymen migrated to Jamaica at the end of 1656.[157] They were allocated to the Port Morant area,

Table 1.1 Population and Acreage of Jamaica, Barbados and the Leeward Islands in the 1670s

Colony	Population						Acreage
	White Males	White Females	White Children	Whites	Blacks	Total	(in square miles)
Jamaica[1] 1673	4,050	2,002	1,712	7,764	9,504	17,268	4,411
Barbados[2] 1676	10,000 (adults) 3,030 (children)	8,695 (adults) and children)	–	21,725	32,473	54,198	166
St Christopher,[3] Nevis, Montserrat, Antigua, Saba 1678	4,760	2,700	3,663	11,123	8,560	19,683	259 (excluding Saba)

Sources:

[1]Jamaica House of Assembly 1784–1791, vol. 1, appendix, 20.

[2]House of Commons Accounts and Papers, vol. XXVI (1789), part IV, Population. No. 3 Barbados.

[3]Charles Higham, *The Development of the Leeward Islands under the Restoration 1660–1688* (Cambridge: Cambridge University Press, 1921), 148.

to the east of the island, in the parish of St Thomas-in-the-East, which had an excellent harbour, fertile soil but poor drainage. In fact, it proved to be one of the worst environments for would-be planters, 300 dying within a month; by March 1657, nearly two-thirds were buried. The hardiest of the survivors succeeded in establishing by 1671 "upwards of 60 settlements".[158] The 1670 survey of St Thomas-in-the-East shows a high proportion of medium-sized properties, forty-nine out of fifty-nine heads of families owning less than 500 acres each, and the average holding containing about 144 acres. But development was slow. St Thomas then contained 590 persons.[159]

At the end of the century, Port Morant proved a particularly vulnerable point for foreign invasion: hundreds of settlers were destroyed by French soldiers in 1694; many were evacuated.[160]

This unhappy precedent did not deter other adventurers; nor did the multiple hazards of Caribbean migration, such as the experience of fifty planters from St Christopher, who were captured in 1660 on their way to Jamaica by two Dutch men-of-war commissioned by Spain.[161] Similarly, a number of Barbadians were intercepted in 1670 in mid-voyage by two sloops from Curaçao, and their slaves and servants commandeered.[162] Sir Thomas Modyford, who dispatched his son Jack in June 1664 to Barbados to fetch his mother, was forced after a few years to give him up as lost somewhere on the inter-island journey.[163]

Barbados lost several hundreds of its colonists to the new frontier, in spite of its Council and Assembly's determined efforts to prevent emigration.[164] Lord Windsor, on his way to Jamaica in 1662 as governor, went off with "many servants and debtors".[165] Modyford, his successor, took an additional 987 persons in 1664, "mostly belonging to composed families".[166] Sir Thomas Lynch, who became Jamaica's governor in 1671, also stopped off in Barbados, where he found the island in an uproar because of the new 4.5 per cent export duty and such was the effect of this taxation "that 200 volunteered to go with them to Jamaica, and as many more were preparing to follow".[167]

Jamaica's official declaration of a policy of religious toleration[168] attracted as well "several Quakers who had been driven from Barbados".[169] Many of these appeared to have moved on to Pennsylvania,[170] but others settled and formed their church communities in Port Royal and Liguanea.[171] The Quakeress, Judith Jordan of Port Royal, left legacies of £20 and £50 sterling in her will of 7 June 1676 for Quaker women's and men's meetings.[172]

Jamaica also became a shelter for Caribbean war refugees. As a result of French raids on Montserrat, 600 of its colonists took refuge in Jamaica. In 1667, they had been "extremely plundered, even to their very shirts, so that many would have perished, had they not been relieved by the charity of the planters".[173] Other war casualties arrived from Suriname. Previously a thriving English settlement, it had a population in the 1660s of about 4,000, predicted as likely to increase "for the women are very prolific and have lusty children".[174] It was reclaimed by the Dutch in 1667 by the Treaty of Breda and the English there were offered the option of evacuation; 105 families, totalling 517 persons, headed for Jamaica in two ships, which were so tightly packed that "they scarce had room to lodge in".[175] In 1675, another group of 250 English colonists, together with 950 slaves, transferred to Jamaica. This batch contained approximately seventy family groupings, including ninety-two adult females. They were on the whole people of moderate means, owning an average of thirteen slaves each. Only eight were substantial slaveholders, having more than twenty-five slaves, the largest holders being two women, Dorothy Wayle and Eliza Render, who together owned eighty-three slaves.[176]

It is impossible to know the precise figure of this inter-Caribbean movement of peoples involving as it did irregular displacements of individuals as well as of households. It constituted the most substantial influx of whites into early Jamaica, and the presence of women in that migratory wave was vital. They were essential to the brief population boost which Jamaica enjoyed in the late 1660s, 1670s and early 1680s, after the devastating mortality of the 1650s and before the decline of the 1690s, which lasted well into the eighteenth century.

Table 1.2   Jamaica's White Population, 1655–1722

	1655[1]	1661[2]	1662[3]	1673[4]	1698[5]	1722[6]
Men	4,510	2,458	2,600	4,050	2,465	–
Women and Children	173	455 women 44 children	645 women 408 children	2,002 women 1,712 children	4,900	
Totals	**4,683**	**2,937**	**3,653**	**7,764**	**7,365**	**7,100**

Sources:

[1]John Thurloe, *A Collection of the State Papers*, vol. 4 (London, 1742), 153–54 [quoted in, Stanley A.G. Taylor, *The Western Design* (Kingston: The Institute of Jamaica Historical Society, 1965), 91].

[2]Calendar of State Papers (CSP Col.) 1661–1668 (31 December 1661), 65.

[3]Jamaica House of Assembly Votes, vol. 1, appendix, 20.

[4]Ibid., 40.

[5]CSP Col. 1679–1698 (13 October 1698), 470.

[6]George W. Roberts, *The Population of Jamaica* (Cambridge: Cambridge University Press, 1957), 33.

The fact that land patents could be taken up as combined family holdings was a persuasive factor behind the mobility of these domestic units in the seventeenth century. It must have helped to promote a spirit of practical planting partnership, some glimpses of which appear in the records. John and Mary Ridway had jointly patented land in the area of the Upper Cobre River, and when they sold 160 acres to Cary Helyar in September 1669 for £20 1s., an additional 14s. was placed on the purchase price for Mary "for her consent to her husband's sale".[177]

This period of family pioneering coincided with that of diversified agriculture, much approved by enthusiastic promoters.[178] They envisaged profitable holdings of from 50 to 600 acres, a modest capital outlay not exceeding £500, a mixed labour force of blacks and whites and a range of crops including cocoa, timber, indigo, tobacco, cotton and ginger, as well as sugar.[179] This corresponded to the reality of the times, when the average landholding was between 100 and 200 acres.[180] The St John's census of 1680 contains a majority of what appeared to be medium-sized estates, only three proprietors owning more than 50 slaves. The others, forty-five owners in all, averaged 9 slaves, 3.5 slave children and 1.5 white servants each. Seven families had no servants either black or white, twenty had no white servants, and eleven had no enslaved Africans.[181]

The white servant, contracted as a bondsman or bondswoman for a period of four to seven years, was a significant member of the majority of early Jamaican households, totalling in the St John's census ninety-five persons, or 38 per cent of the white population of 247.[182] Servants were an essential source of recruitment for Jamaican whites, male and female; like African slaves, they were an integral part of family migration within the Caribbean. They came directly from Britain as well, and it has been roughly estimated that in the 1670s they were entering Jamaica at the rate of over three hundred annually.[183]

The traffic in indentured labour flourished in the seventeenth and eighteenth centuries because of the abundance of land and the shortage of manpower in the Americas. Metropolitan merchants, entrepreneurs from London, Bristol and Liverpool, were geared to provide the valued commodity, labour, for which the colonial planter gladly paid a price profitable both to himself and to the supplier. This human cargo became available for transatlantic shipment, partly because the New World always attracted some

whose financial resources never matched their spirit of adventure; they therefore traded a few years of their working lives for the westward passage. Partly
too because the beggars, vagrants, debtors, convicts, religious and political
refugees of the British Isles were often given by their societies the alternatives
of destitution, death or transportation.[184]

Servants were originally needed in the Caribbean as general labourers in
agriculture, trades and domestic service; but as the number of black slaves
grew, white labour specialized and came to mean almost exclusively supervisory work on estates and artisans' skills.[185] Eventually, as the hazards of imperialist wars threatened the safety of all islands and as the black masses
swamped the white population, white servants became necessary to help protect society from the external and the internal enemy. The late seventeenth
and early eighteenth centuries saw the steady replacement of a purely economic demand for European labour by a compulsion to provide a bulwark
against what whites saw as a frightening racial imbalance.[186] When the criteria for emigration increasingly demanded effective units of defence, women
clearly could not claim priority of passage.

The statistics are fragmentary; they offer no accurate quantitative picture,
but do indicate the regularity of the indentured flow into the island for over
a century. By the 1770s, it had dwindled almost to nothing. Table 1.3 illustrates this. Of these servants approximately one-third were female. Ligon,
describing Barbados in 1673, estimated this to be the prevailing ratio,[187]
which is consistent with the figures for the Leeward Islands in the 1770s[188]
and with a 1,730 estimate from the Jamaican population, namely: 2,171 masters and mistresses, 3,000 white men servants and 984 white women servants.[189]

The white female servant is almost lost to the records by the third quarter
of the eighteenth century. Many had re-emigrated; from as early as in the
1670s, it was noted that a quarter of the servants who arrived had moved
on.[190] The majority of those who remained and who survived graduated in *white*
time to the ranks of the free and the respectable. *female servants*

Jamaica peculiarly favoured the upward mobility of its servant class. Its
code, adopted from Barbados,[191] developed during the 1660s and 1670s into
one of the more liberal in the New World. The coercive element was always
present – an indentured worker for the period of his or her service was
virtually the chattel of the master – but relaxation of punishment, increased

Table 1.3   Movement of Indentured Servants into Jamaica, 1671–1774

Years	Numbers	Point of Departure
1671–1679	Approx. 350 per annum	Barbados, Leeward Islands, Great Britain
1662–1686	468 (total)	Bristol
Sept. 1683–Aug. 1684	72 (total)	London
1720–1732	1,146 (total)	London
1736	169 (total)	London
1773	8 (total)	London

Source: Abbot E. Smith, *Colonists in Bondage, White Servitude and Convict Labour in America 1607–1776* (Chapel Hill: University of North Carolina Press, 1947), 334, 309, 308, 310, 311, 312.

provisions for food, clothing and freedom dues were introduced into the laws, reflecting the unique extent of white Jamaican underpopulation, which gave the bondsmen some bargaining power and forced legislatures into making realistic concessions.[192] Cary Helyar, for instance, who busied himself in the 1660s with promoting the importation of his East Coker countrymen as indentures, faced tough negotiations with a carpenter, Henry Hodges, and his wife, who were determined to reduce their family's period of servitude to the minimum. Helyar eventually granted terms more generous than those in the original agreement.[193]

Opportunities for freedom and advancement were clearly recognized, made available and seized.[194] Serving women in particular were beneficiaries of the frontier society with its marked sexual imbalance. They received better treatment than their male peers.[195] They are significantly absent from the early-eighteenth-century advertisements of runaway servants and slaves. Between 1718 and 1730, a total of sixty-eight runaways listed in the pages of the weekly *Jamaica Courant* include thirty black males, nineteen black females (with two children), one mulatto male, sixteen white males and no white females.[196] John Taylor observed that "those women servants which are kept in the Planters' family are kept somewhat better than the plantation servants, being employed to make and mend their clothes for 'em".[197] If, in addition to her domestic skills, the bondswoman was also "handsome and kind", she could fairly confidently plan to become mistress.[198]

Emigration and promotion to a higher social rank contributed to the eventual disappearance of the white servile group. This phenomenon was linked with the withdrawal of the upper-class female and the decline of the Creole yeomanry, all corollaries of the growth of the plantation system.

IMMIGRATION AND PLANTATION CONSTRUCTION:
ESTABLISHING THE LINK

they solicited small farming families but promoted big plantations served by slaves

The early architects of Jamaica's colonial structure saw no basic contradictions in their criteria for population growth and economic progress. While Marlborough, Modyford and Lynch pushed for the immigration of the poor spinsters of rural England and the small landless men and women of Barbados, they simultaneously represented land monopolization, sugar monoculture and intensified slave trading, all of which turned out to be incompatible with the kind of family pattern from which the white population could spread. Marlborough's proposal of November 1660 for "all willing to transport themselve to Jamaica" also stressed the need "to persuade the Royal African Company to make Jamaica the staple for the sale of blacks".[199]

Modyford's propositions to the Privy Council of 20 and 28 September 1670 for "the speedy increase of people which is the foundation of all, the *causa sine qua non*",[200] detailed some of the incentives to shippers to transport white immigrants, "the price being rates £12 to £15 females, £10 to £12 ready money".[201] His enthusiasm for the thirty-acre man had even led him previously to advocate the setting up of the black farmer as well.[202] He was not only governor, but also the largest property owner in the island. In forwarding his survey of Jamaica's land distribution to Secretary Arlington on 23 September 1670, he found it necessary to explain away the family's acquisition of 11,229 acres in St Andrew, St Catherine and St John's as follows: "Your Lordship will find great quantities of land granted to some persons among whom my son 6,000 acres whose name I made use of for myself having 400 Persons in Our Family and so but one half-acre due."[203]

The leading creole Pooh-Bah of the seventeenth century, as head of the government and uncrowned king of the privateers, as land baron and agent of the Royal Adventurers, he was well placed to ensure that public policy coincided with private interest; and when the official channels of the African slave trade proved too slow for his purposes, he could bypass the Navigation Acts and run in slaves from Dutch Curaçao.[204]

Modyford's fall from power in 1671 did not fundamentally alter the island's course. Privateering profits earned during his regime were merely diverted under Lynch's administration into increased sugar cultivation and increased slaving. The land grabbing also continued, and Lynch ended up the most propertied governor of all. He acquired some 30,000 acres during his term of office and died leaving about 22,000 acres in Port Royal, St Catherine, St Mary, St Thomas-in-the-East, St David, St Elizabeth, St James, Clarendon and a parish, Vere, named for his wife.[205]

Large landholdings dedicated to intensive sugar production based on a highly capitalized labour system made survival of the small to medium farmer precarious. The £500 capital outlay required for establishing a cocoa walk in the 1670s would not, in the same decade, have got sugar off the ground.[206] Cary Helyar costed the assets of his small Bybrook sugar estate in 1672 at £1,858 – his investment in slaves alone was £1,100[207] – and he had been subsidized by Modyford.[208] The small man, outside the corridors of patronage, re-emigrated. By the 1690s, official correspondence had become one sustained whine on the subject of white depopulation. Governor Sir William Beeston on 19 June 1696 wrote: "No people came in, many die, some get away from fear, others because they are in debt . . . so by many ways we decrease."[209] In December 1696, renewed schemes were on foot "to procure and encourage poor tradesmen and others to transport themselves".[210] But that class, within forty years of scouting the frontier, no longer saw Jamaica as the promised land. Barbadian history repeated itself in the Greater Antilles: "the mean people who are the strength get away, as they find opportunity to the northern plantations".[211] "The planters that are left", said Beeston on 27 February 1696, "are rich".[212]

At the same time, Beeston observed that although Jamaica could easily absorb ten thousand men, the British government would have to be prepared to finance any such mass migration, "for the planters would contribute nothing towards it".[213] Gilbert Heathcote, who presented the petition which pressed for this migration, strongly urged the strict enforcement of the

Deficiency Law by which planters should keep one white servant to every ten slaves; but Heathcote himself admitted that "he spoke this as an Englishman, against his interest as a planter".[214]

The planting interest in the matter was clear. Jamaica's ruling class saw itself as the only planting class: the little man, whether free or bonded, was solicited in time of war and unrest as a militiaman, in time of peace as a tradesman. During the French naval and military threat to Jamaica's security in the 1690s, "being sensible of their weakness", Jamaicans strengthened legislation to attract white servants.[215] With the end of the war and the dissipation of their fears by the Treaty of Ryswick in 1697, the Council of Trade and Plantations shrewdly observed, "the planters will not now think it to their interest to invite others thither".[216] Indeed, in the following year Beeston found it necessary to impose penalties on Jamaican proprietors in order to pressure them into buying white servants.[217]

Projects for re-attracting "the mean people" persisted throughout the eighteenth century. A memorial of the Council of Jamaica to the Council of Trade and Plantations on 13 March 1716 contained one of the more enlightened and comprehensive contemporary statements of the criteria required "to augment the number of provision plantations and small settlements in which and not in great plantations the strength of the planting interest with respect to numbers of white people must consist".[218] The memorial recommended putting a halt to further large land grants, taxing the holders of idle lands, and building up a fund "to give credit to such new settlers for a slave or two for six months provision at least and for proper tools. . . . These newcomers should also be exempted from all taxes and all dutys civile and military (except only in cases of insurrection or invasion) for the first three years."[219]

Immigration schemes of the period attempted, with varying degrees of conviction, to embody some or all of these proposals. None achieved the desired results.[220] Some were conceived as private enterprise ventures but failed to find takers.[221]

The majority were official schemes, depending for implementation on the availability of Crown lands. Attention focused on the parish of Portland, which, being relatively undeveloped in the eighteenth century, seemed to offer the necessary potential. The process of acquiring the required acreage became a thorny issue. Governor Lawes found in fact that most of it had already been patented for "upwards of forty years, although no quit rents [had] been paid for any part of it".[222] When the question of Crown acquisition came up for consideration by Council and Assembly, "private views and interest govern'd".[223] Portland, in any event, was Maroon country; few established creole planters were themselves prepared to tackle the difficult task of its development.

White fear of being a defenceless minority reached a peak during the 1730s when Maroon aggression was at its most menacing. This motivated renewed schemes to procure young children who would grow into loyal creole workers. It was the unanimous opinion of the Assembly in March 1730 that "boys and girls of seven years old and upwards [should be] brought over at the public expense and supported and provided for by the public till bound to the inhabitants as apprentices".[224]

The climate was one of desperation, but the battle against white depopulation was nevertheless being lost, in the words of a contemporary, "by the petulance of the inhabitants or the exorbitant avarice of a few leading men who have eat up all their poor neighbours and expelled them [from] the island".[225]

The strictly limited roles envisaged by the plantocracy for "their poor neighbours" were reflected in the type of package-deal settlement schemes discussed by the Jamaican Assembly and presented to the British government for its approval on the eve of the first Maroon war. The proposal was that "10,000 men, not regular troops, but married men of some trade be raised and sent from England under half-pay officers etc . . . with a promise of a grant of land as soon as the Negroes were reduced".[226] As an incentive for tracking down the rebel blacks, £10 per head was offered for each one taken: "Every soldier who shall go out in this service, having a wife or family, such wife or family shall be subsisted during such soldier's being out in the country's service." Should he be killed or maimed on the job, "a competent provision" would be made for his wife and family.[227] Each soldier who settled down in Jamaica after being discharged would receive £4 per month. The size of his land grant was not spelt out, the suggestion being that the Maroon lands should be divided among the ex-soldiers after the guerillas were quelled.[228] The functions designed for these men, in short, were to rid the island of the black rebels, then take root, service the estates and multiply in numbers adequate to sustain such servicing.

After 1740, when the truce with the Maroons was concluded, it seemed possible to open up the northeast hinterland with safety, and assisted immigration schemes continued.[229] They involved direct land grants and cash advances to newcomers, as well as payments to established planters who introduced more whites.[230] The act of 1749 for "better and more effectual Encouragement of White Families to become settlers and for giving a bounty to certain Artificers to come over and exercise their Trades" provided each immigrant family with free passage, twenty-acre lots of land, a house valued at £50 and a black slave. A planter responsible for settling an immigrant family received £145 and was allowed to claim each member of the family for saving deficiency for four years.[231] Between 1739 and 1754, public expenditure for these purposes totalled £33,609 13s. 8d.[232] Between 1734 and 1754, the Crown made 208 grants of land to immigrants, who came mainly from Great Britain, the Leeward Islands and North America.[233] During this period, fewer than two hundred families settled.[234]

The failure of peace-time policies for encouraging white population growth made it clear that an irreversible socio-economic process (see table 1.4) had, by the mid-century, made the survival of the small developer difficult, if not impossible.

The problems of would-be farmers and planters of the northeast section of the island brought home to the House of Assembly the obstacles in the way of white small-scale settlement. Promotion of this area had been in progress since the 1730s, and the Crown had acquired 30,000 acres of uncultivated land in Manchioneal and Norman's Valley. An act of 1736 offered what seemed relatively liberal land grants which could reach maximum of 300 acres per family.[235] By 1749, it was feasible to do some stocktaking.

Table 1.4   The Growth of Jamaica's Sugar Economy, 1703–1768

Year	White Population	Enslaved Population	Value of Sugar Exports (£'000)
1703	7,000	45,000	287
1739	10,000	99,239	652
1754	12,000	130,000	1,025
1768	17,949	166,914	1,871

The House of Assembly on the 3 May considered the petition "of several inhabitants of Manchioneal, St Thomas-in-the-East".[236] Thirty-three cases were presented. They involved immigrants, nearly all married, who had arrived to attempt settlement, each with an average of between two and three children and about nine slaves. They received capital loans from public funds, which ranged in value from £344 3s. 10d. to £18 16s. 1d. each.[237] Some pursued the trades of bricklayer, shoemaker and carpenter. One or two were employed as overseer or bookkeeper on estates; three kept cattle-pens, and about five tried cane cultivation with "small sugar works". After approximately seven years of pioneering effort they all admitted to insolvency.[238]

The following are revealing cases:

> John Hogg . . . brought a wife, one child and one white man; he hath now a wife and four Negroes; he lived seven years upon the land granted him, but at present he lives at Port Mourant and follows the trade of a shoemaker; he hath no Negroes upon his settlement; he received from the public £88. 2s. 6d.[239]

> William Boyle brought to the island a wife and six children and thirty-two Negroes; . . . he hath now a wife, and eight or nine children and hath but ten Negroes; . . . the said Boyle is now so much reduced by the loss of his slaves that he hath been forced to throw up a sugar-work that he had in great forwardness; he received from the public, £160. 10s. 8d.[240]

> William Hinde . . . brought his wife and five children, and four Negroes; he is dead, but his wife, four children and one negro are living; he quitted his settlement before the seven years expired and resided in Kingston, where he followed the trade of a carpenter and there he died; his settlement is entirely thrown up; he received from the public, £172. 5s. 10d.[241]

> Mary Hooker, widow, brought three children and four Negroes and hath now three children and three Negroes; that she is very poor; she received from the public £89. 19s. 10d.[242]

In these circumstances, the House approved "total remission of all the debts . . . due to the public by the several persons therein mentioned".[243]

Cases of indigent immigrants continued to appear before the House claiming relief of indebtedness.[244] Alice Moon's petition, which came up in November 1753, was a touching one: her husband, Robert Moon, "having heard of the encouragement given by the legislature of this island to persons

indigent white settlers

that shall become settlers", set out from New York in March 1753, leaving behind his wife, who was pregnant, and one child. She was due to follow him as soon as was convenient; but owing to the sickness of her children and the subsequent death of the infant, she did not leave for Jamaica until the following year and arrived there in August 1753 to find her husband had been dead for two months. The House allowed her £40 for herself and her child's passage and maintenance for the period of stay in Jamaica.[245]

On behalf of the Assembly, a committee of accounts in 1758 reviewed the island's "several laws for introducing of white people to the country".[246] They scrutinized in particular the workings of the act passed in 1750 "for the better and more effectual encouragement of white families to become settlers in this island and for giving a bounty to certain artificers to come over and exercise their various trades". They commented on the great public expense involved in implementing such an act, which had nevertheless failed to answer "the ends for which the legislature intended it".[247] The House therefore agreed to its repeal.[248]

WHITE WOMEN IN SOCIETY'S CONSCIOUSNESS

If the white man of limited resources was not easily accommodated by the creole socio-economic system of the eighteenth century, how much more the woman? The white female who was part of the great house complex had her niche assured, limitations not withstanding. But at other levels of society, she appeared irrelevant. By masculine tradition, women had no artisan's skills. Woman as militiaman with striking exceptions, was inconceivable. One such exception was Mrs Mary Woodhouse, widow, who in 1748 earned the approval of the House of Assembly by her spirited stand against Spanish attackers in the midst of yet another European war for New World trade. She petitioned the House to compensate her for the property she had lost during the skirmish and, in examining her case, the committee of the House found an inspiring female epic. Her house had been the object of

> a desperate attack . . . both by firearms and broad axes . . . the doors and windows being much cut with the axes and tore with a shot discharged through the same . . . very good defence was made from the said dwelling house, and the enemy obliged to retire without entering the same – there is good reason to believe of several of

them were dangerously wounded and one of them mortally; . . . on their retiring they carried with them the following Negroes which were in their outhouse, the property of said Mary Woodhouse, 3 men, 2 cattle-boys, 2 women, Benneba and Bess with her sucking child . . .

As a result of her losses, Mary Woodhouse became "greatly reduced in her circumstances and has been obliged to abandon her dwelling and is truly an object of compassion deserving the consideration of the House and the rather, as the resolute defence made will be a means to deter the enemy from the like attempts". The House allowed her £400.[249]

Few fighting women, however, appear on the records. They were much more likely to be in search of aid and protection. The largest number were widows, who in the absence of their menfolk looked to the official paternal machinery to provide them and their families with relief from debt and destitution.[250] As a rule, they received sympathetic responses. On occasion, they even got preferential treatment, as in the case of Sarah Palmer and Mary Harding, widows of St Catherine who petitioned the Assembly on 10 May 1733, "praying relief in regard to their poverty, against the tax on retailers of wine".[251] The House granted their petition and, after debate, further agreed that "widows in general should be relieved against the said tax"; but a similar request from the tavern keepers of Port Royal for tax relief was refused.[252] Such women were obviously regarded as "objects of compassion" and, in the rough context of the time, the male establishment must have seen them as social and financial liabilities rather than as pioneering assets.

Officialdom as a consequence was either lukewarm or negative, where it was not hostile, to female immigration. Female convicts, for example, were rejected by masculine bureaucracy, not so much because they were convicts as because they were women. In the midst of the 1690s depopulation crisis, Jamaican merchants refused to accept an offer of eighty convicts condemned to transportation "because most of them were women and because persons of bad character were not wanted in Jamaica!"[253] On investigating the general immigration policy in the British Caribbean, the Board of Trade discovered that convicts were on the whole unwelcome, female convicts doubly so. The following year, it tried its best to hawk a batch of fifty Newgate inmates in the colonies but found few buyers. Jamaica's position was that it would have the women on condition that 150 men were sent with them.[254] Women, as malefactors, were clearly not the issue: the merchants complained that "they could not prevail with any to go to Jamaica except a few poor families of more women and children than men who would not serve their end".[255]

Jamaica's Deficiency Laws demonstrated how little real concern existed about the size of the female population.[256] They constituted one of the main legislative instruments of the eighteenth century for promoting white increase. The act of 1703 "to encourage the importation of white men" required a planter to keep one white man for each ten slaves, up to the number of twenty, and then one for each twenty thereafter; he was liable to pay a fine for each man of which he was deficient.[257] The 1703 act and similar bills all ignored women as potential immigrants, capable of saving deficiency.

The Council of Trade and Plantations observed this neglect and, on 25 April 1715, advised Lord Hamilton, governor of Jamaica, accordingly: "As the Island can never be peopled without a sufficient number of white women, it seems necessary that all persons should be obliged for every 20 negroes to keep one white woman, or rather that two white women shou'd be reckoned equivalent to one white man."[258]

In the following year, Jamaica's Council echoed the views of the Council of Trade and Plantations. It agreed that in order to redress the "unhappy state of [our] affairs", namely the racial imbalance, it was desirable to consider the role of women in population growth. "Indeed," it wrote, "what seems most defective in these laws is that there is no provision for the encouragement of women which defect we hope may be remedy'd hereafter."[259]

Over a decade passed, however, before a legislative remedy was attempted, during which time the Deficiency Laws became a casualty of the plantation system. The purchase of black slave labour even for the traditional occupations of white labour became the economic practice, and the value of the fine imposed for breaches of the law never equalled the cost to the planter of importing and employing a white man. By the 1730s, the Deficiency Laws were essentially revenue, rather than population measures.[260] In any event, the provision in the 1730 act for encouraging women was based on the calculation of the Council of Trade and Plantations, a calculation that equated one woman to half a man and proceeded to enshrine this in successive acts.[261] And since it was then becoming clear that the immigrants that these laws purported to encourage were really marginal to the colony's needs, by this sort of social arithmetic, women were twice as marginal. Prevalent attitudes of male supremacy had reinforced the values of the plantation and directed immigration policies accordingly. As the eighteenth century advanced, Jamaica, now swept along on the assembly line of cane field, factory and market, had become a business; and the world of business is "a man's world".

Peripheral to the economy, women, particularly of the middle and lower classes, also became peripheral to society's consciousness. Absenteeism, which was primarily a white upper-class phenomenon, has so clouded past and present perspectives on Jamaica as to negate the reality of the non-absentees, black and white, male and female, now being belatedly restored to history. Secondary whites, in fact, never completely disappeared from the scene.[262] Had the island's economic imperatives been otherwise, they might have been more numerous and more visible. Many did however stubbornly persist, and many of them were female. Richard Sheridan points out that in the parish of St Andrew in 1753 there were 154 estates, of which "128 produced no sugar but were engaged on a moderate scale in raising provisions, coffee, ginger, livestock and cotton".[263] A list of Jamaican landholders at about the same period showed 177 women, of whom 133 were medium to small proprietors, scattered mainly throughout St Elizabeth, Westmoreland, Vere and St Andrew.[264] Sheridan estimates that, in the 1770s, the island had "455 sugar plantations and probably a greater number of minor staple plantations, provision farms and cattle pens".[265] Edward Long's calculations at that time make clear that there were always more white women on these lesser estates than on the large sugar plantations.[266]

As long as thousands of acres of Jamaica's land remained "beyond the sugar line", the pioneer domestic farmer never became extinct.[267] Geographically on the fringe, economically and statistically overlooked, the hinterland provided right into the nineteenth century a challenge to the island's historical frontier instincts, its continuum to be ultimately established by a black, family-oriented, hillside peasantry. But slave society cared to project exclusively its vision of the great house and the great house lady. The only white women of whom Long wrote were of this class.[268] That its numbers were infinitesimal was irrelevant; it was its image that mattered.

A significant transformation in contemporary regard for the female character accompanied this increasing focus on the elitist woman. In the seventeenth century, there had been frank recognition of the possibility that a white female could be disreputable. "You shall see a common woman", wrote

[handwritten annotation: prior to this the image of white women was the elite respectable white woman]

John Taylor in 1680s, "only in her smock . . . barefooted without shoe or stocking, with a straw hat and tobacco pipe in their mouths . . . and thus they [go] about their streets in their warlike position, and thus arrayed they will booze a cup of punch easily with anyone."[269]

Mary Carleton, alias German Princess, notorious convict on forced arrival in Kingston in 1671 wondered, with delight, "to see so many of [her] acquaintances".[270] If pregnant female pirates, dressed in men's clothes and sentenced to hang,[271] were possibly unusual even for their time, Port Royal's loose women were commonplace. They were, Taylor maintained, "a crew of vile strumpets and common prostitutes", against whom not the "Cage, whips, nor ducking Stool would prevail".[272] A recently built House of Correction was one hope for their reform:[273] its effects might in time, it was hoped, "somewhat abate the malignity of that walking pest and allay the furies of those hot amazons".[274] But apparently they continued to be irrepressible, even at the turn of the century in the wake of natural disaster.[275]

Impropriety was not the monopoly of the lower classes. The eminent doctor Sir Hans Sloane treated his share of female drunks of all ranks and other women of suspect habits.[276] The leading "scarlet woman" of the time came straight out of the top drawer, and because of her social prominence, the Manning-Beckford domestic scandal of the 1730s was reviewed, in every prurient detail, by the Jamaican House of Assembly. Her misdeeds included interracial "criminal conversations".[277]

The establishment seemed only superficially concerned about its women's conduct. Attempts to flush out prostitutes from the expeditionary forces, after the debacle in St Domingo in 1655, were part of a rearmament campaign, more military than moral in intention.[278] It has been already noted that female criminality could be tolerated under the smoke screen of the male presence.[279] The penalties imposed by law on "such as beget a woman servant with child" unequivocally aimed at compensating the employer's loss of labour, rather than the servant's loss of virtue.[280] No sustained legislative policy for casting out the adulteress, comparable to that of Puritan New England, existed: only the occasional offender caught the official eye and, then, just for the treasurer's books, such as "£1.8.9. by a fine from whorish woman".[281]

There is no evidence of any conscious reformative process at work on the manners and morals of the white woman during the first century of her arrival in Jamaica. Nevertheless, what unquestionably altered, in direct ratio to her dwindling numbers, was society's view of her and with it, no doubt, her view of herself. By the last quarter of the eighteenth century, the drunks and bawds, thieves and adulteresses had practically vanished. The women whom Edward Long[282] and Bryan Edwards[283] saw were all impeccable ladies of quality, modest and temperate. Not only had the Jamaican white woman become genteel, she was also utterly sober and chaste. Long considered few more irreproachable in their actions than creole women and, after considering carefully all the disadvantages which they suffered as a consequence of being creole, concluded that "their virtues and merits seem justly entitled to our highest encomium, and their frailties and failings to our mildest censure".[284] Essentially what had occurred during these first formative hundred years was that the discarded vices of the white woman, like her other hand-me-downs, had fallen to the lot of the black woman.

2   The Arrivals of Black Women

There is an epic dimension to the theme of Afro-American migration, which has – significantly – received impressive treatment in the verse-trilogy of the poet/historian Edward (Kamau) Brathwaite;[1] and yet, profound and wide-ranging as is Brathwaite's perception of the black nomadic experience, his assumptions are almost exclusively those of "the poor, pathless, harbourless spade" who is male. But slavery and the slave trade, providing as they did a crude levelling off of sexual distinctions, ensured that the woman too shared every inch of the man's physical and spiritual odyssey.

WOMEN IN PRE-COLONIAL AFRICA: MYTH VERSUS REALITY

African women were among the original victims of European slave trading. The Portuguese Gomes Bannes de Azurara, whose chronicle contains evidence of the earliest Guinea coast commerce in Africans, tells of the black Moorish slave woman, in 1441, whose male owners allegedly fled, abandoning her to a party of white raiders led by Antom Gonçalvez, the pioneer Portuguese trader. This unexpectedly easy success encouraged Gonçalvez and others to pursue the traffic:[2] apocryphal, perhaps, but suggestive of the centuries of justification which followed that first assault and which implied Africa's precedence and acquiescence in its own enslavement and that of its womenfolk.[3] The facts about pre-colonial African women have been to a great extent distorted in the tales of seventeenth- and eighteenth-century adventurers whose perspectives were masculine and Eurocentric and who, furthermore, seldom had access to Africa's inner life.

For centuries after his first intrusion into Africa, the white man remained a stranger on the threshold.[4] The policy of abstention imposed on foreigners, right into nineteenth and twentieth centuries, evolved naturally out of traditional concepts of the community's relationship to its environment, the lineal ownership of land for instance, governed by powerful religious sanctions, which forbade alienation.[5] Social and domestic institutions, also manifestations of the religious belief system, remained among the main areas of native existence, which were screened from the eyes of the outsider. Women in some countries, such as Benin, which was placed in early contact with the white trader, could only be approached on pain of death.[6]

But even if it had been possible to see her condition in depth, and to assess the African woman accurately, this was not the purpose of the newcomers to the continent. Continuing the apologetics of the Portuguese pathfinder, successive generations of Europeans used what they conceived to be the status of women in "primitive" culture, as the gauge of civilization. Show us, they said, the level of women in society, and we will show you the level of the whole society.[7] This was valid to a point, but was compromised by the need to establish, whatever the evidence, that the female in Africa was degraded, *ipso facto* that Africa was degraded: enslavement then was justifiable.

The notion of masculine superiority inspired the ordering of the social hierarchy in Europe, as in Africa. White men, however, failed to admit their common inheritance with black men in this as in many other respects. Both had in fact developed matrimonial systems reflecting the principle of a double morality. Both, in general terms, legalized and sanctified sexual unions between men and women, imposed strict chastity on the wife under heavy penalties, and permitted the husband freedom with impunity to cohabit with other women.[8] But there were essential differences. European monogamy formalized the ideal of a mutually exclusive alliance between one man and one woman: then under cover of darkness, created a whole class of women "outside the pale", the only conceivable partners in extramarital sex. The fallen woman in extremity was the prostitute, rationalized by masculine thought into a necessary evil. "Remove prostitutes from human affairs," St Augustine had declared, "and you would pollute the world with lust."[9]

Hundreds of years later, E.H. Lecky wrote: "Herself the supreme type of vice, she [the prostitute] is ultimately the most efficient guarding of virtue."[10] With perhaps equal sophistry, but infinitely more compassion, African polygyny organized the right of the husband to move openly from one female to another; but the "other" woman could also be a wife.

European sensitivity was shocked to find the male capacity for multiple mating so institutionalized within marriage. Polygyny became a strong factor in external assessments of man/woman relationships in Africa and a vital measuring rod of the status of the continent. White male observers testified to the widespread incidence of polygyny throughout the countries of west and central Africa from which Jamaican slaves came in the seventeenth and eighteenth centuries.[11] As chief factor for the Dutch at Elmina, William Bosman extensively explored Guinea in the late seventeenth century, and he wrote of the Gold Coast: "Each man marries as many wives as he pleases, or is consistent with his circumstances, though they seldom exceed twenty, but are commonly contented with a number betwixt three and ten and these who would appear very great complete the mentioned number of twenty."[12]

These female symbols of conspicuous male consumption appeared to the European to be also objects of economic exploitation. "Most of these wives", continued Bosman,

> are obliged to till the ground, plant Milhio or Jommes, or otherwise work for their Husbands, and to take care that he finds something to eat when he comes home.
> . . . Whilst the man can only idly spend his time in impertinent tattling (the Women's business in our Country) and drinking of Palm wine which the poor wives are frequently obliged to raise money to pay for and by their labour maintain and satisfy these lazy wretches their greedy thirst after wine.[13]

Another Dutch writer of the same period, Nyendael, speaks of masses of indolent men on the Slave Coast, who lay "the whole burtoen of their work on their wives and slaves, whether it be tilling the ground, spinning of cotton, weaving of cloathes or any other handicraft whilst they, if they have but the least stock, apply themselves to merchandise alone".[14] "The women of Benin", Bosman stated, "are as much slaves as in any place in this Kingdom."[15] Foreign witnesses testified that their servitude implied sexual exploitation as well. "Several Negroes are so brutal that they marry many Wives only to got a good living by them and to wear gilt Horns [they] give their wives full order to entice other men . . . which done these she Brutes immediately tell their Husbands who know very well how to fleece the Amorous Spark."[16]

These unfavourable views of women within the African marriage system became firmly lodged in the European mind, carrying with it serious implications for the subsequent judgment of the Jamaican woman. Polygyny was seen as a repulsive institution, symptomatic of black masculine oppression, and its offshoot, black female debasement. It stood out, as Philip Curtin suggests, as "a special evil, epitomizing the low condition of women and hence the low state of society".[17] an excuse to debase black women in Jamaica

It is fortunate that modern research in a number of disciplines, anthropological, archaeological and linguistic, in conjunction with extensive use of oral traditions, now makes possible the reinterpretation of the old travellers' tales in more rational terms.[18] The dialogue between historian and anthropologist has been especially fruitful in the reconstruction of social institutions which are common to a relatively homogenous West African complex. Their complementary findings give evidence of a cultural continuum which is solidly grounded in a living past. They make it possible to do greater justice to the reality of the African woman who underwent and who survived the Middle Passage.

There is no doubt that plurality of wives reflected the nearly universal acceptance of the theory of male superiority over the female, whose labour could be exploited within the marriage system. The majority of the West African societies were masculine dominated: religious and public, as well as domestic authority and decision-making resided in the man.[19] As head of a patrilocal subsystem, his control extended over an ever widening concentric of kin, composed of wives and their offspring, sons, their wives, grandsons and granddaughters, further spreading out to embrace domestic slaves. It was understood that the woman's reproductive capacity, as well as her labour, were subjects of masculine command; hence her marriage, which effected the transfer of these assets to another male authority, was something outside of her control. The male members of the kin involved usually decided and exchanged her bride-price. The man's vested interest in her fertility and economic value influenced family customs: part of her earnings in some countries, whether by agriculture, craft or trade, belonged to her husband. Female adultery was harshly punished, and the damage assessment was based on conventions concerning encroachment on property. She was disposable after marriage, as well as before. The most uxorious of autocrats, the king of Benin, distributed his wives at will to favourite subjects. Women were more likely than men to be used as pawns in the settlement of debts. Lesser men, as well as monarchs, bequeathed them to their heirs: some, when widowed, were condemned to ritual death.

West Africa was unquestionably a masculine domain; but it was also more than that. It was a cultural milieu, in which a varied range of human associations was carefully identified and carefully regulated. It spelt out in detail its sexual, matrimonial and inheritance patterns, giving precise definition to the woman's status and simultaneously modifying her "subordination" in ways unknown to European male chauvinism.[20] It clarified the man's responsibilities to the woman. The procedure of bride wealth, for example, confirmed his obligations to her, as well as his rights in her. Her pregnancy imposed on him ceremonially prescribed duties owed to her and to the child.[21] The transfer of a man's widow to his sons was not exclusively, or even primarily an act of proprietorship, but fulfilled the deceased man's heritable responsibility to secure her place in a household.[22]

Traditional forms of social machinery not easily assessed by European travellers, in fact, expressed the view of the woman, not so much as inferior to the man but as dissimilar to him. Evans Pritchard's description of the role and function of women in pre-industrial societies is applicable: it was "less a matter of level than a difference of status".[23] West African mores emphasized the woman's complementary, but clearly separate, existence, and proceeded to organize many of its institutions on the premise of her unique attributes and needs.

Feminine biology directed the essential puberty rites of West African peoples,[24] and a girl was not regarded as an adult until she knew how her body functioned. It was assumed that among other things, womanhood implied the capacity for sexual initiatives and response. Sex education was a necessary accomplishment, certain communities seeing it as more appropriate to women than to men;[25] young girls were accordingly initiated, under the skilled guidance of mature women. Female societies were a highly formalized medium of such training. They shielded girls from all male contact, in some cases, for as long as a year. Their novitiate included practices as well in domestic skills, in the intricacies of buying and selling – for trading was stressed among the Ibo, Ashantis and Dahomeans as an occupational prerogative of women, the community's entrepreneurs *par excellence*.[26] The militant Mendes of Sierra Leone looked to their women for expertise in producing war medicines, which they developed in secret female societies.[27] When the young initiate re-entered tribal life, they were equipped for their particular social and economic, as well as marital, responsibilities.

The woman's biological processes, personal to herself, were also important concerns of her kin and household. Menstruation, pregnancy and lactation imposed magico-religious restraints on her physical contact with male members of her family. The Ibo ex-slave Olaudah Equiano remembered how irksome these taboos were to him as a boy. "I was so fond of my mother," he wrote, "I could not keep from her, or avoid touching her at some of these periods, in consequence of which, I was obliged to be kept out with her in a little house made for that purpose till offering was made and then we were purified."[28]

Periodic abstention from sexual intimacies between spouses, in the case of lactation for as long as two or three years, was legitimized by religion and tradition. "Both men and women", wrote Barbot about Sierra Leone, "account it a great crime and infamy to transgress this custom."[29] The polygynous family unit ordered itself accordingly, and the tabooed wife's duties, sexual as well as domestic (for example, the preparation of food), devolved on her co-wives.

Such households illustrate the extent to which the tight, nuclear relationship between husband and wife familiar to the European world was de-emphasized in West Africa within a wide circle of reciprocal rights. The introduction of an additional wife became the affair not only of the men and women and their respective kin, but of the man's co-wives, who also had an economic interest in his increased possessions and the added prestige he enjoyed with each new acquisition.[30] Head wives were often involved in the choice of other wives and ceremonially helped to integrate them into the family.

The story of Baba of Karo, a Muslim Hausa woman, illustrates the many dimensions of a polygynous situation from the female perspective. As the new wife of Malam Maigari, she was taken on her first entry into her husband's compound to the hut of his senior wife who, together with her kinswomen, received Baba. The old and new wives, through the intermediary of their respective sisters and best women friends, exchanged customary gifts of money: the bridegroom gave presents of equal value to his head wife and his bride.[31] Baba continued her story:

> The head wife comes and "buys the bride's speech". She says "there it is; I have bought your mouth!" The bride says "thank you," and they greet one another. Then later on in the morning, when there is no one about in the compound the bride covers her head and goes to the head wife's hut in her best clothes, to greet her. I remember Malam Margari's head wife was cooking nice food – rice and stew – then she sent for me and I went and we ate together. We chatted, then at noon our husband's mother came and brought me ten kolanuts and six hundred cowries; she came to look at the dowry, I covered up my head like this. I used to call her "Mother of Idirisu". She saw the hut looking nice, she was pleased.[32]

It was customary for the groom to spend the first four days in his new wife's hut, while the chief wife prepared the meals. The wives then exchanged roles for the next two days: the bride began to cook, she uncovered her head and by the seventh day she had become "a daughter of the house".[33]

The provision and preparation of the food by the woman for the men and children were fundamental obligations which affected her standing in the domestic hierarchy. The whole concept of sustenance, the support of life, contained a range of hidden meanings which were concretized in the ceremonials and taboos surrounding food. They all contributed to creating a mystique around the food-provider, woman, subtly enhancing her prestige and authority,[34] as well as her economic status.

There was real dispersal of power within the polygynous household, in which the principal wife stood, second in command to the husband, as the lynchpin of domestic organization and harmony. The economic life of the compound, in which the woman farmed, traded, wove, potted clay, represented, not so much exploitation of female labour, as a division of duties between the sexes and the collective as well as the individual effort of women. The Dahomeans allowed the woman to keep her personal earnings, as a result of which some achieved independent wealth.[35] The practical and ritualized roles prescribed for women of the family in the vital phases of the life cycle (birth, puberty, marriage, and death) gave them claims to the community's high regard. The effective cooperation of co-wives in their own common cause *vis-à-vis* the husband was possible, and even genuine affection among such women was not unusual.[36] "The woman who has no friends among her co-wives", says a traditional Yoruba song, "needs good character indeed."

A close personal relationship was possible between the individual husband and wife. Evans Pritchard warns against the tendency to judge the external forms of social arrangements, rather than their "psychological and moral content".[37] Jealousy among wives, for instance, has been widely attested, pointing to a natural envy of the privileges which might accrue to a favourite. It also indicates the crosscurrents of love and hate which were present within the conventional pattern of communal concerns. Baba said of her marriage to Malam Maigari,

> That night Malam Maigari brought one thousand cowries and twenty kolanuts and some perfume when he came to my hut; the children were teasing him, then when everyone was asleep and I had put out the lamp and lain down, he came in. He said, "light the lamp so I can see your eyes." I hid my eyes, I felt shy. When he had lit the lamp he said, "I thank you, I thank you. You have kept your promise. I thank you, I am happy." Then we made our marriage for fifteen years, but we had no children. Then I left him. I loved him very much, I left him because I had to – I had no children.[38]

Baba's life underlines the most important fact about the African woman's condition. Her status as wife, although capable of sustaining deep feelings for a husband, was clearly subordinate to her status as mother. This leads one anthropologist to note that the basic facts about polygyny are that "several mother-child units exist and that one male is responsible for them – circulating among them as it were";[39] whereas "the conjugal tie is variable, . . . the mother-tie is inevitable and given".[40]

Motherhood, the fulfilment of female adulthood, above all else gave shape and meaning to the African woman's life cycle. "What else is marriage for?"[41] Puberty rites celebrated primarily the girl's physical readiness for childbearing, for fertility was her greatest gift. "The Wife", commented Bosman, "who is so fortunate as to be big with child, is very much respected by her Husband and waited on; besides which, if it is the first time, rich offerings are made to the False-God, to obtain her safe delivery."[42] The childless woman was an object of contempt, derision or compassion. Adoption was formalized into an acceptable substitute for natural parenthood. Baba of

Karo was both beneficiary and victim of this valuation of woman's prime function: early in her marriage she adopted a daughter, but her pride would not allow her to remain forever in a household where two other wives had together borne fourteen children, while she remained barren. In spite of her husband's pain at losing her, she insisted on going,[43] thereby exercising the right of wives in some polygynous societies to initiate divorce.[44] She expressed also the customary disapproval of those who held on selfishly to their offspring, refusing to share them. The Fulani were apparently prime offenders, unlike her own people: "We are Habe; we are different. Then too Fulani won't let their children be adopted, they don't like their laughter taken away to another compound; the child is their laughter and pleasure. We give children to our kinsman; if they have none of their own we cannot refuse them."[45]

This elevation of fertility and motherhood grew naturally out of a belief system grounded in ancestral veneration. It saw blood as the life force, through which a man's kin, dead, living and unborn, procured for him integration into his universe. The kinship web lay at the heart of spiritual faith and inspired the social structure.[46] Woman was at the centre of that web, guaranteeing its endless proliferation. If she were "carrier of burdens", she was also "carrier of roots".

Bride wealth was in this context more than the simplistic "purchase" of a wife. As Melville Herskovits pointed out, it included "much that was ceremonial in character, and of little intrinsic value".[47] It became symbolic of the clan's transfer of its most valued possession: the reproductive power of its women, which made its continuity possible. Their functions in this respect were emphasized in those West African societies (notably among the Akan Ashanti peoples) in which matrilineal kinship structures charged women with the responsibility of ensuring succession and inheritance. Ideas of male supremacy, added to matrilineal inheritance, produced a family hierarchy in which the maternal uncle exercised the greatest authority.[48] "The most obvious results of a social organization formed on such lines", says Rattray, "is to raise immediately the status of women in the community, and when matrilineal descent is found in a society which is frankly communistic, we seem to have in these factors in many parts of Africa the key to the importance of women."[49] He continues: "The whole concept of 'mother-right' affords the woman a protection and a status that is more than an adequate safeguard against ill-treatment by any male or group of males. . . . Her children belong to her and her clan, not to that of her husband."[50]

Her kinship connection remained a crucial determinant of her condition and ensured her integrity as an individual. She belonged primarily to her kin, and incidentally to her husband. The bride's virginity, the wife's adultery, was not solely the affair of two persons: it was the proper concern of her subgroup. As Gluckman has pointed out, the weakening of the marital bond was the price paid for membership of a wider group;[51] but this had its rewards, for dispersal of affection and loyalty involved numerous other persons who accepted responsibility for the woman's welfare. Rattray says of the Ashanti, "no woman stands alone, for behind the woman stands a united family, bound by the tie of blood".[52] The strong links that were possible, particularly between sister and brother, were expressed by the Ibo Equiano, in flowery but significant terms:

> When these people knew we were brother and sister they indulged us to be together, and the man to whom I supposed we belonged lay with us, he in the middle while she and I held one another by the hands across his breast all night and thus for a while we forgot our misfortunes in the joy of being together: but even this small comfort was soon to have an end, for scarcely had the fatal morning appeared when she was again torn from me for ever! I was now more miserable, if possible, than before. The small relief which her presence gave me from pain was gone, and the wretchedness of my situation was redoubled by my anxiety after her fate and my apprehensions lest her sufferings should be greater than mine, when I could not be with her to alleviate them. Yes, thou dear partner of all my childish sports! Thou sharer of my joys and sorrows! Happy should I have ever esteemed myself to encounter every misery for you, and to procure your freedom by the sacrifice of my own.[53]

Identification with her kin was carried through to death: observance of dual funeral rites by husband, and by family, symbolized the woman's role as mother/wife, as sister/daughter.[54]

Other relationships, outside of the kinship group, provided security for women. Herskovits directs attention to the value of such associations in Dahomean culture.[55] The segregated rites of puberty underlined the notion of a sisterhood of women – of the particular group of women who had learnt and endured together. Extra-familial bonds of friendship in some societies were as self-consciously ritualized and as powerfully sanctioned as the blood connection. M.G. Smith defines such an institution in its modern Nigerian form as follows: "Formal bond-friendship between persons of the same sex is a symmetrical relation of equals in status and age, with a variety of reciprocal obligations emphasizing the mutual identification of the partners. Between women, such bond friends are known as Kawaye (Kawa), and they exchange gifts on ceremonial occasions."[56] The importance of the best friend, as social, economic and emotional support for the woman, has been movingly demonstrated in the experience of Baba. In one of her many references to her Kawa, she says, "We consult one another, we discuss our affairs, her daughter is my daughter, her son is my son."[57]

Other status-granting criteria cut across sexual distinctions and gave a further lift to woman's position. Older women, like men, shared in the reverence due to age:[58] this was inspired not only by the conviction that wisdom comes with years, but by the customary emphasis laid on the authority of the ancestor, which provided the main focus of cultural unity and identity. Being close to the grave, the old were the living evidence of the ancestral spirits. They were, as well, the community's memory: they were surrounded by an elaborate code of etiquette and given due respect, regardless of their sex.[59]

Some societies endowed women with high priestly office. Bosman writes of the Slave Coast:

> Their religious offices are here celebrated by Men and Women together, both of which are held in such high veneration amongst the Negroes, that they are not liable to Capital Punishment or any crime whatsoever; the women which are promoted to the degree of Priestesses, tho some of them perhaps were but slaves before, are yet as much respected as the Priests, or rather more, insomuch that they pride themselves with the distinguishing name of God's children; and as all other women are obliged to a slavish service to their husbands, these on the contrary exert an absolute sway over them and their effects, living with them perfectly according to their Arbitrary Will and Pleasure; besides which, their Husbands are obliged to shew them so much respect, as they received from their wives before their becoming Priestesses, which is to spead to, and serve them upon their knees. For this reason, the most sensible Negroes will neither marry a Priestess, nor easily consent that any of their wives be raised to that honour. But if notwithstanding it happens, they must not oppose it, for if they did, they would be called to a severe

account for it, and look'd upon as men who endeavour'd to stop the common course of Divine Worship.[60]

Women also occupied high influential positions in public life. African society was highly stratified: enormous gaps existed between rulers and ruled. Women were found at the lowest rungs of society, as lesser wives and as slaves – although "slavery" was to a great extent a misnomer in pre-colonial Africa, being a mild form of domestic feudalism, in no way comparable to New World chattel slavery.[61] But as members of the elite, women could also occupy the highest rungs. They could be pawns or players in the power game. If frequently exploited, some could also exploit, thus upsetting the simple delineation of masculine dominance/feminine subordination; and the woman in fact could be a central figure in native myths of power. Hausa traditions of origin focused on dominant queens, of whom the legendary Amina of Zazzau stood out as a conqueror of vast territories.[62] The Congolese chronicles spoke of "the old mother of the tribe, Mpemba Nzinga", who directed the early mass migration that led to the founding of the kingdom of Kongo.[63]

But the powerful woman was not merely a creature of myth. Women of all civilizations, however inferior their legal status, have applied their personalities in various ways to influence affairs of state. In Africa, this was facilitated by the traditional deference paid to motherhood. The queen mother of the Ashanti, for example, was a figure of awe and fear, who exercised real authority, and her stool was senior to the king's.[64] Benin similarly elevated its dowager queen. "The king's mother", wrote Dapper, "is held in great esteem and has a splendid court, beautifully and magnificently built, where she resides with many women and daughters. She is consulted in all state affairs."[65] The sister of the Congolese king "held a very exalted position".[66] The women of the Dahomean royal household controlled the system of internal taxation.[67] Bosman wrote of Agouma on the Gold Coast, which "hath for some time past been governed by a woman, with as much courage and conduct as other countries are ruled by men. . . . This Governess is so wise, that to keep the Government entirely in her own hands, she lives unmarried."[68] It is significant that in the English attempt to supersede the Dutch at Elmina on the Gold Coast in the first decade of the eighteenth century, Sir Dalby Thomas, the governor, successfully used a woman friend, Aguaba Braffo, as the puppet queen, symbol of the British takeover.[69]

The recurring image of the female as the power behind the throne and at times the throne itself, exercising influence on the destiny of the state, was an additional element contributing to the composite form of African womanhood. European devaluation of that form, as has been suggested, arose from an incomplete understanding of the woman's cultural axis. Let us make no mistake about it: Africa was a black man's world, capable of insensitivity and brutality to women. But it was also a world constructed out of a religion and cosmology, which rationally analysed, deliberately and ceremonially anticipated, a whole host of human apprehensions and antagonisms.[70] Starting with the basic biological reality of women's unique function in the perpetuation of the race, the African mother-child connection became the seminal one: the man, unquestionably master of the universe, was primarily her mate, secondarily her spouse. The potentially neurotic exclusiveness of the European husband-wife partnership had limited relevance in that context. The African woman instead existed within a more extended range of familial and extra-familial interdependence, which widened and deepened the base of her foothold on her society.

White observers, operating from quite different cultural assumptions, motivated by their economic aims, focused almost exclusively on the elements of sexual and economic exploitation that they saw in the African woman's condition. They underrated the traditional network of social and spiritual supports, which served to diffuse the woman's status, giving her respect and self-respect. European enslavement uprooted her from a logical, human value system and threw her into the world of the market. It transformed her into mere cargo, her identity expressed through the transfer of an entry from a bill of lading to an estate inventory.

If indeed, as has been argued, their ancient culture was "the shield which frustrated the efforts of Europeans to dehumanise Africans through servitude",[71] it can also be argued that it was the African woman's perception of herself within that culture, which accompanied her across the Middle Passage and which helped to preserve her from total defeminization in the New World.

The Abominable Trade in Captives: Surviving the Middle Passage

It is particularly difficult to assess the psychic survival rate of the earliest African "arrivants", for whom the journey from continent to Caribbean islands was an extraordinarily broken one. In 1655, the English found approximately fifteen hundred Africans, slaves and ex-slaves, in Jamaica, who had been trickling in under the Spanish since 1513.[72] The majority escaped the net of occupation and initial colonization and could not be tempted from their mountain hideouts even by prospects of Anglo-Saxon citizenship.[73] Seven years after the English arrived, the black population numbered 552, about one-sixth of the whole.[74] "The want of Negroes", declared Sir Thomas Lynch, on 12 February 1665, was "the grand obstruction" to progress; "without them, the Plantation will decline, and people discouraged".[75] Jamaica had, therefore, a powerful interest in promoting the African slave trade by all means, fair and unfair; and although its funds were always scarce and its labour demands seemingly insatiable, by the end of the century, it could point to impressive results.

Between 1655 and 1700, eighty-eight thousand Africans arrived in the island,[76] ten times the volume of previous decades,[77] setting the pace for succeeding black immigration that did not ease until 1807 when the British trade in slaves ended. Unlike the commerce of the eighteenth century, which predominantly involved littoral peoples, the seventeenth-century trade was to a considerable extent of hinterland origin.[78] Approximately fifteen thousand of Jamaica's early slaves were of the large numbers sold to Portuguese and Dutch factors by the long-established Muslim Mandingo merchants who dominated the Senegalese and Gambian trade routes.[79] This meant acquiring slaves from great distances in the interior and transporting them to the coast by the overland slave coffles or by the river, the first hazardous and frequently fatal lap of the journey. This pattern of inland displacement recurred in the experience of thirty-four thousand others, or 39.5 per cent of the earliest arrivals, who came from the inner forest belts of Angola in Central Africa.[80] This area began as a major source in the seventeenth century and tapered off in the eighteenth century, but by the closing years of the slave trade was again proving a virtually endless reservoir of labour for Jamaica.[81]

The other main provenance of Africans in early English Jamaica was the Bight of Benin. This country supplied 24,300, or 27.6 per cent, of the slave population up to 1700.[82] Where the traders got their human merchandise from is not always absolutely clear; but the evidence suggest that here too the forest regions behind the coastal strips were the crucial source areas. James Barbot, for example, describes the three months cruising of a slaver on the Calabar River in 1700 while waiting on the canoes to return from their expedition to inland markets in search of cargo for the Atlantic voyage.[83]

The Middle Passage was therefore the terrible second stage of migration,[84] and not the last. It was, for many, the prelude to a no less terrible vortex of enforced mobility on the other side of the ocean.

Portugal and Spain had made untenable monopolist claims to the East and West Atlantic, the former demanding sole right to sell slaves on the West African coast and the latter the sole right to buy in the Indies. Dutch maritime strength had successfully challenged these presumptions and by the early seventeenth century controlled the Gambian and the Gold Coast slaving posts, extending trade activities from Senegal to Angola.[85] The scale of their enterprise allowed the Dutch to undersell their competitors by as much as 20 per cent.[86] They consequently dominated the slave market in the Antilles from their well-stocked depôts in St Eustatius and Curaçao.[87] Until the 1680s, after the Anglo-Dutch wars, when English traders came into their own,[88] these Dutch islands were for many Africans their first landfalls in the Caribbean.

Spanish inability to make it into their sacred *mare clausam* had resulted in the Caribbean being opened up to international revolution, outside the pale of international law. Rejecting all notions of peace beyond the line, the maritime nations of Europe left off their wars of religion, moved on to wars of trade and joined battle in the Indies for the New World. In their wake came the sea desperadoes who terrorized Antillean waters for over twenty-five years in search of loot, one prize among many being African slaves.[89]

Dutch trade, not having been blessed by Spain, was illegitimate. So it was from the smugglers' entrepôt of Curaçao that cargo was unloaded, sorted, and transshipped to the centres of demand in the mid-seventeenth century. These were the sugar colonies of the Eastern Caribbean, the scene of a revolution within a revolution, the colonial process by which small adventurers bowed out of island after island, leaving the field clear to large adventurers.[90]

For thousands of Africans, the property of white settlers on the move, Barbados, Antigua, St Christopher, Suriname were stopover ports of call on the northward trek.[91] Between 1655 and 1674, one-third of Jamaica's slaves reached by way of Barbados.[92] In 1701, a total of sixteen thousand had travelled the inter-island route, leaving no full record of the shipwrecked and the intercepted.[93]

Arrival in Jamaica was not necessarily the end of journeying. As those early footloose pioneers found themselves forced out, and on to the next colonial venture, the mainland north, they packed their black baggage too. Jamaica, launching pad for raids on Spanish Cuba, Hispaniola and Middle America, became another privateers' paradise, another centre of illicit slave transfers. As English naval strength grew and legitimized itself, it acquired the *Asiento* in 1713, the mercantilist status symbol *par excellence*, the privilege of selling Africans to Spaniards in the Americas.[94] Jamaica replaced the Dutch islands as the leading slave emporium, shipping out almost as many blacks as it retained for its own use.[95] Strategically, the island became a focal point in the colonial wars of Holland, England, France and Spain.[96]

Whether as personal luggage or as contraband, article of trade or booty of war, the first thousands of African men and women circled the Caribbean archipelago, propelled as much by the forces of the new imperialism as by the north-east trade winds.

It is impossible to say what Africans salvaged throughout their turbulent voyagings. At least one aspect, however, of their cultural equipment may conceivably have served as a mechanism of survival. Their civilization had carefully articulated the forms by which the mysteries and dangers of existence were seasonally dramatized and exorcized. The African braced himself or herself for each new and possibly frightening phase of the life cycle (birth, adulthood, parenthood, death) by a *rite de passage,* which often tested physical and spiritual resources to the ultimate. Camara Laye wrote this of the painful ceremony of circumcision, which tribal traditions imposed on boys and girls of many West African countries:[97]

> However great the anxiety, however certain the pain, no one would have dreamed of running away from the ordeal . . . and I for my own part never entertained such thoughts. I wanted to be born, to be born again. I know perfectly that I am going to be hurt, but I wanted to be a man and it seemed to me that nothing could be too painful if by enduring it, I was to come to man's estate. My companions felt the

same; like myself, they were prepared to pay for it with their blood. Our elders before us have paid for it thus; those who were born after us will pay for it in their turn. Why should we be spared? Life itself would spring from the shedding of our blood.[98]

The transatlantic passage could in a sense be seen as such a monstrous but endurable ordeal, a ritualized agony of transition from an old to a new world of experience.[99]

Rebel Women, Guerilla Warfare

Numbers of African women, on arrival in Anglo-Jamaica, entered an estate that was clearly not the one prescribed for them by the captains of slavery and the slave trade. Imported as workers, they became immediately involved in the role of rebel. Imbedded in the slave laws that supported the Spanish colonial system was the unequivocal assertion that "liberty is the natural and proper condition of man".[100] Spanish slavery in Jamaica contained many escape routes to freedom. The Catholic proselytizing mission was an underlying constant, applying to blacks as well, and implicitly projected the human and free will of slave chattels.[101] A great deal was left to the slaves' initiative by the easy-going Spanish colonists relaxing in their townhouses, "leaving their servants and slaves in ye country to manage their cattle, sugarworks, and Cocoa Walks".[102] The economic system drew a very faint line between the open woodman's life of cattle ranching and wild-hog hunting (two of the main occupations of slave labour) and the rugged existence of runaways in the mountains.[103]

In 1611, the island had 1,510 persons, 558 of whom were enslaved and 107 free blacks.[104] In April 1655, the English had their first encounter in St Domingo with free fighting blacks, whom, together with the roving ranchers, formed the nucleus of the defence against the invaders. "If it were not for theas Cowkillers and Negors," wrote Henry Whistler, "the Spaniayards were not able to hoald up his hand against any enemie."[105]

There were approximately fifteen hundred slaves and ex-slaves in Jamaica in 1655, including a black priest, "a discreet negro".[106] Along with mulattoes, they helped to form the colonial garrison and in the view of a Spanish observer, "were the best fighters on the Spanish side".[107] The invasion gave the slave owners urgent cause to free their slaves and solicit their assistance in repelling the newcomers. A handful, some seventy or so, defected to the English, but soon reneged. In January 1656, Sedgwicke complained, "those few Blacks we had amongst us, are run from us, even all but seven or eight, that are now kept with shackles to prevent them".[108] The majority took to the St Catherine and Clarendon foothills and mounted a resistance movement in brief alliance with the Spanish colonists, the first context of Afro-English relations in Jamaica.[109]

The collapse of the Spanish side of the military operations in 1660 left the Africans as sole freedom fighters. It highlighted the true nature and objective of the movement. Much more than defensive manoeuvres against a new foreign intruder, it aimed at the dual emancipation of a black Jamaica, free of the English and free of slavery. Protection of womanhood was a *casus belli*. An English witness, John Paul, testified that the guerilla group known as "Varmahaly Negroes" killed five English hunters who stole away black women.[110] Men and women were partners in resistance. The large band of armed runaways, numbering over three hundred, who wreaked such havoc in St Mary in the mid-1680s[111] included women and children.[112] The female as actual and/or symbolic leader was also recognized; so that the 180 Coromantyn slaves who conspired against Colonel Guy in 1683 in the parish of Vere, "had combined themselves by oath, had chosen them a King and a Queen, and a chief captain, to whom they were to render all due obedience".[113]

Rebel settlements were the microcosm of free black aspirations. Beginning as scattered groups of thirty or forty wandering about the fringes of the coastal valleys, the guerillas eventually established themselves in three main communities: at Lluidas Vale, Los Vermejeles and Los Porus in St John's, St Catherine and Clarendon.[114] Estimates of their numbers are vague. Sedgwicke, in November 1655, admitted his ignorance of the precise size of the enemy:

> Some think most of the Spaniards are gone over to the backside to Cuba and that some of the Blacks and Mulattoes are dead; but certain it is, they meet with our English in the woods and every now and then kill three or four of them together; it is out of doubt there is a considerable amount of Mulattoes and Blacks, and some Spaniards, some say a thousand men, some say two.[115]

John Style, in 1670, was aware of the existence of a large rebel group and assessed them roughly to be more numerous than the loyal slaves; and their numbers increased daily.[116] Governor Trelawney, in 1737, at the height of Jamaica's terror over the damaging raids of Maroons on white plantations, calculated them to be "not less than 2,000".[117]

Natural increase to a limited extent kept the numbers of the bush terrorists buoyant. Black warfare was a corporate family effort; and being communities, as well as camps, rebel polincks all contained women and children. The women were described as "remarkably prolific" because of the healthy outdoor life they lived in fertile areas, exempt from excessive labour.[118] In the 1730s, Guy's Town, a relatively large village stronghold of the Windward Maroons, had more women and children than armed men.[119]

In addition to the first nucleus of Spanish ex-slaves, the fighting population was regularly reinforced and gradually outnumbered by runaways.[120] As slave importations increased over the next decades and the valleys became flooded with new Africans gradually being regimented into the routines of sugar production, there were always maverick spirits who escaped the plantations and found their brothers and sisters in the rebel settlements. Women were regularly found among runaways. During the period 1718 to 1730, for example, a sample of sixty-eight runaways advertised in the *Jamaica Courant* showed thirty black males to nineteen black females, two of whom had fled with their young children.[121] Female slaves were also abducted by rebel mountaineers, although this sometimes had unfortunate results.[122] The frequent association of Maroon men with slave women proved a strong contact point between free and unfree blacks. It operated both as an effective grapevine and as a system of recruitment.[123]

The strategy of survival in villages staked out the indispensable role for the woman as the food provider, whose efforts on the provision grounds complemented the man's functions as hunter and fighter.[124] The Lluidas Vale headquarters of Juan Lubola had some 200 acres of land under intensive cultivation in 1660, the year he and his men transferred allegiance to the English, thus destroying the Spanish cause and dealing a damaging blow to the whole militant movement. He deprived it not only of valued fighting hands, but also of its food basket, at that time the largest single source of local food supply. It is not surprising that after enjoying a few years of freedom and prestige under English patronage, he fell victim to black vengeance.[125] But the type of agricultural production which he had so successfully organized in Guanaboa Vale became the pattern for rebel cultivation. Guerillas still continued to live off the country, playing havoc with both large and small estates, but they also grew their own supplies. Patterson writes of the 100 "well planted acres" of provision grounds which served the Windward Maroons.[126] Guy's Town had not only intensively grown fields, but also "patches of eddoes, plantains and yams scattered in remote areas over the countryside which they used only during periods of retreat and emergency".[127] Agriculture was largely woman's work in such communities.[128]

The chief line of attack of the white Jamaica establishment in the 1730s was to starve out the rebels. Jasper Ashworth, commander-in-chief and commissary of the vigilante parties in Port Antonio in 1733, was most severely censured by a committee of the House of Assembly "for high crimes and misdemeanours by him committed".[129] His most criminal offence, bordering on treason, was to spare "the great plantain walk" of the formidable Windward Maroons at the time of the first successful British assault on Nanny Town, the rebel headquarters in the Blue Mountains that contained about one thousand men, women and children. "To the manifest prejudice of the public, [he] did not order the said plantain walk to be cut down till near six months after the said discovery."[130] As a result of his negligence, "great quantities of eddoes, yams and other provisions remained in the ground in and about the said negro-town and barracks". A female Maroon warned Ashworth that "they were driven to extreme want of provisions, and resolved, rather than perish in the woods, they would attempt to re-take their town, [for] it was better to be killed by the hands of the white men than to die in the woods for want of provisions".[131] They carried out their threat, surprised and recaptured their town: their granary was intact and they held out for another six years.[132] Without the vital labour contribution of women to the resistance movement in the area of agriculture, it is unlikely that it would have the resources to threaten white development to the extent which it did, out of all proportion to its fighting size.

The white establishment recognized the value of the guerilla woman. Like the man, she carried a price on her head. There was a £20 reward for every guerilla man, and £10 for every guerilla woman, taken dead or alive.[133] Several women and children fell victims to the search parties that attempted

to flush them out of their dense hiding places and to collect the bounty.
Simon Booth, a civilian head hunter, with the approval of the colonel and
commanding officer of the regiment in Clarendon and Vere, led a successful
voluntary excursion in the Porus region in June 1729 and "did kill one man
and two women, who were marked TS, with a heart, which was Sutton's
work and supposed to be in Sutton's rebellion which happened about forty
years ago and out ever since: they also killed two other negrowomen, said to
be rebellious".[134] Booth had other prizes of war, the ones he brought home
alive, among them "a negrowoman belonging to Mr Rippon, who was out
about seven years; one other negrowoman, belonging to one Mr Wright, said
to be out above two years; the other an old negrowoman of Colonel Sutton's,
and out since that rebellion; besides seven children, the eldest not above
seven years old". Booth was allowed to keep the children and received as well
"£450 from the country, as reward and encouragement".[135]

Mr Booth's expertise in slave-hunting continued to pay off handsomely. A
year later (June 1730) he put in his claim for five dead rebels (men and
women), eight alive (men and women) and six children under the age of
fourteen. This entitled him to a bounty of £650 and permission to keep the
children.[136] His captives included "a mulatto wench", and the Assembly
agreed that, "inasmuch as she was born in the woods", she should be given to
Booth and his heirs "as a further encouragement" on condition she was
shipped to the northern colonies "for the benefit of the said Mr Booth".[137]

With such incentives being dangled before the eyes of loyal men, blacks
themselves were tempted to betray their own and frequently did. Black
women benefited from the policy of rewarding informers. The enslaved wife
and children of a free black man, Sambo, "who had been very serviceable to
the country", got their freedom in 1732, although with the proviso that their
menfolk would be required at all times to join in search parties "under
penalty of forfeiting their freedom".[138] Colonel Cudjoe's wife, who had been
originally abducted from her estate, betrayed the numbers and location of
the Maroon settlement and was as a result rewarded by manumission in
1737.[139]

It should be noted that in the field of rewards, as in other areas, creole values laid down clear differentials for blacks and whites. Philip, a black man
belonging to Dennis McCrash of St Andrew, was considered by the
Assembly to be a useful subject. He had taken part in several search parties,

he knew the layout of the Maroon stronghold, New Liguanea, "and from thence to old Cotta-wood and Northside"; he had killed and captured several black rebels. He further claimed to know "the hideout of the Maroon women and children" and volunteered to guide a party there. He had up to that time received only a coat in payment. The House agreed to reward him further with the sum of £5 and the promise of his freedom, should he do "any signal service for the country".[140]

The records do not state if Philip did earn his liberty by showing the way to the secret quarters of the rebel families. It was Maroon policy to take special precautions for the safety of women and children. Cudjoe's Leeward band had hidden them in a virtually inaccessible dell in a cockpit at Petit River.[141] The whole process of rounding up concealed families after the fighting was over became an issue in the truce negotiations of the second Maroon war of 1795.[142]

In March 1733, the bounty payable to those "party Negroes as have behaved well" was fixed at £10 per head for "every rebellious negro man, £8 for every rebellious negro woman, and four pounds for every rebellious boy and girl under the age of ten years that shall be killed or taken alive".[143] The Assembly recommended highly nineteen blacks for their "resolution, bravery and fidelity" in the service of the island.[144] Five men were singled out for extra honours: in addition to the prescribed payment, they received "the sum of £5, a common silver laced hat, a good blue baize coat, with a red cross upon the right breast, and ten yards of osnaburgh, . . . such coat and hat, with ten shillings should be given each of them, on 20 December yearly".[145]

One of these men merited official gratitude for his alleged capture of an extremely valuable militant: Williams's Cuffee, "a very good party negro", had distinguished himself, claiming to have "killed Nanny, the rebels' old obeah woman",[146] and the most renowned female warrior/priestess in Jamaica's history. It is not easy to say precisely whether this was a genuine error, or whether it was deliberate misinformation. Nanny was very much alive; she survived the end of the first Maroon war in 1740 and received from the Government of Jamaica a grant of 500 acres of land for herself and her people, a unique achievement for a black woman.[147]

The magico-religious leader always played a strong part in the black resistance movements. Governor Molesworth reported in 1685 that "[the Maroons] having lost one of their conjurers, on whom they chiefly depended, retired".[148] Edward Long also observed about the Maroons that "their priests, or obeah men are their chief oracles in all weighty affairs, whether of peace, war or the pursuit of revenge".[149] This role was associated with the marked dominance of Akan-speaking or "Coromantee" people in the island's slave rebellions, whose procedures reproduced many West African forms.[150] Monica Schuler writes:

> The role of the obeah man in the Akan slave rebellions, for instance, is very like the role of priests and magicians in Ashanti military campaigns. Before military campaigns the principal commanders of the Ashanti army met with the priests at night and participated in a ceremony designed to weaken the enemy each time it was repeated. Priests also recommended propitious days for advancing and attacking, usually after consulting oracles . . . the priests (*esamankwafo*) also accompanied the soldiers on their campaigns and provided them with protective charms and amulets, some of which were believed to make their wearers invulnerable to bullets.[151]

Dallas wrote about Nanny that she was "the only one of that sex known to have exercised the art" of obeah.[152] This, however, is unlikely: the obeah woman was, and still is, well known to Jamaica.[153] Nor was it surprising to find a woman exercising power in communal warfare: West Africans had historical precedence, as had been indicated, for women who were dominant in public affairs.[154] Nanny had her Jamaican precursor in the Coromantee Queen of 1683,[155] and her successor in Cubah of the 1760 slave uprisings.[156] The Maroons, moreover, of all communities in the island, were furthest removed from sustained, direct contact with Euro-Jamaica. They adhered strongly to Ashanti cultural belief and practices,[157] which accepted leadership roles for women.

Nanny's uniqueness lay in the extraordinary effectiveness of her combined magical, military and civic authority. Both the official records of the Jamaican establishment, as well as the oral traditions of her Maroon descendants, pay tribute to her stature.[158] Nanny was of the Ashanti nation, and a free woman, who had never been enslaved. Her brother was Cudjoe, the Leeward Maroon leader. Her husband was a man of considerable prestige among the Windward Maroons, but appears to have taken no active part in the military affairs of their community.[159]

Old Nanny Town was the most important black settlement of the turbulent northeast of the island. It covered over 600 acres of land in the back Rio

Grande Valley of the parish of Portland, strategically sited for its access to the coast. It was governed by Nanny when the white vigilantes first launched their intensive offensives against it in the early 1730s.[160] Nanny's tactical genius dominated the strategies of the guerillas in the ensuing year of the First Maroon War. She herself did not take part in the battles – the fighting chief was Quao – but she blessed and directed the campaigns and exploited to the maximum her people's brilliant mastery of their difficult and dangerous terrain. The Maroon horn, the abeng, as well as African talking drums, were her effective means of communication across the mountains and valleys.[161]

She became celebrated as a great worker of magic. In the words of one nineteenth-century Maroon leader,

> Nanny had more science in fighting than even Cudjoe. . . . After the signing of the treaty, Nanny say that she show them science. She told fifty soldiers to load their guns and then to fire on her. She folds back her hands between her legs and catches the fifty shots. This was called Nantucompong, Nanny takes her back to catch the balls.[162]

She was supposed also to keep a huge cauldron boiling, without the use of fire, at the foot of the precipice where Nanny Town stood. Maroon history has it that when curious soldiers and militia-men came close to inspect this "freak of nature", they fell into the cauldron and were suffocated.[163]

Of all the black resistance leaders of her time, Nanny was foremost among those who resolved never to come to terms with the English. She infected her followers – men, women and children – with this determination, and their aggressiveness became legendary.[164] It is significant that hers was the community which in 1735 carried out what has been described as "a superb tactical manoeuvre":[165] an epic trek by some three hundred men, women and children across the island's most wild and impassable mountains to join forces with Cudjoe's Leeward Maroons. But they were too militant for the guerillas of the west, who were moving towards a policy of peaceful coexistence with whites.[166] Cudjoe accused the Windward blacks of being cruel and insolent to the English, and he probably feared that they were too high-spirited and independent to accept his authority.[167] Attempts at collaboration failed, and the Portland group made their hazardous return march in 1737.[168] Maroon history affirms that in that same year, Nanny took a solemn pledge on the brow of Pumpkin Hill that she and her followers would continue to fight the English raiding parties to the death.[169]

The news of Cudjoe's peace treaty of 1739 was received bitterly in Nanny's Town. Exercising her unquestioned power over life and death in the community, she ordered the execution of the white courier, "the poor laird of Labaret", who brought news of the truce.[170] It is significant that while the men led by Quao accepted a peace agreement, the women mainly carried the grim symbols of defiance. They wore as ornaments around their wrist and ankles the upper teeth of white soldiers killed in battle.[171]

After the conclusion of the truce, the Windward Maroons split into two groups: one went closer to the coast to Crawford Town, with Quao as their chief, and the other to New Nanny Town (now Moore Town), under Nanny's leadership. On 5 August 1740, her land patent was approved, duly granting to "the said Nanny and the people now residing with her, their heirs and assigns a certain parcel of land containing 500 acres in the parish of Portland bounding South and East on King's land and West on Mr John Stevenson".[172] Nanny continued to rule her people in peacetime, exercising a unifying influence for many years on the two Maroon groups in Portland.[173]

Throughout the eighteenth century, women continued to play vital roles in the communal life of Maroon villages, which demonstrated the determination of free blacks to reconstruct their African cultural patterns, even in exile. Women's fundamental occupation as food grower has already been commented on; and when the island became increasingly accommodating to their presence, they pursued as well, with official approval,[174] the traditional occupation of marketing their surplus vegetables, fruit and poultry in the neighbouring towns. Women and children were also exclusively responsible for the profitable manufacture of tobacco. They travelled twenty or thirty miles away to estates to buy the leaves, carried them home, dried and processed them to a stage ready for marketing.[175]

These free black towns contained a recognized hierarchy of authority and a pattern of mating forms, reminiscent of West Africa.[176] Girls' nubile rites, for example, were communally celebrated, marriage involved a ceremonial exchange of gifts between the kinship groups involved,[177] and polygyny carried with it careful organization of the spouses' rights and obligations, breaches of which were frowned on.[178] Maroon men were allegedly reluctant to adopt Christianity and become monogamous. What, they asked, would then become of their responsibilities to their extra wives?[179]

The Jamaican men and women who formed the Maroon population were always few. After the peace of 1739, their activities as fighters for the next fifty years were relaxed and their numbers dwindled relative to the accelerated influx of African slaves. In 1768, when the slave population was between 160,000 and 180,000, Long estimated them to be about "700 men, women and children: of these the men are about 300".[180]

Their importance, however, was always disproportionate to their size. It has already been stressed that their role of watchdog over the frontier was one important element affecting the opening up of the Jamaican hinterland. Later, in their free mountain towns, even when they became official runaway slave hunters, they nevertheless concretized a fact known instinctively to the blacks who laboured in the plains and valleys, viz., that their servitude was neither inevitable nor eternal. "It is something", as one writer has expressed it, "for the island community not to be composed entirely of slave holders and slaves, but to include also a class of black men, who inherited freedom almost from time immemorial, who had made their own terms with the government, and who for generation after generation had lived in their mountain homes a life of recognized liberty".[181]

The women participated as full partners in this life of liberty and, as the eighteenth century advanced, they demonstrated one of the most vital symptoms of a free existence: the capacity of the race to reproduce itself. The relatively high fertility of the Maroon communities was in telling contrast to the record of slave women.[182] Women continued to flee the plantations, although it is possible that after 1740 relatively few of them found their way to the free black villages.[183] They did not need to; they could get lost in the growing towns, in the always receptive slave cabins of other estates. Every missing woman jolted the socio-economic order, however slightly.

In Jamaica, manumission was hard to come by; but some women continued to secure freedom, even (like some enslaved men) through being informers, thus placing them outside the closed system of enslavement and denting the system. Two women slaves, Sylvia and Domingo, were freed at the time of the Trelawny disturbance of 1745 for providing "material evidence in several trials of the Negroes concerned in the late conspiracy".[184] In 1760, Congo Molly, Moll and her son Quaco were given their freedom for discovering "the later conspiracy and rebellions and other faithful service to the public". In addition to providing their purchase price of £60, £50 and £70, respectively, the Assembly voted each an annuity of £5 for the rest of their lives and a circular silver badge each, valued at 40s; their names were inscribed on the badges with the words "freedom, for being honest" on one side and the words "by the country" on the other.[185]

The most gruesome case of profitable betrayal occurred in 1759. Mimba, a free woman, and Sarah, a slave, had been abducted by the rebel chief Ancouma and forced to become his wives. They were probably ill-treated by him, for Mimba, who bore two of his children, aided and abetted Sarah to behead him with a broad axe as he slept. The two women cut off his ears and took them to Foster's estate in Portland "as a proof of their assertion". Sarah's freedom was purchased for £20 by the government, both received annuities – Sarah of £5, Mimba of £10 – having earned "the encouragement and protection of the legislature".[186]

Protégées of the establishment, their very existence as free black women in a slave society were an affront to the establishment. But this was the negative face of violent protest. The positive face of female militancy re-appeared in the widespread slave conspiracy of 1760, which affected at least six parishes, involved nearly all the Coromantees in the island and shook white Jamaica to its foundations.[187] Cubah, a female slave belonging to a Jewess of Kingston, was prominent among the city's branch of conspirators. She was elevated to "the rank of royalty and dubbed Queen of Kingston". At the meetings which were held to plot insurrection, "she had sat in state under a canopy, with a sort of robe on her shoulders, and a crown upon her head". She was tried and ordered to be transported to Cuba, and was in fact shipped off the island. She appears to have persuaded a ship's captain to take her back, for he landed her at Crooke Cove in Hanover, where she "continued for sometime undiscovered, but at length was taken up and executed".[188] Her case provided additional evidence of the extensive nature of the conspiracy that linked scattered parishes in a common cause.[189] It also suggests the strong influence of African civil and military organization, with the probability that Cubah might have been "cast in the role of at traditional Akan Queen Mother".[190]

ECONOMIC EXPEDIENCY, LABOUR IMPORT POLICIES AND EARLY SOCIO-ECONOMIC CONTEXT

Contemporary evidence indicates that African women were present in seventeenth-century Jamaica in approximately equal numbers with men. One contributory factor probably originated in Africa. The Oba of Benin had established in 1615 a system of separate markets for male and female slaves, in which it was always more difficult to negotiate male purchases. The policy may have arisen out of the country's military needs. But as Ryder suggests, "whatever the original purpose may have been, restriction on the export of male slaves developed within a few years into a total embargo which persisted until the close of the seventeenth century".[191] The sex-composition of Jamaica's slaves, 27.6 per cent of whom came from Benin in the seventeenth century,[192] must have been affected by this trend.

The trade otherwise appeared to have operated flexibly, with little of the later insistence on preponderantly male cargoes. Shipments of slaves in the 1670s, showing slight excesses of males, went by without comment. The *Sarah Bonaventura,* which carried Africans from the Gold Coast to Barbados and Jamaica in 1676, had forty-six men and thirty-four women.[193] Similarly, the *Arthur* traded from Guinea in 1677 to 1678 with an average of 175 men to 135 women.[194] Mrs Aphra Benn in 1688 wrote: "Perhaps in one lot that may be for ten, there may happen to be three or four men, the rest women and children. Or be there more or less of either sex you are obliged to be contented with your lot."[195]

This was also the period of migration from the Eastern Caribbean and especially from Barbados, whose regular shipping links with Jamaica facilitated movement of people.[196] The sex ratio of blacks in Barbados and the Leeward Islands was then relatively stable,[197] and this was probably reflected in migrant groups.[198] Of the sixteen thousand slaves who entered Jamaica from Barbados, many may have already survived the dangerous seasoning period, when mortality could be as high as 30 per cent.[199] Bennett found some evidence of lower slave mortality at Bybrook estate in the 1670s:[200] acclimatized creole slaves were better adapted to childbearing. A population whose numbers are topped up by natural increase rather than migration tends to produce a better balance of the sexes, which in turn promotes reproduction. It is likely that Jamaica's creole slave population of the seventeenth century contained potentially more healthy demographic evidence than that of later periods.

Planter demand suggests that the recognition of the slaves' domestic needs, plus a measure of self-interest, encouraged a balance of the sexes. Ligon wrote accordingly about Barbadian slaves in 1657: "We buy them so, as the sexes may be equal; for if they have more Men than Women, the men who are unmarried will come to their Masters and complain that they cannot live without Wives and desire him, [that] they may have Wives."[201] In costing the clothing expenses of a medium plantation, he estimated the slave force at fifty men and fifty women.[202] Blome did a similar calculation for Jamaica in 1672: "The labour requirements of a cocoa walk could be met initially with 3 negro men and 3 negro women to be later supplemented by 5 more of each sex."[203] John Taylor's observations were consistent with this pattern, stating "after a Planter hath purchased some twenty, thirty or more negro slaves he first gives to each man a wife without which they will not be content, or work";[204] this, too, was Sloane's impression more than a decade later. He noted in 1707 that "they [slave men] have everyone his wife . . . the care of the Masters and Overseers about their wives, is what keeps their plantations chiefly in good order, whence they ever buy wives in proportion to their men less the men should wander to neighbouring plantations and neglect to serve them".[205]

Planter inventories of the time confirm this demographic feature of the slave population. Forty-six statements of slaveholders' estates between 1674 and 1676, which were examined, show a total of 461 slaves. The small proprietor far exceeded the big proprietor, and in fact only three men owned more than 40 slaves each; the average holder had 6.5 slaves totalling 274, of which 143 were men and 131 women, a sex ratio of almost 1:1.[206]

One corollary of this was the acknowledgement of slave men and women as functioning family units. So that

> [the planter] gives to each man and his wife an half acre of Land, for them to care for themselves, to plant maize, potatoes, yams, etc, which land they clear [in their leisure hours] and build them a Wigwam on it and they plant it as fast as they can. Then he gives them a sow pig, a cock and Hen to brood on etc.[207]

Taylor clearly perceived the life of seventeenth-century slaves in these domestic terms. When the planter, for instance, dispensed the luxury of rum and molasses, it was to "each negroman and his family".[208] At the end of a day of work and recreation, blacks lay themselves "all round their fire, the whole family together in a confused manner to sleep".[209]

In some respects, conditions for the Jamaican slave woman were less intolerable in the seventeenth than in the eighteenth century. The social structure had not yet become an irreversibly polarized black/white caste system. Remnants of the looser Spanish colonial pattern lingered. The English were compelled to come to terms with more free than enslaved blacks, so that Sir Charles Lyttleton, bargaining for the military support of Juan Luyola and his men, had to promise land and citizenship.[210] D'Oyley had instructions in 1660 to make similar offers,[211] and Modyford, anxious to promote the island's settlement, was prepared at first to be colour-blind.[212]

Other evidence suggests that there may have been slightly more official willingness to admit the slave's humanity. One of the earlier bits of legislation, the act of 1674, which defined African bondsmen and bondwomen as chattels, nevertheless conceded them to be "reasonable creatures and capable of being taught the principles of our [that is, Christian] religion".[213] The Slave Act of 1696, which constituted the basis of Jamaican slave legislation for nearly a century, renewed the principle of encouraging slave baptisms.[214] As is implied above with regards to D'Oyley, Littleton and Modyford, a relatively more favourable view of manumission existed, if only for the purpose of swelling loyalist numbers. The position for the English was then a desperate one, and their liberalism should not be exaggerated; the approach was essentially pragmatic, economic and strategic realities dictating the social relationships.

A fair proportion of whites among the menial working-class group affected also the context in which blacks first functioned. Between 20 and 30 per cent of the labour force in the seventeenth century were white indentures. Ligon's Barbadian ratio in 1657 was 30 servants to 100 slaves.[215] Blome's model cocoa plantation of 1672 contained 4 whites to 16 blacks.[216] Carey Helyar started Bybrook sugar estate in 1670 with 1 servant and 4 slaves.[217] In 1672, his operations had extended, but the racial composition of his workers remained more or less the same: 14 servants to 55 slaves.[218] The St John's census of 1680 showed 95 servants to 527 slaves.[219]

Servants admittedly did mainly artisan and supervisory jobs on estates, but some did field work as well.[220] Their legal status, as contract workers, differed fundamentally from the life-long bondage of blacks; but in respect of some of the concessions, as well as disabilities shared with slaves, they were often lumped together at the bottom of the ladder, and this helped to keep the social/racial situation relatively fluid.[221] They appeared to be both victims of excessive punishment, and the official view was that they needed equal protection from "any inhuman severity which by ill masters or Overseers may be used towards their Christian servants and their slaves".[222] Their living conditions were similarly poor.[223] They slept on floors; and Sloane, as a result, remarked that "ordinary white servants, like Negroes, who lie not on beds, are not said to go to bed, but to go to sleep".[224] Some owners like Helyar fed servants better than slaves. The official standards laid down, however, were the same: masters were "obliged to furnish their servants both whites and blacks with three pounds of salt-beef, pork or fish, every week, besides Cassado Bread, Yams and Potatoes, which they eat on bread".[225] It has been suggested that the use of white men as artisans in the early stages of West Indian development helped the slave physically by forcing the planter to spare more acreage from sugar cane for provision crops.[226] The two groups obviously maintained contact with each other, much frowned on by some contemporaries, who regarded such association as the ruin of servants;[227] certainly they shared some of the social stigma, which at a later period was almost exclusively reserved for blacks.

Economic expediency in the seventeenth century had not yet become the sole overriding consideration of things Jamaican: subsistence planting did not immediately give way to commercial agriculture. Not that the sugar industry was not taking formidable shape. Trapham, writing in 1679, already saw it as a dominating entity

> on the margin of the rising hills which still terminate our dexterous aspects; the most remarkable sugar-works allure us thither: the stranger is apt to ask what village it is (for every completed sugar-work is no less . . .) for besides the more large mansion house with its offices, the works, such as the well contrived Mill, the spacious boiling house, the large receptive curing houses, still house, commodious stables for the grinding cattle, lodging for the over-seer, and white servants, working shops for the necessary smiths, others for the framing carpenters, and coopers: to all which when we add the streets of the Negroes houses, no one will question to call such completed sugar-work a small town or village.[228]

But sugar production did not become a virtual monopoly of the island's agricultural effort until the eighteenth century. Rear Admiral Benbow in 1701 saw the island primarily in terms of an unused hinterland. "It is", he wrote to the Board of Trade, "well known to be a large island, and not a tenth part inhabited, and those promiscuously over the land, except that of Legane, Withiwood and Spanish Town".[229]

The open, half-free life of hog hunting persisted in Sloane's time, when he noted that "wild hogs haunt the more unfrequented, woody inland part of the island"; their flesh formed a staple food for the inhabitants and was procured by hunters. "These hunters, are either Blacks or Whites, and go out with their dogs, some salt and bread, and lye far remote from houses, in huts, with woods, for several days, in places where swine came to feed on the fruits."[230]

Jamaica had the quality of a still moving frontier, blocked by shortage of capital, shortage of labour and by the pockets of rebels lurking on the outskirts of the plains. The adjustment of African women was accordingly conditioned by the less intensive level of agricultural labour which was required in the period preceding the large-scale regimented field and factory processes of sugar manufacture. In Barbados in 1657, says Ligon, "the work which women do is most of it weeding"; and although this was "a stooping and painful" occupation,[231] it could not be compared with the hoeing, digging and cane cutting which was later demanded of women labourers. Cary Helyar in 1672 was busy building up his slave stock for future use in a fully equipped sugar estate, and in the meantime, his slaves' tasks were "comparatively light".[232]

Certain very broad generalizations can therefore be made about the slave's condition in early Jamaica, the age of the small settler, as compared to a later period, when the big planter dominated the scene. A higher incidence of creolized slaves probably prevailed, and the sexes were more evenly balanced, with implications of lower mortality and higher fertility. Women's work was less demanding, social status, influenced to some extent by the presence of white servants, was less degraded. This relative social and demographic equilibrium of the 1660s, 1670s and 1680s must not be overstated.[233] It was short-lived. It was soon to be agitated by the momentum of highly capitalized export monoculture, which pushed labour and population patterns in the directions charted by its needs.

The turning point was the 1690s. The Slave Act of 1696 significantly cod-ified the status of the African as unequivocally that of permanent chattel. In case doubt lingered, it made clear that even the transformation of pagan into Christian was no passport to freedom. Whereas the term "slave" in previous official documents could be used interchangeably for black or white, after 1696 "the term Negro was invariably identified with slave".[234]

Like the law, the pattern of the slave trade reflected the changing eco-nomic circumstances. In 1698, a slave consignment of the *Dragon,* which sailed from Old Calabar, revealed a marked alteration in its sex ratio, 102 men to 53 women.[235] In 1700, the discrepancy was even more pronounced in a shipment from the Congo of 65 men to 16 women.[236] At the same time Jamaican plantations showed a widening sex ratio of 415 men to 349 women in a sample of 42 inventories.[237]

In 1710, Sir Dalby Thomas at the Cape Coast Castle referred to the *Pindar's* load of 207 men to 99 women;[238] and by 1713 the official directive from the British slave purchasing agency, the South Sea Company, to the buyers, the Royal African Company, spelt out precise specifications for a cargo of 4,800 slaves to be obtained at Whydah, Cape Coast, Windward Coast, Gambia and Shabro:

> Negroes from the Ages of Sixteen years to the Ages of Forty Years at the price of ten pounds sterling per head, and Negroes from the ages of ten years to the ages of Sixteen years at the price of Six pounds Sterling per head and that two thirds parts at least of the said Negroes to be delivered shall be males . . . .[239]

The rejection of a catch-as-catch-can market policy was re-emphasized in 1714,[240] the sex ratio again carefully stated, and subsequent correspondence insisted that the requirements for human cargo be scrupulously met.[241] By the 1720s, Jamaican estates clearly mirrored this market preference for men. A sample of forty-three inventories for the years 1726 to 1728 contained a total of 2,332 slaves, of whom 1,342 were male and 990 were female.[242] Additional refinements were from time to time included for the model labour unit. In 1717, the South Sea Company, in reference to a cargo of 400 Angolans, tagged on a further provision that "the Women should be as near as possible to being virgins".[243] Details of skin colour were laid down: slaves should be "very black and handsome".[244] Light skins, associated with European fragility, were clearly second priority for labourers in the tropics, and girls in particular should not be "too much in the yellow cast".[245] The age limit was repeatedly emphasized: children under ten were of little economic value, and nine-tenths of most cargoes were to be between sixteen and forty years of age. Barbadian factors in 1683 complained to the Royal African Company that one-third of a recent cargo were too young, "most of them no better than suckling children . . . and the most part of those small ones not worth above £5 per head".[246] The Jamaican factors were rapped on the knuckles in 1716 because "1 woman and 4 children did not in respect to their ages conform to the Charter party".[247] They were instructed to give "timely notice" should any future deviations from the stated guidelines be necessary.

Some of the implications of current import policies concerning ages apparently escaped the traders' and the planters' notice. Their insistence that young children be rejected as far as possible was of course dictated by their need for sturdy manpower on the estates. The majority of human imports were, as a consequence, young adults already initiated into the essentials of their African culture. Girls, for instance, had already undergone their puberty rites and were thereby better equipped to preserve their ethnic integrity in a foreign land; were better equipped perhaps, to question their status as chattels.

The basic principle of selecting larger numbers of male slaves persisted unaltered into the 1770s. The mercantile firm of Robert Hibbert, who regularly supplied Jamaica with slaves, shipped 10,149 African males and 6,105 females between 1760 and 1774.[248] Edward Long stated the situation in its most extreme terms: "of the slaves shipped from the coast, not a sixth part are women".[249]

The rationale behind sex-selective slave trading was a simple one – although, as will be subsequently discussed, its apologists of the late eighteenth century made every attempt to complicate the issue.[250] The planter's calculation saw slaves as units of labour and initially measured labour output exclusively in terms of physical potential: women clearly could not rate as equals of men when the measure of worth was maximum, unbroken capacity for strenuous activity.

Actually, West Indian policy with regards to female labour proved capricious in the extreme. Women were first tolerated because the trader/planter had little choice, and in any event their presence kept their menfolk more or less content on the estates. The planter, in time, learnt more precisely what he required of his workforce: only a man then seemed strong enough to meet his major needs, and women became second priority. Rejected in theory, on the grounds of their physical frailty, women ended up, nevertheless, as the chief manual labourers on the plantation.

Estate work in the seventeenth century was allocated roughly along the following lines: white servants supervised blacks and undertook all skilled, technical occupations; male slaves bore the brunt of the agricultural task; female slaves supplemented male labour in the lighter jobs and staffed the planters' houses.[251] With their opportunities for social mobility and their propensity to migrate, the proportion of white servants on estates dwindled, and with them went their skills. But the Jamaican sugar estate was an agro-industrial complex, requiring much more than brute force; male slaves were therefore promoted into the expert skills essential for keeping estates in operation. Effect came to be seen as cause: the increasing number of black male artisans was given as a prime factor in white depopulation. To attract small white settlers, it was felt necessary to deny slaves access to the higher levels of training.[252] But the economic imperatives making for a black/white imbalance made it impossible to recall the white artisan. A proportion of male slaves continued to acquire skills and trades, and to join the ranks of the most valuable and specialized members of the estate workforce, to occupy positions unavailable to women.

In the inventories of the seventeenth century, few or no details of slaves' occupations appear, but in the 1726–28 inventories, forty-six men were singled out as artisans doing the work of bricklayers, carpenters, canoe-men, blacksmiths, coopers, wheelwrights, sawyers, block makers, coach men, postilions, grooms. Eight non-praedial women were distinguished by the titles of a buttery keeper, a seamstress, a washerwoman, a nanny, three cooks and "a mulatto".[253]

Sheridan presents the data for Richard Beckford's Roaring River sugar plantation in Westmoreland in 1756: there were 176 adult slaves, of whom eighty-four were men and ninety-two women. Thirty-eight men were drivers and tradesmen, twenty-eight were field workers and there were eighteen others whose jobs were unlisted. Seventy of the women worked in the field, twenty-two others fell into an unspecified category.[254] A similar pattern of male/female work distribution existed at that time on Beckford's Hartford Cattle Pen, in which seven out of twenty-four men were field workers, the majority of the others being tradesmen and cattle tenders, while six out of seven women were field-hands and the seventh was a "house wench".[255]

Godfrey Shreyer's estate in St Mary in 1764 was valued at over £20,000, and contained 179 slaves. Eight of his men worked in the great house, forty-six in the field, and fifty were artisans, gardeners, fence-cutters and watchmen. His skilled workmen included his highest priced slave, a mason worth £150. One of his slave women was a water carrier, seven worked in the great house and the remaining sixty-seven in the field (none worth more than £60).[256] Frances Burnett of St Thomas, in the same year, owned fifty-six male slaves, thirty-one of whom were artisans and housemen, leaving twenty-five field workers; all of her twenty-nine female slaves, except one cook, were field workers.[257]

Edward Manning's sugar estate, St Toolies in Clarendon, had 242 slaves in 1766. The adult working population contained eighty-five males and fifty-six females. Thirty-five males (or 41 per cent) were classified as skilled or semi-skilled artisans. The remaining fifty (or 59 per cent) were unskilled field workers. Of the fifty-six women all (or 100 per cent) were field workers.[258] In 1769, Robert Arcedeckne of St Catherine had a slave force of thirty-six male artisans and thirty-nine field-men, four house women and fifty-five field women.[259] It appeared that as some black men moved upwards within the slave hierarchy, acquiring greater expertise over a broader span of tasks, the vacuum they left at the bottom of the occupational ladder was filled by their women. A labour pattern was emerging in which it seemed not only that the majority of black women were field workers, but, more significantly, that the majority of the field workers were black women.

APOLOGISTS FOR SLAVERY AND REPRESENTATIONS OF THE BLACK WOMAN

Imported as worker, assuming on her own initiative the role of rebel, the black woman was also tacitly expected to be always available for her master's pleasure. In the 1730s, Leslie spoke of the established custom of black/white concubinage and of the black female favourites "of young squires, who keep them for a certain use".[260] The creole mind found itself by the third quarter of the century fully committed to a socio-economic system supported by black slavery, and ripe for its apologists, who were thereby forced to the indefensible. Every known sophistry came into use, including the distortion of the female image, black and white. To justify the plantation system and all its creatures, to support the case for white physical and moral superiority, the black woman, partner in interracial sex, had to become insatiable temptress, sole agent of the white man's fall from grace. In the face of the facts, the white woman became the more plausible torch-bearer of purity.

The distance Jamaica had journeyed in a hundred years can be measured, not only by comparative statistics of acreage and output, imports and exports, but also by the racial perspective of Ligon, Taylor, Sloane and Leslie on the one hand, and Long and Edwards on the other.[261] In the earlier period, the economy, the society, was still playing it by ear. If the writers of that time found no white goddesses, they found few black she-devils. Slave men and women in Ligon's time went frequently without clothes; but nevertheless, he commented: "chaste they are as any people under the sun".[262] He had, moreover, "strong motives to cause one to be of that persuasion, that there are honest, faithful and conscionable people amongst them, as amongst those of Europe or any other part of the world".[263] John Taylor was generally ethnocentric, but seldom saw the black woman outside of the role of a "kind and honest" wife;[264] his sharpest strictures applied to the "Lazie Strumpets (white) of which there are many".[265]

Sloane, the most careful observer of Jamaican life during this period, is detached: he made little distinction between his black and white female patients, frequently lumping them together: "['T]is very ordinary for servants, both whites and blacks, to pretend or dissemble sickness of several sorts . . . ."[266] He found both equally liable to drunkenness, abortion, debauchery, venereal diseases; if anything, he defends black nurses from the planters' charge that their unhealthiness might infect their children, as he "he never saw such consequences".[267] Leslie saw Jamaican society with little emotional involvement. He found black female nudity shameless, but on the other hand had few compliments to pay to white women.[268]

There is nothing in seventeenth-century creole literature, not even the least favourable perception of the female sex on the slave coast in Bosman's and Barbot's time, which can parallel the sick venom which inspired Long's denigration of the African and Jamaican slave woman in the 1770s. He stated it as "a common known proverb, that all people on the globe have some good as well as ill qualities, except the Africans . . . devoted, . . . in short, to every vice that came in their way, or within their reach".[269] Africans, according to Long's scale of the natural order of beings, were closely related to the orang-utang;[270] their bestiality, and particularly that of their females, was therefore not surprising. This and other vile qualities accompanied them to the New World, where the women became notorious as "common prostitutes".[271]

 It should be noted that Long's racism exercised wide influence outside of creole Jamaica. His *Candid Reflections* on black sexuality, published in London in 1772, made an impact on English thinking on the subject.[272] His conjecture on the affinity of apes for Hottentot women was reprinted in the *Colombian Magazine* of 1788 and made a substantial contribution to the then-current discussion in the United States on the real nature of black men and women:[273] it became, as Curtin points out, "a support for later American racism".[274]

But Long's poison pen, powerful as it was, could not completely negate life. The dichotomy between the concept and the reality of women's charac-ter and condition remained to be seen by all who had eyes to see. The inter-racially promiscuous witch of Rose Hall, the most enduring creation of Jamaica fantasy,[275] next to the spiderman Anansi, by all the rules of the creole game should have been black, not white. By confounding society's postu-lates, her existence, mythical/historical, hints at suppressed truths.

But there was at least one area in which the Jamaican psyche did not need to play guessing games with fact and fiction. The plantation value system, of such impressive economic, social and ideological force, clearly had some tri-umphs to sustain it. If black and white women frequently insisted on evad-ing their stereotypes, the creole ethos could at least point to its truly native product, the brown female, at whose conception image and reality met and fused.

3   The Growth of the Mulatto Group

PRECEDENCE: MULATTOES IN WEST AFRICA

Miscegenation was already a limited but significant part of West African social experience from as early as the fifteenth century. The first Portuguese traders/explorers mated with African women, both free and slave, and produced mulatto families. This occurred in Upper Guinea, along the coastal areas between Senegal and Gambia, on the Cape Verde Islands, and on the Gold Coast.[1] As Portuguese and mulatto traders proceeded to penetrate the interior of Upper Guinea, following the riverain courses, they often settled inland and bred more mixed groups.[2] Portugal's adventures in the Congo in the sixteenth century left a similar trail of half-caste children,[3] as did her commercial activities in Angola.[4]

By the mid-seventeenth century, Portuguese monopoly of West African business had been breached. France was installed in Senegal, and England in the Gambia. Their factors continued the Portuguese pattern of relationships with African women.[5] The status of these relationships was not always "illegitimate": the guidelines for European conduct were in fact often laid down by Africans themselves, consistent with the "landlord-stranger" contracts which characterized early Afro-European dealings.[6] Walter Rodney points to the emphasis placed by seventeenth-century Portuguese travellers on the fact that "flirting with women was the worst crime that a white could commit, and would always cost loss of goods and even loss of life". The Corubal region south of the Gambia was singled out as "an area where it was advisable to keep at a very respectable distance from married women".[7]

High official approval was frequently given to mixed marriages, as well as to concubinage. The superiors of the French Company of the Indies at home tried to discourage such liaisons for fear that their employees on the spot would then be inveigled into trading with their in-laws at the expense of the company's interests.[8] On the other hand, some of their representatives in Senegal "were glad to encourage interracial menages as likely to produce a more stable community, [for] French men provided with home comforts were less likely to desert and set up as private traders".[9]

Indigenous matrimonial forms were frequently observed for cementing such liaisons. Although unrecognized by European churches, they often nevertheless received formal status. The Danish, for instance, on the Gold Coast, drew up definite regulations governing these unions, including the provision for an African woman to join her husband in Europe if and when he should return.[10] Other companies arranged for the wife's welfare and maintenance if the man departed leaving her behind.[11] Factors of the Royal African Company regularly charged their wives' living allowance to the company's accounts.[12]

Barbot describes a widow of such an approved alliance: "Donna Catalina, a black lady of a good presence and a very jovial temper, widow to a Portuguese of note and a Roman Catholick, invited me to a dinner at Rio Fresco, where she then lived in great esteem among the Blacks, but always dressed after Portuguese fashion."[13]

White fathers more often than not accepted responsibility for their mulatto children, sometimes to the extent of sending them to Europe to be educated. Edward Barter, whom Bosman met as an influential mulatto trader on Cape Coast in the early eighteenth century, had been schooled in England.[14]

At least one such half-breed became a European celebrity during the regime of Louis XIV, the Mooress Louisa Marie Theresa, who was alleged to have been the king's daughter and apparently his protégée. When Voltaire saw her in 1716, she had then been living in a convent at Moret since 1695 on a royal pension of three hundred livres a year and "exhibited a haughty spirit of which her superiors complained".[15]

African mulattoes were never a large group, for the Europeans entered the continent in small numbers. They tended to be scattered in pockets. In 1678, Elmina on the Gold Coast had about two hundred families of Afro-Portuguese descent.[16] British Senegambia in the 1760s had a little over one thousand coloureds centred in St Louis.[17] Sierra Leone had the largest mixed population, reaching twelve thousand by the end of the eighteenth century.[18] Their significance in West Africa was unrelated to their numbers. Because of the shortage of whites, they attained positions in the Army and in the Roman Catholic Church. In 1684, the Crown of Portugal ruled that racial discrimination was tabooed in military appointments, and this opened up the way for Afro-Portuguese officers in the garrison in Angola.[19] Similar policies operated in colonial churches, and mulatto priests were frequently ordained.[20]

Berlin   Houston?

But it was primarily in the world of trade that the mulattoes established dominant places for themselves. A handful of white factors and administrators on coastal ports, steadily infiltrating a huge continent, without overt political takeover, found the services of a more or less neutral group invaluable for their purposes. Their linguistic mobility alone made them an asset: they became the bridge between two economies. Ideal middle people, they climbed the ladder of commerce, starting first as minor functionaries of the European companies, moving upwards to become merchants and traders in their own right. They were gradually acknowledged to be shrewd and skilful men and women of business, handling, in some instances, considerable capital and deeply involved in the slave trade.[21]

Edward Barter of Cape Coast was outstanding but not unique:

> He hath [wrote Bosman] a greater power on the Coast, than all the three English agents together (in whom the chief command of the Coast is vested jointly). . . . He is become so considerable that he can raise a large number of Armed Men, some whereof are his own slaves, and the rest Free-men, that adhere to him. . . . So that his interest is at present so great that he is very much respected, honoured and served by the principal People about him: and whoever designs to trade with the English must stand well with him before he can succeed.[22]

The Afro-English clan of Tuckers in seventeenth- and eighteenth-century Sierra Leone wielded equivalent commercial power. So too did the influential Vaz family of the Upper Guinea Coast,[23] whose most formidable member was the female mulatto merchant Bibiana Vaz. A tough, not over-scrupulous businesswoman, she traded in every section of the littoral regions with the Papels, the Banhuns, the Mandingos and the English. It was said that, "with her own two masted vessel and other smaller craft, she was able to exploit the coastal and riverain trade to the full".[24] She became the spearhead of a movement in the 1680s that set out to resist the attempted Portuguese monopoly of the Atlantic trade. Such a monopoly if successful, would have crushed the Afro-Portuguese middle people. The episode was full of melodrama. It included the imprisonment of Captain Major Jose D'Oliveira, head of the Portuguese administration, for fourteen months in Bibiana's house, her own subsequent arrest, exile and eventual reinstatement; all of which demonstrated the initiative and effective solidarity of "a whole new class articulating a well-defined set of commercial interests".[25]

A fundamental aspect of their economic strength was their native base. In Bibiana Vaz's case, it made possible her wealth, influence and survival. The Portuguese administration could not, much as they would have liked to, levy on her property, because it was too far in the African interior.[26] The governor of Cape Verde found that he could not take on the uncertain business of arresting subversive mulatto leaders because they had the protection of neighbouring African tribes.[27] On the other hand, mulattoes could just as easily, when necessary, exploit their European links. Certainly they gained financially from their white ancestry: in many instances, they received their original trading capital from their European fathers.[28]

The sixteenth and seventeenth centuries saw a relatively even balance of the two racial influences; but with the mushrooming of European commercial activities, and particularly with the opening up of slave trading, white cultural values exercised the greater magnetism. Mulattoes tended to live apart from their original tribal kin, to rely increasingly, in entrepôts like Elmina, on the patronage and protection of Europeans.[29] They underplayed their black heritage and stressed their white. Their adoption of Christian religions underlined their alienation from their African roots. "Because they christen and marry by the help of a priest", wrote one European observer of the eighteenth-century Euro-Mandingoes of Cape Verde, "they reckon themselves still as well as if they were actually white, and nothing angers them more than to call them Negroes".[30]

Their position, however, was inherently equivocal. Moving away from the native compound, emphasizing their extra-tribalism, they were never fully embraced by European civilization. Bosman, for example, spoke contemptuously of this

> race begotten by Europeans upon the negroes, and Mulatto Women. This bastard strain is made up of a parcel of profligate villains, neither true to the negroes' norms, nor indeed dare they trust one another: so that you very rarely see them agree together. They assume the name of Christians, but are as great Idolaters as the negroes themselves. . . . I can only tell you whatever is in its own nature worst in the European and Negroes is united in them, so that they are [a] sink of both.[31]

Women came off worst in the assessment of the half-caste. Conspicuously fashionable, "most of the women", declared Bosman, "are Public Whores to the Europeans, and private ones to the Negroes; so that I can hardly give them a character so bad as they deserve".[32] This became the stereotype of the "mongrel" breed of nearly all continents, both cause and effect of the ambivalent quality of the mulatto, offspring of two cultures, citizen of neither.

The Portuguese, the earliest and most persistent of European miscegenators, went to great lengths to give interracial mingling "moral dignity and equalitarian significance".[33] Their most eloquent apologist has been the Brazilian Gilberto Freyre, who saw it, in retrospect, as a special quality of the Iberian colonizing genius. He listed the many gifts to world civilization which "those hybrid descendants of Europeans and autochthonous people" could bring. He rhapsodized in these terms:

> The very value of beauty, particularly as regards the beauty of types of women, would thus come to be enriched, when to the classic Greaco-Roman forms of that type of shape, new substance, and even new forms and especially new colours were added, through the great adventure of miscegenation . . . as a result of which they [the Portuguese] now have like peace islands in the midst of a world divided by racial wars, Timor, Macau, Angola, Mocambique, Guinea . . . .[34]

The "great adventure" has, however, been observed differently by other historians. More careful research into the assimilationist policies of the Portuguese have demonstrated that sexual contact between blacks and whites could and did exist side by side with racial intolerance and discrimination.[35] Similarly in Jamaican development, ostensibly liberal treatment of some coloured peoples did not conceal a deep-seated regard for them as unequal to white. Miscegenation in African has in fact been defined, with greater credibility, as "erotic expediency" arising from the simple fact that European wives did not as a rule accompany their husbands to West Africa in the sixteenth, seventeenth and eighteenth centuries.[36] The image of Africa was, physically and culturally, a hostile one: the view expressed of Senegal in the eighteenth century, applied widely, namely, "another Siberia, fit only for male-factors and libertines";[37] no place for white women.

JAMAICAN BEGINNINGS

In Spanish Jamaica, self-indulgence, as much as expediency, may have brought the coloured group into being. Extra incentives were offered to white settlers with wives and children, in preference to unmarried men.[38] There is evidence of strong domestic attachments among those who had families: concern for their safety recurs throughout the Spanish records.[39] Nevertheless, in 1650, a member of one of the leading families, Don Francisco de Leyba Ysassi, island treasurer and married, was known to have had a liaison with a mulatto woman for more than sixteen years.[40] A student of the Seville papers came to the conclusion that Don Christoval de Ysassi, who led the Spanish resistance, "was in some degree related to the Negroes who fought under him".[41] Example of interracial unions came even closer home to the English: there was still on the island a handful of survivors from the raiding excursion of 1635 led by General William Jackson,[42] and one of these Englishmen converted to the Roman Catholic faith and married a slave of Don Joana de Fuentes.[43]

The fate of the Afro-Spanish mulattoes whom the English found is not absolutely clear. Like the blacks they were an integral part of the colonial garrison – there were, for example, two companies of mounted mulattoes and free Negroes.[44] At one stage, they were identified with the remnants of the fugitive Spaniards and were hunted down by the African allies of the English.[45] Some perished, some escaped to Cuba, others survived, linked with the rebel blacks and "lived by robbing and hunting, committing many murders".[46]

When free coloureds agitated for civil rights in the nineteenth century, they claimed that Jamaica's early constitutional edicts had granted them the status of full citizenship, of which they had been subsequently deprived. This status, they maintained, was therefore theirs by natural right: they were asking for nothing new.[47] It was a good debating stance, for which there was partial justification. In the first desperate days of occupation, English efforts to buy more black fighting hands did, at times, have a ring of racial liberalism, soon however, to be silenced. When mulattoes claimed constitutional rights as inherent in the royal proclamation of 1661, which granted to "all children of any of our natural-borne subjects of England, to bee borne in Jamaica . . . the same privileges, to all intents and purposes, as our free-borne subjects of England",[48] they were on even less certain ground. They were arguing, retroactively, that since they were not black, they should have been assumed white. The whites, also retroactively, were arguing the reverse. It is inconceivable that early Jamaica settlement, a classic case study of colonization by improvisation, could have legislated for a class who did not then exist, even if their ultimate appearance could have been predicted.

Harking back to the past reflected less of seventeenth-century realities, and more of the actual role which free coloureds gradually came to assume, that of the traditionalists, never the radicals of the society. They were obviously not numerous enough in the seventeenth century, and even the first decades of the eighteenth, to qualify as a class, and they are not differentiated as such in the few population estimates of that period.[49] Neither of the two most discerning writers of the late seventeenth century, Sir Hans Sloane and John Taylor, makes reference to them. Apart from their identification with the resistance, they appear on the occasional estate inventory of 1675 and 1676,[50] serving only to indicate that from an early stage mixed blood placed the individual, although enslaved, in a separate racial category from blacks. The earliest discrimination acts of 1711 and 1713, banning mulattoes from public office and from managerial posts on estates, did not single them out as special victims, but covered all potential aliens, namely, Negroes, Indians and Jews.[51] Marginal to the consciousness of Jamaica's founding fathers, it was only when the Afro-English became visible as more than a scattered handful that they began to be observed as problem children of the society, requiring special handling.

The peculiarity of the mulatto situation is demonstrated in one of the first available case histories of a member of that group. In 1672, the fortunes of Cary Helyar were beginning to look up. His sugar enterprise seemed about to pay off. He planned a life of gentility, requiring a new house and a wife. First, he had to set aside his brown mistress, the mother of his two sons. She was promised an annuity of £32, "on consideration she would save him harmless from the parish and never trouble him". He was then free to marry Priscilla. A few months later Helyar died, leaving his ex-mistress the untidy task of suing his estate for her annuity. With some difficulty, the Court accepted the testimony of her mother, "the old Grandum", on her behalf. She nevertheless lost her plea, although the judge, Sir Thomas Modyford, seemed to favour her cause. With such a powerful patron, she eventually succeeded not only in getting employment in his household, but with his assistance arrived at a private settlement with Helyar's executor for the maintenance of her sons.[52]

Ambivalence was inherent in interracial alliances. The female partner, member of an inferior caste, was expendable; on the other hand, the relationship created responsibilities which were acknowledged and provided for in a variety of ways. In a perceptive and provocative article on mulattoes in the British American colonies,[53] Winthrop Jordan points to the mainland where the offspring of mixed unions were indeed the skeletons in the family cupboard, denied public recognition. "On the continent, unlike the West Indies," he writes, "mulattoes represented a practice about which men could only feel guilty. To reject and despise the production of one's own guilt was very natural."[54] North American law and custom tended therefore to classify mulattoes as "Negroes", and so maintain the fiction that whites had had no part or lot in their being.

West Indians, and particularly Jamaicans, were less guilt-ridden: mulattoes came to be a real part of the social scene, their distinctive presence recognized, albeit with contradictions and reservations.

The difference in attitude between the continent and the island was influenced by demography. The imbalance between the sexes in white Jamaica was always high, the most extreme in Anglo-America. Men outnumbered women in ratios of from 1:26 to 1:2 in the seventeenth century[55] – a period when the black sex ratio was evenly balanced.[56] Granted the fact of "biological inevitability", granted the power of the master over his slave, it is easy to understand the pace at which Englishmen embraced black women. As the importation of Africans gathered momentum, accompanied by a relative decline in white female numbers, this practice grew.

In 1722, when whites numbered seventy-one hundred and blacks numbered eighty thousand, it was estimated that there were eight hundred free coloureds.[57] This figure does not include a crucial statistic of miscegenation, the number of mulattoes who legally retained the status of their slave mothers, and had not therefore joined the ranks of the freed. It is impossible to give the number of mulatto slaves in the seventeenth and early eighteenth centuries, but it is fairly certain that they outnumbered free coloureds. The early social scene suggests that they would have been fathered by a relatively large proportion of lesser planters and servants, financially less able to purchase their enfranchisement. As the century advanced, the majority of mulattoes were more favourably placed to become free men and women. In 1768, Long estimated the free coloureds at approximately thirty-seven hundred; mulatto slaves numbered seventeen hundred.[58]

Tolerance of mulattoes throughout the British colonies tended to relate to the size of their black communities. Starting with the most stringent laws against interracial mingling in New England, with its 3 per cent black minority, increasingly relaxed legislation can be traced throughout the mid-colonies (8–15 per cent), North Carolina (25 per cent), Georgia (40 per cent), South Carolina (60 per cent), Barbados (75 per cent), the Leeward Islands (80 per cent), and the most interracially permissive area in Anglo-America, Jamaica, with a black preponderance of 90 per cent. Here, no legislation against mixed unions, either marital or extramarital, existed, as on the mainland.[59] In addition to manumission, there were special legislative procedures in Jamaica for elevating the offspring of such unions.[60] Jordan implies that the overwhelming racial and sexual imbalance had forced the white Jamaican by the eighteenth century, unlike the continental, to abandon hope of maintaining his physical and cultural integrity, hence the recognition and upgrading of the mulatto. "Jamaica," he asserts, "with the highest proportion of Negroes and the highest sex ratio of all the English colonies, was unique in its practice of transforming Negroes into white men."[61]

It is debatable, however, how much fundamental dissimilarity existed between the racial objectives of the mainland and those of the island. All the weight of evidence points to a Caribbean oligarchy, which also saw its world as a white world. The Jamaican creole also sensed "that continued racial intermixture would eventually undermine the logic of the racial slavery upon which his society was based;" and that "the presence of mulattoes blurred the essential distinction" between white and black, a distinction absolutely vital to the preservation of this social order.[62] But the local climate would dictate different solutions, so that if ostracism of mulattoes on the continent was essentially part of white design to retain its superiority, it can be argued that the partial integration of mulattoes was applied in Jamaica towards the identical end.

The Jamaican white remained, throughout slavery, an intractable racist and pragmatist. If erotic imperatives resulted in the presence of a brown breed, those browns could be bleached into a condition of usefulness to the white establishment, could supplement the shortfall in white numbers, could become surrogate whites. Long voiced the realistic creole stand in the matter, as follows: "It will be of some advantage, as things are circumstanced, to turn unavoidable evils to that benefit of society, as the best preparation that can be made for this breach of its moral and political institutions."[63]

The strategy of selected co-option of mulatto offspring to the cause of the master/father was applicable in Long's time; it had had peculiar relevance from the early eighteenth century, when white depopulation and black rebellion threatened white survival. It is significant that legislation in 1738, which aimed at rendering "free Negroes, Mulattoes, and Indians more useful" for the island's military purposes,[64] coincided with more liberal policies towards individual mulattoes and a generally more conscious regard for the browns as a group.[65] These policies unfailingly reflected the establishment's need to make a virtue of necessity: reflected always the basic ambiguities of the subject in hand, as well as the white creole's determination never to lose control of social relationships; so that whatever was conceded with one hand, was almost instantly snatched away with the other.

INHERITANCE, LEGISLATION AND THE "MULATTO PROBLEM"

Douglas Hall deftly describes the crux of the mulatto problem: "the master possessed a woman who was a slave and who bore him a child who was a chattel".[66] Both individual and official action attempted the resolution of this anomaly. Where the mother of a mulatto was a slave woman, the child, by law, was automatically a slave; but as offspring of a free white man, it had at least one foot through the door of the white world. Early evidence appeared of the will and authority of the white parent to gain for his offspring at least qualified admission into that world.

In theory, a slave, black or brown, was a slave: the law made no distinction between the status of mulatto and black chattels. But custom did: mixed blood was increasingly seen to be a determining factor in the condition and occupation of mulatto slaves. Planters tended to remove them from the lowest category of workers, to make tradesmen out of the males, to promote females from the field to the great house.[67] Preferential treatment, designed to make white allies out of brown slaves, applied particularly to women, who as domestics and housekeepers served many functions. Even the female mulatto Maroon captive, as has been noted, was regarded differently. A brown slave was embarrassment enough, just capable of acceptance by being a privileged slave. But a brown female rebel virtually baffled solution: removal from the local scene seemed the logical fate.[68] And so early precedents were established, even within the slave hierarchy, for the brown woman to be somewhat special and capable of a unique type of mobility.

A more fundamental step was, of course, enfranchisement. Of the eight hundred free coloureds in the 1720s, some may have purchased their freedom themselves (the most unlikely means at this stage of Jamaican development), or have been born of free black or mulatto mothers, or have been manumitted by their fathers. In either of the two latter cases, white male initiative was important, as is clearly demonstrated in seventeenth-century wills.[69] The House of Assembly's report of 1762 on free-coloured Jamaicans also made evident a longstanding pattern of white men arranging for the manumission of their black/brown mistresses and/or their coloured children.[70] The mere act of manumission, however, was just the first technical step towards creating more whites, for it implied essentially the master's relinquishment of his property in the slave. It conferred no rights as such on the enfranchised.

The process of coloured enfranchisement was carried even further. Official policy made clear the point at which adequate infusions of European blood could make black white. If blacks proceeded to mate white enough, long enough, eventually ethnic and legal problems would take care of themselves. The law of 1733 confirmed that "mustifinos" and lighter-skinned coloureds, namely, those persons above three degrees removed in a lineal descent from a black ancestor, were deemed white and enjoyed the status of English citizenship.[71] The genetic process of producing more creole whites worked: the early records deal with the first generation hybrids, that is, mulattoes (in the strict sense, offspring of black and white).[72] By the end of the eighteenth century, a high incidence of quadroons (that is, offspring of mulatto and white) and of mustees (offspring of quadroon and white) indicates that the population had taken seriously legal encouragement to move from one race to another in three generations.[73] But that took time.

Speedier and more effective methods of assuring free mulattoes at least partial integration into the social order were the acquisition of property and the enjoyment of specially legislated privileges.

By the 1760s, when free-coloured Jamaicans numbered approximately thirty-five hundred,[74] the property which they held had become a matter of serious official attention. On 16 March 1762, Mr T. Gordon reported to the House of Assembly on the findings "of the Committee appointed to enquire into what exorbitant grants and devises had been made to Negroes and Mulattoes or the illegitimate issue of the Negroes or Mulattoes within the fourth degree".[75] The committee found it impossible to cover all such grants, and what it presented to the House was merely an abstract of some of these devises. The sums of money which they listed represented mainly the value of slave and of personality, not of reality, which was estimated to be at least half the amount of the personality. On this assessment, individual mulattoes were possessed of considerable property. Their combined holdings, excluding much of their real estate, totalled in value over £230,000.[76]

There were fifty devisees in all, including twenty-eight women, fifteen of whom, at least, had been the mistresses of testators. The race and legal status of these women were given: four were slaves (three black and one mulatto); eleven were free (eight black and three mulatto).[77] The implication is that enslaved women were usually manumitted as a result of these associations. In addition to gaining their liberty, provisions were nearly always made for their support; and in most instances, they were left comfortably off. John Patoun bequeathed legacies adequate to maintain them for the rest of their lives to the three women with whom he had cohabited: one free mulatto, one free black and one slave. Thomas Golding, owner of a sugar work in Vere and a pen in Clarendon, left his household furniture and an annuity of £50 each to two free black women, the mothers of his six mulatto children. Mary Thomson, a free women (her race unspecified), received 40 acres of Thomas Orgill's estate in St Mary, plus eleven blacks for life. Lucius Levermore, Esq., bequeathed the use of his pen, Great Pimento, as well as three blacks, for life, to his housekeeper Elizabeth. Jennerson, a free black woman, received through the will of Samuel Seagrove "his household goods, kitchen furniture, wearing apparel, plate, rings, chaise, and best saddle horse, one hundred pounds, four houses in Kingston, two in Lamb-lane, and thirteen blacks for life, if she remained single. An annuity of 50 and a year's residence in his house in Kingston."[78]

Susanna Augier, mulatto spinster, had been granted her freedom in 1738 as a result of her alliance with Peter Caillard, Esq., who left her in his will a life interest in a valuable pen in St Catherine, a profitable mountain at Wag Water in St Andrew, and sundry houses in Kingston and St Jago. She had also borne two children for Gibson Dalzell, Esq., who owned personal property at his death worth £6,854 1s. 3d., in addition to considerable realty, including a sugar plantation.[79] When she died in 1760, she left personality valued at £1,097 14s. 8½d. Her belongings reflect something of her lifestyle: she left among other things crested plate, silver and ivory-handled cutlery, marble-topped tables, a mahogany dresser, a gold-headed cane, a chariot, a pair of horses, thirty-five head of stock (mules and cows) and eight slaves.[80]

The chief beneficiaries, however, were the mulatto and quadroon children and in some instances grandchildren of these unions, some thirty-seven in all.[81] The majority appeared to be already free, no doubt following the status of their mothers; for the handful left enslaved, as in the case of Lucius Levermore's four mulatto children, the request was made that their freedom be purchased.

Substantial portions on the whole accrued to the legatees. Levermore's estate was in fact a modest one, his inventory amounting to £2,103 17s. 6d. William Foster, merchant of Spanish Town, on the other hand, died, "seized of a very considerable estate, consisting among things of a sugar plantation in St John's, called Watermount; one very valuable pen, called Dirty-Pitt, one other pen, called Hog-Hole; and divers houses in the towns of Kingston and St Jago de la Vega". Foster's inventory was valued at £56,301 4s. 6¼d., devised to his daughter Anna Petronnella, "the issue of a negro woman slave".[82]

The solid base provided by this sort of inheritance became, for individual free mulattoes, their launching pad for an even better life. The peculiarly Jamaican device of a private Act of Privilege was the passage to improvement. The legislative process was frequently started by the white father, but could be set in motion by the black or mulatto mother or by the coloured offspring themselves. A petitioner for a private bill, which would entitle him or her to special privileges equivalent to those of whites, had to state carefully the qualifications for such privilege. The basis of eligibility was property, with Christian education and membership in the Anglican church as important added requirements.

Elizabeth Rogers, a quadroon, on 14 May 1747, petitioned the House of Assembly on behalf of herself and her daughter, Mary Bagnet. She was the daughter of Dr Rogers by one Rachel, a free mulatto woman. She owned a freehold consisting of 48 acres of land, and four blacks valued at £350. She had been educated in the principles of the Christian religion and was in the communion of the Church of England. Her daughter Mary, ten years old, was the child of a white man, was christened, was attending school and owned fourteen slaves. The committee of the House which investigated these claims, found the petitioners to be "fit objects of public regard".[83]

Another typical plea was that of Stephen Lost, a St Catherine merchant, who presented the case for his five children's advancement in August 1756. These children by Mary Ricketts, a free mulatto, deceased, had been baptized, and were to receive instructions in the principles of the Christian religion and in the communion of the Church of England. He had sent three of his children, including his daughter Elizabeth, to England to be educated, and he planned to do the same for the other two. He himself, he stated, owned a considerable fortune, which he proposed to distribute among his children, as soon as they came of age.[84]

Acts of Privilege, which totalled 128 in the eighteenth century,[85] invariably involved more than one petitioner. Thirty-nine, for example, which were passed between 1737 and 1769, accounted for a total of 145 persons, 68 males and 78 females.[86] They do not, however, reflect the prevailing economic condition of the majority of Jamaican mulattoes, a large number of whom remained, as has been indicated, in the category of dispossessed slaves, although relatively less dispossessed than their black peers.

The circumstances of the average free coloured, black and brown, are probably more accurately reflected in the few inventories found of this class; for example, Jane Enguston, a free black woman of Kingston, was worth £178 12s. 6d. when her estate was assessed on 12 September 1764. It included some thirty-seven items of old furniture and clothes valued at £9 10s., jewellery at £2 10s., three hundred pounds of coffee priced £9, cash to the value of £1 13s. 9d., a credit note of £13 and her most valuable asset, three slaves (two of them children) worth £110.[87]

Another free black woman, Elizabeth Huggins, owned a house at Jew Alley in Kingston, valued at £190. Her personal effects were worth £5.[88] Rebecca Robinson, a free mulatto woman of St David's, had an estate on 29 July 1766 worth £173 5s. 7½d., which included three slaves, valued at £130, and miscellaneous small stock and poultry.[89] Such persons, and they were in the majority, were worlds removed materially from the heiresses to estates of men like Lost and Foster.

But not even for these fortunate few did the acts establish their full equality with whites. Their very terminology, it has been observed, makes clear that free coloureds were regarded not as a class entitled to the same "rights" as white citizens but as a class which could, from time to time, produce special individuals, on whom selected "privileges" could be bestowed by an establishment prompted first by expediency, secondarily by charity and rarely, if ever, by egalitarianism.[90]

A study of the original manuscript laws of the eighteenth century has shown that the Jamaican Assembly seldom granted "all the rights and privileges of English subjects born of white persons" for which the petitioners applied. These private bills spelt out in detail which in particular of the essential rights of citizenship, whether of suffrage, of office holding, of testimony in judicial procedure and so on, would be conceded the individual petitioner. In fact, "only 4 of the 128 laws provided for the grant of all of the rights of white men, including suffrage and office holding (subject, as in the case of whites, to property and religious qualifications)".[91]

The Lost brothers and sister, for example, and any "such children as they or any of them have or may hereafter have . . . born of white women or begott by white men", were granted equality with whites in all judicial proceedings; but were excluded from holding public office, serving on juries, sitting in the Assembly and voting.[92]

Anna Petronnella Woodard's private act sounded more generous than it actually was. She was granted, like the Losts, full freedom of the courts: no reservations ostensibly entered her act, which stated her entitlement to "enjoy all and every the Rights Privileges and Immunities of White Persons . . . in the same manner as if she, had been born of White Parents".[93] But since only men could vote, hold public office, sit in the Assembly or serve as jurors, this left almost no other rights or privileges that a woman could claim; disabilities of sex replaced those of colour.

The true value of these acts, with their hand-picked privileges, conferred on hand-picked individuals, lies in the extent to which they mirror faithfully the white oligarch's concept of the marginal brown's place in a white/black complex. They dealt with a vulnerable class, which, belonging nowhere, could be manipulated by the prospect of belonging somewhere. The acts also made clear that the brown puppets should be in no doubt as to who pulled the strings.

The procedure adopted for the passage of these acts emphasized this point: requests for private bills were carefully vetted by a small committee of the House of Assembly, usually three eminent members of the plantocracy, who, in a small society, knew precisely who or what the petitioner was:[94] Mr Gordon, for example, in presenting his report on mulattoes, admitted to the Speaker that one source of his information on the colour and illegitimacy of the legatees was "the notoriety of the fact".[95] It was unusual for the House to reject the recommendations of its committee: the civic status and future prospects of the mulatto was thus seen to rest on the grace and favour of a few creole patrons and scrutineers.

The case of the Elletsons further illustrates how the attitudes and procedures governing the fate of the mulatto worked. On 4 October 1760, Jane Harris, free mulatto woman, and her children, John and Dorothy Elletson, the reputed son and daughter of John Elletson, Esq., of St Thomas-in-the-East, petitioned for a private Act of Privilege. The children were suitably endowed with a Christian upbringing; John Elletson had been schooled in England, and was possessed of a very good estate, consisting of a sugar plantation and of divers lands and slaves. His sister was at that time in England, "for the benefit of her education", and was entitled to a considerable fortune. Their mother's condition, however, clearly gave the Assembly some thought: they debated her eligibility for privilege and eventually rejected the bill in the form presented on 6 October 1760. A revised version of the bill reappeared before the House on 24 October, carefully omitting mention of Jane Harris, and was duly passed.[96]

It is interesting that this case coincided with the beginning of the Assembly's consideration of the extensive holdings of mulattoes.[97] The conspicuous wealth of the Elletsons and the embarrassment they appeared to create may well have played a part in triggering off the debate. The controversy which followed it resulted in the major legislative act of the eighteenth century aimed at determining precisely how far the mulatto would be permitted to advance within the white structure. The Devises Act of 19 December 1761 observed that the numerous and valuable bequests to mulattoes "tend greatly to destroy the distinction requisite and absolutely necessary to be kept in this Island between white Persons and Negroes, Their issue and offspring". The fear was that in time such large coloured holdings might be "the means of decreasing the number of white inhabitants". Since it was the "Policy of every good Government to restrain individuals from disposing of property to the particular prejudice and detriment of their heirs and relations and to the Injury and Damage of the Community in general", a restraint was therefore placed on any gifts to mulattoes, Negroes or other illegitimates, of land, cattle, slaves and money exceeding the value of £2,000.[98]

Ambiguity continued to dog the mulatto condition, for individual white fathers still proceeded to prepare special petitions to grant them the freedom to dispose of their property to their coloured children as they chose, notwithstanding the Devises Act of 1761.[99] In other vital areas of existence, the creole policy of elevating the coloured, within limits, went hand in hand with their policy of downgrading him or her, within limits.

Occupationally, the free coloured were neither landed proprietors, nor chattel workers. They tended to drift into the towns and slid into the no man's land of petty local entrepreneurship, became the artisans, lesser middlemen and women of the economy.[100] Brown female innkeepers, traders, rum distillers, seamstresses, hirers of slaves, met the "service" needs of Port Royal, Kingston, Spanish Town, Montego Bay, Falmouth. The establishment was alert to such activity and insisted, at least in theory, that these marginal occupations should be reserved for secondary whites. There were, presumably, other fields, unspecified, in which mulattoes could or should be better engaged: hence the legislation of 1730, which was designed "to render free Negroes and Mulattoes more useful", restricted their hawking and peddling.[101] In fact, lesser whites continued to migrate, and free coloureds to service the domestic economy.

The act of 1733 to secure the freedom of elections, which had made clear that selected racial mating could produce ethnically and legally acceptable citizens, also made it equally clear that mulattoes could not vote.[102] In 1748, Act 153 granted free blacks, Indians and mulattoes, for the first time, the right to give evidence in court against each other; but a firm distinction was made between the specially endowed individuals who had benefited from Acts of Privilege and "lesser freed persons" (that is, those without the blessing of a private act). These were required to prove that they had been enfranchised for at least six months before claiming the right of the evidence of their equals in the courts.[103]

The Jamaican plantocracy thus awkwardly applied itself to the task of keeping the mulatto in his or her place, simultaneously revealing its awareness that he or she had no predetermined place in the socio-ethnic order.

No member of the mulatto group was more subject to the paradoxes and tensions of the circumstances than the woman. Officialdom had made Christian respectability an imperative for citizenship, but simultaneously, the electoral law of 1733, as well as Acts of Privilege contained a clear invitation to blacks and browns to improve the lot of their future generations by mating white;[104] and this, in the eighteenth-century creole context, meant for the woman extramarital mating.

Not that mixed marriages did not take place. Sarah Shreyer, a free mulatto, was the wife of Godfrey Shreyer, "the elder planter of the parish of St Mary, a white man". They had five children, and when Shreyer died in 1764 he left a substantial estate, valued at £20,092. Of the 179 slaves whom he left, twenty-two were the personal property of his widow.[105] Elizabeth Cadogan, a free mulatto, had been formerly married to "a gentleman", Lawrence Cole. One of her sons was, incidentally, married to a white woman in the town of Kingston.[106] Samuel Du Fresnay, who was married to a free mulatto woman, Ann Du Fresnay, appears to have been white.[107] So too was William Wyllis, bookkeeper of Kingston, the husband of Lucea, the daughter of a free mulatto carpenter, William Gregory;[108] and there were a few others.[109] But these were the cases that stand out in the records because of their rarity. Marrying white was almost too much for the brown woman to aspire to; she settled for the role of concubine.

The status of concubine obviously held out hopes of cons rewards. Whites, always hopelessly outnumbered by blacks, needed browns; and as long as white female absenteeism prevailed to the extent to which it did, white men would need brown women most of all. Such women, even though relegated to extramarital associations, could still maximize the opportunities thus offered to them.

The woman could not fail to see that she was the key person in the process of upward mobility. It was her initial mating pattern which set in motion the exodus of certain blacks, legally and ethnically, out of the servile class. Once this trek started, the tendency, as has been suggested, was for mixed families to continue to lighten their complexions through their women's selection of suitable sex partners.

Personal, familial and public pressures inevitably made of the mulatto a social and psychological hybrid. The brown woman who narrowly escaped death in the 1760 slave uprising in St Mary lived precariously in limbo: she was raped by rebellious blacks for being a white overseer's mistress. Her life, however, was spared because it was remembered in time that, in the past, she was alleged to have interceded for her slave brothers and sisters. The real facts seem to have been that her white lover, afraid to appear weak to his slaves, had attributed to her a leniency which was really his.[110]

She would be extraordinary indeed if the values, so authoritatively imposed from above, did not sink deeply into her subconscious. The blueprint for citizenship – property, Christianity, education (English style) and the white mate – implied rejection of the slave heritage, which had none of these gifts to offer. The black side was the negative, inhibiting side, best forgotten. If the mulatto nursed a resentment against the white society that would never fully accept her, she bore an even greater resentment against the black ancestry which made her unacceptable. If, on the one hand, she could exploit her command of white male attention, on the other, she could exercise the extreme of prejudice and discrimination against her black kin. In a crisis, she could be relied on to throw her lot in with the white interest, which always promised promotion, which accommodated, albeit uneasily, the brown skin, as long as it wore its white mask.

Part Two

CREOLE SLAVE SOCIETY, 1770–1834

4   The White Woman in Jamaican Slave Society

King's House, Spanish Town, Jamaica, was thought to be, wrote Edward Long, "the noblest and best edifice of the kind, either in North America or any of the British colonies in the West Indies".[1] Governor Lyttleton had then recently spent £30,000 on rebuilding and redecorating it. The resulting effect was "an air of grandeur".[2] It was an appropriate seat for the most prestigious governorship in the British New World in the late eighteenth and early nineteenth century.[3]

The combined positions of head of the civil establishment and commander-in-chief of the Jamaican military forces carried handsome emoluments, estimated at between £8,500 and £10,000 yearly,[4] with attractive prospects of added trading fees and prizes for seized vessels.[5] The perquisites included the use of Government Penn, a short distance from Spanish Town, which contained 300 acres of land and an elegant villa, as well as a provision farm in the mountains "with a comfortable mansion house". From both of these places, the governor and his family were supplied with "hay and corn, mutton, milk, poultry and provisions for [their] domestics, creating a saving in [their] housing expense of at least £1,000".[6]

Birth and influence in the mother country determined appointment to this colonial prize. The Jamaican posting proved a windfall to Sir Basil Keith, the governor from 1774 to 1777. In the 1760s, his family was concerned about his financial difficulties. They pledged themselves to "plot, project and plan" for the restoration of "his ragged fortunes".[7] Their efforts procured him the governorship and a wealthy wife. The one initially subsidized the other. His outlay for the job, in spite of "all the attention possible to the strictest economy consistent with his situation", was nearly £6,000, which included, among other things, the cost of his horses and £500 for the purchase of his commission. It would have been impossible for him to meet these expenses without his marriage settlement.[8] But the investment seemed to him fully justified. Indeed, he was "positively determined to realize all again before [I] leave Jamaica": he was confident about the "good desirable purchases we may buy in the West Indies".[9]

The position of the king's representative and his lady was actually not as exalted in the eighteenth and early nineteenth century, as it became in the days of Crown Colony government, when constitutional arrangements trimmed the wings of the Jamaican plantocracy. But truculent and self-assertive as the native oligarchy could be, it was a small and imitative community, obsessed with status and with the metropolitan image. It accommodated itself to the expatriate elite, who, on the whole, met local expectations: King's House set as its standard "a little aping of England's court life".[10]

There was unabashed curiosity shown by creoles, white and black, high and low, when the new incumbents came into residence. There was something of the ceremonial exercise of a nation's right to satisfy itself of the authenticity of its "royal family". Maria Nugent described her first formal meal in the ballroom of King's House in Spanish Town. She could scarcely call her company "guests, as these dinners were given to us by the public out of the entertainment vote. . . . All the population, I believe, both white and black, were admitted to walk round the table and stare at me after dinner."[11] After this followed, as a rule, "a kind of public entry into Kingston". There the festivity continued, with the custos and the inhabitants "who usually made a subscription purse for the purpose, attempting to outdo the capital in lavish entertainment".[12]

Life, for the governor's wife, then settled into a round of levees, in the drawing-room and in the bedroom; regular inspections of troops, a retinue of young officers always in attendance, grand progresses through the island (pregnancy notwithstanding), gracious endurance of varied ceremonials, mingled with boredom, fatigue and discomfort.

Spanish Town came alive at the judicial and legislative sessions, and particularly between the months of October and December, when the Assembly sat.[13] Mrs Brodbelt, the wife of a Spanish doctor and councillor, and occasional dinner guest at King's House, voiced native enthusiasm for the social whirl, when the whole tempo of life quickened with the influx of the many friends and acquaintances from the "distant parishes".[14]

Long described fashionable Jamaican society at its high season:

> [A]t these times, universal gaiety prevails; the balls, concerts, and routs, alternatively hold their reign: the Governor, according to ancient custom, gives a ball and entertainment once a year at the King's House, in honour of His Majesty's birthday: the appearance of company on this occasion is generally brilliant, the ladies vying with one another in the richness of their dresses: everyone makes a point of exhibiting a new suit of finery, and this regulation is so lavishly indulged that such a ball is seldom attended with less than three or four thousand pounds expense to the guests, which however is so far excusable, as it is laid out in British manufacture.[15]

Mrs Nugent was all splendour when she attended the grand ball held in her honour by the Council on 25 November 1801:

> [P]ut on my smartest dress, with a gold tiara and white feathers and made myself look as magnificent as I could. At 8, was received at the entrance at the House of Records by the Members of the Council, some of the Assembly, and some military. Was conducted to a sort of throne covered with pink silk and draperies festooned with flowers. The declarations of the room were beautiful and the supper was superb: one dish I shall never forget; it was a roasted peacock placed before me, with all the feathers of the tail stuck in, and spread so naturally, that I expected every minute to see him strut out of the dish. Danced myself almost to death, to please both civil and military, Army and Navy, and stayed till 1 o'clock.[16]

The Spanish Town festivities in honour of the English naval victory over the French at the Battle of the Saints on 12 April 1782 were among the most memorable of the period.[17] Subsequent anniversary celebrations to "the memory of the valiant Rodney" continued to be social landmarks. In 1792, the "whole was climaxed with an elegant Ball to the ladies in the evening, given by the newly-elected members of the Council and the Assembly".[18] Another grand event was the knighting of Governor General Williamson in 1795 by his successor, Lord Balcarres, before his departure for St Domingue:

"A vast concourse" of people flocked to Spanish Town, and the creole debutante Mary Ricketts, being the only privy councillor's daughter present, opened the gala ball.[19]

Local families with social pretensions would not in any circumstances be left out of these glittering occasions, especially as they offered opportunities for their daughters to meet eligible young officers. Only Mrs Henry Lynch struck a slightly sour note: "the stiffest parties that I have been to are the dinners at King's House". But even she conceded that it was "a noble place for dancing";[20] and when Governor Williamson's wife died, Mrs Brodbelt wrote regretting that the Spanish Town season had closed, to "the very great disappointment [of] those who are fond of dancing and dress".[21]

There was a tacit agreement between the occupants of King's House and the island elite. As an outsider, the governor's wife was allowed the privilege of being a little different, a little remote, even a little eccentric. But she was not expected to initiate or to exert conspicuous individuality or to develop relationships in depth: local jealousies and the average short term of office, a couple of years, would in any event inhibit close involvement. Maria Nugent was, in these respects, a very nearly perfect governor's wife. She tactfully avoided "cabals",[22] had only her immediate family as intimates, and only once or twice did she rock the native boat, gently.[23] She admitted probably only to "her dear N." and to her journal that gubernatorial duty could be distasteful, but, *noblesse oblige*. If a "political" dance, as she termed it, was required of her, she would be as agreeable about it as she could.[24] Being proper and pious by instinct and upbringing, she disapproved of the creole Simon Taylor's multicoloured household; but he was the island's leading sugar baron and her husband needed his support. She therefore took the correct wifely stance, offered hospitality to the powerful man, accepted his, and made him proxy godfather to her daughter Louisa.[25]

Respect for local sensitivities was really what the post of governor's wife demanded. If, for example, King's House had not originally set the pattern for Jamaica's superior rating of planter over merchant, it certainly perpetuated it. Mrs Lynch observed: "We have an exclusive system even in this far off corner of the world, and it is seldom that anyone in the merchant's offices at Kingston can get entrée at the King's House."[26] Certainly, few members of the commercial classes appeared on the Nugent's guest list; and the question of black or brown did not arise.

Jamaica's colonial society, structured on a black/white, slave/free dichotomy, devoid of its own innate dignity, imported the form and trappings of a mini-court for the benefit of the chosen creole few. As with bona fide royalty overseas, the person of the monarch scarcely mattered, so that even the scruffy Earl of Balcarres served the island's purpose.[27] But it was generally agreed that a gracious adornment to His Excellency's entourage undoubtedly helped.

CREOLE WHITE WOMEN: DEMOGRAPHIC PROFILE

The female consorts of the military, naval and administrative elite would always be a transient handful: their creole peers were scarcely more numerous. Indeed, white women were always a small minority in Jamaica during the last sixty years of slavery, in relation to the black and brown population of both sexes, as well as in relation to white men. In the 1770s, there were between 17,000 and 18,000 whites, these figures reaching a peak of about 30,000 in the 1820s, and declining to 15,776 in 1844, the date of the first official census.[28] Blacks' numbers throughout this period moved from 230,000 in 1780 to 346,150 in 1817 and fell in the 1820s, reaching a figure of 311,100 in 1834, but sustaining throughout the period a ratio of approximately ten blacks to every white person.[29]

Sex ratios for whites can only be guessed at: whereas the Registry Bill of 1816 made sex data for slaves obligatory information on the triennial returns, no such official ruling produced accurate figures for whites.[30] The restless movement of families between Jamaica and England made them an elusive group. Many of their births, baptisms, marriages and deaths went unrecorded right into the era of compulsory registration.[31] The census of 1844 gives the first reliable statistics, showing a sex ratio of 143.2 males per 100 females.[32]

The statistics of parish populations which exist support, without exception, the prevailing impression of the white creole woman's scarcity. These data probably underestimate her presence, for they were very largely based on calculations made for the purposes of tax assessment or for militia counts.[33] But with this reservation in mind, the sex disparities indicated are very striking.

The parish of St James in 1774 contained, according to Edward Long's estimates, sixty-two sugar plantations, with a total white population of 433 persons, of whom 283 were men and 150 women and children.[34] In 1785, St David's deficiency list showed 93 white persons (79 men and 14 women). In 1790, there was an overall increase of 144, but the sex ratio remained virtually unchanged, 117 men to 27 women.[35] Clarendon in 1788 was estimated to have 418 men and 182 women,[36] and this kind of sex ratio is found in other fragments of parish data, as shown in tables 4.1, 4.2 and 4.3. The sexual imbalance seemed greatest in the young adults, as is indicated in some of the age-group figures available (table 4.2). A similar pattern recurs in a ten-year series of population figures for the parish of Portland during the period 1812–22.

Table 4.1   The White Population in Select Parishes, 1812, 1825–1829

Year	Parish	Male	Female
1812[1]	Portland	217	96
	St George	257	55
	St David	116	10
	Westmoreland	432	129
	Vere	249	110 women & children
	St Thomas	369	49
1825–1829[2]	Westmoreland	560	149
	Port Royal	205	124
	Vere	130–140	12–15
	Manchester (1829)	253	73

Sources:
[1]*PP*, vol. VI, 1814–15, no. 14, Jamaica.
[2]*PP* 1831, Slave Population Papers.

Table 4.2   White Inhabitants in Clarendon, 1788

Age Group	Males	Females
1–10	36	35
10–20	29	33
20–30	105	35
30–40	194	42
40–50	33	20
50–60	14	10
60–70	4	7
Totals	418	182

Source: Add. MSS 12435: Long Papers, Inventory of Sugar Estates in St James, 1774.

Table 4.3   Parish of Portland: Population Returns (White), 1812–1822

Years	Males under 10 Years	Females under 10 Years	Males over 10 Years	Females over 10 years
1812	36	22	169	73
1813	30	18	176	71
1814	32	20	171	74
1815	28	17	173	73
1816	24	16	171	73
1817	21	18	163	72
1818	23	18	168	70
1819	18	16	154	69
1820	18	17	172	70
1821	20	16	147	68
1822	16	20 1	53	66

Source: PP, vol. VII, 1823, Population Returns.

Several Jamaican plantations throughout the island had no resident white females. At the time of Long's count in September 1774, this was true of nineteen of the sixty-two St James sugar estates listed.[37] St David's deficiency returns of 1785 listed thirty out of forty-one estates without white women. Only one had as many as four, and this was one of the larger slaveholding units of Llandewy, Rhyddersh and New Ramble, with 187 slaves, which were regarded as one agricultural complex and which contained seven white persons. It was the only estate of the parish shown to have a larger number of white women than men, a ratio of 4:3. Isolated women stood out in the records of St David's. Albion estate, the largest in the parish, containing 296 slaves, had five white men in residence and one woman, Elizabeth Croder Millward. Colus Valley, next in size with 271 slaves, had four white men and one white woman, Mary Parker.[38]

These were the women who could not be found when Maria Nugent did her grand island tour in 1802. She travelled from Spanish Town eastwards, through the parishes of St Andrew, Port Royal, St David's, St Thomas-in-the-East, northwestwards into Portland, enjoying great-house hospitality en route,[39] and reached Bog Estate near Port Antonio, eight days after setting out, before meeting her first white lady, Mrs Cosens, "a very pleasing young woman".[40]

This was consistent with Edward Long's findings in 1774 on the other side of the island. The higher up the socio-economic scale, the larger the estate, the greater the scarcity of white women. Long distinguished three categories of St James settlers, according to the number of slaves and stock they owned. The first category of seventy-three larger estates, all sugar-growing, had an average of 172 slaves each and 128 head of stock; the white population numbered 332 men and 155 woman and children. The second degree of settlers were coffee and pimento growers, pen keepers, owners of jobbing slaves, professionals, artisans, representing 63 economic units in all. Each contained an average of 47 slaves and approximately 17 head of stock; there were 90 men in this group and 112 women and children. The third degree of settlers, 91 in all, covered the same occupational range as the second, but had smaller operations. They averaged 14 slaves and approximately 3 head of stock: their white population totalled 71 men and 86 women and children.[41]

A further breakdown of the St James sugar estates, reinforces a probable correlation between large industrial enterprises and high white sex ratios: not only did the sugar estates in the parish have proportionately fewer white women than other economic units, but larger sugar estates had fewer even than small sugar estates, both relatively and absolutely. Whereas the eight smallest estates in the sample, that is, those which produced less than sixty hogsheads of sugar in the month of September 1774, had a white population of 32 men and 20 women, the eight largest estates, each of which produced over two hundred hogsheads of sugar, together contained 53 white men and 13 white women.[42]

It is this fugitive minority of persons who nevertheless have traditionally been projected as the arbiters of female creole manners and morals, evidence of the overwhelming effectiveness of the great house image in obscuring all other features of the island's landscape.

The Planter Household: Fiction versus the Domestic Norm

The planter household became Jamaica's dominant domestic norm. Its structure and functioning are documented in an endless flow of contemporary accounts, expressing the view either of the resident or of the passerby, but all attesting to a fairly uniform pattern of living. A rarely expressed perspective is that of the young women of the house. Margaret Cowper, of a Trelawny estate near Rio Bueno, writing in 1820, saw the routine of herself and her sister in this light:

> I will give you a journal of a day at Baron Hill, which is not often much interrupted being an Establishment just calculated to admit of certain deviations, such as one or more acquaintance calling in perhaps to breakfast, to dinner or to sleep. . . . [W]e rise generally at ½ past 6 and breakfast a little after 7 (all early hours for meals in this country) guests or no guests – After Breakfast Mary & myself resort to our own chamber where we pursue the occupations of the day, either needle work, writing or reading till two o'clock when we alter our dress & go downstairs about a quarter before three – at three we dine. The afternoon we mostly sit upstairs also, & then one of us generally reads aloud to the others (as often too in the forenoon when my mother has finished her inspection of household matters which she chuses entirely to see about, ever tenderly considering us – & believing herself better qualified to direct according to my Father's Approbation) Mama being then always with us – at

six o'clock when the sun is declining, Mary & myself visit the garden or ramble about elsewhere till quite dusk & then till candles, walk or sit in the Piazza – when it is time for them we repair to the Hall & generally occupies the Harp, the other reading, also Mama, till supper about ½ past nine, and after supper we chat . . . till we chuse to retire – my Father except when anybody is here seldom sits up later than eight o'clock.[43]

The Cowper family did not belong to the hard core of the local plantoc-racy. Their estate grew, not sugar, but pimento and coffee; their family links were more numerous in Savannah, Georgia, than in Britain, and they had not been living long in Jamaica. But their lifestyle was generally that of the creole elite, reflecting many of its characteristic features.[44]

The physical background to planter domesticity was, with few exceptions, neither elegant nor luxurious, but comfortable.[45] Interiors, in particular, were fitted for the use and enjoyment of a leisurely class. Long found that "the furnishings of some of them is extremely costly: and others constructed in so magnificent style, and of such durable materials as to shew that they were not intended for mere temporary residence".[46] Edward Manning's elab-orately equipped house at Up-Park-Camp in Kingston in the second half of the eighteenth century may have been more representative of the very wealthy planter class in the town than in the country. It contained furniture and other household effects valued at about £2,300 and included items such as ebony and ivory-inlaid mahogany bureaus and bookcases, gold-laced and velvet-fringed dressing tables, damask-curtained mahogany bed-heads, car-pets, hundreds or articles of china (Delftware), crystal, silver, as well as a handsome library of books.[47]

More typical perhaps was that of Ann Halliburton of St Andrew, whose household inventory of 9 February 1773 was valued at £413 10s. and indicated a substantial living standard. Prized among her possessions was her silver col-lection of coffee and tea sets, candlesticks, tankards and the like, weighing 287 ounces in all, at 8s. 9d. an ounce.[48] The fashionable furniture firm of Waring and Willow Limited of Lancashire, England, shipped several con-signments of goods to Jamaica between 1770 and 1788. Their business trans-actions showed a regular consumer demand for domestic items of high quality.[49]

It was the exteriors of planter homes which often suggested that other cri-

teria besides taste and comfort dictated creole domestic style. Estate buildings were usually the outstanding works of construction, whereas the façade
of the family house was sometimes "mean and ramshackle". More than one
writer was struck by the incongruity between the form and the setting of
planter life.⁵⁰ An architectural annex to the sugar factory, the great house,
too, was often a kind of fortress:

> A creole of former days, in building his country-house, had two principal objects in
> view, namely stability against the shock of hurricanes, and security in the event of
> an insurrection of the slaves. Accordingly, the massy stone walls of the lower story of
> his house were perforated with loop-holes for musquestry; while the superstructure
> (of one story), surmounted with a considerably inclined roof, was formed of the
> most substantial hard timber.⁵¹

This was particularly true of north coast estates, where, in addition to
internal risks, privateers would land "in order to plunder the inhabitants of
their negroes".⁵² Most of the houses in the parish of St Ann, as Long pointed
out, "are made defincible with loop-holes". He expressed regret that too
many inland houses were not similarly designed, "either through negligence
or an impudent contempt of danger".⁵³

Isolation was inherent in agricultural and social organization founded in
vast, scattered, relatively self-sufficient land units. It was a corollary also to a
racial/caste system which inevitably inhibited vertical relationships: the hor-
izontal ones, for whites, as statistics indicate, were missing. Northside plantations, hemmed in between the Caribbean sea and the mountains, in an age
of poor inter-island communication, were particularly lonely places for
planter families. It was in this area of the island that the largest agglomera-
tion of the black population was to be found: Hanover, St James, Trelawny,
St Ann and St Mary, each contained double or more the number of slaves to
be found in many other parishes, only St Thomas-in-the-East equalling
them in this respect.⁵⁴

The Cowper sisters felt acutely the absence of their equals. A young male
visitor would naturally cause a flutter in the dull lives of young girls:

> We had a smart English beau in our neighbourhood a week or two and several times
> here – a partner in the house of Bryan Edwards, of the name of Wilders, with all the
> modish nonchalance, and agreeable enough to permit our casting a look at Bryan

Castle sometimes when there, but not so formidable as for his departure to require more than a little phylosophy.[55]

The sense of being cut off from civilization, geographically, racially, motivated the creole view of the white stranger at the gate and underlay the famous planter welcome. The military officer in the 1760s, on his islandwide inspection of barracks, was struck by "the extremely civil and remarkable hospitality of the gentlemen of property", which made inns redundant.[56] Young William Hickey found a generous reception during his whirlwind rake's progress through planter society in the 1790s.[57] Bernard Senior maintained that all the newcomer needed was "an introduction to one respectable family in a parish", which would then be regarded as "a passport to the whole".[58] And the visitor in return might only need to sing for his supper. Cynric Williams joined the daughter of the family in the evening's entertainment after dinner at the home of his host at Orange Grove estate. He noted: "They sang and danced quadrilles and allemandes: one of them excelled on the pianoforte, and my squeaking voice was put under contribution for the bass of a glee . . . . One gentleman favoured us with a negro dance, to a negro tune, both original and diverting and to myself unintelligible."[59]

Long distances and bad roads made it impossible for visits to be casual, hence the elaborate and extended visits exchanged by planter families, lasting days and weeks.[60] Stewart commented:

> Not many years ago it was no unusual thing for one or more families to pay a six weeks visit to their relations, for the purpose of showing the warmth and cordially of their regard. One family of these visitors might consist of from twenty to thirty, including domestics for whom a suitable entertainment was to be provided every day during their stay; so that, instead of a visit, this might more properly be termed a visitation. . . . Before the term of their visit had expired, not a turkey, pig, fowl, or duck, fit for the kitchen, was left on the place, and even the vegetable substance was almost totally consumed.[61]

It proved an increasingly expensive way of having company, but apparently persisted. Even the unexpected "migration" continued to be welcome. Senior, writing in 1835, observed that "the kindness with which they were met, can only be equalled by the friendly entertainment they receive: themselves, their servants, and quadrupeds, invariably find a cordial welcome and substantial fare".[62] If costly, it must nevertheless have been worth it. It served to maintain local family and social links, it helped to preserve the image of an opulent, lavish ruling class, it assisted, temporarily, the illusion of redressing the racial imbalance. But it was only an illusion: each white visitation, inseparable from its "cavalcade of blackies",[63] only served to re-emphasize the dependence of the minority elite on its massive black base.

If the evidence of many contemporaries is to be believed, one might conclude that planter ladies had little or nothing to do in between dispensing hospitality. Long conceded that they were "remarkably expert at their needle, and indeed every other female occupation taught them"; but he admitted, although with great reluctance, that they "yield too much to the influence of a warm climate in their listless indolence of life".[64] James Stewart, writing in 1808, commented that Jamaican ladies considered it "vulgar and ungenteel to rise too early in the morning".[65] He is, in some respects, less critical of them in his later account of 1823, but still, like Long, observed in them, "a languor, listlessness, and disposition to self-indulgence, to which the females of more northern climates are strangers".[66] Bryan Edwards found that, apart from dancing, "in which they delight and excel, they have no amusement or avocation to impel them [to] too much exertion of either body or mind. . . . To a stranger newly arrived, the ladies appear as just risen from the bed of sickness."[67] One supposed female correspondent to a local journal defended "gossipping visits" as necessary relief to those "condemned to lead a miserable, insipid round of life in an obscure part of the country". What, otherwise, she or he asked, were they expected to do with their time, "unless it was to eat half of the day, and sleep the other half".[68]

It was also well known that creole ladies seldom walked.[69] Certainly, there is no contemporary writer who observed in the Jamaican lady anything of the energy and industry which Mrs Carmichael found in the planter wives of the Eastern Caribbean — although what she described was really a plantocracy falling on hard times and gradually descending into the class of a yeomanry. It had practically become, she maintained, "a farmer for the British merchant".[70]

The image of the Jamaican lady who seldom soiled her hands grew out of the context of a numerous black household staff. The Reverend Bridges, Anglican minister of St Ann, describes the compulsion of the newcomer to conform to the creole domestic pattern.[71] On his first arrival in Jamaica, having neither "the inclination nor the ability to purchase servants", he hired his first family "helps", but "their ill-service was a source of continual vexation, labour and expense". Whereas he had been accustomed to make do in England with three servants, he soon found eight inadequate in Jamaica. Besides, the cost of hiring, £320 per annum, was beyond his means. His wife struggled for four years "in trouble and anxiety" when "motives connected with the welfare of my children, induced me to purchase twelve domestics. . . . They are all occupied in no other service than that of the house, for I have no land, and I trust have not exchanged for the worse, by becoming members of my family."[72]

Long confirmed that planter families employed "too numerous a tribe of domestic servants . . . from twenty to forty servants is nothing unusual". He classified them:

1 Butler	1 assistant
2 Footmen, or waiting men	1 key, or storekeeper
1 Coachman	1 waiting-maid
1 postilian	3 house-women
1 helper	3 washer-women
1 cook	4 seamstresses[73]

The great house at Worthy Park, when Rose Price was resident in the 1790s, used from eleven to seventeen slaves.[74] The Jackson estate at Mount Pleasant in Hanover in 1787 had eight domestic slaves listed on its inventory:[75] Beckford's estate at Dank's in Clarendon in 1780 listed twelve.[76] Inventories would fall short, however, of the real size of the domestic retinue, many of whom carried no professional label; for each child in the family tended to have its own nurse, "and each nurse, her assistant boy or girl".[77]

Nor were these all. Senior observed:

Independent of these regular servants already specified, there are invariably a few little pensioners about every house, sons and daughters of a steady waiting man, or of a well behaved cook or house-woman, who get themselves insinuated by some means or other, and are seen employed in sweeping out the fowl-yard, helping the cook, cleaning the knives and forks, or drawing the cart horse of "young massa" or "little missis".[78]

The occasional local family employed its white housekeeper to supervise this army of black helps, but this was rare.[79] As a result, the lady of the house, some maintained, was the sufferer. Sarah Dwarris described her plight thus:

> As to slavery it is only the name for I don't know what great slaves they are, one Servant in England will do as much as four of them, you can't keep house here without five or six of them and notwithstanding you have so many you must look to everything yourself or you will not have one thing decent about you. I am sure the Mistress of a house in this country is the Slave and not her negroes.[80]

Domestic pandemonium was not unknown, such as Mrs Nugent observed at General Rose's house at St Ann's Bay in March 1802:[81]

> This is really a most uncomfortable house, the servants awkward and dirty, the children spoiled, and screaming the whole day. As for the ladies, they appear to me perfect viragos; they never speak but in the most imperious manner to their servants, and are constantly finding fault. West India houses are so thin, that one hears every word, and it is laughable, in the midst of the clamour, to walk out of my room, and see nothing but smiles and good humour, restored to every countenance in an instant.[82]

Long thought creole ladies were very indifferent economists in their household affairs.[83] So did the Reverend William Jones, who wrote: "Domestic economy, one would suppose, had in it something which scared them; they detest its appearance."[84] It is hard to say how well Mrs Cowper, for instance, organized her home, as it seemed appropriate that her daughters should be kept idle and ignorant of domestic matters.[85] Mrs Brodbelt was equally reticent about her household duties, only once, over a long period of correspondence with her daughter Jane, referring, guardedly, to what she had to attend to "below stairs".[86]

There is other evidence suggesting that, if not the girls, women of the house had chores. One writer found that at least in the parish of Vere, ladies turned their hands to independent money-making activity: Indian corn was grown there in abundance, and pigs were widely reared. The pork was marketed in Spanish Town and Kingston "and form a source of comfortable revenue to some small settlers and to the wives of some of the richer planters, who are careful to fill a private purse".[87] The Kings, members of a large Portland planting family, were hardworking women. Louisa King, an unmarried sister helped to care the small stock, while her sister, Harriett,

Mrs William Thompson, wrote frankly to her sister, Isabella, about her financial circumstances: "we, alas, are no better off in the world than when you left us: I work hard to raise stock and live within ourselves".[88]

Women's personal ownership of slaves must also have involved them in their practical management. Legislation of the 1820s prohibited public officials from holding all except domestic slaves; they were required to part with their plantation slaves at the earliest opportunity. But there was nothing to prevent their wives being slave proprietors. Thirteen out of thirty-one officials, including the chief justice, assistant judge, attorney general and ministers, declared either joint or exclusive women's ownership of the family's slaves. The Reverend Lewis Bowerbank, for instance, declared 190 to 200 slaves by right of his wife, who had one-fifth of an interest in the sugar estate Dunbarton in St Ann, "not subject to [his] interference or control".[89] Self-interest might have led to positive exertion.

It would seem that, in actual fact, more ladies busied themselves than was assumed; but no one proclaimed that fact too loudly, as this would not accord with the role which society prescribed for them and which they accepted. Mrs Henry Lynch was rare in questioning the prevailing custom of screening genteel white women from financial reality:

> Ladies in the West Indies have no money cares: not that they do not sympathize with their husband on pecuniary difficulties, but they have no purchase to make concerning eating and drinking: they have no pestering cares, such as bow down the spirit of an English housekeeper, to buy good things, and yet keep within the bounds of, perhaps very restricted means. . . . [W]ith regard to clothing for herself and all of us, papa gives my father access to two or three of the principal stores in Kingston, and Payment for the things received is not her part of the matter. . . . How can girls, brought up in this way ever become what is called in England, good managers? How can they ever prove careful and economical English wives?[90]

Even where the stereotypes did not always apply, contemporary concepts projected the planter female in the role of ornament. Never as doll-like and precious as their American sisters of the slaveholding south, Jamaican gentlewomen were nevertheless seen by many contemporary writers as not quite real. Their "scrupulously correct"[91] conduct at all times, their "habitual temperance and self-denial", "the calm and even tenour of their lives", impressed observers.[92] They possessed a "native goodness of heart and gentleness of disposition" which "combined with their system of life and manners (sequestered domestic and unobtrusive)".[93] The result was that "no women on earth [made] better wives or better mothers".[94]

These women existed at two levels: at that of a largely masculine consciousness of them as delicate beings, requiring masculine protection, and as good creatures, always charitable and forgiving of masculine frailties. Then, there was as well the level of their own actual existence, which often fell short of that idealized perfection.[95]

FAMILY, FERTILITY, MOTHERHOOD AND MORTALITY: THE ELITES

Motherhood constituted a major part of the lives of creole women, although precisely how major, it is impossible to say. Figures on the average size of the white Jamaican family are even more fragmented than on sex ratios. Two critical indices of childbearing, the incidence of stillborn deliveries and of infant mortality, are virtually unrecorded. One suspects that the little family tragedy which the Archers experienced sometime in the 1820s was exceptional only in catching posterity's eyes: "On Monday morning at 9½ o'clock my beloved Mary was confined, after a severe labour delivered of a stillborn male child – the image of her first born 'Jim' – the infant was buried in the garden between the 2 large cocoa trees . . . at 6 p.m."[96]

Hardly one Jamaican family whose surviving papers have been examined during this period failed to record the death, or deaths, in some instances after brief and sudden illnesses, of infant or child. Maternal mortality, too, was grim in the century before childbed pain and infection came under control. The life expectancy of England's ruling class had risen from 32.7 years in the seventeenth century to 49 years in a sample generation of the late eighteenth century.[97] A very crude cross section of Jamaica's elite, those who could afford permanent memorials, shows an average age at death of females buried in the St Andrew Parish Church between 1770 and 1840 to be approximately 33, in Kingston Parish Church 24 years old.[98] The physical vulnerability of childbearing was always a real and influential factor.

But however grave they might have been, the risks of pregnancy and childbirth for the upper-class white woman would have been minimal in comparison to those to other women in the society. With the traditional creole table, laden with "flesh, fish, fowl, game",[99] her diet, for one thing, need never have been protein-starved. Sarah Dwarris's main worry was that some tropical calamity, like the seasonal hurricanes which frequented the 1780s, might coincide with her delivery, for it would then have been impossible for her to get professional help;[100] as it turned out, her baby's arrival just escaped the hurricane by a few days.[101]

Lying-in expenses could be high, estimated at £20 by Sarah Dwarris, who appealed to her parents in England to help out. The midwife's fees alone, she indicated, were £15, "there being but two midwives they pick and chuse who they like",[102] but were apparently worth it. Mrs Hayes, who attended her, proved "a most excellent nurse".[103] Maria Nugent describes

> some of the *agrémens* of a Creole confinement. First, the heat is so dreadful, that it is impossible to go to bed. Then, to mitigate it a little, the blinds are kept closed. Then, the dark shade of the room brings swarms of musquitoes. With these teasing, tormenting insects I am half buzzed out of my senses, and nearly stung to death. Then, the old black nurse brought a cargo of herbs, and wished to try various charms, to expedite the birth of the child, and told me so many stories of pinching and tying women to the bed-post, to hasten matters, that sometimes, in spite of my agony, I could not help laughing, and at others, I was really in a fright, for fear she would try some of her experiments upon me. But the maids took all her herbs from her, and made her remove all the smoking apparatus she had prepared for my benefit.[104]

The birth of her second baby eleven months later was less eventful: it took place within an hour, before the doctor's arrival, and she "was actually speaking, and walking towards the sofa, the instant before it was all over".[105]

In view of the strong resentment expressed in planter circles about black mothers' prolonged nursing of their babies,[106] one would hardly expect to find the practice favoured for whites. Edward Long, knowledgeable in this, as in many other things, declared "a proper age for weaning . . . should not be thought of till most of its teeth are cut".[107] Maria Nugent reluctantly started her baby's weaning at eleven months,[108] and Sarah Dwarris nursed both her babies well past their first year.[109] William Dwarris, seldom given to husbandly compliments, was obviously proud that his wife fed her infants herself, "which I assure you", he wrote, "is rather uncommon here".[110] Sarah

Dwarris regarded breastfeeding as a means of birth control, which she recommended to her sister.[111] She also expressed disapproval of the creole custom of black and mulatto wet-nurses: "I should be very unhappy to have him suck a Negro, there is I think something unnatural in seeing a white child at a black breast besides that of being obliged to put up with their ill manners for fear of hurting your child."[112]

Long shared her disgust: he regarded the practice as self-indulgence, most discreditable to creole ladies, barely tolerable in England where it had originated, but perverted in Jamaica into a "shameful and savage custom".[113] It was the beginning of the decline in health, and worse, of many creole children, he believed.

In Long's opinion, Jamaican mothers, in other respects, applied a good deal of "maternal good sense" to the rearing of children:

> From the time their infants are a month old, they are allowed no other bed than a hard mattress, laid upon the floor: and, instead of a sheet, they repose on a smooth sheep-skin, which is occasionally shifted for the sake of cleanliness. They are clad loose and light, go without the encumbrance of stockings, and bathed regularly in water every day, and exposed freely to the air.[114]

The island was fortunate in having for years benefited from the original research work done on the treatment of two contemporary killer diseases, measles and smallpox, by Dr John Quier of Worthy Park estate.[115] But lingering prejudices against inoculation survived into the nineteenth century: there was, in fact, still some trial and error involved in perfecting the use of cowpox in vaccinations. Maria Nugent was on edge for both her infants, importing her own vaccine virus from England, and never relaxing until they were safely past the worst.[116] As late as 1831, there were still irregularities and hazards in vaccination practices. Dr Archer had conscientiously, between May and August, inoculated over thirty-four children on a number of estates in St Ann, only to find an outbreak of smallpox on his hands in December: "10 December 1831 . . . saw several cases at Retirement where Gatchan's daughter and several of the Negroes had smallpox, including Ophelia, by Gatchan's absurdity of inoculation without medical concurrence."[117]

It was the mysterious tropical fevers, however, which took the greatest toll of young life, and haunted the creole consciousness. Enough had been observed about these "malignant, putrid fevers" to cause peculiar doubts, and fear: they were no respecter of age, but were most fatal to the child and infant. Often they came without warning and could bring death within hours. They were clearly endemic to the low-lying lands, but not exclusively so. They created havoc among newcomers, but also ravaged residents, and did least harm to blacks.[118] There was not enough known about the capacity of peoples to build up strong immunities in their native disease environments to explain the greater resistance of creoles, black and white, to certain tropical afflictions. Even less was known about malaria and yellow fever, and the relatively greater resistance of some African nations, which knew these fevers, although in rather different forms from the New World versions they subsequently met.[119]

The mosquito was widely seen as a particularly unpleasant local pest, but no contemporaries came near enough to seeing its significance, although Long came pretty close:

> In the West Indies, such low swampy spots, are still more fatal; and they are infested with muskeetos, which seem as if placed there by the hand of Providence to assault with their stings, and drive away, every human being, who may ignorantly venture to fix his abode among them.[120]

Maria Nugent wrote:

> The very night my dear baby was born, it was nearly devoured by the mosquitoes, in spite of all my care, . . . and, for a day or two, his dear little eyes were almost closed up.[121] . . . [T]he mosquitoes were more intolerable than ever. They are indeed in such swarms, that it took more than an hour last night to get them out of my darling George's net, who could not sleep for their tormenting him.[122]

Mrs Nugent, a naturally neurotic person, was not however the only worried Jamaican mother; their anxiety unquestionably was fed by the helplessness of doctors to diagnose, much less to cure, while their infants died.

White mothers were as strongly criticized for overindulging their children as black women were for neglecting theirs. One explanation was that they knew they did not have them for long; if they survived infancy, they very soon left home. Certainly, they appeared to start by overfeeding them: when Long's sister, Mrs Hemming, lost her little girl during her teething stage, he declared that she had "overacted the mother's part and was never satisfied unless the child was crammed like a capon".[123] Mrs Nugent, too, was critical of creole child-feeding practices and on occasion pitied the poor things "for being so stuffed with all sorts of unwholesome food".[124]

Spoiling was associated in some minds with the presence of black menials, who were all subject to the dictates of the children of the household:

> Miss Skinner's little Bonella is a sweet child, and so spoiled that I am afraid she will be a little tyrant. Mrs S. like all creole ladies, has a number of servants with her, and all are obliged to attend to any caprice of the little girl, as well as her mamma.[125]

Stewart discusses at length the damage which slavery did to the young child's character and personality: they became so conditioned to seeing blacks whipped, that this became a source of amusement to them, and naturally soft-hearted girls acquired harsh and domineering ideas about dealing with subordinates.[126] From an early age, the child of the house had her own little Negress, "destined to be her future waiting-maid; her infant mind cannot conceive the harm of a little vexatious tyranny over this sable being, who is her property; and thus are arbitrary ideas, gradually engrafted in her nature".[127] There were no corrective influences to arrest these unhealthy trends, certainly not the parents, "who are too fond and indulgent to check these indications of spirit in their darlings, while, should the little black retaliate the ill usage she meets, she is immediately chastised for her impatience".[128]

All was not well either in the area of their formal education: Jamaican girls were either taught at home, or they attended the few private schools, or they went abroad. None seemed the ideal system. The main problem of local education was how to insulate young creoles from vulgarizing contact with blacks. When they were boys, and very young, parents could be easy-going:

> Our dearly little fortune grows an entertaining companion, and says but everything – it would amuse you and my Mother to hear his little tongue talk half negro like which is the worse thing attending children here, but as they are always playing with the negro children they learn their ways and language, notwithstanding my being particular.[129]

Mrs Nugent was still tolerant even after returning to England, when her family was amused by her small children's "little funny talk, and Creole ideas and ways".[130] But continued negligence with girls' upbringing could produce results such as appalled refined tastes like those of Maria Nugent herself,[131] or

Edward Long. The latter paints the most notoriously unflattering picture that there is of those girls "who have had no opportunity of forming themselves either by example for tuition"; they were creatures "truly to be pitied".[132]

A cautionary tale on the perils of the Jamaican girls' education, or lack of it, appeared in a local journal in 1812. It saw the home-bred product in this light:

> Eliza remained at home under the protecting wing of a foolishly fond mother, who LOVED her to such excess that she never thwarted a wish of her heart, but allowed her to pursue in everything the free bent of her own inclinations. Insensible to the blessings of mental cultivation herself, this INDULGENT mother would not even force reading and writing upon this her darling, FURTHER THAN SHE HERSELF LIKES . . . so that by time that Eliza had arrived at womanhood she knew but little, and that little imperfectly and but by halves.[133]

The Elizas of creole society, in Long's opinion, ended up as hopeless and helpless wives "unfit to be the companions of sensible men, or the patterns of imitation to their daughters".[134] The Reverend William Jones was equally critical: "All the Breeding these seem to have is affected. As untaught, and almost as indelicate, as are those hapless Negroes they imagine themselves born to trample on."[135] These grew into the ladies whom the governor's wife was obliged to entertain on occasion and whom Maria Nugent found "completely stupid. All I could get out of them was 'Yes, ma'am – no, ma'am,' and now and then a simper or a giggle. At last, I set them to work stringing beads, which is now one of my occupations, and was heartily glad when their carriages came at 2 o'clock."[136]

Girls fortunate enough to have a governess from England of the quality of a Mrs Annabella Smith[137] could turn out to be "agreeable and well-behaved".[138] One such governess apparently was successful in curtailing all conversation between her charges and the blacks: as a result it was impossible to tell from their accents "but that they had been brought up at some genteel boarding-school in England".[139] But there is not much evidence that this sort of teacher was widely found in Jamaican homes.

Those who lived in the towns had slightly better advantages, both from their wider contact with Europeans and from the education offered in the few private schools found, for example, in Kingston:[140]

Kingston, June 10, 1791.

Boarding School

Mrs Robinson begs leave to acquaint the Ladies and Gentlemen of this Island, who are Parents and Guardians, that the proposes on Monday the 20th of June, to open a BOARDING SCHOOL for the reception of Young Ladies, at her house the South east corner of the Parade, nearly opposite to Wolmer's Free-School, conducted on the same plan as those in England, Ms Robinson having for many years been engaged with her fittness? In that business, in the city of Canterbury, she flatters herself she is perfectly acquainted with the tempers and dispositions of children; therefore ensures those who may honour her with the education of their children or wards, that their morals and health will be as carefully [attended] to, as those elegant accomplishments which are taught in schools.

The following are her terms:

Boarding and washing including English, and all the elegant and fashionable works which are now taught at the Boarding Schools in England, such as Embroidery, Felagree, Flower-Making, Landscapes, Maps,

Wafer and Cloth work	...	per ann.	£10
Entrance	...	per ann.	10
Day Boarders	...	per ann.	25
Entrance	...		1
Day Scholars	...	per ann.	6
Entrance			1

No Gratuity expected but at Christmas, which will be 1 Pistole.
No entrance will be required for such Ladies who have paid it at any other School.
Proper masters in French, writing, drawing, music and dancing will be engaged.[141]

The ideal was a genuine English education, not the copy, and this, rather than local schooling, became the norm for planter families. Stewart describes it in the 1820s as the "now universally prevailing practice for both boys and girls".[142] Creole children were despatched at an early age to England, girls apparently even earlier than boys: they left home at five, six, nine, ten, twelve years old. "Some go off without friends but the person they are consigned to with the sugar and rum."[143] Richard Vassal's account with a Miss Richards for the living and educational costs of a young girl in England totalled £177 17s. 6d. for the years 1772, 1773 and 1774. Boarding bills were sixteen guineas, and dancing lessons £3. Christmas and Whitsuntide holiday expenses cost £3 12s. each year; miscellaneous items included 7s. for pocket money, 7s. for a new prayer book and 4s. for hair cutting for one year.[144]

Mrs Brodbelt seemed eager that her daughter Jane, who went to England to school at the age of nine, should be able to ride, sing, play the piano and speak French. Embroidery also was a nice accomplishment, as long as it was not such fine work as to ruin the eyes.[145] It was Dr Brodbelt who showed a serious and sustained concern that Jane should be a really educated young woman: he attempted conscientious long-distance guidance of her reading and arithmetic, among other things.

> 8 September 1793. When Mrs Fenwick thinks you sufficiently qualified in draw-ing, I will be obliged to request of her to have you taught drawing in the Botanical way, and I wish you had it in your power to learn a sufficiency of Botany to make you a good Florist.[146]

> 25 November 1793. Have you any turn for making of Verses?[147]

> 19 February 1794. Let me know if you can calculate interest and how far you are advanced in Arithmetick. I hope you read History with great attention, and study Geography constantly, both which will improve your mind, and render you a very pleasant companion.[148]

> 20 May 1794. [B]e obliged to [Mrs Fenwick] to make you read with the greatest attention the best books on Musick, so as to teach you that science systematically, and make you a mistress of the Technical words, and to have you taught properly to tune the Harpischord and grand Piano Forte . . . pay great attention to your handwriting . . . in the two last you were very careless. . . . When you have occa-sion to make a large T or a large F do not turn them up in the very ugly way you do.[149]

> 4 October 1795. I wrote to you last month by the *Halifax* and desired you to · purchase Whitaker's Real origin of Government: when you have read it over 2 or 3 times buy the "History of the Clergy during the French Revolution" by the Abbe Barruch, Almoner to the Princess of Conti and give that one or two careful readings.[150]

Dr Brodbelt's anxiety over the development of his daughter's mind was no doubt well-placed. His older daughter Nancy had returned from school in England in 1794 and showed little signs of being equipped for any kind of meaningful existence in Jamaica. Overseas education successfully finished the possibility of creole girls having any serious commitment to the island on their return. The cultural gap between mother country and colony seemed unbridgeable: local society was viewed with condescension, if not contempt. This worried Dr Brodbelt: "It is really a grievous, heartbreaking business to see how very ignorant and supercilious most all the young ladies return to Jamaica from school."[151] Mrs Nugent voiced a similar concern:

> The extent of Mrs Israell's travels has been to Kingston, and she is always saying, "When I was in town;" she says too, that frost and show must be prodigious odd things. The daughter has been brought up at the *Queen Square Boarding School,* and is much looked to by her mamma; and she, in return, is in constant anxiety, for fear they should be guilty of some mistake, etc. This difference of education is, I think, a real and mutual misfortune.[152]

Williams had a similar view of such young ladies, educated to become misfits:

> She is a very nice amiable girl, sensible and accomplished, and has a rooted antipathy to the island of Jamaica and the islanders. . . . An education in England has unfitted her for society here. At Kingston, or Spanish Town, she might be happier; but a society of overseers and bookkeepers, uneducated or half-educated, and cigar-smokers, has no charm for an accomplished woman or a person of fine feelings.[153]

Melissa complained to the local press about the crude level of social behaviour she was forced to put up with on her return:

> I observed two or three young men of a so-so appearance, but not one of them had the politeness to ask me to dance – instead of which, a set of lowbred awkward creatures came up to me (one or two of whom appeared to be flustered with liquor) and had the presumption to ask me to be their partner; while girls that I thought far beneath me, both in rank and education, seemed to engross the attention of those beaux![154]

Island life, when it was not repellently vulgar, was unbearably dull; letters home spoke endlessly of tropical tedium. Nothing seemed adequate to fill the empty days of these young belles: "We have not yet practised much on account of the Instrument wanting strings, nor have I drawn a single flower, tho I see many I should like to give a sketch of, had I much turn that way –

I have no paints or brushes either."[155] Nancy Brodbelt could not even be induced to ride the "excellent Horse which [her] Dear and Best of Fathers made her a present of".[156]

In the towns, the Kingston and Spanish Town periodic whirl of dancing, horseracing, theatre-going, frenzied seeking out of the more acceptably polished male, the visiting officer – all seemed excitingly time filling. Fashion became an obsessive interest – London fashion:

> They do not scruple to wear the thickest winter silks and satins; and are sometimes ready to sink under the weight of rich gold or silver brocades. Their head-dress varies with the one at home; the winter fashions of London arrive here at the setting in of hot weather and thick or thin caps, large as an umbrella, or as diminutive as a half crown piece, are indiscriminately put on, without the smallest regard to the difference of climate.[157]

What was important was that one wore the exact replica of what was latest on the English scene; to do otherwise would be to "appear ridiculous".[158] A great disappointment was not to have the "fine cloaths" arrived in time for the activities at the sessions.[159] But even then, at the height of the season, ennui persisted: "I have been spending ten weeks with Mary Ricketts at a Pen over Kingston, we were very gay there, a continual round of dancing, indeed so much that I was heartily tired of it."[160]

For however busy the social round, it could never compare with England. Mrs Brodbelt sent greetings to their friend Mr Raymond who had left the island; they wished he were still with them, but apologized for the thought: "I much doubt whether he would thank me for wishing him in a country so greatly inferior in point of pleasures to those he enjoys in England."[161] Melissa also: "Need I tell you how many dull and cheerless movements I am doomed to lead in the absence of those dear amusements which has so often enchanted me on the other side of the Atlantic."[162]

Nancy Brodbelt probed more deeply than she knew the source of cultural deprivation:

> You cannot imagine how forcibly I felt your attention in being so particular in your description to one of Powis Castle as you knew I was always so fond of antiquity. It must be really a delightful pile of building, and such is my partiality for Castles, Abbeys, etc. that I declare I had rather see a ruin of those than go to the first amusement in the world.[163]

The parvenu creole universe, whatever its rewards, could never compensate for its absence of historic ruins, symbols of a cherished civilization, now out of reach. The model on which the Jamaican lady fashioned her lifestyle was to be found overseas. She confirmed this in her nostalgia for all things English. It was reflected in her attempts to reproduce the world of Anglo-Saxon landed upper classes, their stately homes, gracious exchanges of social courtesies between peers, respectful tenants and numerous dignified retainers. The creole reality never measured up to that ideal, and a crucial question for the planter lady was: To which England, in fact, did she belong? An essentially bourgeois slaveholding class playing it manorial had no transatlantic equivalent. It was no wonder that the English were unable to dissociate her from her plantation, that agrarian factory manned by black bondsmen and women. The metropolitan saw the creole as alien. As the cockney in the play expressed to the young West Indian heroine: "Miss Prissy, I wonder you are not ashamed of yourself: but this is the breeding you got in the plantations – you know you was turned out of Hackney boarding-school for beating the governess – I believe you think you have got among your blackamoors."[164]

Neither emotionally nor occupationally grounded in the island's soil, its ruling class continued to pursue its European inheritance. But the smear of black Jamaica, starting at birth, spread and coloured the life patterns of white Jamaica, made its members into reluctant creoles. The most displaced creoles of all, the ladies of quality, hovered anxiously between two worlds, unable fully to inhabit either.

The "Secondary Whites"

Brathwaite's study of Jamaican creole society between 1770 and 1820 has done much to bring to the surface the submerged "lesser" whites, the middle and lower-middle strata of the society. They were about four times as many as the planter elite, numbering in the early nineteenth century between eighteen thousand and twenty-four thousand.[165] Social divisions in the white group were on the whole fluid: the Cowpers, for example, who were "border line" planter stock, declined financially and socially after their father's death.[166] On the other hand, in the case of a young Kingston lawyer, William Dwarris, and his wife Sarah, insignificant struggling relatives of an eminent creole family, it was just a matter of time before their contacts and their determined ambitions assured them arrival at the top.[167] Lower down the scale were the Doves, who moved from the Kingston paupers' house to solid artisan's status within a few short years.[168]

Secondary whites covered a wide range of incomes and occupations: they included the professional and the estate owner of moderate circumstances, the pimento farmer, the hillbilly coffee grower of Port Royal and Portland, the tavern keeper, teacher, Vestry employee, pensioner; and in every category women could be found.

At these levels of society, the rural woman was more likely than the lady of quality to be her husband's working partner on the estate and in the field. Senior describes, for example, a Scottish couple who had settled on land near Catadupa in St James: he, his wife and grown-up daughter "all worked daily in the grounds, in the preparation of tobacco, for market, and in making straw hats and baskets at which wife and daughter were extremely skilful".[169]

Coffee was an attractive crop to the farmer of limited means: the capital outlay required on slaves, stock and equipment was perhaps half that of sugar.[170] Promising markets opened up for the Jamaican producer when the black revolution in St Dominique closed that source of European supply.[171] The small to medium settler pioneered the new crop in the interior uplands, with varying degrees of success. The Nugents stayed in the Portland mountains with one such family, who were clearly making good:

> We found Mrs Sheriff, her mother Mrs Strachan, and a Miss Cumming, dressed ready to receive us, all in their best. Mrs S. is a fat, good humoured creole woman, saying dis, dat, and toder; her mother is a vulgar old Scotch dame; and Miss C. a clumsy awkward girl. The house is a good one, quite new, and every thing neat about it. It is situated in the midst of the mountains, out of which issue abundant streams of water; all up the sides of the mountains are plantain and cocoa-nut trees, and coffee bushes. . . . Went to the coffee works, and saw the process of preparing coffee.[172]

But the small white settler image was not always one of industry. Williams is one of the few contemporaries who describe Jamaica's shiftless poor whites during slavery. He found them in a coffee walk in the Blue Mountains:

> He was a stout squat Scotsman, with red hair and whiskers; his beard, which seemed a week old, was a trifle darker. . . . His dress consisted of a huge pair of canvas

trousers and ragged boots, with a no less ragged shirt, and an old buff waistcoat. He wore no coat or neckcloth. His wife was in as elegant a dishabille as himself, with her long locks straggling down her back, half sandy, half grey; she was at least as old as her husband, a circumstance of which he was fully sensible. The piazza, about five or six feet wide, and about five-and-twenty long contained three broken chairs and a bench, a round table of some white wood, an old chest of rusty tools, and a fiddle with two strings. There were three white children running about, all rather sluttish and dirty, eating unripe maize, and teasing the parrot, who had taken his station on a perch. Mr M'——y poured me a glass of punch from an old broken tea-pot, which politeness induced me to put to my lips.[173]

Mrs George Archer, on the other hand, pimento grower of St Ann, appeared a model of thrift. She was the widow of a doctor/planter of an old West Indian family, with members in Barbados: the Jamaican branch was scattered throughout Hanover, St Ann, Westmoreland, St Andrew and St James. One of her deceased husband's cousins, also George Archer, was a military surgeon in the 1820s; another was the curate of Highgate in St Mary. Mrs Archer herself was a creole, had been a Hodge of Trelawny. She lived at Breadnut Hill estate near her son, James Henry Archer, a busy country doctor, who serviced many estates in the parish. They both planted pimento: she had eleven or twelve slaves, and she emerges from the pages of her son's diary as an independent and hardworking woman.[174]

She and James Archer alternately pooled or divided their slave forces – he owned an average of seventeen slaves – for the daily allocation of work tasks. For example:

> 8 March 1828. I engaged this day my mothers people to job for me, and they began Fencing in Cedar Valley bottom – 12 in bottom.[175] 12 February 1829. Mother's Negroes joined mine in billing bush in right hand side of Maddock Hill.[176] 15 September 1829. . . . my mother's Negroes assisted my own in cleaning pimento walk Cedar Valley Bottom.[177] 10 August 1830. . . . sent Charlotte, Lavinia, Rebecca Archer and Thos. Reid to pick pimento for mother at Breadnut Hill at 2/6, she giving me pickers here instead.[178]

Mother and son clashed more than once about the work arrangements, discipline of their slaves and about family finances.[179] The detailed care with which their small task force was deployed, the scrupulous attention paid to every minute household expenditure and every labour transaction[180] showed a family husbanding its resources with the greatest economy. "My mother", wrote Dr Archer with feeling, "required her Pimento to pay taxes and clothe and feed herself".[181]

Pimento was a non-prestige crop, requiring little labour and capital, and by the 1820s virtually monopolized by the free coloureds.[182] Bryan Edwards in 1801 observed its extreme vulnerability to the fluctuating British market and predicted its collapse: there was so little certain profit that, as he pointed out, "many beautiful walks [are] being cut down, and the land appropriated to the cultivation of sugar".[183]

The Cowper family at Baron Hill experienced the current hazards of pimento cultivation in the uncertain Caribbean economic climate of the beginning of the nineteenth century. Their father died in June 1802, leaving his widow and two daughters with a heavily encumbered estate. They planned to leave Jamaica, but first had to sell Baron Hill, and were unsure "whether the property is only just to pay its own immense debts or whether by time and success we are to have a clear and sufficient competence".[184] They tried to be optimistic about the future but realized that they were very much at the mercy of weather and climate: "We are still parched up for want of Rain, but have the River running thro our own land and not more than a miles distance and that is a great blessing. We begin Pimento crop next week, the dry season has injured and retarded its growth."[185]

Drought set them back again the following year:

> There has prevailed a destroying drought some months and still continues here – it has hindered the Pimento crop from being near so good as the profusion of Blossoms promised, in many parts it is totally lost, but we are told ours is more tolerable than we could have expected, I suppose it will be about the usual quantity – it is now the busiest time of picking – Fine rains within the last week have just come in time to save the coffee from materially suffering in the mountains.[186]

But their finances continued depressed:

> Our debts are so immense they cannot be paid unless by a sale of the lands, and that is out of all reason to think of when nobody has money or hardly confidence in any person or thing, and the West Indies in particular at a low ebb of credit, the income then from these Properties must go to pay the annual interest. . . . [F]rom whence then is to come our support in another country? [W]e are destitute . . . of a single farthing of our own independent.[187]

Margaret Cowper, however, found one bright spot in all their gloom:

> I am sole mistress of a carpenter Negro by name Frank he is it is true but a rough
> artist however will bring me in nearly £20 per annum – now would you not think
> this really handsome? For a single woman? Perhaps indeed considerable enough to
> attract some honest swain?[188]

When overseas markets rose and fell, when all else failed, there were slaves; and for countless women on their own, who had no other source of capital or income, this was no light-hearted matter. Slaves were Jamaica's most pervasive currency, at times more accessible than currency itself, and more liquid than land: certain to depreciate with time, but until then, returns on investment were sure, for labour and skills continued increasingly throughout this period to be in short supply.

Any claims that white women might have made to economic independence, or security in their old age, rested solidly on ownership of slaves. This was particularly true of lesser white women, who were without the background of landed wealth, but who on the whole projected an image of greater self-sufficiency than the ladies of the upper class. Whereas, for example, all the prestigious agricultural holdings in St James in 1774 – sugar estates – were male owned, the pattern or proprietorship altered perceptibly as one descended the social scale. In the lowest economic classification, eleven women settlers were listed, their slaveholdings representing a significant part of their substance.[189] They were:

Table 4.4 Women and Property-Holding, St James, 1774

Name	Property	Number of Enslaved
Elizabeth Burke	Pimento Walk	7
Alice Brown	Midwife	9
Rebecca Chambers	Pen/Jobber	24
Margaret Hickey	Washerwoman	7
Ann Jameson	Widow	11
Deb Mead	Widow	6
Millie Markhan	Widow	13
Elizabeth McFerguer	Widow	23

Source: Add. MSS 12435, Long Papers, Inventory of Sugar Estates in St James, 1774, 3.

St Ann in 1792 had twenty-two female slave owners, who together owned 679 head of stock and 943 slaves; three of these held them jointly with male relatives.[190] Westmoreland in 1812 had a white female population of 129, of whom thirty-one, as slave owners, handed in returns to the vestries on the increase and decrease of their slaves; none appeared to be large proprietors.[191]

Many more white women owned slaves than owned real property. Few women took out original land patents, one only, for example, in the whole island in 1778;[192] and the law of primogeniture inhibited land transference to the female by inheritance. In a sample of forty Jamaican wills of the late eighteenth century, representing a wide range of incomes, only two testators bequeathed land to a widow and daughter, whereas at least thirteen made clear their legacies of slaves to their heiresses – mainly daughters, but mother and common-law wife also included.[193] A sample of eighteen white women's inventories in the years 1772–73 and 1803 showed slaves to be the most valuable portion of their personal property.[194] This was true of a relatively affluent woman, like Ann Halliburton, widow of St Andrew, whose household furnishings (already mentioned), stock, chaise and harness totalled £674 10s.,[195] while her slaves were worth £5,216; or of Tabitha Goulbourne, widow of St Ann, whose inventory was worth £4,929, of which £4,395 represented slaves.[196]

It was equally true of less well-off women. The other sixteen listed among the inventories of these years were all of moderate means, their estates averaging in value about £900 and some as modest as that of Rebecca de Pass, of Kingston, worth £142 2s. 6d.[197] For two women, slaves represented their all: Rebecca Deacon, a widow of Portland, whose six slaves accounted for her total estate of £200,[198] and Sarah Demetrius, a widow of Clarendon, whose sixteen slaves were her complete estate, worth £1,530.[199] For ten other women, slaves constituted between 60 and 95 per cent of their property, for two women, less than 50 per cent. In only one instance, that of Sarah Green, widow of Kingston, did her other personal effects exceed the value of her slaves by any considerable amount: her twelve slaves were worth £465, her inventory totalling £3,218 10s. ½d.; from all appearances, she was an innkeeper.[200]

Not that women were completely excluded from land ownership. The parish of Manchester in 1819 had twenty-five women on its rolls paying land and road taxes, and owning a total of 4,402 acres, an average holding of 176 acres.[201] The St Thomas-in-the-Vale tax roll of 1789 had approximately 10 per cent of its taxpayers women, twelve in all, assessed at the parish rate of ½d. per acre. These women together owned 5,027 acres of land, an average of 419 acres each. These same women, it was observed, also paid taxes on their slaves and livestock, at the rate of 2s. 6d. per slave and 9d. per head of stock. They totalled between them 321 slaves and 156 stock, and paid into the Vestry that year £46 14s. 6d. The parish contained a total of 7,367 slaves and 5,573 stock, and it collected £1,129 17s. 3d. in taxes from all ratepayers.[202]

Where women did own land on a moderate scale they appeared marginal as taxpayers and land developers – as the discrepancy between the size of landholding and slave-/stock-holding in St Thomas-in-the-Vale would suggest. One obstacle would undoubtedly have been that of management, to which Brathwaite most relevantly directs attention. The provisions of the Deficiency Law, which required landholders to maintain a certain ratio of white personnel to black slaves, or pay a fine, were seen as

> peculiarly oppressive to white females possessing small properties, the whole income of [which] barely yield[ed] a sufficient sum to defray the expense of a white overseer, for whom they would be compelled to maintain a separate establishment on their properties, as it could not reasonably be expected that a female could introduce a single man to reside in the same dwelling with her.[203]

Slaves, however, could be hired out and income assured for their owner without the headaches of supervision – even Mrs Archer, it would seem, hired out her slaves to her son at least as often as she used them for her own cultivation. Mary McKay, a widow of Kingston, had, among her seven slaves, one washerwoman worth £80, one seamstress worth £90, four skilled men, sailmakers, two of whom were valued at £250, and one at £230 – all clearly representing income-earning investments. Her seventh slave, "a negro wench washerwoman and drudge", was probably for her own personal use.[204]

Hiring out one's slaves had its own headaches. Jobbing slaves usually had appalling work conditions, worse than those of the slaves attached to their estates;[205] but they were comparatively mobile, often required even to do their own job-hunting and inclined as a result to become "uppitty".[206] Slaves also ran away frequently, and the temptation to flout the control of single women-owners must have been very great. The widow Sarah Davis of St

Mary had a troublesome time in 1809. Quaca, her slave, was indicted at the Port Maria Slave Court on 24 April for running away and being absent for more than six months. He was found guilty and transported for life: she received compensation of £50. At the same court another of her slaves, the more valuable Caesar, worth £87, was also convicted and transported: he had been "charged with rebellion, by frequently resisting the lawful commands of the White People who had him in charge". On the same day another widow, Sarah Knaggs, had her slave, Cuffee, also indicted and transported for running away.[207] In the following year the courts found a slave guilty of the manslaughter of another slave, Dick, the property of Sarah Knaggs.[208] Other widows and gentlewomen appear regularly in the records of the courts and in advertisements of runaways, plagued in a variety of ways with the trials of slave ownership.

But this was the calculated risk of investment in human chatteldom. Lesser whites, moreover, particularly in the countryside, were conditioned to the peculiar hazards of creole Jamaica, which mitigated against them more strongly than against the planter class. They faced drought, hurricane, runaway slave raids, militia billeting, shortage of credit and appealed, often with little success, to an establishment dedicated to its own cause, which was essentially the cause of the big sugar producer.

At least thirteen of the forty-five small settlers of Hanover and Westmoreland who applied for government aid after the terrible hurricane of 1780 were women.[209] After the devastation followed drought and yet another fierce storm in August 1781, which "totally blasted hopes of recovery".[210] The people of these parishes then fell victims to a bureaucratic machinery, which only obstructed and corrupted, where it did not completely ignore, their claims for relief. A large portion of the House of Commons vote of £40,000 for the rehabilitation of storm victims found itself into the pockets of "very many persons of rank, figure and fortune".[211] Food provisions ear-marked to alleviate a condition of near-famine were similarly misappropriated: "the distresses of the people [of St Elizabeth] have been aggravated by the whole crop of corn being bought up by the opulent Attorneys from Leeward".[212]

WORKING-CLASS WHITE WOMEN

Jamaica's cost of living, highly vulnerable both to acts of God and of men, weighed heavily on the lower classes. Unlike women of the planter elite, housewives of more modest establishments were concerned, in practical detail, with the exorbitant and fluctuating prices of basic domestic necessities.[213] William Dwarris and his wife found it difficult to make two ends meet in the 1780s:

> 10 February 1782. I only wish I had £200 p. ann. in old England I would never more quit it on any account whatsoever, indeed a person may with frugality live there with that sum, as with a £1,000 p. ann. here. . . . [O]ur Mutton has risen to twenty pence p. pound, and our Butchers begin to think themselves entitled to a shilling for beef – but I am in hopes they will be kept down at 10 pence fish thank God remains cheap and plentiful. . . . [T]imes are so hard and cash almost impossible to be got. . . . My uncle has never assisted me, but we frequently honor him with eating a good hearty dinner with him.

> 10 April 1782. [W]e are here in daily expectation of the French and Spanyards martial law as been on for some time and nothing but millitary operation. . . . [N]o business carry'd on and all kinds of provision so excessive dear that it is almost impossible to keep house. 8 July 1782. . . . [E]very day Provisions get higher and higher. . . . Beef 1/3 Mutton 1/10½ Veal 1/8 Pork Fish 1/8 Turtle 1/3 most of these formerly at a bitt and ½ Capon per pair £1 and a good turkey cock £2 but things are not even to be got at these extravagant rates the navy give any price and overbuy the town people.

> 11 August 1787. [M]oney is so scarce and everybody distress'd we think it very great, to be able to keep house, and now and then pay off an old debt.

> 27 January 1788. [W]e are going to move in a few days lower down town. . . . I hate moving it is so troublesome, but the house we are going to is so much more convenient for Business that my Uncle wishes Mr Dwarris to have it although we are to pay eighty Pounds a year which is a great deal of money.

> 1 June 1788. I have got five guineas by me and I want a good many things, I had rather sent it to England than pay it out here, everything is so dear . . . [in Jamaica] they make me pay a bit for two or three rows of pins and you cannot get a little nutmeg for less than tenpence . . . I am sure it is not possible to be more frugal than we are, for we have but one dish when we are by ourselves and that in

this country is nothing as Clark will have two or three but notwithstanding all our frugality we do no spend less than five hundred a year.[214]

Women in this, and the lower strata of society, needed income-earning occupations; but outside of moderate-to-minimal agricultural enterprises that they attempted, the economic activities available to them were restricted.

Creole opinion had by the late eighteenth century turned its back firmly on the notion of white domestic service, which had previously absorbed a fair proportion of working women. Long condemned them as a class that in Britain was notoriously insolent and unmanageable. How much more in the West Indies, where they would very soon discover that

> by the policy of the country, there subsists a material distinction between them and the Negroes. If they could chance to meet with any black servants in the same family, they would impose every part of the drudgery of service upon these poor creatures, and commence ladies and gentlemen. The females would attend to no work, except pinning their lady's handkerchief; and the men, to no other than laying the cloth for dinner, and powdering their master's hair.[215]

Mrs Brodbelt advised her daughter Jane, who due to return to Jamaica from England, that she should engage a brown or black female travelling companion: "you may hire one of that description for a trifle" in preference to a white servant, "for you will not know what to do with her after you arrive here".[216] It became accepted practice that white domestics were almost exclusively to be found at King's House. Mrs Nugent relied heavily on her wet-nurses and her personal maid; but even here they were social misfits, and soon married out of the service.[217] The tendency, therefore, was for governors "to get quit of them, and fall into the modes of the country".[218]

This left a few equally limited areas, such as midwifery, sewing, teaching, innkeeping and shop-keeping. Dr Archer noted in his diary the services of the local midwife, when his eldest child was born on 16 July 1823. He wrote: "Mrs Thompson whose age appears to be about 52 came to attend my beloved Mary in her approaching confinement. She is a white woman, very charitable and wellspoken of, the sister of George Lloyd of Mt. Hermon."[219] Black "nanas" were probably, however, used on a wider scale: at a later childbirth, on 10 December 1831, Archer paid "old Kitty for attention to my poor Mary £2.13.4 after her accouchement for assistance".[220]

Sewing provided a decent living for some women: mantua-makers and seamstresses from time to time took in young apprentices.[221] Official sewing orders were probably few but, where available, quite profitable. Lucy Gallant of Montego Bay earned a steady income making cartridge bags and sundry regimentals for the militia and for the paupers' home, receiving regular payments; for example, April 1812, £56; April 1815, £34; April 1818, £80.[222] There were some openings too for the milliner or embroiderer:

Kingston April 22, 1791

Mrs ROBINSON
Milliner and Embroiderer

From the House of Mrs Lott, Pattern Drawer,
Embroiderer, and Flower Maker, to Her Majesty
Begs leave to inform the Public, that she
Proposes executing the above Business in all its
Branches; and at the same time instructing YOUNG
LADIES in those fashionable and elegant accomplishments on
the same terms as in London.[223]

May 14, 15 & 21 May, 1791

. . . she also makes up, crimps, and dresses
Baby-Linen in the same manner as is used in
The Child-Bed Linen Warehouse in London.[224]

Ladies of means, however, tended to look down on local handiwork. For them, the only fashionable gown or bonnet was London-made, and they accordingly imported their finery when they could: "The Ladies dress very expensively as most of them have everything of that kind from England."[225]

There were a few white lodging keepers: William Hickey, for instance, spoke highly of "the elderly widow lady" with whom he stayed in High Street, Kingston, in 1775.[226] Mrs Conway of Church Street regularly advertised for paying guests:

Kingston, April 8, 1791

Mrs CONWAY

offers her respectful thanks to the Public
in general for the past Favours which she

has received. She has fitted up her House
in Church-street in a genteel manner, proper
to accommodate six or eight Gentlemen with
BOARD.

A few cool airy LODGING ROOMS to be let,
By the year or quarter, on reasonable terms.[227]

But by the early nineteenth century, this was practically the monopoly of brown women.[228]

Governesses were employed in a few wealthy households:

Kingston, March 4, 1791

WANTS A PLACE, a Person who can take charge of
two or three children, can teach Reading, Writing,
and all kinds of Needle and Tembour Work, can
teach French, and several kinds of Music: has no
objection to live with a single lady – A line
addressed to B.B. to the care of J. Smith, Stay-maker,
King-Street, will in two or three days be
punctually attended to.[229]

Neither in fact nor in fiction was it an attractive profession. Mrs Annabella Smith was frank about the financial exigencies which forced her to take employment with a family in Dry Harbour, St Ann. She wrote on 13 June 1812: "At a period when I would thankfully consign my bones to the grave have I undertaken the charge of the Education of three children for which I have 70 currency about 50 st. and that paid me in pimento."[230] As she pointed out later in the same letter, the island "had never experienced greater hardships, from the want of markets for their produce".[231] Prices for pimento, rum and sugar were then at rock bottom levels. Many planter families were hard hit by these periods of depression and those who were most likely to be able to afford governesses, preferred to send their daughters abroad. Some women, as has been already mentioned, turned their hands to running private schools, day or boarding, but, as with governesses, their most likely clientele were metropolitan-oriented. A handful of women were employed as teachers in public institutions.[232]

Trading provided a relatively wide opening for white women's enterprise. Even those of upper-class aspirations like Sarah Dwarris engaged in buying and selling. Her father was a merchant in Coventry, who sent her consignments of goods from time to time. On one occasion, she lost her expected profits on a cargo of potatoes which had been kept too long on board ship: "they were rotten in two days after they were open'd I only made twenty shillings of them, the flour was likewise quite frusty – it sold for little or nothing".[233] Retailing in a variety of small items was a regular means of livelihood for women in the towns, in particular Kingston and Montego Bay:

Kingston, July 2, 1790

MARY PHILLIPS

East end of Harbour Street, ACQUAINTS her
Friends and the Public that she PRESERVES
all Kind of SWEETMEATS, including PINEAPPLES,
in Spirits, and otherwise:[234]

Twenty out of forty-six members of the shopkeeper class appearing on the Kingston deficiency list of 1782 were women.[235] Rum was a common commodity handled by these women: eleven out of the twenty-five persons who took the oath of allegiance required by the rum licensing law in Kingston in 1782[236] were women; in 1821, they numbered eighteen out of 101.[237] In Montego Bay, three women out of twenty-five persons in 1793,[238] six out of thirty in 1808,[239] twenty out of thirty-six in 1818 were granted licences "to retail spirituous liquors".[240] A fair proportion of Jewish women fell into this category, both in Kingston and Montego Bay.

It is doubtful that they ever made fortunes in this line. On 28 July 1784, the Kingston Vestry advertised the names of those persons whose hawking and peddling licences were in arrears during the years 1781 to 1984: it listed twenty-four women (of whom twelve had Jewish names).[241] The Vestry took a lenient view of small struggling female shopkeepers; it saw their petty trading activities as alternatives to destitution. On occasion, it voted the funds to set them up in business: on 19 February 1810, it paid to "Elizabeth Hudson a poor woman with a large family the sum of thirty pounds to enable her to take out a licence for retailing spirituous liquors for the present year".[242] In the following year, the city fathers again subsidized Elizabeth Hudson and extended their indulgence as well to one Edward Peyton and to three other women, Sarah Yarworth, Mary Ann Campbell and Margaret Shaw, "being all persons in indigent circumstances".[243]

Any legal means of earning an income was preferable to having white women fall below a certain poverty line. Individual white creoles, women included, had for a long time showed concern for what they saw as the most vulnerable members of their society – poor white females – and charitable bequests had from time to time singled them out for benefits.[244] The Reverend John Venn, rector of the parish church of St Catherine, remembered them in his will. He left instructions for his own modest burial, insisting "that no covering of any kind be placed on his coffin – in lieu of that idle piece of Human Vanity – £20 to be given to 4 poor widows on the day of his burial".[245] Matthew Gregory, also of St Catherine, tried to give more long-term help: he left a trust yielding a yearly income of £230 for the relief of "any distressed object of this Island coming to St Jago de la Vega / to bind out poor children to trades / and to Portion Orphan Girls at Marriage".[246] But arbitrary displays of charity by private persons could not be relied on to relieve this class, and government machinery had to take on the responsibility of keeping white female destitution from reaching embarrassing proportions.

The Vestry: Rescuing the Disreputable and Underprivileged

Officialdom could not always impose propriety on lower-class women who appeared before the courts for a variety of disreputable acts. Intoxicated army wives became embroiled in assaults, leading in one instance to death.[247] At least one offender sold rum without a licence and was duly indicted.[248] The Montego Bay Resident Magistrate's Court, whose records in this respect are the fullest, had at least ten cases between 1793 and 1808 in which white women were charged, in some instances with black and brown women, for assault; or violent assault, on men, on women, or for keeping "a disorderly house". They were either fined or bound over to keep the peace.[249] What the establishment could do to keep this sort of scandal to the minimum was to find an honest means of livelihood for women at risk. Facilities to keep them off the streets, and in the course of performing its essential duty of running the parish, the local Vestry, the most paternalistic institution of creole Jamaica, kept a special eye on white women's needs.

It distributed to them what jobs it could. The St James Vestry appointed Elizabeth Farley as matron of the hospital and work house in 1807 at a salary of £80 per annum.[250] In 1810, the duties of matron were combined with those of nurse of the Negro hospital with an additional honorarium of £30 per annum.[251] The tutor to the charity girls, one Mrs Sharp, received £70 in 1807.[252] The organist, Mrs Walker, was the highest paid Vestry employee, receiving £200 per annum;[253] when she resigned in May 1814, there were two candidates in the running for the vacant post.[254] Rebecca Cunningham was appointed sextoness by the St Thomas-in-the-Vale Vestry in February 1790, at £20 per annum, and was granted an additional allowance of £10 for the support of her child.[255]

The Kingston Vestry was the largest local government employer: its female establishment for the year 1823 was:

Table 4.5   Women and the Kingston Vestry, 1823

Name	Job	Remuneration
Ann Galbraith	Church organist	130 p.a.
Elizabeth Ross	Keeper of Court House	40 p.a.
Elisa Lawrence	Matron/Parish House	140 p.a.
Mary Charles	Tutoress/Parish House	30 p.a.
Mary Charles	Tutoress/Wolmers Free School	20 p.a.
Elizabeth Campbell	Matron/Public Hospital	100 p.a.

Source: Kingston Common Council Proceedings, 1820–1828, List of Parish Officers, 1823.

The matron's salary in 1823 was an improvement on the past. In the 1780s, when Janet Guthrie had been governess (matron) of the poor house, she was paid £50;[256] nevertheless, when the post became vacant, three persons applied to fill it.[257]

Other parish jobs which women held in Kingston included pound keeper and caretaker of the beef market: Elena Androuin received a salary of £20 per annum in the latter post in 1770, but as she had a large family to support the acting warden granted her 10s. weekly towards their subsistence.[258] In 1781, Mrs Barbara Twist was appointed to clean both the beef and fish markets for £40 per annum.[259] In 1786, Mary Wright was given her late husband's job as keeper of the town clock.[260] Ione Felsted, as beadle at £20 per annum, was required to give written notices of all Vestry meetings and to attend them herself.[261]

The jobs white women did for local government, with the exception of teaching (which was one of the lowest-paid occupations), were either institutional extensions of their traditional house skills and/or barely disguised forms of poor relief. The salary scarcely differed from the allowances paid out to pensioners and was sometimes less. Westmoreland, for example, was giving its paupers in 1781 sums of £20, £50, £70 and £75 each per annum.[262] Recruitment to parochial posts was, in fact, often made from the paupers' roll: pensions and salaries doled out were intended in many instances to supplement each other.

The Vestry also gave openings to those on its pay sheet to top up their wages by a miscellaneous variety of services to local institutions. Mrs Elizabeth Lee, matron of the Kingston parish house, supplied bonnets for the inmates and was accordingly paid £14 in 1808.[263] Elizabeth Farley, matron of St James hospital and work house, supplemented her salary of £80 by hiring a slave nurse to the slave hospital at £7 10s. per quarter and by doing needlework for the hospital.[264]

The Kingston Council played a positive part in the "success" story of the Love family. In July 1781, Malcolm Love, a blacksmith, his wife and children, "poor persons", received from the Vestry 20s. weekly towards their support.[265] In the following year Love was given the job of repairing the city's fire engines, for which he was paid £15 18s. 9d.[266] On 17 February 1883, Love and his wife were off the paupers' roll, leaving only their three children on relief.[267] By the next month, that relief was discontinued, "he being in good business".[268] In April, he was appointed captain of fire engine No. 1[269] and shortly after was paid £51 5s. 10d. for repairing two fire engines for the parish.[270]

Having made appointments, the Vestry responsibly exerted efforts to get service in return. It threatened to fire Mrs Allen if she continued to neglect keeping the Kingston court house "perfectly and constantly clean".[271] Mrs Wall, matron of the Kingston Public Hospital, was dismissed from her post in 1809, after a report on its operations revealed "a most shameful expenditure in the necessaries for this institution".[272] The Committee of the Council did not accept her explanation that the large discrepancy between the quantity of beef purchased, and the quantity served, represented shrinkage in cooking.[273] Intermittent investigations of institutional abuses paid at least lip service to the maintenance of proper standards.[274] Another matron, in one such instance, came off badly: "[She] gets drunk mostly every evening, she associates with them [that is, the nurses – blacks], in consequence of which all is neglect . . . for it cannot be expected that negroes would care anything about a white person who makes a companion of them."[275]

The numbers of local government appointments available were clearly limited, and the extensive use of poor relief, both indoor and outdoor, provided for the welfare of poor women. The majority of pensioners who passed through the Vestry's hands were women and white. Forty-one persons received outdoor relief in January 1781 from the Kingston Vestry, of whom all, except one adult male with his wife, were women and their children; their allowances were 5s. per week for a child, and 10s. for an adult.[276] The pensioners' roll increased to fifty-three in January 1784. There was one adult male, the rest were women on their own, mothers and children, and foster mothers of poor children.[277] St James, on 25 January 1813, had one man on its roll of twenty-two persons;[278] in May 1818, it had four men and twenty women.[279]

Poor relief represented a varying but significant proportion of parish budgets. St James, in 1819, estimated its annual expenditure for the financial year to be £9,803, of which £700 was earmarked for paupers, including £100 for coffins and burial costs.[280] Kingston, always the largest recipient of Jamaica's poor, allocated £3,200 out of its 1788 budget of £15,400 for the expenses of poor house inmates, out-pensioners, clothing and salaries, with an extra £750 for aid to transient poor.[281] In 1820, it allocated £7,728 out of its budget of £33,516 19s. 11d. for the relief of the poor.[282]

The Vestry, strongly motivated by the need to rehabilitate suffering whites, did not undertake its work lightly. The Kingston Council, for instance, would not consider approving Julienne Haynes's application for aid without first warning her husband, Mr Anthony Haynes, that "should she became a burthen to the Parish, the Common Council will direct that he be prosecuted for such charge".[283] It regularly insisted that pensioners justify their case for continued public assistance and, at times, threatened to withdraw aid when recipients did not conform to the regulations, such as the ones requiring them to present themselves weekly in person to collect their dole.[284]

"No person", stated a Kingston Vestry ruling, "[can] be admitted as an out-pensioner, unless recommended by a respectable inhabitant".[285] Some pensioners had in fact known better days: a former rector's daughter in 1783 was on the parish roll.[286] Mrs Priscilla Hales, "an old respectable inhabitant", was paid 12s. 6d. weekly in 1788.[287] Mrs Hannah Jackson, widow of Dr John Jackson, received 30s. weekly for the support of herself and her five children;[288] this was increased by £20 per annum, which made her the largest recipient on the list of fifty-three pensioners in January 1784.[289] In February 1787, she was still on relief; but her two sons were apprenticed out and as a result her allowance was reduced to 20s. weekly for herself and three children, "2 having renounced patronage of vestry".[290]

Within the poor house itself, desired patterns of respectable conduct were carefully regulated: "the house and apartments of the poor with their bedding [were to] be kept clean and in proper order". The house was locked at 8:00 p.m. and everyone expected to retire at that time. Inmates "such as shall get drunk or become riotous" were strictly penalized, the offender locked up and fed bread and water for first offence, for forty-eight hours, for ninety-six hours with a similar diet for the second offence and expulsion for the third.[291] The children's manners and morals were even more carefully supervised: the rules and regulations for the government of the parish house required them to rise at six, the tutoress "to see that their hands and faces are washed, hair combed and cleanly dressed". Prayers were said before breakfast, and those who were old enough went off to Wolmer's Free School, the smaller ones remaining under the care and instruction of the tutoress. They dined together at 2:00 p.m.:

> The Matron and Tutoress are to be at each end of the table to serve them and to preserve due decorum. Grace to be said before and after dinner by one of the children in rotation. . . . The Matron and the Tutoress shall at all times pay due observance to the morals and good behaviour of the children and never allow them to ramble abroad or to play in the Streets.

These rules were to be posted in the schoolroom at the poor house and to be publicly read every week by the parish steward.[292]

Racial exclusiveness was implicit in creole canons of social propriety. A survey of the Kingston local records covering some forty years, between 1769 and 1828, reveal one instance of a mulatto child being admitted into the parish house. Evelina Waldt, the property of one Frances Daly, was brought before the Court of Common Council exhibiting marks of violence and severe ill-treatment. An official inquiry into her circumstances resulted in the decision to send her to the Parish House.[293] This seemed the first breach of a policy which was precisely stated in 1808, in these terms: "Elizabeth Richardson and Libbe Roberts women of colour and therefore considered improper persons to be within the Parish House do receive from the Treasurer weekly the sum of 10s. each."[294]

The Kingston poor house had up to 1781 employed its own tutor, Ann Burton, to teach the children who lived there. But on the establishment of Wolmer's Free School, the children attended there instead. She was then given the responsibility of caring "the said children, and other children in the said parish house, to keep them clean, and from time to time, to mend and make for them".[295] In 1823, the Vestry abolished the post of tutoress to Wolmer's Free School and decided to reinstitute a system of teaching children within the poor house – "the duties of same in future be performed by such of the young women in the Parish House as are competent thereto under the direction and control of the Matron".[296] In the next year, the treasurer of Wolmer's school paid honoraria of £15 each to four young females "late in the Parish House . . . as a reward for their meritorious services in assisting to teach the junior classes in that institution".[297]

The decision to remove charity children from Wolmer's Free School coincided with the conspicuous withdrawal of white children from that school, as its complexion darkened. Its attendance figures are significant (see table 4.6).

However humble the level of existence, race and colour mattered. Whiteness gave its holders special claims even in the administration of charity, suggesting that in Jamaica, as in the Leeward Islands, as Elsa Goveia has demonstrated, "a heavy emphasis on racial particuliarism characterized the entire social order".[298]

The education and work training of the poor were important matters of policy. Charity children were apprenticed to trades when they were old enough. An advertisement was placed in the *Kingston Journal* or in the *Royal Gazette,* as follows:

June 4–June 11, 1791

Clerk of the Vestry's Office, Kingston, May 20, 1791

There being in the PARISH HOUSE several YOUNG WOMEN of a proper age to be
apprenticed out, any person desirous of taking an Apprentice therefrom may apply
to the Vestry (or . . . the same to the clerk of the Vestry) as to the term of years for
which they are to be indented and the amount of the apprentice-fee to be given,
on the execution of the deed of indenture, and the bond for performance of indenture, and the bond for performance of covenants.

By order,
J. Hardwar (Vestry)[299]

In January 1770, Mary Jameson and Ann Fish were bound from the
Kingston parish.[300]

Seamstresses, milliners and mantua makers took young girls in respond-
ing to advertisements or on direct application to the Vestry, which appeared
to keep a vigilant eye on these placements, sometimes insisting that apprentices should have permission to attend school, sometimes withdrawing them
if the arrangements did not turn out to be satisfactory.[301] There was one case
of the Vestry paying for a girl to be bound to her own mother, a mantua
maker, who then received the apprentice fee of £10.[302] In 1820, the city treasurer paid out £42 13s. 4d. for Mary Fogarty to be bound out of the parish
house with one Mrs McGeorge for three years; William Robertson stood
security for the return of the fee to the city, should she not complete her
term.[303] Adults could apparently be also placed by the Vestry but in a rare
case recorded, this proved unsuccessful: within a few months the apprentice,
who had apparently entered domestic service, objected to being bound to
her employer "on account of her keeping a lodging house".[304] The Vestry as a
result declared the arrangement null and void.

The long-term prospects of the underprivileged obviously received serious
thought from the establishment. Mr Ebenezeer Reid, Headmaster of
Wolmer's Free School, was given a special mission when he went on a year's
leave in 1824 to Europe for the restoration of his health: he was asked "to
inquire into the best mode and most eligible situation in any part of Great
Britain where the poor children of this Parish may be sent for the advantage
of their education and acquirement of humble views and industrious habits
to their future welfare".[305]

Table 4.6   Whites and Coloured Children at Wolmer's School, 1814–1825

Year	Whites	Coloureds
1814	87	0
1815	111	3
1816	129	25
1817	146	36
1818	155	38
1819	136	57
1820	110	78
1821	118	122
1822	93	167
1823	97	187
1824	94	196
1825	89	185

Source: J.A. Thome and J.H. Kimball, *Emancipation in the West Indies: A Six Months' Tour in Antigua, Barbados, and Jamaica, in the Year 1837* (New York: American Anti-Slavery Society, 1838), 87; also quoted in Brathwaite, *The Development of Creole Society,* 173–74.

This was consistent with the ultimate in local government's concern for its citizens' welfare its financing of back-to-Europe movements of poor whites. At the Kingston Vestry meeting of 23 January 1770, the Church Warden authorized payment of passages "for such persons as may require to depart the island for the benefit of health (not exceeding £10) and also fit cloathing if required".[306] Margaret Duffus and her two children were among the first considered for such repatriation, and the Vestry allowed them 20s. weekly while they awaited transportation.[307] Fifteen persons were granted passages to emigrate in 1786, seven of them women; one went to Philadelphia and the others to England.[308]

The benevolent parochial bureaucrat inevitably played at times the role of father confessor. Mary Primrose related her sad history to the Manchester Vestry. She had a heritage of female gullibility and, like her mother before her, fell victim to poverty and to masculine persuasion:

[M]ere necessity obliged her to listen to the illicit addresses of Mr Bartlett and she has by him four children in addition to the two she had by her late husband one of whom about seven years had dreadful fits sometimes three times a day. That none of the children know a letter; and unless some fish are caught, which is [not] often, for went of the means, which Mr B. has not, the children and herself go without a mouthful – that the Mrs Primrose with shame owns she does not live in a creditable connection with Mr Bartlett, but it was dire necessity brought her to it, and had she smallest means would discontinue it tomorrow could she only maintain her four starving children who want food clothes and education. She begs and prays to entreat humans feelings of the magistrate vestry and gentlemen of the Parish.[309]

The archives do not indicate what became of Mary Primrose, but her future was not hopeless. Even for her, mobility was a real possibility. For whiteness guaranteed to even the most depressed member of Euro-Jamaican society, the destitute female, a variety of escape routes from her condition: poor, but white, she could move up or out.

5   The White Woman

Legal Status, Family, Philanthropy and Gender Constraints

A WOMAN'S PLACE? CUSTOM, LAW AND SOCIO-POLITICAL RIGHTS

English law and custom defined the status of the white woman in Jamaica. That status was perceived to be that of a member of the second sex, eligible only for second-class citizenship. She exercised no political rights. An English seventeenth-century statement of the position of women expressed it accordingly: "Women have no voice in Parliament. They make no laws, they consent to none, they abrogate none . . . The common-laws here shaketh hand with divinitye."[1]

The law was in fact imprecise about women's electoral rights. No "positive exclusion" of women from the franchise was spelt out in British law until the Reform Act of 1832 specified that the vote in the new constituencies was confined to "male persons".[2] Nevertheless, women, traditionally, in Jamaica as in Britain, did not vote, did not stand for national or local elections, did not hold public office.[3] Society ordained that any rights or interests in civic matters which they might claim to have were adequately exercised on their behalf by male members of the community.[4] Their place was clearly identified as being not in the world, but in the home.

Law and custom further ensured that their role and functioning in the family were carefully circumscribed. The philosophy of family law was pervaded by the interests of propertied men. As a result, their cardinal concerns in relation to women were most clearly expressed in the laws governing inheritance and marriage, two of their main instruments for conveying property.

The rule of primogeniture was observed in Jamaica in accordance with English convention.[5] The eldest son succeeded by right to all the real estate of a parent who died intestate. An analogous right of succession was frequently given either by will or by marriage settlement. A system of inheritance, which keeps the family assets intact in one hand, perpetuates land monopolization. It was ideally designed to support the creole agricultural system of extensive plantations.[6] Simultaneously, primogeniture emphasized, the legal and financial inferiority of the lesser members, and especially the female members, of the family.

Underlying all legal and customary provisions made for the maintenance of the woman was the presumption of marriage as the natural state of adult females: "all of them are understood either married or to be married, and their desires are to their husbands",[7] said Spruill. Spinsterhood was unnatural, pathetic or, even worse, ridiculous. Although more independent in strictly legal terms than a wife, a single woman existed in a familial vacuum, the stock European figure of pity or of fun. A local review of the play which opened the Kingston Theatre in 1812 echoed what was no doubt the prevailing creole view: "Miss Shaw, as Miss Durable personated antiquated virginity as naturally as if she had in reality already arrived at that state of protracted purity which dubs the neglected fair with the sad and unenvied title of 'Old Maid'."[8] Edward Long breathed a sigh of relief at his daughter's "honourable alliance" to Mr Howard in 1801; for he had "dreaded leaving her at large in the world, either to be subject to the multitude of inconveniences which generally attend the situation of the single woman, or else to experience the mortifications of a state of dependence on someone of their relations".[9] His son-in-law, it is true, did not qualify in "the most necessary qualification" for matrimony, in that he had only a moderate income. But his "expectations were respectable" and, most importantly, he had, after all, married the girl.[10]

Louisa King, the only spinster member of a Portland family, struggled to retain her financial independence *vis-à-vis* her eldest brother. Her whole situation revealed something of the workings of a culture that had no really meaningful place for a woman outside of marriage.[11]

The conspicuous scarcity of the white female did not, as might be supposed, serve to give her much real advantage on the marriage market; for brown and black female/white male concubinage was so deeply entrenched in the creole way of life as to make the white spinster virtually redundant;[12] hence her eager seeking after naval and military officers, the Johnny Newcomer to the island, before they fell captive to the custom of the country.[13]

The much desired marriage, in fact, brought "civil death" to women. It placed them in "coverture", which implied their incapacity to act as free and rational beings and therefore, like minors and idiots, disqualified them from responsibility for their criminal offences, required for them the protection (cover) of a male.[14] Blackstone's dictum circumscribed the life of the wife: "the very being, or legal existence of the woman is suspended during her marriage".[15]

Few other western European systems of jurisprudence, it has been maintained, gave husbands as extensive powers as the English: in France, a concept of community property permitted the woman significant property rights. The recognition of strong parent-child bonds in countries influenced by Roman law similarly modified her subordination. There, "family has a more extended meaning, and woman regains there, in the heightened reverence with which the mother is regarded, all that she loses in the lessened dignity that attaches to the wife".[16] It was in England, above all, that a pattern of conjugal life was perfected "which seemed to reproduce at every fireside the bond of lord and vassal".[17]

As in English law, the personalty of the creole wife, like her personality, was merged into her husband's. He took instant and complete possession of all her personal property, he enjoyed throughout marriage full use of her real estate, and by "curtesy" was entitled after death to its continued use as tenant for life. At her husband's death, the widow was entitled to dower chargeable to her husband's real estate, as well as one-half of the personalty if she alone survived him; but in case of a child or children of the marriage also surviving him, she was entitled to one-third.[18]

This was the basic legal framework: supplementary instruments of disposition, such as wills and marriage settlements, were invoked to express more fully the human realities and relationships involved. Often they genuinely provided for those whom the common law neglected; just as often they merely re-affirmed that women's security rested on masculine caprice.

A sample of forty Jamaican wills drawn up or probated in the late eighteenth century revealed the principle of primogeniture at work. In one instance only did a daughter, in the absence of a surviving heir, inherit all real and personal property. For the rest, primogeniture prevailed. In twenty cases the testators left a natural heir by common law – who in all except three instances received the bulk of the estates.[19] The exceptions occurred with wealthy men, such as William Lewis[20] and the Honourable John Scott,[21] who divided their vast holdings equally among their sons. James Charles Sholto Douglas was unique in making his daughter equal heiress with her five brothers to his landed fortune.[22] Even here, the rationale behind primogeniture was relatively untouched: each unit or property remained large, capable of retaining its indivisible integrity.

Men of substance on the whole took relatively good care of their daughters. In the Jamaican wills analysed, thirty-four girls and women were well provided for. Nearly all received annuities of approximately £100, adequate at that time for decent maintenance. Many received sums varying from £1,000 to £4,000 each, at the age of nineteen or twenty-one or at marriage. Very few, significantly, inherited land;[23] and testators, in some instances, did not even attempt to conceal the grace and favour element in their bequests. William Lewis, for example, made clear the reasons for his daughter Jane's preferential treatment in his will. He testified to "his particular affection and regard for her tenderness, goodness and her partaking in his severe affliction for the loss of her mother as well as her uncommon carefulness and remarkably prudent behaviour (for one of her tender years) towards his motherless children and in other Family affairs". As evidence of his appreciation, he left her £500 in addition to the £2,500 bequeathed to herself and each of her five sisters. She received, as well, an extra five slaves and was made joint executrix-guardian, with her two brothers, for her sisters and for the whole Lewis estate.[24]

Like wills, marriage contracts, which were regularly drawn up by the middle and upper classes, went some way towards filling in the blanks left by the law; but, like wills, their format remained inspired by prevailing social values. Marriage contracts were employed by fathers as much to protect their daughters' interest as they were by husbands to insure the inalienability of the family inheritance. "Every marriage settlement", observed Sinclair, "was a protest against the law: but every marriage settlement was a guarantee for the continuance of the law".[25] So, provisions in the marriage contract for the upkeep of daughter, wife, widow, assured her an income. Arrangements also made clear as a rule that these provisions should not involve the sale or division of the family's lands. The wife customarily brought a lump sum, portion or dowry, into the marriage; the husband paid a jointure, an annual income calculated in ratio to the portion. Both capital and income were flexible, dependent on the relative social and financial strength of the families concerned, and the two sides to the bargain matched their wits in working out the terms most favourable to their respective interests.[26]

Jointures in England, throughout the eighteenth century, tended to get smaller in relation to portions. The wife's dividends declined *vis-à-vis* her patrimony, indicative, it has been suggested, of a virtual glut of mercantile heiresses seeking landed connections; indicative also of an increasingly materialist rationale of marriage.[27] The bride, in bald terms, was buying a husband in a seller's market; the peculiar features of creole Jamaica even further devalued the white bride's portion.

There was very little sentimentality in the administration of these marital agreements. Governor Keith's timely marriage, as he frankly admitted, bailed him out of near bankruptcy.[28] Edward Long, looking back at his family's fortunes, regretted that his father had not been as lucky: Samuel Long's marriage to Mary Tate in 1723 had brought with it a dowry of £3,000, a mere drop in the ocean of his financial embarrassments. Their son commented: "Although my Mother might be a very good match in point of personal and marital accomplishments, and the rank of her family connections, yet she was certainly not a suitable one in point of fortune to a man whose own Estate was so harassed and dismantled, and liable to so many serious encumbrances."[29]

Jamaican testators often repeated in their wills the fact that a wife was legally entitled to a pension (or jointure) under the marriage settlement or to her dower under common law, but not to both. Sir Henry Moore stated it in typical terms: "Catherina Maria Moore dear wife £600 sterling, a year for life from Moore Hall estate in St Mary (provided she relinquishes all claim to jointure settled on her on indenture of 11 January 1750 and now of record in Jamaica)."[30]

A testator, James Egan of Clarendon parish, whose will was written in 1750 and probated in 1781, made clear his obligation to observe the strict letter of the common law and no more: "Alice Egan beloved wife £500 sterling and all plate rings jewels and household furniture whatsoever for over £400 sterling per annum from his Estate in Jamaica for life – but if she claims more dower all bequests void except any contingent estate he may bequeath to her."[31]

One significant variation from English common-law principles was found in Jamaica legislation governing the property rights of the woman. This was in respect of her entitlement to dower in slaves. The creole wife was "entitled to dower of the real estate of her husband as in England and to similar provision (subject to his debts) out of the slave-property indisposed of in his life time".[32] The proviso on slaves was spelt out in the law: "[A]ll slaves assigned for dower shall be liable, proportionately with those belonging to any heir or heirs, to the payment of debts but not of legacies . . . such sale, gift, or disposition (by husband) shall be a perpetual bar to his wife from any claim of dower in such slave or slaves."[33] By English criteria, this was an anomaly and provoked comment from the judicial commissioners, who reported in 1825 on the West Indies legal system: "This seems a very extraordinary departure from the principle of the law of England with respect to dower, under which the wife's title accrues by the act of marriage and becomes a vested interest."[34]

The widow's right to dower, chargeable to her husband's estate, was in fact her most substantial legal claim on the matrimonial property. To partially exempt slave property from the widow's claim was to exempt a portion of the estate which averaged about a third of its customary value.[35] It is not surprising that this perplexed the judicial commissioners. It was, in fact, expedient for Jamaican lawmakers to convert slaves, otherwise regarded as real property, into moveable chattels for purposes of settling debts. A corollary to primogeniture was the holding of estates in tail for future heirs, a system which could frustrate the attempts of planters to make their estate operations viable. The legal procedures required for docking an entail, and thereby permitting the sale of an otherwise inalienable estate, was long and difficult.[36] If slaves could be freed from the restrictions imposed on real property, planter financing was that more flexible. They came therefore by creole practice to be used routinely as easily liquidated assets for payment of debts and for gifts: they were, as well, the conventional form in which the planter rewarded and provided for his black/brown mistress and offspring.

Slaves, moreover, were awkward property: men may have genuinely preferred to spare their widows as much as possible the harassment and expense of managing them. The Reverend John Venn, rector of the parish church of St Catherine, expressed husbandly consideration in his will: he left instructions for all his moveables, including his slaves, to be sold at his death, but strongly advised his wife against purchasing any of them. He wrote: "They will not only diminish her Income but help to consume what remains, she having more of her own than will do her Good."[37]

On the other hand, black labour, although costly to maintain, nevertheless represented the most important source of income for the woman, as has been previously discussed.[38] If there were any masculine intention, conscious or unconscious, of keeping women in a permanent state of financial dependence, fewer more effective means could be devised in creole Jamaica than curtailing her potential ownership of slaves.

The Jamaican white woman, like her continental sister in North America, inherited in general principles the legal status of her English equivalent. But English common law underwent significant alterations on its transatlantic journey, consistent with colonial realities.[39] The circumstances of the western frontier, which made the woman often the co-worker of the man, made relatively liberal modifications in the condition of North American womanhood. New England courts conceded to women rights which were unknown to Blackstone's England.[40] It is significant that the American Married Women's Property Act of 1848, which made the first major breakthrough in the West in the assertion of women's property rights, predated its English equivalent by almost a generation.[41]

No similar emancipating influences appeared in British slaveholding society in the deep south or in the Caribbean. Whatever gains the frontiersman made for the woman in one region, the slaveholder withdrew in another; so that her property rights narrowed, and the marriage noose tightened. Asked by the judicial commissioners whether Jamaica had any jurisdiction competent to pronounce a sentence of divorce, the attorney general replied that there was none and, further, that "there is a positive instruction to the Governor, to withhold his assent to any act of the Legislature dissolving a marriage".[42] The chief justice reconfirmed this fact, and added that "inconvenience must result".[43]

The equity jurisdiction of the Courts of Chancery was available to the Jamaican woman, as to the English, for redressing grievances when the common law proved inadequate. Such jurisdiction covered a range of subjects affecting the woman's condition in many essential ways, for example, dowry settlements, probate of wills, intestacy, and guardianship of minors.[44] But the concept behind equity, as nineteenth-century feminists maintained, was charity, not justice. Besides, the shortcomings of Chancery in Jamaica, as in England, were notorious. Edward Long attacked sharply its lack of guiding principles and procedures, its shortage of trained personnel, its inefficiency, its "tardy process" that made it, in his opinion, "a sanctuary for knaves and malicious litigants".[45] The findings of the judicial commissioners in the 1820s confirmed Long's strong judgement. The evidence of Mary Wright and her sister, two victims of Chancery's tardiness, forced the commission to conclude that the many years' delay they suffered in disentangling their father's estate were, under the rules of the Court of Chancery, "unavoidable". They could only hope that the reforms that they proposed would minimize individual distress in the future.[46]

Traditional disabilities and cumbrous procedures did not entirely discourage women from demanding their legal dues, and the records show numerous cases of women who resorted to the courts for the protection of their interests. For the majority, however, it was the family circle which, fairly or unfairly, provided for their well-being.

"Till Death Do Us Part": Love and Family Relationships

It is evident that the Euro-Jamaican family successfully met the basic needs of its members. Certainly it housed, clothed and fed them, even to excess; it educated them in its way. It provided mutual affection and concern such as are fully documented in diaries, wills and letters. Matthew Lewis, whose insight into Jamaican slave society emerges as one of the more sensitive of the period,[47] inherited a legacy of loving family relationships. The Honourable John Scott respected the wishes of his "First beloved wife", Frances Mary Scott, that she and her husband should share a grave: she died at the age of twenty-seven in 1753 and was buried in the Kingston Parish Church. When John Scott wrote his will on 28 October 1772, he instructed his executors that should he and his "second much beloved wife", Lucretia Favell Scott, the daughter of Matthew Gregory, die in Jamaica and at a reasonable distance from Spanish Town, his first wife's body should be removed from Kingston and "interred with him and his second wife one grave to contain his ashes and those of two good wives whom he truly loved and esteemed – and he to be placed with a Family which he respects and regards".[48]

The Honourable William Lewis of Westmoreland, the grandfather of Matthew Lewis, had married another daughter of Matthew Gregory, and he too spoke highly of his "worthy father-in-law". He also wished to be buried with his "ever dear wife who was a pattern of conjugal affection", in the orchard behind their home at Cornwall Plantation. He asked his children and "their descendants, particularly those who inherit Cornwall Plantation that they keep in good repair the said Monument and the chapel erected over it. The shingle and inside of the chapel are to be painted black and all is to be cleaned out yearly in or before 19 February."[49] When his grandson visited Cornwall for the first time forty-three years later, he found that many old slaves still remembered his grandfather with fondness.[50] The family mausoleum in the heart of an orange grove so impressed him that he felt inclined to repeat his grandfather's wish to be buried there, for "I never yet saw a place where one could lie down more comfortably to listen for the last trumpet".[51]

The sense of grief and desolation which men like Thomas Munro and James Archer expressed at their wives' deaths seemed very deeply felt. Thomas Munro, who poured out his sadness in page after page of his journal, found some small comfort in the thought that theirs had been a happy marriage: "'Tis sweet, 'tis consoling to reflect that as far as it was in our power the lost sharer of our heart knew no cares, that we could prevent, and no happiness that we did not endeavour to increase." It seemed to him that his slaves too felt his loss: "They all loved Misses, and they now as well as Massa weep for Misses too – their drums beat no holiday when Massa is by."[52]

Three generations of Archers – mother, son and granddaughter – in the absence of a wife, linked with the neighbouring Great Pond branch of the Archers, operating as a tightly knit domestic group, their emotional, social, and financial affairs mutually supportive.[53] George Hyde Clarke's will further demonstrates the family's assumption of responsibility for the members in need. He left to Ms Katherine Hyde Clarke, "dear unhappy and much injured niece (wife of George Hyde Clarke, profligate abandoned nephew) £300 to enable her to come to England to see her children".[54] For Louisa

King, otherwise doomed to a "recluse life", it seemed that it was her close and practical involvement with the family circle of married sisters, nieces and nephews, which provided her with a *raison d'être*.[55]

The consciousness of being a small minority helped to develop a strong sense of cohesion and interdependence among white creoles. This trend was strengthened by the entrenched practice of intermarriage among local families. The case of the Archers is an example: James Archer of Spring Mount estate in St Ann and George Archer of nearby Great Pond were cousins. In addition, their wives were sisters, thus facilitating their functioning as virtually one domestic unit.[56] Jamaica had the quality of "a family centred society", dominated by a few families of considerable permanence and power, a pattern also observed in other Caribbean islands.[57]

John Scott's clan from St Thomas-in-the-East, whose holdings spread over eight parishes, linked with the equally large and powerful landowning family of the Honourable John Lewis, custos of Westmoreland, through their respective marriages to the daughters of the influential Gregorys of St Catherine, and thus formed an unbroken chain of dynastic interests stretching across the island.[58] The prolific Barretts of Cinnamon Hill intermarried with their cousins the Goodins and Moultons on adjoining estates and made large acreages in the north coast parishes of St James and Trelawny into virtually a family reservation.[59]

Edward Long represented the classic creole concentration of kinship and influence. His father, Samuel Long, a member of the Jamaican Council and proprietor of Longville estate in Clarendon, had four sons and three daughters. Long's eldest brother died young and his other two brothers were relatively obscure. But his own marriage and those of two of his sisters were significant. His three brothers-in-law, Samuel Hemming, George Ellis and Sir Henry Moore, were all of old West Indian stock, although the Hemmings fell on hard times. Moore's inherited prestige included an English seventeenth-century baronetcy and a creole ancestor who was one of Jamaica's earliest members of its Assembly, Colonel Smart. Smart's daughter was Henry Moore's grandmother. Earlier, Moores and Longs became linked by marriage with an English family of Lowes. Henry Moore, born in Jamaica and educated at Eton, was a landed proprietor who married his cousin Catherine Long in 1751; he was lieutenant governor of Jamaica during the period when Edward Long was chief judge of the Admiralty Court and member of the

Assembly for the parish of St Ann. Moore subsequently became the governor of New York.[60]

George Ellis's marriage to Susanna Charlotte Long in 1754, although brief, nevertheless represented an impressive network of property and power.[61] John Ellis, the founder of the dynasty, had married into the family of Colonel George Nedham, who was Jamaica's first Speaker of the Assembly. The first George Ellis had been chief justice and member of the Assembly in the early eighteenth century. His son, the second George Ellis, Edward Long's brother-in-law, was also a member of the Assembly: his older brother, John Ellis, married Elizabeth, daughter of the chief justice, John Palmer, and their older son, Charles Ellis, became the powerful first Lord Seaford.[62]

The ramifications of these matrimonial links were practically endless; for the Ellisses were also related by marriage to the eminent planter family of Beckfords,[63] and their connections further intertwined when, on 12 August 1758, at the Spanish Town Cathedral, Edward Long married Mary Ballard Beckford Palmer, heiress to the Beckford-Ballard estates, and relict of the wealthy deceased John Palmer of Springvale.[64] Mrs Edward Long, incidentally, was also a member of the Gregory-Lewis family group: her grandmother was a Gregory, the sister of Monk Lewis's grandfather, Matthew Gregory.[65] One of Edward Long's nephews by blood became a governor of Tobago; another married a daughter of Sir Peter Parker, Admiral of the Fleet.[66]

Concentric circles of relatives and friends met each other's needs, especially at society's upper level. Familiar names recur in personal documents as Beckfords, Windes, Gales, Brodbelts, Longs, Morants. They drew up and witnessed each other's wills, became trustees and executors of each other's estates and guardians of each other's heirs. Samuel Hemming's "affairs were too unsettled" for him to make proper provision for his dear wife, Elizabeth Amelia, at his death; but he had "most unbounded confidence in the honour and integrity of his esteemed and worthy friends", John Dalling, lieutenant governor of Jamaica, Sir Charles Price, Scudamore Winde and Edward Long, whom he appointed his trustees, executors and guardians to sort out his tangled finances.[67] Creoles remembered each other in their deathbed bequests, with affection and with gratitude for past services rendered.[68]

These services, often practical and necessary, were required to be performed both in Jamaica and in Britain. The education of children abroad was a major responsibility that made the colonial family strongly dependent on its metropolitan connections. Domestic arrangements for children's holidays, supervision in particular of girls' wardrobe, health, minutiae of deportment, were all delegated to someone in the mother country willing to act *in loco parentis.*[69]

The Reverend John Venn of St Catherine spelt out carefully the grave responsibilities which he placed on his executors and friends Rose, Thomas and Stephen Fuller, and John Morse for the care and upbringing of his four daughters, Mary, Elizabeth, Sarah and Susanna. He left strict instructions that

> they shall never return to Jamaica, but settle in Great Britain. . . . No daughter of mine to remain at a Boarding School after 13 . . . I put it to the conscience of my executors not to board out any daughters of mine in the City or any obscure part of London even with any relation, but to let them be brought up in liberal but frugal manner . . . also hope that Stephen Fuller will next Xmas remove daughter Mary into his own house and find her some other safe establishment till she marries or is of age, and to do so with the others as they attain to 13 . . . .[70]

Favours from abroad were almost indispensable to the running of the creole household. Women relied heavily on relatives and friends, as well as their husbands' business associates, to get their shopping done. This applied not only to their luxuries, but also to items of food, clothing and other basic domestic necessities. Whenever letters and parcels were few and far between Jamaican residents were cut off from family news, and from supplies.

The men of the family were equally dependent on metropolitan goodwill and services of a very personal nature. Jane Brodbelt was go-between for her father's orders of medical supplies and for his professional reading matter.[71] If Edward Long went almost beyond the call of friendship as intermediary in William Ricketts's domestic affairs, he too needed Ricketts on-the-spot help in sorting out his tailor's bills and in putting in a good word for him with his powerful uncle Beeston Long. "[I]f I stand fair", wrote Long, "in my Good Uncle's opinion whom I love and revere as a Parent I must owe a great deal to the friendly representations you have made considering my distance from him and the frequent opportunities which may happen to do me ill-offices with him by accusing me of such things as he is known to dislike."[72]

In the field of professional and political placement, family contacts and family needs were all-important. In fact, government by family patronage was so much the order of the day that comment was sharp when the kinsman failed to pull the necessary strings. Long expressed to Mary Ricketts his surprise and disappointment that her influential brother's ministerial colleagues in the British government had not made more adequate provision for her and for her husband:

> I consider that your friends in power have hitherto done nothing but promise, I want to see them perform, and hope if there is any such thing as sincere friendship among them, and a real desire to serve your brother that they will manifest it by placing you upon some establishment for life, let this be the test of their sincerity: all else is but wind.[73]

Long did not consider the military commission that had been offered to Ricketts as substantial enough, for it had not been accompanied by the concession of clothing the regiment: it had therefore no "material thing to make it of any profit".[74]

As in the handling of domestic matters, so it was in the exercise of colonial patronage: the link with England was invaluable. William Dwarris, who made no attempt to conceal his professional ambitions and who regularly solicited aid from his wife's parents for his advancement, stated bluntly that "applications from Home are more successful – it shows a person had interest in England".[75]

Edward Long's tribute to his deceased uncle Beeston Long is significant:

> His family and connections derived a lustre from his irreproachable character, principles, worth and fortune. When obliged to go to Jamaica, his kindness still followed me thither, and I owe to his voluntary solicitation, the V. Admiralty Patent, which was an act of consideration and Friendship I can never think of but with utmost Gratitude. To Jamaica too his loss is not trivial. He was always a warm friend to the interest of the planters, and a faithful Advocate, upon every suitable occasion. Here too, his known Experience, Judgement, and Candour, were such, that he has been often advised with, and respectfully attended to by some of the ablest Ministers in this Kingdom.[76]

Creole Jamaica was dominated by many Beeston Longs: their family names might have been Price, Ellis, Fuller, Beckford, Dawkins or Holland. The combination of their landed holdings in Jamaica, their mercantile inter-

ests in England and their access to political power in both countries placed
them in strategic positions to influence the fortunes of their relatives and
friends. They embodied the phenomenon of a family/class which spanned
two continents but which functioned in many essentials as one interlocking
entity.[77]

But the transatlantic character of the creole clan made it also a peculiar
domestic unit: if its presence on both sides of the ocean implied dual sources
of support, it also implied a group which was fragmented and therefore
vulnerable.

The basic ingredients of the European-type nuclear family were often
missing. Seldom were mother, father, daughter and son under the same
Jamaican (or English) roof at the same time. Edward Long, for example, was
a member of what was, in this as in many other respects, a characteristic creole home and a "broken" migratory home.

Long describes "the serious and extreme depression" which overcame him
at the age of eleven, when his parents, brother and sisters went to Jamaica,
leaving him alone in England at a very inferior boarding school, which was
all that their financial position could allow at the time.[78] "Years passed away
before I heard further tidings of my absent relatives."[79] Another painful
experience of his youth and early adulthood was the serious estrangement
between his parents, which sprang from his mother's distress at having to live
again in Jamaica. She claimed that her health had been destroyed in her
younger days at Longville in Clarendon,[80] a parish described by Long himself as "undoubtedly the Golgotha of Jamaica".[81] She delayed in joining her
husband: as a result, the breach between them became permanent and they
lived apart until her return to England with one of her daughters, to whom
she was eventually forbidden all access.[82]

It did not matter whether the family saw itself as resident in Jamaica or in
England: in a domestic pattern whose model was the European household,
such gaps and rifts undermined its structural integrity. William Ricketts, in
the last years of his Jamaican exile, had to face the fact that nearly a lifetime's
separation from his family had lost him his children; and when he attempted
a belated Lord Chesterfield letter of advice in March 1780 to his older son
Henry, whom he had scarcely ever seen, it resulted in an admission that he
had abdicated his father's role to his brother-in-law, Lord Jervis. "[E]mulate
your Uncle's example . . . he will lead you to the paths of honour and

glory."[83] He resigned himself as well to writing off his own non-functioning marriage: "I have suffered greatly in my mind and constitution from so long a separation from your excellent mother, it was with a view to serve you and your Brother. . . . I have separated myself from the world, and what was more precious the company and conversation of one of the best women on Earth."[84]

The experience of the Archers further illustrates the implications of the dispersed creole family. James Archer recorded the arrangements for the departure of six-and-a-half-year-old Jim to school in Scotland:

> 14 April 1829, went to Oracabessa and booked passage on Brig. Temple with Captain Midwinter.[85]

> 18 April received Mr Thorpe's draft horse to take Jim to St Ann's Bay to be christened tomorrow . . . went with Jim and Drs. A. to St Pond where he slept.[86]

> 19 April . . . with Mr & Mrs S. Archer went to St Ann's Bay and had Jim christened by Rev. Bridges for which I gave him £5. 6. 8. ret. home to Spring Mount.[87]

Archer went to Oracabessa three days later to see the boat and paid Mrs Pinnock £28 to travel with Jim on the voyage.[88] On 25 April, Jim departed:

> Accompanied by George and his own family Mrs A. Jim and myself went to Oracabessa – and they went on board ship about 10½ a.m. My dear Jim was terribly affected. Oh that Providence will guard him from all the dangers of the deep and send him in health to his friends at home. No Rain, Little wind all day. Mrs John, on our return from Oracabessa went there to see if she could not procure a boat to bring Jim . . . all in vain.[89]

Two and a half months later, when Archer was in Spanish Town, he met a Mr Carr, "who mentioned the diabolical report of the Temple being captured by Pirates".[90] The rumour turned out to be pretty nearly accurate. A note in the margin of Archer's diary states that "Captain Midwinter had been wrecked off Gt. Cayman, rescued by Captain Burlow of the Thetis, nearly captured by pirates off Cuba."[91] Then: "31 August . . . saw in the papers yesterday for the first time the arrival of the Thetis at Gravesend in which my darling Jim went home."[92]

The physical and emotional voids thus created had long-term repercussions. At the time of her marriage in March 1822, Mrs James Archer's father had settled £2,500 on her. James Archer, in their marriage contract, obliged himself and his heirs, executors and successors to secure the sum of £4,000 in favour of himself, his spouse, the longest lived and their children. Both spouses also guaranteed that the marriage settlement should finance the education of the children of the marriage, "in a manner suitable to their stations". Mrs Archer died in 1831, leaving a daughter Mary and her son Jim still at school in Scotland. When Archer remarried in 1838, his interest in the marriage contract ceased, and the provisions devolved on Jim Archer and his sister, thereby setting in motion a chain of family disputes which were still unsettled far into the 1840s.[93]

James Archer, Jr., felt injured in relation to his inheritance in two respects: he claimed that he received nothing from his mother's marriage contract, but was advised by the trustees that his interest in the fund had been exhausted by expenditure on his education and upkeep in Scotland, and the subsequent purchase of his commission in the Army; in fact, they maintained, it was his sister's share which supplemented the cost of his commission. In addition, his father, by his will of 26 July 1846, left all his estate, including Spring Mount that had greatly depreciated in value, to his two daughters (he had had another by his second marriage). To his son Jim, whom it appears he had not seen since 1829, he left £5, "in lieu of all claims as my heir-at-law or otherwise".[94]

MONEY MATTERS

The financial base of the creole family critically determined its *modus operandi*, and this was often most brittle ground. It is difficult to conceive of interpersonal relationships more charged with monetary considerations than are found, for example, in the Dwarris papers. Scarcely any vital human experience – a marriage, a birth, a death – escaped calculation in terms of economic profit and loss. In the extended business enterprise that was plantation Jamaica, emotion seemed to be assigned its column in the ledger book.

A grandmother's death found William Dwarris most reluctant to register grief: "14 January 1782 . . . tis unfortunate for me she had not died before she married, as she was worth £5000 and by will left it to myself and Robt.

Brereton, but when she married she made over to the longest liver however in time I shall learn to bear misfortune like a philosopher." He and his wife had not even received the conventional incentive of a mourning ring or gift of money and, as a result, "had almost resolved not to go into [mourning]", but were prevailed on by their Aunt, "as she thought My Uncle wou'd expect the compliment".[95]

The hope of inheriting their Uncle's estate haunted their otherwise unremarkable nights and days, so that the presence of a young in-law, their aunt's daughter by a previous marriage, seemed, temporarily, to threaten their prospects: "26 June 1782 . . . in the Fleet came Mrs Neufville – my Uncle's daughter-in-law who went off abt. 14 months since for her health – and has spent My Uncles 100 Guineas a Month in England having kept a coach 2 footmen etc. this he told me himself."

Death, however, soon disposed of the rival: "13 September 1782 . . . tis a bad wind that no one gets by . . . very soon after Mrs Neufville's arrival from dining twice a week there we only dined twice in the month before she was taken sick. I most candidly confess I am in no way in the world sorry for the tribute she has paid."

The expectation for their own heir strengthened their position, while adversely affecting their aunt's: "14 November 1784 . . . [Sally's pregnancy] does not seem to afford anything very pleasant to My Aunt Dwarris . . . perhaps concludes My Uncle may alter his will and hurt her son."

Their uncle's future plans remained, however, tantalizingly obscure: "20 March 1785 . . . My Dear Sally was safely delivered of a clever Boy on the 5th inst. . . . My uncle has called every day but gets old and stingy, no present as yet for the Young Stranger."

Their son's death a few months later seriously set back their hopes: "17 July 1785 . . . My Uncle was very fond of him and if it had pleased God he had lived he would I dare say have been a very rich man . . . ."

But nature could provide new heirs, and their second son, the future eminent Sir Fortunatus Dwarris, caught their Uncle's eye, apparently to the unconcealed dismay of Mrs Dwarris, Sr.: "1 February 1787 . . . tis a bitter pill for my Aunt she can scarcely behave with propriety – may God permit him to live, and confound her wishes – my child . . . has best right to his paternal family Estate, which has been in this Country above 100 years in our Possession."

Sarah and William Dwarris may have been a singular couple; they may, on the other hand, have merely projected the deep-seated uneasy creole awareness that the estate which they coveted was really most ramshackle.

The underlying insecurity that characterized so many Jamaican economic undertakings arose out of a complex of financial and commercial arrangements inherent in mercantilism. In particular, certain aspects of plantation financing were affected by and simultaneously affected the family situation within that complex. One such aspect was the irrationally high propensity of colonial slaveholding elites to consume their plantation profits.[96]

The socially induced expenditure of upwardly mobile classes is nearly universal; it frequently accompanies new access to land and money. The goals of status maximization soon outstripped those of profit maximization. In a sense, as Eugene Genovese has pointed out, what seemed excessively conspicuous consumption, might not have been as irrational as it appeared. Among other things, it served the vital function of providing "the ruling class with the façade necessary to control the middle and lower classes".[97] In the Jamaican context, such compulsion would be exaggerated by the need to duplicate the metropolitan and to magnify the distance between white and black.

Status symbols of the tribe are often eagerly adopted by females, themselves, at times, scarcely more than status symbols. The Jamaican lady was in many ways the classic creole consumer of prestige. Steady erosions of plantation income and profits were made by the uneconomic operations of the great house: by feminine extravagance on the superfluous domestic staff, by the overladen table, by the European wardrobe, by the foreign education, by the crossing and recrossing of the Atlantic. One observer remarked that "[the ladies] talk of sending and going to England with much more indifference than you do of a Northern jaunt in Georgia and as if it was not half such an undertaking".[98] The price of exclusiveness and ostentation was high. While his womenfolk pursued their preoccupation with finery, frivolity and travel, Dr Brodbelt wrote to his daughter that, much as he would have liked joining his family in England, "I am obliged to remain here to work for your sister and Brother".[99]

The public, as well as the personal price, was equally high: excessive outflow of plantation income on unproductive consumer expenditure left little over for productive reinvestment in the enterprise – a fact of serious long-term implications for the restructuring of the society/economy on healthy lines. The commitment to "splendour and good living", a process difficult to reverse, meant that, when hard times hit the plantation, the creole lifestyle was purchased with credit. Plantation accounting practices frustrated possibilities of rationalizing its operations. Personal domestic expenses became, by convention, a fixed charge on the plantation books and made difficult any clear line between the needs of the business and the needs of the family. This compromised the calculability of the business and compromised the integrity of the family.[100]

At best, the matrimonial/domestic scene implies sensitive, potentially trying relationships. But, in an age when the rationale for marriage was very largely property acquisition, in a plantation context where property was sacrosanct, but most precariously held, the injection of financial discord could wreak havoc with such relationships. Douglas Hall has described the process out of which this discord so easily developed: "By generous gifts bestowed in times of prosperity and optimism about the continued profitability of sugar, many sugar estates encumbered their properties with charges on expected profits: when profits declined, beneficiaries, accustomed to and often dependent on their gratuities, pressed impossible claims."[101] Production and marketing costs were reducible, but interest on debts and fixed annuities to litigious dependents were not: these were "the millstones around planters' necks".[102]

Those spoilt beneficiaries and litigious dependents pressing their impossible claims were frequently the women of the family. Having little other means of livelihood than what their menfolk handed out, maiden sisters, aggrieved wives, determined widows were prepared to harass the estate for legacies and allowances. They were often in the centre of the vicious circle of economic irrationality that characterized much of the creole scene. Victims of the financial insecurity that surrounded the second sex, their struggles to achieve personal solvency often accelerated the insolvency of the very enterprises they besieged and, in the process, did damage, not only to the business, but to the human beings involved.

Plantation economics, compounded by its constant corollary of absenteeism, contributed towards undermining the Ricketts family. The rot had started to set in early with Mary Ricketts's instant distaste for the Jamaican scene, which resulted in their quick return to England. Then followed their enforced separations, while Ricketts re-visited Jamaica to straighten out his late father's tangled affairs,[103] thus strongly substantiating Hall's observation on absenteeism: "It was not so much true that absentee-owners were residents gone abroad as it was that residents in the colonies were temporarily, they hoped, absentees from Britain."[104] William Ricketts, although of a large, long-established creole clan, saw himself as such a transient tenant, whose visits to oversee his Jamaican business were justified to his wife by his friend Edward Long in these terms:

> A separation of this sort must undoubtedly be very afflicting to you, but you must consider that we are all in the hands of providence. That the nature of our property here must of necessity be always productive of these little interruptions of happiness, for no Man's Estate here is so well taken care of in his absence, as to render it unnecessary for him to have an eye to it himself. I hope this short parting will be attended with happy consequences, in enabling him to settle everything on so dear and proper a footing that he will not be hereafter constrained to the disagreeable hardship of another separation.[105]

In the case of this couple, the partings were painfully prolonged. Ricketts became engaged in Jamaica in the tortuous legal process of breaking the entail on the family property, in order to effect a sale of lands to clear the pressing debts left by his father. He himself became even more deeply indebted, although the exact amount of his indebtedness always appeared obscure. Maintaining a household on each side of the Atlantic caused further financial embarrassment. His creditors had the first claim on his sugar crops, and means had to be devised to circumvent this prior charge, so as to provide an annual allowance for his wife and children in England.[106]

Long, for years, despaired that Ricketts could ever bring order into his affairs. New charges on his estate kept coming to light; and he watched with evident distress as his friend's credit-worthiness disappeared, as his family's claims became increasingly subservient to those of his merchant financiers and as relationships between husband and wife turned sour. He had the unpleasant task of informing Mary Ricketts where she stood:

> [I]f they [that is, Ricketts's creditors] were to observe one half of the yearly produce, or any considerable share of it [diverted?] from their hands, to the subsistence of his wife and children, I have no doubt but the major part of them, if they were to be

asked what sum they thought a sufficiency for their debtor's Family [would] be of opinion, that £50 a year, would be a most generous allowance.[107]

In 1783, Long stated even more clearly to her the hard facts of life:

> I have no expectation that Mr R. (whatever he may have promised) will be able, considering the variety and extent of demands upon him, to permit anything from your use, and as to what the saw-mill may produce, I think it rather to be hoped, than seriously to be depended on . . . take a decisive step . . . resolve to commit yourself entirely to your Brothers' protection and direction. . . . If contrary to my present expectations any supplies should come to you this year from Jamaica, accept it as a prize, but do not stake the tranquility of your life upon such an eventful resource.[108]

It was not until 1797 that the Ricketts' financial problems appeared at last to be resolved. Long wrote Mary Ricketts on 6 May, congratulating her on having reached the end of her adversities and "attaining that comfort and affluence which [she] always merited".[109] This was some thirty years after their transatlantic domestic correspondence and negotiations were first started. William Ricketts died in Jamaica about a year later.

The affairs of the Jackson family represented, as Kenneth Ingram has remarked, "a case study of how inherited encumbrances, natural disasters and the vicissitudes of war served to frustrate the enthusiastic effort of a resident proprietor, who it was clear spent a great deal of time and money putting his estate in order".[110] Here too, family relationships became a significant casualty. John Jackson, barrister-at-law, spent several years managing the Hanover estates of Salem, which was his by purchase, and Mount Pleasant, which his wife owned, entailed from her late father, Thomas Witter, and of which John Jackson was a tenant for life. Mount Pleasant carried among many liabilities a heavy legacy of accumulated annuities payable to Jackson's mother-in-law, Mrs Douglas. In the course of improving and extending the operations of both estates, Jackson relied very heavily on credit advanced by the London merchant house of his father and by his brother, Henry Jackson, who received all consignments of sugar for the estates. The personal/professional dealings of the family in the colony and the metropole, as will be seen, carried risks as well as benefits.[111]

John Jackson made his will on 31 August 1785, leaving his wife, Elizabeth

Eleanor Witter Jackson, an annuity of £600, in lieu and bar of dower, payable out of the rents and profits of his real estate; he made her guardian of his heirs, their children, "convinced from the goodness of her heart and the excellence of her understanding that she is the fittest person to superintend their Education & Morals".[112]

Two years later Jackson, on his deathbed on board the ship *Amity,* repeated his faith in his wife's good sense, appointing her as joint executor of his estate with his brother. He asked that his body be preserved in a puncheon of his own rum should he die at sea. He reminded all whom it might concern that he had left the family linen and silver at Dr Brodbelt's home in Spanish Town "but took no receipt for same", and he died leaving his able wife to protect his inheritance.[113]

This Mrs Jackson proceeded relentlessly to do, not stopping short of open confrontation with her brother-in-law. In his efforts to make both plantations viable, John Jackson had drawn on the assets and credit of Mount Pleasant to finance Mount Salem, as well as to improve Mount Pleasant itself. Eleanor Jackson acknowledged that Henry Jackson was her deceased husband's chief creditor and was prepared also to concede Mount Pleasant's liability in a few instances, such as the payment of her mother's jointure and of some assistance given on the estate by slaves and stock which were John Jackson's personal property. But she was adamant that the accounts of the two estates, Mount Pleasant and Mount Salem, should be strictly separated and that the former, which was Witter's inheritance, should not be chargeable with any debts that were, strictly speaking, the personal responsibility of her late husband. Henry Jackson contended otherwise:

> [T]he whole annual net proceeds of both Est. should be divided into 43 equal parts or shares and [that] twenty of such parts or shares should be annually appropriated to the liquidation of Henry Jackson's demand on his late Brother John Jackson and the interest paid [that] the remaining 23 of such parts or shares be appropriated to the satisfaction of the specific charges & encumbrances, affecting Mount Pleasant and also to the discharge of the debt owing by Mrs Jackson to Henry Jackson.[114]

Since Henry Jackson, as merchant financier, received all proceeds of the estate, this made Elizabeth Jackson the insistent aggressor for her and her children's share of their inheritance. Jackson's refusal, for example, to honour her lodging bills in London, which became her base for litigious activities, created embarrassment.[115] Jackson, driven to distraction by her demands, maintained "she has nearly destroyed the Hen to get the golden Eggs".[116] Personal relationships so deteriorated that Henry Jackson could not even face a joint discussion of their differences in an arbitrator's office: "I lament that she intends attending the next meeting; her Presence can do no Good it may do harm I trust you will prevent our meeting the present temper of my mind is not fit for it."[117]

As women, carefully sheltered from the life of industry and commerce, recipients merely of the plantations' proceeds, female dependents were naturally unconcerned that the sugar crops had failed or that the market had collapsed. Louisa King noted, *en passant,* that her brother Richard had recently made only seven hogsheads of sugar. She hoped for his sake that he would have a good crop, "I assure you that he has great need of plentiful return from the Property to answer all the demands against him."[118] Her own demand, an annuity of £50 chargeable to their deceased father's estate, was paramount to her. She refused to be cast in the role of a dependent, for she saw her allowance not as a "bounty" but as "her just right", and she was even prepared "to take counsel's opinion on it" – which she apparently did. She rallied her sisters round her in bitter condemnation of their brother's "piecrust promises", his failure to live up to "the principle of [their] dear Father" and "his indifference to the welfare of his sisters". They advised their sister, Isabella King, who was then in the United States, against trusting him; if she knew what was good for herself and her son, she would "take [her] Negroes out of the hands they are now in".[119] Legal judgement was pronounced against Richard King: he paid the bankrupt's penalty of imprisonment. When he was sworn "out of gaol" in August 1824, Harriet Forbes wrote to her sister Isabella informing her of the official appointment of assignees to the estate. She was hopeful that "some of the Debts given in his schedule . . . will be recovered, in that case you will get all there is out of it, as you have the prior judgement".[120]

There was an additional element, apart from the purely financial, in the King domestic rift: the family's conviction that Richard King was wasting his money on his mulatto associates. The nature of the association was apparently too shameful for them to spell out. "I could tell you", wrote Louisa King, "a tale of degradation as would shock you beyond conception . . . I will

not soil my Paper with so despicable an account of him."[121] These unmen-
tionable circumstances made his sisters bitter and were a clearly decisive factor in pushing their financial differences to the point of litigation:

> [I]n fact his whole family must feel degraded by his late conduct respecting a parcel
> of Mulattoes which he has lately taken upon him to say he will stand their friend. I
> do assure you he would at any time much sooner assist those kinds of cattle than
> think or trouble himself bout a distressed sister.[122] . . . Were we Mulattoes . . . were
> we Mulattoes, there would be no need of consanguinity to induce him to the ten-
> derest acts of solicitude and to spend thousands on us.[123]

BLACKS IN THE WHITE FAMILY

Slave society introduced "alien" elements into the white family. These elements did, it is true, fill many of the gaps in the creole domestic structures:
so that black retainers took the place, for instance, of the English wet-nurse
or nanny. They became in many households extensions of the family. The
Brodbelts' high regard for Tabby, their old nurse, is clear.[124] Like members of
the family, such retainers often earned respect and affection and, in at least
one instance, an enduring memorial, such as is found on a Trelawny estate:
"Eve, an honest obedient and faithful slave, erected by her affectionate and
grateful master Henry Shirley, 1800."[125]

But black involvement with the white family, and the subtle influences
which accompanied it, were as often resented as welcomed, for they created
awkward problems of accommodation. If corruption of young white morale
by black members of the household is only hinted at in the Jamaican literature,[126] the corruption of the language, as previously noted, was a repeated
source of grievance: whites descended "so low as to join them [blacks] in
their gibberish, and by insensible degrees almost acquire the same habit of
thinking and speaking".[127] Creole speech patterns were the unwished-for
badge of black/white coexistence – an inescapable badge, for the peace of the
white household was endlessly broken by the noise of "talky" blacks. They
ate into the family's substance, encroached on its every private act: they took
part in the household's prayers, slept in its passageways, spilled over into its
inner chambers. As servant or nurse, playmate or bed-mate, there was no
physical limit to black/white intermingling.

The creole family with its half-brothers and half-sisters of various shades was anything but a tidy domestic organism. In fact, the unorthodox pattern often attributed to the black family applied in equal proportions to the white.

Samuel Delpratt, merchant of Kingston, in his will of 17 June 1783, made comfortable settlements on his five lawful sons and daughters and a nephew, as well as legacies for his two sisters in Great Britain. Simultaneously, he provided for his three reputed natural daughters, free quadroons, Sarah Delpratt, Elizabeth Delpratt and Mary Foord, who was at that time living in his house.[128] James Peddar of the parish of St David, in his will of 30 March 1774, bequeathed a life annuity of £50 to his reputed natural daughter Frances Peddar, "begotten on the body of Jane Harris a free mulatto". He left funds in trust for the sons of Frances Peddar, for their maintenance to the age of fourteen; and in the case of one son, he provided for an apprentice fee, "not to exceed £30, and if his conduct is satisfactory £100 sterling". He then left the bulk of his estate to his lawful daughter, "Elizabeth Valette Peddar, dear child" and to "Elizabeth Peddar, beloved wife £200 p.a. for life payable in Bristol and he advises her for her own comfort and health to reside to England".[129]

Even in cases where the testators left no legitimate white children, their mulatto connections clearly touched other white lives. The Barretts of Cinnamon Hill in St James produced brown Barretts in nearly every generation for a century and a half.[130] George Goodin Barrett went as far as to make one of his six quadroon children, a boy of eleven, Thomas Peters, a trustee and executor of his estate, in his will of 7 March 1794.[131] When Peters came of age, he challenged legitimate members of the family for their maladministration of his father's estate.[132] Scudamore Winde's association with the black woman, Sarah Cox, was well attested. A solid citizen of St Catherine, he left her comfortably provided for in his will of 7 August 1774, so that at the time of her death in 1828, at the age of eighty-four, she had acquired the respectable title of Mrs and a tombstone in the parish cathedral.[133] In his will, he also left substantial sums of at least £2,000 each to his three children by Sarah Cox. He left legacies as well to Patt, a Negro woman, and her daughter Mary Winde. At the same time, Winde remembered his sisters and many close friends. To Jane Catherine Long, for example, "daughter of Edward Long, friend" he left 200 guineas for a ring.[134]

However remote the mulatto link, it worked its way into the white family's consciousness and, above all, into its pockets. James Affleck, a carpenter of Hanover, left his Scottish relatives the task of tidying up the legal and financial irregularities he bequeathed them, while simultaneously settling the fate of his brown Jamaican offspring. In his original will of 11 February 1801, he left the bulk of his estate to his mother, brothers and sisters. He also arranged for the manumission of the black woman slave named Molly and for the maintenance and education of the son she had borne him. A year later, he wrote, with a pencil, a codicil in which an additional sum of money was left for his son, Alexander, bringing his inheritance to £1,900. His reputed daughter Sarah was left £800 for her maintenance and education. To both children he left legacies of slaves, as well as his wearing apparel and household furniture. Affleck then "struck through so much of the said devise and bequest of his residuary real and personal Estate as was in favour of his said Brothers and Sisters and directed that the same should go to his said son Alexander Affleck and his children lawfully begotten".[135]

The will with the pencil alterations was duly probated in Jamaica, but was queried in 1807 by Affleck's surviving brother and two sisters and brothers-in-law in Edinburgh. Doubts were raised about the validity of pencil changes in a legal document and of devises exceeding £2,000 to the mulatto Alexander. The Affleck family in Scotland was apparently anxious to avoid litigation. They declared, as well, their concern "that the intentions be fulfilled as far as they can consistently with law have generally agreed". The compromise they arrived at was, essentially, to trade Sarah Affleck's freedom (which had not been proposed in her father's will) for the lion's share of the estate. Alexander's legacy was cut back to £2,000, out of which his sister's manumission expenses were to be charged. Sarah Affleck was allowed the £800 originally left her, as well as the slaves. The Edinburgh branch of the family received the residue of the estate and, "in as much as the Testator has not by his said will and codicil directed the said Sarah Affleck to be manumitted from slavery, they have agreed to execute all proper acts for that purpose"; her deed of manumission was accordingly executed on 9 February 1807.

Not all family situations provided as easy a formula for equating righteousness with monetary gain, and unquestionably, the relative helplessness of the white family to stave off mulatto claims on its economic preserves added stresses and strains to its operations.[136] It served to aggravate the economic dependence of white women and helped to engender the kind of bitterness found in the King papers.[137]

But interracial sex carried deeper and more difficult implications even than the economic ones. Creole Jamaica was a society based on the massive delusion that a man or a woman could be an object; yet it was a society that, at the same time, witnessed daily evidence of most intimate contact between the master race and its enslaved. If the slave were truly a thing, if the African were, by the definition of the creole spokesman Long, close relative to the orangutan,[138] what indeed was the real nature of that sexual encounter between master and slave?

Honest resolution of this dilemma must have been self-lacerating, unless one took flight in fantasy, as many creole men and women clearly did. If the woman could, she would persuade herself that the gap between the races was too great to permit familiarities:

> I don't know how papa allowed himself to be prevailed upon by Captain . . . to compel us to come to this mulatto ball; Mama used to tell me that it was unbecoming a white person to be seen talking in a familiar way with these people; then how can he reconcile coming to meet them like this. I am sure there are many among them, who would consider themselves highly honoured if I would only allow them to enter my dressing room like our waiting maid, to arrange my headdress and here we are obliged to submit to an equality on account of the infernal Union and anti-Unions! Whereupon an old dame replied, "True my dear little creature but do not swear, keep your temper and endeavour to permit things to pass off agreeably, tomorrow we shall know as little about them as we did yesterday."[139]

The male observer found it more difficult to deny all knowledge of the other race; but he too fell victim of the compulsion to compound delusion. He chose, for example, to see an all-forgiving magnanimity in female attitudes towards the custom of the country:

> Men married and single, openly and impudently avowed these cursed connections. Creole ladies are by no means disconcerted at that which is so fashionable among Husbands in this Country.[140]

> If a gentleman pays his addresses to a lady, it is not thought necessary, as a homage to her delicacy, to get rid, a priori, of his illicit establishment, nor is the lady so unreasonable as to expect such a sacrifice . . . the wife may even condescend to

take in good part the occasional calls, inquiries, and proffered services of the ex-favourite, and make suitable returns of kindness to her and her children.[141]

[T]o be surpassed in costly finery by a woman of colour excites no uneasiness in a white female, though she would not wish to be eclipsed by one of her own class.[142]

A sentimental serial in a local magazine projected the image of a creole Griselda who "could not for her soul hate a living creature, and the poor ignorant being who had thus misled her husband, she felt more pity for than abhorrence". The long suffering heroine, Julia, "even privately made up little articles of dress and sent them as presents for a little girl, the reputed daughter of Mr D" (her husband).[143]

Romancing of this kind salved the male conscience and flattered the gentler sex; it also blinded itself to the more credible reaction of a Louisa King. Edward Long implied that some of the blame for male interracial philandering should be attributed to the low level of white female education. Too many creole men, he suggested, were tied to "pretty idiots".[144] His blueprint for the reform of the Jamaican school system placed high priority on provisions for girls. In the boarding seminary he proposed, they would be "weaned from the Negroes dialect, improved by emulation, and gradually habituated to a modest and polite behaviour".[145] They would in time become "objects of love to the deserving youths, whether natives or Europeans, and by the force of their pleasing attractions soon draw them from a loose attraction to Blacks and Mulattoes, into the more rational and happy commerce of nuptial union".[146]

But until such time as the white woman could be groomed for successful competition with her black and brown rivals, her view of race and interracial sex was inevitably charged with feelings of jealousy, fear and insecurity. There are clear innuendoes of sexual fear in Mary Ricketts's hostile view of Jamaica.[147] The King sisters' obsessive interest in the rather flashy lifestyle of one of their sister's mulatto slaves is revealing: "Eleanor is on her own establishment. I assure you she is not a little importance among her own colour. . . . Few Ladies go finer than [she] does." [148]

The physical cruelties to which white women from time to time subjected blacks are also suggestive. Stewart, writing in the 1820s, indicated that this was a thing of the past: "Nothing was more common formerly than for white mistresses not only to order their slaves to be punished, but personally to see that the punishment was duly inflicted!" He felt that only in a rare instance among "the most low and ignorant" did this still occur.[149] However infrequent the incidence, cases were well known in the nineteenth century. Cynric Williams's trek up to the Blue Mountains in 1823 carried him into a scene of moral as well as physical squalor: he was, he alleged, on a rescue mission, to purchase a pretty mulatto slave girl on behalf of his Port Antonio host:

> [She] had complained bitterly of her mistress's cruelty and her master's attentions, amorous attentions or intentions . . . Susanna had spirit enough to resist the gentleman's importunities though she was his slave, but the mistress, instigated by jealousy, gave the poor girl no credit for her forbearance, and used her very shamefully indeed. . . . She told me her mistress sometimes beat her with a horsewhip, on which her master would in turn threaten his wife.[150]

William recaptures in his journal something of the claustrophobic existence of a nearly inaccessible plantation in which enforced intimacy could aggravate jealousies and hatreds.[151] It is significant that the "white witch" legend grew out of the physical context of the remote North coast estates, where the great house lady was pressed in on all sides by inescapable relationships fraught with tension.[152] The most notorious case of sustained white female sadism to slaves during this period is characterized by the high level of society in which it occurred, namely, the wife of the custos of Port Royal, as well as by the very close contacts that existed within the household between the parties involved.[153]

Such relationships, and the disquiet they generated, underlay the white woman's conspicuous evasion of the central moral issue of her society: slavery.

THE WHITE WOMAN'S SOCIAL CONSCIENCE AND MORAL CONCERNS

Before the era of the female vote, women had no institutional framework except the church within which to express moral concerns. Religion in many countries was the approved outlet for the female social conscience, and was powerful enough in some societies to prove a catalyst for reform. It could lead women, individually and collectively, in communities in Britain and some states of North America, even to condemn slavery and to agitate for its abolition.[154]

But Jamaica had few such resources to draw on. The failure of white leadership to provide guidelines for the society was repeatedly commented on. "It had been a very general complaint", wrote a local journalist, "that in the West Indies, religion is known, by the bulk of its inhabitants, only by the name – that it is disregarded by some as an affair of no consequence, sneered at by others as the mere offspring of human invention and utterly neglected by almost every one".[155] The Reverend C.W. Bridges castigated his flock from his pulpit in St Ann for setting low spiritual standards:

> As long as our Church here is empty . . . as long as the galleries remain unoccupied
> – as long as the Sabbath is profaned, the marriage vow disregarded, the baptism of
> children delayed, or too often, altogether omitted, as long as we thus persist in set-
> ting such wretched example to those who look up to us for everything, it is in vain
> that the clergy shall declaim against the vices of the lower orders.[156]

The established clergy was itself frequently held responsible for this condition. Its educational standards were often poor and it was riddled with patronage, and both factors mitigated against its effective pastoral functioning. As an integral part of the plantocratic hierarchy, its interests seemed more secular than spiritual.[157]

The moral welfare of slaves did not become a matter of serious concern until after 1816, when local legislation made some provision for curates to give religious instruction to blacks, and this was after Nonconformist churches had taken the initiative in this field.[158] Anglican clergymen may then have influenced some of their congregation to undertake similar work. But the Church of England creole membership revealed few individual manifestations of strong faith. The Kings' religion made them seek to escape the society, not to alter it. Louisa King wrote accordingly to her sister:

> We look forward most anxiously for the period when we shall be able to pack up
> . . . and quit this Island for good and all, to join you in America . . . where we can
> only spend our lives congenial to our feelings. We have lately taken the Sacrament,
> and Mrs F. is of too religious mind to endure the management of such beings as you
> know the Negroes are after such solemn an act.[159]

Mrs Nugent was a conscientious church-going Anglican, whose piety fell short of accepting the brotherhood of man. She was the prototype of the Jamaica lady whose compassion for the souls of black folks was perfectly consistent with the instinctive social/ethnic responses of a master class/race. Her concern for blacks and her exertion on their behalf were, within their limits, sincere. Very soon after her arrival in Jamaica, she reflected all night upon slavery and decided that her policy would be one of "kindness and indulgence".[160] She kept her word, personally undertook responsibility for their spiritual welfare and found few activities in the island that were as satisfying to her as teaching the blacks their catechism, keeping a tally of the converted, and watching their orderly and correct behaviour in church.[161]

Other creole women also did their pious duty among blacks. They were, however, more likely to be found among members of the non-establishment churches, whose work always contained a greater proselytizing purpose than that of the Church of England.

The earliest missions in the island, those of the Moravians in St Elizabeth in the 1750s, relied heavily on the initiative and support of creole families, who saw the slave as capable of Christian salvation. Without their continued hospitality and patronage, these missions would have had no physical base. Planters provided them with land on their estates on which to build their chapels, schools and homes; they even supplied them regularly with food. The women of a few planter households helped the missions with holding classes and services. They set the example of daily prayers for "people of all colours and ages" in their own homes.[162]

The families of Matthew and William Farquharson of Springvale and Hazle Grove in St Elizabeth gave substantial assistance to the work of the Moravians in the parish. They gave land, timber and money. Isabella Farquharson's contribution to the building of the Springvale chapel in 1830 was £50.[163] Slaves and freemen, black and white, met for "divine service in the large hall on the close piazza of the family mansion which was offered for use by its pious inmates". The "unwearied exertions of the ladies of the family" kept going the school for slave children under the age of eight, who received daily instruction in reading and in learning the catechism and hymns. They also worked in the Sunday school for older boys and girls.[164] Other "kind Christian friends" of the mission, such as Mrs Wright, the owner of a coffee plantation at Kensworth, and Mrs Miller of Malvern were energetic in promoting missionary work.[165]

Mrs Mary Ann Able Smithy, who had come to Jamaica from the United States at the time of the War of Independence, was a member of the class of eight persons who formed Jamaica's first Methodist society.[166] She became renowned for her spirited defence of the Wesleyan leader Mr Thomas Coke in 1789, when he first attempted to introduce Methodism into Kingston. The Reverend Peter Duncan's account of the incident showed her to be a for-midable member of her sex. Coke's meeting was "rudely interrupted by a number of white persons calling themselves gentlemen, who, hating the message of mercy to the perishing heathen, pressed through the congrega-tion to drag him from his place". A near riot followed, which threatened to increase in violence. Mrs Smith intervened, at first unsuccessfully.[167] Then,

> [f]inding that all gentle means were utterly ineffectual, she boldly assumed a threat-ening attitude, and drawing out a pair of scissors she exclaimed to the rioters, "you may now do as you please, but the first man who lays a violent hand upon him [Coke] shall have these scissors thrust into his heart." They saw that this was no empty threat, and therefore they escaped as fast as possible, actually boasting of their great courage while they were running downstairs.[168]

She became one of the most effective leaders in the new church and was regarded as "the mother of Methodism in Jamaica".[169]

Mrs Samuel Moulton Barrett was well known for her efforts aimed at Christianizing blacks. "She was the daughter of a long line of ancestors who had devoted their lives to education and to religion."[170] She accompanied her husband to Jamaica in 1827–28, when he returned to sort out litigation con-cerning the family estates of Cornwall, Cinnamon Hill, Retreat, Oxford and Cambridge. She became the chief patroness of the Presbyterian missionary Hope Waddell, who was based on the Barretts' estates but whose work grad-ually extended through the districts to embrace some eighteen or twenty estates.[171] She influenced her husband to give his personal support to Waddell's mission. She was responsible for starting a school at Retreat Pen, their property in St Ann.[172] She died in 1831. Waddell paid tribute in his writ-ings to "the excellent and beloved lady of Cinnamon Hill, endeared to us and to her people by her endeavours for their temporal and eternal welfare".[173]

Where a sincere evangelical faith inspired women's attitudes, the lives of slaves and slaveholders were humanely affected. But the Jamaican female humanitarian, whether missionary or creole Lady Bountiful, was neither numerous enough nor organized enough to be a movement or to assert effective public pressure. In any event, her aims were strictly limited. Fundamentally, it was to make the slave "religious, decent and orderly" – to make him or her, in fact, a better bondsman or bondswoman – not to make him or her free.

The young female Baptist missionary Mary Ann Hutchins was rare in expressing unreserved joy at emancipation: "Thank God, slavery! Vile slavery is abolished. Like the poor Negro, I can only say, Massa me too glad; such a sun as the first of August sun dese eyes neber 'spected to see on eart."[174] Her evangelical zeal led her into deep involvement with the society for the period of her short mission. She is the only white woman found in Jamaica's slavery records who did not constantly long to be somewhere else. She wrote to her family from Falmouth on 7 April 1834: "I do not wish myself in England again."[175] She saw her life and work committed to her "black brethren and sisters", and she threw herself tirelessly into the task of education and conversion, until her health failed.

But Mary Hutchins's perspective was almost unique during the era of slavery. Other women of good works were careful to maintain the correct distance between themselves and the objects of their charity: Mrs Nugent's indulgence was clearly that of patronizing superiority. Government House blacks received all possible freedom to amuse themselves at Christmas. "Poor things we would not deprive them of one atom of their short-lived and baby-like pleasure."[176] Mrs Nugent shocked the local elites by opening a dance for the governor's staff with "an old negro man". She could not understand the consternation: it was a gesture of patronage which English ladies traditionally extended at "a servants' hall birthday in England", how absurd to confuse this with notions of social and racial equality.[177]

Female benevolence made it necessary to ensure that slaves were not ill-treated. On this point, Mrs Nugent was satisfied: she saw evidence that "generally speaking the slaves are extremely well used". Indeed, she felt they had "reason to be content, for they have many comforts and enjoyments. I only wish the poor Irish were half as well off."[178]

But kindness and smugness never fully concealed the aversion and fear that lay below the surface. The smell of blacks repelled,[179] the proximity of slave revolution in Dominique made blackness threatening; thus, "I am sure the blacks are to be as much dreaded as the French."[180] The ladies of Spanish Town spoke "such horrid things of the savage ideas, etc. of the slaves, on the estates in the interior".[181] The sight of an "Eboe" by the roadside "of Herculean size", with "truly cannibal teeth", caused the lady to shudder.[182] A boatman at Port Henderson, who had previously been seen as humble, became "a horrid black man" who grinned "and gave us a sort of fierce look, that struck me with a terror I could not shake off".[183]

Mrs Henry Lynch too saw blacks as alien and frightening: "It was very foolish of me to be frightened but though I have lived all my life among Negroes, I cannot get over the horror that I have of their wild odd ways."[184] Sarah Dwarris became squeamish at the sight of a black wet-nurse feeding a white infant: she found it "unnatural".[185] The planter Ryland's aunt frankly detested blacks; she had lived among them and knew "their deceitfulness, idleness, hypocrisy and their determined opposition to all good advise".[186] Blacks, being regarded as a race apart and inferior, did not justify having normal criteria of physical well-being applied to them, so that, in comparison with the white underprivileged, they were well off.

Other women repeated Mrs Nugent's favourable comparison of the condition of New World slaves with that of the British working classes. The sprightly, much-travelled Mrs Anna Falconbridge[187] found the Jamaican plantation something approaching rural paradise. It offered black bondsmen a comfort and security from birth to death, unknown to the masses of Europe:

> How very few of our labouring poor can boast, when their mortal bodies become tenants of the grave, that their children have such certain provision secured them, and probably thousands and thousands of themselves may go supperless to bed this very night, and rise tomorrow, not knowing where to get a breakfast, or without means of acquiring a morsel of bread to allay the gnawings of hunger – whether then are their situations, or those of slaves, having Christian masters, most preferable.[188]

Sarah Dwarris wrote in similar terms:

> There are a hundred or more Negro houses with their little Gardens before their doors which really look very pritty, they have every one a piece of Ground to raise their provision if they are not too lazy and if they are, why their Master is obilig'd to feed them, they are the happyest set of people in the world I am sure, much more so than a day Labourer in England for if they are sick they have a Doctor to attend them and are nursed without any truble or exspense to them, and they live as well as

any white people for they raise all kinds of stock and don't think any thing of getting a fine J'onbar Duck for their Dinner, nowhere is the poor person in England that can do . . . .[189]

One could not expect otherwise of the white female. She was the second sex taking her cue from the man. The whole thrust of her upbringing had been to make her "pretty parrot", to add sweetness and charm to public life if she could,[190] but not to interfere or agitate.

Mrs Archer, it is true, objected more than once to her son's handling of their slaves. She stated her disapproval of the punishment he imposed in the field on a female slave. She connived behind his back at the marriage of two slaves, to James Archer's great annoyance.[191] But such spirited defiance of masculine wishes is unique in the documents.

Mrs Nugent was more typical. Bright and articulate as she was, it was clear that she acceded to her "dear N's" wishes in all things. No woman in the records made an original judgement on social and political matters. Mrs Brodbelt's comment on the Maroon War of 1795 was the official and conventional one:

> From the last accounts we have received I hope that the business is drawing nearer to a conclusion in Favour of the Whites than was expected a week ago; if so, everything will be right again, and it may be a very good lesson to others of like description of people to conduct themselves with that respect proper attention which is due to those who are appointed to keep them in peace and quietness . . . .[192]

Mrs Henry Lynch's was an intelligent mind, vulnerable nevertheless to masculine influence. She described the "large, dark room" for confining disorderly Negroes: "Oh! It looked so dismal, with its barred windows but pappa says it is a palace compared to Newgate."[193] Sarah Dwarris was only echoing what had been previously voiced by her husband in defence of slavery.[194]

If Jamaica produced no native humanitarian movement led by white males, it was unlikely that such a movement would be initiated by those conditioned to rock the cradle, not the boat. Slavery, therefore, as a denial of a fundamental human right, was never questioned by women. On the contrary, it could be justified: "Slavery", pontificated a creole lady, "is a Divine institution, expressly recognized by the Mosaic Law, and indeed, by St Paul under the milder Scheme of Christianity."[195] Lady Normanby, in 1833, conceded slavery to be "a wicked and unchristian practice". But emancipation was the worse evil:

> It will set loose a lawless rabble upon a population of women and children, unmanned and defenseless in every way, and I much fear bloodshed of every revolting description will be the consequence. . . . [Slaves] must be amalgamated with a free and superior people before they will be fit to form a population.[196]

White women's unnamed dread of blacks, and the near-hysterical responses this frequently evoked, contained sexual undertones. More physical association took place between white women and coloured men in creole Jamaica than has been commonly assumed. Parish registers reveal the evidence of mixed marriages although by no means in large numbers and seldom with full-blooded black men.[197] Extramarital associations occurred. The Reverend William Jones's entry in his diary of 9 June 1778 repeated local gossip: "I now heard of more than one or two white ladies, within his [an overseer's] knowledge, & cited by name, who had, tho' married, borne children of Negroes."[198] Nancy Morgan, a mulatto woman who was a witness in the murder trial of a mulatto man from St Mary's in 1781, was allegedly "born of a white woman" of that parish.[199]

White males, consciously or unconsciously, fed women's fears of black assault. They appeared quick to cry "rape". Their view of slave rebellions was often charged with the assumption that a prime objective of the black male insurrectionist was to violate the white bed. The establishment's view of the mutiny of black troops in 1808 contained this assumption:

> Q. Are any of the black soldiers married to white women?
>
> A. No.
>
> Q. Do any of them cohabit with white women?
>
> A. Not to my knowledge.[200]

Dread of black virility haunted white perception of the 1831 slave uprising: there was little doubt what was "the Universally acknowledged intention of the rebels, as regarded the white female".[201] This conviction recurred throughout reports, official and unofficial.

> [W]e understood, for a certainty, that Daddy Sharp was their leader, and that every white man's house and property was to be destroyed, in order to force them into the

towns, with their wives and families, and that the last effort was to be a simultane-
ous attack on all the towns, by every Negro in the island, when the houses were to
be set on fire, the males slaughtered, and the females taken as wives to the principal
leaders and officers of the insurrection.[202]

Senior describes in revealing language the rescue of fifteen white women
from a rebel hideout by a party of militiamen in the course of the uprising:

> No pen can describe the forlorn condition of these disconsolate women, or express
> their feelings on first beholding the countenance of their deliverers. So completely
> had they deemed themselves out of the power of release, and with such mental
> agony had they viewed their future prospects, if death should not previously put an
> end to their degradation and sufferings, that some were barely conscious of the sud-
> den change in their state: others rent the air with acclamations of joy for their
> preservation, mingled with screams of horror produced by the recollection of what
> was to have been their fate.[203]

In fact, there were two proven instances of black violence against whites
in the course of the rebellion, neither of them involving women.[204]

Jordan's comments in relation to the North American continent are suggestive:

> White men anxious and guilty over their own sexual aggressiveness were quick to
> impute it to others especially at a time of interracial crisis. One has only to imagine
> the emotions flooding through some planter who had been more or less regularly
> sleeping with some of his slave wenches when he suddenly learned of a conspiracy
> among their male counterparts: it was virtually inevitable that his thoughts turn in
> a torrent of guilt to the safety of his wife.[205]

Such uneasiness, communicated to the woman, could add to her neurotic
regard for the black presence, could make her, like Lady Normanby, see slavery as an institution designed to contain the moral anarchy that threatened
her, an institution to be preserved.

GENDER AND ABSENTEEISM

White absenteeism can perhaps now be viewed from a rather different
stance. Ever since regret for white depopulation was first voiced in the seven-

teenth century, it has been held responsible for nearly every major defect in Jamaica society, from white insolvency to black insurrection. The theme was kept alive by eighteenth- and early-nineteenth-century writers and pursued by a long line of twentieth-century scholars.[206] Only two historians to date have seriously questioned its thesis: Douglas Hall, who started logically, by demanding a relevant definition of absenteeism,[207] and Edward (Kamau) Brathwaite, who modifies the stereotype by establishing real and significant evidence of the "non-absentee".[208] By focusing on the most persistent absentee in the records – the white woman – it may be possible to adjust the historical perspective even further.

Patterson, whose works have broken important new ground in the study of the Jamaican slave system, continues, nevertheless, to regard absenteeism in conventional terms. It appeared to him "the root of all evils" of the society.[209] In particular, the shortage of white women is seen by him as damaging to the social structure. "In the absence of wives, mothers, daughters and sisters, the Jamaican great house", he maintained, "never became the sanctified fortress of Southern gynocracy".[210] This, as a result, robbed the Jamaican of that chivalrous concern for white womanhood which tradition attributes to the Southern gentleman of the United States. He suggests that "the failure of a creole/colonial culture (similar to Southern culture) to develop was largely due to the high sex ratio of the white population",[211] a major contributory factor to Jamaica's "lack of cultural cohesiveness and social will".[212]

His fundamental assumption, that of the non-society lacking distinctiveness and cohesion, of course creates an issue in itself. Other, less negative ways of viewing the West Indian past have been impressively stated by Goveia and Brathwaite.[213]

Absenteeism was mainly a white elitist phenomenon, a conspicuously female elitist phenomenon. From the long historical view of subordinate blacks and browns, who formed the majority of the population, the failure of creoles to develop a cult of the magnolia-like white goddess could, in no way, be seen as evil.

Analysis of female absenteeism involves the relevant but complex question of the relationship between patriarch and racist. The alter ego of that gallant southern male was one of the most intractable Negrophobes in the Western Hemisphere.[214] His view and treatment of the black functioned within a caste system which was firmly embedded in a patriarchal domestic structure, requiring the presence of the women-folk under the family roof.[215] Properly subordinate wives, daughters and maiden sisters in the flesh were essential to substantiate masculine claims of total authority over them as over other human beings: one cannot command women who are not there – as William Ricketts, Francis Brodbelt and every other Jamaican male, deserted by wives and daughters, knew full well. The protective cloak of the southern patriarch extended outwards to embrace the black members of the family, his children too, and all were children, needing permanent care and guidance. It is significant that the ultimate in New World racist apologia evolved out of the social-domestic context of southern patriarchism, the William Fitzhugh perspective, which saw slavery as "the proper relationship of all labour to capital".[216] This attitude has been immortalized in the Ulrich Philips's perspective,[217] updated and sophisticated in the Elkins theory of "the helpless dependents".[218]

The plantation, in this conceptual context, becomes indeed "a civilising factor", needing to be preserved at all cost in the interest of black progress. Phillips commented:

> The patriarchal feature is necessary. The average black person has many of the characteristics of a child, and must be guided and governed, and often guarded against himself by a sympathetic hand. Non-resident ownership and control of plantations will not do. The absentee system has no redeeming virtue for the purpose at hand. With hired, voluntary labour instead of forced labour, it is the Virginia plantation system and not that of the West Indies, which is needed. The presence of the planter and his wife and children and his neighbours is required for example and precept among the Negroes . . . . The average Negro longs for the personal tie: respect, affection and obedience for those who earn and encourage his admiration are second nature with him. . . . What [the Negroes] most need is friendly guidance and control for themselves, and peace and prosperity for the South as a whole.[219]

What black would need an enemy, with a patriarch as friend?

If Jamaica endured the depersonalized brand of bourgeois racism as it functioned on its absentee-owned estate/factory, it was at least spared much of that insidious ethnocentricity disguised as paternal benevolence that characterized and outlived the slavery of the old south.

The West Indian island of Barbados raises interesting speculations about what indeed becomes of social relationships in the long run in a black/white colonial construct when the white settler woman is on the spot. This is one British Caribbean society conspicuous by the fact that the white family has remained in residence for centuries, the closest West Indian model of the patriarchy. This is also the society in which a political scientist has recently observed evidence of English domestic civilization transplanted overseas:[220] in the same breath, he speaks of "the stranglehold of resident whites over the Barbadian blacks".[221] The functional connection between transplanted English domesticity and the continued subordination of the local black, the presence of the white woman and the persistence of a "settler" problem are also duplicated in those countries on the African continent where colonial camp has been transformed into the Englishman's and Englishwoman's home, the castle to be guarded from black intrusion.[222] Whereas, it would appear, the bourgeois investor in the face of black advance, having primarily his profits to protect, may choose to transfer his capital elsewhere and retreat, the seigniorial patriarch digs in to defend a total lifestyle.

The issue is also one of black and brown social mobility. In the masculine sphere, the movement of lesser whites away from the estates provided occupational openings that slave tradesmen were quick to seize. With women something similar occurred, compensating to some extent for their exclusion from skills. Parry and Sherlock made the point clearly: absentee owners, having paid their periodic visit to their West Indian estates, returned to Europe, "and plantation life slipped back into its old slovenly routine. Many of the elegant great houses stood empty most of the time, or were occupied by overseers, often with their slave concubines and a troop of mulatto children."[223]

Nature and society hate vacuums: the space left on the plantation by the departed white was instantly filled by brown and black women – not always on the most exalted conditions, but because they were the women available, they could state some of the terms, if it were only the insistence on occupying the great house. Once the foot was through the door, the inroads into the structure could then follow. The statistics of parishes like St Thomas and St David, with one white woman to seven men, with thirty estates out of forty-one without a white woman, tell a significant part of the story.[224] It is not impossible to sense there the possibilities for self-assertion, if not advancement, for black and brown women who had no reigning white queen to keep them in their places.[225]

The white woman had a special vested interest in keeping Jamaican ⸻ᵇᶫᵃᶜᵏˢ down. She was herself a second-class citizen subject to masculine domination, and her instinctive response was to find an even more inferior target, ripe for compensatory repression. The special economic usefulness of the enslaved group to the white woman, as well as her own understandable sexual jealousy, reinforced prejudice. Where she did not flee the society, she echoed the white man's sentiments on black slavery, she acquiesced in the system, she added her own brand of feminine shrewishness and rarely feminine compassion.

Finally, a word about the implications of absenteeism for the progress of official reforming measures: all social legislation promoting the welfare of Jamaican blacks during slavery originated in England. Local whites were unfailingly outraged at every metropolitan proposal that they ameliorate or put an end to slavery, but not so outraged that they did not ultimately capitulate. Not only did the fragmentation of the ruling creole family/class, inherent in absenteeism, weaken its capacity for strong local action against imperialist dictates, but in addition, to strike out on an independent line against Whitehall was to break the umbilical cord to the English parent: to sever a connection made real by the physical presence of the family on both sides of the ocean.[226] Failing the domestic, cultural, not to mention the military and economic self-sufficiency of other colonial rebels, the Jamaican establishment, however much it raged and threatened, never mustered the resources to relinquish its lifeline to Anglo-Saxon civilization. The price it paid was reluctant acquiescence in the social legislation of the period, culminating in the Emancipation Act of 1833, which opened up new and creative possibilities for black Jamaica. One significant ally of the enslaved masses in this process was the structural weakness of the creole ruling class, the intrinsic abnormality of the plantocratic family, manifested in its absent women.

6 The Black Woman
Demographic Profile, Occupation and Violent Abuse

Populations, left to their own devices and uninfluenced by heavy migration or by unnatural circumstances such as slavery, tend to show a more or less even balance of the sexes, inclining towards a higher proportion of females.[1] The scarcity of women in Jamaica's white population, as has been discussed in previous chapters, resulted from a combination of the low immigration and high emigration rates of females. It has been already noted that a sampling of the relatively immobile free population of England between 1574 and 1821 showed an excess of women.[2]

George Roberts has observed a similar phenomenon among native-born West Indians, whose demographic patterns show a low sex ratio at birth and a male/female mortality differential favourable to females, so that proportionately more creole females are born and more creole males die. This was true both of pre-emancipation and post-emancipation Jamaica. Consequently, according to Roberts, "a preponderance of females in the population is to be expected".[3] With blacks, this trend is even more pronounced than with whites, largely, it would appear, because of low sex ratios at birth. The result, he says, is that "this expected preponderance [that is, of females] is larger than would be secured for non-negro populations in general".[4]

One would expect to find such a tendency during slavery in those groups of blacks whose population structures were least affected by importation or enslavement. The free Maroon communities provide such a model. Being a relatively closed group after the 1740s, they relied far more on their own natural reproductive processes for population growth than on either external or internal migration.[5] Their special constitutional position required official vigilance, which resulted in fairly reliable statistics on their numbers, unlike those available for an elusive group such as the free blacks.[6] The Maroons are a very small sample of the island's population but their relatively even balancing of the sexes suggests the expected demographic norm of a free black people (see table 6.1). This was not the demographic profile of enslaved blacks for the greater part of the period of slavery.

The market preference for men which had been initiated in earlier decades continued unchanged late into the eighteenth century. So that between 1782 and 1788, the firm of Coppells dispatched to Jamaica slave cargoes totalling 6,641 men and 3,739 women; the firm of Rainfords between 1779 and 1783 dispatched 5,254 men and 3,698 women; Mure's and Dunlop during the period 1781 to 1786 shipped 3,849 men and 2,190 women;

Table 6.1   Maroon Population, 1770–1830

Year	Males	Females
1770	261	284
1793	434	497
1799	375	379
1801	256	279
1810	428	426
1820	440	480
1830	551	572

Sources: PP 1789, vol. XXVI (84) 646 (a), part III, Return of Maroons, 20 October 1770; CO 137/91, encl. of 9 March 1793; Robert C. Dallas, *The History of the Maroons, from their Origin to the Establishment of their Chief Tribe at Sierra Leone, Including the Expedition to Cuba for the Purpose of Procuring Spanish Chasseurs and the State of the Island of Jamaica for the Last Ten Years with a Succinct History of the Island Previous to that Period,* 2 vols. (London: T.N. Longman and O. Rees, 1803), 329; George Cumper, "The Demographic Balance of the Maroons" (paper presented to the Fourth Conference of Caribbean Historians, UWI, Mona, 1972), table 2.

Alexander Lindo between January and August of the year 1788 shipped 4,743 men and 2,766 women. These combined shipments contained a total of 20,487 men and 12,393 women, representing an overall sex ratio of 1.7:1 (male to female).[7]

There are no accurate and comprehensive data on the sex ratios of Jamaica's black population throughout the eighteenth century. Several estimates postulate a male excess varying from 2:1 to 3:2.[8] Individual estates were subject to a number of variables, of which male mortality and female fertility were among the most uncertain determining factors. The death rate of men tended to exceed that of women,[9] and this might have had the effect of modifying the original sexual imbalance of new African arrivals. Moreover, female fertility may well have been higher than one might expect, granted the disproportion of the sexes; for, as Philip Curtin has observed, "each slave cargo, with virtually all of its women of childbearing age, could possibly have an initial birth rate much higher than that of a native-born population with a more even sex ratio but also with a more normal age distribution".[10]

But none of these factors was capable of precise assessment on an island-wide basis before 1817 when, by the Registration Act, detailed slave returns became obligatory so that Edward Long in 1788 claimed to know of estates which had three men to one woman.[11] Bryan Edwards, writing in 1801, found there was scarcely a sugar estate "that possess a sufficient number of negro women in proportion to the men".[12] On the other hand, the Clarendon complex of William Beckford's estates in 1780 contained a nearly even balance of the sexes, 649 males to 604 females.[13]

In 1789, a joint committee of the Jamaica Assembly and Council reported to Parliament that the slave population numbered 140,000 men and 110,000 women, a male excess of 30,000.[14] This sexual imbalance became a matter of public interest as the anti-slave trade campaign gathered strength in Britain in the last quarter of the eighteenth century. Among the many evils of the trade that were singled out for criticism was the unequal importation of women and men. The reason for this disproportion would, to an outsider, seem obvious enough. The Jamaican frontier, which continued to expand steadily throughout the eighteenth century, needed masses of labour to clear new land. The physical exertion involved was unsuitable for female workers. Maintaining women, and rearing a native labour force, were calculated to be more expensive than purchasing cargoes of Africans with a guaranteed majority of sturdy males. Regular, and at times prolonged, loss of female working time was an inescapable fact of human biology: the degree of sustained manual output required by the plantation of its labour units was inconsistent with the physical demands made on women by menstruation, pregnancy, lactation, infant and child care. This view of the female worker as an economic liability was fundamental in shaping import policies, although not always as openly acknowledged as it was by, for example, the planter Hector McNeill, who wrote in 1788: "The common practice of purchasing a greater number of males than females [was] on account of the superior strength and labour of the men, and their being much less liable to disease and confinement."[15]

Many apologists of slavery and the slave trade tended to evade this kind of frank admission. Jamaicans, it is true, did not prove as intellectually adroit as those Hispanic slaveholders who attempted to defend their restricted quota of slave women on moral grounds: black celibacy, they were prepared to argue, was healthy and good.[16] But numbers of Jamaicans attempted, in their terms, to explain away sex-selective immigration, and many traders were firm allies in this exercise.

They argued in terms of the social and legal context of the African trade, which, they maintained, left them with no alternative but to take men in larger numbers than women. Witnesses before the parliamentary committee of 1789, which reported on the conduct of the slave trade, contended that the majority of Africans who appeared on the slave market were criminal offenders and were usually male. In addition, the prevailing system of polygyny in most of the west coast countries involved in the traffic made women in short supply both as wives and as labourers, so much so that female convicts, whenever they were held, were often redeemed by males.[17] Captain William Littleton, for example, who had traded for eleven years in the Gambia, maintained "we always find female slaves scarce". As a result, very rarely was more than one-third of his cargo female.[18] Captain John Knox, surgeon on the Windward Coast, Grain Coast and Angola, stated in his evidence that, even if a higher price were offered for women, it would still be impossible to get more, because of the demand for women in the continent's matrimonial system of polygyny. His estimated ratio of male to female slaves was 2:1.[19] Captain Fountain, who had commanded the African Company's troops, had been their factor in Accra and the governor of Tantum, estimated also that

African polygyny dictated the average ratio of one woman to every five men.[20]

On the other side of the Atlantic, West Indians echoed these views. Edward Long explained the heavy male preponderance in these terms: "this happens from there being fewer criminals to be transported, and no female warriors to be taken prisoner".[21] Bryan Edwards also claimed that the high incidence of male criminals as well as the effects of polygyny were responsible. He further argued that "females become unfit for the slave-market at a much earlier period than the males. A woman, through childbearing, may appear a very exceptionable slave at twenty-two, or twenty-three years of age, whereas a healthy well-made man will not be objected to at four or five-and-thirty." Consequently, there was a higher percentage of female rejects: the result of this was that the trader "has not an option in the case".[22]

But it was impossible to escape the realities of the market, the imperatives of planter demand and trader supply. Ship's captain William McIntosh confessed that during his 1778 trip on the Senegalese coast, he could have purchased more women, but did not do so, because as he said, "I thought the men would turn to better account."[23] Long had to concede that "It has never been the planters' care to proportion the number of females to males";[24] and Edwards grudgingly admitted that "a greater number of males" was to "the immediate interest of the planter".[25]

Edwards would certainly have exonerated the creole slaveholder if he could. "This circumstance" (that is, the sexual imbalance), he argued, "has been tortured into a charge of criminal neglect and improvident avarice against the planters of the West Indies, who are supposed from thence to have no wish to making their slaves even as happy as their situation will be."[26] It was, perhaps, enough for planters to acknowledge that they had converted blacks into chattels; to deny them, as well, the opportunity to find themselves mates was a disquieting fact of slavery, difficult to live with.

The sexual disparity, complete with rationalizations, acquired strategic significance as the abolitionist movement advanced. West Indians based their defence of the transatlantic slave traffic on their manpower needs. Without such a trade to provide labour for agro-industrial development, the colonies would perish: a growing slave population meant an expanding economic frontier.

The slave trade was undoubtedly the dominant factor in moving the island's black population from 45,000 in 1703 to 217,584 in 1787.[27] Without steadily mounting African immigration the island could never have maintained this level of growth, for concurrent with heavy black importation was heavy black mortality. Slave deaths exceeded births by as much as 3 per cent in the eighteenth century, evidence of both high mortality and low fertility.[28]

Planters had to face the fact that the low rate of natural increase of their slaves was a most vulnerable plank in their platform. The size and condition of the slave population gradually superseded the conduct of the slave trade as the cardinal concern of the humanitarians.[29] Edwards correctly perceived the issue of slave mortality as one of the most vital and sensitive confronting the white creoles. "The grand and I admit the most plausible accusation against the general conduct of the planter arises from the necessity they find themselves under of having an annual recruit of slaves from Africa to fill up the numbers that perish in the West Indies", he wrote.[30]

Planters preferred to avert public gaze, if they could, from the harsh conditions of the slave plantation as likely factors in depressing population growth. The Jamaican Assembly in 1788 denied those "many general unqualified Allegations, in respect of the Condition and Treatment of the slaves employed in the cultivation of this and others of his majesty's colonies in the West Indies". They continued: "The decrease of our slaves does not arise from the causes alleged in the petitions presented to the British House of Commons, but from various other causes not imputable to us . . . ."[31]

An excess of males, they contended, led to licentiousness in the female, which had moral and physical consequences inimical to a healthy birth rate. The image of the promiscuous African woman, articulated and promoted by persons like Edward Long during this period, supported their contention. These assumptions had pervaded the evidence given by West Indians to the Parliamentary Committee on the Slave Trade, and guided its official findings:

> the natural increase of population, among the slaves in the Islands, appears to have been impeded principally by the following causes:
>
> 1st – The inequalities of the numbers of the sexes in importations from Africa.[32]
>
> 2nd – The general dissoluteness of manner among the slaves and the want of proper regulations for the encouragement of marriages and of rearing children.

Other reasons which followed referred to diseases "which are in some instances attributed to too severe labour or rigorous treatment, and in others to insufficient or improper food".[33]

West Indians were ready to accept and to project the sexual disparity as a prime reason for the stagnation of the black population, for they could claim that that disparity was "not imputable" to them but to circumstances in Africa beyond their control. If they could, however, control those circumstances and ensure that equal numbers of men and women crossed the Middle Passage, they might succeed in preserving intact their system of labour supply.

Hence the willingness of the Jamaican House of Assembly in 1788 to advance the idea of a regulated slave trade which would ensure a healthy balance of men and women "by compelling the said ships to transport an equal number of both sexes".[34] This was also the rationale behind the moderate corrective policy of Henry Dundas, who successfully recommended to the House of Commons in 1792 measures to monitor the slave trade in order to avoid abolishing it. He proposed, among other things, that imported males should not outnumber females.[35] Bryan Edwards, too, stated his support for a sex-selective immigration policy which would, hopefully, defuse the abolitionists' case.[36]

The latter argued back that abolition itself would be the most effective means of achieving that desired balance in the population: William Pitt, prime minister, declared in the House of Commons in 1791 in the debate on William Wilberforce's Abolition Motion, that "when the importation should stop, that disproportion between the sexes, which was one of the obstacles to population, would gradually diminish and indeed our whole colonies in the West Indies would revert to that natural order and course of things by which population and civilization would be promoted".[37]

The prediction proved correct in one aspect. Within ten years of the end of the slave trade, Jamaica's population began indeed to assume normalcy in terms of its sex ratio. The first reliable census of slave numbers, in 1817, showed a declining sexual imbalance. There were 346,150 slaves, of whom 173,319 were men and 172,831 were women, a male excess of 488.[38] It was the last recorded year in which men outnumbered women in the island's population. Native-born blacks were rapidly outstripping importees and accordingly altering the national sex structure. Whereas African-born men still outnumbered African-born women by over 10,000 (58,272 women to 68,631

Table 6.2 The Enslaved Population, 1817–1829

Year	Males	Females	Total
1817	173,319	172,381	346,150
1820	170,466	171,916	342,382
1823	166,595	169,658	336,253
1826	162,726	168,393	331,119
1829	158,254	164,167	122,421

Source: Orlando Patterson, *The Sociology of Slavery: An Analysis of the Origins, Development and Structure of Negro Slavery in Jamaica* (London: MacGibbon and Kee, 1967), 98.

men) creole females already exceeded creole males by nearly 10,000.[39] This was as had been anticipated. But in another important respect, expectations were confounded: reversion to that natural order and course of things did not in fact promote population, and the island's black numbers fell. Table 6.2 illustrates this.

An equalizing of the sex ratio could not, as such, guarantee a natural increase of population: there were clearly other vital considerations.

The size of the black female population was, in fact, only inadvertently of official interest. It was significant only because of its inescapable biological link to population growth. In this respect, such interest as the Jamaican establishment displayed in the subject at this time typified most of the island's policies regarding women: they were, essentially, by-products of other more pressing masculine concerns.

This was true of the series of legislation which started with the Consolidated Acts of 1788 and 1792, continued into the nineteenth century with the Abolition Acts of 1807, the Registry Bill of 1817 and the various ameliorative measures of the 1820s. They all revolved around the economy's manpower needs and as such expressed a kind of population policy, which perforce acknowledged the woman's reproductive function. But their limited terms of reference permitted little more than a marginal regard for her over-all situation. That condition was in fundamental ways determined by the requirements of the white plantation which, seeing her primarily if not exclusively as worker, would nevertheless attempt encroachment on the other roles implicit in her condition as a woman.

Gender, Colour and the Division of Labour

By the 1770s, Jamaica was overwhelmingly a sugar plantation. The national wealth was estimated to total about £18 million sterling, of which approximately £15 million represented the value of sugar property including slaves.[40] About two-thirds of the island's 250,000 slaves in 1789 were estimated to be working on sugar estates.[41] By the 1830s, when blacks numbered 312,876, nearly half worked on sugar plantations and the majority of sugar workers were women, the ratio being 920 males per 1,000 females.[42]

almost in the fields

The sugar estate, dominating so much else in creole Jamaica, set the occupational norms for black women. Allocation of jobs within the slave force during the last sixty years of slavery followed the same trend observed earlier in the eighteenth century. Women were concentrated in most unskilled areas of agriculture to such a considerable extent that even during the period before 1820, when men outnumbered women in the slave population, all evidence suggests that women nevertheless outnumbered men in the most menial and least versatile tasks of the plantation.

Historians have drawn attention to this pattern of work distribution among the sexes on particular estates that they have studied. Craton and Walvin's history of Worthy Park estate in the parish of St John's shows an overall male preponderance in the 1780s, the proportion being 52.5 per cent men to 47.5 per cent women.[43] But they also observed that

> proportionately more women worked in the fields than men. In 1789, 70 women out of 162 worked in the fields compared to 29 men out of a total of 177. Similarly in 1793, although the total slave population had increased, this pattern remained, 107 women out of 244, worked in the field compare to 92 of a possible 284 men . . . while the work of the female slaves was concentrated in the fields the energy and skills of the men had to be channeled into the great variety of functions vital to sugar production.[44]

Orlando Patterson examined the tasks of slaves on Orange River and Green Park estates in Trelawny in 1823 and was "struck too by the fact that male slaves had a much wider range of occupations to choose from than females".[45] He found this tendency equally pronounced at Rose Hall estate in St James in the 1830s. There, the great majority of the women between the ages of 19 and 54 were in the field. The proportion of women in the field was larger than that of the males. This was due partly to the fact that men had a wider range of occupations to choose from and at Rose Hall in particular, they were outnumbered by the women.[46]

These cases are neither isolated nor inadvertent. On the contrary, they reflect implementation of a creole labour policy, an explicit statement of which was made by William Beckford in 1788, as follows: "A negro man is purchased either for a trade, or the cultivation and different processes of the cane – the occupations of the women are only two, the house, with its several departments, and supposed indulgences, or the field with its exaggerated labours."[47]

Additional estate samplings taken at various periods in fact confirm an extensive Jamaican pattern of work distribution based on the use of unskilled agricultural female labour in excess of male.[48] James Reid's slave force of 180 slaves in the parish of Hanover in the 1770s contained 90 adult males and 66 females, of whom 42 men, or 47 per cent, and 42 women, or 64 per cent, worked in the fields.[49] Nutt's River plantation, the property of Sir Thomas Champnoys in the parish of St Thomas, took an inventory of its 56 slaves who were under mortgage in 1786. Of the 15 adult females listed, 12 of them (or 80 per cent) were field women: of 25 adult males, 12 (or 50 per cent) were field men.[50] In 1790, another Nutt's River inventory was taken, this time of 153 slaves. Eight of the 52 adult males (or 15 per cent) were field workers, in contrast to 41 of the 54 adult females (or 76 per cent).[51]

Inventories of the Jackson estates of Salem and Mount Pleasant in Hanover show that in 1787 the field force at Mount Pleasant totalled 10 men out of a total of 44 (or 22.7 per cent), and 23 women out of a total of 44 (or 52.3 per cent). Plans to expand sugar cultivation involved purchasing more labour during the year. These additions brought the field contingent up to 47 men out of a total of 89 (or 52.8 per cent), and 50 women out of a total of 79 (or 63 per cent). By 1802, after John Jackson's death, which had been followed by family disputes over the properties, the slave population had declined, but the sex ratio on the combined properties of Salem and Mount Pleasant indicated a continued preference for women in the field gangs: 25 men out of a total of 69 were field workers (or 36 per cent), and 40 women out of a total of 66 (or 60.6 per cent).[52]

In 1787, in the parish of St Catherine, an inventory of Wakefield sugar estate, the property of the deceased Charles Bowles, showed a total of 113 slaves, comprising 57 males and 56 females, of whom 30 women (or 54 per cent), and 16 men (or 28 per cent), were field Negroes.[53] Spring Vale estate in the parish of St Mary combined coffee growing with livestock rearing. In 1792, it contained 477 head of stock and a slave labour force of 51 men and 51 women. Of these, 25 (or 50 per cent) were field men, and 31 (or 61 per cent) were field women.[54] The official compensation evaluation of Amity Hall estate in St Thomas in 1834 showed a slave population of 242, containing 114 males and 128 females. Sixty-three males, or 35 per cent, as compared with 105 females (or 82 per cent) were classified as field workers (see table 6.3).[55]

Barry Higman's comprehensive survey of the Jamaican slave population on the eve of emancipation included an analysis of labour organization on a number of estates: Master's and Whim sugar estates in St Mary, Maryland coffee plantation in St Andrew, and Irwin, Montpelier and Rose Hall sugar estates in St James. All revealed the dominance of female workers in the field gangs, even at Master's and Maryland, which contained more males than

Table 6.3 Percentages of Male/Female Field Workers on Seven Jamaican Estates, 1773–1834

Year	Estate/Owner	Males			Females		
		Total adult males	Total field workers	%	Total adult females	Total field workers	%
1773	James Reid	90	42	47	66	42	64
1786	Nutt's River	25	12	50	15	12	80
1790	Nutt's River	52	8	15	54	41	76
1787	Wakefield	57	16	28	56	30	54
1787	Mount Pleasant	89	47	53	79	50	63
1792	Springvale	51	25	50	51	31	61
1802	Salem and Mount Pleasant	69	25	36	66	40	61
1834	Amity Hall	114	63	55	128	105	82

Sources: Egerton MS 2134: Nutt's River Plantation Inventory of Slave Population; Add. MSS 19049: Wakefield Plantation Inventory; MS 236: Green Park and Spring Vale Estate Book, 1790–1795; G.S. Ramlachansingh, "Amity Hall 1760–1860: The Geography of a Jamaican Plantation" (MSc thesis, University of London, 1966), 99–100.

females.[56] Higman's analysis of the Montpelier estates over a longer period in the nineteenth century (1817–32) led him to conclude that all male slaves had more flexible occupational openings than female, brown female slaves had the first option on domestic work, "thus only aged or invalid black females could expect to escape labour in the field".[57]

The slaveholdings in the 1780s of another William Beckford, the absentee planter and Lord Mayor of London, demonstrate also the heavy participation of women in the "exaggerated labours of the field". This large complex of estates provides additional valuable evidence of a labour force consciously deployed in accordance with contemporary criteria of what was appropriate occupation for the sexes. It offers useful evidence, as well, of some of the effects of such labour policies on the condition of black women.[58] Beckford's Jamaican properties included thirteen estates scattered over the three parishes of Clarendon, Westmoreland and St Ann. The Clarendon holdings comprised eight units, seven of which were largely engaged in sugar growing, with some livestock. These were Danks, Rock River, Lime Hall, Kays, Moore, Mamie Gully and Retreat; cattle was raised at Bodles Pen. They contained a total slave population in 1780 of 1,253, of whom the men and boys totalled 649, the women and girls 604. Adults numbered 479 men and 458 women. The combined task force in the field comprised 143 men and 263 women.

Bodles Pen had an expected high proportion of workers engaged in the care of livestock, which resulted in its purely agricultural activity left almost exclusively in the hands of women. Of 62 slave women at Bodles, 32 were in the field, compared with 4 male field labourers out of a male adult population of 94; or, to state it another way, 88.8 per cent of the Bodles field contingent were women. The St Ann estates of Drax Hall and Esher in the same year combined 606 slaves, of whom 200 were adult females and 233 adult males. The field gangs contained 114 men and 110 women. In 1780, Beckford's Westmoreland properties of Bog and Retrieve contained 345 slaves, including 100 adult males and 120 adult females. Thirty-four of these men and 71 of these women were field workers.[59] To summarize, this complex of twelve estates containing 2,204 slaves revealed that in 1780, 36 per cent, or 291 out of 802 men, and 57 per cent, or 444 out of 778 women, were field workers.[60]

A varied range of skills, as William Beckford implied, was possible for the male slave. Nutt's River estate, for example, with twenty-five males, had

Table 6.4   Percentage of Male/Female Field Workers on William Beckford's Estates in Jamaica, 1780

Estates	Male Adult Total	Male Adult Field Workers	% of Male Workers	Female Adult Total	Female Adult Field Workers	% of Female Workers
Clarendon						
Rock River	60	25	41.6	85	52	61.2
Danks	74	30	40.5	86	60	69.8
Kays	76	31	40.8	82	44	53.6
Moore	41	21	51.2	55	27	49.1
Retreat	46	19	41.4	52	27	51.9
Bodles	94	4	4.2	62	32	51.6
Mamie Gully	12	4	8.3	10	6	60.0
Lime Hall + mountain tradesmen	30 46	9	30.0	26	15	57.0
Parish Total	479	143	29.2	458	263	57.4
Westmoreland						
Bog	59	22	37.3	71	45	63.5
Retrieve	41	12	32.4	49	26	53
Parish Total	100	34	35.4	120	71	59.2
St Ann						
Drax Hall	111	58	52.2	103	60	58.2
Esher	112	56	50.0	97	50	51.5
Parish Total	223	114	51.0	200	110	55.0
Total of 12 Estates	802	291	36.0	778	444	57.0

Source: CO 107/43, Public Record Office, London.

fourteen artisans who included sawyers, carpenters, stone masons and boilers, as well as a blacksmith, a farrier and a cooper.[61] The occupational openings for the men on the Beckford estates were even wider, for, in addition to
the categories of work found at Nutt's River, they had on their 1780 establishment slaves classified as bricklayers, wheelwrights, distillers, fishermen,
wharf-men, tailors and doctor's assistants; a high proportion were also
engaged in the care of livestock.[62] Male workers sometimes combined agricultural and non-agricultural work, so that on Esher estate, for instance,
three men listed as field workers, Bob, Cudjoe and Caesar, were also respectively a boiler, a wainman and a distiller. On Bog Estate, Frank, Charles and
Adam were simultaneously field men and sawyers. Drax Hall estate had six
male field workers who also combined the skill each of either a boiler or a
distiller.[63]

In contrast, women were confined within a considerably more restricted
area, and field women were exclusively field women. Indeed, often when
women were listed in other categories of work apart from that of the field, a
closer look reveals that they were in fact engaged in ancillary field tasks
requiring little or no special skills. So that, for example, in addition to the
444 women on the Beckford estates in 1780 who were classified as "field
negroes", there were nineteen who cut grass, worked in the estates' provisions
garden and hoed fences. Other jobs allocated to women demanded little
expertise: a further ten women did miscellaneous tasks, they carried water or
watched gates or worked on the road. Seven women were drivers of field
gangs.[64] The care of poultry, pigs and sheep engaged thirty-three women, or
8 per cent of the adult female population.

Domestic work was the most significant work category next to agriculture, and accounted for fifty-nine women, or 13 per cent of the total sample.
Within this group were to be found fifteen washerwomen, eighteen housewomen and twenty-six cooks. Eighteen of these cooks were assigned to the
field gangs and prepared meals on the work site; half of the house slaves
(nine in all) were mulattoes.[65] Goveia's observation on the occupational rating of domestics in the Leeward Islands is here relevant: she noted that the
female house slave on the plantation was more a "favoured" than a "skilled"
worker.[66]

Women with "skills" numbered thirty-four, or 8 per cent. They included
seven midwives, eight doctresses, five field nurses and fourteen seamstresses.

Table 6.5 Miscellaneous Occupations of Enslaved Women

Occupations	Danks	Kays	Moors	Mamie Gully	Rock River	Retreat	Bodles Pen	Sub-total	Retrieve	Bog	Sub-total	Esher	Drax	Sub-total	Totals
Drivers	1	1	1		1			5		1	1	1		1	7
Grass Cutters	1		1		2		3}								
Sugar Work					2		}	15	1	1	2	2		2	19
Garden	1				1	1	}								
Hoes Fences			2				}								
Hogs/Sheep	1		1		2	1	}								
Shepherdess	2	2					1}						8	2	10	33
Small/Meats							}	19	3	1	4				
Stock					6		}								
Fowl House	1					1	1}								
Water Carrier			1		2		}	7	1	2	3				10
Gate Washer							3}								
Road	1							1							1
Midwife	1	1			1	1		4		1	1	1	1	2	7
Doctress	2	2	1		1	1	1	6		1	1	1		1	8
Field Nurse			1		1		1}	3							
Child's Nurse							}	4		1	1	1		1	5
Seamstress	1	1			2	1	1	8	1	1	2	3	7	10	14
Washerwomen	2	1	1	1	1	1	1	3	2	1	3	2	3	5	15
Housewomen							3	12	2	1	3				
Housewife	1	2	2		1	2	4	5	1	1	2	1		1	18
Cooks	1	1	1	1		1	1	5	1	1	2	1		1	8
Field Cooks	1	2	1		2	3	3	12	1	1	2	3	1	4	18
								104			22			37	163

Source: CO 107/43, Public Record Office, London.

This proportion of non-praedial female workers overrates the black woman's access to special expertise, for mulattoes dominated as seamstresses – eleven out of the group of fourteen – and the labels of "doctress", "midwife" and "nurse" were often euphemisms for superannuated field workers. Stewart comments on a widely attested phenomenon: "When the slaves are rendered unfit, by age or infirmity for field labour they are employed in occupations that require little bodily exertion; the men are placed as watchmen over the canes and provisions and the women to take care of the children, or in other light employment."[67]

Estate inventories do not give much information about the training in skills, if any, which was made available to young female slaves. The only instances in all the samples (tables 6.4 and 6.5) which suggest a period of apprenticeship are: Dido, aged fourteen, at Bodles Pen, who was learning to be a washerwoman, Essey, "a fine healthy mulatto girl" at Nutt's River, who was learning to be a seamstress, and Sophia, a young girl at Mount Pleasant in 1787, who was "with the midwife".[68]

Market prices of slave men and women reflect the contemporary creole assessment of their respective skills. On Wakefield plantation in 1787, the most highly priced women were Oriah and Cumba, each worth £100, and Mimba, Cretia and Rebeck Peggy, each worth £95, all of whom were field women. The most expensive field men were valued at £110 and £120. The most highly priced slaves on the estate were six tradesmen worth between £120 and £160 each.[69] The highest value of a woman slave was normally that attached to a strong and able field worker, in contrast to the man, whose price instantly rose as he acquired a trade. The woman's alleged expertise as doctress, nurse or often even as midwife added little to her valuation. The instances of a female professional who was worth more than a female field worker are rare: the midwife, in theory a valued person, in fact was often so elderly as to be in a state of decline, physically and hence monetarily.[70] Domestic service, often regarded as a more prestigious type of female occupation, was rated on the slave market approximately the same as that of a field slave.[71]

John Jackson's valuation of the Mount Pleasant slaves in 1787 demonstrates this. His head driver, coopers, carpenters and boilers ranged in value between £150 and £200, his healthy field men between £90 and £100. Able field women ranged from £70 and reached a maximum value of £100. His doctress and midwife were worth £90 and £80 respectively: a house slave was £90, a cook, £50.[72]

In 1791, Jackson purchased 111 slaves. The most costly were the field men, whose price started at £100 and ranged to £130, one fisherman valued at £120 and three young able carpenter's apprentices worth £130 each. The most highly priced woman was the field woman Princess, who cost £100. The other field women cost between £70 and £90; Nancy, who "attended the women in labour", was bought for £90.[73]

With so few levels of expertise in the creole system to which she could aspire, the black slave woman was irretrievably the unskilled labourer in the field and, in the hierarchy of the "outer" plantation, no one ranked lower.[74] Male slaves with advanced skills could become "important personages of great responsibility" on the estate.[75] Distinction as "a good workman" earned authority and privilege.[76] In contrast, the black woman, trapped in an occupational cul-de-sac, was the least able of all slaves, and of all women, "to attain positions of status and relative independence".[77]

The importance of the work situation in determining the individual social niche inevitably received excessive emphasis in New World slave societies organized towards a single economic goal. The possession of skills opened up opportunities for profitable employment over and above what the individual estate could absorb. Surplus labour could purchase material goods, even comforts, could do more, for with the use of one's trained hands it was possible to purchase freedom. Exclusion of female slaves from the higher ranks of labour cut her off from this avenue to independence.

An indicator of the despised rating of field labour, especially when associated with sugar cultivation, was its regular use as punishment. The demotion of a house slave to gang work, or the transfer of a pimento picker to the tasks of the cane field, was a recognized penalty for misdemeanours, and a standard means of humiliating women. A domestic slave, the nurse of a planter's children in Vere, was guilty of "misbehaviour such as obliged her Master to turn her out of his House and she was ordered to work among the field negroes".[78] James Archer entered in his diary on 3 April 1830, the return of all of his Negroes, the majority female, from Great Pond estate to which they had been sent "as a punishment to dig cane holes".[79] "Common labour" in the field was a threat constantly held over the heads of house slaves who resisted white male advances.[80]

In this context, not surprisingly, as one contemporary witness expressed it, "most Negroes conceive it more or less a degradation to work in the Fields".[81] But a large majority of black slave women had no alternative. Craton and Walvin wrote:

> On the whole, the more arduous tasks on sugar plantations fell to the male slaves, though at Worthy Park at least, women also worked hard in the fields. It was the men, however, who bore the brunt of the heavy work of cane cutting and boiling, and men alone tended the blistering operation in the factories.[82]

Contemporary evidence, however, indicates that the task force of Worthy Park may have been more typical than its chroniclers imply, and that the more arduous tasks both of field and of factory were not always confined to men.[83]

The severe routine of plantation agriculture with its paramilitary regimentation in gangs is widely documented. Descriptions of these gangs seldom distinguish the tasks assigned to male as opposed to female workers. Youthfulness and physical fitness were the prime criteria on which manual labour was distributed. The first, or great gang, of the workforce was "the flower of all the field battalions".[84] It contained "the most healthy and robust of the men and women, whose chief business it is, out of crop-time, to cut the canes, feed the mills, and attend the manufacture of the sugar".[85]

Female labourers received the same work implements as male.[86] Equipped with their bills and hoes, they dug cane holes, they trashed, cut, tied and carted canes, they made lime kilns, they built roads, they carried manure,[87] they worked from sunrise to sunset; in crop-time they worked at night as well. We learn the following from William Taylor's evidence before the parliamentary committee of 1832:

Q. Are the women employed for the same number of hours as the men?

A. Yes, except the women who have the children at the breast.

Q. And at the same description of labour as the men?

A. Almost entirely, there are of course different branches of labour which they cannot undertake; they cannot undertake the management of cattle; they are excused from night work out of crop in watching.

Q. Are they employed in digging cane holes?

A. Yes.

Q. In gangs with men?

A. Yes.

Q. And exposed to the same degree of labour?

A. Yes.[88]

Planters admitted their policy of exacting equal work output from women as from men. Bickell, for instance, wrote of the determination of estate managers not to part with hard-working females: "as to that young woman, she will work as well as any man I have got".[89]

Women were fully involved in the less technical tasks of the factory. Matthew Lewis described the crop-time activities of his estate: when "the ripe canes are brought in bundles to the mill, where the cleanest of the women are appointed, one to put them into the machine for grinding them, and another to draw them out after the juice has been extracted, when she throws them into an opening in the floor close to her".[90] Thomas McNeil, attorney for Lord Holland's estates in western Jamaica, observed that during slavery "females have been required to perform several duties more fitted for males such as driving cattle in the mills, attending the pans in which the cane juice is first treated in Boiling Houses".[91]

Thomas Cooper commented as follows:

> [T]he slaves capable of the labour are, with some necessary exceptions, divided into two gangs or spells, which, besides being both fully occupied in the various occupations of the plantation during the day, are engaged the whole of the night, on alternate nights, in the business of sugar-making. Their labour, during crop-time, is thus equal to six days and three nights in the week. And in the exaction of this labour, no distinction is made between men and women; both are subjected to the same unvarying rule.[92]

Women were also to be found in jobbing gangs, which consisted usually of twenty to forty "stout male and female negroes".[93] They were hired out by managers and overseers to do the heaviest tasks on estates and to repair roads. Their living and working conditions were notorious. They might be employed several miles from their homes and remained on their work-site from Monday morning until Saturday evening. Jobbing mothers might have to leave their infants and children behind for this period or carry them with them to their transient assignments. They travelled with their ground provisions and they constructed shaky sheds by the roadside or on the estates to which they were assigned, as temporary shelters.[94]

This extensive use, and abuse, of unskilled female labour was the product of a universal attitude, still prevalent, which saw women as having little capacity for acquiring skills. This was reinforced by plantation economics, which functioned in a vicious circle of poor technology and labour exploitation. The vast corps of captive human power represented as much as 30 per cent or more of the capital investment in a plantation enterprise:[95] economy demanded that it be put to maximum use. "Slavery required all hands to be occupied at all times",[96] female hands included.

The plantation dictated the particular use to which female hands were put. The dominance of one-crop export monoculture left little room for the mixed farming activities, dairy production or cottage/craft industries, which often engaged rural female labour in other types of economies. No scope or demand existed for the Jamaica woman slave to vary or upgrade her occupational potential.

Female labour, moreover, was expensive labour because of its inevitably high rate of absenteeism, and slaves, whether at work or not, had to be maintained. So, unless she was breeding additional work units in adequate numbers to compensate for her absence from the field gang, the female slave could offer very minimal returns on capital outlay. To offset her high cost and the losses she incurred, she had to be heavily utilized. With the abolition of the slave trade and the tapering off of the sexual imbalance, she swelled the numbers of estate hands who at any given time were non-effective, at the same time as she came to represent an even greater proportion of capital outlay.[97]

The need to extract maximum manual output from black women influenced the plantation's willingness to rationalize its techniques. Long had, in the 1770s, made a vain plea for the wide use of the plough on Jamaican estates. He estimated that one plough could do the work of one hundred slaves; those interested in good husbandry, he felt, should be concerned about this, for "no other work in a plantation is so severe and so detrimental as that of holing or turning up the ground in trenches with . . . hoes".[98] Mr Ashley, a witness before the parliamentary committee of 1788, confirmed how difficult it was to get overseers to replace slave labour with the plough: "they have a Prejudice against [its] use".[99] At Amity Hall estate in St

Catherine, where there was ideal ploughing soil, managers for years stubbornly resisted advice to mechanize. On that estate, the managers' vested interest in their labour holdings was an influential factor: they owned gangs of jobbing slaves whom they hired profitably to the estate for holing, hoeing and planting.[100]

There were always some humane and practical planters prepared to update their agricultural techniques. Matthew Lewis, for example, was anxious to use the plough on his estate and to "substitute the labour of oxen for that of Negroes, whenever it can possibly be done".[101] But planters obviously viewed the slave as a special kind of equipment, a "multi-purpose", flexible capital asset which, unlike machinery, could be deployed for any use at any time.[102] So, as long as the most occupationally backward (but versatile) section of the labour force, namely slave women, continued to service the plantation in such proportions, technological progress was inhibited. As long as creole agriculture failed to advance technologically, women continued to be used in overwhelming numbers as substitutes for animals and for machines.

HEALTH AND WELL-BEING

The demanding toil of the estate took a heavy toll on women's health, so that their physical condition was generally very poor. The Beckford sample of 1780 illustrates this (table 6.6). Its total of 604 women and girls found on the Clarendon estates contained 188[1] (or 31 per cent) in various stages of physical malaise, indicated either by the specific ailment or variously labelled "sickly", "weakly", "infirm", "distempered" or "invalid". In addition there were thirty women who were simply listed as either "superannuated" or "useless".[103]

Poor health was prevalent among the elder women: of the 199 women over forty years old, 136 (or 68 per cent) were below par. The majority of "superannuated" women, twenty-four in all, were sixty years and over. The remaining six of this "useless" group were in their forties and fifties, which indicates that uselessness implied not only increasing age but literally the potential for working, which these women physically did not have, whereas a few older women, in spite of their years, were still able physically to perform certain duties and therefore were not written off. So that Leslie Grace,

Table 6.6 Incidence of Illness among Enslaved Females on William Beckford's Clarendon Estates, 1780

Name of Estate	Table 1			Table 2			Table 3			Table 4		
	Total No. of Women of All Ages	Total in Poor Health	% of Total	Total No. of Women over 40	Total in Poor Health	% of Total	Total No. of Field Workers of All Ages	Total in Poor Health	% of Total	Total No. of Field Workers 15–40	Total in Poor Health	% of Total
Clarendon												
Danks	106	30		30	24		68	8		56	6	
Lime Hall	38	9		11	8		15	4		9	2	
Rock River	113	35		44	25		54	12		31	5	
Kays	107	45		36	27		59	15		39	12	
Moors	78	25		25	15		30	9		23	2	
Retreat	70	36		15	13		28	15		13	11	
Bodles Pen	81	43		2	20		33	1		22	–	
Mamie Gully	11	4		6	4		7	1		4	–	
Totals	604	188	31%	199	136	68%	294	65	22%	197	38	20%

Source: CO 107/43, Public Record Office, London.

the doctress at Rock River, was sixty-two; Prue, the overseer's cook at Mamie Gully, was sixty-three; old Juba at seventy-four was still working in the dry sugar works of Moors Estate; the midwife at Moors, Suzanna, was seventy-one; and Bridget of Bodles Pen, although "very weak", still functioned at the age of seventy-seven as midwife. It was possible to find also "fit and able" women over the age of fifty. Creole Joba, age fifty-six, and Bollinda, age sixty, of Bodles Pen, were both "able field-women". But these were rare.

It was the condition, however, of the young adults, in what would normally be the prime of life, which was the real indicator of slave morbidity. Women between the ages of fifteen and forty totalled 274, or 45 per cent of the total female population. Seventy-eight of them, or 28 per cent, were in poor shape. The healthiest women on an estate were allocated to the field gangs. As already noted, 294 field women of all ages were found on these estates, and would be expected to be in good condition to carry out the strenuous tasks allotted to them. But in fact 65 of the total field force, or 22 per cent, were physically below par. One would also look within the prime age group of that field force to find the physically fittest, the cream of the female population, the adults aged fifteen to forty, of whom there were 197. Here too their health record was poor, 38, or 20 per cent, being in poor shape (see table 6.6).

Table 6.7 indicates, which the nature of women's illnesses, was in some instances detailed: four cases of yaws were identified, one at Rock River, one at Bodles Pen, and two at Moors, as well as three cases of venereal disease. There were three cases of bone-ache, one of sore eyes, and fourteen of sores and sore legs. Slaves tended to suffer from festering cuts, which they received while cutting cane and grass; their feet were especially vulnerable, as they were barefooted. Some whites maintained that slaves would not care to wear shoes even if they had them.[104] The majority of unwell women had no diagnosed disease. Their condition was referred to in 11 instances as "distempered", and in 119 instances as "infirm" or "weakly", which suggests the general debility associated with, among other things, excessive exertion and poor care.

An examination of the slave women responsible for providing health and welfare services to other women is revealing. Such persons were required to cook for the field gang, attend the babies of mothers who worked in the field, and staff the slave hospital as doctresses or midwives. Their own physi-

Table 6.7   Female Ill-Health: Beckford Estates, 1780–1781

				Kinds of Ailments				
Estates	Yaws	Venereal Disease	Sore Legs	Sore Eyes	Bone-Ache	Weakly	Distempered	Superannuated
1780								
Danks			3	1		23	1	2
Lime Hall		1	2			10		1
Rock River	1	1		3	2	15	2	8
Kays	2					17	6	17
Moors	2	1				14		8
Retreat		1	2			24		9
Bodles Pen	1		1			11	1	6
Mamie Gully						5	1	
Totals	4	3	14	1	2	119	11	51
1780								
Bog	3		1			9	5	6
Esher	1	1				21		24
Drax Hall	1		4	1		9		30
Totals	5	1	5	1		39	5	60
1781								
Bog	4		2			11	5	6
Retrieve	1		3			9		7
Drax Hall				1		17	8	34
Ackendown	1					9	1	7
Totals	6		5	1		46	14	54

Source: CO 107/43, Public Record Office, London.

cal condition was almost invariably unsatisfactory. Four cooks were listed at Mount Pleasant estate in 1787. One was "very old", one was "weakly" and one of the two others who cooked daily for the Negroes had "a very bad sore". John Jackson in 1791 purchased a lot of slaves for the estate. It contained one woman, Violet, who was allocated to kitchen work, but she was "very weakly". Nancy, who was "rather weakly", had the task of attending the women in labour. The black population on Henry Jackson's estates of Mount Pleasant and Salem in 1802 contained two field cooks, one of whom was old, the other weakly; of the three children's field nurses, two were "weakly" and one was "middling". The field hospital nurse was "weakly", so was Mimba the doctress; Daphny the midwife was "old".[105]

The more detailed age data available for the Beckford slave women is even more significant: there were twenty-one cooks listed in 1780 on the Clarendon plantations. Their ages ranged from twenty to fifty-four years. Of these, ten were "weakly" and nine were "able" women; of the remaining two, one had lost a hand and one had sore eyes. Four of the Bodles Pen's "able" cooks were aged thirty-five, thirty, thirty-one and forty-two and worked, not in the field, but in the attorney's house.[106]

The nursing personnel totalled twelve women, whose condition was as follows: two nurses, aged fifty-nine and forty-four, were both "weakly"; there were six doctresses, of whom two, aged twenty-six and fifty, were "able", and four, aged fifty-six, sixty-two, sixty-five and seventy-seven, who were "weakly". Midwives numbered four, aged fifty-five, sixty-one, seventy-one and ninety-two, all of whom were "weakly".[107]

Slave midwives and nurses were held responsible for maternal and infant sickness and mortality. The frequently fatal lockjaw from which Jamaican babies suffered was attributed to the "the want of skill or inattention of the black midwives who like their fair sisters in Europe are always illiterate, generally careless and often intoxicated". They neglected to take proper care of the babies' umbilical cord or to provide for the comfort of the mother "who is generally exposed to cold by lying in the wretched hut".[108] Their unhygienic practices were deplored. Dr James Williamson expressed strong views about their habits, which he saw as being "barbarous", "cruel" and "ignorant".[109] He recommended that they should be trained. "It would", he wrote in 1817, "be a wise measure to establish under legislative provisions a course of lectures and a lying-in hospital at which a professional gentleman ought to

Table 6.8   Physical Condition of "Professional" Enslaved Females, 1780 and 1781

Estates	Occupation	Age	Physical Condition
1780			
Danks	Midwife	61	Weakly
	Doctress	56	Weakly
	Doctress	26	Able
Rock River	Nurse	44	Weakly
	Midwife	72	Weakly
	Doctress	62	Weakly
Moors	Nurse	59	Weakly
	Midwife	71	Weakly
Retreat	Midwife	55	Weakly
	Doctress	65	Weakly
	Doctress	77	Weakly
	Doctress	50	Able
1780			
Bog	Nurse	41	Able
	Doctress	30	Weakly
Esher	Midwife	55	Infirm
	Doctress	55	Able
Drax Hall	Midwife	74	Invalid
1781			
Bog	Nurse	42	Distempered
	Nurse	54	Able
	Midwife	69	Able
	Doctress	36	Weakly
Ackendown	Doctress	20	Able

Source: CO 107/143, Public Record Office, London.

instruct a certain number of women from estates to take care of those in childbed."[110]

There is some counter-evidence to suggest that black nurses/midwives were not always regarded as totally without knowledge and expertise. Lady Nugent risked having one present at her first lying-in.[111] Dr Archer paid "old Kitty" for assisting at his wife's childbed.[112]

What is here relevant is that it was clearly the accepted policy to give aging women or young women in frail health, who could not labour in the fields, the responsibility of preparing food for the working gang and for attending mothers, infants and sick slaves. As a consequence, the health needs of the women, children and patients receiving such services could only be inadequately met.

Before the advance of modern medical knowledge, illness was seen as one form of divine retribution, visible testimony of God's judgement on sinful man and woman. Blacks, always perceived by whites as especially sinful, were accordingly severely judged. By their many delinquencies and debaucheries, by their women's immoralities, they brought sickness on themselves. "There is no doubt", declared a committee of the Jamaican Council in 1789, "but the Negroes in Jamaica would live healthier and for a much longer term than they do in general, if it were not for their vicious and irregular Practices".[113]

Moral diagnoses were almost inseparable from medical diagnoses. Estate hothouses were places of confinement for both the sick and the erring slave.

Bryan Edwards claimed that the greatest debt which West Indian slaves owed their masters, was for their "liberality . . . of medical attendance and accommodation when sick".[114] Doctors paid daily or weekly visits to estates. They received retainer fees, averaging 6s. for each slave, sick or well. They charged additionally for specialized services, such as inoculations and difficult child-bed deliveries. Some doctors resided on the property; and every plantation was provided with "a sickhouse or hospital, divided into different apartments".[115]

Matthew Lewis gave much thought to the hospital facilities at Cornwall Plantation, and ruled in March 1816 that

> a new hospital for lying-in women, and for those who might be seriously ill, should
> be built, and made as comfortable as possible, while the present one should be

reserved for those whom the physicians might declare to be very slightly indisposed, or not ill at all: the doors being kept constantly locked, and the sexes placed in separate chambers to prevent it being a place of amusement by the lazy and lying as is the case at present.[116]

In February of the following year, although the new building was unfinished, it was nevertheless declared open. It was christened with Madeira wine, and the toast of "Health to the new hospital and shame to the old lazy house" was drunk by whites and blacks alike.[117]

Florence Nightingale's first requirements of a hospital (a revolutionary concept in 1859, when she first advanced it) was that "it should do the sick no harm".[118] There is no sure evidence that estate hospitals did blacks much good. Their physical environment left much to be desired. Inadequate drainage facilities, water supplies and refuse disposal on estates caused illness to spread.[119] Dr John Quier, who worked for years at Worthy Park estate in the late eighteenth century, had major problems of epidemic control. Outbreaks of measles, for instance, which were especially dangerous to women, sometimes affecting fifty to sixty slaves (including the nurses), were caused by the contagion of improperly disposed-of bodily waste matter.[120] Plantation hospitals during slavery were breeding grounds of disease and suffering in an era before medical science could effectively counter germs and pain.

The vigilance and competence of white doctors were often questionable.[121] Harmful methods of treatment, such as excessive purging and blood letting, were still widely used up to the 1840s. Dr James Archer bled his patients and himself regularly.[122] He treated one female patient with a chest infection by bleeding,[123] another with a threatened abortion,[124] and when the slave woman Ann Brown of Unity Valley received a blow from a stone, "I bled her", wrote Archer.[125]

In the course of developing his measles and smallpox vaccines, Dr Quier experimented extensively on the slaves of Worthy Park. He admitted that some of his methods were drastic: he relied heavily on purgatives such as calomel, emetic tartar, jalap mixed with cream of tartar, and the like, as preliminaries to inoculation.[126] The physical stamina of many of Dr Quier's guinea pigs was, however, low: "they [could not] bear frequent repetitions of strong purgatives. The consequence of such copious evacuations is almost always a tendency to dropsy."[127] Quier was on the whole, extremely satisfied with his results, but identified the Negroes' "want of strength" as a big obstacle to creole medical research.[128]

The slaves' weak physical stamina was seldom attributed to the circumstances of their environment, which many planters saw as eminently satisfactory. If slaves failed to respond to the care and facilities provided for them, they were held to blame. Matthew Lewis, in spite of the up-to-date and humane arrangements which he considered had been made in the interest of his slaves' well-being, ended in a state of exasperation: "Say what one will to the Negroes, and treat them as well as one can, obstinate devils, they will die!"[129]

The unbalanced diet of slaves was a large factor in their debility. "Roots and other vegetable substances . . . at all times make up the greatest part of their nourishment, such as yams, cocos, or eddoes, potatoes, plantains, bananas."[130] They received "seven or eight herrings per week" from their masters and "about eight pounds of salted codfish once or twice a year".[131] They were provided with "animal food, only when sick".[132] The view was expressed that, as blacks so seldom had meat in their diet, they had no desire for it.[133]

As Genovese has aptly pointed out, it is not the adequacy of food bulk that is at question, but "the finer questions of dietary balance".[134] The nutritional deficiencies implicit in the slave diet had special relevance for the health of nubile women and for their capacity to bear and rear healthy children.[135] The plantation routine was indiscriminately harmful to the health of male and female slaves alike. The survival rate of women was slightly better than that of men, their life expectancy was greater.[136] They were, on the other hand, uniquely susceptible in their reproductive function. Dr Quier did not, for instance, find that black women, as was sometimes suggested, enjoyed any "immunity from the evils of child-bearing". In his experience, "the accidents attendant on child-birth happen fully as often to these people, as to the rustic part of their sex in Europe".[137]

Estates claimed to provide pregnant and lying-in women with special treatment appropriate to their condition, such as exemption from hard labour, medical and nursing care, and supplementary diet.[138] But as has been observed, the physical condition of women, even in the potentially fittest age group of the slave population, was so alarmingly impaired as to minimize greatly their prospects of healthy pregnancies.[139] So that a population of 274 women of childbearing age on the Beckford Clarendon estates, as table 6.9 shows, produced nineteen live infants in 1780. In that same year, deaths numbered thirty-four.[140] The natural decrease of the slave population was an islandwide phenomenon, estimated to be approximately 2 per cent per annum in 1770s and 1780s.[141]

The abolitionist campaign gained momentum in this depressing demographic context. The hard facts of slave decrease and the mounting humanitarian agitation resulted in the emergence of population methods which, although containing some elements of concern for black welfare, were pri-

Table 6.9 Births and Deaths on William Beckford's Estates, 1780

Estates	Total of Each Estate	Nos. of Women Ages 15–40	No. of Births	No. of Deaths
Clarendon				
Danks	214	61	7	8
Lime Hall	81	15	2	2
Rock River	198	47	5	8
Kays	224	47	2	6
Moors	140	33	1	7
Retreat	129	37	1	1
Bodles Pen	193	30	1	1
Mamie Gully	28	4	–	1
Totals	1,207	274	19	34
St Ann and Westmoreland				
Bog	225	55	3	14
Esher	267	49	2	8
Retrieve	116	20	2	4
Drax Hall	339	73	5	12
Totals	947	197	12	38

Source: CO 107/143, Public Record Office, London.

marily motivated by the need for adequate labour supplies. This was embodied in some of the clauses of the Consolidated Slave Acts of 1792 which "gave all possible encouragement to the raising of negro children". Legislation thus, for the first time, gave some official cognizance of the role of the female in population growth.[142]

Clause XXXV of the act provided for overseers to receive annually £3 for each newly born slave who represented an increase in the slave force of the estates for that year. The owner would gain a deduction from his public taxes for each such bonus paid to the overseer.[143] Clause XXXVI provided that every female slave with six living children would be "exempted from hard labour in the field or otherwise", and that her owner would be exempted from paying poll-tax or any other kind of tax for her. Slave owners would also receive a deduction from their taxes for such women in the case of an annual increase of the number of slaves, provided proof was given, on oath to the satisfaction of the local justices and vestry, that the requisite number of children were alive, that the mother was not at work and that she was "provided with the means of an easy and comfortable maintenance".[144]

The abolition of the slave trade in 1807 made the question of labour supplies even more urgent, and the metropolitan government tried earnestly to impress on planters how much it was to "their true interest" to concentrate on the care of the slave.[145] The high incidence of infant mortality caused great concern and demanded corrective policies. Jamaica's governor was instructed from Downing Street to investigate the circumstances of the mother in relation to the child's death rate: "Should it upon examination appear that the Disorder [that is, tetanus] in infants arises from working the mother too severely during gestation or too early after childbirth or from such causes as might be remedied by Legislative Provision, etc.", appropriate action should be taken.[146]

The 1816 Slave Act extended rewards for slave births to mothers, midwives and nurses, so the £3 bonus previously provided for overseers was to be "divided in equal proportions among the mothers of the surviving children, the midwife and the nurse or nurses attending such children".[147] For the further encouragement of population growth and "the protection of negro infants", clause XII of the act extended the work exemption afforded to mothers of six children to adopted mothers "having raised from infancy and during the period of nurture, a child or children of deceased mothers".[148]

Tax remissions to slaveholders, and work exemption for women with over six children, thus remained the substances of official natality policies until emancipation. Individual planters devised their own incentive schemes. It became customary for nursing mothers to be allowed an extra hour off at the beginning and at the end of their working day;[149] extra food allowances were usually given to such women.[150]

William Ricketts welcomed the Consolidated Slave Act of 1792 and was optimistic about the benefits that would flow from it, as well as from the measures which he personally took at Canaan estate. He wrote sometime in the 1790s observing that "the Negroes [were] much happier" and the women already more prolific: "By giving my women a distinguishing coat who have raised children they have taken to breeding, and by having a room near my dwelling House, I have raised 6 children since Feby, and have 9 more women ready to lye in here."[151]

Matthew Lewis established an elaborate "order of honour" for the fertile women on his estates:

> I then gave the graundee and the mothers a dollar each, and told them, that for the future they might claim the same sum, in addition to their usual allowance of clothes and provisions, for every infant which should be brought to the overseer alive and well on the fourteenth day; and I also gave each mother a present of a scarlet girdle with a silver medal in the centre, telling her always to wear it on feasts and holidays, when it should entitle her to marks of peculiar respect and attention, such as being one of the first served, and receiving a larger portion than the rest; that the first fault which she might commit, should be forgiven on the production of this girdle; and that when she should have any favour to ask, she should always put it round her waist, and be assured, that on seeing it, the overseer would allow the wearer to be entitled to particular indulgence. On every additional child an additional medal is to be affixed to the belt, and precedence is to follow the greater number of medals.[152]

To emphasize the favoured status of prolific women, Lewis declared a "play day" for the whole estate, at which the mothers were the honoured guests. He also ensured that all the slaves were informed that they owed their good fortune of a holiday to "the piccaninny mothers, that is for the women who had children living".[153]

A year later Lewis could only express bewilderment and dismay at the stagnant birth rates on his estate. "Among upwards of 350 Negroes, and with a greater number of females than men, in spite of all indulgences and inducements, not more than twelve or thirteen children have been added annually to the list of the births."[154]

At about the time when Lewis wrote,[155] the enslaved black population throughout the island had reached its numerical peak and was beginning its decline.[156] Natal and ameliorative legislation, however well intentioned, touched merely on the fringes of the slave's condition, in many cases introduced no new benefits and left essentially untouched the harsh environment of the plantation in which the woman laboured.

Even Edward Long, who was inclined to dissociate the natural decrease of the slave population from the circumstances of enslavement, did on one occasion reluctantly conceded a co-relationship. "I will not deny", he wrote, "that those Negroes breed the best, whose labour is least, or easiest. Thus the domestic Negroes have more children, in proportion than those in pens: and the latter, than those who are employed in sugar-plantations."[157]

Excessively demanding field work, especially that of the sugar estate, was seen by others apart from Long as a major deterrent to maternal and infant well-being. And the demands on female workers was in no way mitigated during the period of amelioration. In the view of a local contributor to the *Jamaica Magazine* in January 1814, the first step which had to be taken towards improving the health of slave children was to relieve pregnant women from the tasks of "carrying heavy loads and cutting cane holes".[158]

On 6 June 1823, the bookkeeper Charles Talbot, from Low Layton estate in the parish of St George, testified before the magistrate in Buff Bay courthouse that "[p]regnant women do work in the great gang till about seven months or pregnancy".[159] Witnesses such as William Taylor in 1832 repeatedly maintained that if women were "exempt from cane hole digging and the night work", then there was some hope that "the decline of the slave population might be arrested".[160]

These contemporary observations have been fully substantiated by modern demographic analysis of the slave data in the period immediately preceding emancipation. Not only did Jamaica's sugar estates have the highest death rates, but they also had the lowest birth rate. When all other factors such as sex ratios, age structures, proportions of Africans and creoles, and the like, have been assessed, the inescapable conclusion is that "the natural decrease was related to the labour-requirements of sugar".[161]

The last years of slavery represented the period of maximum natural decrease of Jamaica's black population.[162] Economically, it was a period characterized by the amalgamation of agricultural units into fewer and larger complexes.[163] It was the period that marked the peak of dominance of the vast sugar estate. Higman's convincing conclusions on the high correlation between sugar estate labour and the natural decrease of the slave population emphasize the harsh circumstances of the majority of the island's black women. Excessive, regimented physical exertion, poor diet and few supportive services took a heavy toll of black lives. These conditions on the outer plantation combined to shorten the slave's life span, to age and weaken women before their time and to reduce their capacity to be healthy mothers. By subjecting them constantly to even more demeaning kinds of physical abuse, the plantation further attempted to deny them their womanhood.

VIOLENCE AGAINST BLACK WOMEN

Both law and custom facilitated acts of violence against the black woman. Colonial codes gave to the master and to the magistrate the power of corporal punishment over male and female slaves found guilty of misconduct, and they provided few effective restraints on the exercise of that power. The law, moreover, until 1826, gave the female slave no protection from sexual attack. For the greater part of slavery, in fact, the only recognition in the penal system of her special circumstance as a woman was expressed in the regulations governing capital punishment: a pregnant woman condemned to die would not be executed until "a reasonable time after delivery".[164]

The slave woman, in this context, not surprisingly, was subject to deliberate brutality, public and private, legal and illegal. She was branded, she was placed in the stocks and she was whipped. Flogging as a means of correction had been gradually controlled in law throughout the eighteenth century.[165] By 1788, the amount of physical punishment which the slave could legally receive in the work house or on the estate was limited to not more than ten lashes at one time for one offence, unless the owner of the estate, the attorney or the supervisor of the work house was present, in which event a maximum of thirty-nine lashes was permitted.[166]

Flogging was regularly ordered by magistrates as one of the penalties imposed in slave courts, often as an adjunct to imprisonment and/or to hard labour.[167] Twenty-five cases involving slave women appear on the records of the St George's Slave Court between 1822 and 1831. Eighteen resulted in convictions, and whipping was ordered for five of the women found guilty.[168]

Margaret James had stolen "five handkerchiefs, one chemise, one frock and one under-petticoat, of the value of two shillings" from another slave on Kildare estate. She was sentenced to three months' hard labour and was ordered to receive "thirty-nine lashes when the medical man who attends the said institution [that is, the work house] declares her fit to receive it".[169] One of these whippings was to be administered publicly. Harriet, who was described as "a notorious and incorrigible runaway and evil person", was sentenced to "three months' hard labour: she was also due to receive two dozen lashes on her bare back with a cat-o-nine tails in the market-place of Buff Bay on 3 February 1827 and again on her discharge".[170]

Between 1819 and 1834 the Port Royal Slave Court handled 150 trials involving women. One hundred and twenty resulted in verdicts of guilty, of which 28 included floggings for the women convicted; 12 of these were public floggings.[171] One such case concerned the female slave Julia. She had lodged a complaint against her owner that she had not received her "negro grounds" allocated to her by law for cultivating her provisions. Her master, I.P. Levy, produced a witness, a Negro driver, who testified against her. The magistrates found her complaint to be without foundation, to be frivolous, and "in consequence of the delicate appearance of the woman, and her having a young child, their worships sentenced her only to 20 lashes publicly, then to be discharged".[172]

"The gangs", wrote the Reverend Thomas Cooper in 1824, "always work before the whip, which is a very weighty and powerful instrument. The driver has it always in his hand, and drives the Negroes, men and women, without distinction, as he would drive horses or cattle in a team."[173]

The whip was seen as an indispensable instrument of estate management, necessary to maintain both discipline and productivity, applicable to men and women alike. The driver,

> who is generally a Black man . . . has the power not only of stimulating the slaves under him to exertion, by application of the whip to their bodies while they are proceeding with their work, but he has the power also of prostrating them (women as

well as men) on the ground, causing them to be held down by other Negroes when he may inflict upon the bare posteriors such a number of lashes as he may deem the fault to have merited.[174]

Women were special targets of the whip, being often perceived as more difficult to handle than men.[175] Every morning delinquent slaves, either late-comers, or returning absentees, were flogged: "They were laid down in the filthiest place the driver could find . . . this was done especially to women and was the general practice throughout Jamaica."[176] Whiteley witnessed, in St Ann in 1832, the flogging of a young woman who left her field tasks ahead of her scheduled time to visit her sick child in the estate hot-house.[177] James Archer, the majority of whose slaves were women, entered in his diary on 31 March 1830, the fact that he had flogged "all [my] own people except Margaret for general idleness and bad conduct"; three days later he confined them to the stocks.[178] Idleness and low work output were cardinal crimes. Whiteley also described the punishment of two young girls who received thirty-nine lashes each because their pimento baskets were not full.[179]

Neither age nor pregnancy exempted women from corporal chastise-ment,[180] which, on estates, might be administered in the full gaze of blacks and whites, men and women.[181] Chloe, a slave of Amity Hall plantation near Savanna-la-Mar, was flogged by her overseer, Moore, for harbouring in her house, without permission, her common-law husband William Madgett, a smallpox patient. Chloe explained to the Council of Protection, before whom the matter subsequently appeared, that she felt her punishment was deserved.[182] The secretary of state, Lord Goderich, thought otherwise, and commented:

> [I]t is true that the woman avowed at the Council of Protection her opinion, that she had been justly punished, and declared that she had no complaint to make. But what does this prove except that she either did not venture to complain or had become insensible to the claims which her sex and her peculiar relation to the sick gave her upon the sympathy of those she addressed. I fear that it may be very true that in inflicting this punishment the Law of the Island was not infringed, but it is no less true that this was such an exercise of power as no man of ordinary humanity can contemplate without disgust.[183]

With the law sanctioning so much that was inhumane, inevitably a cli-mate of opinion existed in which extralegal acts of physical brutality to women were commonplace.[184] Some creole observers would not agree. Bryan Edwards, for instance, regarded the treatment of West Indian slaves as "generally mild, temperate and indulgent". If instances of cruelty did occur, he was confident that they were "universally reprobated . . . and were severely punished".[185]

Illegal offences against female slaves did appear regularly before the local courts. The charges were initiated by slave women themselves and were usually supported by other slaves, male and female. And the occasional case in which the slave woman received redress for her complaint was sufficiently publicized to satisfy the conscience of those creoles who claimed to see "the most perfect regard to impartial justice displayed at these slave trials".[186]

The Jamaica *Royal Gazette,* for example, carried a report of the case of Joseph Boyden, who was tried by jury on 19 January 1818, in the Surrey Assizes, for branding and maltreating a female Sambo slave, Amey. He was found guilty, was very severely admonished and sentenced to imprisonment for six months; the slave woman Amey was freed. Other guilty slave owners, John Batiste Cadou, in the Surrey Assize Court of 14 August 1823, and William Lee, a blacksmith, in the Grand Court of 22 October 1824, were similarly convicted, and the female slave victims granted their freedom.[187]

The main business of local courts in relation to slaves was, however, not to appease, but to control them, and the overwhelming majority of such cases dealt with offences committed, not by whites, but by blacks. Eighty cases appeared before the Port Maria Slave Court between 1806 and 1812. In three instances were the defendants free persons (one white and two free coloureds); all other defendants were slaves.[188] And when slaves did seize the initiative, as is recorded in the parish of Port Royal, for instance, between 1819 and 1834,[189] the scales of creole justice were so heavily weighted against them as to make these judicial processes, on the whole, mere travesties.

Between the years 1787 and 1812, the Kingston court of quarter sessions found twenty-two instances in which slaves had been maltreated, an average of less than one verdict of guilt per annum.[190] Twenty-one complaints of ill-treatment were brought by female slaves before the Port Royal magistrates between 1819 and 1834. In only one instance was a white defendant convicted.[191] The essential facts of creole legal and judicial systems were that magistrates were members of the white slaveholding class, and slaves could not give evidence in courts of law against whites.[192]

Attempts were made to reform both the law and its machinery in ways that might result in improved treatment of slaves and especially of female slaves. The initiative came from Westminster. The humanitarian Thomas Buxton introduced a resolution in the House of Commons in May 1823, demanding substantial reforms in West Indian slave laws leading to the gradual abolition of slavery. It included the proposal that female slaves should not be whipped. Buxton's recommendation were supported by Lord Canning, foreign secretary and leader of the House of Commons, and communicated by Lord Bathurst, the secretary for the colonies, to all the West Indian governments for local implementation.[193]

Bathurst was optimistic about achieving humane changes in the area of women's punishment. He felt that no difference of opinion existed on that subject:

> [B]eing single in its nature [it] may be at once adopted, viz., an absolute prohibition to inflict the punishment of flogging under any circumstances on female slaves. The system of ameliorating the condition of slaves to which His Majesty's Government stands pledged by these resolutions, cannot better commence than by the adoption of a principle which by making a distinction of treatment between the male and female slaves cannot fail to raise this unfortunate class generally above their present degraded level and to restore to the female slave that sense of shame which is at once the ornament of and the protection of their sex, and which their present mode of punishment has tended so unfortunately to weaken if not to obliterate.[194]

The ameliorative measures also included provision for gradually emancipating all female children born after a certain period, with a view to "the ultimate extinction of slavery progressively and almost imperceptibly at some definite and distinct period".[195]

Bathurst's optimism about the uncontroversial nature of his proposal was unjustified. Jamaica's governor advised him in November 1823 that the local House of Assembly was not interested in any substantial improvement in the condition of slaves and was emphatically not ready to put an end to the use of the whip.[196] Unlike the Crown Colony of Trinidad, for instance, which had no alternative but to accept an Order-in-Council abolishing the use of the whip on women, the independent Jamaican House of Assembly was constitutionally able to resist metropolitan pressure.[197]

The Trinidad Order-in-Council was recommended as a model to the

Jamaican Assembly in November 1824, but again the proposals it contained received a negative response.[198] Nor would it even consider the subsidiary recommendation that women's bodies should not be indecently exposed for punishment.[199] The result was that the Slave Act of 1826, ostensibly a significant measure of amelioration, excluded the recommendations either to abolish or to regulate flogging.[200]

The reason given for creole intransigency on the issue was bluntly stated by John Baillie to be "Prejudice".[201] Another observant and concerned contemporary, William Taylor, went closer to the heart of the matter. "Think," he stated, when asked his opinion on the abolition of flogging females, "that if you will have Slavery, you must have cruelty . . . if you endeavour to incorporate Humanity and Religion with the System, that will not do; the System will not take it."[202]

There were individual slave owners who voluntarily put an end to corporal punishment for women on their estates;[203] but it continued, right up until emancipation, to be a routine feature of estate management, seen by many as an inseparable aspect of the labour system.[204] Pressure was again exercised on the system in 1831 to humanize its treatment of women, and it again made clear that it was incapable of accommodating decency. But by 1831, it was almost time for the system to capitulate. The governor, on the insistence of Westminister, on 27 October 1831, brought to the attention of the Jamaica House of Assembly Lord Huskisson's despatches of 22 September 1827 and 22 March 1828 on the inadequacy of the 1826 Slave Act. Among its many shortcomings was its failure to exempt women from punishment by flogging. In this, as in other respects, "the provisions of [the] act fell short of the recommendations of his majesty's government".[205]

In an atmosphere of high black expectation of freedom and extreme white nervousness, the Assembly placed the subject on its agenda on 22 November 1831. The motion was put to the House that "a Committee be appointed to inquire and report on the Expediency of abolishing the flogging of Female Slaves". The House divided on the subject of whether the matter should be debated, and the Negroes gained an overwhelming majority of twenty-five to three in the affirmative.[206]

These proceedings took place behind closed doors but nevertheless leaked out. "Parts of the Discussion were conveyed in the usual Form to the Public at large; so that, while no actual concealment was observed the attempted secrecy rendered the whole proceeding obnoxious to vague and alarming suspicions."[207]

The white establishment attempted to divide the movement for freedom by finding the male slave chauvinist to support its stand.[208] But feelings against the flogging of women, which had always seemed an outrage to male and female slaves alike,[209] were not easily diverted.

The legislature's obstinacy on the issue triggered off "much excitement".[210] It added fuel to the fire of black unrest, which exploded in December 1831, spelling the end of slavery. Attempts to reform the judicial machinery dealing with the ill-treatment of slaves proved as futile as attempts to abolish flogging. The Consolidated Slave Act of 1792 had confirmed the procedure by which the slave suffering from physical abuse had the right to apply to any justice of the peace, who could authorize protective custody for the complainant in the nearest work house, at which time they could constitute themselves a Council of Protection to examine the charges. After full examination of the circumstances, including examination of the slave's physical condition, the Council could order prosecution in the Supreme Court or in the Assizes. An accused found guilty could be fined up to £100 or imprisoned for a period not exceeding twelve months. The injured slave, for his or her future protection, might be declared free.[211]

Two major factors obstructed the impartial administration of this process. For the greater part of the period of slavery, the evidence of a slave was inadmissible in a court of law against whites. This was in fact seen, even by members of the creole plantocracy, as the "great" defect of slavery. It was, in addition, regarded as "incurable".[212] Moreover, local justices, vestrymen and jurymen were either appointees or members of the slaveholding classes, whose prejudices were deeply entrenched. Legal redress for slaves was known to be difficult, especially in some districts of the island, "where the Council of Protection was composed of the intimate Friends and Associates of the accused Party".[213]

Bathurst's reform measures of 1823 reflected some concern for these defects.[214] His recommendation in relation to slave evidence was, however, limited to cases in which the crime against the slave was punishable by death. His proposal to replace the Council of Protection by a protector or guardian of slaves, such as was instituted in Trinidad by an Order-in-Council in 1824, was more substantial.[215] It would have established "an independent functionary", neither slave owner nor slave manager, who would have the potential for making the law less of "a dead letter" than it was.[216] Neither of these measures was, however, acceptable to the Jamaican establishment.[217]

No improvement in the treatment of women was discernible in the later period of slavery. Her condition, in fact, may even have worsened. British colonial officials sensed, for instance, reactionary elements in the last of the slave codes, that of 1831. Viscount Goderich, the secretary for the colonies, pointed out to the governor of Jamaica, on 10 June 1831, a turn of phrase in the new law which seemed to reflect a "less humane" approach to the women. Whereas the 1826 law exempted mothers of six living children "from all hard labour in the Field or otherwise", they were, by the equivalent 1831 clause, "exempted merely from hard labour".[218]

It is not improbable that a hardening of creole attitudes towards slave women did occur in the latter decades of slavery, proportionate with their increasing numerical dominance of the labour force and the plantation's reliance on their reproductive capacities to sustain that labour force. The black woman was, under neonatal "ameliorative" policies, a main recipient of the indulgences that the period grudgingly afforded slave mothers, evidence of her critical role in agricultural output. She was not only a costly work-unit, she could hold the estate to ransom by not working or not breeding. The slave woman, strategically placed after abolition to confound the expectations of the outer plantation, could not hope to escape the full brunt of its frustration.

It is significant, for instance, that Whiteley, who witnessed twenty floggings of slaves in the year 1832 in St Ann, recorded one case in which the punishment exceeded the legal limit of thirty-nine strokes. That case was of an elderly woman, married, the mother of several children, who received fifty lashes and the stocks for allegedly having stolen a fowl.[219]

The most highly publicized cases of slave brutality occurred in the last years of slavery, and in most cases the victims were women. The case of Kitty Hylton, a slave belonging to the Reverend Bridges of the parish of St Ann, was infamous:[220] Bridge's vindictiveness and violence towards her reduced her to a physical condition that led one witness, a white man, to declare that he had never seen "a woman so ill-treated".[221] Bridges nevertheless was completely exonerated by the creole magistrates who heard the case in May 1829. From his position in Downing Street, Goderich, who found no extenuation for Bridge's "repeated and persevering cruelty", could "only lament that the ends of justice have been defeated and that the crime of Mr Bridges must be left unpunished".[222]

The case of Eleanor James classically illustrated the futility of attempts, either by statutory or by customary machinery, to ensure justice for the enslaved in a slave society. Eleanor James was an elderly female slave, attached to Low Ground estate in Clarendon, the property of James Wildman. Accompanied by another slave woman, Joanna Williams, Eleanor James on 28 November 1829 went to a nearby estate, North Hall, to collect payment for a pig which she had sold to the proprietor, one McDonald. The latter instructed two of his drivers to flog her; she was afterwards raised and washed with salt pickle. The next day McDonald sent her two dollars and ordered her to leave the property.[223] Joanna Williams subsequently swore that she watched the beating in concealment and counted two hundred lashes being administered.[224]

Eleanor James sought redress through the Council of Protection, which made three abortive efforts to convene between January and March 1830. It finally met on 19 April and resolved that "the subject matter is not properly cognizable by the Council of Protection". The Council advised that Eleanor James's owner had recourse to action against the drivers responsible for the punishment, either in the slave court or by indictment in the grand court.[225]

William Taylor, who was James Wildman's attorney, attempted an indictment against the two drivers by means of the only accessible legal witness, McDonald's sister, who had seen the incident and had tried to intervene but, before her deposition could be taken, "she had sailed for Great Britain". Attempts to produce another witnesses, McLeavy, a young white man, who had been present at the beating, also failed: McLeavy "professed utter ignorance of the material points".[226]

Taylor in reviewing the circumstances re-emphasized the fact that "so long as slave evidence is rejected by law, the slave has scarcely the shadow of protection from ill-treatment".[227] Goderich concluded, from his examination of Eleanor James's case, that "a stronger illustration can scarcely be supposed of the inefficiency of the law in force in Jamaica for the protection of slaves by the instrumentality of a numerous and irresponsible Council".[228]

In the following year, yet another case of brutality to women provided an even stronger illustration. The custos of Port Royal and senior magistrate,

Mr Jackson, and his wife, reacted most viciously towards a domestic slave in their household, who in very strong language, objected to a harsh beating given her daughter (also a domestic slave) by Mrs Jackson. The custos and Mrs Jackson then inflicted on mother and daughter a campaign of excessive beatings, combined with field work and confinement in the stocks, sustained over a period of nearly six months, from January to June 1831.[229] As a result of the women's official complaint, Jackson, as custos, appointed his brother, a junior magistrate, to investigate the circumstances. The women reluctantly stated their case before him. He recommended its referral to a Council of Protection, while at the same time declaring the charges "vexatious and frivolous". The Council – of local magistrates who all owed their appointments to the custos – met on 11 June and found that no sufficient grounds existed for prosecution: "neither the Letter nor the Spirit of the Law had been infringed" and "the Duration of the Punishment was not limited by Law". A good deal was made by the Council of the "insolent and indecorous language" of the complainants.[230]

The governor then ordered the attorney general to prefer a bill of indictment, which met the customary stumbling block of the inadmissibility of slave evidence. The grand jury, on 1 August, claimed to have no substantive facts relating to the alleged charges and ignored the bill.[231]

Viscount Goderich stated disbelief that "in the contracted society of Jamaica, the grand jury was unaware of so remarkable an occurrence"; that is, "Perseverance for several months together in Cruelties of the most scandalous character. . . . [O]ne of the offenders was the Chief Magistrate of the District, the other was the Magistrate's Wife." Goderich strongly condemned as well the Council of Protection, whose members had dismissed the charges brought before them "with a sentence full of harsh Expressions respecting the conduct of the injured Party".[232]

Both the Council's and the grand jury's actions in relation to the injured slave woman reflected the white creole regard of her. The image of the black female as an easy target for physical humiliation was so deep-seated and pervasive that it penetrated the attitudes of many more than the Bridges, McDonalds and Jacksons of the society.[233] It underlay and influenced any attempts made to eliminate the particular indignity of flogging to which she was constantly subjected and which no existing judicial machinery could restrain.

Sexual exploitation and violence were also inescapable features of the black woman's condition. Although the rewards to the female slave for cohabiting with white males were, by creole standards, considerable and must have induced many women into voluntary associations, the element of coercion was nevertheless a very real one.[234] Slave women who objected to the sexual advances of masters/overseers/drivers were subject to victimization and physical abuse.[235] "Punishment was not confined to the resisting female herself, but was extended to her parents and relatives and especially when they were suspected to encourage her to retain her chastity inviolate."[236]

Until the last few years of slavery, there was no redress against sexual attack for slave women in the courts. The law against carnal abuse and rape that operated in Jamaica was the statute of 18 Elizabeth ch. 7.[237] It protected only those females who were white and/or free. The earliest record of its application to Jamaica dated back to 1731. The rape trials which took place subsequently involved only white persons. It was not until April 1817 at the Surrey assizes that, for the first time, an indictment was heard implicating a white man and a slave. The prisoner was acquitted and the question of the application of the law did not arise.[238]

In 1822, Thomas Simpson, a white planter of Fyffes Pen in St Elizabeth, was tried in the Cornwall Assizes, convicted and sentenced to hang for committing rape on the body of a female slave child under ten years of age.[239] Simpson petitioned for mercy, and the attorney general, William Surge, together with the chief justice, William Scarlett, examined the legality of the trial and the sentence. They concluded that the English statute in use had no force in Simpson's case, as the victim was a slave.[240] Scarlett voiced his concern that no provision existed in the colony's laws for an offence of such magnitude.[241] Burge recommended that "a legislative remedy might be obtained for such a defect in our criminal code".[242]

This, as it turned out, was the only legislative reform, out of many ameliorative measures proposed in 1823, which the Jamaican Assembly was prepared to concede without a struggle.[243] The governor in Council consented in 1823 to the bill "to take away clergy from offenders in rape on slaves".[244] In 1826, it was enacted in the Jamaican slave laws "as a consequence of Simpson's case" that offences of carnal knowledge and rape committed on female slaves were punishable by death.[245]

7 The Black Woman

Agency, Identity and Voice

NOT JUST A WORK UNIT: WOMEN'S AGENCY

The reality of the black slave woman has been overshadowed by the monolithic structure of the plantation that defined her working life. It has been further negated by orthodox historiography, which has been largely masculine and white. Her vital role in the epic of black Jamaica's survival and growth has consequently been unchronicled, and her right to her own identity unacknowledged. In the age of black New World self-awareness, which contains important elements of creative feminism,[1] her historical significance can now make valid claims for reinstatement. From these perspectives, one reviews the conventional sources of Caribbean history, which open up new emphases and new interpretations relating to her. One also looks to the world of the slaves' inner experience, wherever it reveals itself, for further evidence of her functioning, not as work unit, but as woman.

The black woman asserted in a variety of ways that, beyond the boundaries of the estate, she had another life. It was a life which was lived in cultural antithesis to that of the white plantation. In the one, she was a fixed unit of labour and breeder of units of labour; in the other, she could be a dynamic producer/entrepreneur/person.

Of necessity, that black world kept its secrets to itself; they are only now beginning to be decoded. As new disciplines and new insights come imaginatively to grips with these codes and, hopefully, begin to shift the parameters of traditional historiography, the complex language of Afro-Caribbean culture begins to surface.[2] As it does, it increasingly reveals a black mass communications media of word, drum, horn, chant and dance refined to near perfection in order to ensure the viability of the enslaved community.

The woman was always central to the preservation of that community. It was clear that she did not see herself throughout that process as static and devoid of choice. Her capacity for action, reaction and aggression held firm in the face of determined white domination. She was among the most articulate in the slave community and used to great effect what an exasperated West Indian official described as "that powerful instrument of attack and defence [her] tongue, which is exerted in insufferable insult".[3] It was the noise and quarrelsomeness of the female slave virago that provided the rationalization for those who insisted that without the threat of the whip, field women were uncontrollable.

Some of the more trying cases of slave management with which Matthew Lewis dealt on his Jamaican visits in 1812 and 1815 concerned the hot-tempered and sharp-tongued slave "vixens", for whom words became pointed means of self-assertion.[4] Records of slave trials confirm the incidence of female verbal aggressiveness. Of 150 cases, in which slave women appeared at the Port Royal Slave Courts between 1819 and 1834, 42 cases involved language offences, described as "indecent", "scandalous", "outrageous", "insulting", "abusive", "threatening"; they were directed against free persons, coloured and white.[5]

Mary and Betty of Round Hill estate were tried on 4 April 1820 for behaving "rudely" and "contemptuously" to the overseer. Betty was sentenced to four months' confinement with hard labour. Maria was given "a good character" and was admonished to behave better in future.[6] Clementina displayed her disrespect for her betters even in the courtroom. She was found guilty on 20 August 1832 of using abusive language to a free person and was given thirty days' hard labour. When sentence was passed on her, she used such "contemptuous language" that she was given an additional punishment of thirty lashes.[7]

Women created and led one of the most important forms of black verbal expression: the song.[8] They used this medium as they worked in the fields, with artistry, often with malice, making penetrating statements about themselves or heaping pure ridicule on the whites.[9] "The style of singing among the Negroes", wrote William Beckford, "is uniform, and this is confined to the women; for the men very seldom, excepting upon extraordinary occasions, are ever heard to join in chorus."[10]

Women knew the subjects of their songs well:

> New-come buckra
> He get sick,
> He tak fever
> He be die
> He be die
> New-come buckra.[11]

They revelled in exposure of buckra's other frailties:

> Hi! de Buckra, hi!
> You sabby what for he da cross de sea
> Wid him long white face and him twinkling yeye.
> He lub, make lub, as he preach to we,
> He fall on his knees, but he pray for me,
>
> Hi! de Buckra, hi!
> Massa w-f-e da come ober de sea,
> Wid him roguish heart and him tender look,
> And while he palaver and preach him book,
> At the negro girl hi'll winkie him yeye.
> Hi! de Buckra, hi![12]

But they also satirized their own impossible condition:

> If me want for go in a Ebo
> Me can't go there!
> Since dem tief me from a Guinea,
> Me can't go there!
>
> If me want for go in a Congo,
> Me can't go there!
> Since dem tief me from my fatta
> Me can't go there!
>
> If me want for go in a Kingston,
> Me can't go there!
> Since massa go in a England
> He can't go there.[13]

To be immobilized, however, was not to be silenced.

> Tink dere is a God in a top
> No use me ill, Obisha!
> Me no horse, me no mare, me no mule,
> No use me ill, Obisha.[14]

Slaves knew that their strength lay in numbers and generally displayed "a most lively *esprit de corps* whenever anyone [was] illegally punished or oppressed.[15] Their manner of address in such cases, Cynric Williams maintained, was sometimes almost "bordering on impudence".[16] Slave mothers, in particular, had many grievances in common, and the chorus of "the Picaninny Mothers"[17] clamouring for redress was not easily subdued.

Blacks were "most tenacious and jealous of their rights",[18] and black women in a body insistently besieged the local courts for their due. On 8 April 1823, eighteen slaves from Dallas Castle plantation in the parish of Port Royal, fifteen of whom were women, complained to the justices of the slave court that they had been severely and cruelly treated by the overseer of the property. The magistrate's investigations revealed that two female slaves, Elizabeth Craig and Margaret Dallas, had had inflicted on them more flogging than the slave law permitted. The overseer was fined £20 for each offence.[19]

Bessy Chambers's case against Mr Prudden, overseer of New Layton estate, was presented by twenty-four slaves from her estate before the magistrate at the St George's General Slave Court on 6 June 1823. They accused the overseer of having had her so excessively punished as to cause a miscarriage. After hearing the bookkeeper's evidence, the magistrate declared that there was "no certain proof of Bessy Chambers having been in a state of pregnancy and no evidence of her miscarriage". The case was dismissed, and three of the male slave complainants were sentenced to two weeks' hard labour and thirty-nine lashes each.[20]

Female slave complainants responded quickly to injustices. At the Buff Bay Court, on 23 July 1826, a group of slaves from Windsor Castle estate lodged a complaint of oppressive treatment to the magistrate Kirkland against their overseer, Saunders. Kirkland persuaded the slaves that their charge was not serious, and they agreed to return to work. On the following day, when they turned out in the field, Saunders selected a number of those

238 — A Historical Study of Women in Jamaica

who had reported him and had them punished, including the slave women Eliza Oliver, Susan Irvine, Cardina Wilson and Harriet Buckmaster. They promptly returned to the court with their grievance and Kirkland reprimanded Saunders for

> causing [the slaves] to fear that they have no right of appeal . . . in cases of grievances or conceived ill-usage. We have communicated to the complainants their right of application of redress to any magistrate, always bearing in mind that they will be held liable and subject to punishment by the magistrate in cases of wanton and fault accusations.[21]

No doubt aware that the odds were heavily against them, female slaves nevertheless exercised "their rights of application for redress". In twenty-one cases of grievances lodged by women slaves against their overseers or owners in the Port Royal courts in 1820s, eighteen were thrown out as being "trifling", "groundless", "fault" or "malicious". The complainants in a few instances were discharged. The majority were punished by flogging, imprisonment or both. Only in three cases did the complainant appear alone in court; approximately 170 slaves were involved in these twenty-one group appeals to law.[22] They achieved virtually nothing in terms of legal remedies. The appeals were significant as demonstrations of black solidarity, giving, in particular to the slave woman, the certain group base of her black sisters, and brothers, from which to claim justice. They were evidence too of the potential, at times the effectiveness, of black verbal skills for obstructing the operations of the plantation. Complaining slaves, large numbers of whom were women, took up the magistrates' time and forced owners and overseers to appear in court and answer for their actions. While these proceedings lasted, precious labour was lost. The nuisance value to the white establishment was incalculable.

Not surprisingly, at least one slave owner retaliated. Mr Wilson of Good Hope estate was the complainant before the Port Royal court on 19 October 1833: the accused were his nineteen slaves, of whom ten were women. They had left the property, without his permission, to accompany an aggrieved member of their group to a previous sitting of the court. The magistrates considered it necessary to take punitive action. He selected two men and two women as examples. The men received twenty lashes, the women ten days' hard labour; the rest were reprimanded.[23]

The records give the occasional fleeting glimpse of someone who might have been a female ringleader of dissension, for example, Dido. She was among a group of slave mothers appearing as complainants against the trustees of Orchard Plantation on 4 December 1820. Their charges were dismissed. Five weeks later, Dido, this time alone, was harassing the courts for "having been severely flogged and otherwise ill-treated". On the evidence of "two of the white persons belonging to the property", the accusation was found to be "untrue . . . the complainant was a very bad character" and was, as a result, sentenced to fourteen days' hard labour, on the expiry of which she was to receive twenty-four lashes.[24] In the Windsor Castle fracas of 23 July 1826, the overseer, Saunders, maintained that the particular women whom he had singled out for punishment had been the instigators of the group complaint made about him to the magistrate on the previous day.[25]

Slave women, at times, did not hesitate to down their tools.[26] On 26 January 1812, the women on Matthew Lewis's estate went on strike:

> It seems that this morning, the women, one and all, refused to carry away the trash (which is one of the easiest tasks that can be set), and without the slightest pretence: in consequence, the mill was obliged to be stopped, and when the driver on that station insisted on their doing their duty, a little fierce young devil of a Miss Whaunica flew at his throat and endeavoured to strangle him: the agent was obliged to be called in, and at length, this petticoat rebellion was subdued and everything went on as usual.[27]

But this was not the last of the work stoppages with which the women confronted Lewis. On the very next day, he had yet another "petticoat rebellion", and it took him a long lecturing to "the most obstinate and insolent of the women"[28] before they could be persuaded to return to work.

The slave woman's withdrawal of her labour was usually more subtle. She became mistress of the art of malingering, joining the large number of slaves who daily challenged slaveholders to deal with the problem of "a lilly pain here, Massa" or of "a bad pain we know nowhere, Massa".[29]

Matthew Lewis again fell victim to this form of plantation sabotage:

> On Saturday morning there were no fewer than forty-five persons (not including children) in the hospital; which makes nearly a fifth of my whole gang. Of these, the medical people assured me that not above seven had anything whatever the matter with them, the rest were only feigning sickness out of mere idleness, and in order to

sit doing nothing, while their companions were forced to perform their part of the estate-duty. And sure enough, on Sunday morning they all walked away from the hospital to amuse themselves, except about seven or eight: they will, perhaps, go to the field for a couple of days; and on Wednesday we may expect to have them back again, complaining of pains, which (not existing) it is not possible to remove. Jenny (the girl whose hands were bitten) was told by the doctress, that having been in the hospital all the week, she ought not, for very shame, to go out on Sunday. She answered, "She wanted to go to the mountains, and go she would." "Then," said the doctress, "you must not come back again on Monday at least." "Yes", Jenny said, "she should come back;" and back this morning Jenny came. But as her wounds were almost completely well, she had tied packthread round them so as to cut deep into the flesh, rubbed dirt into them and in short, had played such tricks as nearly to produce a mortification in one of her fingers.[30]

In self-defence, the slave owner tried out strategies for cutting down on hospital picnics:

> I directed the head-driver to announce, that the presents which I had brought from England should be distributed to-day, that the new-born children should be christened, and that the Negroes might take possession of my house, and amuse themselves till twelve at night. The effect of my prescription was magical; two thirds of the sick were hale and hearty, at work in the field on Saturday morning, and to-day not a soul remained in the hospital except the four serious cases.[31]

Planters exaggerated the extent to which slaves either pretended illness or made themselves and their children ill in order to avoid work. The majority of bondsmen and bondswomen were so greatly overworked, ill-fed and generally physically abused, that there was a high proportion who were either genuinely sick or chronically weak. This situation obviously could be – and was – exploited by them. Feminine biology aided women in devising subversive techniques which were uniquely theirs and which were devastating to the estates' operations. Few female acts caused as much irritation to managers as the slave woman's failure to wean her baby in accordance with the estate's timetable. While nursing she was entitled to extra food allowances and time off at regular intervals from the field in order to feed her infant.[32] But the planter, anxious for her maximum work output, offered counter rewards for speeding up weaning. The black mother was, however, not easily tempted to give up suckling her child and regularly nursed it for periods of two to three years.[33] John Baillie testified in 1832 that he had promised his nursing mothers two dollars each for weaning their infants within twelve months, "and I see by my returns that since 1807 not one has applied for these two dollars".[34]

Women were even prepared to use local legal machinery for retaining their maternal rights in this respect. On 14 December 1820, the slave women Dido, Lizzy, Augusta and Yuba, who belonged to Orchard plantation, complained to the magistrate of the Port Royal Slave Court that the trustees of the property had directed their children to be taken from them and weaned from the breast. The women declared that the babies "were too young for weaning". The court's findings were that "the whole of the children were at least twelve months old each, the women were reprimanded and directed to proceed back to the property to work".[35]

The black woman no doubt sensibly assessed the value of late weaning to the physical and emotional well-being of her infant and herself. Prolonged breastfeeding was a meaningful affirmation of womanhood. It was as well a weapon in the female protest armoury, not only because of the work exemption which it earned her, but because of its likely depressive influence on her fertility. Modern research on lactation as a factor in population control confirms that this "primitive form of birth control"[36] contains a high probability of effectiveness. "There is a considerable basis of fact in the view that conception is unlikely as long as lactation proceeds."[37] Both Anglo- and Afro-Jamaicans would have known this well.[38]

In so far as her work environment, especially on the sugar estate, was hostile to childbearing and child rearing, the black woman's reproductive functions fell involuntary victim to the plantation regime. But this did not entirely rule out some conscious exercise of will in this area of her life; and within the limits of the knowledge available to her at that time, she probably practised abortion as well as lengthy breastfeeding, as matters of choice.

Spontaneous miscarriages must have been frequent among female slaves,[39] and especially those in the field gangs. But induced abortions seemed also to have been widespread;[40] and the midwife, who was held in such suspicion in the estate hospital, came into her own in the slave quarters, where she was chief manipulator of black birth processes. She was a person of authority. "She belonged", according to Roughley, to "a most fearful fraternity".[41] Midwives were said "to impress by the nature of their office . . . such an awe and reverence for them on the minds of all classes of slaves, that few practising doctors wish to encounter them, or to be called in to assist at a birth, or give relief to a female slave in travail, which those harpies attend".[42]

Sir M. Clare, MD, testified to the "very general perpetration of Abortion by the Midwives". He witnessed in one instance the effective administering by a midwife of "the wild Cassava, which is a Drastic of the most violent kind" to a young woman who was two or three months' pregnant. He described the midwife involved as an African who, having been in Jamaica a long time, was then passing as a creole.[43] The midwife, or grandee, as she was called, epitomized the fact that the black population never ceded total control of its life processes to the white plantation.[44] Whether the slave woman interrupted her pregnancies in her own personal interest or in order to frustrate the estate's labour needs, the effect was the same: the proprietor was touched in his most vulnerable spot. Matthew Lewis owned more than 150 women on his Cornwall estate. They were, he claimed,

> all well clothed and well fed, contented in mind . . . overworked at no time and when upon the breeding list [were] exempted from labour of every kind . . . In spite of all this and their being treated with all possible care and indulgence, rewarded for bringing children, and therefore anxious to have them, how they manage it so ill I know not, but somehow or other certainly the children do not come.[45]

Women's physical make-up and maternal responsibilities may have limited their participation in some forms of black assertion. The records do not give evidence of their extensive participation in plots and conspiracies that involved armed uprising. The case of Venus of the parish of St George in 1824 stands out. Along with eight men, she was concerned "in a rebellious conspiracy to kill and murder the white inhabitants and to subvert and destroy the present government". All the conspirators were found guilty, some were sentenced to hang, others, including Venus, were transported for life.[46]

In the great slave uprising of western Jamaica in 1831, which shook the island's establishment and was a precursor of emancipation, some female rebels were identified as incendiaries. One woman at Palmyra estate surrendered with her male accomplice:[47] and she may have been one of the two women who were tried and convicted in the Montego Bay Court on 2 January 1832.[48] Major General Cotton described them as being among "some villainous Ringleaders, who have proved to have been the most active Incendiaries".[49] Two men had their sentence of execution immediately carried out; the "Women [were] respited till Pleasure".[50] Yet another female incendiary, whose husband, her co-conspirator, had been shot, was tried on the following day.[51] Richard Barrett, the custos of St James, regretted that the life of a female activist should be spared, as "I think she should be hanged".[52]

Women may have helped to provide a front for the male strategists while they organized. Investigations into the mutiny of black troops of the Second West India regiment on 27 May 1808 uncovered activities centred on the Negro dance halls and yards of Kingston. They were frequented by male and female slaves and by free Negroes, who made merry while the mutineers in their midst planned subversion.[53]

The woman's initiative in plots was more likely to be aimed at the individual free person, and she was often well placed to do mischief in the white household. Matthew Lewis declared that "the negroes' worst fault was the facility with which they are frequently induced to poison to the right hand and to the left".[54]

Poisoning appeared to have been fairly widely practised by blacks and even more widely feared by whites.[55] It could be the very nearly perfect crime. Creole lifestyles offered blacks and coloureds maximum access to vulnerable whites. Tropical diseases could be so sudden and mysterious, diagnoses so uncertain, that death by foul means was not always easily detected. The suspected as well as the proven cases of poisoning must have served to keep white terror alive.

It was, for instance, alleged that Caroline Biggs, a black slave woman of Lenox estate in St George, "willfully, maliciously, and feloniously did put verdigris into the Decanter of Rum on the sideboard of the Dwelling House with intent to poison Thomas Spicer, Attorney of the estate and the inhabitants of the Dwelling House". No prosecutor appeared, however, and she was discharged.[56]

The Port Maria Slave Court in St Mary, between July 1807 and August 1808, convicted five slaves for attempting to poison white persons. Damsel and Sarah, together with a male slave, were found guilty of giving poison to Thomas Hettington and were transported off the island for life. Two separate attempts were made on the life of a planter Robert Hazzard: one by a mulatto slave Molly, who was tried and convicted on 21 April 1807, for putting poison in his rice, and the other, Baker, a Negro woman who poisoned peas soup for the same victim and was similarly convicted on 29 August 1808. Both women were sentenced to hang.[57]

Physical manifestations of aggressiveness in women appeared more in individuals, or small groups, rather than in organized concerted action, and were quite extensive. As with verbal violence, they were directed at free people, some of whom were whites, but the majority of whom were free coloureds.[58] In the relatively high proportion of urban cases in the Port Royal samples of 1819 to 1834, a thin line seemed to be drawn between individual aggression and civil disorder, and "rudeness" was often escalated into "riotousness". Venus, Hannah and Sandy were charged with "riotous" conduct on the streets on 18 November 1820, Hannah and Harriet similarly on 17 July 1821; all were warned to keep the peace. Dido, Else and Betsey, caught misbehaving in the latter part of December of that year, were accused of being "riotous" and were locked up for five days. Grace's and Jackey's "riotous" behaviour at night was regarded rather more seriously, and on 12 September 1826, the courts sentenced them to three weeks' hard labour.[59]

Harmless-seeming acts of black self-expression produced nervous reactions from the white establishment. Rosanna, Phoebe, Else, Mary and Fanny, who joined male slaves in beating drums and dancing in the slave yard at night, were charged for these activities and reprimanded by the magistrates.[60]

Next to the armed rebel, perhaps the most dangerous black activist was the runaway.[61] The slave who "pulled foot", for whatever reason, made one of the strongest statements during slavery about his or her rights as a viable human being. Runaways represented those slaves who had the maximum motivation and the maximum number of opportunities for seeking a free life, whether temporarily or permanently. Women with children had natural limits imposed on their mobility. But equally important was the fact that slaves without skills, the majority of whom were women, had the least economic hopes of making it in an open system. And in this latter respect, data on runaways demonstrates the extent to which the slave woman's occupation of chief field worker influenced not only her current existence, but also her future prospects for escaping that existence.

Schuler has done a breakdown of the 514 slave runaways who were either advertised for by their owners or were listed in the island's gaols between

Table 7.1   Sex Distribution of Runaways, 1 May 1779–1 April 1780

Gender	Numbers	
Adult males	379	
Adult females	107	
Young boys	17	
Young girls	2	
Children who accompanied mothers		5 boys
		1 girl
		3 sex unspecified

Sources: Monica Schuler, "Slave Resistance and Rebellion in the Caribbean during the Eighteenth Century" (seminar paper, Department of History, University of the West Indies, 1966), 74. Compare Higman's findings for the period 1829–1832: of 124 slaves transported for running away in these years, 13 were females; of 255 committed to work houses, 29 were females ("Slave Population and Economy in Jamaica at the Time of Emancipation" [PhD diss., University of the West Indies, 1970], 201–3, tables 31 and 32).

1 May 1779 and 1 April 1780. The sex distribution is shown in table 7.1. The occupations of 55 of these runaways were indicated: they covered a variety of skills; only 5, however, were listed as field slaves.[62]

With the weight of the plantation pressing the woman down into a state of permanent subjection, the phenomenon of the female runaway is remarkable. Numbers of them throughout slavery still managed to get out from under it, fled, and featured prominently in Jamaica's fugitive population as bold and resourceful persons.

Runaways were individualists, who dared to move out of the regimentation and anonymity of the plantation. But their enterprise was grounded in the whole complex of a black subculture whose intricate communications system sustained the runaway and made escape a feasible alternative to enslavement. Ostensibly without subterfuge, some mothers with their children braved the free world together. Well-known local personalities brazenly risked exposure. Husbands headed for their wives' estates and vice versa. But art and subtlety were clearly present, for forged documents and changed identities were not unusual. The hiding places of runaways were often known to their owners, but this did not guarantee capture. Slaves were in touch with each other the length and breath of the island, and distances seemed to vanish once they were in flight. An identifiable black under-ground existed, and it functioned effectively. Women helped to make it, and a relatively small, but nevertheless significant, number of them used it.

Runaways included females of all ages. Sally, a child of six, was taken up at Passage Fort in March 1780, while running away from her owner to find her mother in Kingston.[63] Princess was a black teenaged girl of the Mongola country, who originally came from Kingston, but was being harboured on a sugar estate in the parish of St George.[64] The *Royal Gazette* reported that "a little humped-back old woman, marked on both breasts, A.M. speaks no English, owner and country unknown, 4 feet 6½ inches high", was held in 1791 in the Morant Bay work house as a runaway;[65] that Betsey Bennett, alias Elizabeth Anderson, a young creole black woman, who was held in the St Andrew's work house in October 1829, referred to three past owners. She gave "an indifferent account of herself, and stated that she had been a run-away from a child".[66]

The female runaway was often described as "artful" or "plausible", imply-ing resourcefulness and a facility with words (spoken and sometimes writ-ten), which were assets in the free world where she might be required at any time to explain her presence. The *Royal Gazette* tells us that

> a Sambo Woman, named Hannah Phillips, about 45 years of age . . . was often seen in the parish of St David and its vicinity. Also her daughter, Nancy McNeil, a Mulatto, about 21 years of age . . . The above Slaves will endeavour to pass them-selves as free persons, and are very artful in using fictitious names.[67]

Mary Ann Shaw, from an estate in St Thomas-in-the-East, was allegedly using another name,[68] and Jane Brown of Quebec Castle in St Mary was sup-posedly a cover for Eliza James of Dover Castle in St Thomas-in-the-Vale.[69] The "creole black woman named Benny, alias Benneba", exploited available escape techniques. She originated in Kingston, where her owner advertised for her on 17 September 1813.[70] She was well known in St Thomas-in-the-East, where she had relatives and a husband, who were supposed to be har-bouring her. She had been seen vending goods between Morant Bay and Manchioneal and had made use of an old letter, which was addressed to her ex-owner, to protect herself from being taken up.

Mental alertness and job expertise were valued qualifications for survival in the open society. We are told that the washerwoman, "Friendship, a short stout wench, rather elderly", was "well known in Kingston", but nevertheless eluded capture.[71] So did "Nelly of the Chamba country", who was a baker by trade, and who presumably might have been identified by her yellow complexion and "her country marks on her face".[72] "[A] Creole negro Girl, named Fanny, yellow skin, slim made, has lost some of her upper front teeth, stutters occasionally, . . . is an excellent seamstress"[73] was also among the runaways.

John Spencer's black slave woman, Esther, was obviously well equipped for an independent life. She was

> 37 years of age, a very good seamstress and washerwoman . . . has been frequently seen at the house of Mr Robert Pitcairn senior in this town, who was paid the Subscriber [that is, John Spencer] hire for the said negro named Esther; she is well known in this town Kingston, and Port Royal where she has practised hiring herself out without the subscriber's consent.[74]

When opportunities for mobility presented themselves, women like Esther seized them; and although the existence of the jobbing slave, especially the rural jobbing slave, could be harsh and uncertain, it could also be a tempting invitation to take flight. Its risks were seen by slave owners. The King sisters of Portland, who kept a watching brief on their absent sister's slaves, were always nervous about the quasi-independent lifestyle of slaves who hired out. Susan, Elenor, Jane, Ann and Bell were left behind by Isabella King to earn their wages. They wandered about at large in Port Antonio, fast becoming uncontrollable. They did "very little, having no supervision . . . and pretended to be sick almost all the time". Their owner's agents had difficulty in collecting wages from them. Bell, for instance, paid nothing for eighteen months, "pretending to be sick and taking care of her children". Jane had been "selling cakes and bread in the street", which was a source of great distress to the family: they doubted that she could ever be "a serviceable servant again" for "as a breadseller she would be utterly ruined".[75]

It was an easy step from freelancing to freedom. A black girl named Esther, when advertised for by her owner in July 1817, had already been gone for two years. She was of a very yellow complexion, about 20 years of age, and well known in this city [that is, Kingston] for vending Cakes and Pies. She is full breasted, and has the mark of X on each side of her cheeks, occasioned by the rind of a cashew nut. She has lately changed her name to that of Nancy, and is supposed to be about Stony-Hill.[76]

Sally Williams had fled nearly a year previously from her owner in the parish of St Andrews, before she was advertised for. She too was "well known in Kingston, having been employed for several years in selling vegetables and fruit". She was supposed to be harboured by a black man on an estate in Blue Mountain Valley in St Thomas-in-the-East.[77]

The professional mobility of the higgler put her in easy touch with would-be runaways. The case of the creole black girl Sue, alias Susanna, illustrates this. She was about fifteen years old and was originally from Kingston, but was purchased by a new owner who lived in St George. She was apparently enticed back to the city by a Sambo girl, a higgler, "who lives in St George's Lane, Kingston, with whom she was seen on the road to Town; and it is strongly suspected she knows where the said girl is secreted".[78]

Runaways were able to cover long distances because they had points of contact all along the escape routes. The harbouring of the fugitive, whether a relative or not, was an accepted fact of black lifestyle. Only communal and/or kinship feeling of a high degree would, for instance, have made possible the trans-island survival of Margaret, alias Amey, and her family. They had absconded from the far-western parish of Hanover sometime in 1812 and had found their way to Kingston, over a hundred miles away. The group included Margaret,

> a black woman, slender make, large eyes, prominent forehead and a straight nose, and marked GH or MH; Eliza Arnold, her daughter, a slender black girl with very large eyes, and thin visage, without any mark. Richard McLeod son of Margaret or Amey, aged 18 years, about five feet five inches high, large eyes, thick lips, the remains of a wen under one of his ears.

The trio was described as "very plausible" and "concealed somewhere in the neighbourhood of Kingston, where they probably will pass themselves as free people".[79]

A young female runaway, Grace, and her five-year-old son, John Elkins, from the parish of St Mary, were also receiving sanctuary somewhere in Kingston.[80] So was the slim black girl Lean, from St Elizabeth, who had been apparently caught, but was "rescued by a negro man", and was hiding out with relatives in the city.[81] The creole woman Fanny, from a St Andrew's estate, was being harboured by her husband on another estate in the same parish.[82]

Slaves who gave food and shelter to escapees knew the risk and penalties which they incurred. Women, as well as men, faced the courts for harbouring:[83] Fanny, of the parish of St Elizabeth, who was tried on 24 April 1810 for concealing the slave Belmore, "knowing him to be a runaway", was lucky to be acquitted.[84]

Female audacity found full expression in the world of escape. At least one bold woman took part in a work house break: "Madam, a creole 5 feet 2½ inches, thick lips, no mark", joined a party of nine men in escaping through a window from the Morant Bay work house, where they were being held as runaways.[85]

The garrison at Fort Augusta attracted adventurous women. In August 1813, the local press reported the presence in the Kingston work house of nearly seventy black and other runaway women who had been found in the barracks. Fort Augusta was condemned as having been "for several years . . . a great nuisance to all the neighbouring properties, from the numbers of runaway women continually harboured in it, some of whom are at this moment under sentence of transportation for having absented themselves from their owners for years".[86]

An intrepid minority of female escapees was prepared to risk the high seas. On 19 April 1788, eleven fugitive slaves set out in a canoe from Dover Castle estate, the property of Dr Richard Martin, in the parish of St Mary on the north coast. Three of the fugitives were female, "two wenches, and a girl about seven years of age". They spent six days at sea before reaching Cuba, and there found refuge in Havana. Dr Martin's son went after them and was allowed to search the port of Trinidad, where he found "a great number of runaway Negroes known to be the property of several inhabitants of Jamaica". The Spanish authorities refused to hand over either Martin's slaves or any other Jamaican runaways. The official claimed that they had fled to Cuba to become Catholics, which gave them full protection in Spanish law.[87]

Maria was a slave woman, the property of John McGregor, who with five male slaves became Catholic on reaching Cuba. She was reported by her ex-master to have expressed regret at her escapade and her willingness to return. In the course of McGregor's bitter battle to recover her, he promised her forgiveness "on the word and honour of a gentleman". But the obstinacy of the Spanish governor provided no opportunity for testing his good faith.[88]

Runaways who returned either voluntarily or otherwise faced certain punishment by imprisonment or by transportation. The Slave Court in Port Maria tried six runaways over the period 1806 to 1811. Cynthia of Cardiff Plantation got off the lightest with three months' hard labour; the rest were transported.[89] Penalties increased in severity with repeated escapees. Harriet, the habitual offender of the parish of St George, was sentenced to imprisonment for three months and public beatings.[90] Other "incorruptible runaways" of that parish were Ann Wright, Sarah Henry (who had disappeared for four years), Nancy Thompson of Spring Garden estate, Congo Nancy of Craig Hill estate and French Becky, all of whom received life imprisonment with hard labour.[91]

"Bush, bush no have no law", the slaves maintained.[92] Slaves did not necessarily escape a life of regimentation to enter one of anarchy. Black runaways often had to mobilize their scant resources in a disciplined communal strategy for survival. This was especially true when men and women took to the "bush", where as outlaws, they lived outside of white laws but within their own.

The free existence led by Maroon women and their families in their mountain villages was not seen by estate blacks as either unique or unattainable. From time to time, runaway communes of men and women, reminiscent of the original freedom fighters, came to light. In 1819, the white establishment caught three hundred escaped slaves who had formed a settlement "of considerable extent" in St Catherine "on hills contiguous to the sea". They did not, according to creole officials, have "any horrible designs against the peace of the country" but, rather, "contemplated an establishment similar to the Maroons".[93]

The parish of Trelawny in the 1820s had a remarkable runaway settlement in the mountains on the edge of Maroon territory. It was named "We no sen' they no come", which expressed accurately the intention of its inhabitants "not to stir from home, not to be seen, not to attract notice".[94] They succeeded in their design so well that between 1812 and 1824, while keeping in close contact with the slaves of their former estates, they managed without disturbance to establish a flourishing district. From all reports, they had 200 acres "of very fine provisions, in full bearing, with abundance of hogs and poultry".[95] The settlement contained fourteen houses "of considerable magnitude, well built", wattled and thatched, with "terraced floors . . . few under 25 feet long". They had what seemed a communal meeting place "70 feet long and open in the centre". Their numbers were allegedly "very great".[96]

They suffered two attacks in 1824 from a combined party of white militiamen and Maroons. The second raid surprised a group of nine men, eight women and four children, in the preparation of their evening meal. Two members of the group were fatally wounded. One of the women was "fired at without effect", and as she ran away with the remaining black settlers to seek safety in the woods, she voiced the community's anger at the white invasions.[97]

SOCIAL CUSTOMS, FAMILY AND CULTURAL IDENTITY

African values of kinship and community were implicit in the traditional conditioning of the thousands of forced migrants who entered the Caribbean, having already undergone their transition into adulthood. Massive infusions of African culture continued without interruption for nearly two centuries. Twenty-five years after the abolition of the slave trade, when slavery approached its end, a quarter of Jamaica's population, all adults, was African.[98]

Maroon communities in Jamaica continued, into the late eighteenth and nineteenth centuries, to reflect clearly the transatlantic origin of its family systems,[99] to the extent that they consciously rejected Christian monogamous marriages.[100] Outside of free Maroon villages, the imperatives of the outer plantation obviously inhibited the free functioning of any type of family, whether polygynous or otherwise. Unions between black men and women, whether in or out of Christian wedlock, had major obstacles to surmount; obstacles which, by challenging the slave's human need to retain a domestic identity, may well have served to strengthen structure and relationships well known in Africa, which existed in the black Jamaican family and which are too often underrated.[101]

The white establishment did not always underrate them. In acknowledging, and indeed exploiting the vulnerability of black feelings and forms of kinship, it simultaneously paid tribute to their positive force in black New World existence. The Society of West Indian Merchants and Planters, at their meeting in London of 27 June 1795, expressed the gravest concern at the recommendation of Jamaica's governor, the Duke of Portland, that a black regiment should be formed, comprising six thousand slaves. It seemed to them "a measure pregnant with the most fatal consequence"; and if it were to be implemented, the Society demanded that it should only apply to those slaves "upon whom their Masters can have the most perfect reliance and who have their wives and families and productive ground on the estates of their masters as pledges of their good conduct and fidelity".[102]

"The attachments of the negro to his family, his home, and the grave of his ancestors is well known", said William Taylor in evidence before a committee of the House of Lords.[103] It was to the interest of whites fending off humanitarian attacks to project black domesticity as near-idyllic. So Jamaica's committee of the Council, which reported on the state of slavery in the West Indies in 1789, for instance, observed that Negro men and women "do not marry . . . but they much more frequently live and grow old together, when their Children and Relations through a strong Family Attachment that generally prevails amongst them, furnish them with their care and Assistance, in addition of their Masters".[104] The reality, however, was not without form, purpose and emotional support, which gave significant dimensions to the life that was lived outside of the white orbit, in the "hidden freedom"[105] of the black slave quarters, only partially perceive by whites.

"When I entered", wrote Cynric Williams in 1823,

> I saw a negro woman squatting on the floor attending the cookery of her husband's dinner, which was simmering in an iron pot, and consisted of ochro and cocos, picked crabs and salt fish with a bit of salt pork. The lady was peeling a few plantains to roast and the lord of the mansion was inhaling the fumes of tobacco from a short junko pipe, as he lolled at his ease in his hammock, suspended from one of the rafters to within two feet of the floor . . . I must not forget to mention three young children, fat and sleek as moles, that were playing about the house and garden, which contained plantain suckers, an alligator pear tree, mangos, two or three coconut trees, orange trees, a few coffee bushes and many other fruits and vegetables; and a pineapple fence separated it from the adjoining garden. There was a pigsty in one corner, occupied by a sow and her family.[106]

Higman's survey of the data on Old and New Montpelier estates in St James between 1817 and 1832 indicates that nearly half of the slaves lived in households approximating that of the elementary family of a man, a woman and her children. This was especially true of Africans.[107] The spatial evidence of Higman's material, although admittedly tentative, also points to the emergence of a residential pattern based on patrilocal rules, that is, "men may have played a greater role than women in the establishment of co-resident unions".[108]

Contemporary observers certainly presumed black masculine presence and, in some instances, black masculine authority bordering on patri-archism.[109] Moreton saw the slave couple "as mutual helpmates to each other", dividing their domestic responsibilities, with the woman performing personal services for her spouse.[110]

Edward Long described the male heads of slave families as disciplinarians exercising "a kind of sovereignty over their children, which never ceases during life, chastising them sometimes with much severity".[111] They had a dominant say in the disposal of the black family's property.

> The grandfather, or father directs in what manner his money, his hogs, poultry, furniture, cloaths and other effects and acquisitions shall descend or be disposed of after his decease. He nominates a sort of trustees or executors from the nearest of kin who distribute them among the legatees, according to the will of the testator.[112]

Senior observed that "the strictest laws of primogeniture" prevailed in cases of sudden death when no previous provision had been made for the disposal of the slave's property.[113]

One important corollary of male proprietary rights was male responsibility for other members of the family. Male slaves, some of them artisans, succeeded in acquiring their freedom and then worked for the purchase of their relatives. They sometimes had to bargain hard for the freedom of their wives and children: "very exorbitant prices [were] often demanded and paid".[114] Some were frustrated in their attempts. The slave Samuel Swiney tried to redeem his wife, who was being sold at public auction, but although he bid as high a sum as £230, he lost her to a higher bidder.[115] Others were more fortunate. Richard Brown of Falmouth worked and saved and succeeded in purchasing his own freedom for £250, as well as his wife's for £80.[116] Pike, a slave shoemaker of Kingston, gave a sum of money to the Reverend John

Barry to hold for the purchase of his son. Barry advised him to purchase his pregnant wife instead. "However his desire was stronger to purchase his son, because he said he could work and he would do something to aid him in purchasing the rest of his family." Barry negotiated on Pike's behalf with the slave proprietor involved and secured a deal by which both wife and son were freed.[117]

The male slave at times took full responsibility for the maintenance of his spouse and family. Such was the position of a Kingston tailor, whose master allowed him to hire himself out and to pay from his wages $12.00 weekly for himself and 10s. for his wife.[118] The estate as well acknowledged the male slave's greater obligation for his family's maintenance by giving him an extra allotment of half an acre of provision land.[119]

The paternal head might have to accept the grave responsibility for the whole family's misconduct, as happened in the case of the slave Felix. He, together with his wife, Lucky, and their nine children accused the overseer of Pleasant Hill in the Port Royal Slave Court of improper treatment, of flogging, of confinement and of not allowing them sufficient provision for a family of that size. Their case was dismissed as "fallacious and groundless". Lucky and their children were admonished, and Felix was sentenced to receive fifty lashes.[120]

Such relationships were clearly supported by individual and communal sanctions, although the precise ceremony accompanying slave mating is not always fully communicated by contemporaries. Significant fragments surfaced, however. Matthew Lewis, for instance, witnessed what appears to have been a courtship dance.

> The dances performed tonight seldom admitted more than three persons at a time: to me they appeared to be movements entirely dictated by the caprice of the moment; but I am told that there is a regular figure, and that the least mistake, or a single false step is immediately noticed by the rest. I could indeed sometimes fancy that one story represented an old duenna guarding a girl from a lover; and another, the pursuit of a young woman by two suitors, the one young and the other old; but this might be only fancy. However, I am told that they have dances, which not only represent courtship and marriage but being brought to bed.[121]

Edward Long made reference to the significance of the cotta (a circular pad of cloth or bark worn by women) in common-law unions. He wrote:

"On the voluntary divorce of man and wife, it is cut in two and each party takes half; as the circle was a symbol of eternity, and the ring of perpetual love or fidelity, so this ceremony perhaps is meant to express the eternal severance of their mutual affection."[122]

Sexual taboos reminiscent of West African customs were observed during pregnancy by couples in polygynous associations.[123]

At the death of a wife, "the husband lets his beard remain unshaved, and remains rather negligent in his attire, for the space of a month; at the expiration of which, a fowl is dressed at his house, with some messes of good broth, and he proceeds, accompanied by his friends, to the grave".[124]

The bonds cementing these relationships were only in the minority of cases those of Christian marriage. It was not until the 1820s that planters began to pay lip service to the promotion of slave marriages, primarily in the interest of population growth.[125] Such marriages could only be performed for baptized slaves according to the rites of the established church, which was a strong deterrent in a situation where the Nonconformist missionaries were much closer to the slave's personal life. The Moravians tried to deal with this difficulty by "private" ceremonies, whose legality was doubtful.[126] The custom of seeking the slave owner's permission to marry was made into law by the Slave Act of 1826.[127] Permission was not always forthcoming, and opposition from the white master was sometimes bluntly stated: "You may live as I am living myself."[128] James Archer's rationalizations on the subject did not conceal his rejection, or fear, of legal black unions. He clashed with his mother for conniving at the marriage of one of his slaves without his knowledge. He wrote indignantly on 5 December 1831:

> George Archer obtained from my Mother, *unknown to me,* and as he always knew, against my inclination, a paper to Mr Bridges to be married to Hannah belonging to my niece – he was read in church three Sundays and on Sunday last 4 December he went down to the Bay and was married – my Mother very improperly gave him the paper, and never told me of the circumstance until after the marriage was contracted and solemnized, though she as well as George knew that it was always against my wish, on no other account but because the 2 slaves did not belong to one owner, and in case of their moving, or being separated, it would be cruel to have kept them asunder from each other. It was very wrong to have given them a paper.[129]

To consolidate a relationship by marriage in the face of these odds required a sense of familial responsibility, personal commitment and initiative, which growing numbers of slaves revealed in the latter years of slavery. The support of the Nonconformist churches encouraged them to challenge the obstacles placed in the way of legalizing concubinage. John Baillie's estate of 350 slaves witnessed nine slave marriages in 1826 and forty-nine in 1830.[130] The Moravian congregation at Fairfield in the parish of Manchester recorded fifty-two slave marriages during the years 1830 to 1834. In the last five months of 1834, immediately following abolition, sixty marriages took place.[131]

Growing evidence of structured domestic associations,[132] increasingly legitimized during slavery by Christian marriage, places the status and relationship of slave men and slave women in a rather different context from the stereotype of formless promiscuity.

The image, for instance, of the dominant black woman in slave society that is often projected, with its corollary of a mainly absent, powerless and demoralized black male,[133] requires challenging. It fails to take adequately into account the context of a black family in which the male was clearly neither invisible nor functionless. Respect for the black man within the slave family was reinforced by the leadership roles that he was able to assume within the whole community. Afro-Jamaica had its folk heroes, the male slaves who waged successful warfare on the white plantation, whether they were the master craftsmen who seized white techniques and their freedom, by purchase or by flight,[134] or the chief preachers and dread obeah men who defied creole laws or the legendary captains of armed rebellion, Tacky, Kofi, Three-Finger Jack, "Daddy" Sharp.[135]

If the plantation did admittedly undermine the capacity of the male slave to function fully as *paterfamilias,* it attempted equally to usurp the role of *materfamilias.* The estate pressed for early weaning, for if not "the child becomes accustomed", wrote one slaveholder, "to too much tenderness unsuitable to its station".[136] Black children, declared another white creole, "should not be made to depend upon their mothers for food".[137] William Ricketts saw his responsibilities to his black "family" in this light:

> [B]y having a room near my dwelling house I have raised 6 children. Feby and I have 9 more women ready to lye in here – I have now 26 from 3 years old to the breast at this place besides a swarm at my mountain, and I make it a rule to have them fed from my own table every day and in my sight which pleases their parents . . . .[138]

It is also suggested that the slave woman's unique access to "the source of all power in society" earned her special rewards.[139] This may have some significance in determining the status of the mulatto woman, the real beneficiary of creole sexual collaboration, who started as the darling of the plantation and became the city's leading courtesan.[140] It has less relevance for the black woman. It is inconceivable that the white slave master, who so degraded the black female, could offer any meaningful gifts of power of privilege with which to elevate her. Whatever dignity, respect or positive status she salvaged as a bondswoman was derived from elements within the black family/community, which allowed her to perform worthwhile functions as a worthwhile member.

The sense of a black extended family group was epitomized in the position of the slave who died intestate and without children. The community became his or her heir. "They have all connections, more or less, the Africans; they call one another Brothers and Sisters, and so on. Those who are their countrymen, they claim it."[141]

These "connections" wove themselves into a network of mutual supportiveness and concern, providing for the woman a broad kinship base to which she gave and from which she derived strength. It involved the large numbers of men who travelled miles nightly to visit their wives on distant estates,[142] and large numbers of women whose male relatives felt resentment for the improper approaches made to them by white men[143] and for the corporal punishment inflicted on them;[144] these same men and women who ensured that no woman need appeal for justice alone, and the fugitives who always knew where shelter could be found. The kinship net embraced as well the large numbers of slave children who knew no greater offence than abuse of "either of their parents".[145] In particular, they would tolerate no disrespect towards their "mammies".[146]

Respect for the parent, male and female, was linked with the traditional African regard for the elders, which continued to be a strong element in slave society. Affection and veneration for the aged found practical expression within the immediate family group, where adult slaves found time not only to support themselves by exertion in their grounds, but to support their elderly relatives as well.[147] This extended into the wider community creating mutual obligations of discipline and care:

In addressing such of their fellow-servants as are considerably advanced in years they always prefix to their names the appellation of ta and ma, which signify father and mother, by which appellation they express the sentiments, not only of filial reverence, but of esteem and fondness. Nor is this regard confined to outward ceremonies, or mere terms of respect. . . . The whole body of Negroes on a plantation must be reduced to a deplorable state of wretchedness (indeed) if any time they suffer their aged and infirm companion to want the common necessaries of life, or even many of its comforts.[148]

A passage from Matthew Lewis's journal inadvertently provides insight into the desires and concerns of the black community in relation to its members. As he walked through the slave village on his estate, numerous slaves approached him:

[O]ne wanted an additional supply of lime for the whitewashing of his house, another was building a new house for a superannuated wife (for they have all so much decency as to call their sexual attachments by a conjugal name) and wanted a little assistance towards the finishing it; a third wanted a new axe to work with; and several entreated me to negotiate the purchase of some relation or friend belonging to another estate, and with whom they were anxious to be reunited.[149]

The woman was an integral part of that pattern of mutual concern; and as she advanced in years, seniority added even more affection and respect to her role of mother, always one of high regard. She reciprocated that regard: "The affections between the mothers and even spurious offspring are very powerful as well as permanent."[150] She held on to her young infant as long as the estate would allow her, and longer.[151] She placed herself protectively between her children and the plantation, when it attempted to oppress them.[152] She took her stand against separation from them.[153] She actively, determinedly, promoted their advancement.[154]

THE SEARCH FOR ECONOMIC AND SOCIAL AUTONOMY

Woman's important function as a producer served to ground her firmly into her community. The plantation, ironically, gave her the basic resource, namely the provision plot and there she put to her own, her family's and her community's service, the main skill which the New World offered her. There she laboured hard and profitably in her own field.

Like the male, the female was entitled by law to "a sufficient quantity of land" as her "proper ground".[155] The master was required to allow each slave "sufficient time to work the same, in order to provide him, her or themselves, with sufficient provisions for his, her or themselves, with sufficient provisions for his, her or their maintenance".[156] The alternative policy of slave subsistence was for the masters to "make good and ample provisions for all such slaves as they shall be possessed of, equal to the value of two shillings and sixpence currency per week for each slave".[157] With the considerable amounts of "backlands" available on most plantations, managers found it in their interest to farm out the responsibility for maintenance to the slaves themselves.[158]

Contemporaries maintained that "the negroes have in all Plantations an unbounded liberty to cultivate as much land as they please".[159] Certainly, there seemed few limits placed on their land use;[160] plots varied in size according to the agricultural effort of which each individual was capable. "Some negroes", wrote Senior, "who are industrious cultivate from a rood to an acre, or even more, changing to a new spot, as the old ground gets poor."[161]

These grounds were usually sited on the slopes surrounding the valleys; and as estate cultivation expanded, the slave's field shifted higher into the hills, placing longer distances between the plot and the plantation.[162] Provision grounds were especially vulnerable to storms and hurricanes, which frequently ravaged "the plantain walks"[163] where so much of surplus slave energy went; but this did not prove a deterrent to effort.

Slaves were widely acknowledged to be "diligent and industrious in their provision ground".[164] They revealed there a level of "exertion which was seldom obvious in the master's work",[165] and this was true of both sexes. Women, it was observed, "worked just as much on their provision grounds as men",[166] frequently as part of a family enterprise.[167] "The females . . . married, or living constantly with a man, they often unite their grounds and conjointly labour for themselves and families, till the children arrive at a certain age, when they must provide for themselves."[168]

The pooling of land and labour was seen, for instance, in the case of male slave wharf workers in Kingston. They had no plots of their own, but their wives on neighbouring estates did: so they worked in their spare time on those grounds which "in right of their wives, they might be said to possess".[169]

Lord Seaford's estates of Old and New Montpelier and Shettlewood, in the parishes of Hanover and St James, offer valuable evidence of this area of combined black activity.[170] In 1825, their slave population totalled 864 persons who lived in 301 household units. Fifty-nine houses contained single occupants and all others except eight were occupied by both males and females. Each domestic unit worked a provision ground and accounted for a total acreage under cultivation of approximately 641 acres.[171] The main crops were plantains, cocoas, yams and corn. The slave community owned 291 head of cattle, 522 hogs and 1,728 poultry.[172]

Most plots showed signs of skill and care: 182 of the 301 grounds fell into categories ranging in description from "fair/middling" to "very good".[173] In contrast, slave huts were on the whole in poorer condition, a large number requiring repairs.[174] This may have been as much due to the shortage of materials for effecting such repair, as to shortage of work time. It suggests that the prospects of economic returns on agricultural effort determined the slave's allocation of his or her time and physical energy.

In the one day off per fortnight the law permitted the slaves for labouring on their grounds,[175] they succeeded not only in deriving "the greater part of their subsistence", but they fed as well the local free population.[176]

"A Kingston Negro market", wrote James Kelly,

> was to me, a newcomer, a scene of the liveliest interest. Several thousand Negroes, generally seated on the ground, without much regularity, with basket, or little heaps or ground provisions, yams, cocoas, plantains. I was curious to know the prices and made a cursory calculation that amounted to fifteen or two thousand dollars. . . . It is a remarkable fact, well worth noticing, that a very considerable portion of the ground provisions, fresh pork, eggs, fruits, etc., consumed in the towns, or supplied to the shipping is the growth and produce of the slaves.[177]

A modern attempt to assess with some precision the value of ground provisions on the basis of per capita starch food consumption has arrived at the sum of £847,000 (at current prices) for the year 1830,[178] which, excluding the value of poultry and stock, represents an underestimate of the slave's contribution to the creole domestic economy.

Long distances separated provision grounds from markets. The opportunity for legitimate movement outside of the plantation and into a lively, colourful world of commercial and social exchange motivated blacks to travel weekly as many as five to twenty miles each way to Sunday market.[179] The market place became the distinctive and profitable creation of black Jamaica, dominated by women, who thereby kept the internal trading and communications systems viable. They carried into creole economic organization a strong precedent of African female entrepreneurship.[180] Slaves apparently had no "regular price for anything, but asked as much as they could get".[181] Women were considered to be "more eloquent in making bargains".[182] As a consequence, stated one contemporary, "the greatest numbers are Women that one sees on the Market".[183]

A number of factors thus combined to place the black woman firmly in the centre of the island's free enterprise system. Her functions as food producer and food distributor developed in the complex of a family's corporate agricultural activity. Out of this activity were derived the resources with which she could make the slave hut a home.

Slave dwellings represented a practical demonstration of black technical expertise, ingenuity and communal effort, for they built them either by themselves or, frequently, through voluntary group organization.[184] They became the shelters within which the family jealously guarded its privacy. "I never did", testified John Baillie,

> nor did any Proprietor I know attempt to go into a Negro House without asking permission, and they are very tenacious upon that Point . . . I have known in Jamaica, and have myself attempted the building of Barracks for Negroes with Stone, and made them a far superior Description of House to the ordinary Negro House; and the Negroes have refused to occupy them, stating that they were so much exposed to their Neighbours, they did not like to let them know what they were doing on all occasions.[185]

The black population would understand fully the special nature of the family site, which became sacrosanct as the resting-place of the ancestral spirits. Slaves buried their dead within reach of their living: the graves of their "near and dear relatives"[186] were in the garden plots that normally "adjoined their House, which makes the House go to the Family as it were".[187] They lavished on these houses the rewards of their independent labour.

Many contemporaries gave an inflated view of the standard of domestic living of the slaves, in order to prove how well off an energetic black could become. "Slaves", wrote Mrs Normanby, "are ridiculously well off."[188]

What is undeniable, however, was their "excessive attachment" to any of the fruits of their own work,[189] chief of which was the furnishing of their cottages. Matthew Lewis claimed that he saw no slave house which did not have "a four post bedstead and plenty of bed clothes".[190] William Taylor saw numerous slaves living in conditions of great poverty and misery, but he also observed "in many houses great neatness, great cleanliness and great attempts at style, that is to say articles of furniture and plates and things of that sort".[191] Some, he maintained, had mahogany furniture, crystal decanters and pictures, all purchased from the slaves' own earnings.[192]

Women saw their economic activity not only in terms of the family's pool of resources, but in terms of their own individual productivity, which earned them personal rewards.[193] Their labour was the currency with which all slaves laid claim to property and especially to land. Their proprietary rights to their provision grounds were recognized by creole convention, as having been earned by the work put into them.[194] Since the woman too participated fully in the free agricultural process, she could also stake her claim, as a member of the family and at times, it would appear, by virtue of her own right as an individual producer. One contemporary advanced the opinion that the black woman did not forfeit her ownership of her personal possessions. This caused disappointment to a particular slave spouse who apparently embarked on marriage with great expectations of inheriting. His wife's son, however, a "head Hospital Man" on John Baillie's estate, seemed to have the stronger claim.[195]

Slaves were the chief craftsmen and women of Jamaica. They practised their skills in their own time outside of the plantation's schedule. They supplied the local consumer with "mats out of their useful palm tree";[196] they made wicker chairs and baskets (some ornamental), straw hats,[197] as well as "neatly constructed jars and pans for which they found a ready sale".[198] They frequently manufactured "earthenware utensils . . . and a variety of little articles of that kind".[199] Women were especially gifted in pottery making and employed the techniques of the traditional Akan ceramic artists, who were predominantly women.[200]

Women allocated a fair portion of the returns from their creative/productive/marketing activities towards purchasing their clothes and finery. The colour and flair of black women's fashions attracted regular attention from contemporary observers. They bought out of their private earnings dresses "of a very superior description"[201] and wore their hats, handkerchiefs and gold and coral jewellery with striking style, to market, to church and on holidays.[202] John Baillie had to come to terms with the fashion consciousness of slave women:

> On going out to Jamaica the last time, I took out Printed Cotton as Presents for my Women and Children; I arrived shortly before Christmas, and I employed the House Women and some of the Field Negroes, Women, to make it up into Gowns for them. On Christmas Day it is usual for the Negroes to come up and ask their Master how he does, and wish him a merry Christmas; they come up dressed. On this occasion they did not, except some of the very old Women. I asked one of those Women how it was; she said, "You will see by and by;" I could not elicit any other Answer. A Second Woman came up; she told me the Negroes had turned Fool; I asked her what she meant, and she said, "Massa, it is not the Fashion to wear Printed Cotton; the Fashion is White." I asked who led the Fashion; they told me the Noble Lord's Negroes upon the adjoining Estate, Lord Seaford's Negroes, had. That evening they came up and danced in their white Dresses; in compliment to myself they wore Red Sashes, some of them being Creole; others wore Blue, as they said my Father was a Scotchman; they appeared in White principally; the next Day they did appear, however, in their Printed Gowns.[203]

If slaves' actual possession of material goods was frequently exaggerated by whites, their aspirations for them were not. Acquisition was limited only by economic opportunity. In the parish of St Thomas in-the-East, with no large busy town, it was noticeable that slaves spent Sunday market-day not in trading, but in church-going.[204] In Mountain Clarendon, judging from the appearance of the slaves, they were poor compared with the slaves in Vere.[205] The reason attributed to this was that the remote sugar district of Clarendon was difficult to access, thirty miles from Spanish Town, had no market and slaves had no facility for turning their provisions into money.[206]

In contrast, the slaves of the parish of Vere had better economic prospects. It was corn-growing country, which made poultry rearing easy and profitable. Both land and sea transport, and marketing outlets, were within easy reach: "hucksters [came] from Kingston, and there [was] considerable trade carried on by the ship masters and the hucksters at Kingston with the Vere negroes in poultry". As a consequence, the slaves of that parish were described as "exceedingly well off". The women were well known for their expensive clothes: they wore to church muslin dresses and Leghorn bonnets.[207]

They made a splendid showing at the many creole festivities, in which they were chief among the merrymakers. These celebrations coincided largely with the seasonal Christian holidays of Christmas, Easter and Whitsuntide. These brought slaves out in vast numbers from their quarters, in a blaze of colour, into the streets and often into the great houses, where they took brief possession. "Superbly dressed" women participated in, and often led the singing, dancing and masquerade. The visual impact of their finery and their movements dominated the creole carnival scene.[208]

Slave women's ambitions went beyond externals. Within their total situation of overwhelming oppressiveness, but also of hopeful possibilities, they showed a constant capacity for assessing the options available to them and for making shrewd choices. They recognized education, such as was available in slaveholding Jamaica, as a path of advancement; and in spite of the odds against them, many reached after it, for their children primarily, but also for themselves. "The parents of the [slave] children take a manifest interest in the education of their children and show a desire that they should to be taught to read."[209] This interest was said to apply to "immense numbers" of slave parents.[210] The fulfilment of this "very great desire"[211] was obviously obstructed by the absence of educational facilities, the plantation work demands on young and old and the powerful prejudice that many planters showed against any form of secular and religious learning for blacks.

It is impossible to say to what extent this became a subversive activity, dependent on the individual slave's initiative and determination, and conducted, like so many other vital aspects of slave life, apart from white scrutiny. On the question of slave instruction, William Taylor commented that "the proprietors and the landowners know very little about it; it goes on in the negro's own cabin".[212]

It is probable, therefore, that the relatively few slaves who were known to attend the missionaries' classes passed on their learning. "A Negro", Taylor further noted, "may have his child taught in the evening by another Negro on the Estate without the knowledge of the Overseer, and with which he is perfectly unacquainted. In that case the Negro Parent exercises control."[213]

Missionaries naturally took full credit for black achievements in formal learning. The Reverend Duncan wrote with pride, "I have known an old

African woman of nearly 80 years of age in a few months by attending our schools alone, able to read short lessons."[214]

Whatever learning was transmitted to slaves certainly involved males and females. The attendance register, for instance, of the school run by the Church Missionary Society at Papine estate in St Andrew showed eleven males and fourteen females in the adult evening class for the study of the Bible, psalms and spelling in 1827. The children of the estate took time off in shifts from their work tasks for lessons from 7:00 to 9:00 and 10:00 to 12:00 in the mornings, and 2:00 to 5:00 in the afternoons. They numbered twelve boys and thirteen girls. Over a period of several months, they seldom missed a lesson. The star pupil of Papine school was Harriet Wildman (perhaps a captive student). She was the domestic slave of the missionary Reverend Jones and his family, had a record of 100 per cent attendance from April to July of 1827, and was soon recruited into teaching other slaves.[215]

Women had essential educational and socializing functions to perform inherent in their role of mother. So the wise old woman of black creole folklore, a "Mammy Luna", moralized and reminded a forgetful young generation of the correct values of truthfulness, courtesy and respect for the elders.[216] She was acknowledged as the transmitter of much of the community's magical and religious beliefs and customs. Her authoritative presence as midwife at the childbed has already been discussed.[217] The knowledge she displayed of herbal medicine and of the rituals of birth strengthened her position as a repository of folk wisdom.

No person was held in greater awe in New World black society than the obeah man and obeah woman, whom the white establishment tried, futilely, to control:

> It is very common among these People, who have so small a Portion of human Endowments, for some to pretend to supernatural Powers, and thereby to practice upon the imagination of those, who believe they can be protected by them from the Harms of this Life. This practice of Witchcraft is commonly called Obeah, and is always made an offence punishable with Death.[218]

This was the white perspective, which saw the obeah woman as a practitioner of witchcraft, poisoning and subversion. As such, she was liable to pay the penalty for her alleged crimes.[219] But from the African perspective, such a person was "doctor, philosopher and priest",[220] who commanded communal respect and enjoyed the status of an "oracle" whom blacks consulted "with the most implicit faith" on all occasions.[221] Her power was closely associated with the strong healing element in her activities, an inseparable element from African religious observance.[222]

A most striking feature of black creole religious organization was, and is, the massive involvement of women, both as leaders and as celebrants. Modern musicological research, for instance, interpreting the ritual sounds of drum and chant, has dug deep into the island's past and traced a long unbroken history of the woman's high status as keeper of black religious traditions.[223]

When the white society looked to the black woman to assume religious responsibilities and leadership, it was acknowledging a position already validated by her own community. The minister of the Salt Savannah church in 1832 needed "to discover if any [other] sincere Christians" could be found among the blacks: he called on one of his female communicants to be his contact and informant.[224]

Black spiritual experience in the New World was formalized at the level of the Nonconformist Christian norm, which missionaries struggled to keep orthodox. It coexisted with African beliefs and with forms which blacks observed very much within their own private domain,[225] but which often spilt over into the wider creole world.

"During the sermon", the Moravian John Lang wrote,

> a heathen woman began to twist her body about, and make all manner of grimaces. I bore it for some time till she disturbed the congregation when I desired one of the assistants to lead her out, thinking she was in pain. When the service was over, I inquired what ailed her, and was told, that it was a usual thing with the negroes on M. estate and called by them Conviction.[226]

Women were possessed by, and in possession of, a spiritual realm whose full dimensions still remain to be explored in the New World,[227] where their endurance and survival seemed beyond rational explanation. Sarah Anderson was a native of Guinea, of the Congo country, who died a free black woman in 1813 at Providence Grove in St John's parish:

> She came to the island during the government of the Duke of Albemarle and according to her own statement, was then a young woman of 14. She was bedridden

for the last three years, but retained a good appetite and could hear, see and converse with cheerfulness to the last moment of her existence. She has left fifty-five children, great grandchildren and great great grandchildren, twenty-five of whom attended her to the grave. Had her life extended a few months longer, she would have seen her fifth generation.[228]

Nothing in the ideology and organization of the outer plantation was designed to preserve for the black woman her integrity as a woman. Yet, grounded as she was in her own community, she found there inner resources of wisdom, corporate strength and deep spiritual experience on which to draw, and throughout slavery she drew on them with confidence. Matthew Lewis, struck by the physical presence of black dancing women, conveyed something of the essence of their resilient spirit and their unquestioned sense of their own human dignity. They moved through the streets of Black River with precision, ease, grace and elasticity; his attention was caught and held by "the lofty air with which they carried their head".[229]

8   The Mulatto Woman in Jamaican Slave Society

NUMBERS, OCCUPATIONAL AND SPATIAL DISTRIBUTION

The mulatto population, both enslaved and free, continued to increase in size throughout the period of slavery. Between the 1770s and 1830s, it grew from approximately 23,000 to over 60,300.[1] These, however, are rough estimates, precise demographic data being almost impossible to ascertain for a group whose ethnic and legal condition tended to be fluid. The free coloureds, moreover, were self-conscious about their marginal status and at times deliberately evaded enumeration, which they regarded as a degrading process.[2]

The system of slave registration, which was enforced after 1817, makes it possible to assess more accurately the numbers of enslaved mulattoes in the latter years of this study. Long had calculated them to be about 1,700 in 1770, which would have been approximately 1 per cent of the slave class.[3] Barry Higman's recent careful demographic analysis of the years 1829 to 1832 shows them to have been more numerous than is usually assumed: their total in 1832 was 34,000, or 11 per cent of the slave population.[4] Almost two slave births in every ten were coloured, a total of 4,041 being registered in the years 1829 to 1832, representing an average of 18.4 per cent of all slave births.[5]

There was significant regional variation in their incidence. The urban concentration of Kingston and St Catherine had the largest registration of coloured slave births, over 34 per cent and 26 per cent respectively of all slave births,[6] equalled by the parish of Hanover, also with over 26 per cent,[7] and followed closely by the other western parishes of St James, Westmoreland, Trelawny and St Elizabeth.[8]

Miscegenation was at its highest peak wherever an excess of females occurred.[9] In such a situation, black and brown slave women, outnumbering black men, found more white or coloured mates and so increased the coloured population. This phenomenon was a conspicuous feature of the urban scene, and in rural areas it occurred most markedly in those parishes with the largest estates, which tended to be characterized by high levels of white absenteeism, especially female absenteeism.[10] Miscegenation, as Higman's findings confirm, was lowest on medium-sized plantations, which grew lesser crops such as coffee and pimento and where white masters and mistresses were likely to be resident.[11]

The mulatto slave enjoyed a position of relative privilege on the plantation. "The slave of colour", wrote Richard Barrett, "from the day of his birth, is absolved by custom from the worst features of slavery."[12] Their white connections combined with the prevalent identification of a pale skin with physical frailty to earn mulattoes exemption from the most menial estate tasks, so that they were rarely found in the fields. "It is a custom", Matthew Lewis wrote, "as to the mulatto children, that the males born on an estate would never be employed as field negroes, but as tradesmen: the females are brought up as domestics about the house."[13]

The weeding gang of twenty-nine boys and girls at Nutt's River Plantation in 1790 contained fourteen young black females, nearly all described as "fine and healthy", and one mulatto, Margaret. The other young mulatto slave girls on the estate were Judy, "a small weakly girl" who was a seamstress, Essey, "a fine healthy girl" who was learning to be a seamstress, and Caroline Anne Champnoys, "a fine young mulatto child" who "did nothing".[14]

The pattern persisted into adulthood. The only female mulatto slave on Edward Manning's estate at St Toolies in the parish of Clarendon in 1768 worked in the house.[15] The classification of the twenty-six mulatto slave women among William Beckford's slaves in Clarendon in 1780, was as follows: eleven seamstresses, six housewomen, three superannuated (ages sixty-eight, sixty-eight and eighty-six), two invalids, two who did "no work" (ages twenty-six and thirty), one washerwoman and one field woman.[16]

This correlation between colour and occupation, the association of a light complexion with non-praedial tasks, continued to be a strong feature of slave labour organization right up to emancipation. It was particularly marked at Rose Hall estate, for example, which in the 1830s had a relatively high ratio of mulatto slaves (about 18 per cent) who, with the exception of one child, were all non-praedials.[17] The identical pattern prevailed at that time on the coffee plantation of Maryland in St Andrew, and the St James sugar estates of Irvine and Old and New Montpelier.[18] Roehampton estate had twenty-six brown people in 1832, eight of whom were female, "and these are all considered domestic".[19]

The position of the house slave was by no means one of unqualified privilege. Her physical freedom was greatly circumscribed by the round-the-clock demands of the household. She was the steady target of daily harassment and petty complaints. She was held responsible for breakages and losses and often forced to replace them by extra labour.[20] Interpersonal stresses and strains could be aggravated by close contact and could erupt into ugly conflict.[21]

But life under the slave owner's roof had its compensations. It represented a less physically arduous and a less regimented routine than that of the field gang. The fifteen-year-old mulatto girl Susanna, whom Cynric Williams rescued, had the advantage of a relatively light schedule: she looked after the children, fed the poultry and did needlework.[22] The task load of mulatto female slaves, as house servants or washerwomen, wrote one observer, "was nearly synonymous with being entirely idle, so little work was required of them".[23]

Housework always held out the promise of promotion to the position of housekeeper, which almost invariably involved a relationship of concubinage with a white. On rural estates, the mistresses of white men below the rank of planters (bookkeepers, for instance) were usually slave women and, conspicuously, brown slave women.[24] Like the highly trained male artisans of the sugar factory, these women formed part of the slave aristocracy and enjoyed status and authority. Their offspring, even if enslaved, might also claim special respect.[25]

The majority of mulatto slaves were found, however, not on rural plantations, but in urban households and small business places. The town offered the brown female slave an even more flexible way of life than had been possible for her on the plantation. Her occupations covered mainly a variety of personal services such as laundering, sewing or hawking, domestic work in private homes, in lodging houses and in taverns. She had easier access even to religious worship, for domestic slaves in towns were allowed to attend services "without having such time abstracted from their own".[26]

She was sometimes a jobbing slave with responsibility for finding her own employment and thus enjoyed some freedom of movement, as long as she handed over her wage regularly to her owner. Mrs Isabella King's slave women, Jane, Susan, Ann and Elenor, hired themselves out in Port Antonio during her absence from Jamaica. Elenor was a mulatto. Her occupation was dubious, but apparently profitable. "Few ladies", commented Mrs Harriet Thompson, "go finer than Elenor does." But since she paid in her dollar weekly to her owners, as required, she was apparently left to "her own establishment".[27]

Whatever advantages they may have enjoyed either in town or country did not prevent female mulatto slaves from regularly appearing on the records as wrongdoers. They committed assaults on other slaves or on free persons of all colours, they were found guilty of "violent obscene and threatening language", they became drunk and they refused to work.[28] Ann Goodman's crime was the gravest of all: she did "feloniously, wickedly, maliciously and knowingly mix and give or cause to be mixed and given some poisonous drug or drugs to Mary Murray (of same parish [that is, St George], a free woman of colour) with intent to cause her death". The jury recommended mercy in view of evidence of her repentance, but she was nevertheless sentenced to hang.[29]

COLOUR AND ACCESS TO FREEDOM

Colour was a significant determinant of manumission. Although coloured slaves represented approximately 11 per cent of the total slave population in the latter years of slavery (1829 to 1832),[30] yet during this same period, 1,363 slaves were manumized, of whom 797 (or 58 per cent) were coloured.[31] Jamaican manumissions were also always heavily weighted in favour of females. In 1826, for example, a total of 309 slaves were freed, of whom 92 were male and 217 female. Between 1817 and 1829, a total of 2,566 females were freed, in contrast to 1,445 males.[32] Of the 1,363 slaves who were freed between 1829 and 1832, 804, or approximately 60 per cent, were females; 450 were coloured women.[33]

Female slaves unquestionably benefited from their intimate associations with whites, which facilitated the granting and the purchasing of freedom. Manumissions by will often reflect these relations. The terms of some bequests are significant:

> It is my will that my daughter do purchase and set free a certain mulatto girl slave named Jane Green, to be paid for out of the legacy hereby left my daughter.[34]

> I will and bequest what property I may die possessed of towards the freedom of my reputed child and in the event of a sufficiency remaining, such residue to be applied towards the freedom of the mother Isabella Heron.[35]

> It is my positive desire that my executors as soon as possible after my decease, set free and manumize my housekeeper Ann C. Clarke, now belonging to K. Schaw.[36]

In the year 1826, 309 slaves were manumitted by deed. Of these, 92 were male and 217 were female. A total of 110 manumissions in that year were by will, the testators making a variety of provisions for the freeing of the particular slave or slaves. Thirty-nine of the slaves so favoured were male, seventy-one were female.[37]

The white man's sense of obligation towards his coloured dependents has been exaggerated. The majority of white fathers did not in fact manumit their coloured children as has been sometimes suggested.[38] Over four thousand coloured slave births were registered in the last years of slavery, but it has been already observed that only 797 manumissions were effected. The less-well-off fathers could not easily afford the price of manumission, hence the request made by some testators that other slaves on their estates be hired out and their earnings earmarked for the purchase of their "reputed mulatto children".[39]

A testator, for example, requested that his estate be converted by his executors into a fund for the support of his two children. He continued: "and if my executors should deem the said fund sufficient to obtain their freedom, I leave it in the power of my executors to appropriate it to that purpose".[40] Or, alternatively: "Should I not have it in my power to manumize and set free a negro woman named Olive Gray, I request my executors may do so, and to the progency she is now pregnant with."[41] Or the grant of freedom might even be left to the discretion of the testator's wife left behind.

It took the overseer of Amity Hall estate eight years to negotiate the purchase of his mulatto family of seven. He offered at first to exchange his own slaves for members of his family, but was refused by the estate's attorney, and the cash transaction that was eventually executed in 1818 cost £760.[42]

Men of more independent means did not always place the enfranchisement of their illegitimate sons and daughters high among their priorities.[43] Where white men did arrange freedom for their coloured mistresses and their coloured offspring, it was more likely to be in a rural than an urban environment.[44] In the relatively closely woven fabric of plantation life, the white parent may have had a stronger sense of responsibility to at least some of his coloured relations, than in the more flexible environment of a town, where relationships could be more transient and less demanding. Gratuitous manumissions were as a consequence more likely to be found on rural estates, and they strongly favoured the women. This is borne out in the high proportions of coloured female manumissions registered in the large-scale sugar plantation parishes of St James, Trelawny, St Elizabeth, St Mary and St Ann.[45]

The brown slave woman's occupation as a non-praedial, and particularly as a domestic non-praedial, was clearly of economic relevance, but it was difficult to disentangle precisely her sexual/familial associations. William Shand expressed the creole view of the house slave as someone who, being in close contact with whites (who were "superior in every respect, and more civilized than the slave himself"), was more likely to improve.[46] The pinnacle of slave "improvement" was enfranchisement.

William Taylor observed that "the greatest number of manumissions are amongst household servants", and this he attributed to the "greater facilities" they enjoyed.[47] Owners, on leaving the island, tended to free domestics in preference to other categories of slaves.[48] Manumission was as much a function of patronage, as of kinship: the significant element was often the opportunities offered to the house slave for relatively easy contact with well-disposed whites. Taylor also testified that domestic servants had access to the friends of their masters for intercessions on their behalf, and, he stated, "gentlemen of Kingston were often known to give their instrumentality to lead the way to freedom".[49]

It is worth noting, however, that where economic opportunities were roughly equal, colour and contact played a less dominant part. In the city, where the black slave had nearly the same access as the brown to skilled and non-praedial occupations, the mulatto slave had less of an edge over her black sister in acquiring freedom.

Manumission patterns suggest that the urban slave was more likely to purchase than to receive freedom, for the operative factors outside of the plantation were not so much colour and ties of blood as occupation and earning capacity. In such a context, a less racially discriminatory situation could, in a way, prevail. Manumission figures for Kingston for the years 1829 and 1832 show more black than mulatto female slaves acquiring freedom: 122 blacks, compared with 51 coloureds.[50]

This, however, did not alter the overall island picture: the mulatto slave could not only use whatever opportunities existed for buying her freedom, she was, as well, more likely than the black, or the male, to receive her liberty as a gift.

LEGAL DISABILITIES, URBAN LIFE AND SOCIO-ECONOMIC STATUS

Statistics for the free-coloured population during slavery are incomplete. All estimates, however, point to a steady increase in numbers between the 1770s and the 1830s, during which period mulattoes and other mixed groups grew from approximately forty-five hundred in 1775 to approximately thirty-five thousand in 1834.[51] Existing fragments of their sex ratios indicate a roughly even balance of males and females with a trend towards an excess of females. Some parish examples illustrate this (see tables 8.1 and 8.2).

Free-coloured women suffered all the legal disabilities of their group.[52] Until 1823, they shared, for example, with coloured men the handicap of being unable to give evidence in courts of law, which was a severe restraint against their capacity to protect their persons and their property.[53] Some disabilities had relatively less significance for women than for men. Until 1831, free coloureds "were not eligible as Vestrymen, jurors, Members of Council or Assembly: they could not vote in elections, hold public office or even hold commissions in the black and mulatto Companies of the Militia".[54] But this

Table 8.1   Persons of Colour in Eight Parishes, 1812 and 1829

Year	Parish	Men	Women	Boys	Girls
1812[1]	Westmoreland	138	266	175	191
	St Thomas	207	142	–	–
	St George	63	97	163	80
	Portland	73	58	23	26
	St David	5	11	–	–
1829[2]	St George	233	279		
	Port Royal	303	420		
	Vere	120	90		
	Westmoreland	502	548		
	St Elizabeth	883	1,035		

Sources: [1]*PP,* vol. VII, 1814–1815: No. 14, Jamaica.
[2]R.M. Martin, *Statistics of the Colonies of the British Empire* (London: W.H. Allen and Co., 1839). Age specifics for the parish of Portland are interesting (see table 8.2 below).

Table 8.2   Portland: Free-Coloured Population, 1812–1822

Years	Males		Females		
	(under 10 yrs)	(over 10 yrs)	(under 10 yrs)	(over 10 yrs)	Total
1812	18	74	22	69	83
1813	23	82	27	78	210
1814	25	89	28	77	219
1815	31	102	30	81	244
1816	28	111	10	76	255
1817	26	95	10	78	209
1818	18	86	13	80	197
1819	16	85	10	81	192
1820	18	87	14	86	205
1821	20	86	17	87	210
1822	21	91	10	89	217

Source: PP, vol. XVII, 1823, 17 March 1823.

also applied to all women, regardless of colour. In these respects, mulatto females were no worse off than white.

Other disabilities, however, may have borne more heavily on them. Mulatto women, as has been discussed, had always been specially favoured beneficiaries of white men's bequests.[55] The 1761 Act of Devises, which limited the value of such legacies, would have specifically affected them as a group. Relatively few white benefactors took advantage of the legislative procedure available for modifying this restriction.[56] Even fewer mulatto women themselves had the resources to initiate such a procedure on behalf of their heirs.

Sarah Morris's was an extremely rare case. A free quadroon of Kingston and

> owner of considerable real and personal property, she petitioned the Assembly on 23 November 1784 in the interest of Charlotte, her natural daughter by the late Robert Stirling, late member of the Jamaica House of Assembly. Charlotte had received a liberal education in England, where she was then living under the immediate care and patronage of William Stirling, esquire, of Keir, her uncle.

She planned to make England her home. Mother and daughter were already entitled to privileges; the mother was now anxious to make "an ample and handsome provision for her said daughter", but was hampered by the Devises Act of 1761. She appealed to the House for the relaxation of its terms so that she could dispose of her estate without restraints.[57] Her petition was granted.

In the economic sphere, free coloureds, men and women, suffered disabilities, especially in rural Jamaica. It is true that some free mulatto women engaged in agricultural activity and made their living from some of the island's lesser crops. "Many [coloured] men and some women", wrote Bickell, "have small coffee mountains, some few to a large extent."[58] Free black and brown farmers were found in the Claremont district of the Port Royal mountains, where they cultivated small plots of land "with all kinds of vegetables" and "all kinds of Indian corn". They also raised small stock and, by regularly supplying the markets in Kingston with their produce, made themselves a decent livelihood.[59] The large estates dared not harbour goats that were "so prone to trespass on the young canes", so that fell to the lot of small settlers, including brown women, who reared them in "great numbers

. . . for the purpose of supplying the inhabitants with milk". With "four or five milch-goats a brown woman can manage to support herself and family very comfortably".[60] Among the third degree of settlers whom Long identified in St James in the 1770s were three mulatto women, who between them owned twenty-two slaves.[61] Sarah Gardner was a livestock farmer of St Elizabeth, whose twenty-three slaves and stock totalled in value £241.[62] Susannah Brown owned 81 acres at Cherry Gardens in St David, with fourteen slaves. Alice Brown in the same parish managed Hampstead estate with ten slaves.[63]

Creole society did not, however, on the whole, have many places for women in profitable agriculture.[64] Its laws, moreover, discouraged all would-be farmers who were not white. Jamaica's Deficiency Laws, designed to keep the island's racial disparity to the minimum and to provide an adequate white militia, required each slave owner to employ one white male for every twenty slaves and to pay a fine for each person in which he or she was deficient. It discriminated against all coloureds, who normally found it difficult to employ whites and who, unlike whites, were not permitted to save deficiency themselves on their own estates.[65] Legislation of 1813 relaxed this restraint on coloured males, but kept a disabling clause in relation to females.[66] The inability of coloureds to save deficiency on plantations had always inhibited their agricultural activities;[67] the "reform" measures of 1813 must have been a further stimulus to women to move out of rural Jamaica and into its towns.

The greater economic opportunities and the freer lifestyle of the town are always more accommodating than a rural environment to the needs of a marginal class. Throughout the New World, women of all colours, like other subordinate groups in search of personal liberty and achievement, have gravitated towards the melting pot of cities.[68] The free mulatto female became, to a considerable extent, a town dweller. Kingston, Port Royal and St Ann's Bay had large concentrations of free coloureds.[69] Montego Bay, according to Long's estimate in 1774, contained more than half of the registered coloured inhabitants of the parish of St James;[70] and the free-coloured group, as has been noted from parish samples, contained a constantly high ratio of females.

The lure of the town apparently drew mulatto women even from as remote settlements as those of the Portland Maroons, whose population contained about 10 per cent coloured males and females.[71] There were always a number of Maroons who did not remain constantly in their communities; of these a most regular migrant was the mulatto female.[72] This floating group commuted between the hills and coastal districts: Jenny Burke, mulatto, when not in Scots Town, could be found at Fort George at Port Antonio.[73]

The dynamics of the town helped to shape the dominant image of the free brown woman, an image of someone economically active and viable. They were acknowledged to be leading domestic entrepreneurs of accommodation. White male visitors were their chief customers. Travellers of the period seldom failed to spread the word about the quality of the service which they offered. There was the courteous, lively Miss Polly Vidal of Falmouth,[74] Miss Bessy McLean in Black River,[75] Eliza Thompson in Rio Bueno,[76] and the highly praised Judy James of Montego Bay. "Inns", declared Matthew Lewis, "would be powers of paradise if they were all rented by mulatto landladies like Judy James."[77] Elizabeth Sutton of Kingston obviously ran a substantial lodging house. Her personal inventory of 1803 recorded seven bedrooms fully equipped with over 100 household items, including several articles of mahogany furniture. Also listed were new buildings with additional bedrooms. Her personalty was worth £2,821 7s. 3d.[78]

Spanish Town provided profitable business at the time of the Assembly and the grand courts of February, June and October, which brought an influx of jury men, suitors and witnesses into the town and created a demand for entertainment and accommodation.[79] Miss Charlotte Beckford's lodging house at the corner of Whitechurch and Ellis Streets was so well known that Governor Nugent arranged for some of his official French guests to sleep there in July 1803 and to take their meals at Government Pen.[80]

In the 1780s, the traveller paid about 6d. each night for a bed.[81] The landlady often supplemented her income by holding dances, which were great social and financial successes, sometimes "more crowded than the first assembly".[82]

The grog shops of Trelawny's towns "were entirely in the hands of brown persons, mostly women".[83] As an occupational group they contributed between £2,000 and £3,000 annually in parish taxes from the sale of liquor.[84]

Mulatto women were retailers of general goods:[85] they brought their share of new commercial activity into Kingston at the time of the Haitian Revolution, when coloured females were prominent among the group of

French immigrants to Jamaica. The influx of exiles included 193 white males, 107 white females, six coloured males and 105 coloured females, all of whom had property and were also businesswomen.[86]

Coloured women were found among those who earned their living by hiring out slaves. Some of the dock labourers in Port Royal, for example, appeared to have been hired out by their mulatto mistresses.[87] It is very likely that a woman like Elizabeth Sutton of Kingston not only kept a lodging house but also hired out skilled slaves. Her personal property included five valuable artisans: one mason valued at £250, two carpenters valued respectively at £250 and £210, one mulatto mason's apprentice worth £160 and one mulatto tailor worth £100.[88]

The industry and evident success of a significant number of coloureds led some contemporaries to overlook the poor circumstances of others. The Reverend Thomas Cooper, for instance, maintained that he had "never seen a brown man or woman in such distress as to require relief", and he attributed this to their great energy and affluence.[89]

The coloureds themselves, however, acknowledged poverty in their midst, and in 1792 petitioned for their fair share of public assistance. After all, they maintained, they paid taxes, but when in "a state of want and indigence [they were] precluded the advantage of common support".[90] The vestries were certainly less inclined to give assistance to brown paupers than to whites, and this must have discouraged individuals from making their destitution officially known. They were normally prohibited admission to the Kingston poor house for indoor relief, so that Elizabeth Richardson and Libbe Roberts were granted, on 21 November 1808, the weekly sum of 10s. as outdoor relief; for being "women of colour", they were therefore "improper persons to be within the Parish House".[91] Similarly, outdoor rather than indoor relief was granted on 22 January 1821 to Sarah Preston James, "a poor female of colour".[92]

The Assembly, for obvious reasons of national policy, dealt relatively generously with the cases of Mary Watkins, "free mulatto woman". The House in its session of 1796 was "pleased to grant her 20d. per annum for support and maintenance on account of the loss of her only son, who supported her previously, to the Trelawny Maroon war, in which he was killed".[93] But this, too, was rare.

The incidence of mulatto debtors in the island's jails substantiates the observations of other contemporary writers who did not share the Reverend Cooper's opinion and stated that the majority of coloureds were in fact poor.[94] Elizabeth Verdon, a brown female, was confined in the jail of Surrey in 1822 for fifteen days, Ann Brown was confined for seventy-nine days: they were the two brown female debtors out of the twelve mulattoes who were being held at that time.[95] In 1827 and 1828, there were eight brown debtors serving time, of whom four were female.[96] The Kingston debtors' jail in that year contained fifty-five brown debtors, of whom sixteen were women.[97] While in confinement they were entitled to the Vestry's maintenance allowance of 2s. 6d. per day.[98]

Free brown women were involved in a variety of skirmishes with the law. They appeared in cases of disorder, with slaves, on their own as victims or as perpetrators of violence, verbal and/or physical. They were guilty of drunkenness, obscenity and assault; they were present among the society's vagabonds.[99] The career of Susanna, a free brown woman of Port Royal, "a notorious vagrant", was conspicuous in the records.[100] So also was that of Jane Norice, who was variously described as "a thief", "a most abandoned character", "a common vagrant". She was regularly imprisoned, but was clearly "incorrigible".[101]

Rural districts also contained free mulatto women in depressed conditions, at the lowest levels of society. The parched plains of southern St Elizabeth housed communities of poor coloureds. When the Moravian missionaries Ellis and Torn visited Burnt Savannah in January 1829, they found it "settled chiefly by brown persons who live in little huts hid among the log wood and are in a most deplorable state of ignorance and depravity. They are said to run from the presence of a white person to conceal themselves in the bushes, to be much addicted to stealing and to other nefarious practices".[102]

These "poor degraded free people" were seen by the missionaries as proud and indolent, refusing to cultivate their grounds, preferring to move to the sea-shore, where they lived "in caves or little huts" and subsisted on easy catches of fish.[103] Those who remained in the mountains were chiefly the old and infirm, "or those who priding themselves on their fairer skin live with the slaves on the adjoining properties and leave them to work for them".[104]

The women were described as especially shiftless, their "incontinence [was] well known". They neglected their children, who became too chigoe-infested to attend the missionary school.[105] The Moravian ministers Zorn and Pfeiffer attempted to improve the habits of a group of females at Somerset School, but in spite of their degraded circumstances and their religious ignorance, which was equal to that of slaves, "much they plume themselves on their superiority as free brown people".[106]

LIFESTYLE AND "SEXUAL POLITICS"

Not unlike the white women in similar circumstances, the brown woman, however disadvantaged, appeared to see herself and to be seen as always capable of self-advancement, by sole virtue of her colour. Many vital facets of her existence may be validly assessed in the context of her "natural", if not "legitimate", entitlement to many of the good things of creole life. The interracial sexual activity and the domestic establishments in which she was so frequently involved may be observed in this light.

William Hickey was captivated by the lovely but expensive young mulattoes and quadroons who attended a Spanish Town ball. "Girls of this description", he wrote, "are frequently to be procured, though at a monstrous expense, far exceeding what frail ones in London cost."[107] Whether in reference to an unequivocal commercial encounter or to a more intricate domestic relationship, contemporary observers testified to the acquisitive nature of the mulatto female. She, together with her kith and kin, in the words of Edward Long, "fastened upon her keeper like so many leeches, while she, the chief leech, conspires to bleed him *asque ad deliguin*".[108] The bookkeeper Longbey, in the novel *Marly*, learnt the hard way how costly it could be to keep a coloured mistress. He had ignored the warning words of experience, namely, "you would not be advised for your own good, but you must have a brown lady forsooth, but she, I believe made you repent of your choice, after spending nearly two years of your salary".[109]

"A host of Mulattoes, Mustees, Quadroons and Mawkish Whites", wrote Hector McNeill in 1788,

> swarm in every town, and every corner, to the great detriment of the Negro population, and the general disadvantage of the community; for, independent of these free women being the drones of society, they occasion an additional consumption of Negroes, whose services might be applied to much more important purposes. Each lady, for instance, on being admitted to share the bed of her lord, generally receives a New Negro Slave, as a Bridal Gift, which is often doubled, or trebled, according to

the fondness and folly of her lover. Upon this fair one's becoming the mother of a still fairer race, additional servants must be procured for little Master and Miss, who, in their turn, often receive similar donations; so that in the course of fifteen or twenty years, a brown lady may be in possession of twenty or thirty negroes.[110]

She was said to be accomplice, if not instigator, in the common estate practice of appropriating slaves' allowances of clothing, blankets, salted herrings and so on "to her own use".[111] Such a woman was, allegedly, interested only in material possessions and had few scruples about how her property multiplied. She was prepared, some claimed, to profit from the immoral earnings of her female slaves.[112]

The mulatto female was relatively well placed in creole society to name a high price for her favours. For the dominant male group, applying its racist aesthetic made it clear that browns, being closer in physical appearance to whites than blacks, were the more desirable mates.[113] In the absence of white women, the law of supply and demand thus gave mulatto women some bargaining power.

Brown/white concubinage often therefore contained a realistic acknowledgement of the fact that a deal had been struck by the parties concerned and mutual advantages negotiated. The parents of brown females were even known it some instances to initiate these negotiations. "I have known an instance of a woman", testified Reverend Barry, "as fair as I am who voluntarily surrendered her daughter for a consideration in doubloons, and handed her into the chaise with her own Hands."[114]

The brown mistress provided a family and a home away from home, in which her housekeeping skills were generally conceded to be considerable.[115] In a tropical environment of high morbidity and death, her services as resident nurse rated highly. A seasoned bookkeeper recommended a mulatto housekeeper to the newly arrived Marly in the interest of his health. "Your girl", he promised, "will be the most attentive of nurses, far more so than can be expected from strangers."[116] In return, she got her share of the commodities which the society valued.

Brown women frequently outdid white women in ostentatious display. "On public occasions, such as races, reviews, etc., they drive in their curricles, gigs, etc., in a smart and dashing style, as if anxious to leave behind their fairer competitors in the race of fashion, gaiety and pleasure."[117] Maria

Nugent also described the elaborate wardrobe of fine muslin lace and flow-ered hats worn by several of the "half-black progeny of some of the Governor's staff".[118] To her, these hybrids seemed pitiable and "unfortu-nate".[119] But she failed to perceive that their outward show was their badge of relative good fortune, visible evidence of their state of near-equality to whites.

The mistress of a well-off white man at times got partial acceptance by his peers. She might receive, for example, the professional medical care due to a wife.[120] When Dr Archer visited Mr Watkin's "*Chére amie* Gordon", she was introduced to him as "Mrs" Gordon.[121] If she was not allowed by local con-vention to preside openly over her own table,[122] she enjoyed some compensa-tory social preference in the form of an occasional white visit. "I have known", wrote the Reverend Bickell in 1826, "some married ladies pay visits to the kept mistresses of rich men, who were not relatives, though they would not look upon a more respectable woman of the same colour, who might be married to a brown man."[123] Respectable white ladies sometimes stood as godmothers to the children of mulatto/white unions.[124] Brown women of the great house could even claim intimate audience with a gover-nor's wife who was not above being a houseguest in such a menage.[125]

Admission to at least some of the rights of citizenship through private acts of legislation was one of the strongest incentives to mulatto women to strive after liaisons with whites, to recommend a similar course to their daughters and, in the process, to reaffirm how favoured they were above others in the society. The clear concepts of privilege and preference continued to be enshrined officially in the petition process of these acts. Frances Bower Baker, a free mustee of Westmoreland, and her eight children, were granted civic status in 1790, their material condition being such as to ensure "that their situation will be more respectable than that of free people of colour in general".[126] Their comfortable circumstances were guaranteed by the peti-tioner, Robert Baker, who declared his real and personal property as ade-quate to maintain Frances Baker and her children of whom he was the father.[127] In the year 1783, eleven acts confirmed the entitlement of forty-two coloured persons (twenty-three female and nineteen male) to "the same rights and privileges with English subjects, under certain restrictions". Five of these acts identify clearly the mothers of the petitioners, who in four instances were free mulattoes and in one instance a free Negro.[128] In that year, two fathers, William Wright and Thomas Wynter, also successfully petitioned for the right "to settle and dispose of their estates . . . in favour of their natural children", notwithstanding the act of 1761.[129]

Arrival at the peak of coloured aspirations for civic identity is illustrated in the success story underlying a private bill of 1789, enacted in favour of one Sarah Wallace, a free mulatto of Kingston. Rights and privileges of English subjects were granted to her two surviving quadroon daughters, Jane Fraser and Elizabeth Delpratt, their seven mustee children, and her four other mustee granddaughters who were the offspring of a deceased daughter. Sarah Wallace and her three daughters, by consistently mating white, had elevated fourteen persons to the status of citizenship. Five of her mustee grandchildren were girls. With such a pattern of family miscegenation, there was strong motivation for these girls also to find white lovers and produce full citizens within the next generation.[130]

The ultimate reward of concubinage was a guaranteed pension in old age. Robert Nisbett's will of 7 June 1787 demonstrates the kind of provision that was customarily made for the maintenance of the brown mistress after the death of her keeper. Nisbett was a planter of the parish of Westmoreland. Aimey Gordon, a free mulatto woman who had been recently manumized by William Beckford, was left by Nisbett all his household furniture, eleven slaves, and 15 acres of land at Cave in Westmoreland. The estates' executors were further instructed to build her a house not exceeding £100 in value, for her use during her lifetime. Her daughter, Elizabeth Gordon, a free mulatto, received a legacy of a girl slave "with her increase for life". Nisbett's two sons by Aimey Gordon were each to receive £2,000. A final provision for her maintenance underlined the quasi-contractual nature of the relationship between the creole planter and his common-law wife: Aimey Gordon was also left an annuity of £30, which was, however, to be discontinued "if she connects herself with any person who shall seem to them [that is, the executors] improper".[131]

Not all settlements were as comfortable as Aimey Gordon's. May Campbell of St Ann's parish was probably more representative of a larger class of women who exchanged their sexual favours and domestic expertise for only a moderately secure old age. In his will of 1780, John Lawrence left her an annuity of £30. Their two sons were, however, better taken care of: each received £50 per annum for their maintenance and for the cost of their apprenticeship "to some mechanical or other profession". After the completion of their apprenticeship, each was to receive £500 to start in business.[132]

The reputed acquisitiveness of the mulatto woman was probably exaggerated by whites jealous of any attention and benefits bestowed on members of an "inferior" group. A few contemporaries perceived the basic insecurity of the brown mistress, who could at any time be superseded by a white bride. The Reverend Bickell observed that "the poor woman of colour, feeling and duly considering the precariousness of her situation", placed her long-term material welfare high among her goals.[133] Bickell on the whole saw her not as a mercenary exploiter, but as a victim of creole sexual politics. His sympathies went out to vulnerable coloured women, unable to resist "the white man's gold and fine promises".[134] Moravian missionaries felt the need for "particular vigilance and caution" in their pastoral care of local women, who were "generally much exposed to the scouting snares of white men".[135]

The mulatto male in the novel *Marly* spoke with equal compassion of his "woefully ill-treated" sisters. Their illegal alliances, in his opinion, sprang not from any inherent immorality, but from the society's standards, which made conspicuous success possible from "a connexion with a white man".[136]

The Jamaican plantation system could be held responsible for the unfavourable image of the brown woman. Coloured/white concubinage, whether involving black or brown women, slave or free, had its roots in the institution of slavery. The prevalence of sexual coercion has already been discussed above.[137] The Reverend John Barry stated the position, as he saw it, in these terms:

> Q. "Do you mean", he was asked, "that the state of slavery gives to the proprietor that extent of wealth or property which enables him to corrupt the women that are there?"
>
> A. "I mean particularly that it invests him with unlimited power over the body of his female slave."
>
> Q. "But is it not the fact that he has not that power over the free woman, who you say constitute, upon the whole, a large proportion of the mistresses?"

The Reverend Barry was more explicit.

> A. "No, but I attribute the existing state of morals (as to its origin) to slavery, in consequence of the looseness of morals that must necessarily have been produced by the master's indiscriminate intercourse with his servants."

Q. "Then you think that the example arising from the master's intercourse with the servants corrupts the morals of the free people?"

A. "I certainly do".[138]

Religion, Education and Civic Identity

If interracial sex was in creole society one approved means of brown upward mobility, religion, as the other end of the moral spectrum, was frequently another. For conversion, like concubinage, conferred significant social benefits. An avowal of Christianity in a society with a large "pagan" mass could be a passport to a civic identity. Jamaica's private Acts of Privilege throughout the eighteenth and early nineteenth centuries required that the beneficiaries should be baptized in the Church of England.[139]

Penelope Brewer's religious qualifications, as stated in her petition of 14 November 1789, were the typical formula: she had been "baptized, educated, and instructed in the principles of the Christian religion and in the communion of the Church of England as by law established". As a consequence, she received privileged status, like many others similarly blessed.[140]

Under a relieving act of 1796, free coloureds, in order to be eligible to give evidence in the courts in certain limited cases, had to be baptized in the Anglican Church.[141] Baptism remained a qualification for a witness in 1813 when the restrictions on coloured evidence were further relaxed, and it was not finally removed until 1823.[142]

The religious requirement for citizenship received less emphasis in the latter years of slavery. As Sheila Duncker has pointed out: "After 1823 there was less mention of the Christian upbringing; obviously the only relevant fruit of a Christian standard was, in this context, the realization of the binding quality of an oath, and since free-coloured evidence was accepted after 1823 without question, there was no need to claim a specifically Christian attitude."[143]

But free coloureds continued to be "constant attendants at places of worship", turning increasingly to the non-established churches.[144] Genuine religious faith unquestionably motivated numbers of mulatto churchgoers.[145] In relation to whites, they were an inferior group in the society, subject to discrimination and in need of spiritual refuge. They turned mainly to those dissenting churches which, being outside the ecclesiastical establishment, also suffered disabilities.[146]

British Nonconformism was strongly oriented towards salvation as manifested in achievements here and now. Culturally and socially, it aimed at the *ne plus ultra* of the bourgeois ethic, namely, respectability.[147] It found a wide response in coloured creoles striving for material success and social acceptance.

Missionaries took credit for diverting women of colour from the primrose path. This proved a challenge to the authority of the church, as well as to the character of the convert. Backsliding was inevitable and was firmly dealt with: "from time to time the bejeweled free coloured women were disciplined for their love of ornament".[148] Nevertheless, they opted in large numbers for the more austere and pious life. The Reverend Barry spoke with professional pride of Jamaica's "several hundreds of fine young women", who, having been brought under the influence of religious instruction, turned their backs on their old ways and could not be tempted to return even by "the greatest inducements offered by their former keepers".[149]

Religion too had its inducements, and within the constraints of the less prestigious churches, coloured congregations had much to gain. The Wesleyan Methodist church in particular provided for the marginal class of mulattoes an outlet not only for the their religious needs, but for their organizational and leadership potential. It gave to brown women active and fulfilling roles which were denied by other creole institutions to non-whites and to females.

Mary Sutliffe was a free-coloured class leader attached to the Wesleyan missionary society in Kingston in the 1820s. She appeared as a witness in 1828 before the committee of the House of Assembly appointed to investigate the financial operations of the colony's sectarian and dissenting groups. She gave instructions in the principles of religion to a class of ninety-eight persons who included thirteen slaves, the others being "respectable persons of colour, with the exception of a few free blacks".[150] She took pride in the voluntary nature of her work and declared that she would refuse payment for her services to the church, if offered.[151] The Wesleyan church leaders and stewards in Kingston and Port Royal in 1825 and 1826 numbered 142, of whom 88 were female.[152]

Their femininity may have been exploited in promoting the church's cause. Augustus Beaumont recalled being approached for contributions in a Kingston store some time in 1824 or 1825 by "a very handsome Wesleyan mulatto girl with a subscription list which she was carrying about to raise money for some such purpose [that is, founding chapels and the like]".[153] Enterprising females, higglers and small traders, showed great zeal in collecting money for the support and expansion of the missions.[154]

Coloured women's work in fund raising, as well as in proselytizing and in teaching, was fully acknowledged and approved. The Reverend Peter Duncan paid great tribute to the exertions of a number of outstanding women in the cause of Jamaican Methodism. Catherine Ffrench's contribution in the parish of St David was significant. She was

> a coloured female of earnest piety, and remarkable for her uncommon zeal and intelligence. She was born in slavery, and belonged to a Mrs Geoghegan, a white lady, who gave her freedom in infancy, and brought her up with great tenderness. She joined the Society in Kingston; and possessing many advantages she became noted for piety and usefulness. After a number of years, her kind benefactress was under the necessity of removing from Kingston, and settling on a property of her own, called Pomfret (in the aforesaid parish of St David's), which was situated about eight miles westward from Morant Bay. The thought of separating from her religious associates was extremely painful; but she felt she could not part from one to whom she was under so many obligations, who had brought her up with maternal kindness, and with whom she had resided from her birth. She therefore accompanied her, in the hope that the Lord would make her useful amongst a people who knew nothing of the way of salvation. She soon succeeded in forming a class of serious enquirers after religion; and, to her unspeakable joy, was rendered instrumental in the conversion of Mrs Geoghegan herself, who met along with her for religious exercises, and profited by her instructions. The house of that lady was now opened for the preaching of the gospel, and the hall was fitted up with benches for the accommodation of all who chose to attend. Pomfret became connected with Morant Bay, and was visited by the missionaries as often as their engagements would allow. This continued for two or three years; when, on the death of Mrs Geoghegan, the property was sold and the house could no longer be occupied. A temporary hut was however erected at no great distance from it, large enough to accommodate between two and three hundred hearers and the ordinances of God were administered as before.[155]

Miss Mutton, a coloured woman of some substance, was the moving spirit behind the foundation of a Methodist society at Grateful Hill, in northern St Andrew.[156] Miss Sarah Racster, also a coloured woman of

means, gave thirteen years' service to the Kingston society early in the nineteenth century; she was "one of its brightest ornaments".[157] She led two
female classes in Kingston and one in Port Royal; her generosity was well
known.[158]

Mrs Wilkinson of Manchioneal was acclaimed as a remarkable religious
pioneer. Her district, at the beginning of the nineteenth century, had apparently been a spiritual desert: "she saw no way but to perform the duties of the
clergyman herself, and she actually married several couples, which were
among the first negro marriages, solemnized on the island".[159] Her religious
work among the slaves apparently "excited the suspicions of the principal
inhabitants", and she decided to move to Kingston, where she continued to
be one of the most energetic foundation members of the chapel there.[160]

Free coloureds constituted half of the membership of the Wesleyan missions in Kingston. They outnumbered slaves in the Port Royal and Spanish
Town congregations.[161] They served as officials and as lay preachers and kept
the societies together. They gave substantial financial support.[162] In 1827, the
Kingston mission collected between £2,500 and £3,000, subscribed by
"many affluent persons of colour belonging to [the] society [who] contribute
from £4 to £8 a year".[163] Interest-free credit for chapel building was sometimes advanced by coloured church members: Miss Catherine Jervis of Ocho
Rios sold land and premises to the mission in 1829 for £450; and was still
without payment three years later, when the premises were destroyed.[164]

In the campaign of harassment and persecution of sectarians and dis-
senters, waged in the 1820s and 1830s by the creole clerical and planter establishment, free-coloured women too were targets. Miss Jervis together with a
Robert Watkis, a mulatto and a Wesleyan, appeared in October 1826 before
the St Ann's Bay Court of Quarter Sessions, for breaches of the law governing sectarians. She was accused of being engaged in religious exercises in her
house after dark. She was found not guilty of any offence and dismissed.[165]

Missionaries valued coloured church sisters an indispensable patrons,
activists, even martyrs, in the cause. But there were limits to their esteem: it
did not extend to close personal relationships. It became a cardinal tenet of
the evangelical behaviour code that missionaries should avoid contact with
mulatto women, lest they too, like so many of their flock, fall into sinful
creole ways. They therefore received instructions to treat the brown ladies
of their congregation "with the utmost reserve and prudence".[166]

Considerations of colour, as much as those of morality, appeared to be the factors underlying this taboo. Missionaries accepted creole racial conventions that ruled out legal unions between whites and mulattoes.

> It never entered into the imagination, I suppose, of a Missionary in this island to take one of them, although as to mental and religious requirements many of them are not perhaps behind most of them that might become missionary's wives; and their persons and manners also agreeable. Yet we are too well acquainted with the policy of this country to sanction a marriage of that kind which would be a weapon in the hands of our enemies to chastise us; for this would be the case even if their previous lives had ever been virtuous.[167]

As a consequence, the young Methodist missionary Mr Langslowe, who, "while convalescent, succumbed to the charms of his free coloured nurse", had to resign from his district in order to marry her. His resignation was accepted with regret, but he was later allowed to become a lay preacher.[168]

Religious involvement did, however, offer professional, if not matrimonial openings to brown women. The churches made full use of their coloured female members as teachers in the Sunday and day schools.[169] They were always short of personnel and the burden of teaching tended to fall heavily on mission wives. The employment of women also served as a relief on the always scarce church funds, for they were paid less than men.[170] The Moravians, for instance, regularly used coloured women at a small salary in their schools for free children.[171] In the 1820s, they considered the training of local teachers, and this led to the establishment of a normal school in 1833 at the Fairfield mission, whose first two brown female pupils had their fees paid by patrons who wished to save them from concubinage.[172]

Bryan Edwards, writing in 1801, estimated that not "one in fifty of the unhappy [coloured] females could read or write".[173] This was not surprising in view of the scant provisions made for local education. Few free schools existed, Beckford's in Spanish Town, Mannings in Savanna-la-Mar, Wolmer's in Kingston and Rusea's in Lucea, and these were "second-class schools for the children of poor second-class whites".[174]

Such educational facilities as developed before emancipation, and indeed after, received their momentum from the initiative of the Nonconformist bodies, starting with the early Moravian estate Sabbath schools of the eighteenth century and developing, by the 1820s, into institutions such as the new Baptists' school in Kingston, which opened in January 1826 with 224 scholars, 90 of whom were girls.[175] Free coloured attendance was approximately 50 per cent.[176]

Education was a prerequisite for citizenship. Jamaica's private privilege bills were every much "in favour of such persons of colour as have been educated".[177] An English education was rated highly for this purpose, but this was the prerogative of the sons and daughters of wealthy men, a very privileged handful.[178] Long implied that overseas schooling was wasted on mulattoes, as they would still suffer racial discrimination and ostracism from white Jamaicans.[179] Mulattoes certainly never saw their position as immobile and irredeemable. When educational facilities, however limited, became available locally, they were quick to grasp them.

They promoted learning among their children[180] and sent them in large numbers to the missionary schools.[181] It has been already noted that when the doors to Wolmer's School, hitherto the preserve of whites, was first opened to them in 1814, they entered in large numbers, crowding out white pupils and radically altering the complexion of the island's largest free school within one decade.[182] Ebenezeer Reid, the headmaster of Wolmer's in the 1830s, reported that "since the admission of coloured children in 1815 to 1837, a period of twenty three years, 842 children have been educated".[183] Table 8.3 shows the number of schools in Kingston and their enrolment in 1832.

Table 8.3   Schools in Kingston, 1832

Schools		Scholars
Wolmer's	2	472
National	1	260
Gentlemen's private	31	1,169
Ladies' private	41	856
Sunday	8	981
Totals	**83**	**3,738**

Source: James A. Thome and Joseph H. Kimball, *Emancipation in the West Indies: A Six Months' Tour in Antigua, Barbados, and Jamaica, in the Year 1837* (New York: American Anti-Slavery Society, 1838), 355.

It is fairly certain that the whites attempted to keep these institutions, especially the private ones, exclusive, but in the city this would have been difficult. Thome and Kimball observed in 1837 that there were "no segregated schools in Kingston".[184]

REPRESENTATIONS AND INTERRACIAL TENSION

In the mulatto woman's struggle for status in creole slave society, she exploited available opportunities in the domestic economy, in religion, in education, in her sex. In particular, she maximized the rewards of her association with the dominant group: the white male. This tended to place her in a relatively favourable position *vis-à-vis* other members of the society. White men gave her the local prize of Paris. White women, too few, too remote, and not at their best in the tropics, did not qualify.

Edward Long dismissed blacks' claims to good looks with predictable venom.[185] The coloured woman, by much wider consensus, became the full-blown creole beauty, her infusions of white blood significantly shaping her aesthetic rating. Tributes to her physical qualities characterize the records.[186] The period novel *Hamel, the Obeah Man* contains a rhapsody on her near-white gifts:

> What a sweet face! . . . Can the Eastern Houris surpass its loveliness – or even the beauties of Great Britain? Praxiteles himself could not have desired a more enchanting model. How beautiful is the blush upon her cheek! It is almost as deep as the rose-colour of her silk handkerchief. And her skin – how smooth and delicate, and how fair! Who would suppose her to be the descendant of an African black – of one whose skin was as sooty as that of Hamel? And where are the thick lips, and the flat nose, and the woolly hair? Not even Joanna herself could surpass her in any of the externals of beauty.[187]

Another writer stated: "The vanity of female [mulatto] slaves is raised to an unbounded degree to be chosen objects of their master, . . . managers are obliged to pamper and indulge them like goddesses."[188] They became "intolerably insolent"[189] to others who did not, like themselves, enjoy the favours of the male creole elite. They were domineering to subordinate white men: "woe betide a poor overseer if he affronts one of them".[190]

White women viewed them as "serpents" that exercised sinister authority over susceptible white men;[191] and white men acknowledged their power. "These ladies", Dr Williamson wrote in 1817, "became the greatest tyrants that can be imagined: so much so that the most despotic in matrimony with their own colour have seldom reached such uxorious oppression."[192] Governor Nugent saw few prospects for the successful immigration into the island (as was being proposed in the early nineteenth century) of Irish female settlers, because "the Mulatto women have too much ascendancy over every class of settlers to leave any hope of disposing of the Females described in your letter in any manner".[193]

A focus of interracial tension, the brown woman's poor relationships extended to blacks[194] and to brown men. She held herself aloof from slave festivities:[195] she engaged in independent social activities, the popular mulatto balls, for instance, from which all non-white men were excluded.[196] She considered it a "degradation to marry black"[197] and an unwelcome last resort to mate with brown.[198] In this context, coloured men's self-respect and status were compromised. The Speaker of the Jamaican House of Assembly in 1828 underlined the distinction white society made in its dealings with brown men and women: "[W]e have been used from infancy to keep mulatto men at a distance."[199] John Campbell, a wealthy St James mulatto, in his "humble memorial" of 1823 to Earl Bathurst, the secretary of state, lamented the helplessness of coloured men who had no safeguards against the seduction of their wives and daughters.[200]

With brown men "helpless" and brown women "ascendant", creole conventions operated to make coloured females very much their own domestic bosses. Their predilection for white men ruled out for many the possibility of legal and/or stable unions. Even on rural estates, where settled relationships between brown females and white males existed, this did not necessarily mean a recognized family unit under one roof. Evidence such as exists of brown slave households suggests the contrary. Higman's studies of Old and New Montpelier estates revealed that domestics, the majority of whom were female and brown, tended to live in families dominated by women. "Slaves of colour", he observed, "formed households in which slave men had no part but were tightly organized round the maternal connection".[201]

These findings are especially meaningful in light of the pivotal role of the woman in creating a free creole dynasty.[202] One may see here emerging something of a true profile of the creole matriarch. Such a woman may have originated as a domestic slave: some of her group reached the top of the local ladder, carrying with them their sons and daughters and grandchildren, claiming the rights of full citizenship. Many of them made this progress without a visible permanent spouse, of whatever colour. The evidence of their children's complexion, however, made clear that their mate, or mates, had not been black, or even brown.

Grace Elizabeth Robertson, a free quadroon, in 1789 had civic rights and privileges granted to herself and her several mustee children, five in all, born of four different fathers.[203] So did Frances Peddar, a free quadroon woman, and her five mustee children, the products of three fathers.[204] Sarah Fisher was a free mulatto woman: one of her daughters and five of her sons were fathered by the St Ann planter William Hull, another son and another daughter by the planter Robert Craig, also of St Ann. All eight of her children benefited from her petition in 1786.[205] The free mulatto Susanna White of St George, like Sarah Wallace,[206] took three generations with her into citizenship, namely her brother, her sister, her sons by one father, her daughter by another, her daughter-in-law and two grandchildren.[207]

Women of interracial unions, heads of their households, frequently engaged in multiple mating, guiding the upward mobility of their families and in the process inculcating socio-racial values applicable to a much wider world than that of the domestic circle. From the perspective of the ruling group in the society, such women were persons of influence and authority. Insofar as females who were non-white had any access to power in a power structure that was white and male, they were these women. The original creole matriarch may well have been not black, but brown.

Part Three

POSTSCRIPT, 1834–1844

9   *The Beginning of a Free Society,*
1834–1844

The first decade of free Jamaica coincided with the advent of Victorian England, on whose manners and morals the Jamaican upper and middle classes predictably modelled themselves. Beginning with the rambunctious mood of the 1830s, Regency England gradually sobered up and did its best to make its image worthy of its lady monarch. The hypocrisy, prudery and snobbery which eventually became the hallmarks of the age grew directly out of its rough origins. "It is easy", wrote Duncan Crow,

> to despise Victorian hypocrisy and the whole euphemistic approach that went with it, forgetting that this blinkered attitude was adopted to hide the proximity of the abyss in which seethed the primitive society the Victorians were struggling away from. Their only defence against slipping back into the slime was, it seemed, to ignore the immoralities and horrifying cruelties that surrounded them, and to adopt the canons of ultra-propriety.[1]

This was peculiarly relevant to colonial societies whose vulgarities and immoralities had not been abolished by imperial act of Parliament. The Euro-Jamaican female had been conditioned to blot out, if she could, the dark realities around her and to pursue gentility.[2] Metropolitan culture, which increasingly penetrated free Jamaica through religion and education, reinforced this myth. The post-emancipation period saw attempts to refine a colonial blueprint for the ideal woman in the ideal family setting.

Industry, temperance, piety and domesticity were necessary virtues for the new society. If they did not thrive naturally in creole society, like so much else, they could be imported. The period of the 1830s and 1840s saw earnest efforts to provide the population with overseas models of the happy white family who worked hard and prayed hard. These models entered the society as missionaries and as labourers/settlers, intended to play some part in the re-arrangement of creole mores and relationships.[3]

The local anti-abolitionist movement of the 1820s and 1830s had also been a movement against sectarianism and against evangelical work among blacks.[4] The passage of the Abolition Bill of 1834 facilitated the religious activism both of the established and of the dissenting churches, and Jamaica entered a period of "a missionary boom" that lasted into the 1840s.[5]

The work of religious conversion and moral regeneration required exemplary practitioners: a family unit was a necessity. William Barrett, indefatigable minister of the London Missionary Society, wrote from his station in Four Paths, Clarendon, on 20 February 1839: "many mighty reasons induce me to say that a missionary ought to be married – economy – usefulness – respectability all demand it".[6] Marriage was acknowledged by most church societies to be crucial to the adjustment and survival of a missionary. The temperament and character of his wife, the nature of his family relationships, could be major factors in his effectiveness in the field. So fiancées and wives were usually assessed in advance, and applicants for work abroad had to show that their wives were pious and "zealous for the mission cause".[7] The ministers of the London Missionary Society wrote to their headquarters in February 1838 about their good fortune in getting the services of an American brother, Reverend Ingraham, a Congregationist minister of twenty-five years of age, and "married to a pious young person of suitable qualifications, both educated at Oberlin Manual Labour College in the state of Ohio". Satisfied of "their self-denying zeal and energetic character", the society appointed Reverend Ingraham as schoolmaster at Liguanea and as assistant missionary to Reverend Woodridge.[8]

John Gibson gave to the mission's secretary the credentials of the lady he proposed marrying, namely that she was

> zealously devoted to the cause of the Redeemer, she is a member of the Wesleyan Body and has been engaged as a class leader and Sabbath School Teacher. She bears

an excellent character, and is beloved by those who know her. I have every reason to believe that she will prove a good help-meet and co-worker with me in the school.[9]

With some half-a-dozen religious societies in action in Jamaica,[10] the work of salvation was a competitive one: nearly all missionary hands counted. Women were needed not only to build Christian homes, but also to be working partners. Women's zeal in collecting money was well established, both in Britain and in Jamaica, and in the process of fund raising, they served as propagandists of the faith.[11] They gave religious instruction to women: Mrs Hope Waddell supplemented her husband's work by her classes for female converts. We are told that "so much depends on them as wives and mothers in maintaining peace and godliness in the family, that Mrs Waddell instituted special female Prayer meetings in several places to give them suitable instruction and teach and encourage them to conduct meetings for religious exercises among themselves".[12] In Chapelton, the Reverend Robert Jones had a group of ninety-six "inquirers" on weekday evenings, too large a group for him to attend properly, so Mrs Jones worked with the women.[13]

Missionary women were indispensable in the running of Jamaica's church schools. Mrs Hodge, whose husband was stationed at Morant Bay, ran the Sunday School of about fifty adults.[14] Mrs Alloway at Williamsfield taught twenty very young children who attended the missionary infant school five days a week.[15] The Reverend James Howell's wife, also of Morant Bay, superintended the girls' school in the needlework department ("except for a short period of childbirth").[16] The Reverend and Mrs Woodridge, while waiting for a schoolhouse at Shortwood to be built, conducted classes together under the piazza of their home.[17] The Reverend Barrett, who was devoted and effective in his educational and pastoral work in Four Paths and Porus, relied heavily on his wife and sister in the schoolroom and the church.[18]

Missionary wives who worked received no salaries. Some church women were specially recruited as teachers and could be paid less than their male colleagues, so that Reverend Ingraham received £100 per annum, and Miss Georgina Squires, who taught at Porus, was hired at £50 annually (although she received no pay for 1840) and her sister Jemima Squires was paid £50.[19] "Without wishing either to unfold or eulogize our manner of life", wrote Reverend Barrett, "I may mention what under other circumstances I would not have done, that Mrs Barrett has for some time past denied herself of tea and coffee and sugar, and has devoted the saving thereby effected to the funds of the Society."[20]

Missionary women were the least self-indulgent and the most socially concerned white females in post-emancipation Jamaica. They had something in common with another small group of new arrivals: the families of stipendiary magistrates, who had the official responsibility of ensuring justice for all in the transitional era of apprenticeship.[21] The magistrate's ostensible function of impartial adjudicator tended to develop into a special concern for the ex-slave and to make him often a "watchdog of apprentice welfare".[22] This brought him closer to the position of the missionary, whose first care was indeed black spiritual welfare.

The men's terms of reference in relation to blacks tended to set their families in a category apart from that of other white interest groups with whom they appeared to have little contact. Missionary families appeared to live their social lives very much within the close orbit of the island's mission community. Women's deep involvement with their husband's work allowed them to share certain levels of black experience and to make their presence felt at very significant levels, and this, even though their numbers were relatively small.[23] But their activism was inhibited by the ills to which all white women in Jamaica fell prey. They were seldom really at ease in the island. They were plagued with the high cost of creole living, with sickness and with death, and in this respect their domestic grievances and tragedies were identical to those of every other white woman who found Jamaica physically hostile. "In October", wrote Reverend William Slayter, from Nightingale Grove in Porus, in 1836, "I had a severe attack of inflammatory Fever which disabled me for the service of our Lord and Master three weeks, during which period Mrs S. was unexpectedly confined. After two days' residence in this vale of tears God took our little one to himself."[24]

The Reverend Matthew Hodge wrote from Morant Bay during the same period:

> just recovering from fever for last 12 days . . . my dear wife at same time suffering as much as myself and even more, but luckily, now convalescing . . . Present an unhealthy season. Fever prevailing in every direction and laying many in the dust. The Methodist Minister stationed here died last week, the sixth Methodist Minister

to die within a very few months . . . these events have not a little affected me. They seem to speak with a voice of thunder . . . when we think of the vastness of our work, the opposing influence of the climate in undermining our energies and cutting short our life . . . we need the prayers of our friends at home.[25]

Their distresses were aggravated by their very restricted financial means, bordering almost on poverty.[26] The Reverend Howell, who was stationed in Morant Bay, was concerned about his inability to pay a bill of between £15 and £20, which he was expecting to receive for the medical expenses of himself and his child incurred during the previous summer. When his wife fell ill on Christmas Eve with "an alarming attack of fever" which lasted four days, he did not call the doctor "in view of the heavy charges and [his] poor circumstances". Luckily, with the help of friends and his own home remedies, she recovered.[27]

The vulnerable financial base from which missionaries operated made it difficult for them to be independent of the ruling creole whites. Some genuinely resisted absorption into planter society, in the interest of their pastoral work with ex-slaves. When Reverend Barrett, for instance, first arrived in the parish of Clarendon, he was offered two rooms in the overseer's house on the estate of the leading planter in the area, Mr Bravo. He was expected in return to minister exclusively to Bravo's apprentices. In addition, Barrett complained,

he expected us, as those paid under obligation to him, to associate with him, and join his dinner parties, which would not only have been incompatible with the Missionary character, but at the same time retarded our usefulness amongst those to whom we were directly sent. Indeed one of the most intelligent negroes on the property assigned as his reason for not coming to hear me that "Massa minister was too near Busha."[28]

Reverend Barrett moved from the property and settled in Old Harbour, but, significantly, required Bravo's assistance to effect the change.[29]

Missionaries, on the whole, unable to dispense with white patronage, consciously promoted values and policies agreeable to the creole establishment. The education which they advanced among blacks was valued for "its acceptableness to the Planters".[30] It was "the combination of common school education with agricultural instruction and labour. It is of great consequence to us here at present to make field labour honourable." The Reverend James

Thomson, on 31 December 1834, advised the secretary of the London Missionary Society that such educational programmes "would much ingratiate [missionaries] with all the people of Jamaica".[31]

The racial perspective of many missionaries was ambivalent, and this, too, compromised their potential as catalysts of social reconstruction. They knew well the local conflicts of race and colour. "The white population", observed Reverend Barrett, "have the most inveterate prejudice against the least vestige of African blood – and the Negroes dislike the brown people extremely."[32] As for the browns, "no inducement could make them associate in a class with the negroes. . . . [T]he coloured people imbibe prejudice against the blacks, from their earliest infancy."[33]

Missionaries, however, did not see it as their function to disturb the creole status quo. Not unlike local whites, who promoted coloureds from time to time for their own purposes, missionaries favoured the browns whose services they needed. The Reverend Henry Russell had in his church at Claremont over 120 apprentices in the Sabbath school, and was grateful that "the three Misses Ingrain brown ladies continue to lend us their valuable aid as teachers on the Sabbath and they often assist in the evening school. We also find them with their Aunt very kind and friendly neighbours. I meet them once a week as a Bible class."[34] Reverend Barrett expressed pleasure when the Mico Charity supplied them with two teachers, both coloured, one, "Miss Steadman, an excellent young person", who boarded with the Barretts at their home in Four Paths.[35] In arguing the need for a larger and better mission building than the one then in use, Barrett had pointed out previously to his London superiors that "the appearance of the place, and the circumstance of its being open all round, prevents many of the brown so-called respectable from attending, who perhaps would attend in a better looking place".[36]

Mulattoes were thus seen by missionaries as "a distinct class",[37] who were destined "on account of their parentage [to] occupy a more respectable and influential station in life than many".[38] It was hoped that their influence in the society would be directed "in a proper channel".[39] In order to ensure this, they were given special attention, both in church and school, involving, if necessary, arrangements which kept them apart from blacks. While Mr and Mrs Barrett taught between fifty and fifty-six children of apprentices in the school at Four Paths, Miss Barrett had

10 brown children, more respectable, whose parents are able and willing to pay for their education – and by this means to keep them separate from those whose skins are tinctured with a darker hue than their own. Thus the means of religious instruction is offered to those who would otherwise be deprived of it by the pride of their parents.[40]

Relationships between blacks and missionaries, male and female, were not made easier by the critical evangelical view of ex-slaves as pagans whose sexual irregularities were particularly undesirable. Blacks had, as a result, to be re-shaped with great difficulty into the desired mould of English morality. "We have taken some pains also", wrote the Reverend Woolridge on 12 March 1838,

> that boys and girls should be kept entirely separate from each other, except while in the school under the master's eye. This is a matter of very great importance, which has not in this country been duly considered. There is a most grievous Deficiency, almost everywhere observable, and such arrangements tend to preserve that delicacy, which especially in the female sex, is so important an outpost of morality.[41]

"The painful state" of the black congregation drove evangelists to a point of near despair; and their punitive policies towards their would-be converts showed wide and virtually unbridgeable gaps in understanding. Members of the Moravian flock at Mesopotamia were strongly judged in 1834 for having "again taken a share in the heathenish Christmas festivities and revelling". By the usual regulations of the church, this would have invoked the expulsion of the whole slave congregation, so a compromise was agreed: "Those who had gone to the Great House or Overseer's House to dance should only be seriously admonished, but those who allowed such practices in their own house, should be excluded."[42]

MORAL OBJECTIVES OF WHITE IMMIGRATION

The task of moral regeneration also involved transforming ex-slaves into obedient and industrious workers, patterned after a probably mythical British working class. Public and private schemes for white immigration in the 1830s and 1840s were prompted by the need to redress the customary racial imbalance, a need which was seen to be even more urgent under a free system. Critical visitors to Jamaica in the late 1830s observed "a mania for immigration . . . as if there were a charm in a European birth and a white complexion".[43] Influxes of whites would also serve the vital purposes of solving problems of labour shortages and providing ex-slaves with models of industry.

Thomas McNeil, custos of Westmoreland and attorney for Lord Holland's estates in western Jamaica, designed a cottage suitable for such immigrants and their families. It was 32 feet long by 16 feet wide, with one bedroom 9 feet by 10 feet for the parents, two bedrooms 9 feet by 7 feet 3 inches each (one for male and one for female children), one pantry 9 feet by 4½ feet, and one hall 16 feet by 12 feet, and it was estimated to cost £60. It would be placed on a half-acre garden plot, and have close by one acre of good provision land which would be cleaned and planted with cocos, yam and plantains, adequate to support a family of five or six.[44] McNeil's first choice for recruitment was Scotland whose labourers had a reputation of being "more tractable, domesticated and sober than their European counterparts"; they paid more attention, he maintained, "to the little family wants" and spent less of their earnings "in the alehouse".[45] Preferably, the elders and ministers of their parishes should recommend them for Jamaica.[46]

Immigrants who were accustomed in their countries of origin to "wheaten flour animal foods and beer" would be too expensive to maintain, and McNeil therefore advised against such costly importees.[47] This was another argument in favour of the potato-eating Scottish labourers, who would take more easily to the African diet of yams, cocos and plantains: "the cheap feeder will in the end be the most fitting person for this country".[48] The presence of their wives was stressed: creole blacks, it was felt, would benefit greatly by "the example of thriftiness in domestic arrangements and housekeeping generally pursued by the poor persons in that part of Scotland" (that is, Galloway).[49]

The visitors to Jamaica, Sturge and Harvey, found six "excellent and wholesome" Scotsmen answering McNeil's criteria in 1837, in the new white settlement proposed for Altamont in the Portland mountains. They were all married, with young families. They had apparently been handpicked by a minister in Aberdeen. The men were "fine athletic peasants", the children were happy and laughing, the "wives however, generally appeared homesick".[50]

Nearly five thousand such white immigrants entered Jamaica between 1834 and 1843, under the regulatory legislation of 1836 and 1840.[51] The majority of the newcomers originated in Great Britain and Germany. The Germans who were settled in Seaford Town in Westmoreland had approximately even numbers of men and women.[52] In 1836, the first batch contained eighty-four men, seventy-two women, forty-five boys and forty-eight girls.[53] The men had a variety of artisan skills and attempted cultivation as well. The women helped to some extent with "cleaning provisions". They also were engaged in cotton picking and were said to be skilled in spinning the cotton into threads with which they made stockings and gloves, glowingly described by an optimistic immigrant official as "excellent and durable".[54] The settlement deteriorated over the next few years in health, in numbers and in agricultural activity.[55] Little improvement took place on the houses and plots provided for them.[56] They showed "little inclination to perform agricultural labour on neighbouring properties".[57] Thomas McNeil saw the problem to be one of "too many handy craftsmen and too few field labourers".[58]

The women were significant casualties. In 1837, the records showed eight female deaths and sixteen cases of weakly or ulcerated women out of a total of fifty-three.[59] It was alleged that in order to avoid agricultural work, women were induced by their husbands to travel about the countryside "under the plea of destitution" and so claim relief.[60] They were seen by some as an "unfortunate and betrayed" group of persons, to whom Jamaica proved "most cruel and inhospitable".[61] The emigrant women of the 1830s and 1840s did not emerge as a superior model of domestic economy for the black working classes. The survivors tended to withdraw into lighter-skinned enclaves, never fully integrating into the black majority of the society,[62] never became pace setters. Neither the female evangelist nor the would-be yeoman's wife proved dynamic enough to alter substantially the *modus operandi* of white women in free Jamaica. Missionary women undoubtedly brought elements of greater concern for the welfare and education of ex-slaves. Essentially, however, the status and role of white women in the society had been too firmly established during slavery to be affected by legislation that gave blacks a new legal status but which left white superiority fundamentally untouched.

The white influx of the post-emancipation decade served primarily to give a brief boost to white numbers. The year 1844, the date of the first census of the Jamaican population, marked the peak of white occupation. Around 15,766 whites were registered in that year and represented 4.2 per cent of a population of 377,433 – the largest proportion recorded before or since, in the island's history. The ratio subsequently declined steadily.[63]

The gender imbalance of the white group also reached its summit at that time, with 1,432 males to 1,000 females.[64] It fell over the next few decades and equalized itself by the twentieth century. It has been suggested that this may not have been a genuine demographic phenomenon, but rather a sociological one, due to "more of the female coloured population electing to class themselves as white, presumably because of the enhanced social status such identification usually assures".[65] Implicit in such a process was the continued negative rating of the newly emancipated black majority.

VOTING WITH THEIR FEET: FREED WOMEN'S ACTIONS DURING AND AFTER APPRENTICESHIP

The reluctance of ex-slaves, females included, to engage in estate field labour was widely attested after emancipation.[66] The question was asked, and answered itself, namely: "Does a considerable portion of the population, especially of the females, look with dislike on that description of labour to which they were peculiarly devoted when slaves, and which is inseparably associated in their minds with the idea of torture, oppression and degradation?"[67] The planter's constant fear of a labour shortage, especially on sugar estates, was aggravated by the black woman's stance. Lord Holland's estates of Friendship and Greenwich, for which Thomas McNeil was responsible, contained in 1836 a majority of female apprentices, ninety-seven women and eighty-four men.[68] They showed extreme unwillingness to continue estate work, and McNeil threatened them with eviction from their houses and plots. The men were reluctantly persuaded to turn out to work, but "only a few of the females", McNeil wrote, "have consented to return to the cane field".[69] It was clear to him that the estates could not operate profitably with such minimal numbers of field women. Even if the men put in sustained labour, it would be, he declared in September 1838, "quite impossible to continue sugar cultivation to give any remuneration to the proprietors unless the Females also be induced to labour regularly".[70]

A month later, McNeil had a more favourable report to give on the size of his labour force, namely, that "a fair proportion of the females now go daily to work in the canefields".[71] But he was by no means optimistic about the long-term prospect of women's participation in essential field tasks. He wrote accordingly:

> I have no hopes of our succeeding in again having the services of more than a small proportion of the Females in the canefields and without which we will experience very great difficulty in getting off the small crops which will be made, for during the progress of crop the greater number of the males are required about the Factories and as cartmen and mulemen.[72]

The excess of women on the Holland estates immediately after emancipation was fairly typical of the population.[73] Their withdrawal in large numbers from estate labour could significantly affect the island's economy. The planter's policy designed to avert this alarming possibility was to apply a variety of coercive measures for keeping women in the field. The harassment of the black female became one of the most notable features of the first years of a free society. The apprenticeship system as instituted by the Emancipation Act of 1834 facilitated this harassment. By attempting to phase out slavery in gradual stages,[74] apprenticeship turned out to be "an impossible compromise", productive of bitter friction between ex-masters and ex-slaves.[75]

A select committee of the House of Commons that investigated the workings of the system in 1837 condemned the act on which it was based as a "vague and imperfect piece" of legislation.[76] Its greatest weakness was that it entrusted to the colonial legislature the detailed subordinate arrangements necessary for implementing the law. This procedure proved "wholly inadequate to secure the rights and immunities given to the apprenticed labourers".[77] The areas of the law that fell under the authority of creole policy makers touched closely on the personal welfare of the apprentice and could be manipulated by a vengeful plantocracy to make life especially intolerable for the black female.

The whole subject of allowances was one on which the Abolition Act was held to be "defective" and ambiguous.[78] The act, for instance, required the planter to continue issues of clothing and salted fish to apprentices, but the legal status of such issues was unclear. The ex-slave saw them as rightful "allowances"; the planter, as "indulgences"; and estate managers, in some instances, required that apprentices work in their own time to earn these prerequisites.

Women were vitally affected by this conflict. Not only were they, as members of the labour force, involved in the disputes about the customary entitlements claimed by all workers, but as the traditional beneficiaries of maternal privileges, their status and their rights became especially controversial. The partial work exemption of pregnant and nursing mothers, the total work exemption of women with more than six children, became sore issues. There was, unfortunately, "no particular law upon the subject".[79] Planter criteria of their own needs tended to prevail, and abuses were rampant.

"Very great hardship", testified the stipendiary magistrate Madden in 1836, "[was] suffered by pregnant women in consequence of being called on to work up to the last month of their pregnancy, which before the first of August they were not called upon."[80] Stipendiary magistrate Brown maintained that on several occasions when he attempted to protect women in an advanced state of pregnancy from excessive labour, he was threatened with action for damages by their owners.[81] James Archer's attitude was typical: he nearly dismissed his headman for allowing Amelia Bogle to arrive late to work in the mornings after a four-week confinement. She must, he insisted, turn out to work at 7:00 a.m. or be reported to the magistrate.[82]

Governor Sligo attempted in 1836, through instructions to the special magistrates, to give clear administrative guidelines about the liability of female apprentices to repay time spent away from work during pregnancy, lactation and children's illnesses. On the subject of pregnancy, he conceded that "sickness is a lawful cause of neglecting the employer's work". This principle he considered applicable to "the sickness of childbed", and he concluded that women therefore did not appear liable to repay the time lost in this way. In spite of these official directives in favour of maternal claims, abuses continued.

The position regarding sick children also made women vulnerable. Lord Sligo's imprecise instructions on this point did not assist much in resolving the variety of subjective interpretations evident. He declared that it had never been the intention that the rights of an employer should "supersede the paramount obligations of a mother to her offspring", and that clearly it would be unreasonable to punish a mother who neglected her employers' duties in order to attend her sick child. But on the other hand, he continued, so much depended on

> the reality and nature of the illness, and the extent of time devoted to that duty in each particular case. . . . If such as apology be untruly alleged as an excuse for idleness, or to deprive the employer of the time he is entitled to, it will become a case to be dealt with as any other unfounded pretext for avoiding duty.[83]

This was a clear invitation to proprietors like James Archer to decide what was the reality of an illness and to manifest his spite against female apprentices. In October 1836, he issued his most harsh warnings again to his head constable, William Murray, and to the apprentice Mary Ann, for failing to observe strict isolation of her child, who was a yaws patient and thereby propagating "this loathsome disease". He was prepared, moreover, to demand time lost to him by any of his female workers whose children contracted the disease, as he held the mothers responsible for spreading contagion.[84] He accused one woman in particular, Kitty, of deliberately exposing her child to its risk, in order that she, Kitty, might stay home:

> [There is] from the neglect which I have this day seen an evident wish to get the children with yaws . . . under the idea that they will be permitted to sit down and mind their children. I shall certainly allow no time of mine to be lost in their attendance and the consequences which will follow on such obstinacy of belief will not, I tell you, be such as Kitty and others can possibly have well thought of.[85]

The policy of extracting the maximum labour from women meant, in many instances, the reversal of the policy of work exemption for slave mothers with over six children. Such women were sent back to the field, to work in the second gang. In addition, there were widespread cutbacks in the provision of "welfare" services, which served the planter's purpose of economizing in his overheads and adding to his field-labour force. The special magistrate Brown testified that in the parishes of Vere and Clarendon, which were under his jurisdiction, the planters "took away all the cooks, they took away all the midwives, and they took away all the water-carriers".[86]

It was a source of great black concern that in some instances midwives were sent back to the field.[87] Deprived of welfare personnel and services and pressured to give maximum work time to the estate, women had often to carry their infants and young children into the work gangs and lay them "beside the trenches where they were digging".[88] Special magistrate Edward Baynes predicted that one "melancholy result" of apprenticeship would be a further decrease of the black population caused by "withdrawing the mother from the care of her children and compelling her to labour because they are free".[89]

Planters applied the economic squeeze to male and female apprentices alike in their determination to keep them tied to estate work. They used the strategy of imposing high rentals on the cottages and plots that ex-slaves continued to occupy. Charlotte Morrison, of a Hanover estate owned by Sir Simon Clarke, was an example of a woman who, before the Abolition Act, would have been exempt from estate labour. She was the mother of nine children and stayed home to "wash, cook, and mend" for her aged African mother and children, five of whom worked on the property at 1s. 3d. daily. The estate manager demanded three days' work weekly from her in lieu of rent; she was unable to provide it, and as a result she was presented with a bill for three months' rent under the threat of immediate eviction.[90]

Planters also put economic pressure on ex-slaves in relation to their provision grounds, and this, too, critically affected women. Dr James Archer, for example, gave peremptory orders to his head constable, William Murray, for regulating the use of ground allotments, and he harassed and threatened Murray for his failure to police the arrangements effectively.[91] On 19 January 1837, Archer spelt out in detail the terms on which apprentices could grow yams, cocoas and other crops, at the same time imposing strict taboos on the cultivation of plantains, bananas and tobacco "which [would] impoverish the soil".[92] His labour injunctions were designed to create hardships for women and for men, who worked normally as a family unit. "Whoever applies for and is permitted", he declared,

> to cultivate such land, is not to employ any other individual or person belonging to this property, or family, or friends, for the purpose of assisting. . . . The person, male or female, who has any sanction to work such land must work the same himself, or herself, no brother, sister, or any other person to assist, or enter therein without my sanction being applied for, and obtained under the certainty of their being turned off such land at a notice to quit within thirty days after.[93]

The women in the apprentices' family provoked punitive action from the white establishment not only because they could withhold their labour in numbers sufficient to embarrass the estates' operations, but, as mothers, they could as well subvert planters' expectations for their future labour force. Under the Abolition Act, children under six years of age were to be free, and as they became of age to be apprentices, could be employed with their parents' consent.[94] Planters never lost sight of young blacks as a source of potential manpower. Their cooperation with missionaries in the religious and secular instruction of apprentices' children contained this hard element of self-interest. Thomas McNeil, for example, recommended that in the siting of chapels and schools, it should be a matter of policy "[t]hat all wants of such a nature should be supplied at home, the less cause for the children or others going off their properties".[95]

Women stood in the way of these hopes. The overseer of Joseph Gordon's estate in St Andrew observed to Sturge's visiting group in 1837 that "a greater insult could not be offered to a mother than by asking her free child to work".[96] At Silver Hill estate in the same parish, the party also learnt that "not a single free child worked on the estate". The overseer asked a woman in their presence "to let her eldest child, a boy of eight years, do light work for his clothing, and allowance, but she replied that the child was free, and she did not wish to bind him".[97] Only a year previously, special magistrate Pryce from the parish of Trelawny had written to Lord Sligo on 29 March 1836, complaining of the women's lack of cooperation:

> [T]he female apprentices generally (and who outnumber the men) have not behaved so well as could reasonably have been expected of them . . . . They almost defy all authority and shew an ungrateful feeling with insulting conduct quite opposite to that of the male apprentices. The women are on all occasions the most clamourous, the most troublesome and insubordinate and least respectful to all authority. None of their freed children have they in any instance apprenticed to their former masters or otherwise.[98]

The establishment's response to female protest was physical brutality to women on a scale paralleled only by the worst atrocities of slavery. The Abolition Act had expressly forbidden the whipping of women in the field under any circumstances.[99] As a result of this sanction being removed, women became, in the opinion of the House of Commons' Committee on Apprenticeship, "the principal sufferers" in the punitive policies which were devised during this period.[100]

Excessive harshness was facilitated by the conflict which developed between the Abolition Act and the Jamaica Gaol Act of 1834, which gave "any ordinary justice" power to "correct" prisoners, male and female, by corporal punishment. It was acknowledged that the whipping of female apprentices in work houses was a breach of the spirit of the Abolition Act, but it was not so clearly admitted that it was a breach of the law.[101] While this area of uncertainty existed, the authority of the Gaol Act was exploited to flout the Abolition Act, and "women, who could not be whipped in the field [were] scourged in the workhouse".[102]

Women stood firm: only nine free children who had been less than six years old on 1 August 1834, were released by their families to become apprentices.[103] Black men, women and their families were seeking, and finding, viable alternatives to the regimentation of the outer plantation. In February 1839, Thomas McNeil already knew of "about 200 Families [from the parish of Westmoreland] who have removed and are preparing to remove from the Sugar Estates to their own small properties".[104]

"Infinitely more land" was being cultivated in the mountains of Trelawny and St Ann in 1836 than in 1834, in the opinion of the stipendiary magistrate J.A. Dillon. The Falmouth and Browns Town markets were well supplied with provisions: "almost all the apprentices", wrote Dillon, "grow, yams, cocoas and other vegetables greatly to exceed domestic consumption, which was not the case in 1834. . . . Indeed, with a few, very few idle exceptions, Plenty may be said to preside in every Hut, and content in every face."[105]

Freed blacks were effectively becoming the yeomanry of creole dreams and schemes, using the greater mobility which emancipation brought to develop further their economic potential. Emancipation meant also increased freedom for evangelical bodies such as the Baptists, and allowed ex-slaves to enter with them into productive partnerships of faith and enterprise, which, significantly, made the establishment nervous. "I am satisfied", wrote Thomas McNeil, in 1839, "ten years will not pass over before these squatters become formidably dangerous to the peace and quiet of this island, this rage for the purchase of Lands is much encouraged by the Baptist Ministry."[106]

At Sligoville in the parish of St Catherine, Joseph Gurney saw in 1840 the free black Baptist settlement located on a lofty hill, . . . surrounded by 50 acres of fertile mountain land. The property is divided into 150 freehold lots, 50 of which had been already sold to the emancipated Negroes . . . some of them had built good cottages, others temporary huts; and others again were preparing the ground for building. Their gardens were cleared, or in the process of clearing; and in many cases, already brought into fine cultivation . . . the people settled there were all married pairs, mostly with families.[107]

Jamaica's new peasantry developed its agricultural/marketing activities on a domestic base, which was often consolidated by Christian marriage. In the first twelve months of freedom, it was calculated that the Baptist missionary J.M. Phillippo married about three hundred apprentices in the Spanish Town area.[108] Between 1830 and July 1834, the Moravian Church at Fairfield in Manchester solemnized fifty-two marriages of its members. In the five months following the Abolition Act, it solemnized sixty marriages and performed a total of 712 between 1830 and 1840.[109]

The exodus of numbers of black women out of the estate environment and into the independent existence of a family-oriented village had important implications for the economy and the society. It was the beginning of an even larger process, which gained momentum as the century advanced. By leaving the traditional plantation system, women were substantially altering the main occupational feature of slavery – that is, the impressment of all able-bodied persons, females conspicuously so, into employment.[110] Jamaica's census of 1844 showed approximately 234,500 persons occupied, in contrast to 255,300 at the time of the compensation claims of 1834.[111]

Black women were not only moving into free villages, they were beginning to move into towns. The statistical evidence of female internal migration is not available for the 1840s, but it is certain that black female urbanization, which became one of the most remarkable demographic features of modern Jamaica, was almost immediately accelerated by freedom. Certainly by 1861, the population of the towns reflected a markedly growing increase in the proportion of black women[112] in areas that had traditionally been the preserve of brown women.

Mary Seacole: The Mulatto Woman after Slavery

The history of Jamaican mulatto women steered them towards careers of highly visible achievement. The house slave who became the plantation's favourite, the citizen flourishing a bill which granted privileges, the splendidly gowned *chère amie* of a local dignitary, the successful entrepreneur of the city, all served to create differences of status within the relatively small group of browns. But they also provided incentives to all members of the group to aspire similarly. The determined upward thrust of Jamaica's browns continued to be embodied in the women of the post-emancipation era: it informed the mystique of the century's most eminent creole heroine, Mary Seacole.

Most accounts of her career stress her great nursing services in Panama, in Jamaica and in the Crimea.[113] She saw herself as a "female Ulysses" who grew "in consequence" as the century advanced.[114] She arrived at the pinnacle of colonial ambition: public acclamation in Britain.[115]

Her native town was Kingston, her father was an officer, whose legacy of "good Scotch blood" was, she maintained, the source of her "energy and activity".[116] Her mother's race was unacknowledged but implied.[117] She was in fact reticent about most of her family circumstances, and as a child she shuttled between her maternal home and the care of a "patroness".[118] Her autobiography seems the product of a liberal nineteenth-century education, and this she may well have acquired locally, for by the 1840s, mulattoes were prominent in the Jamaican school system both as teachers and as students.

It has already been observed that mission schools relied heavily on the services of mulattoes. Joseph Sturge and Thomas Harvey noted this repeatedly on their extended tour of Jamaica in 1837. The Reverend Phillippo had apparently thought it impossible to run the Baptist girls' school of about ninety pupils in Spanish Town without a European teacher. But when Sturge and Harvey visited it, its principal teacher was a young coloured woman, an ex-slave, whose grandfather (himself still an apprentice) had purchased her freedom. She had, among her pupils, fourteen coloured girls sent from a neighbouring estate to be trained to become teachers in the estate's schools.[119]

The Report of the Charity Commissioners of 1844 gave evidence of coloured girls taking increased advantage of the island's public educational facilities. Manning's Free School in Westmoreland had sixty-five boys and thirty-seven girls as foundation scholars.[120] Since 1823, it had accepted children of "all colours". Smith's Free School in St Catherine, founded in 1830 "for the instruction of the poorer classes of all colours", had seventy-six boys and fifty-four girls.[121] Titchfield Free School had children of "all religions and all colours". It had in its upper school fifty-five boys and in the lower school seventeen boys and thirty-seven girls.[122]

The island's leading school, Wolmer's, in the 1840s had a ratio of ten coloureds to one white. The headmaster, Ebenezeer Reid, spoke highly of his brown pupils, who were surpassing the whites in academic performance. His curriculum included not only the traditional elementary subjects, but also the physical sciences, French and Spanish.[123] In 1837, Sturge and Harvey were "inclined to pronounce [it] the best school [they had] seen in the West Indies".[124] In March 1844, it had an enrolment of 269 boys and 238 girls.[125] In addition to the free schools, Kingston by 1837 had increased its number of ladies' private schools to sixty-three, with a total of 1,525 scholars.[126]

Mary Seacole learnt the skills of boarding-house keeping and nursing from her mother, who kept a lodging house in Kingston and was "like very many of the Creole women an admirable doctress".[127] Her mother's clients and patients were nearly "all invalid officers and their wives who came to her house from the adjacent camp at Up-Park and the military station at Newcastle".[128] She paid two visits to England during her girlhood, one lasting a year and the other two years. She is vague about the purpose of her first visit, when she travelled with a companion darker skinned than herself; it is likely that they went as ladies' maids. Her second visit marked the beginning of her trading enterprises: she took with her "a large stock of West Indian preserves and pickles for sale".[129]

She worked hard at developing her entrepreneurial skills. On returning to Jamaica she made business trips to Haiti, Cuba and New Providence, "bringing home a large collection of handsome shells and rare shell work which created quite a sensation in Kingston and had a rapid sale".[130] Her account of her marriage made clear who was the dominant partner.

> I couldn't say "no" to a certain arrangement timidly proposed by Mr Seacole, but married him and took him down to Black River, where we established a store. Poor man, he was very delicate. . . . I kept him alive by kind nursing and attention as long

as I could; but at last he grew so ill that we left Black River and returned to my mother's house at Kingston. Within a month of our arrival there he died.[131]

Mr Seacole could have been white. Contemporary observers noted a marked decline in local prejudices against white men marrying their coloured mistresses. The Marriage Act of 1840, which retrospectively legitimized the offspring of such associations, may have been both cause and effect of that trend.[132] Mary Seacole continued after widowhood to combine successfully three of the main occupational preferences of mulatto women: trading, nursing and innkeeping.

Most of her wonderful adventures took place outside the period of this study: only a fragment of her book, in fact, covers her life in Jamaica. Its marked outward orientation makes it, in one sense, less relevant to Jamaican historiography than, for example, the journal of Maria Nugent, a visitor, who nevertheless recorded in acute detail the manners and morals of all groups in the society. In another sense, however, Mary Seacole's autobiography is valuable for creole studies. Its external perspective indicates the intensified Anglicizing of the coloured middle class, which in greater proportions than any other racial or social group, moved into the school system of free Jamaica, absorbing imported English culture.[133]

Mary Seacole admitted the Eurocentric focus of her upbringing: "I was never weary of tracing upon an old map the route to England and never followed with my gaze the stately ships homeward bound without longing to be on them and see the blue hills of Jamaica fade into the distance."[134] Whether in Jamaica, or abroad, she served mainly foreign clients: American adventurers in Panama and British military personnel in Jamaica[135] and in the Crimea. It was the tug of her English and Scottish associates, the officers of the Jamaican garrison who were her customers, patients and friends, which drew her to the Crimea.[136]

Her attitude to race and colour is of interest. It was in some respects atypical. Mulatto prejudice towards blacks, if anything, hardened after emancipation.[137] But Mary Seacole was relaxed on the subject. She referred to her black mother only with respect and affection,[138] while priding herself on the fact that she was "only a little brown".[139] She described without rancour incidents in her career in which her colour set her apart for special comment or treatment. Her confident sense of achievement provided for her a strong buffer against such slights. Moreover, these "racial" incidents occurred mainly in Panama and involved Americans. She interpreted them as manifestations of Yankee uncouthness and therefore alien to the Anglo-Saxon milieu in which she moved with ease.[140]

It is not surprising that it is the mulatto, Mrs Seacole, who has been lifted out of the pages of history as the embodiment of the creole success story, enshrined as a model of and for Jamaican womanhood. She fulfilled the society's expectations of her, maintaining a comfortable balance astride potentially conflicting races and classes. She, and others of her group, could guarantee society its status quo. Not so the white woman, whose alienation, spiritual and physical, dislocated creole arrangements and created awkward breaches; unquestionably not the black woman, the most oppressed of the blacks and of the women. She, in fundamental and unique ways, kept alive forces antithetical to the nice balance of the creole world, thereby preserving for it much of its dynamic. The black woman presented free Jamaica with the great challenge of lifting her oppression and releasing her considerable creativity and resourcefulness for the better ordering of the whole society. The challenge is yet to be met.

Afterword

Recollections into a Journey of a Rebel Past

L u c i l l e   M a t h u r i n   M a i r

In the early 1960s I started to seek out the women of Jamaica's past during the period of slavery, women of all classes and of all colours – black, brown, white. I had no feminist motivation, or at least none that I recognized. I was motivated mainly by intellectual inquisitiveness, the usual ambition of the doctoral candidate to investigate virgin territory, which it was at that time. There was almost nothing to guide such a search. There was, in fact, nothing in modern historical scholarship about the women who came before me. But this was not surprising, for historiography, which has for centuries been a male academic preserve, has been stunningly devoid of a consciousness of women as significant beings.

So feminist historians have been faced with the methodological challenge of excavating women from layers of distortion and obscurity; of getting beyond and behind the formal roles conventional history has accorded them and in the process, perhaps, even transforming the discipline of history.

Digging into the lives of the small minority of free white women in Jamaican slave society takes one along a relatively straightforward route.

Reproduced from Lucille Mathurin Mair, "Recollections into a Journey of a Rebel Past", in *Caribbean Women Writers: Essays from the First International Conference,* ed. Selwyn R. Cudjoe (Wellesley, Mass.: Calaloux Publications, 1990).

There is a substantial body of data to be found in contemporary histories and accounts by residents and travellers. There is even more valuable material in legal documents, in wills, in diaries, and in the volume of transatlantic and inter-American correspondence that has been preserved in the papers of planter families. Letters and diaries of women of this class reveal some of the personal and domestic implications of absentee proprietorship, an alienating phenomenon that has been distinguished throughout most of Jamaica's history by the nostalgia of its white elite for all things English, an intensely female nostalgia that is communicated through the pens of women with perturbing immediacy.

Other approaches are required to recover the feelings of brown and black women and to gain insight into the multidimensional nature of their lives. Until the very recent development of indigenous scholarship, the Caribbean researcher's main reference point was the Eurocentric, ethnocentric historiography of the colonizer and the slaveholder, which is incapable of addressing the humanity of transplanted Africans labelled chattel, identified for the historical record in an entry on a bill of lading or an estate inventory, and rendered voiceless. The state of slavery further compounds the methodological challenge in that women and slaves, as oppressed groups, themselves frequently suppress their objective reality. Their words, if we could only hear them, may have been designed not to reveal but to conceal, not to inform but to misinform.

In attempting to decode the mysteries of the black female condition, the Caribbean scholar is at greater risk than her Afro-American counterpart, who can study collections of slave narratives, with opportunities for testing their authenticity. Nothing has surfaced to date in the Jamaican records comparable to the statements of a Sojourner Truth or a Harriet Tubman, or the remarkable testimony of the slave woman Harriet Jacobs, whose autobiography has only recently come to light.[1]

Only one woman of colour has left a strong imprint on the pages of Jamaica's past, leaving literary evidence of her lively existence: this was Mary Seacole [see pp. 314–17 above]. Her autobiography, a classic of its kind, entitled *Wonderful Adventures of Mrs Seacole in Many Lands,* was first published in England in 1857.[2] It is a vivid, witty account of a life of a spunky mulatto woman who labelled herself a "female Ulysses". Her ambition and wanderlust took her as an innkeeper, huckster and nurse to Haiti, Cuba, the

Bahamas, Panama, England and the battlefield of the Crimea, where she became celebrated as the "brown Florence Nightingale". Her portrait dominated the platform of the Hall at the University of the West Indies in Jamaica, where I lived and worked during the years of my research.

Mary Seacole's "wonderful adventures" occurred during the post-emancipation period and, therefore, fell for the most part outside of my research time-frame, but I expected to meet her on my journey. I did, and certainly she came alive through the picture she drew of herself. Today's Caribbean women writers will be intrigued to explore the value of her contribution to our literary heritage, for her autobiography is both a historical document and a creative work, a unique expression of the female mulatto syndrome.

Nanny of the Maroons was more enigmatic. For as long as I can remember, she has been somewhere in the Jamaican consciousness but without acquiring solid flesh and blood. Was she actually an Ashanti chieftainess who wielded power over her people in the Portland mountains of eastern Jamaica and kept the establishment at bay for years as she led the war of black liberation, frustrating colonial designs to make the island free for King Sugar? Or was she a creature of legend, summoned up by the Maroons from the spirit world to sustain their struggle for freedom?[3] The supernatural powers attributed to her in popular sayings seemed so bizarre as to produce scepticism about her humanity. I did not know precisely how much I would discover about this heroic but insubstantial figure; and if one rejected the folk memory as a valid base for scholarly theses, was there any certainty of finding incontestable evidence that she had really lived?

The twilight zone Nanny inhabited symbolized the hazy state of our knowledge about our black foremothers. Records existed, most of them the result of the very nature of the slave society and economy. Estate papers and slave registration returns are rich in the demographic data complied by proprietors and managers to keep account of the size, age, physical condition, occupation and other attributes of their human property. Colonial Office and parliamentary reports provide prime evidence of the strategic and commercial interests of imperialism, which shaped the island polity and made precise prescriptions for the functioning of each racial group and, above all, of each unit of the work force. There are data in abundance, but there is very little about the inner lives of slaves.

Clearly, one must probe deeply into the conventional sources of

Caribbean history to find those missing women, to attempt new interpretations, and imaginatively to bring new insights to the task of opening up the
slaves' private world, where black women lived in cultural antithesis to the
white plantation. The historical, sociological and creative writings of
Orlando Patterson and Edward Kamau Brathwaite in the 1960s and early
1970s indicated how and where one might find that Afro-Caribbean world.
As Brathwaite expressed it, "history becomes anthropology and sociology,
psychology and literature and archaeology, and whatever else is needed to
make the fragments whole".[4] In the 1960s, however, we were a long distance
away from refining multidisciplinary scholarship.

Understandably, I was nervous about embarking on my venture with such
undeveloped professional tools. But I was inspired and supported by a friend
and teacher, that great woman, Elsa Goveia; and there could be no more
appropriate occasion than this historical gathering of Caribbean women
writers at which to pay tribute to her shining spirit and towering intellect.
She was a native of Guyana, the first female professor and the first professor
of West Indian History at the University of the West Indies. Sadly, she died
too soon, at the age of fifty-five. But what a legacy she has left us! Her first
major publication in 1956 was a study of the historiography of the British
West Indies.[5] In it she dissected with a cool and devastating critique the
racialist and authoritarian ideologies of those historians who, under the guise
of academic objectivity and humanist values, previously attempted to record
the Caribbean past. Nine years later, she produced her landmark history,
*Slave Society in the British Leeward Islands at the End of the Eighteenth
Century*.[6] In his annual lecture in her memory at the University of the West
Indies, Professor Franklin Knight aptly described that work as "magisterial".[7]

Professor Goveia's piercing vision and rigorous scholarship brought fresh
understanding of the complex historical forces that have shaped our island
societies. Brilliantly, meticulously, she analysed the decisive force of race and
colour in constructing Leeward Islands society, demonstrating how "the
social order of the whole community hung upon the distinctions established
between the constituent races". Simultaneously, she identified the propensity
of those same constituents to destabilize the social order. Her thesis tempted
me with prospects of an exciting dialectical exploration to illuminate the
buried lives of women: if the fact that she was black or white or brown
ascribed to a woman her status, her functions, and her subversive potential,

would her being female make a difference? In short, how far would her sexual identity diminish or enhance her capacity to conform or to resist?

It took time, of course, to find answers, and a great deal of patience, like that of the gold prospector, sifting through tons of material in search of the occasional nugget of enlightenment. But fragments of women's lives came to light increasingly out of the shadows of the archives, and the contours of black, brown, and white women's stories took shape.

The combined ideologies of white supremacy and patriarchalism laid down clear guidelines for the status and functioning of white women in a plantation colony. The majority, conditioned to accept such concepts, performed accordingly, but not all did. Some proved capable of flouting convention, of engaging in economic activities that did not fit the white female stereotype, of indulging in unbecoming social conduct, of violating interracial sexual taboos. Women of the plantocracy struck out with even more spirit, in some ways, than did women of lesser classes, making definitive statements of white female distaste for Creole norms. Many came, saw, and fled, leaving behind awkward social and domestic gaps that threatened to undermine the nice designs of the establishment.

Coloured women had their allotted place, initially a marginal one. But selective co-option carried some to the status of surrogate whites, who served partially to defuse the racial imbalance – ten blacks to one white – the highest in the transatlantic plantations and a terrifying spectre to the white establishment. Numbers of brown women exploited openings in creole society, carving out for themselves significant roles that had not been previously prescribed, virtually inverting the social order. Such processes, within the context of Jamaica's sexual and racial demography, have important implications for brown women's assertive capacity to influence the shaping of a society. But under the close scrutiny of research, the black slave woman emerged as the most aggressive of women: she took centre stage as rebel.

Rebels on the run are usually the first to catch posterity's eye, for as valuable property that had to be recovered when they fled their estates, they made copy in the local press. That liberating act of "pulling foot" gave them names, faces and identities. They became conspicuous in the fugitive population, confounding customary perceptions of the passive sex, whose physical mobility is constrained by motherhood. The female runaway often made sure her children joined her escape from bondage in what was one of the most threatening forms of protest; for each missing person, man, woman or child, jolted the system. A family, such as that of Margaret, alias Amey, stands out in the rogues' gallery [see p. 248 above]. She was a "slender black woman, with a large eye, prominent forehead and straight nose, and marked CH or MK"; her daughter Eliza Arnold was also "slender, with very large eyes, and a thin visage"; and her son Richard McLeod, aged eighteen, accompanied them. Described in the advertisement for their capture as a "plausible trio", they had crossed the length of the island from the north-western parish of Hanover and were hiding somewhere in the city of Kingston in the southeast. They and others like them moved through a black underground that sustained fugitives for long periods, over long distances, in the countryside or in the busy subculture of the island's growing towns.

Women featured prominently among the "incorrigible" slaves who ran away again and again, risking recapture and punishment, which increased in severity for each repeated offence. When caught and returned to the plantation, they made common cause with an equally "incorrigible" band of rebels: the industrial saboteurs. Women had the power and the will to destabilize the plantation's labour productivity through a variety of single or collective acts, some blatant, some devious, but all ultimately damaging to the economic enterprise. I developed a special feeling for one such subversive activist, a slave woman of Port Royal, whose owner was so misguided as to name her "Industry". She could not resist that challenge: "For refusing to work and setting a bad example to other negroes on the property by her contumacious conduct", Industry was sentenced by the magistrate to two weeks' hard labour [see p. 239 above and p. 405n26].

Women were highly visible in the go-slows and work stoppages that were endemic on the plantations. For example, a "petticoat" rebellion of those assigned to carry cane trash halted the operations of the sugar mill at Matthew Lewis's Cornwall estate in the parish of Westmoreland during the early nineteenth century [see p. 239 above].[8] Such open sabotage was frequently supplemented by more equivocal strategies such as pretending illness. When admitted to the hospital, the malingerers would settle in for a long stay, to the detriment of the estate's output.

Women often used their reproductive power to erode the productive functions demanded of them. The plantation looked to them increasingly after the abolition of the slave trade in 1807 not only to provide massive inputs of labour but also to replenish the labour force. But slave birth rates declined steadily in the later years of slavery until emancipation in 1834, partly because of the arduous tasks and the physical and sexual abuse to which slave women were often subject, but partly also because women willed it so. They aborted regularly with the expertise of that formidable figure of the slave community, the midwife, who was knowledgeable in the use of folk medicine and who projected an image of having almost supernatural gifts. When they did give birth, slave women exercised their maternal prerogatives to the maximum. Few female acts provoked more frustration and rage in estate managers than women's insistence on nursing their infants for as long as they could and too often for the estate's liking, often for as long as two years. It was an effective strategy because slave laws provided nursing mothers with time off and special allowances, all charged to the estate's accounts.

Women were clearly determined to retain control over their reproductive and maternal rights. During the last years of slavery and the interim period of apprenticeship preparatory to full emancipation, when the fear of labour shortage haunted the plantocracy, women's withdrawal of that labour and that of their children seriously threatened the viability of sugar plantations [see p. 311 above and p. 429n97]. One official report gave evidence: "Negro mothers have been known to say, pressing their children to their bosoms, we would rather see them die than become apprentices." During the four years of apprenticeship, from 1834 to 1838, of the thousands of slave children who were eligible, only nine were released by their mothers for recruitment into the estate work force.

The other side of such reluctant and minimal effort for the plantation was the remarkable industry and productivity of women and their families on their provision grounds. There they laboured long, hard hours, travelled miles weekly to nearby towns to sell their crops and made themselves indispensable to the domestic economy. The profits from such enterprise provided them with the means to acquire possessions for home and person, including the colourful clothes in which women took pride. Personal property represented a degree of economic autonomy which slaves jealously guarded and defended in courts, where they pressed their legal rights to their own time for cultivating their plots. And there another band of determined rebels made their presence felt, the habitual litigants, among whom women were conspicuous. They stormed the courts, claiming their maternal privileges, and they protested excessive physical abuse and punishments, raising their voices loud and clear, displaying black verbal skills to great effect.

Women's voices, clamorous and ceaseless, were a marvellous medium for affirming their identity and for expressing their "magnificent discontent". Words are tools to which everyone has access. They can be explicit or insidiously shrouded in *double entendre*. Exasperated whites described woman's tongue as a "powerful instrument of attack and defence, exerted in insufferable insult" [see p. 235 above]. With malice and artistry their work songs in the field explored Buckra's frailties, which many women had reason to know well. The use or misuse of the master's language developed into sharp and enduring weapons for resistance which received added force from the mystique that surrounded African cultural perceptions of language and the word.

Far more than the written word, the spoken word established Nanny's awesome reality. Close examination of the official records verifies her status as the civic, military and religious leader of a free community in the mountains of eastern Jamaica during the period of the first Maroon war of the 1730s. The records also show how false was an often-quoted allegation that she died in 1733 at the hand of Cuffee, "a very good party negro" [see p. 62 above]. It is not clear whether this is mistake or misinformation; but she certainly lived and continued to defy the colonial establishment until 1740, when she reluctantly accepted a truce. The land patent she received from the British Crown in 1741 can be found today in the National Archives in Spanish Town. It granted to her and her people 500 acres in the parish of Portland, land they still inhabit.

Such documents are invaluable for the reconstruction of Jamaica's history. Of equal value are the oral traditions of the Maroons. Like other Afro-Caribbean groups, they carry their past in their heads. Their storytellers are charged with the sacred and professional responsibility of preserving the historical narrative intact. They have done so with such seriousness and consistency from generation to generation that modern scholarship increasingly acknowledges the ability of the folk memory to validate the authority of the printed page. To do justice to the actual and symbolic presence of a Nanny, as Brathwaite has stated, implies "the commitment of the researcher to undertake an investment in the veracity of our oral traditions and enlist those traditions in the reconstruction of a broken legacy".[9] It is a broken but hardy legacy, not easily lost by the millions of young female adults who for nearly two centuries crossed the Atlantic carrying, if nothing else, their certainty of being African and being women. The majority, before enslavement, had undergone the rites of passage their societies required of them, which ceremonially expressed a civilization's clear perceptions of the truths and joys as well as the mysteries and dangers of existence. Each new and potentially frightening phase of the life-cycle was realistically confronted and exorcized, in the process invoking ordeals that tested physical and spiritual resources to the ultimate and challenged the human will to address, survive and transcend pain, always seeking and drawing strength from a pantheon of deities whose power and wisdom resided with the ancestors – the guarantors of society's integrity.

Female status within such cultures was clearly articulated and structured to ensure respect and self-respect. Motherhood, sisterhood, age and healing gifts assumed supreme significance in African women's world view. It was a view perpetuated through chant and drum and dance, languages virtually impenetrable to the outsider or slaveholder but full of meaning for generations of the enslaved, and increasingly for the musicologists, linguists and other cultural explorers of today, without whom that world view could not be reconstructed. Among its main references is a history of regal women, not unlike Nanny of the Maroons.

Wonderful things happened on the journey into that rebel past, of which Nanny became the permanent, powerful icon. I can here only briefly indicate the personal process of self-growth it meant. No one could spend so many years in the company of such women and remain the same. The expansion of one's emotional and intellectual resources, the deepened pride in one's inheritance and in one's womanhood were inevitable, and are subjects for another article.

More relevant was the great occasion when a personal conviction about Nanny's profound significance to the Jamaican psyche became a public reality. I advanced it as an opinion and a recommendation, and in 1975 the Jamaican government proclaimed her Right Excellency and thereby enshrined her among the galaxy of national heroes: Paul Bogle, George William Gordon, Marcus Garvey, William Bustamante and Norman Manley.

Somewhere along the way, I noted that Brathwaite's great verse trilogy of the African diaspora, *The Arrivants,* is inspired by the almost exclusive assumption of a "poor, pathless, harbourless spade", who is male.[10] The next epic creation of this historian-poet-visionary was his *Mother Poem,* which met the challenge splendidly.[11] Brathwaite also invited me to join him in filling a vacuum in the existing literature by editing a special volume of the journal of the Caribbean Artists Movement, *Savacou,* on Caribbean women's writing, and for the first time, such a collection appeared in 1977.[12] It contained contributions, among others, by participants of this conference such as Merle Hodge, Lorna Goodison and Opal Palmer.

It also contained Maureen Lewis's article "The Nkuyu: Spirit Messengers of the Kumina", an essay of seminal importance in the growing body of Caribbean literature that acknowledges the integrity of the oral tradition and finds a respected place for "groups like Queenie's Kumina bands which today attempt to preserve a sense of historical continuity through spiritual and cultural means". This pioneer publication was dedicated to the memory of the Jamaican poet and playwright Una Marson, another precious and precocious spirit. She would have been at home with her wayward ancestors, those fractious females who ridiculed their masters, downed their tools, harassed the courts, placed themselves between their children and the slave driver, refused to give birth on order, planted their food crops, walked ten miles to market, flaunted their bright finery and disappeared in the melting pot of towns, where they joined the men in plotting poison, arson and rebellion.

One might ask, where on earth did such women, the "subordinate" sex, get this nerve? Perhaps it came from their very subordination – the moral force of the powerless confronting the powerful – and also from their ability to draw strength from that inheritance of ancestral spirits from the other side of the ocean. The militant acts and words of Afro-Jamaican women were neither isolated nor inadvertent. They constituted a political strategy that took different forms at different times but at all times expressed the conscious resolve of the African enslaved to confront the New World plantation's assault on their person and their culture. "Victimization", as Herbert Aptheker has written, "does not simply make victims: it also produces heroes."[13] We might add, "and heroines too". Women expressed the will to resist with an intensity fuelled by their outrage at the sexual violence in their lives. The passion and persistence of their heroic acts of self-affirmation and rebellion rescued them from silence and invisibility, and embedded the meaning of those acts in a people's memory.

Many Caribbean women writers today, also engaged in their acts of conscious self-affirmation, explore history, myth and memory, seeking cultural continuities. Refusing to pursue futility, they seldom lament the absence of ruins. On the contrary, they celebrate their presence, not the presence of fragmented, desolate remnants that signify nothing, but valued monuments, human artefacts, ready to receive vibrant new forms through the genius of those pens which are today busily creating praise songs for Caribbean women. And here, of course, is where the journey has brought me.

Appendix

Population: St James Parish

"Sugar Estates and other Properties in the Parish of St James as they were in the month of September 1774 showing the number of white people residing in said Parish particularizing those able to bear arms, the number of Slaves and Stock, and the number of hogsheads of Sugar made on the several Estates in the Crop of the year 1774."

List I   64 estates, viz.:
210 men able to bear arms
150 women and children
11,732 slaves
8,897 stock
8,618 hogsheads of sugar

List II   7 estates, now settling that will make sugar in the crop of 1773 and 1776, viz.:
22 men able to bear arms
8 women and children
803 slaves
367 stock

List III   "Settlers in the parish of St James next in Degree to Sugar Planters consisting of Pens, Coffee Planters,

Jobbers, Millwrights, Carpenters, Masons and such Like", viz.:

Penkeepers	8	(1 female)
Jobbers	14	
Penkeepers/jobbers	13	
Overseers/jobbers	10	
Surveyor/jobbers	1	
Coffee/grower	1	
Coffee/pimento grower	1	(1 female)
Pimento grower	1	
Millwrights	4	
Carpenters	4	
Masons	4	
Merchant	1	
	63	

90 men able to bear arms
112 women and children
3,044 slaves
1,000 stocks

List IV   "The third degree of settlers in the parish of Saint James possessing Slaves and Stock, particularizing as before the number able to bear arms", viz.:

Coopers	2
Pimento growers	7
Carpenters	12
Doctors	3
Butcher	1
Midwife	1
Overseers	7
Merchants	9
Penkeeper/jobber	1
Jobbers	10
Tailor	1
Free mulattoes	4

Wharfingers	5
Masons	2
Coppersmith	1
Millwright	1
Blacksmiths	2
Fisherman	1
Washerwoman	1
Shopkeepers	5
Jack of all trades	1
School teachers	3
Attorney	1
Planters	2
Cabinet maker	1
Widows	4
Parish clerk	1
	91

71 men able to bear arms
86 women and children
1,033 slaves
252 stock

Source: British Museum, Add. MSS 12435, Long Papers, 3–4.

Notes

ABBREVIATIONS

Add. MSS	Additional Manuscripts
C	Chancery
CO	Colonial Office
CS	Colonial Secretary
CSP	Colonial Calender of State Papers (Colonial America and West Indies)
LMS	London Missionary Society Correspondence
PP	*Parliamentary Papers*

INTRODUCTION

1. See Douglas Hall, ed., *In Miserable Slavery: Thomas Thistlewood in Jamaica, 1750–1786* (Kingston: University of the West Indies Press, 1999); Philip Wright, ed., *Lady Nugent's Journal of Her Residence in Jamaica, 1801–1805* (Institute of Jamaica, 1966; repr., Kingston: University of the West Indies Press, 2002); Matthew Gregory Lewis, *Journal of a West Indian Proprietor* (1834; repr., Oxford: Oxford University Press, 1999); Cynric Williams, *A Tour Through the Island of Jamaica, From the Western to the Eastern End, in the Year 1823* (London: Hunt and Clark, 1824).

2. See article by Jean Stubbs, "Gender in Caribbean History", in *General History of the Caribbean,* vol. 6, *Methodology and Historiography of the Caribbean,* ed. B.W. Higman (Paris: UNESCO, 1999), 95–135.

3. Joan Wallach Scott, *Gender and the Politics of History* (New York: Columbia University Press, 1988), 2.

4. Jenny Sharpe, *The Ghosts of Slavery: A Literary Archaeology into Black Women's Lives* (Minneapolis: University of Minnesota Press, 2003).

5. Lucille Mathurin Mair, "Recollections into a Journey of a Rebel Past", in *Caribbean Women Writers: Essays from the First International Conference,* ed. Selwyn R. Cudjoe (Wellesley, Mass.: Calaloux Publications, 1990).

6. Eric Williams, *Capitalism and Slavery* (Chapel Hill: University of North Carolina Press, 1944).

7. See Orlando Patterson, *The Sociology of Slavery: An Analysis of the Origins, Development and Structure of Negro Slave Society in Jamaica* (London: MacGibbon and Kee, 1967), and Edward [Kamau] Brathwaite, *The Development of Creole Society in Jamaica 1770–1820* (Oxford: Clarendon Press, 1971).

8. Mathurin Mair, "Recollections into a Journey".

9. See Lucille Mathurin (Mair), "A Historical Study of Women in Jamaica from 1655 to 1844" (PhD diss., University of the West Indies, Mona, 1974), 123.

10. Ibid., 473.

11. See A. Gautier, "Les Esclaves Femes aux Antilles Françaises 1635–1848", *Reflexions Historiques* (1983): 409–33; Bernard Moitt, "Women, Work and Resistance in the French Caribbean during Slavery", in *Engendering History: Caribbean Women in Historical Perspective,* ed. Verene Shepherd, Bridget Brereton, Barbara Bailey (Kingston: Ian Randle, 1995), 155–74; Digna Castañeda, "The Female Slave in Cuba in the First Half of the Nineteenth Century", in *Engendering History,* ed. Shepherd, Brereton, Bailey, 141–54; and Félix Matos Rodríguez and Linda C. Delgado, eds., *Puerto Rican Women's History: New Perspectives* (Armonk, NY: M.E. Sharpe, 1998).

12. Bridget Brereton, "Text, Testimony and Gender: An Examination of Some Texts by Women on the English-Speaking Caribbean, from the 1770s to the 1920s", in *Engendering History,* ed. Shepherd, Brereton, Bailey, 63–93.

13. A.C. Carmichael, *Domestic Manners and Social Conditions of the White, Coloured and Negro Population,* vol. 2 (New York: Negro Universities Press, 1969); Wright, *Lady Nugent's Journal*; Charles Leslie, *A New History of Jamaica, from the Earliest Accounts, to the Taking of Porto Bello by Vice-Admiral Vernon* (London: Printed for J. Hodges, 1740); Edward Long, *The History of Jamaica; or, General Survey of the Ancient and Modern State of that Island: With Reflections on its Situations, Settlements, Inhabitants, Climate, Products, Commerce, Laws, and Government* (London: T. Lowndes, 1774); Williams, *Tour Through the Island of Jamaica.*

14. See David Eltis, Stephen D. Behrendt, David Richardson, and Herbert S. Klein, eds, *Transatlantic Slave Trade: A Database on CD-ROM* (Cambridge: Cambridge University Press, 1999).

15. F. Tannenbaum, *Slave and Citizen: The Negro in the Americas* (New York: Alfred Knopf, 1946); Giberto Freyre, *The Masters and the Slaves: A Study in the*

Development of Brazilian Civilization, trans. Samuel Putnam (1933; New York: A.A. Knopf, 1946).

16. See Barry Higman, *Slave Population and Economy in Jamaica, 1807–1834* (Cambridge: Cambridge University Press, 1976); Kenneth Kiple and Virginia Kiple, "Deficiency Diseases in the Caribbean", in *Caribbean Slave Society and Economy: A Student Reader,* ed. Hilary Beckles and Verene Shepherd (Kingston: Ian Randle, 1991), 173–82; Meredith John, *The Plantation Slaves of Trinidad, 1783–1816: A Mathematical and Demographic Enquiry* (Cambridge: Cambridge University Press, 1989); and Richard Sheridan*, Doctors and Slaves: A Medical and Demographic History of Slavery in the British West Indies, 1680–1834* (Cambridge: Cambridge University Press, 1985).

17. Lewis, *Journal of a West Indian Proprietor.*

18. Brathwaite, *Development of Creole Society.*

19. Mary Turner, ed., *From Chattel Slaves to Wage Slaves: The Dynamics of Labour Bargaining in the Americas* (Bloomington: Indiana University Press, 1995).

20. See Nigel Bolland, "Proto-Proletarians? Slave Wages in the Americas", in *From Chattel Slaves to Wage Slaves,* ed. Mary Turner (Bloomington: Indiana University Press, 1995).

21. Barbara Bush, *Slave Women in Caribbean Society, 1650–1838* (Kingston: Heinemann, 1990); Marrietta Morrissey, *Slave Women in the New World: Gender Stratification in the Caribbean* (Lawrence, Kansas: University Press of Kansas, 1989).

22. Higman, *Slave Population and Economy;* Barry Higman, *Slave Populations of the British Caribbean, 1807–1834* (Baltimore: Johns Hopkins Press, 1984); Lorna Simmonds, "Slave Festivities and Leisure-Time Activities in Jamaican Towns" (seminar paper, Mona, 1984); Pedro Welch, *Slave Society in the City: Bridgetown, Barbados, 1680–1834* (Kingston, Jamaica: Ian Randle, 2002).

23. See Sheena Boa, "Free Black and Coloured Women in a White Man's Slave Society: Jamaica, 1760–1834" (MPhil thesis, University of the West Indies, Mona, Jamaica, 1988); Trevor Burnard, "Inheritance and Independence: Women's Status in Early Colonial Jamaica", *William and Mary Quarterly* 1 (1991): 93–115; and Kathleen Butler, *The Economics of Emancipation: Jamaica and Barbados, 1823–1843* (Chapel Hill: University of North Carolina Press, 1995).

24. See Moira Ferguson, ed., *The History of Mary Prince, A West Indian Slave Related by Herself* (1831; repr., London: Pandora, 1987).

25. Butler, *The Economics of Emancipation.*

26. See, for instance, articles in Verene Shepherd, ed., *Slavery without Sugar* (Gainesville: University Press of Florida, 2002).

27. See Bush, *Slave Women in Caribbean Society,* and David Barry Gaspar, "From 'The Sense of Their Slavery': Slave Women and Resistance in Antigua, 1632–1763", in

More than Chattel: Black Women and Slavery in the Americas, ed. David Barry Gaspar and Darlene Clarke Hine (Bloomington: Indiana University Press, 1996).

28. Claire Midgeley, *Women against Slavery: The British Campaigns, 1780–1870* (London; New York: Routledge, 1992).

29. Trevor Burnard, *Mastery, Tyranny, and Desire: Thomas Thistlewood and His Slaves in the Anglo-Jamaican World* (Kingston: University of the West Indies Press, 2004).

30. Woodville Marshall, " 'We Be Wise to Many Tings': Blacks Hopes and ✔ Expectations of Emancipation", in *Caribbean Freedom: Economy and Society from Emancipation to the Present,* ed. Hilary Beckles and Verene Shepherd (Kingston: Ian Randle, 1993); and Swithin Wilmot, "Emancipation in Action: Workers and Wage Conflict in Jamaica 1791–1820", in *Caribbean Freedom,* ed. Beckles and Shepherd.

31. Nancy Prince Gardener, *A Narrative of the Life and Travels of Mrs Nancy Prince* (Boston: The author, 1853).

32. See Thomas Holt, *The Problem of Freedom: Race, Labour and Politics in Jamaica and Britain, 1832–1938* (Baltimore: Johns Hopkins University Press, 1992); Diana Paton, *No Bond but Law: Punishment, Race, and Gender in Jamaican State Formation, 1780–1870* (Kingston: University of the West Indies Press, 2004); and Swithin Wilmot, " 'Females of Abandoned Character'? Women and Protest in Jamaica, 1838–1865", in *Engendering History,* ed. Shepherd, Brereton and Bailey.

33. Patricia Mohammed, *Gender Negotiations Among Indians in Trinidad, 1917–1947* (New York: Palgrave in Association with Institute of Social Studies, 2002); Rhoda Reddock, "Indian Women and Indentureship in Trinidad and Tobago, 1845–1917: Freedom Denied", *Caribbean Quarterly* 32 (1986): 27–47.

34. See, for instance, Bridget Brereton, *Race Relations in Colonial Trinidad, 1870–1900* (Cambridge: Cambridge University Press, 1979).

35. Jean Besson, "Land Tenure in the Free Villages of Trelawny, Jamaica: A Case Study in the Caribbean Peasant Response to Emancipation", *Slavery and Abolition* 5 (1984): 3–23.

36. See Lord Sydney Olivier, *The Myth of Governor Eyre* (London: L. and Virginia Woolf, 1933) and Geoffrey Dutton, *In Search of Edward John Eyre* (South Melbourne: Macmillan, 1982).

37. Gad Heuman, *"The Killing Time": The Morant Bay Rebellion in Jamaica* (London: Macmillan, 1994); Clinton Hutton, "Colour for Colour; Skin for Skin": The Ideological Foundations of Post-Slavery Society, 1838–1865 – The Jamaican Case" (PhD diss., University of the West Indies, Mona, Jamaica, 1992); Wilmot, "Females of Abandoned Character".

CHAPTER I

1. Gabriel Debien, *Les Femmes des Premiers Colons des Antilles, 1635–1680* (Extrait de la revue *La Porte Oceane,* nos. 89 et 90 [November–December 1952]), 1.

2. Ibid., 4–10. See also Arthur W. Calhoun, *A Social History of the American Family from Colonial Times to the Present* (New York: Barnes and Noble, 1945), 1:215–27; Julia Cherry Spruill, *Women's Life and Work in the Southern Colonies* (1938; repr., New York: Russell and Russell, 1969), 3–19; Andrew Sinclair, *The Better Half: The Emancipation of the American Woman* (New York: Harper and Row 1965), 14–15; Philip Greven, "Family Structure in Seventeenth-Century Andover, Massachusetts", *William and Mary Quarterly,* 3rd ser., 23, no. 2 (April 1966): 234–56.

3. C.H. Firth, ed., *The Narrative of General Venables, With an Appendix of Papers Relating to the Expedition to the West Indies and the Conquest of Jamaica, 1654–1655* (London: Longmans, Green, and Co., 1900), 102; Vincent Harlow, *A History of Barbados, 1625–1685* (Oxford: Clarendon Press, 1926), 112.

4. Firth, *Narrative of General Venables,* 155–57. See also p. 168, appendix E, Extracts from Henry Whistler's Journal of the West India Expedition: "16th May, 1655 (Jamaica) . . . [t]hayer Gennerale now had a longing desisor to goe for England . . . his lady doth remaine with him, But the Armie is very much awary of her, but cannot tell how they may be rid of her, for she doth Act verie high"; Charles Leslie, *A New History of Jamaica, from the Earliest Accounts, to the Taking of Porto Bello by Vice-Admiral Vernon* (London: Printed for J. Hodges 1740), 62.

5. Captain Edmund Hickeringill, *Jamaica Viewed; With all the Ports, Harbours, and their Several Soundings, Towns and Settlements Thereonto Belonging. Together, with the Nature of it's Climate, Fruitfulnesse of the Soile, and its Suitablenesse to English Complexions: With Several Other Collateral Observations and Reflexions upon the Island* (London: Printed for John Williams, 1661), 84.

6. Ibid. Hickeringill censured Venables severely for letting the male side down: "[H]e's unfit to be Pater Patriae that is not Domus Dominus, nor to head an Army that must kneel at his own Fire-side" (ibid., 90).

7. Calender of State Papers (Colonial America and West Indies, hereafter cited as CSP Col.) 1574–1660, 20 September 1655, 429.

8. Firth, *Narrative of General Venables,* 102.

9. C.H. Firth, *Cromwell's Army: A History of the English Soldier during the Civil Wars, the Commonwealth and the Protectorate,* 4th ed. (London: Methuen, 1962), 262, 298.

10. Firth, *Narrative of General Venables,* 102.

11. Ibid., 11.

12. Ibid., 102

13. Ibid.

14. See Edward Long, *The History of Jamaica; or, General Survey of the Ancient and Modern State of that Island: With Reflections on its Situations, Settlements, Inhabitants, Climate, Products, Commerce, Laws, and Government* (1774; repr., London: Frank Cass, 1970), 1:224. For other discussions of the secrecy, intrigues, and mixed motivation behind the project, see Harlow, *History of Barbados*, 104–6; C.M. Andrews, *The Colonial Period of American History* (New Haven: Yale University Press, 1937), 3:7–12; and A.P. Newton, *The Colonising Activities of the English Puritans: The Last Phase of the Elizabethan Struggle with Spain* (New Haven: Yale University Press, 1914), 314–21.

15. Firth, preface to *Narrative of General Venables,* xli, also 36.

16. For example, Richard Pares, *Merchants and Planters,* Economic History Review, supplement 4 (Cambridge: Published for the Economic History Review at the University Press, 1960), 3.

17. Ibid.

18. See Long, *History of Jamaica,* 1:244–51; S.A.G. Taylor, *The Western Design: An Account of Cromwell's Expedition to the Caribbean* (Kingston: Institute of Jamaica and the Jamaica Historical Society, 1965), 9–10, 87–90; Harlow, *History of Barbados,* 106; Firth, *Narrative of General Venables,* 30, 40, 100. Venables probably exaggerated the poor quality of the human material with which he was equipped, in order to excuse his own inadequacies. Similarly, the English commissioners tended to attribute "their lack of progress in colonization to the disinclination of the soldiers to work on the land, rather than to their own failure to drive out the Spaniards". See "Two Spanish Documents of 1656", translated and edited by J.J. Pietersz and H.P. Jacobs, with a commentary by S.A.G. Taylor, *Jamaican Historical Review* 2, no. 2 (October 1952): 6 and passim.

19. [Editors' note: Archaeologists and historians are now using Taino as the correct name for these indigenous peoples.]

20. H.P. Jacobs, "The Spanish Period of Jamaican History", *Jamaican Historical Review* 3, no. 1 (March 1957): 79–93, especially 86–87; also Frank Cundall and Joseph Pietersz, *Jamaica under the Spaniards, Abstracted from the Archives of Seville* (Kingston: Institute of Jamaica, 1919), 33–38, 49–50; Robert Wallace Thompson. "Vasquez de Espinosa and Jamaica", *Jamaican Historical Review* 3, no. 2 (March 1959): 63–65; Sylvia Wynter, "Bernardo de Balbueno, Epic Poet and Abbot of Jamaica, 1562–1627", *Jamaica Journal* 3, no. 3 (December 1969) and 4, no. 1 (March 1970).

21. MS 159: History and State of Jamaica under Lord Vaughan, 1679–1680, compiled for William Blathwayt. The Spanish colonists were said to be "not above 500 men, 600 women, and 1500 Negro Slaves". Also John Thurloe, *A Collection of the State Papers of John Thurloe, Containing Authentic Memorials of the English Affairs*

from the Year 1638, to the Restoration of King Charles II (London: Printed for the Executor of F. Gyles, 1742), 4:30.

22. Thurloe, *Collection of the State Papers,* 3:507.

23. Irene Wright, ed., *The English Conquest of Jamaica; an account of what happened in the Island of Jamaica, from May 20 of the year 1655, When the English Laid Siege to it up to July 3 of the year 1656, by Captain Julian de Castilla.* Camden Miscellany, vol. 13 (London: Offices of the Royal Historical Society, 1924), 12; also MS T4: Henry Barham, Manuscript History of Jamaica, 1670, 48.

24. Wright, *English Conquest,* 11.

25. Ibid., 13; John Taylor, writing in the 1680s, maintained that Jamaica in 1655, "Inhabited by Perfidious Spaniards", was "governed by the Marquenoss Signora Margareta Perez de Susman an Ancient Lady of Spain". See Taylor MS: "*Multum in Parvo,* The Present State of Jamaica, 1688", 251, 258. This fact is not, however, corroborated by other sources.

26. Jacobs, "Spanish Period", 84–85.

27. Sir Hans Sloane, *A Voyage to the Islands Madera, Barbados, Nieves, S. Christophers and Jamaica, with the Natural History of the Herbs and Trees, Four-footed Beasts, Fishes, Birds, Insects, Reptiles, &c. of the Last of those Islands; to which is Prefix'd an Introduction, Wherein is an Account of the Inhabitants, Air, Waters, Diseases, Trade, &c. of that Place, with some Relations Concerning the Neighbouring Continent, and Islands of America.* (London: Printed by B.M. for the author, 1707), lxxiii.

28. Firth, *Narrative of General Venables,* 140.

29. Wright, *English Conquest,* 16.

30. Taylor, *Western Design,* 83.

31. Ibid., 103.

32. Pietersz and Jacobs, "Two Spanish Documents", 30.

33. Ibid., 24, 29; Wright, *English Conquest,* 27; MS T4: Barham, Manuscript History, 48; Thurloe, *Collection of the State Papers,* 5:474.

34. MS 159: History and State of Jamaica, 15

35. MS T4: Barham, Manuscript History, 48, 57–58, and passim.

36. Cundall and Pietersz, *Jamaica under the Spaniards,* 34–38; Wynter, "Bernardo de Balbueno", 21.

37. CSP Col., 1574–1660, 26 September 1655, 429.

38. See, for instance, Richard Hill, *Eight Chapters in the History of Jamaica from AD 1508 to AD 1680, Illustrating the Settlement of the Jews in the Island* (Kingston: M. Decordova, McDougall and Co., 1868), 26 and passim; Richard Dunn, *Sugar and Slaves: The Rise of the Planter Class in the English West Indies, 1624–1713* (Chapel Hill: University of North Carolina Press for the Institute of Early American History and Culture at Williamsburg, 1972), 183–84.

39. Pietersz and Jacobs, "Two Spanish Documents", 14, and passim; Taylor, *Western*

Design, 15; Orlando Patterson, "Slavery and Slave Revolts: A Socio-Historical Analysis of the First Maroon War, 1655–1740", *Social and Economic Studies* 19, no. 3 (September 1970): 290–325.

40. Andrews, *Colonial Period,* 37–45.
41. Ibid.
42. See A.P. Thornton, *West India Policy under the Restoration* (Oxford: Clarendon Press, 1956), especially chapter 3 on Jamaica and Anglo-Spanish relations, 67–123.
43. Phillip Wright, *Monumental Inscriptions of Jamaica* (London: Society of Genealogists, 1966), 119–20, no. 1125.
44. CSP Col., 1669–74, 28 September 1670, 105–9.
45. Taylor, *Western Design,* 91–92.
46. Ibid., 92.
47. CSP Col. 1574–1600, 19 December 1655, 434.
48. Ibid., 23 July 1656, 446.
49. Ibid., 10 December 1657, 461.
50. Ibid., 8 April 1658, 465.
51. Ibid. 489.
52. J.G. Young, "The Beginnings of Civil Government in Jamaica", *Jamaican Historical Review* 1, no. 1 (June 1945): 49–53; David Buisseret, "Edward D'Oyley", *Jamaica Journal* 5, no. 1 (March 1971): 6–10.
53. Michael Craton and James Walvin, *A Jamaican Plantation: The History of Worthy Park, 1670–1970* (London: W.H. Allen, 1970), 27; also Phillip Wright, "Materials for Family History in Jamaica", *Genealogist's Magazine* 15, no. 74 (September 1966): 239–50.
54. Thurloe, *Collection of the State Papers,* 3:676.
55. Firth, *Cromwell's Army,* 198–99.
56. Thurloe, *Collection of the State Papers,* 3:675.
57. Firth, *Cromwell's Army,* 199 no. 2; see also Thurloe, *Collection of the State Papers,* 4:603.
58. For examples, see CSP Col. 1574–1660, 13 September 1655, 428; 11 January 1656, 435, 436; 26 March 1656, 438; 18 August 1659, 475.
59. Firth, *Cromwell's Army,* 41.
60. Ibid., 122.
61. Michael Pawson, "The First Civil Council of Jamaica", *Jamaica Historical Society Bulletin* 5, no. 5 (March 1970): 63.
62. An anonymous clergyman wrote with some malice on this subject in 1730, as follows: "[A]nd so our tavern keepers, tailors, carpenters, joiners, are infallibly Colonels, Justices of Peace, as soon as they purchase plantations and our printer, in his papers, styles them every man Esqs., and Lieutenant Colonels, and Honourable . . . ." Wright, "Materials for Family History", 248–49.

63. CSP Col. 1661–68, 17 June 1661, 37.

64. CSP Col. 1669–74, 23 September 1670, 99–104.

65. Land Patents, Liber 1, 1661–62, 298.

66. CSP Col. 1669–74, 23 September 1670, 103.

67. Ibid., 102.

68. Ibid., 99 and passim.

69. Colonial Office (CO) 1/45.

70. See p. 9 above. See also Robert M. Howard, ed., *Records and Letters of the Family of the Longs of Longville, Jamaica and Hampton Lodge, Surrey* (London: Simpkin, Marshall, Hamilton, Kent, 1925), 1:3–9.

71. Ibid.

72. Ibid. Henry Morgan, in his will dated 17 June 1688, left the bulk of his property to his wife for life, and after her death in succession to the Byndloss and Archibould nephews and nieces.

73. Ibid., 3. It is also interesting to note that after Johanna Archibould's death in 1668, Archibould took as his third wife Amy Lawes, whose son by her previous marriage, Nicholas Lawes, became governor of Jamaica and whose granddaughter married into the powerful family of Longs, and so on. Howard, *Records and Letters,* 1:61 and passim; see also Frank Cundall, *The Governors of Jamaica in the Seventeenth Century* (London: The West India Committee, 1936); Richard Sheridan, "Planter and Historian: The Career of William Beckford of Jamaica and England 1744–1799", *Jamaica Historical Review* 4 (1964): 36–58.

74. Thurloe, *Collection of the State Papers,* 3:635.

75. CSP Col. 1669–74, 99–104; also W.A. Claypole, "Land Settlement and Agricultural Development in the Liguanea Plain 1655–1700" (MA thesis, University of the West Indies, 1970), 29, 74 and passim.

76. Taylor MS: "*Multum in Parvo*", 491–500.

77. H.J. Cadbury, "Conditions in Jamaica in 1687", *Jamaica Historical Review* 3, no. 2 (March 1959): 54. The warehouse inventory of a Port Royal merchant in 1670 indicates something of female consumption patterns in jewellery, clothing, furnishings and the like: see G. Yates and J. Belfield, "A Port Royal Merchant", *Jamaica Historical Society Bulletin* 3, no. 15 (September 1964): 243–45; also J.D. Buisseret, "Port Royal 1655–1755", *Jamaica Historical Review* 6, nos. 1–2 (1966): 24–26.

78. Richard Blome, *A Description of the Island of Jamaica* (London, 1672), 35–36; also Taylor MS: "*Multum in Parvo*", 509–10.

79. For an interesting discussion of this phenomenon, see Eugene Genovese, *The World the Slaveholders Made: Two Essays in Interpretation* (London: Allen and Unwin, 1970), chapter 1 and 2, especially 28–34.

80. Richard Sheridan, *The Development of the Plantations to 1750: An Era of West*

Indian Prosperity, 1750–1775, Chapters in Caribbean History (Barbados: Caribbean Universities Press, 1970), 41. Sugar tonnage totalled 670 in 1673 and 3,586 in 1684.

81. Richard S. Dunn, "The Barbados Census of 1680: Profile of the Richest Colony in English America", *William and Mary Quarterly*, 3rd ser., 26, no. 1 (January 1969): 25. (This article is also incorporated in Dunn's *Sugar and Slaves.*)

82. Ibid., 24.

83. CO 1/45.

84. Dunn, *Sugar and Slaves*, 328–32.

85. Cundall, *Governors of Jamaica*, 17.

86. Wright, *Monumental Inscriptions*, 110, nos. 1034, 1035.

87. Ibid., 134, no. 1264.

88. Ibid., 133, no. 1262.

89. Ibid., 18, no. 141 (Kingston Parish Church).

90. Sloane MS 2723, Letter to Mary Weekes from R. Powell, Port Royal, 1680, 35. For Powell's official position see, for example, Elizabeth Donnan, *Documents Illustrative of the History of the Slave Trade to America* (Washington, DC: Carnegie Institution of Washington, 1930), 1:274.

91. Sir William Beeston, *A Narrative of the Descent on Jamaica by the French, 1694* (St Jago de la Vega, 1800), 249–51.

92. Ibid., 255.

93. CSP Col. 1696–97, 13 March 1697, 403.

94. Thurloe, *Collection of the State Papers*, 4:605.

95. Add. MSS 12429: Mr Nevil, The Present State of Jamaica, 1677.

96. John Wilson, Wilson Family Papers, *c.*1692–1770 (Broomhead, Yorkshire), 3 December 1756.

97. Wright, *Monumental Inscriptions*, 121, no. 1135; also Patterson, "Slavery and Slave Revolts", 298–99; Dunn, *Sugar and Slaves*, 259–61; Robert C. Dallas, *The History of the Maroons, from their Origin to the Establishment of their Chief Tribe at Sierra Leone, Including the Expedition to Cuba for the Purpose of Procuring Spanish Chasseurs and the State of the Island of Jamaica for the Last Ten Years with a Succinct History of the Island Previous to that Period* (London: T.N. Longman and O. Rees, 1803), 1:34; CSP Col., July 1711 to June 1712, 204.

98. CSP Col. 1685–88, 29 August 1685, 83.

99. Patterson, "Slavery and Slave Revolts", 299; also Taylor MS: *"Multum in Parvo"*, 551, 554.

100. *Journals of the Assembly of Jamaica* 3 (1731–45): 513.

101. In 1746, there were 112,428 slaves in the island; the white population then numbered 10,000. See George W. Roberts, *The Population of Jamaica* (Cambridge: Cambridge University Press for the Conservation Foundation, 1957), 33, 36.

102. CSP Col. 1730, 10 May 1730, 416

103. Add. MSS 12435: Long Papers, Inventory of Sugar Estates in St James, 1774; see also Lowell J. Ragatz, "Absentee Landlordism in the British Caribbean, 1750–1833", *Agricultural History* 5, no. 1 (January 1931).

104. Vere Langford Oliver, ed., *Caribbeana: Being Miscellaneous Papers Relating to the History, Genealogy, Topography, and Antiquities of the British West Indies* (Oxford and London: Mitchell Hughes and Clarke, 1910), 3:60; Howard, *Records and Letters,* 107.

105. Add. MSS 30001: General Correspondence and Papers of Families of Ricketts and Jervis, 1726–1842, f. 1. Compare MS 1069: Irwin and Tryall Estates, Mrs Bosley to Thomas Hall, 1760–1771. Mrs Bosley of the parish of St James wrote to Thomas Hall, 28 May 1761: "This country grows more disagreeable every day."

106. Add. MSS 30001: General Correspondence, f. 1.

107. Ibid., f. 5.

108. Ibid., f. 7.

109. Ibid., f. 10.

110. Ibid., f. 12.

111. Ibid., and passim; also Ricketts Family Papers, 1758–1834 (University of the West Indies Library), reel 421.

112. Add. MSS 30001: General Correspondence, 22.

113. Firth, *Cromwell's Army,* 298.

114 Ibid., see also petitions above.

115. CSP Col. 1574–1660, 11 January 1656, 435.

116. Ibid., 19 September 1659, 476.

117. Harlow, *History of Barbados,* 112.

118. See, for instance, Firth, *Narrative of General Venables,* 33.

119. Claypole, "Land Settlement", 28–29; Taylor, *Western Design,* 120–28.

120. CSP Col. 1661–68, 17 June 1661, 37.

121. Ibid., 14 December 1661, 62.

122. Thurloe, *Collection of the State Papers,* 3:153; also 455, where it was estimated that in early 1656, the mortality was "fifty every week".

123. CSP Col. 1587–1660, November 1660, 492.

124. Thurloe, *Collection of the State Papers,* 3:454; see also Pietersz and Jacobs, "Two Spanish Documents", 31.

125. Firth, *Cromwell's Army,* 35.

126. CSP Col. 1661–68, 31 December 1661, 65.

127. *Journals of the Assembly of Jamaica* 1 (1663–1709): appendix, Stat. Papers, 20.

128. Thurloe, *Collection of the State Papers,* 4:23–24.

129. Ibid., 3:44.

130. Ibid., 4:40.

131. See Abbot E. Smith, *Colonists in Bondage: White Servitude and Convict Labour in*

America, 1607–1776 (Chapel Hill: University of North Carolina Press, 1947), 169–70.

132. For instance, Joseph J. Williams, *Whence the "Black Irish" of Jamaica?* (New York: L. MacVeagh, Dial Press, 1932), 33.

133. Thurloe, *Collection of the State Papers*, 3:41.

134. CSP Col. 1574–1660, no. 1660, 491–92.

135. Ibid.

136. J.Harry Bennett, "Cary Helyar, Merchant and Planter of Seventeenth Century Jamaica", *William and Mary Quarterly*, 3rd ser., 21 (January 1964): 75.

137. Bryan Edwards, *The History, Civil and Commercial of the British Colonies in the West Indies* (London: J. Stockdale, 1807), 1:216–18.

138. Young, "Beginnings of Civil Government", 53.

139. Land Patents, Liber 1, 1661–62.

140. Ibid., f. 298.

141. Ibid., f. 290.

142. Ibid., f. 316.

143. Ibid., ff. 131, 137, 197, 240, 290.

144. CSP Col. 1669–74, 23 September 1670, 99–103.

145. CO 1/45.

146. CSP Col. 1574–60, 26 September 1655.

147. Ibid.

148. Thurloe, *Collection of the State Papers*, 5:148.

149. Ibid.

150. Major-General J.H. Lefroy, *Memorials of the Discovery and Early Settlement of the Bermudas or Somers Islands*, vol. 1, *1515–1685;* vol. 2, *1650–1685* (London: Longmans, Green, and Co., 1877–79), 2:99.

151. Ibid.

152. Ibid., 100.

153. Ibid., 1: appendix 5, 718.

154. See table 1.1; also Dunn, *Sugar and Slaves,* 107, 127, 327 and passim; J.A. Williamson, *The Caribbean Islands under the Proprietary Patents* (London: Oxford University Press, 1926), 8–13; C.S. Higham, *The Development of the Leeward Islands under the Restoration, 1660–1688; A Study of the Foundations of the Old Colonial System* (Cambridge: University Press, 1921), 148. Interesting, relevant aspects of the subject of the dynamics of early colonial family structures are also raised in Greven, "Family Structure"; Calhoun, *Social History;* David Rothman, "A Note on the Study of the Colonial Family", *William and Mary Quarterly,* 3rd ser., 22, no. 4 (October 1966): 627–34.

155. Thurloe, *Collection of the State Papers,* 5:68.

156. Ibid.

157. Taylor, *Western Design*, 117.

158. Ibid., 118–19.

159. CSP Col. 1669–74, 99.

160. Taylor, *Western Design*, 119; Beeston, *Narrative of the Descent*, 255.

161. CSP Col. 1574–1660, 16 October 1660, 490.

162. CSP Col. 1669–74, 17 October 1672, 422.

163. Cundall, *Governors of Jamaica*, 22; A.P. Thornton, "The English at Compeachy, 1670–1672", *Jamaica Historical Review* II, no. 3 (December 1953): 37: "[Jonas Clough] saw in ye prison at Lyma an English Gent called Don Juan whoe has been prisoner there many yeares and is supposed to bee St Thomas Modyford's son" (17 June 1681).

164. Harlow, *History of Barbados*, 106–8, 139–40, 152–57; Barbadians feared the competition from another sugar-growing colony.

165. CSP Col. 1661–68, 14 August 1662, 346 and passim.

166. Ibid., June 1664, 219.

167. Harlow, *History of Barbados*, 207.

168. CSP Col. 1574–1660, November 1660, 491; Taylor MS: "*Multum in Parvo*".

169. Long, *History of Jamaica*, 1:278.

169. Ibid.

170. Taylor MS: "*Multum in Parvo*", 513; CSP Col. 1669–74, 1 September 1670, 84. Jamaica's reputation for religious liberalism (or indifference?) helped to retain and increase its original Jewish population too. John Taylor wrote of the presence of Jews in large numbers in Port Royal in 1680 (499) and of many wealthy ones in Vere (515–16). The Anglican clergyman of Port Royal, Rev. Francis Crow, saw religious tolerance as necessary to promote immigration in a new colony, "considering the multitude of Jews upon the Point, and the many Quakers there are, both here and in the country plantations" (Cadbury, "Conditions in Jamaica in 1687", 54).

171. G. Yates, "The Spencer Tombstone at Lacovia", *Jamaica Historical Society Bulletin* 1, no. 1 (March 1965): 13–14.

172. CSP Col. 1661–68, 4 April 1667, 459.

173. Ibid., 1 November 1663, 166.

174. CSP Col. 1669–74, 16 January 1672, 319.

175. CSP Col. 1675–76, 22 September 1675, 285–86.

176. Bennett, "Cary Helyar", 61; see also J.G. Young, "Nicolas Lyssons and His Family", *Jamaica Historical Review*, no. 2 (December 1940): 168–71.

177. For example, Blome, *Description of the Island of Jamaica*, 5, 6, 10–15, 59 and passim; Hickeringill, *Jamaica Viewed*, 10, 16–22.

178. Blome, *Description of the Island of Jamaica*; also *Journals of the Assembly of Jamaica* 1 (1663–1709): appendix, 28.

179. See CSP Col. 1669–74, 23 September 1670, 99–103.
180. CO 1/45.
181. Ibid.
182. Smith, *Colonists in Bondage,* 334; also *Journals of the Assembly of Jamaica* 1 (1663–1709): appendix, 42. Approximately 150 servants yearly entered Jamaica between 1672 and 1675 from Bristol; in 1702, they were estimated to total 1,307 (ibid., 255).
183. Smith, *Colonists in Bondage,* parts 1 and 2, discuss this theme fully.
184. Ibid., 257; Leslie, *New History of Jamaica,* 305.
185. CSP Col. 1701, 23 July 1701, 357. The Council of Trade and Plantations recommended to the governor of Jamaica that "all Planters and Christian servants be well and provided with arms".
186. Richard Ligon, *A True and Exact History of the Island of Barbadoes* (London, 1673; repr., London: Frank Cass, 1970), 115.
187. Smith, *Colonists in Bondage,* 334. The Leeward Islands in 1720 had 731 men servants and 222 women servants.
188. CSP Col. 1730, 10 May 1730, 416.
189. *Journals of the Assembly of Jamaica* 1 (1663–1709): appendix, 42.
190. Smith, *Colonists in Bondage,* 228.
191. Ibid., 230, 231, 236–37.
192. Bennett, "Cary Helyar", 70–71.
193. Taylor MS: *"Multum in Parvo"*, 506; Leslie, *New History of Jamaica,* 248; Long, *History of Jamaica,* 2:292; Smith, *Colonists in Bondage,* 295. See also Nicholas Lysson's will of 13 November 1677, which provided for the freedom of his sister's children, "should any of (them) come Servants" (Young, "Nicolas Lyssons and His Family", 169).
194. A. Smith, *Colonists in Bondage,* 259, 274, 302.
195. *Jamaica Courant,* issues of 30 July 1718, 5 August 1718, 15 April 1719, 28 June 1721, 22 March 1722, 20 June 1722, 2 November 1726, 24 April 1728, 25 March 1730, 24 June 1730.
196. Taylor MS: *"Multum in Parvo"*, 536.
197. Ibid.
198. CSP Col., November 1660, 491.
199. CSP Col. 1669–74, 20 September 1670, 94.
200. Ibid., 28 September 1670, 106.
201. CSP Col. 1661–68, 10 August 1664, 223. Modyford recommended that the "King be prodigal in giving away the first million of acres, allowing 30 acres per head to men, women and children, white or black".
202. CSP Col. 1669–74, 23 September 1670, 97; also Andrews, *Colonial Period,* 3:44n.
203. Bennett, "Cary Helyar", 62–63.

204. Cundall, *Governors of Jamaica*, 54–55.
205. Blome, *Description of the Island of Jamaica*, 16–21.
206. Bennett, "Cary Helyar", 74.
207. Ibid., 57–58.
208. CSP Col. 1696–97, 19 June 1696.
209. Ibid., 31 December 1696, 288.
210. Ibid., 13 March 1697, 403.
211. Ibid., 27 February 1697, 386.
212. Ibid., 18 October 1697, 638.
213. Ibid.
214. CSP Col. 1697–98, 4 November 1697, 9.
215. Ibid.
216. Ibid., 6 June 1698, 265.
217. CSP Col. 1716–17, 13 March 1716, 114.
218. Ibid.
219. George Metcalf, *Royal Government and Political Conflict in Jamaica 1729–1783*, Royal Commonwealth Society Imperial Studies no. 27 (London: Longmans, 1965), 78–79; F.G. Spurdle, *Early West Indian Government, Showing the Progress of Government in Barbados, Jamaica and the Leeward Islands 1660–1783* (Palmerston North, New Zealand: The author, 1962), 143–46; Frank W. Pitman, *The Development of the British West Indies, 1700–1763* (New Haven: Yale University Press, 1917; repr., Frank Cass, 1967), 50–56, 108–26.
220. For instance, CSP Col. 1702–3, December 1703, 921. The hope was to get "some fit person to raise 2 or 3,000 Scotchmen to have free passages and £3,000 amongst them on arrival and to be settled on some 50,000 acres between the N.E. side of Rio Grandy and the S.E. side of Port Mourant: each man to have 7 or 8 acres allotted to him, etc.".
221. CSP Col. 1720–21, 20 April 1721, 193–95; *Journals of the Assembly of Jamaica* 3 (1731–45): 9–10.
222. Ibid., see also Spurdle, *Early West Indian Government*, 144.
223. *Journals of the Assembly of Jamaica* 2 (1709–31): 706. Nothing came of this proposal or of the resolution passed by the Assembly on 10 June 1731, that "extraordinary encouragement be given to masters of vessels to bring over boys and girls from nine to fifteen years of age". See *Journals of the Assembly of Jamaica* 3 (1731–45): 14.
224. CSP Col. 1733, 28 October 1733, 229.
225. Ibid., 27 April 1733, 90.
226. *Journals of the Assembly of Jamaica* 3 (1731–45): 49–50.
227. Ibid., also CSP Col. 1733, 27 April 1733, 90.
228. Metcalf, *Royal Government;* Spurdle, *Early West Indian Government;* Pitman,

Development of the British West Indies; Journals of the Assembly of Jamaica 3 (1731–45) and 4 (1745–56), passim.

229. Pitman, *Development of the British West Indies,* 121.
230. Ibid.
231. Ibid., 121–22
232. Ibid.
233. Ibid.
234. Ibid., 120.
235. *Journals of the Assembly of Jamaica* 4 (1745–56): 168–69.
236. Ibid.
237. Ibid.
238. Ibid., 169.
239. Ibid.
240. Ibid.
242. Ibid., 168.
243. Ibid., 169.
244. For example, *Journals of the Assembly of Jamaica* 4 (1745–56): 256–57, the case of Barbara Stevenson of Seaman's Valley; *Journals of the Assembly of Jamaica* 5 (1757–66): 97, 100, and so on, the cases of "divers of new settlers at Norman's Valley, Manchioneal and Portland".
245. *Journals of the Assembly of Jamaica* 4 (1745–56): 438–40.
246. *Journals of the Assembly of Jamaica* 5 (1757–66), 4 November 1758, 97.
247. Ibid.
248. Ibid.
249. *Journals of the Assembly of Jamaica* 4 (1745–56).
250. For examples, see *Journals of the Assembly of Jamaica* 3 (1731–45): 133, 134, 261, 265, 372, 513.
251. Ibid., 163.
252. Ibid.
253. CSP Col. 1696–97, 28 December 1696, 271.
254. Smith, *Colonists in Bondage,* 104–6.
255. CSP Col. 1696–97, 15 January 1697, 303.
256. The inconsistencies in creole population policies did not only apply to women. Jews were prohibited from purchasing white (Christian) servants. On 15 August 1734, they petitioned the Assembly to have the law revoked so that those who lived in "remote and exposed settlements" could hire more white people; if not, they feared they might be "obliged to dessert their settlements". Their petition was refused: see *Journals of the Assembly of Jamaica* 3 (1731–45): 261, 265.
257. Pitman, *Development of the British West Indies,* 50.
258. CSP Col. 1714–15, 25 April 1715, 155

259. Ibid. 1716–17, 13 March 1716, 113.
260. Pitman, *Development of the British West Indies,* 52–53.
261. Ibid., also CSP Col. 1730, 10 May 1730, 105.
262. Edward [Kamau] Brathwaite, *The Development of Creole Society in Jamaica 1770–1820* (Oxford: Clarendon Press, 1971), chapter 10, 135–50. Brathwaite's study of "Other Whites" apart from the elite indicates that they comprised about four-fifths of Jamaica's 30,000 whites in the early nineteenth century.
263. Sheridan, *Development of the Plantations,* 45.
264. Add. MSS 12436: Long Papers, List of Landholders in Jamaica, 1750.
265. Sheridan, *Development of the Plantations,* 98.
266. Add. MSS 12435: Long Papers, Inventory.
267. Brathwaite, *Development of Creole Society,* 146–50.
268. Long, *History of Jamaica,* 2:271–86.
269. Taylor MS: "*Multum in Parvo*", 504.
270. Mary Carleton, *News from Jamaica in a Letter from Port Royal Written by the German Princess to her fellow Collegiates and Friends in New Gate* (London, 1671), 3: her only fear about Jamaicans was that she might "be drowned in their over-flowing cups". She was hanged at Tyburn in 1672. See Cundall, *Governors of Jamaica,* 36.
271. CSP Col. 1720–21, 12 June 1721, 335.
272. Taylor MS: "*Multum in Parvo*", 504.
273. Ibid., 493
274. Ibid., 504, also 497, 502
275. "Dreadful earthquake at Jamaica 1692", *Gentleman's Magazine* 20 (1750): 212–15. A clergyman writing on 22 July 1692 observed that "those audacious whores who remain still upon the place are as impudent and drunken as ever" (ibid., 214). See also Leslie, *New History of Jamaica,* 100, 163.
276. Sloane, *Voyage to the Islands,* 1: introduction, c, cxix, cxiii, cxxvii, cxl, cxliii, cxlvii, cxlviii.
277. *Journals of the Assembly of Jamaica* 3 (1731–45): 478–84.
278. Long, *History of Jamaica,* 1:232; Thurloe, *Collection of the State Papers,* 3:507.
279. See pp. 36–37 above.
280. Long, *History of Jamaica,* 2:291: the offending male was required to serve in the woman's stead double the time which she owed her master or mistress.
281. Kingston Parish Accounts, 1722–59, 5 July 1736.
282. Long, *History of Jamaica,* 2:271–86.
283. Edwards, *History, Civil and Commercial,* 2:12–14.
284. Long, *History of Jamaica,* 2:286.

CHAPTER 2

1. Edward [Kamau] Brathwaite, *Rights of Passage; Masks; Islands* (London: Oxford University Press, 1967, 1968, 1969).

2. Donnan, *Documents Illustrative,* 1:18–20.

3. For instance, Long, *History of Jamaica,* 2:388–94, 401–3; Edwards, *History, Civil and Commercial,* 2:80–83.

4. Kenneth G. Davies, *The Royal African Company* (London: Longman's, Green and Co., 1957), 46–47; Hugh A. Wyndham, *The Atlantic and Slavery: A Report in the Study Group Series of the Royal Institute of International Affairs* (London: Oxford University Press, 1935), 4–7 and passim.

5. Kenneth Onwaka Dike, *Trade and Politics in the Niger Delta, 1830–1885: An Introduction to the Economic and Political History of Nigeria* (Oxford: Clarendon Press, 1962), 6–7.

6. H. Ling Roth, *Great Benin: Its Customs, Art and Horrors* (1903; repr., London: Routledge and Kegan Paul, 1968), 37. The seventeenth-century Dutch writer Olfert Dapper observed about the Kingdom of Benin: "a white man or a Christian can hardly get a public woman there in the country for fear of punishment, as such a thing is prohibited under penalty of death". Trading between Benin businesswomen and Europeans was also tabooed (ibid., 135).

7. Philip D. Curtin, *The Image of Africa: British Ideas and Action, 1780–1850* (Madison: University of Wisconsin Press, 1964), 64, 218–19.

8. Keith Thomas, "The Double Standard", *Journal of the History of Ideas,* no. 20 (1959): 195–216.

9. Ibid., 107.

10. Ibid.

11. William Bosman, *A New and Accurate Description of the Coast of Guinea, Divided into the Gold, the Slave, and the Ivory Coasts* (1701; repr., London: Frank Cass, 1967), 202, 204, 360 and passim; Thomas Hodgkin, *Nigerian Perspectives, An Historical Anthology* (London: Oxford University Press, 1960), 121, 129; Alan F.C. Ryder, *Benin and the Europeans 1485–1897,* Ibadan History Series (Harlow: Longman, 1969), appendix 2, 313–14, and so on.

12. Bosman, *New and Accurate Description,* 198.

13. Ibid., 109.

14. Ibid., 476.

15. Ibid., 463.

16. Ibid.

17. Curtin, *Image of Africa,* 252.

18. J. Vansina, R. Mauny and L.V. Thomas, eds., *The Historian in Tropical Africa: Studies Presented and Discussed* (London: Oxford University Press for the

International African Institute, 1964), 60–76, 101–3; G.I. Jones, "Time and Oral Tradition with Special Reference to Eastern Nigeria", *Journal of African History* 6, no. 2 (1965): 153–60; Joe Ebiegberi Alagoa, "Oral Tradition among the Ijo of the Niger Delta", *Journal of African History* 7, no. 3 (1966): 405–19.

19. The following are some of the sources consulted here: Bosman, *New and Accurate Description*, with notes by J.D. Fage; Jean Barbot, *A Description of the Coasts of North and South Guinea* (London, 1724); Mary Smith, *Baba of Karo, A Woman of the Muslim Hausa, With an Introduction and Notes by M.G. Smith* (London: Faber and Faber, 1954); International Institute of Differing Civilizations (INCIDI), *Report of Third Meeting in Brussels, September 1958, on Women's Role in the Development of Tropical and Sub-Tropical Countries* (Brussels: INCIDI, 1959); Madeline Manoukian, *The Ewe Speaking People of Togoland and the Gold Coast* (London: International African Institute, 1952); Kenneth Little, *The Mende of Sierra Leone: A West African People in Transition* (London: Routledge and Kegan Paul, 1967); Melville Herskovits, *Dahomey, An Ancient West African Kingdom*, 2 vols. (Evanston: Northwestern University Press, 1967); Robert S. Rattray, *The Tribes of the Ashanti Hinterland*, 2 vols. (Oxford: Clarendon Press, 1932); Meyer Fortes, *Oedipus and Job in West African Religion* (Cambridge: Cambridge University Press, 1959); Max Gluckman, *Custom and Conflict in Africa* (Oxford: Blackwell, 1955); Robin Fox, *Kinship and Marriage: An Anthropological Perspective* (New York: Penguin, 1967).

20. See, for instance, Rattray, *Tribes of the Ashanti Hinterland*, 1:77–84.

21. For example, Barbot, *Description of the Coasts*, 117.

22. Ibid., 119–21.

23. E.E. Evans-Pritchard, "Position of Women in Primitive Societies and in Our Own" (The Fawcett Lecture, 1955–56), published as *The Position of Women in Primitive Societies and other Essays in Social Anthropology* (London: Faber and Faber, 1965); also Paul Bohannan, *African Outline* (Harmondsworth: Penguin, 1966), especially chapter 10 on African families.

24. Little, *The Mende of Sierra Leone*; Rattray, *Tribes of the Ashanti Hinterland*; Herskovits, *Dahomey*; Smith, *Baba of Karo*, and so on.

25. For example, Herskovits, *Dahomey*, 1:282.

26. Ibid., 56–62, 86–87; Roth, *Great Benin*, 132; Manoukian, *Ewe Speaking People*, 19.

27. Walter Rodney, *A History of the Upper Guinea Coast, 1545 to 1800* (Oxford: Clarendon Press, 1970), 65–67.

28. Olaudah Equiano, or Gustavus Vassa, the African, *The Interesting Narrative of His Life, Written by Himself* (1789; repr., abridged and edited by Paul Edwards, as *Equiano's Travels*, London: Heinemann Educatonal Books, 1967), 63–67. See also Philip Curtin, ed., *Africa Remembered: Narratives by West Africans from the Era of the Slave Trade* (Madison: University of Wisconsin Press, 1967), 63–67.

29. Barbot, *Description of the Coasts,* 117, 364.
30. Herskovits, *Dahomey,* 1:86.
31. Smith, *Baba of Karo,* 112–17.
32. Ibid., 117.
33. Ibid.
34. See, for example, Smith, *Baba of Karo,* 41–42, 52–54 and passim.
35. Herskovits, *Dahomey,* 1:86–87.
36. For example, Smith, *Baba of Karo,* 119–20, 210–18.
37. Evans-Pritchard, "Position of Women in Primitive Societies", 40.
38. Smith, *Baba of Karo,* 118.
39. Fox, *Kinship and Marriage,* 39.
40. Ibid., 40. See also Frank Lorimer, *Culture and Human Fertility: A Study of the Relation of Cultural Conditions to Fertility in Non-Industrial and Transitional Societies* (Paris: UNESCO, 1954), 69–90; and Meyer Fortes, "A Demographic Field Study in Ashanti", in *Culture and Human Fertility: A Study of the Relation of Cultural Conditions to Fertility in Non-Industrial and Transitional Societies,* ed. Frank Lorimer (Paris: UNESCO, 1954), 253–320.
41. Fortes, *Oedipus and Job,* 37.
42. Bosman, *New and Accurate Description,* 208; Barbot, *Description of the Coasts,* 242.
43. Smith, *Baba of Karo,* 118, 231 and passim.
44. Ibid., 231; see also Herskovits, *Dahomey,* 1:343–49. With the Dahomeans, "a general principle governing divorce . . . is that a man may never divorce his wife, but must be divorced by her, since it is believed that vengeance for his taking the action will be exacted of him by the spirits of the ancestral founders of his family, whose decree he has violated". The Dahomean word for divorce, *asugbigbe* ("husband-refuse") reflects this injunction (ibid., 343–44).
45. Smith, *Baba of Karo,* 142, see also 128.
46. I.A. Akinjogbin, *Dahomey and Its Neighbours, 1708–1818* (Cambridge: Cambridge University Press, 1967), 16–17; M. Fortes and G. Dieterlen, eds., *African Systems of Thought: Studies Presented and Discussed at the Third International African Seminar in Salisbury, December 1960* (London: Oxford University Press for the International African Institute, 1965); see Fortes, "Some Reflections on Ancestor Worship in Africa", in *African Systems of Thought,* ed. Fortes and Dieterlen, 122–41.
47. Herskovits, *Dahomey,* 1:85.
48. For example, Bosman, *New and Accurate Description,* 534, note by Fage.
49. Rattray, *Tribes of the Ashanti Hinterland,* 1:78; For the communalism of pre-colonial African society, see, for example, Walter Rodney, *How Europe Underdeveloped Africa* (London: Bogle L'Ouverture, 1972), 43: "[T]he predominant principle of social relations was that of family and kinship associated with communalism. . . . Land (the major means of production) was owned by groups such as family or

clan." See also Herskovits, *Dahomey,* chapter 5 on property, 1:78–95.

50. Rattray, *Tribes of the Ashanti Hinterland,* 1:78.
51. Gluckman, *Custom and Conflict,* 74–75.
52. Rattray, *Tribes of the Ashanti Hinterland,* 1:79.
53. Equiano, *Interesting Narrative,* 20–21.
54. Fortes, "Some Reflections on Ancestor Worship", 126–27: "[A] wife on her death is given two funerals, a primary funeral in her conjugal settlement where she is mourned by her husband and her children, as wife and mother, and a secondary one when she is 'taken back home' to her paternal lineage. There she is mourned as daughter and sister and is besought to 'reach' her own fathers and forefathers."
55. Herskovits, *Dahomey,* 1:254–55.
56. M.G. Smith, "The Beginnings of Hausa Society AD 1000–1500", in *The Historian in Tropical Africa: Studies Presented and Discussed,* ed. J. Vansina, R. Mauny and L. Thomas (London: Oxford University Press for the International African Institute, 1964), 33.
57. Smith, *Baba of Karo,* 192, also 197–99, 200–205.
58. "In all parts of the Niger delta old men and women are held in high regard and play varying roles" (Alagoa, "Oral Tradition", 406). This "enthronement of the aged" characterized all West African societies; see Manoukian, *Ewe Speaking People,* 43; Curtin, *Africa Remembered,* 63; Herskovits, *Dahomey,* 1:351, and so on.
59. Alagoa, "Oral Tradition", 406.
60. Bosman, *New and Accurate Description,* 383–84; Rodney, *History of the Upper Guinea Coast,* 103.
61. See, for instance, Rodney, *History of Upper Guinea Coast,* 260–63; Smith, "Beginnings of Hausa Society", 22; Mary Smith, *Baba of Karo,* 38–43 and passim; Herskovits, *Dahomey,* 1:79–80, 97–104; Bosman, *New and Accurate Description,* 189–91.
62. Smith, "Beginnings of Hausa Society", 349; see also 340.
63. D. Birmingham, "Speculations on the Kingdom of Kongo", *Transactions of the Historical Society of Ghana* 8 (1965): 8; Ryder, *Benin and the Europeans,* 4.
64. Rattray, *Tribes of the Ashanti Hinterland,* 1:81, 84.
65. Roth, *Great Benin,* 119.
66. Birmingham, "Speculations", 7.
67. Herskovits, *Dahomey,* 1:110–13. Herskovits maintains that "it is impossible to comprehend the fiscal system of Dahomey without an understanding of the position of these women" (ibid., 1:110); their unquestioned allegiance to the king made them the most effective watchdogs over his internal revenue.
68. Bosman, *New and Accurate Description,* 63; Wyndham, *The Atlantic and Slavery,* 27; see also Ryder, *Benin and the Europeans,* 4; Rodney, *History of the Upper Guinea Coast,* 66.

69. K.Y. Daaku, "The European Traders and the Coastal States 1630–1720", *Transactions of the Historical Society of Ghana* 8 (1965): 21–22; Wyndham, *The Atlantic and Slavery,* 30.

70. Gluckman, *Custom and Conflict,* is especially enlightening on the subject of the anticipation and resolution of conflict in African life.

71. Walter Rodney, "Upper Guinea and the Significance of the Origins of African Enslavement in the New World", *Journal of Negro History* 54, no. 4 (October 1969): 345.

72. MS T4: Barham, Manuscript History, 46; MS 159: History and State of Jamaica, 10–11; Donnan, *Documents Illustrative,* 1:15–16.

73. See p. 16 above; also CSP Col. 1661–68, 1 February 1663, 122: "That Juan Loyola and the rest of the Negroes of his Polenque, on account of their submission and services to the English shall have grants of land and enjoy all the liberties and privileges of Englishmen, but must bring up their children to the English tongue. That other Negroes in the mountains shall enjoy the same benefits, provided they submit within 14 days after receiving this notice." Issued by Governor Lyttelton.

74. *Journals of the Assembly of Jamaica* 1 (1663–1709): appendix, Stat. Papers, 20.

75. CSP Col. 1661–68, 12 February 1605, 277.

76. Philip D. Curtin, *The Atlantic Slave Trade: A Census* (Madison: University of Wisconsin Press, 1969), 160, table 46.

77. Ibid., 119. Curtin had estimated that between 1651 and 1675, about 8,000 Africans were imported into Jamaica; between 1676 and 1700, the number was 77,100.

78. Davies, *Royal African Company,* 215–16. The earlier European explorers of North Guinea cherished "a dream of an interior country, rich in gold" and reconnoitred the lands which lay far back from the coast, in search of gold, slaves and ivory. Similarly, on the Gold Coast, little coastal trading took place: slaves came from within three hundred to four hundred miles of the sea (ibid., 226).

79. Walter Rodney, "Jihad and Social Revolution in Futa Djalon in the Eighteenth Century", *Journal of the Historical Society of Nigeria* 4, no. 2 (June 1968): 276.

80. Curtin, *Atlantic Slave Trade,* 160; Basil Davidson, *Black Mother* (London: Gollancz, 1968), 106–8; Orlando Patterson, *The Sociology of Slavery: An Analysis of the Origins, Development and Structure of Negro Slave Society in Jamaica* (London: MacGibbon and Kee, 1967), 128.

81. Ibid.

82. Curtin, *Atlantic Slave Trade,* 160; Patterson, *Sociology of Slavery,* 124.

83. Donnan, *Documents Illustrative,* 1:454–56.

84. The death rate on the Middle Passage in the 1680s was estimated at 23 per cent; see Davies, *Royal African Company,* 292.

85. James Duffy, *Portugal in Africa* (Harmondsworth: Penguin, 1962), 31–36; Wyndham, *The Atlantic and Slavery,* 8–33; Daaku, "European Traders", 11–23.

86. R.B. Le Page and David De Camp, *Jamaican Creole: An Historical Introduction to Jamaican Creole* (London: Macmillan, 1960), 58–59.

87. Ibid.

88. Ibid., 66–67.

89. John Esquemeling, *The Buccaneers of America: A True Account of the Most Remarkable Assaults* (1678; repr., London: Allen and Unwin, 1951); Alan Burns, *History of the British West Indies* (London: Allen and Unwin, 1954), chaps 11–15; A.P. Thornton, "The Modyfords and Morgan", *Jamaica Historical Review* 2, no. 2 (October 1952): 36–60.

90. See pp. 22–25 above; also Curtin, *Atlantic Slave Trade,* 117.

91. Ibid. For instance, 950 slaves accompanied 250 white refugees from Surinam in 1675 (see chapter 1); also Higham, *Development of the Leeward Islands,* 153.

92. Curtin, *Atlantic Slave Trade,* 38.

93. Ibid., also, Beeston, *Narrative of the Descent,* 251; MS 159: History and State of Jamaica, 20; CSP Col. 1661–68, 10 March 1662, 80; Cary Helyar's first business enterprise in Jamaica came about because he was able to salvage 132 slaves from the wreck of the slaveship *Panther* in 1669: see Bennett, "Cary Helyar", 56.

94. Le Page and De Camp, *Jamaican Creole,* 65–68.

95. Ibid., also Curtin, *Atlantic Slave Trade,* 25–26.

96. Burns, *History of the British West Indies,* chapters 13–15; Pitman, *Development of the British West Indies,* chapters 10–14.

97. Bosman, *New and Accurate Description,* 353; Barbot, *Description of the Coasts* 333, 365; Equiano, *Interesting Narrative,* 12; Smith, *Baba of Karo,* 128, 148, and so on.

98. Camara Laye, *The African Child* (London: Collins, 1954, 9th impression 1965), 93–94.

99. See, for instance, Edward [Kamau] Brathwaite, *The Arrivants: A New World Trilogy* (London: Oxford University Press, 1973).

100. Elsa Goveia, *The West Indian Slave Laws of the Eighteenth Century,* Chapters in Caribbean History (Bridgetown: Caribbean Universities Press, 1970), 13.

101. Frank Cundall and Joseph Pietersz, *Jamaica under the Spaniards, Abstracted from the Archives of Seville* (Kingston: Institute of Jamaica, 1919), 1.

102. Blathwayt, *History and State of Jamaica,* 11; also Taylor MS: "*Multum in Parvo*", 250.

103. S.A.G. Taylor, *Western Design,* 26–42; Jacobs, "Spanish Period", 88–89; Long, *History of Jamaica,* 1:237–38.

104. Cundall and Pietersz, *Jamaica under the Spaniards,* 35.

105. Firth, *Narrative of General Venables,* 156.

106. MS T4: Barham, Manuscript History, 30.

107. Wright, *English Conquest,* 10.

108. Thurloe, *Collection of the State Papers,* 3:456.

109. Patterson, "Slavery and Slave Revolts", 294–95.
110. CSP Col. 1661–68, 28 March 1668, 555.
111. See pp. 16–17 above.
112. Taylor MS: "*Multum in Parvo*", 554.
113. Ibid., 549–50.
114. Patterson, "Slavery and Slave Revolts", 295.
115. Thurloe, *Collection of the State Papers,* 3:154.
116. CSP Col. 1669–70, 2 May 1670, 65.
117. CSP Col. 1737, 30 June 1737, 192.
118. Dallas, *History of the Maroons,* 1:32.
119. Patterson, "Slavery and Slave Revolts", 303.
120. Dallas, *History of the Maroons,* 1:29; A.E. Furness, "The Maroon War of 1795", *Jamaica Historical Review* 5 (November 1965): 31; CSP Col. 1669–74, 2 May 1670, 65; CSP Col. 1685–88, 28 September 1686, 281: Governor Molesworth reported that the black insurgents of the parish of St George's had been originally formed sixteen or seventeen years previously by a group of slaves who had been saved from a shipwreck "on the easternmost part of the Island", had since "associated with themselves other runaways" and made themselves "plantations in the mountains from which they descend into the plains in great numbers for provisions, often doing much mischief in obtaining the same". On 13 February 1733 it was reported that the continued "desertion of numbers of the plantation slaves on the north side" had thrown the inhabitants "into despair". *Journals of the Assembly of Jamaica* 3 (1731–45): 220.
121. See pp. 28–29 above.
122. See pp. 66–67 above.
123. Patterson, "Slavery and Slave Revolts", 303; Dallas, *History of the Maroons,* 1:99.
124. Dallas, *History of the Maroons,* 1:108–9.
125. Patterson, "Slavery and Slave Revolts", 296; Taylor, *Western Design,* 99, 186–87, 191–92.
126. Patterson, "Slavery and Slave Revolts", 302.
127. Ibid., 303.
128. Edwards, *History, Civil and Commercial,* 1:539.
129. *Journals of the Assembly of Jamaica* 3 (1731–45): 132.
130. Ibid.; compare similar objectives of the white establishment during the second Maroon War, Furness, "Maroon War", 39–41.
131. *Journals of the Assembly of Jamaica* 3 (1731–45): 132.
132. Ibid.
133. *Journals of the Assembly of Jamaica* 2 (1709–31): 71.
134. Ibid., 683; see Patterson, "Slavery and Slave Revolts", 299, for the uprising on Sutton's plantation in 1690.

135. *Journals of the Assembly of Jamaica* 2 (1709–31): 683.

136. Ibid., 714.

137. Ibid.

138. *Journals of the Assembly of Jamaica* 3 (1731–45): 87.

139. Ibid., 404.

140. Ibid., 62.

141. Dallas, *History of the Maroons,* 1:49–50; Edwards, *History, Civil and Commercial,* 2:565; also the policy of the Windward Maroons, for example, CSP Col. 1733, 173.

142. Dallas, *History of the Maroons,* 2:138; Furness, "Maroon War", 45–47.

143. *Journals of the Assembly of Jamaica* 3 (1731–45): 121.

144. Ibid., 122.

145. Ibid.

146. Ibid.

147. Land Patents, Liber 22, 1741, 16.

148. CSP Col. 1685–88, 29 August 1685, 82.

149. Long, *History of Jamaica,* 2:473.

150. Monica Schuler, "Akan Slave Rebellions in the British Caribbean", *Savacou* 1, no. 1 (June 1970): 8–28.

151. Ibid., 16.

152. Dallas, *History of the Maroons,* 1:74.

153. See, for example, Martha Beckwith, *Black Roadways: A Study of Jamaican Folk Life* (1922; repr., New York: Negro Universities Press, 1969), 106, 124–25. One English military officer who took part in the Windward Maroon truce negotiation of 1739 made reference to the presence of "obea woman". See Philip Thicknesse, *Late Lieutenant Governor of Land Guard Fort . . . Memoirs and Anecdotes 1788,* 1:120.

154. See p. 52 above.

155. See pp. 58–59 above.

156. See p. 67 above.

157. Dallas, *History of the Maroons,* 1:92–94; J.J. Williams, *The Maroons of Jamaica,* Anthropological Series of the Boston College Graduate School (Chestnut Hill, Mass.: Boston College Press, 1938), 383–84.

158. For example, *Journals of the Assembly of Jamaica* 3 (1731–45): 122, 155; CSP Col. 1735, 27 February 1735, 383–85; Land Patents, Liber, 22, 1745; Thicknesse, *Late Lieutenant Governor;* Williams, *Maroons of Jamaica,* based largely on interviews with modern maroon chronicler/chiefs. Beverley Carey, "The Windward Maroons after the Peace Treaty", *Jamaica Journal* 4, no. 4 (December 1970) and *Portland and Rio Grande Valley* (Montego Bay, Jamaica: Public Relations Advisory Service, 1970). The validity of oral evidence for reconstructing much of the Afro-Caribbean past is increasingly acknowledged. Scholars whose research has made significant advances in this field include the linguist Maureen Lewis, the musicol-

ogist Olive Lewin, and historians Edward [Kamau] Brathwaite, Monica Schuler and Beverley Carey. This author is particularly grateful to Beverley Carey, a Maroon, and a generous chronicler of her community's history.

159. CSP Col. 1735, 385.

160. For example, *Journals of the Assembly of Jamaica* 3 (1731–45): 155.

161. Thicknesse, *Late Lieutenant Governor,* 1:114–18, 120; Carey, "Windward Maroons", and so on.

162. Williams, *Maroons of Jamaica,* 389.

163. Carey, "Windward Maroons"; see also Alan Teulon, "Report on Expedition to Nanny Town" (unpublished, July 1970).

164. For example, Thicknesse, *Late Lieutenant Governor,* 1:119; Nanny Town women were commissioned to help carry away spoil and to burn the town if the militia parties proved too strong for them. CSP Col., 1733, 173.

165. Patterson, "Slavery and Slave Revolts", 308; also CSP Col. 1735–36, 383–85.

166. Patterson, "Slavery and Slave Revolts", 309.

167. Ibid.

168. Ibid., 310.

169. Carey, "Windward Maroons".

170. Thicknesse, *Late Lieutenant Governor,* 1:121. Nanny was said to have declared "him (I.E. the laird) bring becara for take the town, so cut him head off". See also ibid., 126.

171. Ibid., 120. Labaret's underjaw was allegedly "fixed as an ornament to one of their hornsmen's horn".

172. Land Patents, Liber, 22, 1741, 22.

173. Carey, "Windward Maroons".

174. Dallas, *History of the Maroons,* 1:60: Freedom to market their surplus agricultural produce in nearby towns was guaranteed to Maroons under the terms of the peace treaty.

175. Dallas, *History of the Maroons,* 1:3.

176. Ibid., 99.

177. Ibid., 115.

178. Ibid., 110.

179. Ibid., 113.

180. Add. MSS 18959: Long Papers, Misc., 3.

181. C.P. Lucas, *A Historical Geography of the British Colonies,* vol. 2, *West Indies* (Oxford: Clarendon Press, 1905), 109.

182. George Cumper, "The Demographic Balance of the Maroon Communities in Jamaica 1799–1830" (paper presented at the fourth Conference of Caribbean Historians, University of the West Indies, Mona, April 1972), 5, 11.

183. Ibid., 12.

184. *Journals of the Assembly of Jamaica* 3 (1731–45): 704.
185. *Journals of the Assembly of Jamaica* 5 (1757–66): 235.
186. Ibid., 148; see also cases of other manumized informers, Venus and Affiba, in *Acts of Assembly*, I, 1681–1768, 231.
187. Long, *History of Jamaica*, 2:447–63; Schuler, "Akan Slave Rebellions", 15–17.
188. Ibid.; also *Journals of the Assembly of Jamaica* 5 (1757–66): 233–34.
189. Long, *History of Jamaica*, 2:455.
190. Schuler, "Akan Slave Rebellions", 15.
191. Ryder, *Benin and the Europeans*, 45; Bosman wrote: "Nor is it allowed to export any Male Slaves that are sold in this country, for they must stay here; But females may be dealt with at everyone's Pleasure." Bosman, *New and Accurate Description*, 462, also Fage's comment, 572.
192. Curtin, *Atlantic Slave Trade*, 160.
193. Donnan, *Documents Illustrative*, I:221.
194. Ibid., 230–32.
195. Ibid., 156n.
196. MS 159: History and State of Jamaica, 66: "Between Barbados and Jamaica there are two or three vessels constantly plying and afford convenient transportation from one place to another."
197. Higham, *Development of the Leeward Islands*, 148: In 1678, there were 3,227 black adult males, 3,120 black adult females and 2,313 black children in the islands of St Christopher, Nevis, Montserrat, Antigua and Saba. Barbados in 1676 had 16,352 black males (men and boys), and 16,121 black females (women and girls) (22, 1789 Part 4. Population, No. 3 Barbados); see also Dunn, *Sugar and Slaves*, 316, table 27.
198. As Curtin points out, however, this can only be conjecture, for "the extent to which planters removed 'seasoned' and Creole slaves from Barbados is unknown" (*Atlantic Slave Trade*, 58).
199. Edward Littleton, *The Groans of the Plantations: or, A True Account of their Grievous and Extreme Sufferings by the Heavy Impositions upon Sugar, and other Hardships* (London: Printed by M. Clark, 1689), 17.
200. Bennett, "Cary Helyar", 69; also Dunn, *Sugar and Slaves*, 322–23.
201. Ligon, *True and Exact History*, 47.
202. Ibid., 115–16.
203. Richard Blome, *A Description of the Island of Jamaica* (London, 1672), 18.
204. Taylor MS: "*Multum in Parvo*", 538.
205. Sloane, *Voyage to the Islands*, 18.
206. Inventories, Liber 1, 1674–76: this is also consistent with Dunn's findings (see *Sugar and Slaves*, 251).
207. Taylor MS: "*Multum in Parvo*", 538, also 542.

208. Ibid., 540.

209. Ibid., also Dunn, *Sugar and Slaves*, 251.

210. See p. 54 above.

211. Patterson, *Sociology of Slavery*, 90.

212. See p. 29 above and Thornton, "Modyfords and Morgan".

213. Patterson, *Sociology of Slavery*, 86.

214. Ibid.

215. Ligon, *True and Exact History*, 115–16.

216. Blome, *Description of the Island of Jamaica*, 16–21.

217. Bennett, "Cary Helyar", 62.

218. Ibid., 74.

219. CO 1/45.

220. Taylor MS: "*Multum in Parvo*", 536, 539.

221. Ibid.; the term "slave" is used throughout the text of the Act of 1681 for regulating servants; see *Acts of Assembly*, 1681–1768, 1:1–5.

222. CSP Col. 1701, 23 July 1701, 59.

223. Taylor MS: "*Multum in Parvo*", 537.

224. Sloane, *Voyage to the Islands*, 31.

225. Ibid., 15.

226. Bennett, "Cary Helyar", 69n.

227. Leslie, *New History of Jamaica*, 204.

228. Thomas Trapham, *A Discourse of the State of Health in the Island of Jamaica* (London: R. Boulter, 1679), 26.

229. CSP Col. 1701, 2 January 1701, 13.

230. Sloane, *Voyage to the Islands*, 16.

231. Ligon, *True and Exact History*, 48.

232. Bennett, "Cary Helyar", 69.

233. It was a period which was also marked by most brutal treatment of the slave offender, as is attested in the writings of Taylor, Sloane and Leslie; see also Patterson, *Sociology of Slavery*, 74–75, 82–84; Dunn, *Sugar and Slaves*, 238–46; R.W. Smith, "The Legal Status of Jamaican Slaves before the Anti-Slavery Movement", *Journal of Negro History* 30 (July 1945). The fear of black guerrilla activity strongly influenced the penal system of this period: see, for instance, the sadistic punishments inflicted on runaways and rebels, Taylor MS: "*Multum in Parvo*", 541, 553.

234. Patterson, *Sociology of Slavery*, 74, also 84; Dunn, *Sugar and Slaves*, 243–44; Smith, "The Legal Status of Jamaican Slaves", 293–94, 298–99.

235. Donnan, *Documents Illustrative*, 1:419.

236. Ibid., 455.

237. Inventories, Liber 5, 1699–1701.

238. Donnan, *Documents Illustrative*, 2:114.
239. Ibid., 159.
240. Ibid., 177.
241. Ibid., 204, 215, 294.
242. Inventories, Liber 14, 1726–28.
243. Donnan, *Documents Illustrative*, 2:215.
244. Ibid., 445.
245. Ibid., 459.
246. Ibid., 1:306–7; also 2:159, 177, 204.
247. Ibid., 2:204.
248. *PP* 1789, XXVI: 646 (a); also vol. III, Jamaica, nos. 1–5.
249. Long, *History of Jamaica*, 2:385.
250. See pp. 192–95 above.
251. For example, Taylor MS: "*Multum in Parvo*", 539.
252. *The Laws of Jamaica passed by the Assembly in 1683 and a Short Account of the Island*, 81. An act encouraging the importation of white servants imposed a fine of £20 on any one who used slaves in the "Trades or Exercise of Coopers or Porters"; CSP Col. 1716–17, 13 March 1716, 111–15; the Council considered "the most effectual means of putting an end to Negro tradesmen", and so on.
253. Inventories, Liber 14, 1726–28.
254. Sheridan, "Planter and Historian", 51.
255. Ibid., 48.
256. Inventories, Liber 44, 37–41.
257. Ibid., 25.
258. C 109/338.
259. Inventories, Liber 46, 1766, 216–18.
260. Leslie, *New History of Jamaica*, 35.
261. The most valuable discussion of this subject is found in Elsa Goveia, *A Study on the Historiography of British West Indies to the End of the Nineteenth Century* (Mexico: Instituto Panamericano de Geografía e Historia, 1956).
262. Ligon, *True and Exact History*, 47.
263. Ibid., 53.
264. Taylor MS: "*Multum in Parvo*", 542.
265. Ibid., 493.
266. Sloane, *Voyage to the Islands*, 142; see also p. 39 above.
267. Ibid., 143.
268. Leslie, *New History of Jamaica*, 35, 37; see also Goveia, *Historiography*, 49–53.
269. Long, *History of Jamaica*, 2:353–54.
270. Ibid., 371.
271. Ibid., 436: also 370, 383, 409, 425, 433.

272. Richard West, *Back to Africa: A History of Sierra Leone and Liberia* (London: Jonathan Cape, 1970), 13–14, 345; David Brion Davis, *The Problem of Slavery in Western Culture* (Ithaca: Cornell University Press, 1969), 260, 460–61.

273. J.C. Greene, "The American Debate on the Negro's Place in Nature", *Journal of the History of Ideas* 15 (1954): 386–88.

274. Curtin, *Image of Africa*, 45, also 36, 228.

275. Glory Robertson, "The Rose Hall Legend", *Jamaica Journal* 2, no. 1 (December 1968): 6–12.

CHAPTER 3

1. F. Mahoney, "Notes on Mulattoes of the Gambia Before the Mid-Nineteenth Century" *Transactions of the Historical Society of Ghana* 8 (1965): 120; Duffy, *Portugal in Africa*, 34; Wyndham, *The Atlantic and Slavery*, 10, 13, 14.

2. Rodney, "Upper Guinea", 332–33.

3. Duffy, *Portugal in Africa*, 37–44.

4. Ibid., 53.

5. J.D. Hargreaves, "Assimilation in Eighteenth-Century Senegal", *Journal of African History* 6, no. 2 (1965): 178–79; Wyndham, *The Atlantic and Slavery*, 24.

6. V.R. Dorjahn and Christopher Fyfe, "Landlord and Stranger: Change in Tenancy Relations in Sierra Leone", *Journal of African History* 3, no. 3 (1962): 391–97.

7. Rodney, *History of the Upper Guinea Coast*, 201.

8. Hargreaves, "Assimilation", 183.

9. Ibid., 178.

10. Curtin, *Africa Remembered*. See chapter 3 on Philip Quaque of the Gold Coast, with notes by Margaret Priestly, 116.

11. Ibid.

12. Rodney, *History of the Upper Guinea Coast*, 216–17.

13. Barbot, *Description of the Coasts*, 50.

14. Bosman, *New and Accurate Description*, 51; Priestly, "Philip Quaque of the Gold Coast", 116.

15. Shelby McCloy, "Negroes and Mulattoes in Eighteenth Century France", *Journal Negro History* 20, no. 3 (July 1945): 279–81.

16. Wyndham, *The Atlantic and Slavery*, 16.

17. Ibid., 52.

18. Rodney, *History of the Upper Guinea Coast*, 216.

19. C.R. Boxer, *Race Relations in the Portuguese Colonial Empire, 1415–1825* (Oxford: Clarendon Press, 1963), 31, 39.

20. Ibid., 39; Wyndham, *The Atlantic and Slavery*, 9.

21. Ibid.; Mahoney, "Notes on Mulattoes", 122–23.

22. Bosman, *New and Accurate Description,* 51; also Davies, *Royal African Company,* 280–81.
23. Rodney, *History of the Upper Guinea Coast,* 216–18.
24. Ibid., 210.
25. Ibid., 212.
26. Ibid.
27. Ibid.
28. Mahoney, "Notes on Mulattoes", 125.
29. Wyndham, *The Atlantic and Slavery,* 10, 13, 14.
30. Mahoney, "Notes on Mulattoes", 122; see also Hargreaves, "Assimilation", 181.
31. Bosman, *New and Accurate Description,* 141.
32. Ibid.
33. Duffy, *Portugal in Africa,* 126.
34. Gilberto Freyre, *The Portuguese and the Tropics: Suggestions Inspired by the Portuguese Methods of integrating Autocthonous Peoples and Cultures Differing from the European in a New, or Luso-Tropical, Complex of Civilisation,* trans. Helen M.D'O. Matthew and F. de Mello Moser (Lisbon: Executive Committee for the Commemoration of the Fifth Centenary of the Death of Prince Henry the Navigator, 1961), 266; see also Wyndham, *The Atlantic and Slavery,* 3–4.
35. Boxer, *Race Relations,* 32, 40.
36. Ibid., 31; Duffy, *Portugal in Africa,* 34; Rodney, *History of the Upper Guinea Coast,* 201; Barbot, *Description of the Coasts,* 37; Davies, *Royal African Company,* 5.
37. Hargreaves, "Assimilation", 177.
38. Cundall and Pietersz, *Jamaica under the Spaniards,* 14.
39. For instance, Wright, *English Conquest,* 7, 10, 12, 27.
40. Cundall and Pietersz, *Jamaica under the Spaniards,* 47.
41. Irene Wright, "The Spanish Resistance to the English Occupation of Jamaica, 1655–1660", *Transactions of the Royal Historical Society,* 4th ser., 13 (1930): 119.
42. MS T4: Barham, Manuscript History, 6.
43. Wright, *English Conquest,* 16.
44. Cundall and Pietersz, *Jamaica under the Spaniards,* 49.
45. Thurloe, *Collection of the State Papers,* 4:601; MS T4: Barham, Manuscript History, 48, 57.
46. MS T4: Barham, Manuscript History, 58; CSP Col. 1669–74, 2 May 1670, 65.
47. Sheila Duncker, "The Free Coloured and Their Fight for Civil Rights in Jamaica, 1800–1830" (MA thesis, University of London, 1960), 22, 177.
48. Edwards, *History, Civil and Commercial,* 1:216.
49. See, for instance, the official population estimates of 1662 and 1673 in *Journals of the Assembly of Jamaica* 1 (1663–1709): appendix, Stat. Papers, 20 and 40; also Douglas Hall, "The Role of the Free Coloured Population during Slavery in

Jamaica" (typescript, University of the West Indies, 1970), 2, estimates of population from 1658 to 1861.

50. Jamaica Archives, Inventories, Liber 1, 1674–76.
51. Laws of Jamaica, 1:133, 137.
52. Bennett, "Cary Helyar", 75, and n. Helyar's mistress was the daughter of a white man and a free Brazilian Negress who had married after living together some seven years in Barbados.
53. Winthrop D. Jordan, "American Chiaroscuro: The Status and Definition of Mulattoes in the British Colonies", *William and Mary Quarterly*, 3rd ser., 19 (1962): 183–200.
54. Ibid., 195.
55. See table 1.1, p. 23 above; Jordan, "American Chiaroscuro", 197.
56. See pp. 69–70 above.
57. Hall, "Role of the Free Coloured Population", 2.
58. Add. MSS 18959: Long Papers, Misc.
59. Jordan, "American Chiaroscuro", 193–96.
60. Ibid.
61. Ibid., 199.
62. Ibid., 200.
63. Long, *History of Jamaica*, 2:333. Long was recommending "the enfranchisement of every Mulatto child". It was "absurd", in his opinion, to expect that white men would ever refrain from interracial intercourse: the only recourse of the wise physician then "was to change an acute distemper into one less malignant". Enfranchising mulattoes, "affording them instruction in Christian morals, and obliging them to serve a regular apprenticeship to artificers and tradesmen, would make them orderly subjects, and faithful defenders of the country" (ibid.).
64. J. Samuel and Edith F. Hurwitz, "A Token of Freedom: Private Bill Legislation for Free Negroes in Eighteenth Century Jamaica", *William and Mary Quarterly*, 3rd ser., 24, no. 3 (July 1967): 428.
65. Ibid., also 426–27.
66. Douglas Hall, "Slaves and Slavery in the British West Indies", *Social and Economic Studies* 2, no. 4 (December 1962): 313.
67. Dunn, *Sugar and Slaves*, 254–55.
68. See pp. 61–62 above.
69. Dunn, *Sugar and Slaves*, 254.
70. *Journals of the Assembly of Jamaica* 5 (1757–66): 376–77.
71. *Acts of Assembly*, 1681–1768 (St Jago de la Vega, 1769), 179–81.
72. *Journals of the Assembly of Jamaica* 3 (1731–45) and 4 (1745–56), Private Acts.
73. Brathwaite, *Development of Creole Society*, 172.
74. Hall, "Role of the Free Coloured Population", 2; Roberts, *Population of Jamaica*, 39.

75. *Journals of the Assembly of Jamaica* 5 (1757–66): 376.
76. Ibid., 376–77.
77. Ibid.
78. Ibid., 377.
79. Ibid., 376.
80. Inventories, Liber 39, 99–100. The Augier women, all mulatto spinsters of Kingston, did rather well for themselves. Susannah's sister Mary and her four children were the beneficiaries of an Act of Privilege in 1747 (see *Journals of the Assembly of Jamaica* 4 [1745–56]: 67). When she died, her inventory of March 1764 was valued at £2,636. 4s. 3d., the bulk of which was a legacy from the late William Tyndall, Esq. (Inventories, Liber 44, 35–36). Another sister, Jane Augier, with her four children, successfully petitioned for a private Act of Privilege (*Journals of the Assembly of Jamaica* 4 [1745–56]: 84). Her inventory of 25 October 1766 included a comfortably equipped house, and twenty-five slaves valued at £907; her total personal estate was valued at £1,225 2s. 10½d. (Inventories, Liber 46, 81).
81. *Journals of the Assembly of Jamaica* 5 (1757–66): 376–77.
82. Ibid., 377.
83. *Journals of the Assembly of Jamaica* 4 (1745–56): 92.
84. Ibid., 579.
85. Samuel and Hurwitz, "Token of Freedom", 424.
86. *Journals of the Assembly of Jamaica* 3 (1731–45), 4 (1745–56) and 5 (1757–66).
87. Inventories, Liber 44, 209.
88. Ibid., 1.
89. Inventories, Liber 46, 22.
90. Samuel and Hurwitz, "Token of Freedom", 423–25.
91. Ibid.
92. Laws of Jamaica, 4:149.
93. Ibid., 27.
94. *Journals of the Assembly of Jamaica* 4 (1745–56): 92.
95. *Journals of the Assembly of Jamaica* 5 (1757–66): 376.
96. Ibid., 168, 169, 178, 179, 274.
97. Ibid., 273.
98. Laws of Jamaica, 5:67.
99. For instance, the private act of George Brooks of the parish of St Elizabeth, who in 1775 was enabled to settle his estate as he pleased. See *Acts of Assembly*, 1770–83, 15.
100. See, for instance, *Journals of the Assembly of Jamaica* 3 (1731–45): 653; *Journals of the Assembly of Jamaica* 4 (1745–56): 67; Inventories, Liber 44, 53, and so on.
101. *Journals of the Assembly of Jamaica* 2 (1709–31): 708.
102. *Acts of Assembly*, 98, 179–81.

103. Ibid., 153, 290; Samuel and Hurwitz, "Token of Freedom", 429.
104. Act 98, of 1733, stated that "no Person who is not above Three Degrees removed in lineal Descent from the Negro Ancestor exclusive, shall be allowed to vote or poll in Elections, and no one shall be deemed a Mulatto after the third Generation, as aforesaid but that they shall have all the Privileges and Immunities of his Majesty's white subjects etc.".
105. *Journals of the Assembly of Jamaica* 3 (1731–45): 703; Inventories, Liber 44, 37–41.
106. *Journals of the Assembly of Jamaica* 4 (1745–56): 39.
107. *Journals of the Assembly of Jamaica* 3 (1731–45): 443.
108. Ibid., 569.
109. For example, ibid., 655; *Journals of the Assembly of Jamaica* 5 (1756–66): 377, and so on.
110. Long, *History of Jamaica,* 2:449.

CHAPTER 4

1. Long, *History of Jamaica,* 2:7.
2. Ibid.
3. J. Stewart, *A View of the Past and Present State of the Island of Jamaica* (1823; repr., New York: Negro Universities Press, 1969), 131.
4. Edwards, *History, Civil and Commercial,* 1:269.
5. Maria Nugent, *A Journal of a Voyage to and Residence in the Island of Jamaica* (1839; rev. ed., ed. Philip Wright, Kingston: Institute of Jamaica, 1966), xv.
6. Edwards, *History, Civil and Commercial,* 1:269.
7. Metcalf, *Royal Government,* 182–84.
8. Add. MSS 35506: Hardwicke Papers, Governor Keith's Correspondence, 24 October 1770, 142.
9. Ibid.
10. Mrs Henry Lynch, *Years Ago: A Tale of West Indian Domestic Life of the Eighteenth Century* (London: Jarrold and Sons, 1865), 52.
11. Nugent, *Journal of a Voyage,* 12–13.
12. Long, *History of Jamaica,* 2:11.
13. Ibid., 33.
14. Geraldine Mozley, ed., *Letters to Jane from Jamaica 1788–1796* (London: Published for the Institute of Jamaica by the West India Committee, 1938). Mrs Frances Brodbelt wrote to her daughter Jane on 20 October 1793: "Your dear Father and Sister are both well, the latter in high expectation of a Gay session (for this is the season of gaiety here, when the Assembly meet and most families come to Town)" (ibid., 70). Also letter of 12 November 1792, 45–47; Lynch, *Years Ago,* 18.

15. Long, *History of Jamaica*, 2:33.

16. Nugent, *Journal of a Voyage*, 41.

17. Brathwaite, *Development of Creole Society*, 107–8.

18. Mozley, *Letters to Jane*, 24 December 1792, 48.

19. Ibid., 25 May 1795, 3.

20. Lynch, *Years Ago*, 52.

21. Mozley, *Letters to Jane*, 12 October 1794, 95.

22. Nugent, *Journal of a Voyage*, 30, 197.

23. Ibid., 156: She opened a King's House servants' dance with an old Negro man, which so shocked her creole guests, the Misses Murphy, that they nearly fainted, and "could hardly forbear shedding a flood of tears, at such an unusual and extraordinary sight". See also ibid., 203.

24. Ibid., 154.

25. Ibid., 64, 65, 69, 73–74, 181. On 22 August 1804, Maria Nugent wrote: "A most kind note from Mr Simon Taylor with a present of grapes and other fruits. Took the opportunity in reply, of being equally kind and flattering, and so I do hope, if he is not an active friend, he will not be an implacable enemy to my dear N. the next session" (ibid., 212). Nugent himself, significantly, had written, on 5 December 1802: "Mr Simon Taylor appears to be a most determined opponent of every useful and advantageous Measure to Government, and I have no hopes of influencing him: his character being that of an opinionated bitter Enemy, altho' to some as a warm friend" (CO 137/109).

26. Lynch, *Years Ago*, 52.

27. Balcarres was Nugent's predecessor in office; he successfully directed the military campaign against the Maroons in 1795–96. For his personal habits and the state of his menage, see Nugent, *Journal of a Voyage*, 11, 12, 15, 17.

28. See Brathwaite, *Development of Creole Society*, 105; Roberts, *Population of Jamaica*, 33, 41–42, 64–65.

29. Brathwaite, *Development of Creole Society*, 151–52; Patterson, *Sociology of Slavery*, 96–98.

30. Roberts, *Population of Jamaica*, 2–3, 70–71.

31. *PP* 1814–15, VI, no. 14, Jamaica. Governor Morrison pointed out to Earl Bathurst on 28 January 1813, that he knew "no mode by which the Number of the White and Coloured Population could be ascertained with any tolerable accuracy" (ibid., 103).

32. Roberts, *Population of Jamaica*, 73. Compare the sex ratio of 100 English communities between 1574 and 1821, which showed a figure of 91.3 males per 100 females; see Peter Laslett, "Size and Structure of the Household in England over Three Centuries", *Population Studies* 23, no. 2 (July 1969): 215, table 7.

33. *PP* 1814–15, VI, no. 14, Jamaica.

34. Add. MSS 12435: Long Papers, Inventory, 10.
35. St David Vestry Minutes, 1785–93.
36. Add. MSS 12435: Long Papers, Inventory, 41, and table 2.
37. Ibid., 3–4.
38. St David Vestry Minutes, 1785–93.
39. Nugent, *Journal of a Voyage,* 64–71.
40. Ibid., 72; compare Governor Nugent's comment: "In most of the parishes there is scarcely a white Family among the Proprietors . . . the Western parts of the island are much better peopled than the Eastern" (CO 137/110, 15 January 1803).
41. Add. MSS 12435: Long Papers, Inventory, 3–4 (see the appendix above).
42. Ibid., 10.
43. MS Cowper-McQueen MacKay, 1800–1816, letters written by Margaret and Mary Cowper, Jamaica, to their cousin Eliza McQueen MacKay, Savannah, Georgia. Margaret Cowper, 23 May 1800.
44. Compare the account of a typical great house day by Bernard M. Senior, *Jamaica, As It Was, As It Is, and As It May Be, by a Retired Military Officer* (1835; repr., New York: Negro Universities Press, 1969), 24–26.
45. Brathwaite, *Development of Creole Society,* 122–26.
46. Long, *History of Jamaica,* 2:22.
47. C 109/338.
48. Inventories, Liber 53, 42–44.
49. Kenneth E. Ingram, "The West Indian Trade of an England Furniture Firm in the Eighteenth Century", *Jamaican Historical Review* 3, no. 3 (March 1962): 22–35.
50. Edwards, *History, Civil and Commercial,* 4:9–10; Nugent, *Journal of a Voyage,* 58; Matthew Gregory Lewis, *Journal of a West India Proprietor Kept during a Residence in the Island of Jamaica* (London: J. Murray, 1834), 63.
51. Stewart, *View of the Past,* 34; Rev. John Riland, *Memoirs of a West India Planter* (London: Hamilton, Adams, 1827), 2; Jeannette Marks, *The Family of the Barretts, A Colonial Romance* (New York: Macmillan, 1938), 159.
52. Long, *History of Jamaica,* 2:100.
53. Ibid.
54. Barry Higman, "The Demography of Slavery in Jamaica, 1817–1834" (typescript, University of the West Indies, Mona, Jamaica, 1971), table 1.
55. Cowper MS, Margaret Cowper to Eliza McKoy, 18 May 1800. The Nugents dined at Bryan Castle on 2 April 1802: Mrs Nugent described it as follows: "It really is a beautifully place; the house is a good one, and tolerably well furnished, and has a Turkey carpet in the drawing room – an extraordinary sight in this country. The house stands rather higher than Arcadia, and is surrounded by pimento (allspice) groves, so laid out, as to make the prospect of the sea and the country more picturesque, through vistas." Nugent, *Journal of a Voyage,* 83, and n.

56. King's MS 213: Journal of an Officer.

57. William Hickey, *Memoirs 1749–1782*, ed. Alfred Spencer, 10th ed. (London, 1948), 2:43–44, 88, and so on.

58. Senior, *Jamaica, As It Was*, 23.

59. Cynric Williams, *A Tour Through the Island of Jamaica, From the Western to the Eastern End, in the Year 1823*, 2nd ed. (London: T. Hurst, E. Chance and Co., 1827), 9.

60. Cowper MS, Mary Cowper to Mrs R. MacKay, 10 April 1800; Mozley, *Letters to Jane*, 19 October 1795, 122.

61. Stewart, *View of the Past*, 213; also Senior, *Jamaica, As It Was*, 30–32; Brathwaite, *Development of Creole Society*, 117–18.

62. Senior, *Jamaica, As It Was*, 30.

63. Nugent, *Journal of a Voyage*, 168.

64. Long, *History of Jamaica*, 2:280.

65. J. Stewart, *An Account of Jamaica and Its Inhabitants by a Gentleman* (London: Printed for Longman, Hurst, Rees and Orme, 1808), 190.

66. Stewart, *View of the Past*, 177.

67. Edwards, *History, Civil and Commercial*, 2:12.

68. *Jamaica Magazine* 3, no. 5 (May 1813): letter to "The Observer" from Barbara Blanc.

69. Mozley, *Letters to Jane*, 4 April 1793, 56; P. Marsden, *An Account of the Island of Jamaica* (Newcastle: Printed for the author by S. Hodgson, 1788), 8; John Williamson, *Medical and Miscellaneous Observations Relative to the West India Islands* (Edinburgh: Printed by A. Smellie for the author, 1817), 1:259.

70. A.C. Carmichael, *Domestic Manners and Social Condition of the White, Coloured and Negro Population of the West Indies*, 2 vols. (London: Whittaker, Treacher and Co., 1833).

71. Rev. G.W. Bridges, *Dreams of Dulocracy; or the Puritanical Obituary* (London: Whitmore and Fenn, 1824), 17–18.

72. Ibid.

73. Long, *History of Jamaica*, 2:281–82; Stewart, *View of the Past*, 210.

74. Craton and Walvin, *Jamaican Plantation*, 139.

75. C 110/141.

76. C 107/143.

77. Long, *History of Jamaica*, 2:282.

78. Senior, *Jamaica, As It Was*, 29.

79. Nugent, *Journal of a Voyage*, 84, 86, 193.

80. Sarah Dwarris, letters written from Jamaica, letter of 9 November 1788; Stewart, *View of the Past*, 172.

81. Nugent, *Journal of a Voyage*, 80. Only a week before, she had commented on the house at the Sherriff's coffee estate in Portland: "This house is perfectly in the

Creole style. A number of negroes, men, women and children, running and lying about, in all parts of it" (ibid., 76).

82. Ibid.

83. Long, *History of Jamaica,* 2:282.

84. Rev. William Jones, *The Diary of the Rev. William Jones, 1777–1821,* ed. O.F. Christie (London: Bretano's, 1929), 31.

85. See pp. 109–10 above.

86. Mozley, *Letters to Jane,* 12 April 1788, 18.

87. Williams, *Tour Through the Island of Jamaica,* 195.

88. MS 93: letters from members of the King family in Jamaica to Mrs Bryan King in the United States, 1812–1833, letter, n.d. 1818; also Louisa King to Isabella King, 15 October 1815, and so on.

89. *PP* 1826–27, XXII, no. 7, Jamaica, encl. 1, Returns of Slave-Holding Officials.

90. Lynch, *Years Ago,* 9–10.

91. Stewart, *View of the Past,* 178.

92. Edwards, *History, Civil and Commercial,* 2:12.

93. Ibid., 13.

94. Ibid., 14; see also Robert Renny, *A History of Jamaica: With Observations on the Climate, Scenery, Trade, Productions, Negroes, Slave Trade, Diseases of Europeans, Customs, Manners, and Dispositions of the Inhabitants: to which is Added, an Illustration of the Advantages Which are Likely to Result from the Abolition of the Slave Trade* (London: Printed for J. Cawthorn, 1807), 325.

95. J.B. Moreton, *Manners and Customs in the West India Islands. Containing Various Particulars Respecting the Soil, Cultivation, Produce, Trade, Officers, Inhabitants, &c., &c. With the Method of Establishing and Conducting a Sugar-Plantation; in which the Ill-practices of Superintendents are Pointed Out. Also the Treatment of Slaves; and the Slave-trade* (London: W. Richardson, 1790). Moreton saw another side of the seemingly correct and virginal white creole female and wrote at some length, rather scandalously, on the subject; for example, ibid., 108–21.

96. Add. MSS 27970: James Henry Archer, MD, Accounts, Drafts of Letters, Business and Private Memoranda 1822–1845, vol. 1, 369.

97. D.V. Glass and D.E.C. Eversley, *Population in History: Essays in Historical Demography* (London: Edward Arnold, 1965), 16–17.

98. Wright, *Monumental Inscriptions;* Dunn's estimate, based on the same data, for an earlier period, produces similar results, although he rightly points out the "built-in statistical defects" of "tomb-counting", see Dunn, *Sugar and Slaves,* 329–30.

99. For instance, Stewart, *View of the Past,* 210; Lewis, *Journal of a West India Proprietor,* 103–4; Nugent, *Journal of a Voyage,* 64, 68, 70, 79.

100. Dwarris, letters, 16 July, 1786, 6 November 1786.

101. Ibid., 6 November 1786.

102. Ibid., 1 October 1784.
103. Ibid., 27 January 1788.
104. Nugent, *Journal of a Voyage,* 124.
105. Ibid., 175.
106. See chapter 7.
107. Ricketts Family Papers, including letters from Edward Long to Mr and Mrs W. Ricketts 1764–1813, 12 December 1764.
108. Nugent, *Journal of a Voyage,* 175–76.
109. Dwarris, letters, 9 December 1786, 27 January 1788.
110. Ibid., 20 March 1785.
111. Ibid., 9 November 1788.
112. Ibid., 24 April 1785.
113. Long, *History of Jamaica,* 2:276.
114. Ibid., 273.
115. J. Quier et al., *Letters and Essays on the Small-Pox and Inoculation, the Measles, the Dry Belly-Ache, the Yellow, and Remitting, and Intermitting Fevers of the West Indies* (London: Printed for J. Murray, 1778); Craton and Walvin, *Jamaican Plantation,* 132–33.
116. Nugent, *Journal of a Voyage,* 176–79, 181, 185.
117. Add. MSS 33293: Journal (1828–1846) of James Henry Archer, MD, of Spring Mount, St Ann, 84.
118. Stewart, *View of the Past,* 40–52.
119. A most useful discussion of this is found in Philip D. Curtin, "Epidemiology and the Slave Trade", *Political Science Quarterly* 83 (1968): 190–216.
120. Long, *History of Jamaica,* 2:506.
121. Nugent, *Journal of a Voyage,* 124.
122. Ibid., 162, also 22, 40, 59, 122, 179, and so on.
123. Ricketts Family Papers, 12 December 1764.
124. Nugent, *Journal of a Voyage,* 154, also 231; Williamson, *Medical and Miscellaneous,* 1:263, 284, 285; 2:21, 53.
125. Nugent, *Journal of a Voyage,* 146.
126. Stewart, *View of the Past,* 170–72.
127. Ibid., 171.
128. Ibid.
129. Dwarris, letters, 6 September 1788; Jones, *Diary,* 16; Mosley, *Letters to Jane,* 19 July 1795, 116.
130. Nugent, *Journal of a Voyage,* 259.
131. Ibid., 52, 76. "Many of the ladies, who have not been educated in England, speak a sort of broken English, with an indolent drawing out of their words, that is very tiresome if not disgusting" (ibid., 98).

132. Long, *History of Jamaica,* 2:279.
133. *Jamaica Magazine* 2 (June 1812).
134. Long, *History of Jamaica,* 2:279.
135. Jones, *Diary,* 31.
136. Nugent, *Journal of a Voyage,* 31.
137. Letter from Mrs Annabella Smith, governess, of Tripoli, Dry Harbour, St Ann's, to Lt Col Archibald Campbell of Argyllshire, 13 June 1812; see also advertisements, for example, supplement to *Royal Gazette* 13, no. 12 (1791): 9.
138. Long, *History of Jamaica,* 2:278.
139. Ibid. Mrs Henry Lynch's father, on the other hand, did not approve of governesses, whom he regarded as husband seekers, so his children were taught "at home", apparently by himself. Lynch, *Years Ago,* 2.
140. Long, *History of Jamaica,* 2:278; Stewart, *View of the Past,* 203.
141. *Royal Gazette* 13, no. 26 (1791): 6.
142. Stewart, *View of the Past,* 168, also 203; *Jamaica Magazine* (June 1812): 229–30 and (September 1813): 680.
143. Dwarris, letters, 28 June 1784; Long, *History of Jamaica,* 2:246.
144. Add. MSS 51806: Holland House Papers; 1775 Richard Vassal's a/c with Miss Richards. Elizabeth Vassal, the daughter and heiress of the wealthy creole planter Richard Vassal, married Henry Richard Fox, the third Lord Holland, in 1797, and dominated Whig social life in London from Holland House.
145. Mozley, *Letters to Jane,* 4 May 1795, 105.
146. Ibid., 70.
147. Ibid., 73.
148. Ibid.
149. Ibid., 86.
150. Ibid.
151. Ibid., n.d. 1795, 117.
152. Nugent, *Journal of a Voyage,* 58.
153. Williams, *Tour Through the Island of Jamaica,* 265.
154. *Jamaica Magazine* 4, no. 2 (August 1813): 608. Melissa was a rare creole feminist, whose criticisms of Jamaican men produced a firm reprimand from the columnist "The Observer". Melissa herself, he informed her, was "the true cause of all her unhappiness:" she was obviously suffering from "a sort of sickly sensibility, or rather fastidiousness;" he recommended the example of "an amiable young friend of (his), whose good sense, gentleness, and affability, render her the delight of all her acquaintance". He hoped that contemplation of "this lovely picture", would serve to correct "Melissa's pride and self-love".
155. Cowper MS, Margaret Cowper, 15 January 1800; see also letters of 18 and 23 May 1800, and 27 December 1803.

156. Mozley, *Letters to Jane,* 17 October 1795, 118; also November 1792.

157. Long, *History of Jamaica,* 2:522. Long regarded this taste for European fashion as "improper, ridiculous, and detrimental, in a hot climate".

158. Mozley, *Letters to Jane,* 13 November 1794, 98. Fashion was the most frequently recurring theme in the Brodbelt correspondence.

159. Ibid., 10 December 1793, 78.

160. Ibid., 19 October 1795, 122.

161. Ibid., 12 November 1792, 48.

162. *Jamaica Magazine* 4, no. 2 (August 1813): 608.

163. Mozley, *Letters to Jane,* 19 October 1795, 121; Stewart, *View of the Past,* 218.

164. Wylie Sypher, "The West Indian as a 'Character' in the Eighteenth Century", *Studies in Philology* 36 (1939): 516, also 512–15.

165. Brathwaite, *Development of Creole Society,* 135–37.

166. Cowper MS, Margaret Cowper.

167. Dwarris, letters.

168. Kingston Vestry Proceedings, 1781–88.

169. Senior, *Jamaica, As It Was,* 268.

170. Stewart, *View of the Past,* 114; Renny, *History of Jamaica,* 143.

171. Alan Furness, "The Jamaican Coffee Boom and John Mackeson, a Blue Mountain Coffee Planter 1807–1819", *Jamaican Historical Review* 3, no. 3 (March 1962); Brathwaite, *Development of Creole Society,* 146–48.

172. Nugent, *Journal of a Voyage,* 76.

173. Williams, *Tour Through the Island of Jamaica,* 322–23.

174. Add. MSS 27970: Archer accounts; Add. MSS 27971: James Henry Archer, MD, Jamaica, collections by son J.H. Lawrence Archer; Add. MSS 33293: Archer journal.

175. Add. MSS 33293: Archer journal, 34.

176. Add. MSS 27970: Archer accounts, 234.

177. Ibid., 245.

178. Add. MSS 33293: Archer journal, 66.

179. Ibid., 11, 33, 79, and so on.

180. For example, Add. MSS 27970, Archer accounts: payment to "my beloved Mary for candles, 2s/1d; Rebecca Archer borrowed to buy fish, 5d; Paid Mother in part of pimento picking, £3; my dear Mary for nursing me well, 10d, 2 cutlasses, 5/–", and so on.

181. Ibid., 284.

182. Anton Long, *Jamaica and the New Order, 1827–1847* (Kingston: Institute of Social and Economic Research, special series no. 1, 1956), 6, 77.

183. Edwards, *History, Civil and Commercial,* 2:372.

184. Cowper MS, Margaret Cowper, 7 August 1802.

185. Ibid.

186. Ibid., 30 August 1803.

187. Ibid., 27 December 1803.

188. Ibid.

189. Add. MSS 12435: Long Papers, Inventory, 3.

190. Ibid., 47

191. *PP* 1814–15, VI, no. 14, Jamaica, 110–13.

192. Land Patents, Liber 34, 87.

193. Add. MSS 34181: Abstracts of Jamaica Wills, 1625–1792.

194. Inventories, Liber 53 and 100.

195. Ibid., 53, 42–44.

196. Ibid., 212.

197. Ibid., 78.

198. Ibid., 31.

199. Ibid., 100, 177.

200. Ibid., 209.

201. Manchester Vestry Minutes, 1816–24.

202. St Thomas-in-the-Vale Vestry Minutes, 1789–1802.

203. Brathwaite, *Development of Creole Society,* 146–47.

204. Inventories, Liber 100, 94.

205. Rev. Richard Bickell, *The West Indies As They Are; Or, A Real Picture of Slavery: But More Particularly as it Exists in the Island of Jamaica in Three Parts* (London: Printed for J. Hatchard and Son, 1825), 50.

206. For instance, King MS T93: King Letters, 1812–1833, Mrs William Thompson to Isabella King, 1818.

207. *PP* 1814–15, VI, no. 14, Jamaica, 126.

208. Ibid.

209. Brathwaite, *Development of Creole Society,* 138, 149–50.

210. CO 137/81.

211. Brathwaite, *Development of Creole Society,* 150.

212. CO 137/81.

213. Stewart, *Account of Jamaica,* 156.

214. Dwarris, letters.

215. Long, *History of Jamaica,* 2:282.

216. Mozley, *Letters to Jane,* 1 February 1796, 129.

217. Nugent, *Journal of a Voyage,* 3, 77, 95, 238, 240.

218. Long, *History of Jamaica,* 2:282. Governor Nugent parted with his valet, Forbes, soon after his arrival in Jamaica, and appointed a mulatto man, named Rogers, in his stead. Nugent, *Journal of a Voyage,* 14.

219. Add. MSS 27970: Archer accounts.

220. Ibid., 5.

221. See pp. 146–47 above.
222. St James Vestry Minutes, 1807–25.
223. Postscript to the *Royal Gazette* 13, no. 17 (1791): 17.
224. Ibid., supplement no. 21, 12; also *Royal Gazette* 35, no. 20 (1813): 14 and so on.
225. Cowper MS, Margaret Cowper, 10 April 1800; also Lynch, *Years Ago,* 10.
226. Hickey, *Memoirs,* 2:20.
227. Supplement to *Royal Gazette* 13, no. 16 (1791): 14, and so on.
228. See chapter 7.
229. Supplement to *Royal Gazette* 13, no. 12 (1791): 9.
230. Governess Smith, letter.
231. Ibid.
232. See pp. 141–45 above.
233. Dwarris, letters, 11 May 1983.
234. *Royal Gazette* 13, no. 26 (1791): 6.
235. Kingston Vestry Proceedings, 1781–88, 3 January 1782.
236. Ibid.
237. Kingston Common Council Proceedings, 1820–28, 12 February 1821.
238. St James Court of Quarter Sessions Calendar Book, January 1793 to July 1841, January Court, 1793.
239. St James Vestry Minutes, 1807–25, 9 January 1808.
240. Ibid., 9 February 1818.
241. Kingston Vestry Proceedings, 1781–88, 28 July 1784.
242. Kingston Common Council Proceedings 1803–15, 19 February 1810.
243. Ibid., 26 February 1811; and similarly to Eliza Pranch on 4 March 1811.
244. For instance, a list of charitable devices and donations registered with the island secretary in 8 July 1737 (see *Journals of the Assembly of Jamaica* 3 [1731–45]: 417).
245. Add. MSS 34181: Jamaican Wills, 133.
246. Wright, *Monumental Inscriptions,* 100, no. 940.
247. *Jamaica Magazine* 1, no. 1 (March 1812): 66; Nugent, *Journal of a Voyage,* 189.
248. St James Court of Quarter Sessions, January 1793–July 1841, 20 April 1793.
249. Ibid.; also July 1793, September 1794, October 1796, and so on.
250. St James Vestry Minutes, 1807–25, 10 February 1807.
251. Ibid., 19 February 1810.
252. Ibid., 11 April 1807.
253. Ibid., 19 February 1810.
254. Ibid., 16 May 1814.
255. St Thomas-in-the-Vale Vestry Minutes, 1789–1802, 13 February 1790, 28.
256. Kingston Vestry Proceedings, 1781–88, 17 January 1781.
257. Ibid., 23 August 1785.
258. Ibid., July 1769–October 1770, 15 January 1770.

259. Ibid., 1781–88, 17 January 1781.
260. Ibid., 7 August 1786.
261. Ibid., July 1769–October 1780, 15 January 1770.
262. Westmoreland Vestry Minutes, 1780–81.
263. Kingston Common Council Proceedings, 1803–15, 3 October 1808.
264. St James Vestry Minutes, 1807–25, 10 February 1807, 10 October 1807, 9 January 1808.
265. Kingston Vestry Proceedings, 1781–88, 16 July 1781.
266. Ibid., 7 September and 16 December, 1782.
267. Ibid., 17 February 1783.
268. Ibid., 11 March 1783.
269. Ibid., 5 May 1783.
270. Ibid., 19 June 1783.
271. Ibid., 19 July 1787.
272. Kingston Common Council Proceedings, 1803–15, 3 April 1809.
273. Ibid., the difference was 692 pounds of beef.
274. Ibid., 1820–28, 15 July 1822.
275. Brathwaite, *Development of Creole Society,* 288–89.
276. Kingston Vestry Proceedings, 1781–88, 17 January 1781.
277. Ibid., 26 January 1784.
278. St James Vestry Minutes, 1807–25, 25 January 1813.
279. Ibid., 25 May 1818.
280. Ibid., 14 April 1819.
281. Kingston Vestry Proceedings, 1781–88, 7 April 1788.
282. Kingston Common Council Proceedings, 1820–28, Statement of salaries and accounts 1819–20.
283. Ibid., 22 January 1821.
284. For instance, "Margaret Holmes an out-Pensioner having neglected to attend at the parish house, the 24 January last, her weekly allowance was in consequence thereof stopt, but having appeared this Day, and given satisfactory reasons for such her neglect, Ordered that the arrears due her be paid up and that she be continued." Kingston Vestry Proceedings, 1 March 1781.
285. Kingston Vestry Proceedings, 1781–88, 6 February 1786.
286. Ibid., 10 February 1785.
287. Ibid., 7 April 1788.
288. Ibid., 1 April 1783.
289. Ibid., 3 November 1783.
290. Ibid., 1 March 1787.
291. Ibid., 1 February 1787; also Kingston Common Council Proceedings, 1803–15, 28 September 1812, and so on.

292. Kingston Common Council Proceedings, 1803–15, 28 September 1812.

293. Ibid., 1820–28, 2 February 1824, 10 May 1824.

294. Ibid., 1803–15, 21 November 1808.

295. Kingston Vestry Minutes, 1781–88, 17 January 1781.

296. Kingston Common Council Proceedings, 1820–28, 6 October 1823; see also 1 July 1822.

297. Ibid., 4 October 1824.

298. Elsa Goveia, *Slave Society in the British Leeward Islands at the End of the Eighteenth Century* (New Haven: Yale University Press, 1965) 312.

299. *Royal Gazette,* 13, 1791.

300. Kingston Vestry Minutes, 1769–70, 23 January 1770.

301. Ibid., 1781–88, 2 June 1786, 19 June 1786, 24 July 1786, 7 December 1786, 25 January 1787, and so on.

302. Ibid., 1 March 1787.

303. Kingston Common Council Proceedings, 1820–28, 2 October 1820.

304. Kingston Vestry Proceedings, 1781–88, 18 February 1782, 28 May 1782.

305. Kingston Common Council Proceedings, 1820–28, 29 March 1824.

306. Kingston Vestry Proceedings, 1769–70, 23 January 1770.

307. Ibid., 19 February 1770.

308. Ibid., 1781–88, 6 February 1786: see also entries of 3 October 1808, 19 February 1810, 9 June 1825.

309. Manchester Vestry Minutes, 1816–24, 17 April 1823.

CHAPTER 5

1. Spruill, *Women's Life and Work,* 340, quoted from "The Lawes Resolutions of Women's Rights: or the Lawes Provision for Women" (London, 1632).

2. Roger Fulford, *Votes for Women* (London: Faber and Faber, 1958), 27, also 17, 18, 28, 54–58. A test case had arisen in 1733 in a parochial election. Lord Chief Justice Lee guardedly conceded the feasibility of a female suffrage in local elections, but at parliamentary level, he was inclined "to think women have not a right of voting, though they are not positively excluded" (ibid., 17). The first debate in Parliament on the subject took place in 1797 when the Whig statesman Fox declared that "in all the theories of the most absurd speculation, it has never been suggested that it would be advisable to extend the elective franchise to the other sex" (ibid., 19).

3. *Acts of Assembly,* 1770–83: Act 71, 1780, 163–74, cl. 6, 8.

4. Fulford, *Votes for Women,* 18–19; Sheila Rowbotham, *Women, Resistance and Revolution* (Harmondsworth: Penguin, 1974), 24–26, and passim.

5. Ragatz, "Absentee Landlordism", 11.

6. Ibid.; also Calhoun, *Social History,* 1:234–35.

7. Spruill, *Women's Life,* 340.

8. *Jamaica Magazine* 2, no. 9 (October 1812): 292.

9. Ricketts Family Papers, 30 September 1801.

10. Ibid.

11. King's MS 213: Journal of an Officer.

12. Long, *History of Jamaica,* 2:328.

13. See, for instance, the numbers of marriages reported in the local press between creole brides and service men, *Jamaica Magazine* 1, no. 5 (July 1812); *Jamaica Magazine* 3, no. 6 (June 1813), and so on.

14. "Coverture" was the condition of a woman during marriage: she was presumed to be under the influence of her husband, and therefore excused from punishment for crime committed in his presence, except treason, murder and manslaughter. This presumption was abolished from British law by the Criminal Justice Act, 1925 (c.86), s.47.

15. Sinclair, *Better Half,* 84. Quotation from Sir William Blackstone's *Commentaries on the Laws of England* (Oxford: Clarendon Press, 1765).

16. Courtney Kenny, *The History of the Law of England as to the Effects of Marriage on Property and of the Wife's Legal Capacity* (London: Reeves and Turner, 1879), 13.

17. Ibid.; also 7–8; Thomas, "Double Standard", 201–2.

18. *PP* 1826–27, XXIV, First Report of the Commissioner of Enquiry into the Administration of Criminal and Civil Justice in the West Indies, Jamaica (29 June 1827), 309 and passim.

19. Add. MSS 34181: Jamaican Wills.

20. Ibid., 60.

21. Ibid., 73.

22. Ibid., 42.

23. Ibid., passim.

24. Ibid., 60.

25. Sinclair, *Better Half,* 85; also Spruill, *Women's Life,* 364–66; H.J. Habakkuk, "Marriage Settlements in the Eighteenth Century", *Transactions of the Royal Historical Society,* 4th ser., 32 (1950): 15–30; Christopher Clay, "Marriage, Inheritance, and the Rise of Large Estates in England 1660–1815", *Economic History Review,* 2nd ser., no. 21 (1968): 503–18.

26. Ibid., see especially, Habakkuk, "Marriage Settlements"; also Rowbotham, *Women, Resistance and Revolution,* 29.

27. Habakkuk, "Marriage Settlements", 24; Calhoun, *Social History,* 1:56–57; 2:216.

28. See above, chapter 4.

29. Howard, *Records and Letters,* 1:119, also, 74, 76.

30. Add. MSS 34181: Jamaican Wills, 11.

31. Ibid., 29.
32. *PP* 1826–27, XXIV, appendix B.
33. Laws of Jamaica, 1804–1809, 5:48, 3c. 20.
34. *PP* 1826–27, XXIV: 309; also 378.
35. Sheridan, *Development of the Plantations,* 100.
36. See, for instance, Add. MSS 30001: General Correspondence; and Ricketts Family Papers.
37. Add. MSS 34181: Jamaican Wills, 133. The Rev. Venn's concern for Mrs Venn was all-embracing, for he continued, "she is under no restraint but he earnestly advises her as Friend never to marry again – if she does (on the prophetic words of a man near his end), she will be very unhappy".
38. See chapter 4.
39. Sinclair, *Better Half,* 83–84.
40. Ibid.
41. Ibid., 87–88; Duncan Crow, *The Victorian Woman* (London: Allen and Unwin, 1971), 154, 251.
42. *PP* 1826–27, XXIV: 448. For the double standard principle underlying English divorce procedures see Thomas, "Double Standard", 199–202.
43. *PP* 1826–27, XXIV: 448.
44. Long, *History of Jamaica,* appendix, 605.
45. Ibid., 26–29; Bryan Edwards's copy of Long's history, which is now in the library of the University of the West Indies, contains Edwards's marginal comment, viz., "It is not so tardy, however, as the Court of Chancery in England" (ibid., 29).
46. *PP* 1826–27, XXIV: 332–34.
47. Lewis, *Journal of a West India Proprietor.*
48. Add. MSS 34181: Jamaican Wills, no. 100. Frances Scott's remains are still to be found in the nave of the Kingston Parish Church (Wright, *Monumental Inscriptions,* 18, no. 143).
49. Add. MSS 34181: Jamaican Wills, 60; William Lewis died in England in 1774 at the age of 53. In accordance with his wishes, his remains were taken to Jamaica and buried beside his wife (Wright, *Monumental Inscriptions,* 196, no. 1940).
50. Lewis, *Journal of a West India Proprietor,* 89.
51. Ibid., 102, also 161.
52. MS 1: Thomas Munro, Member of Assembly for Trelawny, Memo Book, 1810–1812 (vol. 1, 65). See also Add. MSS 33293: Archer journal. Archer wrote on 11 October 1831: "At 20 minutes after 2 this morning my beloved and more than tenderly attached Mary departed this life leaving her unfortunate and wretched Husband to lament the loss of one of the best of wives"; also subsequent entries.
53. Add. MSS 33293: Archer journal; Add. MSS 27970: Archer accounts; Add. MSS 27971: Archer collections.

54. Add. MSS 34181: Jamaican Wills, 93.

55. King's MS 213: Journal of an Officer.

56. Add. MSS 33293: Archer journal; Add. MSS 27970: Archer accounts; Add. MSS 27971: Archer collections.

57. Richard Sheridan, "The Rise of a Colonial Gentry, Case Study of Antigua 1730–1735", *Economic History Review*, no. 13 (1960–61): 344; Long, *History of Jamaica*, 2:266.

58. See p. 157; Add. MSS 34181: Jamaican Wills.

59. Marks, *Family of the Barretts*, 209–10, 308–11, and so on.

60. Howard, *Records and Letters*, 1: chapters 1–7. See in particular chapter 5, Samuel Long of Longville, and genealogical tables on 120–21, 185.

61. Ibid., 192, also 193–96.

62. Ibid.; Leslie Lewis, "English Commemorative Sculpture in Jamaica", *Jamaica Historical Review* 9 (1972): 116.

63. Ibid.

64. Howard, *Records and Letters*, 1:122, also 123–24; and 2:301.

65. Ibid., 1:10.

66. Ibid., 193.

67. Add. MSS 34181: Jamaican Wills, 22.

68. Ibid., and passim.

69. Mozley, *Letters to Jane;* MS 1069: Irwin and Tryall Estates. Arrangements for her two sons' schooling in England caused Mrs Bosley constant concern; for example, a letter of 28 May 1761 to Mrs Thomas Hall: "Don't, my dr Cousin think I take amiss your refusing to take the care of my son George, when I asked that favour of you." Thomas Hall, however, continued to be guardian; but by 1769, he had had his fill of the Bosley boys, who were frequently described as idle, negligent, backward and extravagant. He wrote Mrs Bosley on 5 November 1769 refusing to take the responsibility for supervising George Bosley's university career in medicine in Scotland.

70. Add. MSS 34181: Jamaican Wills, 133.

71. Mozley, *Letters to Jane*, 1 November 1792, 56.

72. Ricketts Family Papers, 12 December 1764.

73. Ibid., 17 September 1772.

74. Ibid.

75. Dwarris, letters, 12 December 1784, also 11 August 1784, 24 April 1785, 3 July 1786, and so on.

76. Howard, *Records and Letters*, 1:175.

77. See, for instance, Lilian Penson, "The London West India Interest in the Eighteenth Century", *English Historical Review* 36 (1921): 381; Sheridan, "Rise of a Colonial Gentry", 346.

78. Howard, *Records and Letters,* 1:86.

79. Ibid., 96.

80. Ibid., 87.

81. Ricketts Family Papers, 5 October 1768.

82. Howard, *Records and Letters,* 1:108.

83. Add. MSS 30001: General Correspondence, 19 May 1780), 56. William Henry Ricketts, Jr, assumed the surname of Jervis in 1801; he was drowned in 1805, and his younger brother Edward succeeded their uncle Lord Jervis as the Viscount St Vincent. See Oliver, *Caribbeana,* 3 (suppl.): 60.

84. Ibid.

85. Add. MSS 33293: Archer journal, 39.

86. Ibid., 40.

87. Ibid.

88. Ibid.

89. Ibid., 41.

90. Ibid., 9 June 1829, 46.

91. Ibid.

92. Ibid., 54.

93. Add. MSS 27971: Archer collections, 396–404.

94. Ibid., also 485 (James Archer's will).

95. Dwarris, letters, 14 January 1782, and subsequent quotations.

96. Eugene Genovese, *The Political Economy of Slavery: Studies in the Economy and Society of the Slave South* (New York: Pantheon, 1965), 18.

97. Ibid. This was equally true of Great Britain; see, for instance, F.M.L. Thompson, "The Social Distribution of Landed Properties in England since the Sixteenth Century", *Economic History Review,* 2nd ser., 19, no. 3 (1966): 506–17.

98. Cowper MS, Margaret Cowper, 10 April 1800. The Rev. William Jones wrote as follows of creole women's spending habits: "Thoughtless Extravagance and expensive Pomp they are dotingly fond of, come the supplies whence they may". Jones, *Diary,* 31.

99. Mozley, *Letters to Jane,* 25 January 1790. Mrs Brodbelt went to England on 8 August 1790 to fetch Nancy home and returned to Jamaica on 24 March 1792. See also letter of 4 October 1795.

100. Douglas Hall, "Incalculability as a Feature of Sugar Production during the Eighteenth Century", *Social and Economic Studies,* no. 10 (1961): 347–50.

101. Ibid., 350.

102. Ibid., 347.

103. Add. MSS 30001: General Correspondence; and Ricketts Family Papers.

104. Douglas Hall, "Absentee Proprietorship in the British West Indies to about 1850", *Jamaican Historical Review* 4 (1964): 27.

105. Ricketts Family Papers, 6 April 1764, also 5 October 1768.

106. Ibid., passim.

107. Ibid., 17 September 1772.

108. Add. MSS 30001: General Correspondence, 13 January 1783, 61.

109. Ricketts Family Papers, 6 May 1797.

110. Kenneth Ingram, "A Bibliographical Survey of the Sources of Jamaican History 1655–1838 with Particular Reference to Manuscript Sources" (BLitt, University of London, 1970), 763; C 110/141, Mount Pleasant and Salem Plantations, Hanover, Jamaica; 1776–1805.

111. Ibid.

112. C 110/141.

113. Ibid., 13 September 1787.

114. Ibid.

115. Ibid., 31 May 1797.

116. Ibid.

117. Ibid., 23 June 1797.

118. King's MS 213: Journal of an Officer, 3 March 1817.

119. Ibid., 26 April 1817; also 5 August 1817.

120. Ibid., 2 September 1824.

121. Ibid., 21 April 1817.

122. Ibid., 26 April 1817.

123. Ibid., 21 April 1817.

124. Brathwaite, *Development of Creole Society,* 158–59.

125. Wright, *Monumental Inscriptions,* 259, no. 2670.

126. Riland, *Memoirs,* 4.

127. Jones, *Diary,* 16.

128. Add. MSS 34181: Jamaican Wills, 89.

129. Ibid., 43; see also Long, *History of Jamaica,* 2:330.

130. Marks, *Family of the Barretts,* 196–99, 209–11, 310–11, and so on.

131. Ibid., 222, 297.

132. Ibid., 298–99, 306.

133. Wright, *Monumental Inscriptions,* 106, no. 990.

134. Add. MSS 34181: Jamaican Wills, 48.

135. C 107/156, Documents relating to the will of James Affleck, carpenter of Hanover, Jamaica, and of Hawthornden, nr. Edinburgh, 1801–1818.

136. Both Mrs Nugent (*Journal of a Voyage,* 12) and Stewart (*Account of Jamaica,* 200) wrote of the "influence exercised by the mulatto connexions".

137. See pp. 171–72 above.

138. Long, *History of Jamaica,* 2:369–71.

139. M.C. Campbell, "Edward Jordon and the Free Coloureds; Jamaica 1800–1865"

(PhD diss., University of London), 237–38; extract from *The Watchman*, 24 April, 1833, no. 33.

140. Jones, *Diary*, 51.

141. Stewart, *View of the Past*, 175.

142. Ibid., 331.

143. *Jamaica Magazine* 4, no. 4 (October 1813): 747, "The Story of Julia"; also Bickell, *West Indies As They Are*, 104–5. The Marquis of Halifax wrote as follows in the seventeenth century: "Remember, that next to the danger of committing the fault yourself, the greatest is that of seeing it in your husband. Do not seem to look or hear that way . . . . Such an indecent complaint makes a wife much more ridiculous than the injury that provoketh her to it" (quoted by Thomas, "Double Standard", 196). This widely accepted assumption about the relationship of spouses conveniently supported Jamaica's extramarital practices.

144. Long, *History of Jamaica*, 2:284.

145. Ibid., 250.

146. Ibid.

147. Add. MSS 30001: General Correspondence, especially her letter of 6 October 1764, 22.

148. King's MS 213: Journal of an Officer, 26 April 1817.

149. Stewart, *View of the Past*, 172.

150. Williams, *Tour Through the Island of Jamaica*, 327, also 317–18.

151. Ibid.; "[Susanna's] master's house was a very sad place; nobody came there; it was so far out of the world, and there was no road past within sight". See also pp. 129–29 above.

152. Robertson, "Rose Hall Legend"; also Joseph Shore, *In Old St James, Jamaica, A Book of Parish Chronicles* (1911; repr., Kingston: Sangster's Book Stores, 1970).

153. *PP* 1831–32, XLVII; see also Bickell, *West Indies As They Are*, 27; also pp. 231–32 above.

154. See, for instance, Sinclair, *Better Half*, 17, on the influence of "moral reform" church societies on female radicalism in Boston in the 1830s. "Women", he maintained, "learnt the techniques of reform within the churches", and applied these techniques in the cause of the emancipation, both of slaves, and of women. See also ibid., 38–48.

155. *Jamaica Magazine* 3, no. 6 (June 1813); *Observer*, no. 16.

156. Rev. G.W. Bridges, *A Sermon Delivered in the Parish Church of St Ann, Jamaica, 4 November 1827* (n.d.), 16–17; see also Nugent, *Journal of a Voyage*, 54n91, 97, 165, and so on; Brathwaite, *Development of Creole Society*, 24–25.

157. Brathwaite, *Development of Creole Society*, 24–25.

158. Ibid., 25, 260–61.

159. King's MS 213: Journal of an Officer, 7 April 1817.

160. Nugent, *Journal of a Voyage,* 14.

161. For example, 35, 39, 48, 49, 86, 103 and so on.

162. General Church Book for the Missionaries of the United Brethren in Jamaica (MS, beginning 7 December 1754); *Diary of John Lang, 1805–1819;* Periodical Accounts of the Moravian Church; *Diary of the Negro Congregation at Fairfield, 1828–1829.*

163. Periodical Accounts, *c.*1831–1832, 460–61.

164. Ibid., also Add. MSS 51819: Holland House Papers, Misc., 82.

165. Fairfield Diary, 1828, entries of 31 August, 29 December, etc.; Add. MSS 51819: Holland House Papers, Misc., 82.

166. Peter Duncan, *A Narrative of the Wesleyan Mission to Jamaica* (London: Partridge and Oakey, 1849), 10.

167. Ibid., 9.

168. Ibid.

169. Ibid., 11.

170. Marks, *Family of the Barretts,* 350, 381–82.

171. Ibid.; also Rev. Hope Waddell, *Twenty-Nine Years in the West Indies and Central Africa* (London: T. Nelson and Sons, 1863), 27, 32, 34, 43.

172. Waddell, *Twenty-Nine Years,* 82.

173. Ibid., 44.

174. Mary Ann Hutchins, *The Youthful Female Missionary: A Memoir of Mary Ann Hutchins Wife of the Rev. John Hutchins, Baptist Missionary, Savanna-la-mar, Jamaica,* 2nd ed. (London: G. Nightman, 1840), Diary entry of 12 August 1834, 104.

175. Ibid. 93.

176. Nugent, *Journal of a Voyage,* 49.

177. Ibid., 156.

178. Ibid., 53.

179. Ibid., 76, 90.

180. Ibid., 237.

181. Ibid., 240.

182. Ibid., 220.

183. Ibid., 227.

184. Lynch, *Years Ago,* 205.

185. See p. 119 above.

186. Riland, *Memoirs,* 27.

187. A. Mackenzie-Grieve, *The Great Accomplishment: The Contribution of five English Women to Eighteenth Century Colonisation* (London: Bles, 1953), chapter 1; Anna Falconbridge, *Narrative of Two Voyages to the River Sierra Leone, during the Years 1791–1793* (repr., London: New Impression, Frank Cass, 1967).

188. Falconbridge, *Narrative of Two Voyages,* 238.
189. Dwarris, letters, 9 November 1788. Similar views were expressed by Lady Normanby (the wife of Governor Mulgrave), in 1832; see Maria Normanby, *Extracts of Letters from Maria, Marchioness of Normanby,* ed. Georgiana Bloomfield (Hertfordshire, 1892), 7, 16, 18–19.
190. When the Kingston Theatre opened in 1812, the prologue asked the audience to give the actors a silent hearing: he then made a special appeal to the ladies present (*Jamaica Magazine* 2, no. 9 [October 1812]), viz.,

> Come to our aid, ye Fair, that grace our boxes.
> Angels on earth, at least the Angel's proxies.
> Tell these male-folk, noise has no charms for you,
> And help to civilise the boisterous crew.
> Should they persist, Eternal Powers call down,
> And crush the haughty rebels with a frown.
> Should this too fail their errors to beguile,
> Dismiss the frown, and tame with a smile.

The *Jamaica Magazine* constantly reminded women of their role in this respect, while making sharp jabs at their intellectual shortcomings.

191. Add. MSS 33293: Archer journal, 33.
192. Ibid., 5 December 1831, 79.
193. Mozley, *Letters to Jane,* 17 October 1795; Lynch, *Years Ago,* 32.
194. "We are all in amazement here, with respect to your Petitions concerning the African Slave Trade – What will those say who read the History of George the third 50 years hence, that within the course of 12 years the King and People of England first wanted to make Slaves of their own Free Subjects in America – that not being accomplished and loosing a mighty Empire – a similar frenzy took them, and they wanted to make Slaves Free – good by to your Colonies if you pass such a LAW – I am sure I have had some little experience in the course of 17 years residence in this Island and declare upon the whole I conceive is only to be the name of Slavery, that grates an Englishman's Ear – many of them are happier and live much better than your poor People in England, those on the plantations have grounds of their own, which not only yield them the necessaries of life, but superfluities to sell for cash with which they buy better cloaths than your poor can afford, as also Salt fish, Salt pork, Irish beef, &c. &c.". Dwarris, letters, 22 April 1788.
195. Riland, *Memoirs,* 27.
196. Normanby, *Extracts of Letters,* 14, also 18.
197. Brathwaite, *Development of Creole Society,* 188–89.
198. Jones, *Diary,* 33.

199. CO 137/81, 149; Brathwaite, *Development of Creole Society,* 190–91.
200. These questions were put in turn to Sargent Henry Dempsey, Sargent John Green, and drummer Thomas Goodwin, by the committee of the Assembly which was appointed to inquire into the mutiny of the Second West India Regiment on 27 May 1808. Each answered in the negative. *Journals of the Assembly of Jamaica* 12 (1808–15): 107–8.
201. Senior, *Jamaica, As It Was,* 247.
202. Ibid., 196, also 217, 218, 219, 228, 235, 258, 271.
203. Ibid.
204. Mary Reckord, "The Slave Rebellion of 1831", *Jamaica Journal* 2, no. 2 (June 1969): 31; H. Bleby, *Death Struggles of Slavery* (London: Hamilton, Adams and Co., 1853). For other indications of this neurosis in the New World, see, for instance, Herbert Aptheker, *American Negro Slave Revolts* (New York: International Publishers, 1969), 224n. Aptheker writes: "[S]o far as the evidence shows there is no case of rape or attempted rape in the history of American negro slave revolts." Nevertheless, the fear existed. See also Winthrop Jordan, *White over Black: American Attitudes Toward the Negro, 1550–1812* (Chapel Hill: University of North Carolina Press, 1963), 398–99.
205. Jordan, *White over Black,* 152.
206. For example, Pitman, *Development of the British West Indies;* W.L. Burn, *Emancipation and Apprenticeship in the British West Indies* (London: Jonathan Cape, 1937); Ragatz, "Absentee Landlordism"; Patterson, *Sociology of Slavery.*
207. Hall, "Absentee Proprietorship".
208. Brathwaite, *Development of Creole Society.*
209. Patterson, *Sociology of Slavery,* 33.
210. Patterson, *Slavery and Slave Revolts,* 323.
211. Ibid.
212. Ibid.
213. Goveia, *Slave Society;* Brathwaite, *Development of Creole Society.*
214. See, for instance, James W.V. Zanden, "The Ideology of White Supremacy", *Journal of the History of Ideas,* no. 20 (1959): 385–402.
215. Calhoun, *Social History,* 3:281.
216. Genovese, *World the Slaveholders Made,* 100, also 235–37.
217. Ulrich Phillips, *Life and Labour in the Old South* (Boston: Little, Brown, and Co., 1929); Ulrich Phillips, *The Slave Economy of the Old South: Selected Essays in Economic and Social History,* ed. Eugene Genovese (Baton Rouge: Louisiana State University Press, 1968).
218. Stanley Elkins, *Slavery, A Problem in American Institutional and Intellectual Life* (Chicago: University of Chicago Press, 1959).
219. Phillips, *Slave Economy,* 89.

220. Gordon Lewis, *The Growth of the Modern West Indies* (London: MacGibbon and Kee, 1968), 226.

221. Ibid., 229.

222. See, for instance, Basil Davidson, *Africa in History: Themes and Outlines* (New York: Macmillan, 1969), chapters 7 and 8; Roland Oliver and Anthony Atmore, *Africa since 1800* (London: Cambridge University Press, 1967); Rodney, *How Europe Underdeveloped Africa*.

223. J.H. Parry and P.M. Sherlock, *A Short History of the West Indies* (London: Macmillan, 1960), 154.

224. See pp. 106–8 above.

225. Chapter 8 on mulatto women makes clear, however, that brown women were the chief beneficiaries.

226. Genovese's discussion of the origins and structure of the colonial plantocracy is relevant. "The question of resistance", he comments, "cannot be separated from the metropolitan orientation, not to say roots, of the planter class. These men could hardly have been expected to move to the colonies to lead a movement of separation from metropolis that was their home, their nation, and the centre of their livelihood." Genovese, *World Slaveholders Made*, 34.

Chapter 6

1. Roberts, *The Population of Jamaica*, 70–76.

2. See above, chapter 4.

3. Roberts, *Population of Jamaica*, 74.

4. Ibid., 75.

5. Cumper, "Demographic Balance".

6. For instance, *PP* 1814–15, VI, Jamaica. Officials regularly complained of the difficulty of producing accurate returns of free coloureds and free blacks.

7. *PP* 1789 (84), XXVI: 646 (a) part 3, appendix nos. 2, 3, 4, 5.

8. Patterson, *Sociology of Slavery*, 107; Jordan, "American Chiaroscuro", 197.

9. *PP* 1789 (84), XXVI: 646 (a), part 3, no. 13; Patterson, *Sociology of Slavery*, 99.

10. Curtin, *Atlantic Slave Trade*, 41n37.

11. Long, *History of Jamaica*, 2:435.

12. Edwards, *History, Civil and Commercial*, 2:133.

13. C 107/143; also below.

14. *PP* 1790, XXIX: 485.

15. Hector McNeill, *Observations on the Treatment of the Negroes in the Island of Jamaica* (London: Printed for G.G.J. and J. Robinson, 1788), 44.

16. Noël Deerr, *The History of Sugar* (London: Chapman and Hall, 1950), 2:277.

17. *PP* 1789 (83), XXV, Minutes of the evidence taken before a Committee of the House of Commons . . . (on) the circumstances of the Slave Trade.
18. Ibid., no. 643, 222, also rest of evidence 204–31.
19. Ibid., no. 638, 73–111.
20. Ibid., nos. 641 and 642, 160–202. Compare also evidence of Jerome Weuves (no. 640), Norris Robert (no. 633), and so on.
21. Long, *History of Jamaica,* 2:435.
22. Edwards, *History, Civil and Commercial,* 1:139.
23. *PP* 1789 (83), XXV, no. 639: 112–27.
24. Long, *History of Jamaica,* 2:435.
25. Edwards, *History, Civil and Commercial,* 2:139.
26. Ibid., 138.
27. Roberts, *Population of Jamaica,* 36–38; Patterson, *Sociology of Slavery,* 94–98.
28. Roberts, *Population of Jamaica,* 39–40; Patterson, *Sociology of Slavery,* 97–104.
29. Goveia, *Slave Society,* especially chapter 1.
30. Edwards, *History, Civil and Commercial,* 2:174.
31. *PP* 1789 (84), XXVI: 646 (a), part 3, First Report of the committee of the House of Assembly of Jamaica.
32. *PP* 1789 (82), XXIV: 627, Summary of Evidence.
33. Ibid.
34. *PP* 1789 (84), XXVI: 646 (a) part 3, appendix, First Report.
35. Goveia, *Slave Society,* 30–31.
36. Edwards, *History, Civil and Commercial,* 2:181–82, as follows: "Instead of abolishing the slave trade by act of parliament further encouragement should be given to the importation of a greater proportion of African women, until the sexes are become nearly equal; after which it is probable that under the present humane and improved system of laws and manners their numbers may be kept up by natural increase."
37. Eric Williams, ed., *The British West Indies at Westminister, Part 1: 1789–1823: Extracts from the Debates in Parliament* (Port of Spain: Government Printing Office, 1954), 9, also 17.
38. *PP* 1832 (127), Report of the Select Committee of the House of Lords on the Extinction of Slavery, I, 29.
39. Ibid.
40. Sheridan, *Development of the Plantations,* 100–101.
41. *PP* 1789 (84), XXVI: 646 (a), part 3, no. 48.
42. Higman, "Demography of Slavery".
43. Craton and Walvin, *Jamaican Plantation,* 127.
44. Ibid., 138.
45. Patterson, *Sociology of Slavery,* 61.

46. Ibid., 157.
47. William Beckford, *Remarks upon the Situations of Negroes in Jamaica* (London, 1788), 1:14.
48. See table 6.3.
49. Inventories, Liber 53, 1772, 162–64.
50. Egerton MS 2134: Nutt's River Plantation Inventory of Slave Population, 54–55.
51. Ibid.
52. C 110/141.
53. Add. MSS 19049: Wakefield Plantation Inventory.
54. MS 236: Green Park and Spring Vale Estate Book, 1790–1795.
55. G.S. Ramlachansingh, "Amity Hall 1760–1860: The Geography of a Jamaican Plantation" (MSc thesis, University of London, 1966), 99–100.
56. B.W. Higman, "Slave Population and Economy in Jamaica at the Time of Emancipation" (PhD diss., University of the West Indies, 1970), 393–418. Higman, rather like Patterson, found the preponderance of women in the field to be the most distinctive occupational feature of Rose Hall estate, where more than half of them, as contrasted with one-eighth of the men, were praedials (ibid., 395). Higman also calculated that women worked longer in the field than men: the average age of a female field hand was thirty-four years, the average age of a male was twenty-three.
57. B.W. Higman, "Household Structure and Fertility on Jamaican Slave Plantations: A Nineteenth Century Example", *Population Studies,* no. 3 (1973).
58. C 107/43, Plantation Papers of William Beckford, 1773–1784.
59. Ibid. The Beckford papers also contain data on the Westmoreland properties of Ackendown, Bog and Retrieve in 1781: these had a total of 324 adult slaves, 135 males and 189 females. Fifty-one men and 119 women were field workers. The data for Ackendown in 1780 is incomplete.
60. Ibid.
61. Egerton MS 2134: Nutt's River Inventory.
62. C 107/43. Two hundred and seven men, or 25.8 per cent of the adult male total, fell into the category of skilled or semi-skilled non-praedials.
63. Ibid.
64. Ibid.
65. Ibid.
66. Goveia, *Slave Society,* 229.
67. Stewart, *View of the Past,* 231; also see pp. 212–16 above.
68. There were nine cases of young males apprenticed, respectively, to the trade of a boiler, cooper, wheelwright, mason and carpenter.
69. Add. MSS 19049: Wakefield Inventory.

70. *PP* 1789 (84), XXVI: 646 (a), part 3, Jamaica A no. 29. An official valuation of "able field Natives" was given as follows:

Negro Men		£80–£100 currency
Negro Women		75–85
Carpenters	}	
Mill-wright	}	
Wheel-wright	}	140–300
Cooper	}	
Sawyer	}	120–200
Distiller	}	
Wainman		120–140
Blacksmith		140–200
Bricklayer		140–200
Midwife		150–200
Head drivers		120–140
Boilers		100–120
Muleman		100
Cattlemen		100
Tradesmen		100–200
Inferior prices	{superannuated {Men and Women	5–40

71. Even the mulatto house slave: see, for instance, the Rose Hall valuation in Shore, *In Old St James,* 110–13.

72. C 110/141: Compare also Wakefield Plantation's slave pricing of the same period, for example, Add. MSS 19049: Wakefield Inventory. In the 1820s and 1830s the criteria of valuation remained unchanged: see, for instance, Senior, *Jamaica, As It Was,* 45; Shore, *In Old St James,* 106–13.

73. C 110/141.

74. See, for example, Goveia, *Slave Society,* 233–34: "No other group of slaves was so completely subject to the harsh necessities of slavery as an industrial system. The life of the ordinary field slave was characterised by coercion and dependence. . . . The gangs of field slaves were worked for long hours under the discipline of the whip; . . . Since the field slaves had fewer opportunities for earning a cash income than most other slaves, they relied heavily on the master for the necessities of life. . . . [They] were maintained by their owners on the bare margin of subsistence. Though they did the most laborious work, their standard of living was generally lower than that of any other group of slaves." Also Edwards, *History, Civil and Commercial,* 2:165. Brathwaite aptly supplies the terminology "the outer plantation" to the world of regimented slavery dominated by whites; in contrast, "the inner plantation" was the blacks' own world. See Edward [Kamau] Brathwaite, *Caribbean Man in Space and Time* (Kingston: Savacou, 1974).

75. Thomas Roughley, *The Jamaica Planter's Guide; or, A System for Planting and Managing a Sugar Estate, or Other Plantations in that Island, and Throughout the British West Indies in General* (London: Printed for Longman, Hurst, Rees, Orme and Brown, 1823), 79–87.

76. Ibid.

77. Higman, "Household Structure", 7.

78. *PP* 1789 (84), XXVI: 646 (a), part 3, Jamaica no. 24: The demotion of a female slave and her daughter from domestic service to field work was a bitterly provocative element in the notorious Jackson case of 1831 (see pp. 231–32 above).

79. Add. MSS 33293: Archer journal, 56.

80. Benjamin McMahon, *Jamaica Plantership* (London, 1839), 185.

81. *PP* 1832 (127), Report of the Committee of the House of Lords on the Extinction of Slavery, I, 16 (John Baillie's evidence), also 62 (William Taylor's evidence); Lewis, *Journal of a West India Proprietor*, 199, and so on.

82. Craton and Walvin, *Jamaican Plantation,* 128.

83. Craton and Walvin also note that the field force in 1789 of no fewer than eighty-nine women were "quite capable of weeding and carrying, and perhaps hoeing and holing but surely not the strenuous monotony of cutting the cane" (ibid., 102). Surprisingly, these authors place on the page facing the text two contemporary prints of holing and cutting, in which at least a half, or more, of the cane cutters are clearly female. A print of a boiling house facing page 59 shows women there too engaged in its "blistering operations".

84. Roughley, *Jamaica Planter's Guide,* 99. "They are drilled", wrote Roughley, "to become veterans in the arduous field undertakings, furnish drivers, cattlemen, mulemen, boilers an distillers. . . . This gang, composed of a mixture of able men and women, sometimes amounting to an hundred, should always be put to the field work, which requires strength and skill in the execution, etc." (ibid., 100).

85. Edwards, *History, Civil and Commercial,* 2:156–57. See also Bickell, *West Indies As They Are,* 48; Stewart, *Account of Jamaica,* 231: "The first gang consists of both sexes, from fifteen to about fifty years of age, and are employed in the most laborious of the work"; McNeill, *Observations on the Treatment,* 5; Lewis, *Journal of a West India Proprietor,* 86–88; Thomas Cooper, *Facts Illustrative of the Condition of the Negro Slaves in Jamaica: With Notes and an Appendix* (London: J. Hatchard and Son, 1824), 2–3, 16.

86. See, for example, Add. MSS 27970: Archer accounts, 228, 232, 235 (James Archer's workers).

87. Ramlackhansingh, "Amity Hall"; McMahon, *Jamaica Plantership,* 33; Henry Whiteley, *Three Months in Jamaica in 1832, Comprising a Residence of Seven Weeks on a Sugar Plantation* (London: Printed for the Anti-Slavery Society, 1832), 3–4.

88. *PP* 1832 (127), I: 27, also 28, 44, 507 (William Taylor's evidence).

89. Bickell, *West Indies As They Are*, 34.

90. Lewis, *Journal of a West India Proprietor*, 86. *Jamaica Magazine* 2 (June–December 1812) reported the inquest into the death of a Negro girl of Palmetto Grove, St Mary, who lost her life when she was drawn into the rollers of the mill which she was feeding with cane.

91. Add. MSS 51816: Holland House Papers, Correspondence, 158, 16 October 1838. William Taylor also testified in 1832 that boiling houses required the services of at least one pan woman, and two women at the mill. *PP* 1832, I (127): 42.

92. Cooper, *Facts Illustrative*, 2–3.

93. Bickell, *West Indies As They Are*, 50.

94. Ibid.; also Stewart, *View of the Past*, 234–35; Edwards, *History, Civil and Commercial*, 2:248n; McMahon, *Jamaica Plantership*, 218–25; H.T. De la Beche, *Notes on the Present Condition of the Negroes in Jamaica* (London: T. Cadell, 1825), 34; Cooper, *Facts Illustrative*, 60–64.

95. Sheridan, *Development of the Plantations*, 100.

96. Genovese, *Political Economy of Slavery*, 49.

97. Hall, "Slaves and Slavery", 305–9. By the beginning of the 1830s, West Indian planters, under pressure from emancipationists, were forced to take a close look at their production costs: they estimated in detail, for instance, the loss of women's labour during childbirth, medical attention, and so on (ibid., 307).

98. Long, *History of Jamaica*, 2:44.

99. *PP* 1789 (84), XXVI: 646 (a), part 3, no. 9.

100. Ramlachansingh, "Amity Hall", 44. Thomas Sampson, who managed Amity Hall estate from 1803 to 1818, was an offender in this respect. See also Mr Ashley's evidence (*PP* 1789 [84], XXVI: 646, part 3, no. 9) in which he expressed the view that overseers with jobbing slaves did not find it in their interest "to Abridge the Labour of Slaves".

101. Lewis, *Journal of a West India Proprietor*, 201, also 324–25.

102. Ramlachansingh, "Amity Hall", 45; also Hall, "Slaves and Slavery", 368–69.

103. The health pattern of these estates was typical. See, for instance, the condition of the slave population at Spring Vale estate, a coffee and livestock pen, in 1791. Of forty-five females, twenty-three were either diseased or weakly; this number included fifteen in their twenties and thirties who were suffering from yaws and sores. Sixteen of the total number were over the age of forty; of these older women, five were in good health, ten were disabled, weak and/or diseased (one insane), and the health of one was unspecified. MS 236: Green Park and Spring Vale.

104. *PP* 1832 (127), I: 146–47 (John Baillie's evidence); also Long, *History of Jamaica*, 2:412; Quier et al., *Letters and Essays*, 59–60; Williamson, *Caribbean Islands*, 77, 106.

105. C 110/141.

106. C 107/43.

107. Ibid., See also the condition of the women similarly occupied at the other estates in 1780 and 1781 (table 6.7).

108. Renny, *History of Jamaica,* 207; see also *PP* 1789 (84), XXVI, no. 6, Dr Chisholme's evidence; *PP* 1833, I (127): 274–75, Sir M. Clare's evidence as follows: "they do much damage internally and danger Women's life".

109. Williamson, *Caribbean Islands,* 1:63, 197, 237–38, 246, 274, 346; 2:59–60, 202; Long, *History of Jamaica,* 2:436; *PP* 1789 (84), XXVI: 646 (a), part 3, Jamaica, nos. 6, 8: Dr John Quier complained of black midwives' "known want of cleanliness arising from the obstinate Attachment of Negro Women to their old customs"; Patterson, *Sociology of Slavery,* 101–2; Roughley, *Jamaica Planter's Guide,* 93.

110. Williamson, *Caribbean Islands,* 1:274.

111. See pp. 117–18 above.

112. Add. MSS 27970: Archer accounts, 5, 10 December 1831. Compare Mrs Henry Lynch's view of "the negro nurse, who in her simple way, knows a good deal about disease [and] who is never more in her element than when in the atmosphere of a sick room". Lynch, *Years Ago,* 128. In the recollections of the Cuban runaway slave, Montejo, Negro wet-nurses and cooks, skilled "with herbs and brews could cure anything"; Esteban Montejo, *The Autobiography of a Runaway Slave* (1908; repr., London: Bodley Head, 1968), 38.

113. *PP* 1789, XXVI, no. 13; also no. 2, namely the Negroes' habit of "rambling to what one called Negro Plays, or nocturnal Assemblie", as well as "their Sensuality and Intemperance", were held responsible for their many illnesses; also no. 15.

114. Edwards, *History, Civil and Commercial,* 2:165.

115. Ibid., 166–67.

116. Lewis, *Journal of a West India Proprietor,* 238–39.

117. Ibid., 342–43.

118. Cecil Woodham-Smith, *Florence Nightingale* (London: Constable, 1969), 257.

119. Ramlachansingh, "Amity Hall", 121–23.

120. Quier et al., *Letters and Essays,* 144.

121. Roughley, *Jamaica Planter's Guide,* 192; Stewart, *View of the Past,* 321.

122. Add. MSS 33293: Archer journal; Add. MSS 27970: Archer accounts; Archer suffered from severe attacks of migraine, and treated himself by bleeding. On 5 January 1828, for instance, he had twelve ounces of blood drawn by one of his slaves "for a continuation of headache". Add. MSS 33293: Journal 1828–1846, 25. The Moravian Missionary John Lang, who worked in St Elizabeth, had to call a halt to the local doctor who attended his second wife. Between 1 and 7 March 1809, she was bled three times, losing in all forty-four ounces of blood. Lang refused to permit a fourth blood letting on 8 April. She recovered temporarily, but

died on 10 August 1809. *Diary of John Lang, 1805–1819;* also Quier et al., *Letters and Essays,* 51, 24; Thomas Dancer, *The Medical Assistant* (Kingston: Alexander Aikman, 1801), 52.

123. Add. MSS 33293: Archer journal, 23.
124. Ibid., 66.
125. Ibid., 59.
126. Quier et al., *Letters and Essays,* 21–23.
127. Ibid., 23.
128. Ibid., 65.
129. Lewis, *Journal of a West India Proprietor,* 388.
130. Quier et al., *Letters and Essays,* 20–21, also 192.
131. Stewart, *View of the Past,* 268; *PP* 1789, XXVI, no. 5.
132. *PP* 1832, I (127), John Baillie's evidence.
133. Ibid., also 198, William Shand's evidence.
134. Genovese, *Political Economy of Slavery,* 45.
135. For instance, Brathwaite, *Development of Creole Society,* 206, and n110.
136. *PP* 1789, XXVI, A, no. 13.
137. Quier et al., *Letters and Essays,* 55.
138. Ibid., also *PP* 1789, XXVI, A, no. 14.
139. See pp. 210–13 above.
140. CO 107/43, also table 6.9. Compare the population of the free Maroon towns which had 754 persons in 1799, were estimated to have thirty-three births and twenty-six deaths, and were showing a rate of natural increase averaging 6 per cent per annum. Their young population also constituted a more significant proportion: there were 220 children up to the age of nine years old, representing 29 per cent of the total community. The Clarendon estates contained 146 children of the same age group, or 12 per cent of the whole. See Cumper, "Demographic Balance", 8, 10 (tables 6.5 and table 6.6). Maroon returns for the year 1801 are a typical sample of their population structure. See Dallas, *History of the Maroons,* 2:329.

1801	Moore Town	Charles Town	Scots Hall	Accompong
Men	53	65 + 7	13	38
Boys	20	30	12	25
Women	83	81	10	47
Girls	12	24	11	11
Children	110	54	–	15
Invalids	–	2	–	–
Totals	278	263	46	136

141. Patterson, *Sociology of Slavery,* 97.

142. Edwards, *History, Civil and Commercial,* 2:187; also Roberts, *Population of Jamaica,* 234–38.

143. Edwards, *History, Civil and Commercial,* 2:206.

144. Ibid., 207.

145. CO 137/121, 18 January 1808. Slave marriages were promoted at the same time in this context.

146. Ibid.

147. An Act for the Subsistence, Clothing and the Better Regulation and Government of Slaves . . . (Jamaica, 1817), clause XI. Overseers continued to receive the bonus as well. The accounts of Lord Seaford's estates at Old and New Montpelier and Shettlewood Pen in 1830 listed the cash rewards paid out to those who were regarded as responsible for the natural increase of the slave population. The sum of £152 6s. 8d. was accordingly distributed as follows: £120 to the three overseers, £32 6s. 8d. to the mothers, nurses and midwives on the three properties. *PP* 1832, I (127): 91.

148. 1816 Slave Act.

149. *PP* 1789 (84), XXVI, Jamaica, no. 7.

150. For example, De la Beche, *Notes on the Present Condition,* 10.

151. Add. MSS 30001: General Correspondence, 48, n.d.

152. Lewis, *Journal of a West India Proprietor,* 125.

153. Ibid., 191.

154. Ibid., 320, also 381.

155. Between 1816 and 1817.

156. See above.

157. Long, *History of Jamaica,* 2:437.

158. *Jamaica Magazine* 4 (January 1814): 891; Whiteley, *Three Months in Jamaica,* 15.

159. St George Slave Court, 6 June 1823.

160. *PP* 1832, I (127): 507, also 27, 28, 44, and so on. Also compare Hill, *Eight Chapters,* 64.

161. Higman, "Demography of Slavery", 11.

162. Higman, "Slave Population and Economy", 238, also 100, 102, 123–24, 126–28, and passim.

163. Ibid., 238.

164. An Act to repeal several Acts . . . for the better order and government of Slaves (St Jago de la Vega, 1788); John Lunan, *Abstract of the Laws of Jamaica relating to Slaves* (St Jago de la Vega, Jamaica: Printed at the Office of the Gazette, 1819); *PP* 1789, XXVI: 646, part 3, Mr Reeves, General View of the Principles of this System of Laws; Edward [Kamau] Brathwaite, "Controlling the Slaves" (typescript, n.d.), especially chapter 1, "Slave Laws", 13–57, 61–64; Goveia, *West Indian Slave Laws,* 18–35; Patterson, *Sociology of Slavery,* 75–79.

165. Ibid.

166. The New Consolidated Slave Act . . . passed 6 December 1789 (London 1789), clause XIII, "in order to restrain arbitrary punishment". See also Brathwaite, "Controlling the Slaves", 41, 51.

167. St George General Slave Court, 1822–31; Port Royal Slave Trials, 1819–34. See also *PP* 1832 (127), I: 571–72, W. Taylor's evidence re: St Andrew Workhouse; Whiteley, *Three Months in Jamaica*, 12, re: slaves from St Ann Workhouse.

168. St George General Slave Court, passim.

169. Ibid., 6 April 1831.

170. Ibid., 31 January 1827.

171. Port Royal Slave Trials, passim. A total of 311 cases were recorded fort this period.

172. Ibid., 27 October 1825.

173. Cooper, *Facts Illustrative*, 16.

174. Ibid., 17; also 18, 56. See also Bickell, *West Indies As They Are*, 27, 48; Whiteley, *Three Months in Jamaica*, 5–9. Cooper commented as follows: "It is well known that the Negroes will make a song out of anything. On one occasion I listened to a party of old women, boys and girls, singing the following in our kitchen!

> O'massa! O'massa! one Monday morning they
> lay me down.
> And give me thirty-nine on my bare rump.
> O'massa! O'massa! (*Facts llustrative*, 17)

The epic of the African diaspora is full of the many survival techniques adopted by blacks in dehumanizing circumstances. See, for instance, the sociological/ historical and creative works of Orlando Patterson and Edward [Kamau] Brathwaite on this theme.

175. *PP* 1832 (137): 204, 239, William Shand's evidence: "Women of low description are more vicious than Men" (ibid., 204); Robert Scott's evidence that female slaves "are generally much worse to manage than the men" (ibid., 337); De la Beche, *Notes on the Present Condition*, 33.

176. McMahon, *Jamaica Plantership*, 19–20, 223; also *PP* 1832 (137), I: 28 (William Taylor's evidence); Bickell, *West Indies As They Are*, 12, 27, 48; Cooper, *Facts Illustrative*, 17; Williams, *British West Indies*, 13; St George General Slave Court, 1824.

177. Whiteley, *Three Months in Jamaica*, 7.

178. Add. MSS 27970: Archer accounts, 234 (5); also Add. MSS 23294, d., 5 December 1831.

179. Whiteley, *Three Months in Jamaica*, 7, also 5–6; *PP* 1832 (127), I: 551, 559, Admiral Fleming's evidence, and so on.

180. Cooper, *Facts Illustrative*, 20; *PP* 1832 (127), I: 46, William Taylor's Evidence.

181. For instance, *PP* 1832 (127), I: 581, William Taylor's evidence, as follows: Q. "Is it not the constant custom that the Wives and Daughters of the Slaves are thus flogged in the presence of their nearest Relatives? A. Yes; they are flogged in what is called in this country, the Farm Land, at the entrance of the Overseer's House; the Punishments take place in the Presence of a Body of Persons." See also 641–42, Rev. P. Duncan's evidence.

182. CO 138/54, encl. 66, 18 November 1831.

183. Ibid. Compare also William Taylor's opinion that "the Overseer has the Power of inflicting a very great Degree of personal suffering upon the Slave without violating the Letter of the Law". *PP* 1832 (127): 569.

184. A local surgeon informed the Rev. Thomas Cooper that "he did not believe any overseer did or could pay any regard to the law for regulating the punishment of slaves". Cooper, *Facts Illustrative*, 59.

185. Edwards, *History, Civil and Commercial*, 2:170.

186. Stewart, *View of the Past*, 143; compare also the opinion of John Baillie that acts of atrocity could not be perpetrated with impunity under Jamaica's laws (*PP* 1832 [127], I: 55).

187. Quoted by De la Beche, *Notes on the Present Condition*, 55–57; Edwards, *History, Civil and Commercial*, 2:170–71ni.

188. *PP* 1814–15, VI, no. 4, Jamaica.

189. Port Royal Slave Trials.

190. *PP* 1814–15, VI, no. 4, Jamaica.

191. Port Royal Slave Trials.

192. Stewart, *View of the Past*, 224–28.

193. W.L. Mathieson, *British Slavery and Its Abolition 1823–1838* (London: Longmans, Green and Co., 1926), 119–28; Burn, *Emancipation and Apprenticeship*, 80–82.

194. Vincent Harlow and Frederick Madden, *British Colonial Documents, 1774–1834: Selected Documents* (Oxford: Clarendon Press, 1953), 560.

195. Ibid., 565.

196. CS 102/5, encl. 10 November 1823; *PP* 1824, XXIV: 452–53; *Journals of the Assembly of Jamaica* 14 (1822–26): 225–29.

197. Although differing constitutional arrangements produced different legislative/administrative results in the colonies, West Indian responses to Bathurst's proposals were remarkably uniform. See Eric Williams, ed., *Documents on British West Indian History, 1807–1833* (Port of Spain: Historical Society of Trinidad and Tobago, 1952), 139–41, 143–44, 210, and so on. For instance, this horrified reaction came from a male supremacist in Trinidad: "I confess that the idea appears to me so monstrous and extraordinary that I hardly know how to approach the subject. Strange indeed it appears to be to bestow on our female slaves prerogatives never to be aspired to our enjoyed by their free sisters in Africa;

and to attempt to arrest an immutable law of nature (subordination of women to men) this would give a superiority to women by a British Order-in-Council" (ibid., 143). Barbadian objections to the same proposal, as voiced in a debate in its Council, were based on the fact that women were flogged in other countries, so that "Even in civilised societies, whenever the gentler sex, have by depravity or vulgarity forfeited their claim to distinction, they are treated with as much harshness as the men . . . . Are not women flogged in houses of correction in England?" (ibid., 140). Furthermore, it was argued, "our black ladies have rather a tendency to the Amazonian cast of character". The Barbadian Council concluded that to abolish the flogging of female slaves would mean "adieu to all peace and comfort on plantations". The flogging of women in English houses of correction had been abolished in 1822. It should be noted that in Jamaica, there was no record of free and/or white women being flogged.

198. *Journals of the Assembly of Jamaica* 14 (1822–26): 263–72.
199. Ibid.
200. The Consolidated Slave Law, passed 22 December 1826 (2nd ed., 1827); *The New Slave Laws of Jamaica and St Christopher Examined* (London: Society for the Mitigation and Gradual Abolition of Slavery, 1828).
201. *PP* 1832 (127), I: 55.
202. Ibid., 593; also 643, Rev. P. Duncan's evidence.
203. Ibid., 43, John Baillie's evidence; 56–57, William Taylor's evidence; 992, William Burge's evidence; De la Beche, *Notes on the Present Condition*, 16, and so on.
204. *PP* 1832 (127), I: 87, Rev. John Barry's evidence.
205. *Votes of the Assembly of Jamaica, 1831*, 16.
206. Ibid., 128; *PP* 1832 (127), II: appendix E, Papers relating to the late Rebellion in Jamaica, 1252.
207. *PP* 1832 (127), II: 1315.
208. Daniel Beckford, a slave from Manchester, testified during the official investigation of the 1831 slave rebellion as follows: "He [that is, Augustus Beaumont] asked me again if I heard that one law came out – one new law that they were not to flog women; I then told him that that person that make that law was a fool, and knew nothing about it. He then said, God Almighty did not make woman's behind to stand da door, because them buckra were bad that make it stand da door. I then told him that we all stand in the field, and work so, no one flesh better than the other and we all the same." *Votes of the Assembly of Jamaica, 1831*, 314; *PP* 1832 (127), II: 1331, 1340. Beaumont, a white creole, was accused of being sympathetic to the cause of emancipation, and of helping to incite black unrest.
209. *PP* 1832 (137): 428, 641; Dallas, *History of the Maroons*, 421, also chapter 8, below.
210. *PP* 1832 (127), II: 732, 1315, 1316, 1252, and so on.
211. Consolidated Slave Act, 1792, clauses X to XIV.

212. Edwards, *History, Civil and Commercial,* 171–72; Stewart, *View of the Past,* 142, 224–28; Goveia, *West Indian Slave Laws,* 34.
213. *PP* 1832 (127), I: 511, W. Taylor's evidence; also *PP* 1831: 5.
214. Harlow and Madden, *British Colonial Documents,* 562.
215. Ibid.
216. *New Slave Laws of Jamaica,* 4–5.
217. Ibid.
218. *PP* 1831, Papers presented . . . in explanation of the measures adopted for the melioration of the condition of the slave population, 6 December 1831, 55–56.
219. Whiteley, *Three Months in Jamaica,* 8–9.
220. *PP* 1831–32, I: encl. 2, 9–13.
221. Ibid., 10.
222. Ibid., 13.
223. *PP* 1832 (127), II: appendix D 1, 1262–71. After the ordeal, Eleanor James testified, she could not speak, "in consequence of having bawled so much, and in consequence of a great hoarseness in (her) Throat" (ibid., 1267).
224. Ibid., 1267.
225. Ibid., 1263, 1265.
226. Ibid., 1267, 1271. The other white witness to the incident was Mrs McDonald who was not "a competent witness against her husband".
227. Ibid.
228. Ibid., Viscount Goderich to the Earl of Belmore, 23 February 1831.
229. Ibid., appendix D 3, 1281–84.
230. Ibid., 1283. Mrs Jackson did not appear innocent in this respect either, as her words were described as "too gross for repetition".
231. Ibid.
232. Ibid.
233. Matthew Lewis, for example, humane and decent by creole standards (although prone to heavy humour), nevertheless commits one of the grossest lapses of sensitivity in the contemporary literature in his obscene joking reference to the physical ill-treatment of black women by white men. *Journal of a West India Proprietor,* 388–89.
234. Winthrop Jordan, in his analysis of the dynamic of interracial sex in the New World, stated it aptly: "White men extended their dominion over their negro to the bed, where the sex act itself served as ritualistic re-enactment of the daily pattern of social dominance." *White over Black,* 140.
235. *PP* 1832 (127), I: 433, Rev. J. Barry's evidence, 554–55, Admiral Fleming's evidence, 641–47, 697, Rev. P. Duncan's evidence; *PP* 1831–32: 266, Rev. W. Knibb's evidence; Williams, *Tour Through the Island of Jamaica,* 317–18; McMahon, *Jamaica Plantership,* 28–29, 130–31, 150, 185, and so on.

236. McMahon, *Jamaica Plantership*, 186.

237. CO 137/153, 5 August 1822; CS 102/5.

238. Ibid.

239. Ibid. The offence was a particularly sadistic one.

240. Ibid.

241. Ibid. Scarlett commented on "the early proceedings of the House of Assembly (which) furnish ample evidence of the dreadful immunities claimed by the planters in their conduct towards the slave population. . . . Early barbarous enactments have long ceased to exist but even at this day the murder of a slave is considered to be punishable by death only under the Consolidated Slave Law, and if the sanction of the Legislature was necessary to authorise that punishment for Murder I know not upon what principle it can in the absence of all usage be inflicted without the same sanction for a mere outrage (however monstrous) on the person."

242. See also Goveia, *West Indian Slave Laws*, 29–33, for the defects and uncertainties of the common law in relation to the protection of the slave; also Stewart, *Account of Jamaica*, 137.

243. CS 102/5, encl. 62, of 23 December 1823: see above.

244. *Journals of the Assembly of Jamaica* 14 (1822–26): 210, 213, 216.

245. Consolidated Slave Law, 1826, para. 32 and 33.

CHAPTER 7

1. For example, *Savacou*, no. 10 (1974) on *Caribbean Woman*; Toni Cade, ed., *The Black Woman: An Anthology* (New York: New American Library, 1970).

2. Orlando Patterson, "Rethinking Black History", *Harvard Educational Review* 41, no. 3 (August 1971); Edward [Kamau] Brathwaite, "The African Presence in Caribbean Literature", *Daedalus* (Spring 1974); Brathwaite, *Caribbean Man*.

3. Williams, *Documents*, 139.

4. Lewis, *Journal of a West India Proprietor*, 139–40.

5. Port Royal Slave Trials; Williams, *Tour Through the Island of Jamaica*.

6. Port Royal Slave Trials (4 April 1820).

7. Ibid., 20 August 1832.

8. Olive Lewin, "The Role of Woman in Jamaican Folk Music", *Savacou* 10 (1974); Moreton, *Manners and Customs*, 152–53.

9. Brathwaite, *Development of Creole Society*, 221–25; Patterson, *Sociology of Slavery*, 253–59.

10. Quoted by Brathwaite, *Development of Creole Society*, 225.

11. Renny, *History of Jamaica*, 241.

12. Williams, *Tour Through the Island of Jamaica*, 297.

13. Moreton, *Manners and Customs,* 153; compare the women's song about being flogged, p. 225 above.

14. Ibid. Compare Anon., *Marly: Or, a Planter's life in Jamaica* (Glasgow: Richard Griffin, 1828), 104.

15. Williams, *Tour Through the Island of Jamaica,* 171–72.

16. Ibid.

17. *PP* 1832 (127), I: 44, Baillie's evidence; see also p. 241 above; Lewis, *Journal of a West India Proprietor,* 321, 331–32, and so on.

18. *PP* 1832 (127), I: 164, Sir J. Keane's evidence.

19. Port Royal Slave Trials, 8 April 1823.

20. St George's Slave Court, 1822–31, 6 June 1823.

21. Port Royal Slave Trials.

22. Ibid., passim.

23. Ibid., 19 October 1833.

24. Ibid., 4 October 1820, 10 January 1821.

25. See pp. 237–38 above.

26. The female slave ironically named Industry was taken before the Port Royal Slave Court on 27 October 1831 by her owner, Mr I.P. Levy, for "refusing to work and setting a bad example to the other negroes".

27. Lewis, *Journal of a West India Proprietor,* 139.

28. Ibid., 140.

29. Ibid., 122.

30. Ibid., 203–4, also 190. Planters also maintained that slaves deliberately infected themselves and their children with yaws in order to escape work. See, for instance, Stewart, *View of the Past,* 303–4; Roughley, *Jamaica Planter's Guide,* 94–95.

31. Lewis, *Journal of a West India Proprietor.*

32. See p. 218 above.

33. For instance, Jones, *Diary,* 33; Roughley, *Jamaica Planter's Guide,* 118.

34. *PP* 1832 (127), I: 51, also 157.

35. Port Royal Slave Trails, 14 December 1820. Compare a case that Matthew Lewis witnessed, when several mothers from Friendship and Greenwich estates complained to their attorney that the overseer obliged them to wean their children too soon. "Some of these children were above twenty-two months old, and none under eighteen . . . of course their demands were rejected and they went home in high discontent." One mother threatened infanticide in retaliation. Lewis, *Journal of a West India Proprietor,* 331–32.

36. Glass and Eversley, *Population in History,* 55.

37. Ibid., 47, also 39, 46, 563.

38. See Lorimer, *Culture and Human Fertility,* for discussions of "a fairly wide prevalence of culturally sanctioned anti-natal measures" in African and other societies.

They include sexual abstention, abortion, lactation, infanticide, and "are entirely congruous with strong cultural emphasis on high fertility". 86–88, and passim. See Roughley, *Jamaica Planter's Guide,* 118; Dr Adam Anderson of the parish of St Ann expressed the view, in 1789, that "great losses are sustained in the increase of Negroes from the Length of Time the Negro Women continue their Children at the Breast". *PP* 1789 (84), XXVII: 646 (a), part 3, Jamaica, no. 7. See also Sarah Dwarris's view, in letters, 9 November 1788, 180.

39. For example, Lewis, *Journal of a West India Proprietor,* 380–81.

40. De la Beche, *Notes on the Present Condition,* 18; Long, *History of Jamaica,* 2:436; Williamson, *Caribbean Islands,* 199–200; *PP* 1832 (127), I: 274–75; *Jamaica Magazine,* 1 January 1814, 891.

41. Roughley, *Jamaica Planter's Guide,* 91.

42. Ibid., 96.

43. *PP* 1832 (127), I: 274–77.

44. The note of fear which is discernible in the adverse judgements made by whites about the African midwife seems to this writer to have emanated from their awareness of her vital, and to them mysterious control over black life cycles.

45. Lewis, *Journal of a West India Proprietor,* 381.

46. St George Slave Court, 20 January 1824.

47. *PP* 1832 (127), II: appendix E, 301.

48. Ibid., 1306.

49. Ibid.

50. Ibid.

51. Ibid., 1309.

52. Ibid., 1310.

53. *Journals of the Assembly of Jamaica* 12 (1808–15): 135–36. Favourite rendezvous for the soldiers were the house of Mrs Saunders, a free black, who lived in a new street in Hannah Town, and of a slave woman, Judy Jackson, who gave "dances and merry-makings", at the upper end of Matthews Lane.

54. Lewis, *Journal of a West India Proprietor,* 149.

55. Monica Schuler, "Slave Resistance and Rebellion in the Caribbean during the Eighteenth Century" (seminar paper, Department of History, University of the West Indies, 1966), 27–36.

56. St George Slave Court, 5 and 6 October 1825.

57. *PP* 1814–15, VI, no. 14, Jamaica, St Mary parish; Lewis, *Journal of a West India Proprietor,* 179, 329–30, and so on.

58. For example, records of the Port Royal Slave Trials contain about thirty-two instances of physical violence of varying degrees. A typical case was that of Eleanor Gibson, who received one month's hard labour in the work house for "beating and otherwise ill treating a free person" (1 February 1832).

59. Ibid., passim.
60. Ibid., 10 December 1819.
61. The Consolidated Slave Law of 1792 defined a runaway as a slave absenting himself or herself for ten days, without a ticket from his or her owner, and found eight miles away from the owner's property. By the 1831 act, the time of grace had lessened to five days.
62. Schuler, "Slave Resistance and Rebellion", 76; Higman, "Slave Population and Economy", 199, and passim; Brathwaite, *Development of Creole Society*, 201–6.
63. Schuler, *Slave Resistance and Rebellion*, 67.
64. *Royal Gazette* 35, no. 30 (1813): 18.
65. *Royal Gazette* 13, no. 13 (1791): 19.
66. *Royal Gazette* 51, no. 43 (1829): 15.
67. *Royal Gazette* 39, no. 30 (1817): 23.
68. *Royal Gazette* 50, no. 51 (1828): 24.
69. *Royal Gazette* 51, no. 16 (1829): 24. Sometimes it was probably "artful" to be inarticulate: "Eliza, a creole of 5 feet 7 inches [had] no brand mark, has several lumps on her shoulders, arms and breast, pretends she has been so long in the woods as to have forgotten the name of her owner or place of abode." *Royal Gazette* 35, no. 1 (1813): 15.
70. *Royal Gazette* 35, no. 44 (1813): 13.
71. *Royal Gazette* 13, no. 16 (1791): 7.
72. *Royal Gazette* 13, no. 26 (1791): 14.
73. *Royal Gazette* 35, no. 35 (1813): 24.
74. *Royal Gazette* 13, no. 14 (1791): 20.
75. MS T93: King Letters, 24 September 1824.
76. *Royal Gazette* 29, no. 28 (1817): 23.
77. *Royal Gazette* 29, no. 35 (1817): 12.
78. *Royal Gazette* 29, no. 51 (1817): 14.
79. *Royal Gazette* 35, no. 36 (1813): 7.
80. *Royal Gazette* 39, no. 10 (1817): 14.
81. *Royal Gazette* 35, no. 36 (1813): 7.
82. *Royal Gazette* 39, no. 10 (1817): 14.
83. *Royal Gazette* 35, no. 35 (1813): 24.
84. *Royal Gazette* 39, no. 52 (1817): 23.
85. *Royal Gazette* 35, no. 43 (1813): 23.
86. *Jamaica Magazine* 4, no. 3 (August 1813): 602. The writer of the news item felt that of the activities implied here, namely running away, and black/white cohabitation, the latter was by far the greater of the two offences.
87. CO 137/88, 30 May 1789.
88. Ibid., See also Schuler, "Slave Resistance and Rebellion", 60–61.

89. *PP* 1814–15: 123–27.

90. St George Slave Court, 31 January 1827.

91. Ibid., 2 April 1828; 7 January 1829, 7 October 1829, 7 July 1830; 6 October 1830, 6 April 1831.

92. Port Royal Slave Trails, 1 October 1831. Robert, a slave from Bellevue estate, threatened to run away into the bush if he were punished. Compare Senior, *Jamaica, As It Was,* 171.

93. CS 102/4, encl. 215, 8 November 1819.

94. *Account of a Shooting Excursion on the Mountains near Dromilly Estate in the parish of Trelawny and island of Jamaica, in the month of October 1824* (London: Harvey and Darton, 1825), 11.

95. Ibid., 9. They apparently had, as well, "near the town, from thirty to forty acres of beautiful coffee, and a large field of canes".

96. Ibid., 8.

97. Ibid., 10: "She was so near as to be heard to exclaim: 'Hy! dem buckra hab impurence to come back!' " The author of the report in the *Cornwall Gazette* was also angered by the incident and condemned the "wanton, cold-blooded excursions, on the part of the white inhabitants in Trelawny to root up a runaway settlement, which had subsisted eleven years without offence or molestation to the neighbourhood". 11.

98. Higman, "Slave Population and Economy", 168.

99. See chapter 2 above.

100. Ibid., also Dallas, *History of the Maroons,* 2:182–83.

101. For example, Patterson, *Sociology of Slavery,* 159–67. Compare, however, Brathwaite, *Development of Creole Society,* 204, as follows: "the slave's sense of family was not as disorganised as some contemporary and modern accounts suggest".

102. West India Committee Minutes, 1769–1833, vol. 4, 27 June 1795.

103. *PP* 1832 (127), I: 61.

104. *PP* 1789 (84): 646 (a), part 3, no. 14.

105. Ivy Baxter, *The Arts of an Island* (Metuchen: Scarecrow Press, 1970), 45 and passim.

106. Williams, *Tour Through the Island of Jamaica,* 100.

107. Higman, "Household Structure", 8–9.

108. Ibid., 25. In this seminal bit of research, Higman finds no evidence of the famed "grandmother" household, and little evidence of the dominance of an exclusively mother-and-child domestic unit among blacks; the latter appeared to be a feature of mulatto households.

109. See below.

110. Moreton, *Manners and Customs,* 150; *PP* 1832 (127), I: 279, Sir M. Clare's evidence: "It is the custom of the wife always to cook his supper for him."

111. Long, *History of Jamaica,* 2:414.

112. Ibid. 410; also Beckford, *Remarks*, 2:323.
113. Senior, *Jamaica, As It Was*, 48.
114. *PP* 1832 (127), I: 127, Rev. J. Barry's evidence; also Bickell, *West Indies As They Are*, 32, 34.
115. *PP* 1831–32: 284, William Knibb's evidence.
116. Ibid.
117. *PP* 1832 (127), I: 74.
118. *PP* 1831–32: 284, William Knibb's evidence; *PP* 1832 (127), I: 172, Rev. John Thorp's evidence, re the case of the slave who supported his blind wife; Rev. Peter Duncan had a slave member of his congregation whose husband "laboured for this family on the Sabbath day". Ibid., 3.
119. Stewart, *View of the Past*, 267.
120. Port Royal Slave Trials, 26 January 1826.
121. Lewis, *Journal of a West India Proprietor*, 80.
122. Long, *History of Jamaica*, 2:413.
123. *PP* 1832 (127): 279, Sir M. Clare's evidence.
124. Long, *History of Jamaica*, 2:421.
125. Ibid. This was the result of sustained promptings from Westminister; see, for example, CO 137/121, 19 January 1808; Harlow and Madden, *British Colonial Documents*, 541.
126. Carmel: Marriage Register, 1827–1840; List of Marriages at Fairfield, 1829–1840.
127. Consolidated Slave Law, 1826, clause 4. The act gave no security against the owner's arbitrary refusal of consent. See *New Slave Laws of Jamaica*, 9–10.
128. *PP* 1831–32: 157, Rev. P. Duncan's evidence, 156, 112; also *PP* 1832 (127), I: 552, Sir A. Fleming's evidence.
129. Add. MSS 33294: Archer journal, 79.
130. *PP* 1832 (127), I: 24, John Baillie's evidence.
131. List of Marriages at Fairfield.
132. See, for instance, Higman, "Household Structure".
133. See, for instance, Patterson, *Sociology of Slavery*, 167–68.
134. Roughley describes the kind of pre-eminence possible for "the negro mechanics". They were sometimes "capital workmen, with great knowledge and skill". White millwrights and carpenters, who were ignorant of Jamaican timber, relied on their expertise. Similarly, masons from abroad without their guidance would have been "totally at a loss how to begin or construct a lime-kiln". *Jamaica Planter's Guide*, 62–63.
135. *PP* 1832 (127), II: appendix E, 1303, 1304, 1305, 1349, and so on. It is perhaps significant that unlike the mulatto woman, whose contempt for brown men is well documented (see chapter 8), the black woman manifested no comparable attitude towards her black mate.

136. Roughley, *Jamaica Planter's Guide*, 118.

137. Beckford, *Remarks*, 36.

138. Add. MSS 30001: General Correspondence, 48.

139. Patterson, *Sociology of Slavery*, 167–68.

140. See below, chapter 8.

141. *PP* 1832 (127), I: 156, John Baillie's evidence; see also Williams, *Tour Through the Island of Jamaica*, 16.

142. Ibid., 279, Sir M. Clare's evidence; 475, Rev. J. Barry's evidence, and so on; Anon., *Marly*, 98, and so on.

143. Roughley, *Jamaica Planter's Guide*, 41–42, 72.

144. Dallas, *History of the Maroons*, 2:421; *PP* 1832 (127), I: 56–57, William Taylor: "he (a male slave) could not endure that his wedded wife should be flogged". Rev. Duncan testified similarly: "it has pained the Minds of decent Male Slaves to have their wives exposed, and both indecently flogged", 641.

145. Ibid., 68, Rev. J. Barry's evidence; Long, *History of Jamaica*, 2:44.

146. Bickell, *West Indies As They Are*, 17, also 19.

147. *PP* 1832 (127), I: 172–73, Rev. J. Thorp's evidence; Lewis, *Journal of a West India Proprietor*, 330.

148. Renny, *History of Jamaica*, 167. See also Dallas, *History of the Maroons*, 2:cx; Brathwaite, *Development of Creole Society*, 215, 238; Lewis, *Journal of a West India Proprietor*, 258 and so on.

149. Lewis, *Journal of a West India Proprietor*, 111. An article in the *Jamaica Journal* of November 1818 significantly describes the Negro compound on Hope estate in St Andrew, as a "family village", 19.

150. Bickell, *West Indies As They Are*, 17.

151. See above.

152. For instance, James Archer had to rearrange the work schedule of his small slave force, "owing to Cornelia being backed by my mother in giving me impertinence in the field because her son Simon was switched". Add. MSS 33293: Archer journal, 33.

153. Bickell, *West Indies As They Are*, 10, 19: "[O]ne woman in particular, a house woman, had six or seven children; two or three of them were seized, and the others escaped, but the youngest, an infant, had been caught, and she wept aloud and very bitterly for it, saying that she must give herself up if the child was not got back, for she could not live separate from it."

154. See pp. 264–65 above.

155. Consolidated Slave Law, 1792, clause 2.

156. Ibid.

157. Ibid., clause 3.

158. See the excellent study of this subject, Sidney W. Mintz and Douglas Hall, *The

Origins of the Jamaican Internal Marketing System, Yale University Publications in Anthropology, no. 7 (New Haven: Department of Anthropology, Yale University, 1960).

159. PP 1789 (84), XXVI, A no. 5, also nos. 9, 11.

160. Senior, *Jamaica, As It Was,* 41.

161. Ibid.

162. Mintz and Hall, *Origins of the Jamaican Internal Marketing System;* also J.H. Parry, "Salt Fish and Ackee", *Caribbean Quarterly* 2, no. 4 (1951): 29–35.

163. *Jamaica Magazine,* no. 1, 1812, for instance, describes the islandwide devastation caused to "the negro habitations on many plantations:" they were "entirely blown down". (238): See Brathwaite *Development of Creole Society,* 4, for the high incidence of hurricanes during this period.

164. PP 1832: 115, Rev. P. Duncan's evidence; De la Beche, *Notes on the Present Condition,* 11.

165. Senior, *Jamaica, As It Was,* 37.

166. PP 1832 (127), II: 993, William Burge's evidence.

167. Stewart, *View of the Past,* 267.

168. Bickell, *West Indies As They Are,* 9.

169. James Kelly, *Voyage to Jamaica and Seventeen Years Residence in that Island* (Belfast: Printed by J. Wilson, 1838).

170. PP 1832 (127), II: appendix F 2, 1376–93.

171. Ibid.

172. Ibid.

173. Ibid., the law required regular inspection of provision grounds.

174. Ibid.

175. For example, Consolidated Slave Law, 1826, clause 4.

176. PP 1832 (127), I: 135, Rev. T. Cooper's evidence; Mintz and Hall, *Origins of the Jamaican Internal Marketing System.*

177. Kelly, *Voyage to Jamaica,* 17; Mintz and Hall, *Origins of the Jamaican Internal Marketing System,* 56–57; Falconbridge, *Narrative of Two Voyages,* 236–37; Normanby, *Extracts of Letters,* 17–18. For a contemporary inventory of a slave produce market, see De la Beche, *Notes on the Present Condition,* 54, appendix A, as follows:

One quart of sugar beans	. . .	from one bit to tenpence, curr.
One quart of peas	. . .	tenpence, currency
Pine apples		{each, sugar-loaf, tenpence; {common, fivepence, currency
Two cocoa-nuts	. . .	fivepence, currency
A large water melon	. . .	tenpence, currency
A large pumpkin	. . .	tenpence to two bits.

Twelve large oranges	...	fivepence, currency
Twelve mangoes	...	ditto
Six star apples	...	ditto
Adozen and a half of neesberries	...	ditto
A large shaddock	...	ditto
Six sweet sops	...	ditto
A quart of cashew nuts	...	ditto
Four large avocado pears	...	ditto
Five good cocos	...	ditto
A quart of ochras	...	ditto
Two cassava cakes		
(made from bitter Cassava)	...	ditto
A large yam	...	two bits.
Three small yams	...	tenpence, currency
Twisted tobacco, per yard	...	fivepence

Numerous fruits, &c., which are sold in the town markets, are not considered of sufficient consequence to be brought to those in the country.

In addition to the above articles, the Negroes very often sell the various allowances they receive from the estate, such as clothes, iron pots, herrings, corn, sugar, rum, &c., not requiring them.

178. Gisela Eisner, *Jamaica, 1830–1930, A Study in Economic Growth* (Manchester: Manchester University Press, 1961), 11.
179. *PP* 1832: 67, Rev. J. Barry's evidence; 115, Rev. P. Duncan's evidence; 35, Rev. T. Cooper's evidence, and so on.
180. See pp. 45–46 and 65–66 above; also A.G. Hopkins, *An Economic History of West Africa* (London: Longman, 1973), chapter 2, on the structure and function of the West African pre-colonial domestic economy.
181. Normanby, *Extracts of Letters,* 1–18.
182. *PP* 1832 (127), II: 993, William Burge's evidence.
183. Ibid.
184. Brathwaite, *Development of Creole Society,* 235–36.
185. *PP* 1832 (127), II: 32–33, John Baillie's evidence.
186. Moreton, *Manners and Customs,* 162; Williams, *Tour Through the Island of Jamaica,* 19.
187. *PP* 1832 (127), I: 338, H.J. Hinchcliffe's evidence; Stewart, *View of the Past,* 267, as follows: "Adjoining to the house is usually a small spot of ground, laid out into a sort of garden, and shaded by various fruit-trees. Here the family deposits their dead, to whose memory they invariably, if they can afford it, erect a rude tomb." Matthew Lewis "rather [wondered] at their choosing to have their dead in their

gardens", but he understood the Negro argument to be "that they need only fear the duppies of their enemies, but have nothing to apprehend from those after death, who loved them in their lifetime" (Lewis, *Journal of a West India Proprietor,* 98).

188. Normanby, *Extracts of Letters,* 16.

189. Lewis, *Journal of a West India Proprietor,* 70; *PP* 1832 (127), I: 85, William Taylor's evidence; 108, Rev. P. Duncan's evidence; 167, Rev. J. Thorp's evidence.

190. Lewis, *Journal of a West India Proprietor,* 110.

191. *PP* 1832 (127), I: 19.

192. Ibid. He did comment, however, that he had never seen a crystal decanter in the home of a field slave.

193. Where women, normally confined to the world of reproduction, find themselves in the world of production, their consciousness is alerted, and their latent ambition and dynamism set in motion. Some aspects of this process are interestingly analysed in Rowbotham, *Women, Resistance and Revolution.*

194. *PP* 1832 (127), I: 119, Rev. P. Duncan's evidence.

195. Ibid., 157–58, John Baillie's evidence.

196. Lynch, *Years Ago,* 36.

197. Ibid.; *PP* 1832 (127), I: 67, Rev. J. Barry's evidence.

198. Lynch, *Years Ago,* 36.

199. *PP* 1832 (127), I: 67, Rev. J. Barry's evidence.

200. Duncan Mathewson, "Jamaican Ceramics: An Introduction to Eighteenth-Century Folk Pottery in West African Tradition", *Jamaica Journal* 6, no. 2 (June 1972): 54–56. This paper is based on the findings of archaeological excavations at Old King's House in Spanish Town. Also Caleine Binns, "From Our Past: A Special Study for the Diploma in Ceramics" (Jamaica School of Arts, June 1972).

201. De la Beche, *Notes on the Present Condition,* 12.

202. Ibid., also Marsden, *Account of the Island of Jamaica,* 12; Williams, *Tour Through the Island of Jamaica,* 3–4; Normanby, *Extracts of Letters,* 16; *PP* 1832 (127), I: 108, Rev. P. Duncan's evidence. See also Brathwaite, *Development of Creole Society,* 232–34, for an informative description of slave women's dress, with its strong African influences.

203. *PP* 1832 (127), I: 37. Brathwaite points out that white is not only a Christian, but also an Akan colour of celebration. *Development of Creole Society,* 233n3.

204. CS 102/4, 24 June 1819, encl. 202.

205. *PP* 1832 (127), I: 19, William Taylor's evidence.

206. Ibid.

207. Ibid.

208. Nugent, *Journal of a Voyage,* 48, 219; Lewis, *Journal of a West India Proprietor,* 51–58. For a full account see Brathwaite, *Development of Creole Society,* 227–32.

209. *PP* 1832: 88, Rev. J. Barry's evidence; 138, Rev. T. Cooper's evidence.

210. *PP* 1832 (127), I: 575, W. Taylor's evidence.

211. Ibid., 171, Rev. J. Thorpe's evidence; C. Campbell, "Social and Economic Obstacles to the Development of Popular Education in Post-Emancipation Jamaica, 1834–1865", *Journal of Caribbean History* 1 (November 1970).

212. *PP* 1832: 52.

213. *PP* 1832 (127), I: 575. Taylor had been asked the question, "Is it possible for a Slave to educate his own Family?" The frequent clever use of written forms of communication by male and female runaways suggests perhaps greater familiarity and understanding by slaves of those forms than the few educational statistics of slavery would imply.

214. Ibid., 106.

215. Church Missionary Society, C/WO 4/4: Papine School Report, 1827. Compare Moravian Records.

216. Lewis, *Journal of a West India Proprietor*, 254–57.

217. See p. 242 above.

218. *PP* 1789, XXVI, Reeves.

219. *PP* 1789, XXVI, nos. 22–26. For example, the case of the celebrated woman of the Popo country, over eighty years old, still hale and active, who had been a practitioner for years, and who was deported to Cuba when "discovered". *PP* 1814–15, VI, and so on.

220. Brathwaite, *Development of Creole Society,* 219.

221. *PP* 1789, XXVI, nos. 22–26.

222. Brathwaite, *The African Presence,* 74.

223. See, for instance, Lewin, "Role of Woman". Women traditionally hold offices of authority in syncretic cults and outnumber male members "by anything from 30% to 80%". Also Edward Seaga, "Cults in Jamaica", *Jamaica Journal* 2, no. 2 (June 1969).

224. CMS Cw 09d/1, 8 May 1932.

225. Their funereal observances, for instance, see Lewis, *Journal of a West India Proprietor*, 96–97; Long, *History of Jamaica*, 2:421–22; Beckwith, *Black Roadways*.

226. *Diary of John Lang, 1805–1819,* 364.

227. Maureen Lewis's linguistic research is opening up important new insights in this field.

228. *Jamaica Magazine* 4, no. 6, October 1813, 807.

229. Lewis, *Journal of a West India Proprietor,* 57.

CHAPTER 8

1. Brathwaite, *Development of Creole Society,* 168; Hall, "Role of the Free Coloured Population", 21; Duncker, "Free Coloured", 1–10; Higman, "Slave Population and Economy", 128–35; Higman, "Demography of Slavery", 3.
2. For example, *PP* 1814–15, VI, Jamaica, 121.
3. Long, *History of Jamaica,* 2:378; he estimated the total slave population at 166,914 (377). In a breakdown of Clarendon's population in 1788, Long reckoned that there were 1,000 mulatto slaves in a slave population of 17,000 in that parish. Add. MSS: 18959 and 18961, Long Papers, Misc.; Add. MSS 12435: Long Papers, Inventory.
4. Higman, "Slave Population and Economy", 128–29.
5. Ibid., 132.
6. B.W. Higman, "Some Characteristics of the Slave Population in 1832" (seminar paper, University of the West Indies, 1969), 3.
7. Ibid.
8. Ibid.
9. Higman, "Slave Population and Economy", 146–49.
10. See pp. 108–9 above.
11. Higman, "Slave Population and Economy", 150–51.
12. R. Barrett, *A Reply to the Speech of Dr Lushington* (London, 1828), 29.
13. Lewis, *Journal of a West India Proprietor,* 74, also 79; Long, *History of Jamaica,* 2:328–30, 332–35; Beckford, *Remarks,* 2:322.
14. Egerton MS 2134: Nutt's River Inventory, 56. The other "five young children" at Nutt's River who were Negroes, were all in the weeding gang.
15. C 109/338.
16. C 107/143; similarly on Worthy Park estate, see Craton and Walvin, *Jamaican Plantation,* 139; Cooper, *Facts Illustrative,* 26; Roughley, *Jamaica Planter's Guide,* 97, as follows: "The house people should always be composed of the people of colour belonging to the property."
17. Shore, *In Old St James,* 106–13.
18. Higman, "Slave Population and Economy", 406–8, 409, 410, 411.
19. *PP* 1832 (127), I: 36, John Baillie's evidence.
20. McMahon, *Jamaica Plantership,* 187–88, and 49–55. See also Patterson, *Sociology of Slavery,* 57–58. An interesting discussion of the situational dimension of slavery in the household is found in Gerald Mullin, *Flight and Rebellion: Slave Resistance in Eighteenth-Century Virginia* (New York: Oxford University Press, 1972), 62–70.
21. See chapter 5; also Nugent, *Journal of a Voyage,* 182.
22. Williams, *Tour Through the Island of Jamaica,* 327.

23. Anon., *Marly*, 95. De la Beche commented similarly: "(They) have in general very little work to perform, many more being required to execute the same work than would be thought necessary in (England)" (*Notes on the Present Condition,* 35).

24. Bickell, *West Indies As They Are,* 104, 112; Nugent, *Journal of a Voyage,* 87.

25. Lewis, *Journal of a West India Proprietor,* 79.

26. *PP* 1832 (127), I: 533.

27. King MS 213: Journal of an Officer, n. 1818, also, 2 September 1824.

28. Port Royal Slave Trials.

29. St George Slave Court, 7 July 1824; compare the case of Molly, a mulatto woman slave of Water Valley estate in St Mary, who was similarly charged and sentenced at Port Maria Slave Court on 21 April 1808, *PP* 1814–15, VI: 125.

30. Higman, "Slave Population and Economy", 190–92, Tables 27 and 28.

31. Ibid.

32. Ibid.; Roberts, *Population of Jamaica,* 71; *PP* 1826–27, XXII, no. 9, Jamaica.

33. Higman, "Slave Population and Economy", 192, Table 28.

34. *PP* 1826–27, XXII, no. 9, Jamaica; also *PP* 1823, XVIII.

35. *PP* 1823, XVIII.

36. Ibid.

37. *PP* 1826–27, XXII, no. 9.

38. For example, Roberts, *Population of Jamaica,* 38; Stewart, *View of the Past,* 333.

39. *PP* 1823, XVIII.

40. Ibid.

41. Ibid.; also Cooper, *Facts Illustrative,* 23.

42. Ramlachansingh, "Amity Hall", 135.

43. For example, James Affleck, see pp. 174–75 above.

44. Higman, "Slave Population and Economy", 192.

45. Ibid.

46. *PP* 1832 (127), I: 204.

47. Ibid., 48; see also Long, *History of Jamaica,* 2:322.

48. *PP* 1832 (127), I: 48, W. Taylor's evidence.

49. Ibid.

50. Higman, "Slave Population and Economy", 192, table 28; see also 191–95.

51. Hall, "Role of the Free Coloured Population", 2; Duncker, "Free Coloured", 9; Brathwaite, *Development of Creole Society,* 168.

52. For these disabilities see CO 137/91; Edwards, *History, Civil and Commercial,* 2:20–24; Duncker, "Free Coloured", 20–36; Brathwaite, *Development of Creole Society,* 169–71, 178, and so on.

53. Ibid.

54. CO 137/91. Encl., 5 June 1793.

55. See above, chapter 3.

56. *Acts of Assembly,* 1774–88 (Kingston, 1788).

57. Jamaica House of Assembly (JHA), 1784–91, 26–28, 30–31, 92.

58. Bickell, *The West Indies As They Are,* 114.

59. PP 1832 (127), I: 196, Admiral Fleming's evidence.

60. Stewart, *View of the Past,* 97.

61. Add. MSS 12435: Long Papers, Inventory.

62. Inventories, Liber 95, 1803, 102.

63. St David Vestry Minutes, 1785–93.

64. Ibid.

65. Barrett, *A Reply,* 30, 41–42; Duncker, "Free Coloured", 30, 119–24.

66. Duncker, "Free Coloured", 30.

67. Ibid., also 119–24; also Lewis, *Journal of a West India Proprietor,* 401.

68. Sinclair, *Better Half,* introduction xxxiii–xxxxx; also Philip Curtin, *Two Jamaicas: The Role of Ideas in a Tropical Colony 1830–1865* (Cambridge: Harvard University Press, 1955), 43–44.

69. Barrett, *A Reply,* 29; Duncker, "Free Coloured", 11–14; Long, *History of Jamaica,* 2:103, 337.

70. Add. MSS 12435: Long Papers, Inventory, 6.

71. *Votes of the Assembly of Jamaica,* 1804, 1814, 1822, and so on. Moore Town, for example, in 1804 contained a population of 300 men, women and children, of whom 32 were mulatto and 4 were quadroon: 7 males, 9 females and 20 children. Ibid., appendix 42, 330–33; also *PP* 1832 (127), I: 167, Major General Sir John Keane's evidence: "(Maroons) are of all colours."

72. Moore Town in 1818 had 372 people, including 37 coloureds; 33 "lived out", and of these 16 were coloured (9 mulatto females): *Votes of the Assembly of Jamaica,* 1818, 232.

73. *Votes of the Assembly of Jamaica,* 1804, 333.

74. Williams, *Tour Through the Island of Jamaica,* 2.

75. Ibid., 85.

76. Lewis *Journal of a West India Proprietor,* 169.

77. Ibid., 65, also 62, 171, 379.

78. Jamaica Archives Inventories.

79. Senior, *Jamaica, As It Was,* 18.

80. Nugent, *Journal of a Voyage,* 168, also index, 287.

81. Marsden, *Account of the Island of Jamaica,* 7.

82. Ibid.; also Williams, *Tour Through the Island of Jamaica,* 63–64, 232; Stewart, *View of the Past,* 329–30; Lewis, *Journal of a West India Proprietor,* 171; H.P. Jacobs, "Port Royal in Decline", *Jamaica Historical Review* 3 (1971): 41–43.

83. Barrett, *A Reply,* 11.

84. Ibid.

85. Duncker, "Free Coloured", 117 and passim.
86. Kingston Common Council Proceedings 1803–15, 31 October 1803.
87. Jacobs, "Port Royal", 42–43.
88. Inventories, Liber 95, 1803, 81.
89. *PP* 1832 (127), I: 137. Rev. Thomas Cooper felt that free coloureds as a group had made a great economic virtue out of necessity: having little or no legal means of enforcing payment from whites who might employ them, they "tended to independent enterprise", thus becoming their own employers. Cooper, *Facts Illustrative,* 136.
90. CO 137/91, 2 December 1792.
91. Kinston Common Council Proceedings, 1803–15, 21 November 1808.
92. Ibid., 1820–28, 22 January 1821. Duncker quotes cases of indoor relief in St Ann ("Free Coloured", 71–76, 171–76).
93. *Votes of the Assembly of Jamaica,* 1804, 35.
94. Stewart, *View of the Past,* 333–34; Lewis, *Journal of a West India Proprietor,* 347; Campbell, "Edward Jordon", 199; Barrett, *A Reply,* 11.
95. *Votes of the Assembly of Jamaica,* 1822, appendix 31, 303.
96. Ibid., 1828, appendix 40, 322–23.
97. Ibid., 1828, appendix 41, 329.
98. Ibid., 1822, appendix 31, 302–3: white prisoners were allowed 3s. 4d. daily.
99. *PP* 1814–15; Port Royal Slave Trials, 1819–34; Montego Court of Quarter Sessions 1797; Montego Bay Slave Court, 1814, and so on.
100. Port Royal Slave Trials; she was arrested five times between January 1821 and September 1824, usually in a state of "excessive intoxication".
101. Port Royal Slave Trials, 17 October 1827, 20 January 1831, 21 May 1832, 19 June 1832 22 May 1834.
102. Diary of The Negro Congregation at Fairfield, 1829, 22 January 1829. Horse stealing was apparently common among them (entry of 17 September 1829).
103. Ibid., 21 May 1829.
104. Ibid.
105. Ibid., also entries of 2 and 16 April. The excessive drought of the region retarded the group's development. The ponds were dried up and prevented the children and their clothing from being properly washed. Their appearance was described by the missionaries as "very sallow and meagre".
106. Ibid., 17 September 1829. It was noted also on 22 March that the free brown people of Southside "think it beneath them to come under our [that is, Moravian] special care in common with the negroes".
107. Hickey, *Memoirs,* 2:28.
108. Long, *History of Jamaica,* 14, 331. See also Stewart, *View of the Past,* 325–27; *PP* 1832: 70, Rev. J. Barry's evidence; Jones, *Diary,* 62; Nugent, *Journal of a Voyage,* 87.

109. Anon., *Marly*, 83.
110. McNeill, *Observations on the Treatment*, 42; see also Jones, *Diary*, 51.
111. McMahon, *Jamaica Plantership*, 190–92; also Moreton, *Manners and Customs*, 130–31.
112. McNeill, *Observations on the Treatment*, 202–5.
113. *PP* 1832: 70, Rev. J. Barry's evidence.
114. *PP* 1832 (127), I: 534, Rev. J. Barry's evidence; also Renny, *History of Jamaica*, 329; Anon., *Marly*, 193–94, as follows: "It is no uncommon circumstance for a father to make these bargains himself, after bringing up his daughter in the best way he possibly can"; Moreton, *Manners and Customs*, 126.
115. Stewart, *Account of Jamaica*, 328; McMahon, *Jamaica Plantership*, 215–16; Edwards, *History, Civil and Commercial*, 2:29; Long, *History of Jamaica*, 2:335; Marsden, *Account of the Island of Jamaica*, 8.
116. Anon., *Marly*, 56; also Moreton, *Manners and Customs*, 131.
117. Stewart, *Account of Jamaica*, 303; Duncker, "Free Coloured", 55n3, also 62.
118. Nugent, *Journal of a Voyage*, 214.
119. Ibid.
120. Duncker, "Free Coloured", 56–57.
121. Add. MSS 33293: Archer journal, 62, also 63.
122. Renny, *History of Jamaica*, 329.
123. Bickell, *West Indies As They Are*, 105; also Stewart, *View of the Past*, 175.
124. Stewart, *View of the Past*, 175.
125. Nugent, *Journal of a Voyage*, 65, 66, 68, 78, 83.
126. *Journals of the Assembly of Jamaica* 8 (1784–91): 578, 580, 581, 584, 628; see also Brathwaite, *Development of Creole Society*, 171–72.
127. *Journals of the Assembly of Jamaica* 8 (1784–91): 578.
128. *Acts of Assembly*, 1774–88 (Kingston, 1788).
129. Ibid.
130. *Acts of Assembly*, 1784–90, iii, index.
131. Add. MSS 34181: Jamaican Wills, 94.
132. Ibid., 101; also 77, Michael Wade's will; 89, Samuel Delpratt's will, and so on; Jones, *Diary*, 51; Duncker, "Free Coloured", 59–60; Craton and Walvin, *Jamaican Plantation*, 182.
133. Bickell, *West Indies As They Are*, 108–9; also 105–6, 113–14.
134. Ibid., 113.
135. Minutes of the Jamaican Missions Conference, 1821–26, May 1822; Edwards, *History, Civil and Commercial*, 2:25; Campbell, "Edward Jordon", 96.
136. Anon., *Marly*, 193.
137. See p. 233 above.
138. *PP* 1832 (127), I: 354.

139. CO 137/91, 5 June 1793.

140. *Journals of the Assembly of Jamaica* 8 (1784–91): 288; also 183 (Sarah Fisher), 416 (Ann Fleming) and so on.

141. Duncker, "Free Coloured", 22–23.

142. Ibid., 24, 32.

143. Ibid., 133.

144. Bickell, *West Indies As They Are,* 114; see also Brathwaite, *Development of Creole Society,* 262–63; *Votes of the Assembly of Jamaica,* 1828, 448: Anthony Gutzmer's evidence of a meeting at the Wesleyan chapel in Thomas Street, Kingston, which was attended "principally by females of colour". See also Mary Reckord, "Missionary Activity in Jamaica before Emancipation" (PhD diss., University of London, 1964).

145. See, for example, Williamson, *Caribbean Islands,* 329–30: coloureds were "devout" worshippers whose conduct in church compared favourably with that of whites, whose behaviour in church was described as "indecent". Nugent, *Journal of a Voyage,* 93–94.

146. Dorothy Ryall, "The Organization of Missionary Societies and the Role of Missionaries in the Diffusion of British Culture in Jamaica during the Period 1834–1865" (PhD diss., University of London, 1959), 145.

147. Ibid., 99, 435–38.

148. Reckord, "Missionary Activity", 166.

149. *PP* 1832 (127), I: 71, also 534.

150. *Votes of the Assembly of Jamaica,* 1828, appendix 9, 407.

151. Ibid., 408.

152. Ibid., 407.

153. Ibid., 432.

154. Ryall, "Organization of Missionary Societies", 167, also 47–48; Reckord, "Missionary Activity", 73.

155. Duncan, *Narrative of the Wesleyan Mission,* 104–5.

156. Ibid., 109.

157. Ibid., 173.

158. Ibid., 174.

159. Ibid., 19.

160. Ibid., 20.

161. Reckord, "Missionary Activity", 173.

162. Ibid., also 62, 69, 154; Ryall, "Organization of Missionary Societies", 184.

163. *Votes of the Assembly of Jamaica,* 1828, appendix 60, 403.

164. Reckord, "Missionary Activity", 72.

165. Duncan, *Narrative of the Wesleyan Mission,* 202–3.

166. Reckord, "Missionary Activity", 29.

167. Ibid., 73.
168. Ibid., 32; see also Ryall, "Organization of Missionary Societies", 184.
169. Reckord, "Missionary Activity", 189.
170. Mavis Burke, "The History of the Wesleyan Methodist Contribution to Education in Jamaica in the Nineteenth Century 1833–1900" (MA thesis, University of London, 1965), 48, 49. Women teachers were paid approximately one-third the salary of men. Reckord, "Missionary Activity", 190.
171. Reckord, "Missionary Activity", 189.
172. Ibid.
173. Edwards, *History, Civil and Commercial,* 2:26.
174. Brathwaite, *Development of Creole Society,* 268.
175. Reckord, "Missionary Activity", 268.
176. Ibid., 192.
177. CO 137/91/ (5 June 1793).
178. Long, *History of Jamaica,* 2:328–29; Stewart, *View of the Past,* 329; Duncker, "Free Coloured", 84.
179. Long ridiculed the whole absurd notion of parents "blind with folly" who think their brown offspring worthy of an expensive overseas education. "Miss is placed at Chelsea, or some other famed seminary: where she learns music, dancing, French, and the whole circle of female *bon ton,* proper for the accomplishment of fine women." When she returns to Jamaica, "she faints at the sight of her relations, especially when papa tells her that black Quasheba is her own mother" (Long, *History of Jamaica,* 2:329).
180. *PP* 1832 (127), I: 73, Rev. J. Barry's evidence.
181. Ibid., 173, Rev. J. Barry's evidence.
182. See chapter 4 above.
183. J.A. Thome and J.H. Kimball, *Emancipation in the West Indies: A Six Months' Tour in Antigua, Barbados, and Jamaica, in the Year 1837* (New York: American Anti-Slavery Society, 1838), 354.
184. Ibid., 356. The Rev. J. Barry declared in 1832 that the free coloureds were "some of the best educated people that he had met in Jamaica". *PP* 1832 (127), I: 73.
185. Add. MSS 1896: Long Papers, 37: "The only possible characteristics of anything like Beauty in a negroe's face are the crystalline humour of the eye . . . . [S]o that nothing in human shape, can possess the attributes of ugliness in greater perfection than a superannuated Negroe." Bryan Edwards's "Ode to the Sable Venus" (*History, Civil and Commercial,* 2:32–38) is a nearly unique contemporary attempt to idealize the black woman's body. Its aesthetic intention is, however, equivocal:

    The loveliest limbs her form compose
    Such as her sister Venus chose,
    In Florence, where she's seen;

> Both just alike, except the white,
>
> No difference, no – none at night,
>
> The beauteous dames between.

186. For example, McMahon, *Jamaica Plantership*, 52; Lewis, *Journal of a West India Proprietor*, 63, 107, 137–38, 169, 171; Williams, *Tour Through the Island of Jamaica*, 306–7, 232–33; Hickey, *Memoirs*, 2:28; Stewart, *View of the Past*, 336; Marsden, *Account of the Island of Jamaica*, 7.

187. Anon., *Hamel, The Obeah Man* (London: Hunt and Clarke, 1827), 1:195–96. Compare the Brazilian Freyre's romantic view of "mixed" beauty (see p. 83 above), or Cynric Williams's extravagant description of the sixteen–year-old quadroon girl Diana, who made him think of "the impression which Caesar might have left at the first sight of the beautiful Cleopatra when she was introduced into his presence by Apollodorus" (*Tour Through the Island of Jamaica*, 53–55).

188. Moreton, *Manners and Customs*, 77.

189. Ibid.

190. Ibid.

191. Nugent, *Journal of a Voyage*, 12, also 98, 171–73.

192. Williamson, *Caribbean Islands*, 42–43.

193. CO 137/110, 15 January 1803; also Long, *History of Jamaica*, 2:170; Duncker, "Free Coloured", 52–53; "[T]hose gypsies", wrote Moreton (*Manners and Customs*, 127), "have a wonderful ascendancy over men, and have injured many, both powerful and subordinate."

194. Her image of "informer" on slaves was significant. She offered "a wretched security" to whites, by conveying to them information about any plots that were being hatched among the slaves; Whiteley, *Three Months in Jamaica*, 19; Moreton, *Manners and Customs*, 131.

195. For example, Williams, *Tour Through the Island of Jamaica*, 27: the mulatto slaves took no part in the John Canoe celebrations at Christmas.

196. Stewart, *View of the Past*, 330; Moreton, *Manners and Customs*, 128.

197. *PP* 1832 (127), I: 73, Rev. J. Barry's evidence.

198. Stewart, *View of the Past*, 325–28, 330. "When one of them gets a child as brown or browner than herself, it is considered a very great blemish in her character." Moreton, *Manners and Customs*, 125.

199. Barrett, *A Reply*, 48; Marsden, *Account of the Island of Jamaica*, 1; See also Hall, "Role of the Free Coloured Population", 26. For the male Barrett's preference for the mulatto female, see Marks, *Family of the Barretts*, 196, 197–99, 220, 222, 297, 310, 614–15.

200. Campbell, "Edward Jordon", 95–98.

201. Higman, "Household Structure", 11.

202. See pp. 274–75 above, for instance.

203. *Acts of Assembly,* 1784–88, 1789, 3.
204. Ibid.
205. Ibid., 1786, 9.
206. See pp. 283–84 above.
207. *Acts of Assembly,* 1784–88, 1785, 8.

CHAPTER 9

1. Crow, *Victorian Woman,* 23.
2. See chapters 4 and 5. The novel *Wide Sargasso Sea* (Harmondsworth: Penguin, 1966) by Jean Rhys, of white West Indian origin, brilliantly analyses the dilemma of the white colonial woman, alienated from her physical and human environment, ultimately alienated from herself. The spiritual displacement of its central character takes place in an authentically reconstructed post-emancipation Jamaica. See also Walton Look Lai, "The Road to Thornfield Hall: An Analysis of Jean Rhys' Novel, *Wide Sargasso Sea*", *New Beacon Reviews* (1968): 38–52.
3. Ryall, "Organization of Missionary Societies"; Douglas Hall, "Bountied European Immigration into Jamaica, with Special Reference to the German settlement at Seaford Town up to 1850" (paper presented at the Fourth Conference of Caribbean Historians, University of the West Indies, 1972).
4. Reckord, "Missionary Activity"; Curtin, *Two Jamaicas,* 80–98.
5. Curtin, *Two Jamaicas,* 158–77; Campbell, "Social and Economic Obstacles".
6. London Missionary Society Correspondence (LMS) Box 2, Folder 4, Barrett to Secretary Ellis (of LMS), 20 February 1839. Compare Rev. Woodridge's comment to Ellis on arranging for a new bachelor missionary/teacher, to be boarded with a family: "I do no know what else could be done for a single man here without exposing him to great personal inconvenience and moral contamination." LMS Box 2, Folder 2.
7. Ryall, "Organization of Missionary Societies", 96, also 178, 186–90.
8. LMS Box 2, Folder 2, 6 February 1838.
9. LMS Box 2, Folder 3, 31 October 1838.
10. The chief ones were the Moravian, Methodist, Anglican (Church Missionary Society), Baptist (black and white), Presbyterian and London Missionary Society.
11. Ryall, "Organization of Missionary Societies", 77–78, 167; also pp. 287–90 above.
12. Ryall, "Organization of Missionary Societies", 375.
13. LMS Box 3, Folder 1, 1 January 1840.
14. LMS Box 1, Folder 2, 31 August 1835.
15. LMS Box 2, Folder 1, 2 May 1837.
16. LMS Box 2, Folder 1, 1 May 1837.
17. LMS Box 2, Folder 1, 9 June 1838.

18. LMS Box 2, Folder 1, 29 October 1838.
19. LMS Box 3, Folder 2, 12 October 1840.
20. LMS Box 3, Folder 3, 20 March 1841.
21. Burn, *Emancipation and Apprenticeship;* Douglas Hall, "The Apprenticeship Period in Jamaica 1834–1838", *Caribbean Quarterly* 3, no. 3 (December 1953).
22. Hall, "Apprenticeship Period", 143.
23. In 1834, there were forty-four missionaries of various denominations in Jamaica, assisted by their wives: Reckord, "Missionary Activity", 15. In 1842, the Methodists listed thirty-two missionaries and 26,000 members: Ryall, "Organization of Missionary Societies", 140.
24. LMS Box 1, Folder 3, 23 February 1836.
25. LMS Box 1, Folder 2, 21 October 1835: there are countless references to family deaths, illnesses and physical discomfort of all kinds in this extensive collection of papers. Another typical item is from the missionary John Vine: "Heard from St Ann's yesterday, Mrs Alloway was very poorly, and Mr A. quite an invalid from mosquito and chigre depredations on his legs and feet. I am also lame of both feet from too-tormenting chigres but am getting better . . . Mrs Vine suffers with many a festering wound from mosquito bites, and rubbing them, from which it is hardly possible to refrain." Ibid. Box 1, Folder 2, 4 November 1835.
26. J. Sturge and T. Harvey, *The West Indies in 1837: Being the Journal of a Visit to Antigua, Monserrat, Dominica, St Lucia, Barbadoes, and Jamaica; Undertaken for the Purpose of Ascertaining the Actual Condition of the Negro Population of those Islands* (London: Hamilton, Adams, and Co., 1838). The residence of the Rev. Vine, about four miles from Stewart's Town, was "in a ruinous condition". It consisted of two apartments and a porch or hall; "in many places the sky (could) be seen through the roof". Sturge and Harvey felt that "nothing but a dedication to their work could enable (Vine and his family) to endure the hardships under which they lived" (ibid., 214).
27. LMS Box 2, Folder 2, 11 January 1838. Special magistrates and their families wrote of identical problems: see Add. MSS 51818: Holland House Papers, Letters from Baynes, Dacres, Edward, Special Magistrates, 1835–1840. Compare the letters of E.D. Baynes to Lord Holland, his patron: "my wife has entirely lost her health and the remainder of my family are subject to almost perpetual fever. I have Doctor's bills now on the table before me amounting to £400." 10 August 1837.
28. LMS Box 1, Folder 2, 23 June 1835.
29. Ibid.
30. LMS Box 1, Folder 1, 31 December 1834.
31. Ibid.
32. LMS Box 1, Folder 2, 23 June 1835.
33. LMS Box 2, Folder 1, 29 October 1835.

34. LMS Box 2, Folder 2, 30 April 1838.
35. Ibid.
36. LMS Box 1, Folder 2, 24 December 1835.
37. Ibid., 28 November 1835.
38. Ibid.
39. Ibid.
40. LMS Box 1, Folder 3, 30 March 1836.
41. LMS Box 2, Folder 2.
42. Minutes of the Jamaica Missions Conference, 1834–36, 22 January 1834.
43. Sturge and Harvey, *The West Indies,* 332.
44. Add. MSS 51816: Holland House Papers, Correspondence, 110, 4 June 1835. McNeil elaborated the rationals for such families as follows: "(They) would allow our apprentices to benefit by the industrious habits and morals example of well selected European labourers, whose presence would infuse a new spirit and more congenial feelings in our Apprentices and also throughout the coloured free population and agricultural labour would the more rapidly cease to be considered (as the slavery system caused to be) a degrading Employment." Ibid.
45. Ibid.
46. Ibid.
47. Ibid., 112.
48. Ibid.
49. Ibid., 132, 28 July 1837.
50. Sturge and Harvey, *The West Indies,* 318–21.
51. Hall, "Bountied European Immigration" 6, table 1, and 7–16.
52. Ibid. The numbers were 2,685 from Great Britain and 1,038 from Germany.
53. Ibid., 19.
54. MS 92: Seaford Town Record Book, 1836–1854.
55. Ibid., for example, 31.
56. Ibid.
57. Ibid.
58. Add. MSS 51816: Holland House Papers, Correspondence, 26 April 1836, 115.
59. MS 92: Seaford Town.
60. Ibid., Report of 30 September 1838 to 30 September 1839.
61. Add. MSS 51818: Holland House Papers, Letters, 20 August 1837, 206–8. Compare McMahon, *Jamaica Plantership,* 26–27: vulnerable young female immigrants were "robbed of their virtue by the wily intrigues of those who afforded them the means of subsistence". Also Sturge and Harvey, *The West Indies,* 323. The German orphan girl Marie Peter was in the care of Amelia Campbell, who received £8 from the St James Parish Vestry for her maintenance. St James Vestry Minutes, 1837–45, 17 July 1837.

62. Hall, "Bountied European Immigration", 31–36.

63. Roberts, *Population of Jamaica,* 65, table 14.

64. Ibid., 73, table 18.

65. Ibid. The autobiography of a Jamaican-born woman makes interesting reading in this context, namely, Lucille Iremonger, *Yes, My Darling Daughter* (Secker and Warburg, 1964).

66. For instance, Add. MSS 51816: Holland House Papers, Correspondence, 152, 153, 155, 170, 172, 173, and so on. Add. MSS 51818: Holland House Papers, Letters, 256, and so on. Also Hall, "Apprenticeship Period", 7, 9.

67. Add. MSS 51818: Holland House Papers, Letters, 256, 6 April 1839.

68. Add. MSS 51819: Holland House Papers, Misc., 52.

69. Add. MSS 51816: Holland House Papers, Correspondence, 153, 4 September 1838.

70. Ibid.

71. Ibid., 157, 16 October 1838.

72. Ibid., 158, 16 October 1838.

73. See pp. 196–97 above.

74. Burn, *Emancipation and Apprenticeship,* 118–20 and passim.

75. Hall, "Apprenticeship Period", 164 and passim.

76. *Negro Apprenticeship in the Colonies: A Review of the Report of the Select Committee of the House of Commons Appointed to inquire into the Workings of the Apprenticeship System* (London: J. Hatchard and Son, 1837), 11.

77. Ibid.

78. *PP* 1836, IV, Report from the Special Committee on Negro Apprenticeship in the Colonies, together with the Minutes of Evidence (House of Commons, August 1836), 499.

79. Ibid., 500, and passim.

80. Ibid., 56, also 482.

81. Ibid., 501.

82. Add. MSS 27970: Archer accounts, 286–87.

83. Ibid.

84. Ibid., 292.

85. Ibid., 293.

86. *PP* 1836, IV: 500.

87. Ibid. Estate medical services were among the many casualties of the first phase of freedom. Although the colonial government did not entirely neglect its responsibility for the population's health, rural medical services, customarily the responsibility of the individual estate, were drastically curtailed and had very largely broken down by 1838. Gurney observed in his travels through Jamaica in 1840 a "grievous want of enlightened medical aid from which the people are now suffering in all parts of the island. The provision which was in this respect made for

them in slavery has now ceased, and they have in general neither the ability nor the wish to employ regular practitioners at the usual prices." Joseph Gurney, *A Winter in the West Indies* (London: J. Murray, 1840), 170; Long, *Jamaica and the New Order,* 87–89.

88. *PP* 1836, IV: 62.

89. Add. MSS 51816: Holland House Papers, Correspondence, 2 September 1837, 210.

90. Marquess of Sligo, *A Letter to the Marquess of Normanby relative to the present state of Jamaica* (London: J. Andrews, 1839), 15–16, also 122, 130; John Candler, *Extracts from the Journal of Candler, John Whilst Travelling in Jamaica,* Part 1 (London: Harvey and Darton, 1840), 20.

91. Add. MSS 27970: Archer accounts, 283–94, especially 285–87.

92. Ibid.

93. Ibid.

94. Burn, *Emancipation and Apprenticeship,* 118.

95. Add. MSS 51816: Holland House Papers, Correspondence, 128, 20 May 1837.

96. Sturge and Harvey, *The West Indies,* 173.

97. Ibid., 61. The Select Committee of the House of Commons which reported in 1837 on the workings of the apprenticeship system interpreted the stance of black parents "as indicative of the just value which the negroes attach to freedom". "Negro mothers have been known to say pressing their children to their bosoms, 'we would rather see them die, than become apprentices' " (*Negro Apprenticeship in the Colonies,* 33).

98. CO 137/215. Compare other views of "the idleness and insolence" of female apprentices, who were identified as "the principal inciters of insubordination", for example, Add. MSS 51818: Holland House Papers, Letters, 181, 25 February 1835; *PP* 1836, IV: 523, William Burge's evidence.

99. *Negro Apprenticeship in the Colonies,* 32.

100. Ibid., 38; See also *PP* 1830, IV: 523–24.

101. Burn, *Emancipation and Apprenticeship,* 284–85; *PP* 1836, IV: 345–46.

102. Ibid.; *Negro Apprenticeship in the Colonies,* 31. Women's hair was cut off in the houses of correction, they were chained together in pairs in penal gangs, whipped on the treadmills, and so on. See also Sturge and Harvey, *The West Indies,* 162, 168, 197, 203–6, 229, 233, 237, 258; Add. MSS 51816: Holland House Papers, Correspondence, 89, 135; Add. MSS 51819: Holland House Papers, Misc., 195, 199, 289.

103. Hall, "Apprenticeship Period", 148.

104. Add. MSS 51816: Holland House Papers, Correspondence, 175, 15 February 1839. This exodus from the estate was projected by McNeil as being to the disadvantage of black women: "having withdrawn themselves to the mountains, and from active life and society . . . the wives will be made the slaves of the husbands, while

the latter spends his time chiefly on his bench or in his hammock by the fireside in half-finished and never-to-be completed hut regardless of the world so long as his wife can provide him with provisions, Rum and tobacco". 173–74; also 152: "his wants are but few and his wife will become his most abject slave".

105. CO 137/215, 9 March 1836.

106. Add. MSS 51816: Holland House Papers, Correspondence, 173–74, 15 February 1839.

107. Gurney, *Winter*, 115–16; compare Candler, *Extracts from the Journal*, 23; also Douglas Hall, *Free Jamaica, 1838–1865: An Economic History* (New Haven: Yale University Press, 1959), 22. Professor Hall writes: "with the possible exception of the present period since the ending of World War II, Jamaicans have never been so alert and enterprising as they were during the first few years of the post-emancipation era, between the ending of slavery and the first decisive step of the British Government in 1846 towards free trade in sugar". Ibid. 18, 157–206, 266, and so on. Also *Jamaica Almanac* 1845, for numbers of small settlements under 10 acres in size in 1844.

108. Sturge and Harvey, *The West Indies*, 196.

109. List of Marriages at Fairfield, 1829–1840.

110. Roberts, *Population of Jamaica*, 85.

111. Ibid., 86–87. The total population had during the decade grown from about 342,000 in 1828, to 377,433 in 1844. Ibid., 41–43.

112. Summary of Census Returns, 6 May 1861.

113. For example, Clinton Black, *Living Names in Jamaica's History* (Kingston: Jamaica Welfare, 1946).

114. Mary Seacole, *Wonderful Adventures of Mrs Seacole in Many Lands* (London: J. Blackwood, 1855), 2.

115. Ibid., 109–10.

116. Ibid.

117. Ibid.

118. Ibid.

119. Sturge and Harvey, *The West Indies*, 181–83.

120. Report of the Charity Commissioners to the House of Assembly: 1844, appendix 6, 194.

121. Ibid., 214.

122. Ibid., 218–19.

123. Ibid., 231–35. Wolmer's Free School was the only one mentioned by the Commissioners as having a school lending library, with "a number and variety of books". The children were permitted to carry them home, on their undertaking to return them. The Commissioners were happy to learn that this was a privilege "much valued and not abused" (235).

124. Sturge and Harvey, *The West Indies*, 281; also Thome and Kimball, *Emancipation in the West Indies*, 353–55.

125. Report of the Charity Commissioners, 234. Before the year was out the school's total numbers had increased to 536, which occasioned the appointment of a tutoress, Harriet Lake, at a salary of £120 per annum.

126. Thome and Kimball, *Emancipation in the West Indies*, 355.

127. Seacole, *Wonderful Adventures*, 2.

128. Ibid., 3.

129. Ibid., 4.

130. Ibid., 5.

131. Ibid., 5–6.

132. Candler, *Extracts from the Journal*, 23; J.M. Phillippo, *Jamaica: Its Past and Present State* (London: John Snow, 1843), 137; Hill, *Eight Chapters*, 64.

133. Campbell, "Social and Economic Obstacles".

134. Seacole, *Wonderful Adventures*, 4.

135. On this subject she wrote: "I think all who are familiar with the West Indies will acknowledge that nature has been favourable to strangers in a few respects, and that one of these had been in instilling into the hearts of the Creoles an affection for English people and an anxiety for their welfare, which shows itself warmest when they are sick and suffering. I can safely appeal on this point to anyone who is acquainted with life in Jamaica. Another benefit has been conferred upon them by inclining the Creoles to practise the healing art, and inducing them to seek out the simple remedies which are available for the terrible diseases by which foreigners are attacked, and which are found growing under the same circumstances which produce the ills they minister to. So true is it that beside the nettle ever grows the cure for its sting." Ibid., 60.

136. Ibid., 8, 73: "When I was told that many of the regiments I had known so well in Jamaica had left England for the scene of action, the desire to join them became stronger than ever."

137. See, for instance, Thome and Kimball, in whose opinion "no white lady of America could speak more disparagingly of the 'niggers' " than a coloured landlady of "good appearance and lady-like manner", whom they met in Morant Bay in 1837; she abused the apprentices and denounced emancipation. *Emancipation in the West Indies*, 377–78). Also Sturge and Harvey, *The West Indies*, 267.

138. Seacole, *Wonderful Adventures*, 2, 6.

139. Ibid., 4.

140. Ibid., 41–42, 45, 47–48, 52, 57–58, 79–80.

AFTERWORD

1. [Editors' note: This observation still remains valid, even though historians have found creative ways to gain access to Jamaican enslaved women's voices, mining the ventriloquized voices evident in historical novels and the first hand accounts of writers like Cynric Williams. See, for example, Bridget Brereton's "Text, Testimony and Gender: An Examination of Some Texts by Women on the English-Speaking Caribbean, from the 1770s to the 1920s", in *Engendering History: Caribbean Women in Historical Perspective,* ed. Verene A. Shepherd, Bridget Brereton and Barbara Bailey (Kingston: Ian Randle, 1995), and Verene A. Shepherd's "Gender and Representation in European Accounts of Pre-Emancipation Jamaica", in *Caribbean Slavery in the Atlantic World,* ed. Verene Shepherd and Hilary Beckles (Kingston: Ian Randle, 2000). The narrative of Mary Prince allows us a glimpse into the inner world of an enslaved woman in the British-colonized Caribbean, though the geographical location is not Jamaica.]

2. Seacole, *Wonderful Adventures.*

3. [Editors' note: For more recent historical data on Nanny, See Beverly Carey, *The Maroon Story: The Authentic and Original History of the Maroons in the History of Jamaica, 1490–1880* (Gordon Town, Jamaica: Agouti Press, 1997).]

4. See Patterson, *Sociology of Slavery,* and Brathwaite, *Development of Creole Society.*

5. Goveia, *Study on the Historiography.*

6. Goveia, *Slave Society.*

7. [Editors' note: This lecture was later published as Franklin Knight, "Slavery and the Transformation of Society in Cuba, 1511–1760", in *Slavery, Freedom and Gender: The Dynamics of Caribbean Society,* ed. Brian Moore, B.W. Higman, Carl Campbell and Patrick Bryan (Kingston: University of the West Indies Press, 2001).]

8. Lewis, *Journal of a West India Proprietor.* [Editors' note: For a more recent analysis of "petticoat rebellions", see Verene A. Shepherd. "Petticoat Rebellions?", in *In the Shadow of the Plantation: Caribbean History and Legacy,* ed. Alvin O. Thompson (Kingston: Ian Randle, 2002).]

9. Edward [Kamau] Brathwaite, *Wars of Respect: Nanny, Sam Sharpe and the Struggle for People's Liberation* (Kingston: Agency for Public Information for the National Heritage Week Committee, 1977).

10. Edward [Kamau] Brathwaite, *The Arrivants: A New World Trilogy* (London: Oxford University Press, 1973).

11. Edward [Kamau] Brathwaite, *Mother Poem* (London: Oxford University Press, 1977).

12. Lucille Mathurin Mair, "Caribbean Woman", *Savacou* 13 (1977).

13. Aptheker, *American Negro Slave Revolts.*

Author's Bibliography

PRIMARY SOURCES

Manuscript Sources

British Museum

Egerton MS 2134: Nutt's River Plantation Inventory of Slave Population.
King's MS 213: Journal of an Officer.
Sloane MS 2723: Letter to Mary Weekes from R. Powell, Port Royal, 1680.
Add. MSS 34181: Abstracts of Jamaican Wills, 1625–1792.
Add. MSS 12429: Mr Nevil, The Present State of Jamaica, 1677.
Add. MSS 30001: General Correspondence and Papers of Families of Ricketts and
    Jervis, 1726–1842.
Add. MSS 12436: Long Papers, List of Landholders in Jamaica, 1750.
Add. MSS 12435: Long Papers, Inventory of Sugar Estates in St James, 1774.
Add. MSS 18959: Long Papers, Misc.
Add. MSS 18961: Long Papers, Misc.
Add. MSS 51806: Holland House Papers; 1775 Richard Vassal's a/c with Miss Richards.
Add. MSS 51816: Holland House Papers, Correspondence.
Add. MSS 27970: James Henry Archer, MD. Accounts, drafts of letters, business and
    private memoranda, 1822–1845.
Add. MSS 27971: James Henry Archer, MD, Jamaica. Collections by son J.H. Lawrence
    Archer
Add. MSS 33293: Journal (1828–1846) of James Henry Archer, MD, of Spring Mount, St
    Ann.

Add. MSS 51818: Holland House Papers, Letters from Baynes, Dacres, Edward, Special
Magistrates, 1835–1840.
Add. MSS 51819: Holland House Papers, Misc.
Add. MSS 35506: Hardwicke Papers, Governor Keith's Correspondence.
Add. MSS 19049: Wakefield Plantation Inventory.

Church Missionary Society, London

Papers Relating to Jamaica 1820–1838.
CW/o 4/4.

Institute of Jamaica

MS T4: Henry Barham, Manuscript History of Jamaica, 1670.
MS 159: History and State of Jamaica under Lord Vaughan, 1679–1680, compiled for
William Blathwayt.
Taylor MS: *Multum in Parvo,* Present State of Jamaica, 1688.
MS 1069: Irwin and Tryall Estates, Mrs Bosley to Thomas Hall, 1760–1771.
MS 236: Green Park and Spring Vale Estate Book, 1790–1795.
Governess Annabella Smith: Letter, 13 June 1812.
Thomas Munro: Memo Book, 1810–1812.
MS T93: King Letters, 1812–1833.
MS 92: Seaford Town Record Book, 1836–1854.

Island Record Office, Spanish Town [now in Twickenham Park]

The Laws of Jamaica passed by the Assembly in 1683 and a Short Account of the Island.
MS Laws of Jamaica, vols. 4, 5.

Jamaica Government Archives, Spanish Town

Land Patents, Liber 1, 1661–62.
Land Patents, Liber 22, 1745.
Inventories, Liber 1, 1674.
Inventories, Liber 5, 1699–1701.
Inventories, Liber 14, 1726–28.
Inventories, Liber 39, 1759.
Inventories, Liber 44, 1764.
Inventories, Liber 46, 1766.
Inventories, Liber 53, 1772–73.
Inventories, Liber 95, 1803.

Inventories, Liber 100, 1803.
Kalender Book, 1793–1841.
CS 102/4.
CS 102/5.
CS 162/5.

Vestry Minutes and Other Parish Records

Hanover Slave Court, 1822–23.
Kingston, Parish Accounts, 1722–59.
Kingston, Vestry Minutes, 1769–70.
Kingston, Vestry Proceedings, 1781–88.
Kingston, Common Council Proceedings, 1803–15.
Kingston, Common Council Proceedings, 1820–28.
Manchester Vestry Minutes, 1816–24.
Manchester Vestry Minutes, 1840–43.
Montego Bay, Resident Magistrate's Court, Quarter Sessions
Port Royal Slave Trials, 1819–34.
St David Vestry Minutes, 1785–93.
St George General Slave Court, 1822–31.
St James Vestry Minutes, 1807–25.
St James Vestry Minutes, 1837–45.
St Thomas-in-the-Vale Vestry Minutes, 1789–1802.
Westmoreland Vestry Minutes, 1780–81.

London Missionary Society, London

Records Relating to Jamaica, 1830–38.

Moravian Church Archives, Malvern, Jamaica

Diary of Negro Congregation at Fairfield, 1829, 1835.
Diary of John Laing, 1805–19.
Minutes of Conference, Mesopotamia, 1798–1818.
Minutes of the Jamaican Missions Conference, 1821–26.
Minutes of the Jamaican Missions Conference, 1834–36
List of Marriages at Fairfield, 1829–40.
Marriage Register, 1829–40.
Carmel Marriage Register, 1840–77.

Public Record Office, London [now the UK National Archives]

C 107/143
C 107/156
C 109/338
C 110/141
CO 1/45
CO 137/85
CO 137/88
CO 137/91
CO 137/99
CO 137/109
CO 137/121
CO 137/147
CO 137/153
CO 137/208
CO 137/214
CO 137/215
CO 138/54

University of the West Indies Library

C 1692–1770. MS.
Ricketts Family Papers, 1758–1834.
William Salt Library MS (Microfilm Reel 421).
Cowper–McQueen MacKay Letters 1800–1816.
Papers relating to the Wilson Family (Broomhead, Yorkshire), *c.*1692–1770.

West India Committee, London

Dwarris, Sarah. Letters, written from Jamaica, 14 May 1781 to 9 November 1788.
West India Committee Minutes, 1769–1893.

Official Documents

Acts of Assembly passed in the Island of Jamaica, 1681–1754. St Jago de la Vega, 1769.
Acts of Assembly passed in the Island of Jamaica, 1770–1783. Kingston, 1786.
An Act to repeal several Acts and clauses of Acts respecting slaves and for the better order and government of slaves. St Jago de la Vega, 1788.
An Act for the Subsistence, Clothing and the Better Regulation and Government of Slaves . . . . Jamaica, 1817.

Calender of State Papers (Colonial, America and West Indies), 1574–1733.

Consolidated Slave Law, 1792. St Jago de la Vega.

Consolidated Slave Law, 22 December 1826 (2nd ed., 1827).

Journals of the Assembly of Jamaica, 1663–1826.

Laws of Jamaica 1681–1816. St Jago de la Vega.

Lunan, J. *An Abstract of the Laws of Jamaica relating to Slaves.* St Jago de la Vega, Jamaica: Printed at the Office of the Gazette, 1819.

Report of the Charity Commissioners to the House of Assembly, 1844.

The New Slave Laws of Jamaica and St Christopher's Examined. London: Society for the Mitigation and Gradual Abolition of Slavery, 1828.

Thurloe, John. *A Collection of the State Papers of John Thurloe, Containing Authentic Memorials of the English Affairs from the Year 1638, to the Restoration of King Charles II.* 7 vols. London: Printed for the Executor of F. Gyles, 1742.

Votes of the Assembly of Jamaica, 1804, 1814, 1822.

Parliamentary Accounts and Papers (Great Britain)

1789 XXIV (24)

1789 XXV (83)

1789 XXVI (84)

1790 XXIX

1810–11 II (409)

1814–15 VI

1816 XIX

1823 VII

1824 XXIV

1826–27 XXII

1826–27 XXIV

1831–32 XLVII

1831, Slave Population Papers

1832, Report of Committee of the House of Commons . . . on the Extinction of Slavery.

1832 (127), Report of the Committee of the House of Lords on the Extinction of Slavery.

1836 IV, Report of the Committee of the House of Commons on Negro Apprenticeship.

Negro Apprenticeship in the Colonies: A Review of the Report of the Select Committee of the House of Commons Appointed to inquire into the Workings of the Apprenticeship System. London: J. Hatchard and Son, 1837.

Summary of Census Returns, 6 May 1861.

Journals, Magazines, Periodicals, Registers

Pre-1900

Jamaica Courant (Kingston)
Jamaica Journal, 1818 (Kingston)
Jamaica Magazine (Kingston)
Royal Gazette (Kingston)
Moravian Periodical Accounts (London)
Jamaica Almanac (Kingston)
Gentleman's Magazine (London)

Post-1900

Agricultural History
Caribbean Quarterly
Daedalus
Economic History Review
English Historical Review
Genealogists' Magazine
Harvard Educational Review
Jamaica Journal
Jamaican Historical Review
Jamaica Historical Society Bulletin
Journal of African History
Journal of Caribbean History
Journal of the Historical Society of Nigeria
Journal of Negro History
New Beacon Review
La Porte Oceane
Political Science Quarterly
Population Studies
Savacou
Social and Economical Studies
Transactions of the Historical Society of Ghana
Transactions of the Royal Historical Society
William and Mary Quarterly

Books

Originally Published 1900 or Before

Account of a Shooting Excursion on the Mountains near Dromilly Estate in the parish of Trelawny and island of Jamaica, in the month of October 1824. London: Harvey and Darton, 1825.

Anon. *Hamel, The Obeah Man.* 2 vols. London: Hunt and Clarke, 1827.

———. *Marly: Or, a Planter's life in Jamaica.* Glasgow: Richard Griffin, 1828.

Barbot, Jean. *A Description of the Coasts of North and South Guinea.* London, 1724.

Barret, R. *A Reply to the Speech of Dr Lushington in the House of Commons on 12 June 1827, on the Condition of the Free Coloured People of Jamaica.* London, 1828.

Beckford, William. *Remarks upon the Situations of Negroes in Jamaica.* London, 1788.

Beeston, Sir William. *A Narrative of the Descent on Jamaica by the French, 1694.* St Jago de la Vega, 1800.

Bickell, Rev. Richard. *The West Indies As They Are; Or, A Real Picture of Slavery: But More Particularly as it Exists in the Island of Jamaica in Three Parts.* London: Printed for J. Hatchard and Son, 1825.

Blackstone, Sir William. *Commentaries on the Laws of England.* Oxford: Clarendon Press, 1765.

Bleby, H. *Death Struggles of Slavery.* London: Hamilton, Adams and Co., 1853.

Blome, Richard. *A Description of the Island of Jamaica.* London, 1672.

Bosman, William. *A New and Accurate Description of the Coast of Guinea, Divided into the Gold, the Slave, and the Ivory Coasts.* 1701; repr., London: Frank Cass, 1967.

Bridges, Rev. George Wilson. *Dreams of Dulocracy; or the Puritanical Obituary.* London: Whitmore and Fenn, 1824.

———. *Sermon Delivered in the Parish Church of St Ann, Jamaica, 4 November 1827.* N.d.

Candler, John. *Extracts from the Journal of Candler, John Whilst Travelling in Jamaica.* Part 1. London: Harvey and Darton, 1840.

Carleton, Mary. *News from Jamaica in a Letter from Port Royal Written by the German Princess to her Fellow Collegiates and Friends in New Gate.* London, 1671.

Carmichael, A.C. *Domestic Manners and Social Condition of the White, Coloured and Negro Population of the West Indies.* 2 vols. London: Whittaker, Treacher and Co., 1833.

Cooper, Thomas. *Facts Illustrative of the Condition of the Negro Slaves in Jamaica: With Notes and an Appendix.* London: J. Hatchard and Son, 1824.

Dallas, Robert C. *The History of the Maroons, from their Origin to the Establishment of their Chief Tribe at Sierra Leone, Including the Expedition to Cuba for the Purpose of Procuring Spanish Chasseurs and the State of the Island of Jamaica for the Last Ten*

Years with a Succinct History of the Island Previous to that Period. 2 vols. London: T.N. Longman and O. Rees, 1803.

Dancer, Thomas. *The Medical Assistant.* Kingston: Alexander Aikman, 1801.

De la Beche, H.T. *Notes on the Present Condition of the Negroes in Jamaica.* London: T. Cadell, 1825.

Duncan, Peter. *A Narrative of the Wesleyan Mission to Jamaica.* London: Partridge and Oakey, 1849.

Edwards, Bryan. *The History, Civil and Commercial, of the British Colonies in the West Indies.* 4 vols. London: J. Stockdale, 1807.

Equiano, Olaudah, or Gustavus Vassa (the African). *The Interesting Narrative of His Life, Written by Himself.* 1789; reprint, abbreviated and edited by Paul Edwards as *Equiano's Travels.* London: Heinemann Educational Books, 1967.

Esquemeling, John. *The Buccaneers of America: A True Account of the Most Remarkable Assaults.* 1678; reprint, London: Allen and Unwin, 1951.

Falconbridge, Anna. *Narrative of Two Voyages to the River Sierra Leone, during the Years 1791–1793.* Reprint, London: New Impression, Frank Cass, 1967.

Firth, Charles Harding, ed. *The Narrative of General Venables, With an Appendix of Papers Relating to the Expedition to the West Indies and the Conquest of Jamaica, 1654–1655.* London: Longman's, Green, and Co., 1900.

Gurney, Joseph. *A Winter in the West Indies.* London: J. Murray, 1840.

Hickeringill, Captain Edmund. *Jamaica Viewed: With all the Ports, Harbours, and their Several Soundings, Towns and Settlements Thereonto Belonging. Together, with the Nature of it's Climate, Fruitfulnesse of the Soile, and its Suitablenesse to English Complexions: With Several Other Collateral Observations and Reflexions upon the Island.* London: Printed for John Williams, 1661.

Hickey, William. *Memoirs 1749–1782.* Edited by Alfred Spencer. 10th ed. 4 vols. London: Hurst and Blackett, 1948.

Hill, Richard. *Eight Chapters in the History of Jamaica from AD 1508 to AD 1680, Illustrating the Settlement of the Jews in the Island.* Kingston: M. DeCordova, McDougall and Co., 1868.

Hutchins, Mary A. *The Youthful Female Missionary. A Memoir of Mary Ann Hutchins Wife of the Rev. John Hutchins, Baptist Missionary, Savanna-la-mar, Jamaica.* 2nd ed. London: G. Nightman, 1840.

Jones, Rev. William. *The Diary of the Rev. William Jones, 1777–1821.* Edited by O.F. Christie. London: Bretano's, 1929.

Kelly, James. *Voyage to Jamaica and Seventeen Years Residence in that Island.* Belfast: Printed by J. Wilson, 1838.

Kenny, Courtney. *The History of the Law of England as to the Effects of Marriage on Property and of the Wife's Legal Capacity.* London: Reeves and Turner, 1879.

Lefroy, Major-General, J.H. *Memorials of the Discovery and Early Settlement of the*

Bermudas or Somers Islands 1515–1685. 2 vols. London: Longman's, Green and Co., 1877–79.

Leslie, Charles. *A New History of Jamaica, from the Earliest Accounts, to the Taking of Porto Bello by Vice–Admiral Vernon.* London: Printed for J. Hodges 1740.

Lewis, Matthew Gregory. *Journal of a West India Proprietor Kept during a Residence in the Island of Jamaica.* London: J. Murray, 1834; reprint, edited with introduction and notes by Judith Terry, Oxford: Oxford University Press, 1999.

Ligon, Richard. *A True and Exact History of the Island of Barbadoes.* 1673; reprint, London: Frank Cass, 1970.

Littleton, Edward. *The Groans of the Plantations: or, A True Account of their Grievous and Extreme Sufferings by the Heavy Impositions upon Sugar, and other Hardships.* London: Printed by M. Clark, 1689.

Long, Edward. *The History of Jamaica; or, General Survey of the Ancient and Modern State of that Island: With Reflections on its Situations, Settlements, Inhabitants, Climate, Products, Commerce, Laws, and Government.* 3 vols. 1774; reprint, London: Frank Cass, 1970.

Lynch, Mrs Henry. *Years Ago: A Tale of West Indian Life of the Eighteenth Century.* London: Jarrold and Sons, 1865.

McMahon, Benjamin. *Jamaica Plantership.* London, 1839.

McNeill, Hector. *Observations on the Treatment of the Negroes in the Island of Jamaica.* London: Printed for G.G.J. and J. Robinson, 1788.

Marsden, P. *An Account of the Island of Jamaica.* Newcastle: Printed for the author by S. Hodgson, 1788.

Martin, R.M. *Statistics of the Colonies of the British Empire.* London: W.H. Allen and Co., 1839.

Moreton, J.B. *Manners and Customs in the West India Islands Containing Various Particulars Respecting the Soil, Cultivation, Produce, Trade, Officers, Inhabitants, &c., &c. With the Method of Establishing and Conducting a Sugar-Plantation; in which the Ill-practices of Superintendents are Pointed Out. Also the Treatment of Slaves; and the Slave-trade.* London: W. Richardson, 1790.

Normanby, Maria. *Extracts of Letters from Maria, Marchioness of Normanby,* edited by Georgiana Bloomfield. Hertfordshire, 1892.

Nugent, Maria. *A Journal of a Voyage to and Residence in the Island of Jamaica.* 1839. Revised edition, edited by Philip Wright, Kingston: Institute of Jamaica, 1966.

Phillippo, James M. *Jamaica: Its Past and Present State.* London: John Snow, 1843.

Quier, J., et al. *Letters and Essays on the Small-Pox and Inculcation, the Measles, the Dry Belly-Ache, the Yellow, and Remitting, and Intermitting Fevers of the West Indies.* London: Printed for J. Murray, 1778.

Renny, Robert. *A History of Jamaica: With Observations on the Climate, Scenery, Trade, Productions, Negroes, Slave Trade, Diseases of Europeans, Customs, Manners, and*

Dispositions of the Inhabitants: to which is Added, an Illustration of the Advantages Which are Likely to Result from the Abolition of the Slave Trade. London: Printed for J. Cawthorn, 1807.

Riland, Rev. John. *Memoirs of a West India Planter.* London: Hamilton, Adams, 1827.

Roughley, Thomas. *The Jamaica Planter's Guide; or, A System for Planting and Managing a Sugar Estate, or Other Plantations in that Island, and Throughout the British West Indies in General.* London: Printed for Longman, Hurst, Rees, Orme and Brown, 1823.

Seacole, Mary. *Wonderful Adventures of Mrs Seacole in Many Lands.* London: J. Blackwood, 1855.

Senior, Bernard, M. *Jamaica, As It Was, As It Is, and As It May Be, by a Retired Military Officer.* 1835; reprint, New York: Negro Universities Press, 1969.

Sligo, Marquess. *A Letter to the Marquess of Normanby Relative to the Present State of Jamaica.* London: J. Andrews, 1839.

Sloane, Sir Hans. *A Voyage to the Islands Madera, Barbados, Nieves, S. Christophers and Jamaica, with the Natural History of the Herbs and Trees, Four-footed Beasts, Fishes, Birds, Insects, Reptiles, &c. of the Last of those Islands; to which is Prefix'd an Introduction, Wherein is an Account of the Inhabitants, Air, Waters, Diseases, Trade, &c. of that Place, with some Relations Concerning the Neighbouring Continent, and Islands of America.* 2 vols. London: Printed by B.M. for the author, 1707.

Stewart, James. *An Account of Jamaica and Its Inhabitants by a Gentleman.* London: Printed for Longman, Hurst, Rees and Orme, 1808.

———. *A View of the Past and Present State of the Island of Jamaica.* 1823; reprint, New York: Negro Universities Press, 1969.

Sturge, Joseph, and Thomas Harvey. *The West Indies in 1837: Being the Journal of a Visit to Antigua, Monserrat, Dominica, St Lucia, Barbadoes, and Jamaica; Undertaken for the Purpose of Ascertaining the Actual Condition of the Negro Population of those Islands.* London: Hamilton, Adams and Co., 1838.

Thicknesse, Philip. *Memoirs and Anecdotes of Philip Thicknesse: Late Lieutenant Governor of Land Guard Fort.* 3 vols. London: The author, 1788.

Thome, James A., and Joseph H. Kimball. *Emancipation in the West Indies: A Six Months' Tour in Antigua, Barbados, and Jamaica, in the Year 1837.* New York: American Anti-Slavery Society, 1838.

Trapham, Thomas. *A Discourse of the State of Health in the Island of Jamaica.* London: R. Boulter, 1679.

Waddell, Rev. Hope. *Twenty-Nine Years in the West Indies and Central Africa.* London: T. Nelson and Sons, 1863.

Whiteley, Henry. *Three Months in Jamaica in 1832, Comprising a Residence of Seven Weeks on a Sugar Plantation.* London: Printed for the Anti-Slavery Society, 1832.

Williams, Cynric. *A Tour Through the Island of Jamaica, From the Western to the Eastern*

End, in the Year 1823. 2nd edition. London: T. Hurst, E. Chance and Co., 1827.

Williamson, John. *Medical and Miscellaneous Observations Relative to the West India Islands.* 2 vols. Edinburgh: Printed by A. Smellie for the author, 1817.

Published after 1900

Akinjogbin, I.A. *Dahomey and Its Neighbours, 1708–1818.* Cambridge: Cambridge University Press, 1967.

Andrews, Charles M. *The Colonial Period of American History.* New Haven: Yale University Press, 1937.

Aptheker, Herbert. *American Negro Slave Revolts.* New York: International Publishers, 1963.

Black, Clinton V. *Living Names in Jamaica's History.* Kingston: Jamaica Welfare, 1946.

Bohannan, Paul. *African Outline.* Harmondsworth: Penguin, 1966.

Brathwaite, Edward [Kamau]. *The Arrivants: A New World Trilogy.* London: Oxford University Press, 1973.

———. *The Development of Creole Society in Jamaica 1770–1820.* Oxford: Clarendon Press, Oxford, 1971.

Burn, William, L. *Emancipation and Apprenticeship in the British West Indies.* London: Jonathan Cape, 1937.

Burns, Alan. *History of the British West Indies.* London: Allen and Unwin, 1954.

Calhoun, Arthur W. *A Social History of the American Family from Colonial Times to the Present.* New York: Barnes and Noble, 1945.

Carey, Beverly. *The Maroon Story: The Authentic and Original History of the Maroons in the History of Jamaica, 1490–1880.* Gordon Town, Jamaica: Agouti Press, 1997.

Craton, Michael, and James Walvin. *A Jamaican Plantation: The History of Worthy Park 1670–1970.* London: W.H. Allen, 1970.

Cundall, Frank. *The Governors of Jamaica in the Seventeenth Century.* London: The West India Committee, 1936.

Cundall, Frank, and Joseph Pietersz. *Jamaica under the Spaniards, Abstracted from the Archives of Seville.* Kingston: Institute of Jamaica, 1919.

Curtin, Philip. *The Atlantic Slave Trade: A Census.* Madison: University of Wisconsin Press, 1969.

———. *The Image of Africa: British Ideas and Actions, 1780–1850.* Madison: University of Wisconsin Press, 1964.

———. *Two Jamaicas: The Role of Ideas in a Tropical Country, 1830–1865.* Cambridge, Mass.: Harvard University Press, 1955.

———, ed. *Africa Remembered: Narratives by West Africans from the era of the Slave Trade.* Madison: University of Wisconsin Press, 1967.

Davidson, Basil. *Africa in History: Themes and Outlines.* New York: Macmillan, 1969.

———. *Black Mother.* London: Gollancz, 1968.

Davies, Kenneth. *The Royal African Company.* London: Longman's, Green and Co., 1957.

Dike, Kenneth Onwaka. *Trade and Politics in the Niger Delta, 1830–1885: An Introduction to the Economic and Political History of Nigeria.* Oxford: Clarendon Press, 1962.

Donnan, Elizabeth. *Documents Illustrative of the History of the Slave Trade to America.* Washington, DC: Carnegie Institution of Washington, 1930.

Duffy, James. *Portugal in Africa.* Harmondworth: Penguin, 1962.

———. *Portuguese Africa.* Cambridge, Mass.: Harvard University Press, 1959.

Dunn, Richard. *Sugar and Slaves: The Rise of the Planter Class in the English West Indies 1624–1713.* Chapel Hill: University of North Carolina Press for the Institute of Early American History and Culture at Williamsburg, 1972.

Eisner, Gisela. *Jamaica 1830–1930: A Study in Economic Growth.* Manchester: Manchester University Press, 1961.

Evans-Pritchard, E.E. "Position of Women in Primitive Societies and in Our Own". The Fawcett Lecture, 1955–56. Published as *The Position of Women in Primitive Societies and Other Essays in Social Anthropology.* London: Faber and Faber, 1965.

Firth, C.H. *Cromwell's Army, A History of the English Soldier during the Civil Wars, the Commonwealth and the Protectorate.* 4th ed. London: Methuen, 1962.

Fortes, Meyer. *Oedipus and Job in West African Religion.* Cambridge: Cambridge University Press, 1959.

Fortes, M., and G. Dieterlen, eds. *African Systems of Thought: Studies Presented and Discussed at the Third International African Seminar in Salisbury, December 1960.* Oxford: Oxford University Press, 1965.

Fox, Robin. *Kinship and Marriage: An Anthropological Perspective.* New York: Penguin, 1967.

Genovese, Eugene. *The Political Economy of Slavery: Studies in the Economy and Society of the Slave South.* New York: Pantheon, 1965.

Glass, David V., and D.E.C. Eversley. *Population in History: Essays in Historical Demography.* London: Edward Arnold, 1965.

Gluckman, Max. *Custom and Conflict in Africa.* Blackwell: Oxford, 1959.

Goveia, Elsa. *Slave Society in the British Leeward Islands at the End of the Eighteenth Century.* New Haven: Yale University Press, 1965.

———. *A Study on the Historiography of British West Indies to the End of the Nineteenth Century.* Mexico: Instituto Panamericano de Geografía e Historia, 1956.

———. *The West Indian Slave Laws of the Eighteenth Century.* Chapters in Caribbean History. Bridgetown: Caribbean Universities Press, 1970.

Hall, Douglas. *Free Jamaica, 1835–1865: An Economic History.* New Haven: Yale University Press, 1959.

Harlow, Vincent. *A History of Barbados, 1625–1685.* Oxford: Clarendon Press, 1926.

Harlow, Vincent, and F. Madden. *British Colonial Developments, 1774–1834: Selected Documents.* Oxford: Clarendon Press, 1953.

Herskovits, Melville. *Dahomey, an Ancient West African Kingdom.* 2 vols. Evanston: Northwestern University Press, 1967.

Higham, Charles S. *The Development of the Leeward Islands under the Restoration 1660–1688.* Cambridge: Cambridge University Press, 1921.

Hopkins, Anthony G. *An Economic History of West Africa.* London: Longman, 1973.

Howard, Robert M., ed. *Records and Letters of the Family of the Longs of Longville, Jamaica, and Hampton Lodge, Surrey.* 2 vols. London: Simpkin, Marshall, Hamilton, Kent, 1925.

Jordan, Winthrop. *White over Black: American Attitudes Toward the Negro, 1550–1812.* Chapel Hill: University of North Carolina Press, 1968.

Le Page Robert B., and David De Capp. *Jamaican Creole: An Historical Introduction to Jamaican Creole.* London: Macmillan, 1960.

Little, Kenneth. *The Mende of Sierra Leone: A West African People in Transition.* London: Routledge and Kegan Paul, 1967.

Long, Anton. *Jamaica and the New Order, 1827–1847.* Kingston: Institute of Social and Economic Research, special series no. 1, 1956.

Lorimer, Frank. *Culture and Human Fertility: A Study of the Relation of Cultural Conditions to Fertility in Non-Industrial and Transitional Societies.* Paris: UNESCO, 1954.

Lucas, C.P. *A Historical Geography of the British Colonies.* 5 vols. Oxford: Clarendon Press, 1905.

Mackenzie-Grieve, A. *The Great Accomplishment: The Contribution of Five English Women to Eighteenth Century Colonisation.* London: Bles, 1953.

Manoukian, Madeline. *The Ewe Speaking People of Togoland and the Gold Coast.* London: International African Institute, 1952.

Marks, Jeannette. *The Family of the Barretts, A Colonial Romance.* New York: Macmillan, 1938.

Mathieson, William. *British Slavery and Its Abolition.* London: Longmans, Green and Co., 1926.

Metcalf, George. *Royal Government and Political Conflict in Jamaica 1729–1783.* Royal Commonwealth Society Imperial Studies no. 27. London: Longman's, 1965.

Mintz, Sidney, and Douglas Hall. *The Origins of the Jamaican Internal Marketing System.* Yale University Publications in Anthropology, no. 7. New Haven: Department of Anthropology, Yale University, 1960.

Mozley, Geraldine, ed. *Letters to Jane from Jamaica 1788–1796.* London: Published for the Institute of Jamaica by the West India Committee, 1938.

Newton, Arthur P. *The Colonizing Activities of the English Puritans: The Last Phase of the Elizabethan Struggle with Spain.* New Haven: Yale University Press, 1914.

Oliver, Vere Langford, ed. *Caribbeana: Being Miscellaneous Papers Relating to the History, Genealogy, Topography, and Antiquities of the British West Indies.* 6 vols. Oxford and London: Mitchell Hughes and Clarke, 1910–21.

Pares, Richard. *Merchants and Planters.* Economic History Review, supplement 4. Cambridge: Published for the Cambridge University Press, 1960.

Parry, J.H., and Phillip Sherlock. *A Short History of the West Indies.* London: Macmillan, 1960.

Patterson, Orlando. *The Sociology of Slavery: An Analysis of the Origins, Development and Structure of Negro Slavery in Jamaica.* London: MacGibbon and Kee, 1967.

Pitman, Frank, W. *The Development of the British West Indies, 1700–1763.* New Haven: Yale University Press, 1917; reissue: London: Frank Cass, 1967.

Rattray, Robert, S. *Ashanti.* 1923; reprint, Oxford: Clarendon Press, 1955.

———. *The Tribes of the Ashanti Hinterland.* 2 vols. Oxford: Clarendon Press, 1932.

Roberts, George W. *The Population of Jamaica.* Cambridge: Cambridge University Press for the Conservation Foundation, 1957.

Rodney, Walter. *A History of the Upper Guinea Coast 1545–1800.* Oxford: Clarendon Press, 1970.

———. *How Europe Underdeveloped Africa.* London: Bogle L'Ouverture Publications, 1972.

Roth, Ling H. *Great Benin: Its Customs, Art and Horrors.* 1903; reprint, London: Routledge and Kegan Paul, 1968.

Ryder, Alan F.C. *Benin and the Europeans, 1485–1897.* Harlow: Longman's, 1969.

Sheridan, Richard. *The Development of the Plantations to 1750: An Era of West Indian Prosperity, 1750–1775.* Chapters in Caribbean History. Barbados: Caribbean Universities Press, 1970.

Shore, Joseph. *In Old St James, Jamaica, A Book of Parish Chronicles.* 1911; reprint, Kingston: Sangster's Book Stores, 1970.

Smith, Abbot E. *Colonists in Bondage: White Servitude and Convict Labour in America 1607–1776.* Chapel Hill: University of North Carolina Press, 1947.

Smith, Mary. *Baba of Karo, A Woman of the Muslim Hausa,* with an introduction and notes by M.G. Smith. London: Faber and Faber, 1954.

Spruill, J.C. *Women's Life and Work in the Southern Colonies.* Chapel Hill: University of North Carolina Press, 1938; reprint, New York: Russell and Russell, 1969.

Spurdle, Frederick G. *Early West Indian Government, Showing the Progress of Government in Barbados, Jamaica and the Leeward Islands, 1760–1783.* Palmerston North, New Zealand: The author, 1962.

Taylor, Stanley A.G. *The Western Design.* Kingston: The Institute of Jamaica Historical Society, 1965.

Thornton, Archibald P. *West India Policy under the Restoration.* Oxford: Clarendon Press, 1956.

Vansina, Jan., R. Mauny and L. V Thomas, eds. *The Historian in Tropical Africa*. London: Oxford University Press for the International African Institute, 1964.

Williams, Eric, ed. *The British West Indies at Westminster, Part 1: 1789–1823: Extract from the Debates in Parliament*. Port of Spain: Government Printing Office, 1954.

———. *Documents on British West Indian History, 1807–1833*. Port of Spain: Historical Society of Trinidad and Tobago, 1952.

Williams, Joseph J. *The Maroons of Jamaica*. Anthropological Series of the Boston College Graduate School, vol. 3, no. 4. Chestnut Hill, Mass.: Boston College Press, 1938.

———. *Whence the "Black Irish" of Jamaica?* New York: L. MacVeagh, Dial Press, 1932.

Williams, J.A. *The Caribbean Islands under the Proprietary Patents*. Oxford: Oxford University Press, 1926.

Williamson, James A. *The Caribbean Islands under the Proprietary Patents*. London: Oxford University Press, 1926.

Wright, Irene, ed. *The English Conquest of Jamaica; an account of what happened in the Island of Jamaica, from May 20 of the year 1655, When the English Laid Siege to it up to July 3 of the year 1656, by Captain Julian de Castilla*. Camden Miscellany, vol. 13. London: Offices of the Royal Historical Society, 1924.

Wright, Philip. *Monumental Inscriptions of Jamaica*. London: Society of Genealogists, 1966.

Wyndham, Hugh A. *The Atlantic and Slavery: A Report in the Study Group Series of the Royal Institute of International Affairs*. Oxford: Oxford University Press, 1935.

Articles

Alagoa, Ebiegreri, Joe. "Oral Tradition among the Ijo of the Niger Delta". *Journal of African History* 3 (1966).

Bennett, J. Harry. "Cary Helyar, Merchant and Planter of Seventeenth Century Jamaica". *William and Mary Quarterly*, 3rd ser., 21 (January 1964).

Birmingham, David. "Speculations on the Kingdom of Kongo". *Transactions of the Historical Society of Ghana* 8 (1965).

Brathwaite, Edward [Kamau]. "The African Presence in Caribbean Literature". *Daedalus* (Spring 1974).

Buisseret, David. "Edward D'Oyley". *Jamaica Journal* 5, no. 1 (March 1971): 6–10.

———. "Port Royal 1655–1755". *Jamaican Historical Review* 6, nos. 1 and 2 (1966).

Cadbury, H.J. "Conditions in Jamaica in 1687". *Jamaican Historical Review* 3, no. 2 (March 1959).

Campbell, Carl. "Social and Economic Obstacles to the Development of Popular Education in Post-Emancipation Jamaica, 1834–1865". *Journal of Caribbean History* 1 (November 1970).

Carey, Beverley. "The Windward Maroons after the Peace Treaty". *Jamaica Journal* 4, no. 4 (December 1970).

Clay, Christopher. "Marriage, Inheritance, and the Rise of Large Estates in England 1660–1815". *Economic History Review,* 2nd ser., no. 21 (1968).

Curtin, Philip D. "Epidemiology and the Slave Trade". *Political Science Quarterly* 83 (1968).

Daaku, K.Y. "The European Traders and the Coastal States 1630–1720". *Transactions of the Historical Society of Ghana* 8 (1965).

Debien, Gabriel. "Les Femmes des Premiers Colons Dux Antilles, 1635–1680". *Extrait de la Revue La Porte Oceane,* nos. 89 et 90 (November–December 1952).

Dieterlen, G. "African Systems of Thought". In *African Systems of Thought: Studies Presented and Discussed at the Third International African Seminar in Salisbury, December 1960,* edited by M. Fortes and G. Dieterlen. Oxford: Oxford University Press, 1965.

Dorjahn, V.R., and Christopher Fyfe. "Landlord and Stranger; Change in Tenancy Relations in Sierra Leone". *Journal of African History* 3, no. 3 (1962).

Dunn, Richard S. "The Barbados Census of 1680: Profile of the Richest Colony in English America". *William and Mary Quarterly,* 3rd ser., 26, no. 1 (January 1969).

Fortes, Meyer. "A Demographic Field Study in Ashanti". In *Culture and Human Fertility: A Study of the Relation of Cultural Conditions to Fertility in Non-Industrial and Transitional Societies,* edited by Frank Lorimer, 253–320. Paris: UNESCO, 1954.

———. "Some Reflections on Ancestor Worship in Africa". *In African Systems of Thought: Studies Presented and Discussed at the Third International African Seminar in Salisbury, December 1960,* edited by M. Fortes and G. Dieterlen. Oxford: Oxford University Press, 1965.

Furness, A.E. "The Jamaican Coffee Boom and John Mackeson, a Blue Mountain Coffee Planter 1807–1819". *Jamaican Historical Review* 3, no. 3 (March 1962).

———. "The Maroon War of 1795". *Jamaican Historical Review* 5 (November 1965).

Greene, J.C. "The American Debate on the Negro's Place in Nature". *Journal of the History of Ideas* 15 (1954).

Greven, Philip. "Family Structure in Seventeenth-Century Andover, Massachusetts". *William and Mary Quarterly,* 3rd ser., 23, no. 2 (April 1966): 234–56.

Habakkuk, H.J. "Marriage Settlements in the Eighteenth Century". *Transactions of the Royal Historical Society,* 4th ser., 32 (1950): 15–30.

Hall, Douglas. "Absentee Proprietorship in the British West Indies to about 1850". *Jamaican Historical Review* 4 (1964).

———. "The Apprenticeship Period in Jamaica 1834–1838". *Caribbean Quarterly* 3, no. 3 (December 1953).

———. "Incalculability as a Feature of Sugar Production during the Eighteenth Century". *Social and Economic Studies,* no. 10 (1961).

———. "Slaves and Slavery in the British West Indies". *Social and Economic Studies* 2, no. 4 (December 1962).

Hargreaves, J.D. "Assimilation in Eighteenth Century Senegal". *Journal of African History* 6 (1965).

Hurwitz, Samuel J., and F. Edith. "A Token of Freedom: Private Bill Legislation for Free Negroes in Eighteenth Century Jamaica". *William and Mary Quarterly,* 3rd ser., 24, no. 3 (July 1967).

Ingram, Kenneth E. "The West Indian Trade of an English Furniture Firm in the Eighteenth Century". *Jamaican Historical Review* 3, no. 3 (March 1962).

Jacobs, H.P. "Port Royal in Decline". *Jamaican Historical Review* 3 (1971).

———. "The Spanish Period of Jamaican History". *Jamaican Historical Review* 3, no. 1 (March 1957).

Jones, G.I. "Time and Oral Tradition with Special Reference to Eastern Nigeria". *Journal of African History* 6, no. 2 (1965): 153–60.

Jordan, Winthrop D. "American Chiaroscuro: The Status and Definition of Mulattoes in the British Colonies". *William and Mary Quarterly,* 3rd ser., 19 (1962).

Laslett, Peter. "Size and Structure of the Household in England over Three Centuries". *Population Studies* 23, no. 2 (July 1969).

Lewin, Olive. "The Role of Women in Jamaican Folk Music". *Savacou,* no. 10 (1974).

Lewis, Leslie. "English Commemorative Sculpture in Jamaica". *Jamaican Historical Review* 9 (1972).

Look Lai, Walton. "The Road to Thornfield Hall: An Analysis of Jean Rhys' Novel, *Wide Sargasso Sea*". *New Beacon Reviews* (1968).

McCloy, Shelby. "Negroes and Mulattoes in Eighteenth Century France". *Journal of Negro History* 30, no. 3 (July 1945).

Mahoney, F. "Notes on Mulattoes of the Gambia before the Mid-Nineteenth Century". *Transactions of the Historical Society of Ghana* 8 (1965).

Mathewson, Duncan. "Jamaican Ceramics: An Introduction to Eighteenth-Century Folk Pottery in West African Tradition". *Jamaica Journal* 6, no. 2 (June 1972).

Parry, J.H. "Salt Fish and Ackee". *Caribbean Quarterly* 2, no. 4 (1951).

Patterson, Orlando. "Rethinking Black History". *Harvard Education Review* 41, no. 3 (August 1971).

———. "Slavery and Slave Revolts: A Socio-Historical Analysis of the First Maroon War, 1655–1740". *Social and Economic Studies* 19, no. 3 (September 1970).

Pawson, Michael. "The First Civil Council of Jamaica". *The Jamaican Historical Society Bulletin* 5, no. 5 (March 1970).

Penson, Lilian. "The London West India Interest in the Eighteenth Century". *English Historical Review* 36 (1921).

Pietersz, J.J., and H.P. Jacobs. "Two Spanish Documents of 1656 Translated and Edited by J.J. Pietersz and H.P. Jacobs, with a Commentary by S.A.G. Taylor". *Jamaican Historical Review* 2, no. 2 (October 1952).

Ragatz, Lowell, J. "Absentee Landlordism in the British Caribbean, 1750–1833". *Agricultural History* 5, no. 1 (January 1931).

Reckord, Mary. "The Slave Rebellion of 1831". *Jamaica Journal* 3, no. 2 (June 1969).

Robertson, Glory. "The Rose Hall Legend". *Jamaica Journal,* no. 1 (December 1968).

Rodney, Walter. "Jihad and Special Revolution in Futa Kjalon the Eighteenth Century". *Journal of the Historical Society of Nigeria* 4, no. 2 (June 1968).

———. "Upper Guinea and the Significance of the Origins of African Enslavement in the New World". *Journal of Negro History* 54, no. 4 (October 1969).

Rothman, David. "A Note on the Study of the Colonial Family". *William and Mary Quarterly,* 3rd ser., 23, no. 4 (1966).

Schuler, Monica. "Akan Slave Rebellions in the British Caribbean". *Savacou* 1, no. 1 (June 1970).

Seaga, Edward. "Cults in Jamaica". *Jamaica Journal* 3, no. 2 (June 1969).

Smith, M.G. "The Beginnings of Hausa Society AD 1000–1500". In *The Historian in Tropical Africa: Studies Presented and Discussed,* edited by J. Vansina, R. Mauny and L.V. Thomas. London: Oxford University Press for the International African Institute, 1964.

Smith, R.W. "The Legal Status of Jamaican Slaves before the Anti-Slavery Movement". *Journal of Negro History* 30 (July 1945).

Sheridan, Richard. "The Career of William Beckford of Jamaica and England 1744–1799". *Jamaican Historical Review* 4 (1964).

———. "The Rise of a Colonial Gentry, Case Study of Antigua, 1730–1735". *Economic History Review,* no. 13 (1960–61).

Sypher, Wylie. "The West Indian as a 'Character' in the Eighteenth Century", *Studies in Philology* 36 (1939): 503–20.

Thomas, Keith. "The Double Standard". *Journal of the History of Ideas,* no. 20 (1959).

Thompson, F.M.L. "The Social Distribution of Landed Properties in England since the Sixteenth Century". *Economic History Review,* 2nd ser., 19, no. 3 (1966).

Thompson, R.W. "Vasquez de Espinosa and Jamaica". *Jamaican Historical Review* 3, no. 2 (March 1959).

Thornton, A.P. "The English at Compeachy, 1670–1672". *Jamaica Historical Review* 2, no. 3 (December 1953).

———. "The Modyfords and Morgan". *Jamaican Historical Review* 2, no. 2 (October, 1952).

Wright, Irene. "The Spanish Resistance to the English Occupation of Jamaica, 1655–1660". *Transaction of the Royal Historical Society,* 4th ser., 13 (1930).

Wright, Philip. "Materials for Family History in Jamaica". *The Genealogists' Magazine* 15, no. 7 (September, 1966).

Wynter, Sylvia. "Bernardo de Balbueno, Epic Poet and Abbot of Jamaica, 1562–1627". *Jamaica Journal* 3, no. 3 (December 1969): 3–12.

Yates, G. "The Spencer Tombstone at Lacovia". *Jamaican Historical Society Bulletin* 4, no. 1 (March 1965).

Yates, G., and J. Belfield. "A Port Royal Merchant". *Jamaican Historical Society Bulletin* 3, no. 15 (September 1964).

Young, J.G. "The Beginnings of Civil Government in Jamaica". *Jamaican Historical Review* 1, no. 1 (June 1945): 49–53.

———. "Nicholas Lyssons and His Family". *Jamaican Historical Review*, no. 2 (December 1940).

Zanden, James. "The Ideology of White Supremacy". *Journal of the History of Ideas*, no. 20 (1959).

Supporting Works

Baxter, Ivy. *The Arts of an Island: The Development of the Culture and of the Folk and Creative Arts in Jamaica, 1494–1962*. Metuchen, NJ: Scarecrow Press, 1970.

Beard, Mary. *Woman as Force in History.* New York: Collier Books, 1946.

Beckwith, Martha. *Black Roadways: A Study of Jamaican Folk Life.* University of North Carolina Press, 1929; reprint, New York: Negro Universities Press, 1969.

Boxer, C.R. *Race Relations in the Portuguese Colonial Empire, 1415–1825.* Oxford: Clarendon Press, 1963.

Brathwaite, Edward [Kamau]. *Caribbean Man in Space and Time.* Kingston: Savacou Publications, 1974.

———. *Rights of Passage.* London: Oxford University Press, 1967.

Cade, Toni, ed. *The Black Woman: An Anthology.* New York: New American Library, 1970.

Crow, Duncan. *The Victorian Woman.* London: Allen and Unwin, 1971.

Davis, David Brion. *The Problem of Slavery in Western Culture.* Ithaca: Cornell University Press, 1969.

Deerr, Noël. *The History of Sugar.* 2 vols. London: Chapman and Hall, 1950.

Elkins, Stanley. *Slavery: A Problem in American Institutional and Intellectual Life.* Chicago: University of Chicago Press, 1959.

Forten, Charlotte. *Journal of a Free Negro in the Slave Era,* edited by R.A. Billington. New York: Collier Books, 1961.

Freyre, Gilberto. *The Masters and the Slaves: A Study in the Development of Brazillian Civilization.* Translated by Samuel Putnam. 1933; New York: A.A. Knopf, 1946.

———. *The Portuguese and the Tropics: Suggestions Inspired by the Portuguese Methods of Integrating Autocthonous Peoples and Cultures Differing from the European in a New, or Luso-Tropical, Complex of Civilisation.* Translated by Helen M.D'O. Matthew and F. de Mello Moser. Lisbon: Executive Committee for the Commemoration of the Fifth Centenary of the Death of Prince Henry the Navigator, 1961.

Fulford, Roger. *Votes for Women.* London: Faber and Faber, 1958.

Genovese, Eugene. *The World the Slaveholders Made: Two Essays in Interpretation.* London: Allen and Unwin, 1970.

International Institute of Differing Civilisations (INCIDI). *Report of Third Meeting in Brussels, September 1958, on Women's Role in the Development of Tropical and Sub-Tropical Countries.* Brussels: INCIDI, 1959.

Iremonger, Lucille. *Yes, My Darling Daughter.* London: Secker and Warburg, 1964.

Jekyll, Walter. *Jamaican Song and Story: Annancy Stories, Digging Songs, Ring Tunes, and Dancing Tunes.* London: Published for the Folklore Society by D. Nutt, 1907; reprint, New York: Dover, 1966.

Jellett, Henry. *The Causes and Prevention of Maternal Mortality.* London: J. and A. Churchill, 1929.

Laye, Camara. *The African Child.* 1954; 9th impression, London: Collins, 1975.

Lewis, Gordon. *The Growth of the Modern West Indies.* London: MacGibbon and Kee, 1968.

Little, Kenneth. *African Women in Towns.* Cambridge: Cambridge University Press, 1973.

Lorimar, Kenneth. *Culture and Human Fertility.* Paris: UNESCO, 1954.

Montejo, Esteban. *The Autobiography of a Runaway Slave.* 1908; reprint, London: The Bodley Head, 1968.

Mullin, Gerald. *Flight and Rebellion: Slave Resistance in Eighteenth-Century Virginia.* New York: Oxford University Press, 1972.

Oliver, Roland, and Anthony Atmore. *Africa Since 1800.* Cambridge: Cambridge University Press, 1969.

Olivier, Lord Sydney. *The Myth of Governor Eyre.* London: L. and Virginia Woolf, 1933.

Patterson, Orlando. *Die the Long Day.* New York: William Morrow, 1972.

Phillips, Ulrich. *Life and Labour in the Old South.* Boston: Little, Brown, 1929.

———. *The Slave Economy of the Old South: Selected Essays in Economic and Social History,* edited by Eugene Genovese. Baton Rouge: Louisiana State University Press, 1968.

Prince Gardener, Nancy. *A Narrative of the Life and Travels of Mrs Nancy Prince.* Boston: The author, 1853.

Rhys, Jean. *Wide Sargasso Sea.* London: André Deutch, 1966.

Rowbotham, Sheila. *Hidden from History: Rediscovering Women in History from the Seventeenth Century to the Present.* New York: Pantheon, 1974.

———. *Women, Resistance and Revolution.* Harmondsworth: Penguin, 1974.

Sinclair, Andrew. *The Better Half: The Emancipation of the American Woman.* New York: Harper and Row, 1965.

Tannenbaum, F. *Slave and Citizen: The Negro in the Americas.* New York: Alfred Knopf, 1946.

West, Richard. *Back to Africa: A History of Sierra Leone and Liberia.* London: Jonathan Cape, 1970.

Williams, Eric. *Capitalism and Slavery.* Chapel Hill: University of North Carolina Press, 1944.

Woodham-Smith, Cecil. *Florence Nightingale 1820–1910.* London: Constable, 1950.

Theses and Unpublished Papers

Binns, Caleine. "From Our Past: A Special Study for the Diploma in Ceramics". Jamaica School of Arts, June 1972.

Brathwaite, Edward [Kamau]. "Controlling the Slaves". Typescript, n.d.

Burke, Mavis. "The History of the Wesleyan Methodist Contribution to Education in Jamaica in the Nineteenth Century, 1833–1900". MA thesis, University of London, 1965.

Campbell, M.C. "Edward Jordon and the Free Coloureds: Jamaica 1800–1865". PhD diss., University of London, n.d.

Claypole, W.A. "Land Settlement and Agricultural Development in the Liguanea Plain 1655 to 1700". MA thesis, University of the West Indies, 1970.

Cumper, George E. "The Demographic Balance of the Maroons". Paper presented to the fourth Conference of Caribbean Historians, University of the West Indies, Mona, 1972.

Duncker, Sheila. "The Free Coloured and Their Fight for Civil Rights in Jamaica, 1800–1830". MA thesis, University of London, 1960.

Hall, Douglas. "Bountied European Immigration into Jamaica with Special Reference to the German Settlement at Seaford Town up to 1850". Paper presented to the fourth Conference of Caribbean Historians, University of the West Indies, Mona, 1972.

———. "The Role of the Free Coloured Population during Slavery in Jamaica". Seminar paper, University of the West Indies, 1970.

Higman, B.W. "The Demography of Slavery in Jamaica, 1817–1834". Seminar paper, University of the West Indies, Mona, 1971.

———. "Household Structures and Fertility on Jamaican Slave Populations". Seminar paper, University of the West Indies, 1973.

———. "Slave Population and Economy in Jamaica at the Time of Emancipation". PhD diss., University of the West Indies, 1970.

———. "Some Characteristics of the Slave Population in 1832". Seminar paper, University of the West Indies, 1969.

Ingram, Kenneth. "A Bibliographical Survey of the Sources of Jamaican History 1655–1838, With Particular Reference to Manuscript Sources". BLitt thesis, University of London, 1970.

Ramlachansingh, G.S. "Amity Hall 1760–1860, the Geography of a Jamaican Plantation". MSc thesis, University of London, 1966.

Reckord, Mary. "Missionary Activity in Jamaica before Emancipation". PhD diss., University of London, 1964.

Ryall, Dorothy Ann. "The Organization of Missionary Societies, and the Recruitment of Missionaries in Britain, and the Role of Missionaries in the Diffusion of British Culture in Jamaica during the Period 1834–1865". PhD diss., University of London, 1959.

Schuler, Monica. "Slave Resistance and Rebellion in the Caribbean during the Eighteenth Century". Seminar paper, Department of History, University of the West Indies, 1966.

Teulon, Alan. "Report on Expedition to Nanny Town". Kingston, July 1970.

Editors' Selected Bibliography

The bibliography above represents Mathurin Mair's original bibliography, which we have not altered, making only slight editorial changes. But the field of Caribbean women's history has advanced tremendously since she completed her PhD dissertation in October 1974, with many students at the University of the West Indies, most in the humanities, following in her footsteps and completing postgraduate research papers and theses on women/gender issues. Mathurin Mair herself continued to write and to deliver public lectures after she did her path-breaking work. We therefore thought that we should include this additional selected bibliography. The first list represents Mathurin Mair's writings. The other lists that follow are by no means exhaustive, but they are intended to illustrate the explosion in historical scholarship on Caribbean women's history since the 1970s. Judging by their citations, many of these works were influenced by Mathurin Mair's work and ideas. For editorial purposes, we have also integrated here the references used in the introduction and which do not appear in any of the other lists.

Published Works of Lucille Mathurin Mair

"Creole Authenticity: A Review of Edward Brathwaite's *The Development of Creole Society in Jamaica 1770–1820*". *Savacou* 5, 1971: 115–20.
The Jamaican Woman under Slavery. Florida: University of Florida Press, 1974.
"The Arrivals of Black Women". *Jamaica Journal* 9, nos. 2 and 3 (1975): 2–7.
"Reluctant Matriarchs". *Savacou* 13 (1977): 1–6.

"Women: A Decade is Time Enough". *Third World Quarterly* (April 1986): 583–93.

"Recollections of a Journey into a Rebel Past". In *Caribbean Women Writers: Essays from the First International Conference,* edited by Selwyn R. Cudjoe, 51–60. Wellesley, Mass.: Calaloux, 1990.

The Rebel Woman in the West Indies during Slavery. Kingston: Institute of Jamaica Publications, 1995.

"Caribbean Woman". *Savacou* 13 (1997).

"Women Field Workers in Jamaica during Slavery". In *Slavery, Freedom and Gender: The Dynamics of Caribbean Society,* edited by Brian Moore, B.W. Higman, Carl Campbell and Patrick Bryan, 183–96. Kingston: University of the West Indies Press, 2001.

A: A SAMPLE OF DISSERTATIONS, THESES AND RESEARCH PAPERS COMPLETED AT THE UNIVERSITY OF THE WEST INDIES ON WOMEN AND GENDER ISSUES SINCE 1974

Ali, Shameen. "A Social History of East Indian Women in Trinidad since 1870". MPhil thesis, St Augustine, Trinidad and Tobago, 1994.

Andrewin-Jenkins, Valerie E. "Early Socialization, Current Sexual Practices and Risk of Sexually Transmitted Diseases of Female Sex Workers in Three Districts in Belize". MA research paper, Mona, Jamaica, 1994.

Antoine, Marlene. "Enhancing the Participation of Women in the Rural Development Process in Trinidad and Tobago". MPhil thesis, St Augustine, Trinidad and Tobago, 2000.

Boa, Sheena. "Free Black and Coloured Women in a White Man's Slave Society Jamaica, 1760–1834". MPhil thesis, Mona, Jamaica, 1988.

Clarke, Richard L.W. "Phallacies: Androgyny, Miscegenation and the Masculine Imaginary". PhD diss., Cave Hill, Barbados, 1997.

Ferguson, Vilma M. "Four Women's Views of Society in the British Caribbean during Slavery". MA research paper, Mona, Jamaica, 1986.

Fido, Elaine Savory. "Crossings: Reading Women Writing Across Culture". PhD diss., Cave Hill, Barbados, 1994.

Forbes, Curdella. "Through the Lens of Gender: A Revisionary Reading of the Novels of Samuel Selvon and George Lamming". PhD diss., Mona, Jamaica, 2000.

Gajraj-Maharaj, Sandra. "The East Indian Woman in Caribbean Writing: Images and Perceptions". MA research paper, Mona, Jamaica, 1989.

Gayle, Dorette E. "The Moravian Church and Women's Roles in Post-Emancipation Jamaica, 1838–1865". MA research paper, Mona, Jamaica, 1988.

Gordon, Erica Donna. "The Representation of Men in Caribbean Women's Writings". MPhil thesis, Mona, Jamaica, 2001.

Gordon-Stair, Angela Ikoline. "Mature Women in Higher Education: Exploring Conflicts and Stresses". PhD diss., Mona, Jamaica, 2000.

Hutton, Clinton. "Colour for Colour; Skin for Skin": The Ideological Foundations of Post-Slavery Society, 1838–1865, The Jamaican Case". PhD diss., Mona, Jamaica, 1992.

Jerrybandan, Prabha. "The World of Lakshmi Persaud: The Empowerment of the Indo-Caribbean Female". MA research paper, St Augustine, Trinidad and Tobago, 2002.

Josephs, Aleric Joyce. "Female Occupation in Jamaica, 1844–1944: Becoming Professional Women". MPhil thesis, Mona, Jamaica, 1995.

———. "Mary Seacole: Her Life and Times". MA research paper, Mona, Jamaica, 1986.

Kassim, Halima-Sa'adia. "Education, Community Organisations and Gender among Indo-Muslims of Trinidad, 1917–1962". PhD diss., St Augustine, Trinidad and Tobago, 1999.

Littlewood, Sita Elaine Dickson. "The Image of the Woman in French Caribbean Literature: Towards a Feminist Theatre". MA research paper, Mona, Jamaica, 1987.

Lynch, Roslyn M. "How Segregated is the Barbadian Labour Market? An Examination into the Extent of Gender Differences in Employment in Barbados, 1946 and 1980". MA research paper, Mona, Jamaica, 1993.

Meade, Herma Joyce Elizabeth. "The Relationship of Personality to Career and Academic Orientation Gender and School Type in a Sample of Jamaican Sixth Form Students". MA research paper, University of the West Indies, Mona, Jamaica, 1994.

McFarquhar, Eugena Louise. "Violence Against Women in Jamaica, a Public Health Concern". MA research paper, Mona, Jamaica, 1994.

Morris, Jeanette Arlene. "Female Secondary School Principals: Career Paths and Management Practice". PhD diss., St Augustine, Trinidad and Tobago, 2000.

Noel, Keith. "Art as Protest: The Work of Sistren Theatre Collective in Jamaica". MA. research paper, Mona, Jamaica, 1988.

Paul, Yolanda. "Making Production: A Case Study of Women in a Garment Factory in St Lucia". MSc research paper, St Augustine, Trinidad and Tobago, 1996.

Pencle, Carmen V. "Students' Perception of Women's Roles Now and in the Future". MA research paper, Mona, Jamaica, 1994.

Phillip, Nicole Laurine. "Women in Grenadian History from Slavery to People's Revolution, 1783–1983". PhD diss., St Augustine, Trinidad and Tobago, 2002.

Robinson, Sharon E.C. "An Investigation of the Perceptions of Selected Fathers as They Relate to Actual Fathering Behaviour". MSc research paper, Mona, Jamaica, 2001.

Russell, Karen Carpenter. "Gender Stereotypes in Jamaican Pre-School Children Towards Personhood". MA research paper, Mona, Jamaica, 1999.

Salter, Veronica Anne. Career Choice in Female Secondary Students". PhD diss., Mona, Jamaica, 1996.

Van Glaanen Weygel, Jeanelle Monique. "Gender Identity and International Relations: A Study of Women's Participation in International Negotiations". MA research paper, St Augustine, Trinidad and Tobago, 1999.

Vassell, Linnette. "Voluntary Women's Associations in Jamaica: The Jamaica Federation of Women, 1944–1962". MPhil thesis, Mona, Jamaica, 1993.

Vendryes, Diane M. "Jamaican Working Class Women's Perception of Female Sex Role Attributes in Relationship to Ego Strength". MSc research paper, Mona, Jamaica, 1982.

White, Blossom Fay. "The Social and Psychological Contribution of Some Jamaican Lower-Income Males to their Families". MA research paper, Mona, Jamaica, 1992.

Williams, Bronty Liverpool. "A Historical Study of Women in Twentieth Century St Vincent and the Grenadines". MPhil thesis, St Augustine, Trinidad and Tobago, 2002.

B: A SELECTION OF BOOKS, BOOK CHAPTERS AND PAPERS ON CARIBBEAN WOMEN AND GENDER ISSUES SINCE 1974

Abbassi, Jennifer, and Sheryl L. Lutjens, eds. *Rereading Women in Latin America and the Caribbean: The Political Economy of Gender.* Lanham: Rowman and Littlefield, 2002.

Abraham, Eva. "Caught in the Shift: The Impact of Industrialization on Female-Headed Households in Curaçao, Netherland Antilles". In *Where Did All the Men Go? Female Headed/Female Supported Households in Cross-Cultural Perspective,* edited by Joan P. Mencher and Anne Okongwu, 89–106. Boulder: Westview Press, 1993.

Acosta-Belén, Edna. *The Puerto Rican Woman: Perspective on Culture, History and Society.* New York: Praeger, 1986.

Acosta-Belén, Edna, and Christine E. Bose, eds. *Researching Women in Latin America and the Caribbean.* Boulder: Westview Press, 1993.

Anim-Addo, Joan, ed. *Framing the Word: Gender and Genre in Caribbean Women's Writing.* London: Whiting and Birch, 1996.

Ansano, Richenel, et al., eds. *Mundu yama Sinta Mira: Womanhood in Curaçao.* Curaçao: Fundashon Publikashon, 1992.

Azize, Yamila. *Luchas de la mujer en Puerto Rico 1898–1919.* Río Piedras: The author, 1979

———. *La mujer en la lucha.* Río Piedras: Editorial Cultural, 1985.

———, ed. *La mujer en Puerto Rico: Ensayos de investigación histórica.* Colección Huracán Academia, Río Piedras: Ediciones Huracán, 1987.

Báez, Clara. *La subordinación social de la mujer dominicana en cifras.* Santo Domingo: Dirección General de Promoción de la Mujer: Instituto Internacional de las Naciones Unidas para la Investigación, Capacitación y Promoción de la Mujer, 1985.

Báez Diaz, Tomás. *La mujer dominicana.* Santo Domingo: Editorial Educativa Dominicana, 1980.

Barbara Bailey. *Issues of Gender and Education in Jamaica: What About the Boys?* EFA in the Caribbean Monograph Series, no. 15. Jamaica: UNESCO, 2000.

————, ed. *Gender Issues in Caribbean Education: a Module for Teacher Education.* Georgetown: Caribbean Community (CARICOM) Secretariat, 2000.

Bailey, Susan F. *Women and the British Empire: An Annotated Guide to Sources.* New York: Garland, 1983.

Bailey, Wilma. *Family and the Quality of Gender Relations in the Caribbean.* Kingston: Institute of Social and Economic Research, University of the West Indies, 1998.

————, ed. *Gender and the Family in the Caribbean.* Mona, Jamaica: Institute of Social and Economic Research, University of the West Indies, 1998.

Bair, Barbara. "True Women, Real Men: Gender, Ideology and Social Roles in the Garvey Movement". In *Gendered Domains: Rethinking Public and Private,* edited by Dorothy O. Helly and Susan M. Reverby, 154–66. Ithaca: Cornell University Press, 1992.

Barceló Miller, Maria de Fátima. *La Lucha por el sufragio femenino en Puerto Rico, 1869–1935.* Río Piedras: Centro de Investigaciones Sociales, University of Puerto Rico and Ediciones Hurancán, 1997.

Barriteau, Eudine. *Engendering Local Government in the Commonwealth Caribbean.* Bridgetown: Centre for Gender and Development Studies, University of the West Indies, Cave Hill, 1998.

————. *The Political Economy of Gender in the Twentieth-Century Caribbean.* Hampshire: Palgrave, 2001.

————. "The State of the Art in Women's Studies in the Commonwealth Caribbean: Women and Gender Studies in the Caribbean Since 1980". Keynote lecture delivered to the Netherlands Association for Latin American and Caribbean Studies, Conference on Women's Studies on Latin America and the Caribbean, Leiden, Republic of the Netherlands, June 1996.

————, ed. *Confronting Power, Theorizing Gender.* Kingston: University of the West Indies Press, 2003.

Barriteau, Eudine, and Alan Cobley, eds. *Stronger, Surer, Bolder: Ruth Nita Barrow – Social Change and International Development.* Cave Hill: Centre for Gender and Development Studies and University of the West Indies Press, 2001.

Barrow, Christine. *Family in the Caribbean: Themes and Perspectives.* Kingston: Ian Randle, 1996.

————, ed. *Caribbean Portraits: Essays on Gender Ideologies and Identities.* Kingston: Ian Randle, 1998.

Batista, Celsa Albert. *Mujer y esclavitud en Santo Domingo.* Santo Domingo: Centro Dominicano de Estudious de la Educación, 1990.

Baugh, Edward. "Lucille Mathurin Mair". In *Chancellor, I Present . . .: A Collection of Convocation Citations Given at the University of the West Indies, Mona, 1985–1998*. Kingston: Canoe Press, 1998.

Beckles, Hilary McD. *Afro-Caribbean Women and Resistance to Slavery in Barbados*. London: Karnak House, 1988.

———. *Black Masculinity in Caribbean Slavery*. Women and Development Unit, WAND Occasional Paper 2/96, Barbados: Women and Development Unit, 1996.

———. *Centering Woman: Gender Discourses in Caribbean Slave Society*. Kingston: Ian Randle, 1999.

———. *Freeing Slavery: Gender Paradigms in the Social History of Caribbean Slavery*. Elsa Goveia Memorial Lecture. Kingston: University of the West Indies, Department of History, 1998.

———. *Natural Rebels: A Social History of Enslaved Black Women in Barbados*. New Brunswick, NJ: Rutgers University Press, 1989.

———. "Property Rights in Pleasure: The Marketing of Enslaved Women's Sexuality". In *Caribbean Slavery in the Atlantic World*, edited by Verene Shepherd and Hilary Beckles, 692–701. Kingston: Ian Randle, 2000.

———. "White Women and Slavery in the Caribbean". In *Caribbean Slavery in the Atlantic World*, edited by Verene Shepherd and Hilary Beckles, 659–69. Kingston: Ian Randle, 2000.

Bell, Beverly. *Walking on Fire: Haitian Women's Stories of Survival and Resistance*. Ithaca: Cornell University Press, 2001.

Benjamin, Esme, ed. *The Caribbean Woman: Her Needs in a Changing Society*. Washington, DC: Caribbean American Intercultural Organization, 1977.

Bilby, Kenneth, and Filomina Chioma Steady. "Black Women and Survival: A Maroon Case". In *The Black Woman Cross-Culturally*, edited by Filomina Chioma Steady, 451–67. Cambridge, Mass.: Schenkman, 1981.

Blackman, Francis. *Dame Nita: Caribbean Woman, World Citizen*. Kingston: Ian Randle, 1995

Bobb-Semple, Leona. *Women in Jamaica: A Bibliography of Published and Unpublished Sources*. Kingston: University of the West Indies Press, 1997.

Bolland, Nigel. "Proto-Proletarians? Slave Wages in the Americas". In *From Chattel Slaves to Wage Slaves: The Dynamics of Labor Bargaining in the Americas*, edited by Mary Turner. Bloomington: Indiana University Press, 1995.

Bolles, Augusta Lynn. *Sister Jamaica: A Study of Women, Work, and Households in Kingston*. Lanham: University Press of America, 1996.

———. *We Paid Our Dues: Women Trade Union Leaders of the Caribbean*. Washington, DC: Howard University Press, 1996.

Brathwaite, Edward Kamau. *Mother Poem*. London: Oxford University Press, 1977.

———. *Wars of Respect: Nanny, Sam Sharpe, and the Struggle for People's Liberation*.

Kingston: Agency for Public Information for the National Heritage Week Committee, 1977.

———. *Women of the Caribbean during Slavery.* Elsa Goveia Memorial Lecture. Cave Hill: History Department, University of the West Indies, 1984.

Brereton, Bridget. "Family Strategies, Gender and the Shift to Wage Labour in the British Caribbean". In *The Colonial Caribbean in Transition: Essays on Postemancipation Social and Cultural History,* edited by Bridget Brereton and K. Yelvington, 77–107. Kingston: University of the West Indies Press, 1999.

———. *Gendered Testimony: Autobiographies, Diaries and Letters by Women as Sources for Caribbean History.* Elsa Goveia Memorial Lecture. Kingston: Department of History, University of the West Indies, 1994.

———. *Race Relations in Colonial Trinidad, 1870–1900.* Cambridge: Cambridge University Press, 1979.

———. "Text, Testimony and Gender: An Examination of Some Texts by Women on the English-Speaking Caribbean, from the 1770s to the 1920s". In *Engendering History: Caribbean Women in Historical Perspective,* edited by Verene Shepherd, Bridget Brereton and Barbara Bailey, 63–93. Kingston: Ian Randle, 1995.

Brodber, Erna. *Perceptions of Caribbean Women: Towards a Documentation of Stereotypes.* Cave Hill: Institute of Social and Economic Research (Eastern Caribbean), University of the West Indies, 1982.

———. *Standing Tall: Affirmations of the Jamaican Male: 24 Self Portraits.* Kingston: Sir Arthur Lewis Institute of Social and Economic Studies, 2003.

Brown, Janet, and Melrose Rattray. *Women in Jamaican Development: An Overview Report Towards Development Strategies.* 1987.

Brown, Jennifer. *Amy Bailey: A Biography.* Kingston: Department of History, University of the West Indies, 1991.

Brown, Wayne. *Edna Manley: The Private Years, 1900–1938.* London: André Deutsch, 1975.

Burnard, Trevor. *Mastery, Tyranny, and Desire: Thomas Thistlewood and His Slaves in the Anglo-Jamaican World.* Kingston: University of the West Indies Press, 2004.

Bush, Barbara. " 'The Family Tree Is Not Cut': Women and Cultural Resistance in Slave Family Life in the British Caribbean". In *Resistance: Studies in African, Caribbean and Afro-American History,* edited by Gary Okihiro, 117–32. Amherst: University of Massachusetts Press, 1986.

———. *Slave Women in Caribbean Society, 1650–1838.* London: James Currey, 1990.

———. "Towards Emancipation: Slave Women and Resistance to Coercive Labour Regimes in the British West Indian Colonies, 1790–1838". In *Abolition and Its Aftermath: The Historical Context, 1870–1916,* edited by David Richardson, 27–54. London: Frank Cass, 1985.

Bustamante, Gladys. *The Memoirs of Lady Bustamante.* Kingston: Kingston Publishers, 1998.

Butler, Kathleen. *The Economics of Emancipation: Jamaica and Barbados, 1823–1843.* Chapel Hill: University of North Carolina Press, 1995.

Castañeda, Digna. "The Female Slave in Cuba during the First Half of the Nineteenth Century". In *Engendering History: Caribbean Women in Historical Perspective,* edited by Verene Shepherd, Bridget Brereton and Barbara Bailey, 141–54. Kingston: Ian Randle, 1995

Celma, Cécile-Marie. "Les femmes au travail à la Martinique XVIIIe–XIXe siècle: Première approche". *Primer Trimestre,* no. 82 (1986): 24–31.

Charles, Mary Eugenia. "The Experiences of the First Female Prime Minister in the Commonwealth Caribbean 1980–1995". Caribbean Women Catalysts for Change Lecture Series. Centre for Gender and Development Studies, University of the West Indies, Cave Hill, Barbados, 3 November 1995.

Chamberlain, Mary. "Gender and Memory: Oral History and Women's History". In *Engendering History: Caribbean Women in Historical Perspective,* edited by Verene Shepherd, Bridget Brereton and Barbara Bailey, 94–110. Kingston: Ian Randle, 1995.

Chaney, Elsa. *Research Migration and Women in Latin American and the Caribbean.* Boulder: Westview Press, 1993.

Chevannes, Barry. *Learning to Be a Man: Culture, Socialization and Gender Identity in Five Caribbean Communities.* Kingston: University of the West Indies Press, 2001.

———. *What We Sow and What We Reap: Problems in the Cultivation of Male Identity in Jamaica.* Grace, Kennedy Foundation Lecture. Kingston: Grace, Kennedy Foundation, 1998.

Cohen-Stuart, Bertie. *Women in the Caribbean: A Bibliography.* Leiden: Department of Caribbean Studies, KITLV, 1979.

———. *Women in the Caribbean: A Bibliography Part Two.* Leiden: Department of Caribbean Studies, KITLV, 1985.

Cole, Joyce. "Official Ideology and the Education of Women in the English-Speaking Caribbean, 1835–1945". In *Women and Education,* edited by Joycelin Massiah, 1–34. Women in the Caribbean Project, vol. 5. Cave Hill, Barbados: Institute of Social and Economic Research (Eastern Caribbean), 1982.

Colón Alice, ed. *Gender and Puerto Rican Women: Third Encounter of Women Researchers.* Río Piedras: Centro de Estudios, Recursos y Servicios para la Mujer/Centro de Investigaciones Sociales, University of Puerto Rico, 1994.

Cooper, Carolyn. *Noises in the Blood: Orality, Gender and the "Vulgar" Body of Jamaican Popular Culture.* London: Macmillan Caribbean, 1993.

Daniel, Judith A., ed. *A Brief History of the Mothers' Union in the Province of the West Indies.* Provincial Mother's Union in the Province of the West Indies, 1997.

Dorsey, Joseph. " 'Women without History': Slavery and the International Politics of Partis Sequiter Ventrem in the Spanish Caribbean". In *Caribbean Slavery in the*

Atlantic World, edited by Verene Shepherd and Hilary Beckles, 634–58. Kingston: Ian Randle, 2000.

Duncan, Neville. *The Changing Global Environment and the Impact on Caribbean Women: An Academic Exploration*. Halifax: Association of Universities and Community Colleges, 2001.

Duncan, Neville C., and Kenneth O'Brien. *Women and Politics in Barbados, 1948–1981*. Cave Hill: Institute of Social and Economic Research (Eastern Caribbean), University of the West Indies, 1983.

Durrant-Gonzalez, Victoria. *Women and the Family*. Cave Hill: Institute of Social and Economic Research (Eastern Caribbean), University of the West Indies, 1982.

Dutton, Geoffrey. *In Search of Edward John Eyre*. South Melbourne: Macmillan, 1982.

Elgersman, Maureen G. *Unyielding Spirits: Black Women and Slavery in Early Canada and Jamaica*. New York: Garland, 1999.

Ellis, Patricia, ed. *Women of the Caribbean*. London: Zed Books, 1986.

———. *Women, Gender and Development in the Caribbean: Reflections and Projections*. New York: Zed Books, 2003.

Eltis, David, Stephen D. Behrendt, David Richardson and Herbert S. Klein, eds. *Transatlantic Slave Trade: A Database on CD-ROM*. Cambridge: Cambridge University Press, 1999.

Emmer, Pieter C. "The Great Escape: The Migration of Female Indentured Servants From British India to Suriname". In *Abolition and Its Aftermath: The Historical Context, 1870–1916*, edited by David Richardson, 245–66. London: Frank Cass, 1985.

Ferguson, Moira, ed. *The History of Mary Prince, a West Indian Slave Related by Herself*. 1831; reprint, London: Pandora, 1987.

———. *Subject to Others: British Women Writers and Colonial Slavery, 1670–1834*. New York: Routledge, 1992.

———, ed. *The Hart Sisters: Early African Caribbean Writers, Evangelicals, and Radicals*. Lincoln: University of Nebraska Press, 1993.

French, Joan. *Colonial Policy towards Women after the 1938 Uprising: The Case of Jamaica*. The Hague: Publications Office, Institute of Social Studies, 1988.

French, Joan, and Honor Ford-Smith. *Women, Work and Organisation in Jamaica 1900–1944*. Kingston: Sistren Research, 1986.

Gaspar, David Barry, and Darlene Clark Hine, eds. *More Than Chattel: Black Women and Slavery in the Americas*. Bloomington: Indiana University Press, 1996.

Gautier, Arlette. *Les soeurs de solitude: la condition féminine dans l'esclave aux Antilles du XVIIe au XIXe siècle*. Paris: Editions Caribéennes, 1985.

———. "Slave Women in the British Caribbean, 1650–1834: A Perspective on Identity, Culture and Resistance". In *Born out of Resistance: On Caribbean Cultural Creativity*, edited by Wim Hoogenbergen, 126–36. Utrecht: ISOR, 1995.

———. "Women from Guadeloupe and Martinique". In *French and West Indian:*

Martinique, Guadeloupe and French Guiana Today, edited by Richard Burton and Fred Reno, 119–36. London: Macmillan, 1995.

Green, Cecilia. *The World Market Factory: A Study of Enclave Industrialization in the Eastern Caribbean and its Impact on Women Workers.* Kingstown, St Vincent: Caribbean People's Development Agency, 1990.

Gregg, V.M. *Jean Rhys's Historical Imagination: Reading and Writing the Creole.* Chapel Hill: University of North Carolina Press, 1995.

Guy, Henry A., and Lavern Bailey, eds. *Women of Distinction in Jamaica: A Record of Career Women in Jamaica, Their Background, Service, and Achievements.* Kingston: Caribbean Herald, 1977.

Hall, Douglas, ed. *In Miserable Slavery: Thomas Thistlewood in Jamaica, 1750–1786.* Kingston: University of the West Indies Press, 1999.

Hamilton, Jill. *Women of Barbados: Amerindian Era to Mid Twentieth Century.* Barbados: The author, 1981.

Haniff, Nesha Z. *Blaze a Fire: Significant Contributions of Caribbean Women.* Toronto: Sister Vision Press, 1988.

Hart, Keith, ed. *Women and the Sexual Division of Labour in the Caribbean.* Barbados: Canoe Press and the Consortium Graduate School of Social Sciences, 1996.

Henderson, Peta, and Ann Bryn Houghton, eds. *Rising Up: Life Stories of Belizean Women by Women of the Orange Walk District.* Toronto: Sister Vision Press, 1993.

Heuman, Gad. *"The Killing Time": The Morant Bay Rebellion in Jamaica.* London: Macmillan, 1994.

Higbie, Janet. *Eugenia: The Caribbean's Iron Lady.* London: Macmillan Caribbean, 1993.

Higman, Barry. *Slave Population and Economy in Jamaica, 1807–1834.* Cambridge: Cambridge University Press, 1976; reprint, Kingston: University of the West Indies Press, 1995.

———. *Slave Populations of the British Caribbean, 1807–1834.* Baltimore: Johns Hopkins University Press, 1984; reprint, Kingston: University of the West Indies Press, 1995.

Hine, Darlene Clark. "Female Slave Resistance: The Economics of Sex". In *Black Women in American History,* edited by Darlene Clark Hine, 657–66. Brooklyn: Carlson, 1990.

Holt-Seeland, Inger. *Con las puertas abiertas: Women of Cuba.* Translated by Elizabeth Hamilton Lacoste, with Mirtha Quintanales and Jose Vigo. Westport: Lawrence Hill, 1982.

Holt, Thomas. *The Problem of Freedom: Race, Labour and Politics in Jamaica and Britain, 1832–1938.* Baltimore: Johns Hopkins University Press, 1992.

Jain, Shobhita, and Rhoda Reddock, eds. *Women Plantation Workers: International Experiences.* Oxford: Berg, 1998.

Jarret-Macauley, Delia. *The Life of Una Marson, 1905–65.* Kingston: Ian Randle, 1998.

John, Meredith. *The Plantation Slaves of Trinidad, 1783–1816: A Mathematical and Demographic Enquiry.* Cambridge: Cambridge University Press, 1989.

Johnson-Odim, Cheryl, and Margaret Strobel, eds. *Expanding the Boundaries of Women's History: Essays on Women in the Third World.* Bloomington: Indiana University Press, 1992.

Johnson, Michelle. " 'Young Woman from the Country: A Profile of Domestic Servants in Jamaica, 1920–1970". In *Working Slavery, Pricing Freedom,* edited by Verene Shepherd, 396–415. Kingston: Ian Randle, 2002.

Kanhai, Rosanne, ed. *Matikor: The Politics of Identity for Indo-Caribbean Women.* St Augustine: University of the West Indies, School of Continuing Studies, 1999.

Kelly, Gail P., and Carolyn M., eds. *Women's Education in the Third World: Comparative Perspectives.* Albany: State University of New York Press, 1982.

Kerns, Virginia. *Women and the Ancestors: Black Carib Kinship and Ritual.* Urbana: University of Illinois Press, 1983.

Kerr, Paulette. "Victims or Strategists? Female Lodging-House Keepers in Jamaica". In *Engendering History: Caribbean Women in Historical Perspective,* edited by Verene Shepherd, Bridget Brereton and Barbara Bailey, 197–212. Kingston: Ian Randle, 1995.

Kiple, Kenneth, and Virginia Kiple. "Deficiency Diseases in the Caribbean". In *Caribbean Slave Society and Economy: A Student Reader,* edited by Hilary Beckles and Verene Shepherd, 173–82. Kingston: Ian Randle, 1991.

Klein, Herbert .S. "African Women in the Atlantic Slave Trade". In *Women and Slavery in Africa,* edited by Claire Robertson and Martin Klein, 29–38. Madison: University of Wisconsin Press, 1983.

Kleysen, Brenda. *Women Small Farmers in the Caribbean.* San José: Inter-American Institute for Cooperation on Agriculture; Washington, DC: Inter-American Development Bank, 1996.

Knight, Franklin. "Slavery and the Transformation of Society in Cuba, 1511–1760". In *Slavery, Freedom and Gender: The Dynamics of Caribbean Society,* edited by Brian Moore, B.W. Higman, Carl Campbell and Patrick Bryan, 76–96. Kingston: University of the West Indies Press, 2001.

Koss-Chioino, Joan. *Women as Healers, Women as Patients: Mental Health Care and Traditional Healing in Puerto Rico.* Boulder: Westview Press, 1992.

Kossek, Briditte. "Racist and Patriarchal Aspects of Plantation Slavery in Grenada, White Ladies, Black Women Slaves and Rebels". In *Slavery in the Americas,* edited by W. Binder, 277–303. Wurzburg: Konigshausen and Newmann, 1993.

Krumeich, Anja. *The Blessings of Motherhood: Health, Pregnancy and Childcare in Dominica.* Amsterdam: Het Spinhuis, 1994.

Lagro, Monique. *The Hucksters of Dominica.* Port of Spain: Economic Commission for Latin America and the Caribbean, 1990.

Latin American and Caribbean Women's Collective. *Slaves of Slaves: The Challenge of Latin American Women*. Translated by Michael Pallis. London: Zed Press, 1980.

Layne-Clark, Jeanette ed. *The Other Sex: Who's Who of Women in Barbados*. Bridgetown: Impact Productions, 1977.

Leo-Rhynie, Elsa. "Gender Issues in Education and Implications for Labour Force Participation". In *Women and the Sexual Division of Labour in the Caribbean*, edited by Keith Hart, 81–97. Kingston: Canoe Press and the Consortium Graduate School of Social Sciences, 1989.

―――. *Gender Mainstreaming in Education: A Reference Manual for Governments and Other Stakeholders*. London: Commonwealth Secretariat, 1999.

―――. *The Jamaican Family: Continuity and Change*. Grace, Kennedy Foundation Lecture. Kingston: Grace, Kennedy Foundation, 1993.

―――. "Tribute to Dr Lucille Mathurin Mair". June 2003

Leo-Rhynie, Elsa, Barbara Bailey and Christine Barrow, eds. *Gender: A Caribbean Multi-Disciplinary Perspective*. Kingston: Ian Randle, 1997.

López Springfield, Consuelo, ed. *Daughters of Caliban: Caribbean Women in the Twentieth Century*. Bloomington: Indiana University Press, 1997.

Lynch, Roslyn. *Gender Segregation in the Barbadian Labour Market, 1946 and 1980*. Kingston: Canoe Press and the Consortium Graduate School of Social Sciences, 1995.

McClaurin, Irma. *Women of Belize: Gender and Change in Central America*. New Brunswick, NJ: Rutgers University Press, 1996.

Mahabir, Noor Kumar. *Indian Women of Trinidad and Tobago: An Annotated Bibliography with Photographs and Ephemera*. San Juan: Chakra Publishing House, 1992.

Maloof, Judy, ed. *Voices of Resistance: Testimonies of Cuban and Chilean Women*. Lexington: University Press of Kentucky, 1999.

Marks, Arnaud. *Male and Female in the Afro-Curaçaoan Household*. The Hague: Nijhoff, 1976.

Marks, Arnaud, and Rene Römer, eds. *Family and Kinship in Middle America and the Caribbean*. Willemstad: Institute of Higher Studies in Curaçao, 1978.

Marshall, Woodville. " 'We Be Wise to Many Tings': Blacks Hopes and Expectations of Emancipation". In *Caribbean Freedom: Economy and Society from Emancipation to the Present,* edited by Hilary Beckles and Verene Shepherd. Kingston: Ian Randle, 1993.

Martinez-Alier, Verena. *Marriage, Class and Colour in Nineteenth Century Cuba: A Study of Racial Attitudes and Sexual Values in Slave Society*. Cambridge: Cambridge University Press, 1974.

Massiah, Joycelin. *Employed Women in Barbados: A Demographic Profile, 1946–1970*. Cave Hill: Institute of Social and Economic Research (Eastern Caribbean), University of the West Indies, 1984.

————. *Manual on the Use of Socio-Economic Indicators of Women's Participation in Development.* Paris: UNESCO, 1982.

————. *On the Brink of the New Millennium: Are Caribbean Women Prepared?* Kingston: Centre for Gender and Development Studies, University of the West Indies, 1998.

————. *Women in the Caribbean: An Annotated Bibliography – A Guide to Material Available in Barbados.* Cave Hill: Institute of Social and Economic Research (Eastern Caribbean), University of the West Indies, 1979.

————. *Women as Heads of Households in the Caribbean: Family Structure and Feminine Status.* Paris: UNESCO, 1983.

————, ed. *Women in Developing Economies: Making Visible the Invisible.* Paris: UNESCO, 1993.

Matos Rodríguez, Félix V. *Women and Urban Change in San Juan, Puerto Rico, 1820–1868.* Gainesville: University Press of Florida, 1999.

Matos Rodríguez, Félix V., and Linda C. Delgado, eds. *Puerto Rican Women's History: New Perspectives.* Armonk: M.E. Sharpe, 1998.

Mayers, Janice. "Access to Secondary Education for Girls in Barbados, 1907–1943: A Preliminary Analysis". In *Engendering History: Caribbean Women in Historical Perspective,* edited by Verene Shepherd, Bridget Brereton and Barbara Bailey, 258–75. Kingston: Ian Randle, 1995.

Méndez-Rodenas, Adriana. *Gender and Nationalism in Colonial Cuba: The Travels of Santa Cruz y Montalvo, Condesa de Merlin.* Nashville: Vanderbilt University Press, 1998.

Midgley, Clare. *Women against Slavery: The British Campaigns, 1780–1870.* London: Routledge, 1992.

Miller, Errol. *Men at Risk.* Kingston: Jamaica Publishing House, 1991.

Mintz, Sidney W. "Black Women, Economic Roles and Cultural Traditions". In *Caribbean Freedom: Economy and Society from Emancipation to the Present,* edited by Hilary Beckles and Verene Shepherd, 238–44. Kingston: Ian Randle, 1993.

Mohammed, Patricia. "The 'Creolisation' of Indian Women in Trinidad". In *Questioning Creole: Creolisation Discourses in Caribbean Culture,* edited by Verene Shepherd and Glen Richards, 130–47. Kingston: Ian Randle, 2002.

————. "Dr Lucille Mathurin Mair: Contributing to the Struggle for Gender Equality". Featured in the 1998 inaugural Lucille Mathurin Mair Lecture "On the Brink of the New Millennium: Are Caribbean Women Prepared?" by Joycelin Massiah. University of the West Indies, Mona. 6 March 1998.

————. *Gender Negotiations Among Indians in Trinidad, 1917–1947.* New York: Palgrave, in Association with Institute of Social Studies, 2002.

————. *The Women's Movement in Trinidad and Tobago Since the 1960s.* Cave Hill:

Women and Development Unit, Extra-Mural Department, University of the West Indies, Barbados, 1985.

————, ed. *Gendered Realities: Essays in Caribbean Feminist Thought*. Kingston: University of the West Indies Press, 2002.

————. *Rethinking Caribbean Difference*. London: Routledge, 1998.

Mohammed, Patricia, and Althea Perkins. *Caribbean Women at the Crossroads: The Paradox of Motherhood among Women of Barbados, St Lucia and Dominica*. Kingston: Canoe Press, 1999.

Moitt, Bernard. "Gender and Slavery: Women and the Plantation Experience in the Caribbean Before 1848". In *Born out of Resistance: On Caribbean Cultural Creativity*, edited by Wim Hoogenbergen, 110–25. Utrecht: ISOR, 1995.

————. *Women and Slavery in the French Antilles, 1635–1848*. Bloomington: Indiana University Press, 2001.

————. "Women, Work and Resistance in the French Caribbean during Slavery" In *Engendering History: Caribbean Women in Historical Perspective* edited by Verene Shepherd Bridget Brereton, Barbara Bailey, 155–74. Kingston: Ian Randle, 1995.

Molyneux, Maxine. *State, Gender and Institutional Change in Cuba's "Special Period": The Federación de Mujeres Cubanas*. London: Institute of Latin American Studies, 1996.

Momsen, Janet. "Gender Roles in Caribbean Agriculture Labour". In *Caribbean Freedom: Economy and Society from Emancipation to the Present,* edited by Hilary Beckles and Verene Shepherd, 216–24. Kingston: Ian Randle, 1993.

————. *Women and Development in the Third World*. London: Routledge, 1991.

————, ed. *Women and Change in the Caribbean: A Pan-Caribbean Perspective*. Kingston: Ian Randle, 1993.

Mondesire, Alicia, and Leith Dunn. *An Analysis of Census Data in CARICOM Countries From a Gender Perspective*. Georgetown: CARICOM, 1997.

Moore, Brian, B.W. Higman, Carl Campbell and Patrick Bryan, eds. *Slavery, Freedom and Gender: The Dynamics of Caribbean Society*. Kingston: University of the West Indies Press, 2001.

Mordecai, Pamela, and Betty Wilson, eds. *Her True-True Name: An Anthology of Women's Writing from the Caribbean*. Oxford: Heinemann, 1989.

Morrissey, Marrieta. *Slave Women in the New World: Gender Stratification in the Caribbean*. Kansas: University of Kansas Press, 1989.

Mota, Vivian, M. "Politics and Feminism in the Dominican Republic: 1931–1945 and 1966–74". In *Sex and Class in Latin America,* edited by June Nash and Helen Safa, 265–70. New York: Praeger, 1976.

Nasta, Susheila, ed. *Motherlands: Black Women's Writing from Africa, the Caribbean, and South Asia*. New Brunswick, NJ: Rutgers University Press, 1992.

Navarro, Marysa, Virginia Sánchez Korrol and Kecia Ali. *Women in Latin America and the Caribbean: Restoring Women to History.* Bloomington: Indiana University Press, 1999.

Neil, Rusty, ed. *Women in the Caribbean: An Overview.* Halifax: Association of Universities and Colleges, 2001.

Nijeholt, Geertje Lycklama à, Virginia Vargas and Saskia Wieringa, eds. *Women's Movements and Public Policy in Europe, Latin America, and the Caribbean.* New York: Garland, 1998.

Norris, Marianna. *Dona Felisa: A Biography of the Mayor of San Juan.* New York: Dodd, Mead and Co., 1969.

O'Callaghan, Evelyn, ed. *Woman Version: Theoretical Approaches to West Indian Fiction by Women.* New York: St Martin's Press, 1993.

Ortiz, Altagracia, ed. *Puerto Rican Women and Work: Bridges in Transnational Labour.* Philadelphia: Temple University Press, 1996.

"Our Women in the Senate". *Daily Gleaner,* 7 March 1991, 16.

Paravisini-Gebert, Lizabeth. *Phyllis Shand Allfrey: A Caribbean Life.* New Brunswick, NJ: Rutgers University Press, 1996.

Paravisini-Gebert, Lizabeth, and Ivette Romero-Cesareo, eds. *Women at Sea: Travel Writing and the Margins of Caribbean Discourse.* New York: Pelgrave, 2001.

Paton, Diana. *No Bond but the Law: Punishment, Race, and Gender in Jamaican State Formation, 1780–1870.* Kingston: University of the West Indies Press, 2004.

Peake, Linda, and D. Alissa Trotz. *Gender, Ethnicity and Place: Women and Identities in Guyana.* London: Routledge, 1999.

Perkins, Althea. "Issues of Class, Race and Gender in the Lives of Three Caribbean Women". In *Selected Issues and Problems in Social Policy: Studies in Caribbean Public Policy 2,* edited by Deryck R. Brown, 30–72. Kingston: Canoe Press, 1998.

Phillips-Lewis, Kathleen. "European Stereotypes and the Position of Women in the Caribbean: An Historical Overview". In *Crossroads of Empire: The Europe-Caribbean Connection, 1492–1992,* edited by Alan Cobley, 64–77. Cave Hill: Department of History, University of the West Indies, 1994.

Poupeye-Rammelaere, Veerle. *The Role of Women in the Development of Jamaican Art.* Kingston: Frame Centre Gallery, 1994.

Powell, Dorian. *Women's Work, Social Support Resources and Infant Feeding Practices in Jamaica.* Washington, DC: International Center for Research on Women, 1988.

Poynting, Jeremy. *East Indian Women in the Caribbean: Experience and Voice India in the Caribbean: Special Commemorative Edition 1838–1988.* London: Hansib, 1987.

Proceedings of the First International Conference on Women Writers of the English-Speaking Caribbean. Wellesley, Mass.: Black Studies Department, Wellesley College, 1988.

Pyne-Timothy, Helen, ed. *The Woman, the Writer, and Caribbean Society: Critical Analyses of the Writings of Caribbean Women.* Los Angeles: UCLA Center for African American Studies, 1997.

Radford Ruether, Rosemary, ed. *Women Healing Earth: Third World Women on Ecology, Feminism, and Religion.* Maryknoll: Orbis Books, 1996.

Ramírez, Rafael L. *What It Means to Be a Man: Reflections on Puerto Rican Masculinity.* Translated by Rosa E. Casper. New Brunswick, NJ: Rutgers University Press, 1999.

Ramírez, Rafael, Victor García-Toro and Ineke Cunningham, eds. *Caribbean Masculinities: Working Papers.* San Juan, Puerto Rico: Research and Education Center, 2002.

Randall, Margaret. *Cuban Women Now: Interviews with Cuban Women.* Toronto: Women's Press, Dumont Press Graphix, 1974

———. *Our Voices, Our Lives: Stories of Women from Central America and the Caribbean.* Monroe, Maine: Common Courage Press, 1995.

———. *Women in Cuba, Twenty Years Later.* New York: Smyrna Press, 1981.

Reddock, Rhoda. "The Early Women's Movement in Trinidad and Tobago, 1900–1930". In *Subversive Women: Women's Movements in Africa, Asia, Latin America and the Caribbean,* edited by Saskia Wieringa, 101–20. London: Zed Books, 1995.

———. *Elma Francois: The NWCSA and The Worker's Struggle for Change in the Caribbean.* London: New Beacon Books, 1988.

———. *Women, Labour and Politics in Trinidad and Tobago: A History.* London: Zed Books, 1994.

———. *Women and Poverty in Trinidad and Tobago.* Cave Hill: Women and Development Unit, University of the West Indies, 1995.

———. "Women in Revolt: Women and the Radical Workers' Movement in Trinidad, 1934–1937". In *The Trinidad Labour Riots of 1937: Perspectives Fifty Years Later,* edited by Roy Thomas, 233–63. St Augustine: Extra-Mural Studies Unit, University of the West Indies, 1987.

Rico, Nieves. *Female Human Resources Development: Growth and Equity as Priorities.* Santiago: United Nations, 1997.

Robaina, Tomás Fernández. *Recuerdos secretos de dos mujeres publicas.* La Habana: Editorial Letras Cubanas, 1984.

Roberts, George W., and Sonja A. Sinclair. *Women in Jamaica: Patterns of Reproduction and Family.* Millwood, NY: KTO Press, 1978.

Rodney, Patricia. *The Caribbean State, Health Care, and Women: An Analysis of Barbados and Grenada during the 1979–1983 Period.* Trenton: Africa World Press, 1998.

Rodriguez, Ana, and Glenn Garvin. *Diary of a Survivor: Nineteen Years in a Cuban Women's Prison.* New York: St Martin's Press, 1995.

Rolfes, Irene. *Women in the Caribbean: A Bibliography, Part Three 1986–1990.* Leiden: Department of Caribbean Studies, KITLV/Royal Institute of Linguistics and Anthropology, 1992.

Rosario Urrutia, Mayra, and María de Fátima Barceló Miller. *Temperancia y sufragismo en el Puerto Rico del siglo XX.* Santurce: Centro de Investigaciones Académicas, Universidad del Sagrado Corazón, 1990.

Safa, Helen Icken. *The Myth of the Male Breadwinner: Women and Industrialization in the Caribbean.* Boulder: Westview Press, 1995.

Safa, Helen Icken, and Peggy Antrobus. "Women and the Economic Crisis in the Caribbean". In *Unequal Burden,* edited by Lourdes Beneria and Shelly Feldman, 49–82. Boulder: Westview Press, 1992.

Saith, Radhica. *Why Not a Woman?* Port of Spain: Paria Press, 1993.

Satchell, Veront. "Women, Land Transactions and Peasant Development in Jamaica, 1866–1900". In *Engendering History: Caribbean Women in Historical Perspective,* edited by Verene Shepherd, Bridget Brereton and Barbara Bailey, 213–32. Kingston: Ian Randle, 1995.

Scott, Joan Wallach. *Gender and the Politics of History.* New York: Columbia University, 1988.

Seacole, Mary. *Wonderful Adventures of Mrs Seacole in Many Lands.* 1857; reprint, edited by Ziggi Alexander and Audrey Dewjee, Bristol: Falling Wall Press, 1984.

Séjourné, Laurette, and Tatiana Coll. *La mujer cubana en el quehacer de la historia.* México: Siglo Veintiuno, 1980.

Senior, Olive. *Working Miracles: Women's Lives in the English-Speaking Caribbean.* Cave Hill: Institute of Social and Economic Research (Eastern Caribbean), University of the West Indies, 1991.

Sharpe, Jenny. *Ghosts of Slavery: A Literary Archaeology of Black Women's Lives.* Minneapolis: University of Minnesota Press, 2003.

Shepherd, Verene A. *Challenging Masculine Myths: Gender, History, Education and Development in Jamaica.* Kingston: Planning Institute of Jamaica, 2002.

————. "Gender and Representation in European Accounts of Pre-Emancipation Jamaica". In *Caribbean Slavery in the Atlantic World,* edited by Verene Shepherd and Hilary Beckles, 702–12. Kingston: Ian Randle, 2000.

————. "Image and Representation: Black Women in Historical Accounts of Colonial Jamaica". In *Stepping Forward Black Women in Africa and the Caribbean,* edited by Catherine Higgs, Barbara Moss and Earline Rae Ferguson, 44–56. Athens, Ohio: Ohio University Press, 2002.

————. "Indian Migrant Women and Plantation Labour in Nineteenth and Twentieth Century Jamaica: Gender Perspectives". In *Women Plantation Workers,* edited by Rhoda Reddock and Shobhita Jain, 89–106. Oxford, New York: Berg, 1998.

————. "Indian Women in Jamaica, 1845–1945". In *Indenture and Exile: The Indo-Caribbean Experience,* edited by Frank Birbalsingh, 100–107. Toronto: TSAR 1989.

————. "Lucille Mathurin Mair's Contribution to Caribbean History, Programme". Featured in the Inaugural Mair Lecture, 1998.

————. *Maharani's Misery: Narratives of a Passage from India to the Caribbean.* Kingston: University of the West Indies Press, 2002.

————. "Petticoat Rebellions: Women and Emancipation in Jamaica". Churches' Emancipation Lecture: Kingston, 2001.

————. " 'Pettitcoat Rebellion'? The Black Woman's Body and Voice in the Struggles for Freedom in Colonial Jamaica". In *In the Shadow of the Plantation,* edited by Alvin Thompson, 17–38. Kingston: Ian Randle, 2002.

————, ed. *Slavery without Sugar.* Gainesville: University Press of Florida, 2002.

————, ed. and comp. *Women in Caribbean History: The British-Colonised Territories.* Kingston: Ian Randle, 1999.

Shepherd Verene, Bridget Brereton and Barbara Bailey, eds. *Engendering History: Caribbean Women in Historical Perspective.* Kingston: Ian Randle, 1995.

Sheridan, Richard. *Doctors and Slaves: A Medical and Demographic History of Slavery in the British West Indies, 1680–1834.* Cambridge: Cambridge University Press, 1985.

Silvera, Makeda. *Silenced: Talks with Working Class West Indian Women about Their Lives and Struggles as Domestic Workers in Canada.* Toronto: Sister Vision Press, 1995.

Silvestrini, Blanca, G. *Women and Resistance: Herstory in Contemporary Caribbean History.* Kingston: Department of History, University of the West Indies, 1990.

Simmonds, Lorna. "Slave Festivities and Leisure-Time Activities in Jamaican Towns". Seminar paper, Mona, 1984.

Simpson, Joanne M. *The Jamaican Woman: A Celebration.* Kingston: Creative Links, 2000.

Sistren, with Honor Ford-Smith, ed. *Lionheart Gal: Life Stories of Jamaican Women.* London: Women's Press, 1986; reprint, Kingston: University of the West Indies Press, 2005.

Skelton, Tracey Lynn. *Women, Men and Power: Gender Relations in Montserrat.* Newcastle upon Tyne: University of Newcastle upon Tyne Press, 1989.

Smikle, Conrad. *Women Food Producers in Jamaica: Technology and Marketing.* San Isidoro de Coronado, Costa Rica: Inter-American Institute for Cooperation on Agriculture, 1996.

Smith, Lois M., and Alfred Padula. *Sex and Revolution: Women in Socialist Cuba.* New York: Oxford University Press, 1996.

Stichting Landelijke. *Surinaamse vrouwen van slavernij naar bevrijding.* Utrecht: Federatie van Welzijnsstichtingen Surinmae, 1977.

Stoner, K. Lynn. *From the House to the Streets: The Cuban Woman's Movement for Legal Reform, 1898–1940.* Durham: Duke University Press, 1991.

————. "Ofelia Domínguez Navarro: The Making of a Cuban Socialist Feminist". In *The Human Tradition in Latin America: The Twentieth Century,* edited by William H. Beezley and Judith Delaware Ewell, 119–40. Wilmington: Scholarly Resources, 1987.

Stoner, K. Lynn, and Luis Hipólito Serrano Pérez, eds. *Cuban and Cuban-American Women: An Annotated Bibliography.* Wilmington: Scholarly Resources, 2000.

Stubbs, Jean. "Gender and Caribbean History". In *General History of the Caribbean,* vol. 6, *Methodology and Historiography of the Caribbean,* edited by B.W. Higman, 95–135. Paris: UNESCO, 1999.

———. "Women on the Agenda: The Cooperative Movement in Rural Cuba". In *Rural Women and State Policy,* edited by Carmen Diana Deere and Magdalena Leon, 142–61. Boulder: Westview Press, 1987.

Symmonds, Patricia. *Women in Politics and Public Life.* Barbados: National Commission on the Status of Women, 1978.

Terborg-Penn, Rosalyn. "Black Women in Resistance: A Cross-Cultural Perspective". In *In Resistance: Studies in African, Caribbean and Afro-American History,* edited by Gary Okihiro, 188–209. Amherst: University of Massachusetts Press, 1986.

———. "Through an African Feminist Theoretical Lens: Viewing Caribbean Women's History Cross-Culturally". In *Engendering History: Caribbean Women in Historical Perspective,* edited by Verene Shepherd, Bridget Brereton and Barbara Bailey, 3–19. Kingston: Ian Randle, 1995.

Thomas, Barbara, and Audrey Michelle Rodrigues. *Women in Guyana: A National Overview.* Halifax: Association of Universities and Community Colleges, 2001.

Trinidad, Josephine. *The Emancipation of the Antillean Woman. Caribbean Women in the Struggle.* Port of Spain: Caribbean Council of Churches, 1975.

Turner, Mary. "The '11 O'Clock Flog': Women, Work and Labour Law in the British Caribbean". In *Working Slavery, Pricing Freedom,* edited by Verene A. Shepherd, 249–73. Kingston: Ian Randle, 2002.

———, ed. *From Chattel Slaves to Wage Slaves: The Dynamics of Labour Bargaining in the Americas.* Bloomington: Indiana University Press, 1995.

Valdés Echenique, Teresa, and Enrique Gomáriz Moraga. *Mujeres latinoamericanas en cifras: República dominicana.* España: Ministerio de Asuntos Sociales, Instituto de la Mujer, 1993.

Vassell, Linnette. *CUSO's Mandate on Women: Problems and Prospects in Jamaica,* 1986.

———. *Voices of Women in Jamaica, 1898–1939.* Kingston: Department of History, University of the West Indies, 1993.

Warner-Lewis, Maureen. *The Nkuyu: Spirit Messengers of the Kumina.* Savacou Publications, no. 3. Kingston: Savacou, 1977.

Welch, Pedro. *Slave Society in the City: Bridgetown, Barbados, 1680–1834.* Kingston: Ian Randle, 2002.

Welch, Pedro L.V., and Richard A. Goodridge. *"Red" and Black over White: Free Coloured Women in Pre-Emancipation Barbados.* Bridgetown: Carib Research and Publications, 2000.

Wilmot, Swithin. "Emancipation in Action: Workers and Wage Conflict in Jamaica

1791–1820", in *Caribbean Freedom: Economy and Society from Emancipation to the Present* edited by Hilary Beckles and Verene Shepherd. Kingston: Ian Randle, 1993.

———. " 'Females of Abandoned Character'? Women and Protest in Jamaica, 1838–1865". In *Engendering History: Caribbean Women in Historical Perspective*, edited by Verene Shepherd, Bridget Brereton and Barbara Bailey, 279–95. Kingston: Ian Randle, 1995.

Wright, Philip, ed. *Lady Nugent's Journal of Her Residence in Jamaica, 1801–1805*. Institute of Jamaica, 1966; reprint, Kingston, Jamaica: University of the West Indies Press, 2002.

Women of Antigua. Antigua: Coordinating Council of Women's Groups in Antigua, 1975.

Yelvington, Kevin A. *Producing Power: Ethnicity, Gender, and Class in a Caribbean Workplace*. Philadelphia: Temple University Press, 1995.

Zaglul, Antonio. *Despreciada en la vida y olvidada en la muerte: Biografía de Evangelina Rodríguez, la primera médica dominicana*. Santo Domingo: Editora Taller, 1980.

C: A SELECTION OF JOURNAL ARTICLES

Agrosino, Michael V. "Sexual Politics in the East Indian Family in Trinidad". *Caribbean Studies* 16, no. 1 (1976): 44–66.

Alexander, J. "The Role of the Male in the Middle-Class Jamaican Family: A Comparative Perspective". *Journal of Comparative Family Studies* 8, no. 3 (1977): 369–89.

Alvarez, Sonia E., Elisabeth Jay Friedman, Ericka Beckman, Maykei Blackwell et. al. "Encountering Latin American and Caribbean Feminisms". *Signs: Journal of Women in Culture and Society* 28, no. 2 (Winter 2003): 537–79.

Antrobus, Peggy. "Crisis, Challenge and the Experiences of Caribbean Women". *Caribbean Quarterly* 35, nos. 1 and 2 (March–June 1989): 17–28.

Ashcraft, N. "The Domestic Group in 'Mahogany': British Honduras". *Social and Economic Studies* 15, no. 3 (1966): 266–74.

Azize-Vargas, Yamila. "The Roots of Puerto Rican Feminism". *Radical Review* 32, no. 1 (1989): 71–79.

Baez, Clara. "Mujer y Globalización en Republica Dominica: Maniqueismo o Complejización" (Women and Globalization in the Dominican Republic: Manicheanism or Complication). *Género y Sociedad* 1, no. 2 (1994): 1–12.

Bailey, Barbara Evelyn. "Gender, the Not-So-Hidden Issue in Language Arts Materials Used in Jamaica". *Caribbean Journal of Education* 17, no. 2 (1995): 265–78.

Baksh-Soodeen, Rawwida. "Issues of Difference in Contemporary Caribbean Feminism". *Feminist Review* 59 (Summer 1998): 74–85.

Balutansky, Kathleen M. "Caribbean Women Writers/Making Men". *Signs: Journal of Women in Culture and Society* 27, no. 2 (Winter 2002): 580–83.

Barnes, Natasha. "Reluctant Matriarch: Sylvia Wynter and the Problematics of Caribbean Feminism". *Small Axe: A Caribbean Journal of Criticism,* no. 5 (March 1999): 34–47.

Barriteau, Eudine V. "The Construct of a Postmodern Feminist Theory for Caribbean Social Science Research". *Social and Economic Studies* 41, no. 2 (1992): 1–43.

————. "Theorizing Gender Systems and the Project of Modernity in the Twentieth-Century Caribbean". *Feminist Review: Rethinking Caribbean Difference,* no. 59 (Summer 1998): 186–210.

Barrow, Christine. "Male Images of Women in Barbados". *Social and Economic Studies* 35, no. 3 (September 1986): 51–64.

————. "Reputation and Ranking in a Barbadian Locality". *Social and Economic Studies* 25, no. 2 (1976): 106–21.

Bell, R.B. "Marriage and Family Difference Among Lower-Class Negro and East Indian Women in Trinidad". *Race* 12, no. 1 (1970).

Bengelsdorf, Carollee, and Alice Hageman. "Emerging from Underdevelopment: Women and Work in Cuba". *Race and Class* 19, no. 4 (1978): 361–78.

Berrian, Brenda F. "Claiming an Identity: Caribbean Women Writers in English". *Journal of Black Studies* 25, no. 2 (December 1994): 200–216.

Besson, Jean. "Land Tenure in the Free Villages of Trelawny Jamaica: A Case Study in the Caribbean Peasant Response to Emancipation". *Slavery and Abolition* 5 (1984): 3–23.

Boa, Sheena, M. "Urban Free Black and Coloured Women: Jamaica, 1764–1834". *Jamaica Historical Review* 18 (1993): 1–17.

Bolles, A. Lynn. "Paying the Piper Twice: Gender and the Process of Globalisation". *Caribbean Studies* 29 (1996): 106–9.

Brana-Shute, Rosemary. "Women, Clubs and Politics: The Case of a Lower-Class Neighbourhood in Paramaribo, Suriname". *Urban Anthropology* 5, no. 2 (1976): 157–85.

Brathwaite, Edward [Kamau]. "Submerged Mothers". *Jamaica Journal* 9, nos. 2 and 3 (1975): 48–49.

Brereton, Bridget. "Searching for the Invisible Woman". *Slavery and Abolition* 13, no. 2 (August 1992): 86–96.

————. "Women and Slavery in the British West Indies". *Trinidad and Tobago Review* 7, no. 11 (1985): 8–11.

Brodber, Erna. "Afro-Jamaican Women at the Turn of the Century". *Social and Economic Studies* 35 (1986): 23–50.

————. "The Pioneering Miss Bailey". *Jamaica Journal* 19, no. 2 (1986): 9–14.

Brown MacLeavy, Jennifer. "Amy Beckford Bailey: A Biography". *Jamaican Historical Review* 18 (1993): 31–39.

Burnard, Trevor. "Family Continuity and Female Independence in Jamaica, 1665–1734". *Continuity and Change* 7, no. 2 (1992).

———. "Inheritance and Independence: Women's Status in Early Colonial Jamaica". *William and Mary Quarterly* 1 (1991): 93–115.

Bush, Barbara. "Defiance or Submission? The Role of the Slave Woman in Slave Resistance in the British Caribbean". *Immigrants and Minorities* 1, no. 1 (1982): 16–38.

———. "White 'Ladies', Coloured 'Favourites' and Black 'Wenches': Some Considerations on Sex Race and Class Factors in Social Relations in White Creole Society in the British Caribbean". *Slavery and Abolition* 2 (1991): 245–62.

Bush-Slimani, B. "Hard Labour: Women, Childbirth and Resistance in the British Caribbean Slave Societies". *History Workshop* 36 (1993): 83–99.

Byron, Jessica, and Diana Thorburn. "Gender and International Relations: A Global Perspective and Issues for the Caribbean". *Feminist Review: Rethinking Caribbean Difference,* no. 59 (Summer 1998): 211–32.

Cobham, Rhonda. "Fictions of Gender, Fictions of Race: Retelling Morant Bay in Jamaican Literature". *Small Axe: AF Caribbean Journal of Criticism* 8 (September 2000): 1–29.

Coppin, Addington. "Women, Men and Work in a Caribbean Economy: Barbados". *Social and Economic Studies* 44, nos. 2 and 3 (June/September 1995): 103–24.

Craton, Michael. "Changing Patterns of Slave Families in the British West Indies". *Journal of Interdisciplinary History* 10, no. 1 (Summer 1979): 1–35.

Cuales, Sonia M. "In Search of Our Memory: Gender in The Netherlands Antilles". *Feminist Review: Rethinking Caribbean Difference* no. 59 (Summer 1998): 86–100.

Dadzie, Stella. "Searching for the Invisible Woman: Slavery and Resistance in Jamaica". *Race and Class* 32, no. 2 (1990): 21–38.

De Groot, Silvia. "Maroon Women as Ancestors, Priests and Mediums in Surinam". *Slavery and Abolition* 7, no. 2 (1986): 160–74.

De Volo, Lorraine Bayard. "Engendering World Politics and Caribbean Studies". *Journal of Interamerican Studies and World Affairs* 38, no. 4 (Winter 1996–1997): 179–88.

Earle, Claudette. "Women in Guyana's Politics". *Caribbean Contact* 5, no. 8 (1977).

Elder, J.D. "The Male/Female Conflict in Calypso". *Caribbean Quarterly* 14, no. 3 (1968): 23–41.

Emmer, Pieter C. "The Position of Indian Women in Suriname: A Rejoinder". *Boletín de Estudios Latinamericanos y del Caribe* 43 (1987): 115–20.

Farrelly, Joan Harrigan. "Gender and Development". *Caribbean Perspectives* (January 1998): 21–23.

Figueroa, Mark. "Making Sense of Male Experience: The Case of Academic Underachievement in the English-Speaking Caribbean". In *YouWe: Quality Education Forum UWI,* no. 8 (May 2002): 11–16.

Fisher Katzin, Margaret. "The Business of Higglering in Jamaica". *Social and Economic Studies* 9, no. 3 (1960): 297–331.

Foner, Nancy. "Women, Work and Migration: Jamaicans in London". *Urban Anthropology* 4, no. 3 (1975): 229–49.

Ford-Smith, Honor. "Una Marson: Black Nationalist and Feminist Writer". *Caribbean Quarterly* 34, nos. 3 and 4 (1988): 22–37.

Francis, Wigmoore. "Nineteenth- and Early-Twentieth-Century Perspectives on Women in the Discourses of Radical Black Caribbean Men". *Small Axe: A Caribbean Journal of Criticism* 13 (March 2003): 116–39.

Franco, Pamela R. "The 'Unruly Woman' in Nineteenth-Century Trinidad Carnival". *Small Axe: A Caribbean Journal of Criticism* 7 (March 2000): 60–76.

French, Joan. "Colonial Policy Towards Women After the 1938 Uprising: The Case of Jamaica". *Caribbean Quarterly* 34, nos. 3 and 4 (1988): 38–61.

Gautier, A. "Les esclaves femes aux Antilles Françaises 1635–1848" *Reflexions Historiques* (1983): 409–33.

Gonzalez, Nacie L. "Multiple Migratory Experiences of Dominican Women" *Anthropological Quarterly* 49, no. 1 (1976): 36–44.

Goosen, Jean Griffin. "The Migration of French West Indian Women to Metropolitan France". *Anthropological Quarterly* 49, no. 1 (1976): 45–52.

Graham, Sheila. "A Revolution of Women: The Cuban Experiment". *Savacou* 13 (1977): 19–27.

Hall, Gwendolyn Midlo. "Women and Slavery in the French Antilles, 1635–1848". *Journal of American History* 89, no. 4 (March 2003): 1499–1500.

Hall, Neville A.T. "Anna Heegaard: Enigma". *Caribbean Quarterly* 22, nos. 2 and 3 (1976): 62–73.

Handler, Jerome S., and Robert S. Corruccini. "Weaning Among West Indian Slaves Historical and Bioanthropological Evidence from Barbados". *William and Mary Quarterly* 43, no. 1 (January 1986): 111–17.

Haniff, Nesha. "Sixty Years of Women Artists in Guyana, 1928–1988: A Historical Perspective". *Concerning Women and Development,* no. 3 (1988): 1–4.

Hellman, J.A. "Making Women Visible: New Works on Latin American and Caribbean Women". *Latin American Research Review* 27, no. 1 (1992): 182–91.

Henry, Frances and Pamela Wilson. "The Status of Women in Caribbean Societies: An Overview of Their Social, Economic and Sexual Roles". *Social and Economic Studies* 24, no. 2 (June, 1975): 165–98.

Higman, B.W. "African and Creole Slave Family Patterns in Trinidad". *Journal of Family History* 3, no. 2 (Summer 1978): 163–80.

Hodge, Merle. "Can Caribbean Women Be Liberated When Our Men Are so Confused?" *Caribbean Contact* 5, no. 6 (1977).

Hodges, Graham. "Reconstructing Black Women's History in the Caribbean: Review Essay". *Journal of American Ethnic History* (Fall 1992): 101–7.

Hoefte, Rosemarijn. "Female Indentured Labour in Suriname: For Better or Worse?" *Boletin de estudios Latinoamericanos y del Caribe* 42 (1987): 55–70.

Jayawardena, C. "Marital Stability in Two Guianese Sugar Estate Communities". *Social and Economic Studies* 9, no. 1 (1960): 76–100.

Kilkenny, Roberta Walker. "Women in Social and Political Struggle in British Guiana, 1946–1953". *History Gazette*, no. 49 (1992): 2–18.

Lamur, Humphrey E. "The Slave Family in Colonial Nineteenth Century Suriname". *Journal of Black Studies* 23 (1992): 344–57.

Le Franc, Elsie, Wilma Bailey, and Clement Branche. "Gender Role Definition and Identity: The Centrality of Primordial Values". *Caribbean Dialogue* 4, no. 1 (January–March 1998): 11–19.

Lewis, Linden. "The Social Relations of Gender and Work". *Caribbean Perspectives* (January 1998): 18–20.

Lobdell, Richard A. "Women in the Jamaican Labour Force, 1881–1921". *Social and Economic Studies* 37 (1988): 1–22.

Lokaisingh-Meighoo, Sean. "Jahaji Bhai: Notes on the Masculine Subject and Homoerotic Subtext of Indo-Caribbean Identity". *Small Axe: A Caribbean Journal of Criticism* 7 (March 2000): 77–92.

MacDonald-Smythe, Antonia. "Gendering the Nation: Author/izing the Caribbean Subject: Review of Belinda Edmondson's *Making Men*". *Small Axe: A Caribbean Journal of Criticism*, no. 7 (March 2000): 127–32.

Mahabir, Diana. "Trinidad and Tobago: Valuing Women's Work". *Caricom Perspective*, nos. 63 and 64 (January–June 1994): 45.

Makward, Christiane P. "Haiti on Stage: Franco-Caribbean Women Remind". *Sites: Journal of the Twentieth-Century/Contemporary French Studies* 4, no. 1 (Spring 2000): 129–37.

Massiah, Joycelin. "Abortion and Public Opinion in Barbados". *Bulletin of Eastern Caribbean Affairs* 3, nos. 11 and 12 (1978): 11–18.

———. "Female-Headed Households and Employment in the Caribbean". *Women's Studies International* (July 1982): 7–15.

———. "Women's Lives and Livelihood: A View from the Commonwealth Caribbean World Development". *World Development* 17, no. 7 (1989): 965–77.

Midgley, Clare. "Anti-Slavery and Feminism in Nineteenth-Century Britain". *Gender and History* 5, no. 3 (1993): 343–62.

Miller, Beth Kurti. "Avellaneda, Nineteenth-Century Feminist". *Revista Interamericana/Interamerican Review* 4, no. 2 (1974).

Mohammed, Patricia. "But Most of all Mi Love Me Browning". *Feminist Review* no. 65 (Summer 2000): 22–49.

———. "Gender Matters in Caribbean Development". *Caribbean Perspectives* (January 1998): 3–8.

———. "Nuancing the Feminist Discourse in the Caribbean". *Social and Economic Studies* 43, no. 3 (1994): 135–67.

———. "Reflections on the Women's Movement in Trinidad: Calypsos, Changes and Sexual Violence". *Feminist Review,* no. 38 (1991): 33–47.

———. "Women's Responses in the 70s and 80s in Trinidad: A Country Report". *Caribbean Quarterly* 35, nos. 1 and 2 (March–June 1989): 36–45.

Morrissey, Marietta. "Women's Work, Family Formation and Reproduction Among Caribbean Slaves". *Review* 9 (1986): 339–67.

Moser, Caroline O.N. "Gender Planning in the Third World: Meeting Practical and Strategic Needs". *World Development* 17, no. 11 (1989): 1799–1825.

O'Brien, Jason. "Women's Voices From The Caribbean: An Annotated Bibliography". *Social Education* 64, no. 2 (March 2000): 97–100.

Paquet, Sandra Pouchet. "The Heartbeat of a West Indian Slave: 'A History of Mary Prince' ". *African American Review,* no. 26 (1992): 131–45.

———. "Surfacing: The Counter Hegemonic Project of Representation, Identification, and Resistance". *Caribbean Studies* 27, nos. 3 and 4 (July–December 1994): 278–97.

Parry, Odette. "Sex and Gender Constructions in the Jamaican Classroom". *Social and Economic Studies* 45, no. 4 (December 1996): 77–93.

Pascal, Phil. "When Will the Church End Discrimination against Women?" *Caribbean Contact* 6, no. 1 (1978).

Pereira, Joseph. "Translation or Transformation: Gender in Hispanic Reggae". *Social and Economic Studies* 47, no. 1 (March 1998): 79–88.

Perez, Luis A. "Women in the Cuban Revolutionary War, 1953–1958; A Bibliography". *Science and Society* 39 no. 1 (1975).

Picó de Hernández, Isabel. "The Quest for Race, Sex and Ethnic Equality in Puerto Rico". *Caribbean Studies* 14, no. 4 (1975): 127–41.

Pollock, Nancy J. "Women and the Division of Labour: A Jamaican Example". *American Anthropology* 74, no. 3 (1972).

Rambchan, S. "The New East Indian Woman". *People* 1, no. 11 (1976).

Reddock, Rhoda. "Alternative Visions: Women and The New Caribbean". *Caribbean Quarterly* 35, nos. 1 and 2 (March–June 1989): 29–35.

———. "The Caribbean Feminist Tradition". *Women in Action* 2 (1991): 8–9.

———. "Caribbean Women and the Struggle of the 1930s: A Pyrrhic Victory". *Caribbean Affairs* 2 (1989): 86–102.

———. "Gender Relations: A Changing Landscape". *Caribbean Perspectives* (January 1998): 9–17.

————. "History and Self-Identity". *Woman Speak!* no. 23 (April 1988): 11.

————. "Indian Women and Indentureship in Trinidad and Tobago, 1845–1917: Freedom Denied". *Caribbean Quarterly* 32 (1986): 27–47.

————. "Women, the Creole Nationalist Movement and the Rise of the Eric Williams and the PNM in Mid Twentieth Century Trinidad and Tobago". *Caribbean Issues: A Journal of Caribbean Affairs* 8, no. 1 (March 1998): 41–65.

————. "Women and Garment Production in Trinidad and Tobago 1900–1960". *Social and Economic Studies* 39, no. 1 (1990): 89–125.

————. "Women's Organizations in the Caribbean Community From the Nineteenth Century to Today". *Woman Spear* 26–27 (1990): 17–24.

————. "Women's Organizations and Movements in the Commonwealth Caribbean: The Response to Global Economic Crisis in the 1980s". *Feminist Review: Rethinking Caribbean Difference* no. 59 (Summer 1998): 57–73.

————. "Women and Slavery in the Caribbean: A Feminist Perspective". *Latin American Perspectives* 12, no. 1 (1995): 63–80.

Robb, Carol, and Alica Hageman. "Let Them Be Examples" *Cuban Review* 4, no. 2 (1974): 19–21.

Roberts, G.W., and L.E. Brathwaite. "Mating Among East Indian and Non-East Indian Women in Trinidad". *Social and Economic Studies* 11, no. 3 (1962): 203–40.

Robinson, Tracy S. "Fictions of Citizenship, Bodies Without Sex: The Production and Effacement of Gender in Law". *Small Axe: A Caribbean Journal of Criticism* 7 (March 2000): 1–26.

Robnett, Belinda. "African-American and Afro-Caribbean Women's Political Struggles: Navigating Courses through White". *Journal of Women's History* 11, no. 1 (Spring 1999): 203–9.

Rowe, Maureen. "The Woman in RastafarI". *Caribbean Quarterly* 13 (1985): 13–21.

Sanders, A. "Family Structure and Domestic Organization Among Coastal Amerindians in Guyana". *Social and Economic Studies* 22, no. 4 (1973): 440–78.

Schlesinger, B. "Family Patterns in the English-Speaking Caribbean". *Journal of Marriage and the Family* 30, no. 1 (1968): 149–54.

Shepherd, Verene. "Indian Females in Jamaica: An Analysis of the Population Censuses 1861–1943". *Jamaican Historical Review* 18 (1993): 18–30.

Simmonds, Lorna. "Slave Higglering in Jamaica, 1780–1834". *Jamaica Journal* 20, no. 1 (1987): 31–38.

Simpson, George Eaton. "Sexual and Familial Institutions in Northern Haiti". *American Anthropologist* 44 (1942): 655–74.

Smyth, Heather. " 'Roots Beyond Roots': Heteroglossia and Feminist Creolization in *Myal* and *Crossing the Mangrove*". *Small Axe: A Caribbean Journal of Criticism* 12 (September 2002): 1–23.

Solien, Nacie C. "Household and Family in the Caribbean". *Social and Economic Studies* 9, no. 1 (1960): 101–6.

Staphorst, Siegmien. "The Economic Role of Surinamese Women before World War II". *Journal of Social Sciences* 2, no. 2 (1995): 5–26.

Steffens, Heidi. "A Woman's Place". *Cuba Review* 4, no. 2 (1974).

Stubbs, Jean. "Gender Constructs of Labour in Prerevolutionary Cuban Tobacco". *Social and Economic Studies* 37, nos. 1 and 2 (1988): 241–69.

———. "Gender Issues in Contemporary Cuban Tobacco Farming". *World Development* 15 (1987): 41–65.

Taylor, Ula Yvette. "Mrs Garvey". *Crisis* 109, no. 5 (September–October 2002): 34–37.

Terborg-Penn, Rosalyn. "Women and Slavery in the African Diaspora: A Cross-Cultural Approach to Historical Analysis". *Sage: A Scholarly Journal on Black Women* 3, no. 2 (Fall 1986): 11–15.

Thomas, Vereen. "Women in Caribbean Society: The Trade Union Movement". *Concerning Women and Development,* no. 2 (1988): 2–4.

Trotman, David V. "Women and Crime in Late Nineteenth Century Trinidad". *Caribbean Quarterly* 30, nos. 3 and 4 (1984): 60–72

Uri, A. "Market Women in Guadeloupe". *Response: United Methodist Women* 9, no. 6 (1977): 12–14.

Valdes, Nelson P. "A Bibliography on Cuban Women in the Twentieth Century". *Cuban Studies* 4, no. 2 (1974) [newsletter].

Verlooghen, Corly. "De vrouw in de wereld en in Suriname". *Span'noe 2,* no. 3 (1975).

Weller, Robert H. "An Historical Analysis of Female Labour Force Participation in Puerto Rico". *Social and Economic Studies* 17, no. 1 (1968): 60–69.

Wertz, Dorothy, C. "Women and Slavery: A Cross-Cultural Perspective". *International Journal of Women's Studies* 7, no. 4 (September–October 1984): 372–84.

White, Averille. "Profiles: Women in the Caribbean Project". *Social and Economic Studies* 35, no. 2 (June 1986): 59–81.

Wilentz, Gay. "Toward a Diaspora Literature: Black Women Writers from Africa, the Caribbean, and the United States". *College English* 54, no. 4 (April 1992): 385–405.

Wilson, P.J. "Reputation and Respectability: A Suggestion for Caribbean Ethnology". *Man* 4, no. 1 (1969): 70–84.

"Woman Speak! Issues of Power for the Caribbean Environment". *Women's International Network News* 18, no. 4 (Autumn 1992).

Index

Abolition Act (1834), 189, 298, 307, 311
abolition movement, 181, 189, 219, 220, 298
  and slave sex ratios, 192, 194, 196–97
abortion, 241, 242, 324
absenteeism, 17–18, 38, 167–69, 185–89
Acts of Privilege, 92, 93–95, 96, 283–84,
  286, 291
Adam (Bog Estate slave), 203
adoption, 48–49
adultery, 39, 44–45
Affleck family, 174
Africa
  cultural practices from, 63, 65, 251, 257–58
  Europeans in, 41, 52–53, 79–83, 188
  families in, 46–48, 49–50, 53
  marriage in, 42, 43–45, 46–47, 53, 80,
    193–94
  miscegenation in, 79–80, 83–84
  mulattoes in, 79–84
  pre-colonial, 41–53
  women in, 41–53, 193–94, 326
agriculture, 13, 59–60, 209–10, 260–61. See
  also specific crops; plantations; provision
  grounds
  in 17th century, 19, 22, 26, 71–72
  livestock, 260, 276–77
  as women's work, 60, 276–77
Allen, Mrs (Kingston Vestry employee), 142
Alloway, Mrs (missionary wife), 299
Allwincle, Widow (Clarendon landowner),
  11
Amey (mistreated slave), 226
Amina of Zazzau, 52
ancestor veneration, 49, 51, 261
Ancouma, 67

Anderson, Sarah, 266–67
Androuin, Elena, 141–42
Anglicans. See Church of England
Angola, 79, 81
Ann (slave of Isabella King), 247, 271
annuities, 167, 169, 171, 284. See also
  pensions
Antigua, 56
apprenticeship (in trades), 144, 145–46,
  388n68
apprenticeship (post-slavery), xxviii, 300,
  306–13. See also slaves
Arawak (Taino) people, 6
Arcedeckne, Robert, 76
Archer family, 117, 129, 157, 158, 163–64
Archer, Mrs George (mother of James),
  129–30, 133, 157, 183, 255
Archer, James Henry, 129–30, 217, 255, 283
  and family, 157, 158, 163–64
  harsh treatment of slaves, 183, 203, 225,
    308, 309, 310
  and midwives, 136, 216
Archibould family, 9–10, 11, 12, 340n73
army. See soldiers
Arnold, Eliza, 248, 323
artisans, 75–76, 201–3, 205, 254, 262, 279
Ashanti, 45–46, 49, 50, 52, 63
Ashley, Mr (parliamentary witness), 209
Ashworth, Jasper, 60
Augier, Susanna (and family), 91, 364n80
Augusta (Orchard estate slave), 241
Azurara, Gomes Bannes de, 41

Baba of Karo, 46–47, 48–49, 51
Bagnet, Mary, 92

Baillie, John, 228, 241, 396n186
Baker, Frances Bower, 283
Baker, Robert, 283
Baker, Susanna, 21
Baker (convicted poisoner), 244
Balcarres, Earl of, 103–4, 105
Baptists, 181, 291, 312–13
Barbados, xxiii, 56, 70, 87, 187–88
  in 17th century, 27, 68
  black women in, 72, 396n197
  settlers from, 19, 22, 24, 68
  white people in, 5, 14
Barbot, James, 46, 55, 80
Barrett, George Goodin (and family), 158,
  173
Barrett, Richard, 243
Barrett, Mrs Samuel Moulton, 180
Barrett, William (and family), 298,
  299–300, 301, 302–3
Barrow, Mrs (St Elizabeth widow), 15–16
Barry, John, 253–54, 287
Barter, Edward, 80, 81
Bathurst, Lord, 227
Baynes, Edward, 310
Beaumont, Augustus, 287–88
Beckford family, 12, 159
Beckford, Charlotte, 278
Beckford, Richard, 75–76
Beckford, William (Lord Mayor of
  London), 201
Beckford, William (planter), 192, 199
Beeston, William, 30, 31
Bell (slave of Isabella King), 247
Belmore (runaway slave), 249
Benbow, Admiral, 72
Benin, 43, 45, 52, 55, 68
Benn, Aphra, 68
Benneba (slave of Mary Woodhouse), 36
Bennett, Betsey, 246
Benny (alias Benneba), 246
bequests, 159. See also inheritance; wills
  to mistresses, 90–92, 284–85
  to mulattoes, 88–89, 90–92, 94–95, 96
Bermuda, 21–22
Besson, Jean, xxix

Bess (slave of Mary Woodhouse), 36
Betsey (Port Royal slave), 244
Betty (Round Hill slave), 235
Bickell, Richard, 208, 283, 285
Biggs, Caroline, 243
birth control, 241–42
black men
  as artisans, 75, 201–3, 205, 254
  family role, 253–54, 256
  as preferred slaves, 73, 74–75, 205–6
  as soldiers, 184–85, 243, 252
black people, 196–97, 216, 229, 244. See also
  black men; black women; slaves
  in 17th century, 54–55
  in 18th century, 192
  in 19th century, 221–23
  as criminals, 226
  as domestic staff, 113–15, 172–77, 203, 205
  education for, 264–65, 301–2, 311
  after emancipation, 312–13
  and family, 251–58
  fear of, 181–82, 184–85
  free, 65–66, 253–54
  and marriage, 65, 289, 313
  and religion, 178, 179, 265–67, 312–13
  as religious leaders, 62–64, 266
  research on, 325–26
  social customs, 251–58
  in society, xxiii, 188
black women, 41–78, 190–267, 313, 317. See
  also black women, enslaved; women
  in Africa, 41–53, 193–94, 326
  agency of, 234–51
  and community, 45–46, 235
  demographics of, 190–97
  economic role, 47, 188, 258–67, 324
  after emancipation, 306–13
  as farmers, 60, 65
  fashions of, 262–64
  free, 66–67, 312–13
  as healers, 265, 266
  historiography of, xxii, 234
  image, 53, 77–78, 195, 232
  language use, 235–37
  as leaders, 58, 62, 63–65, 67

as litigants, 237–39, 324–25
as rebels, 57, 58–67, 242–43, 322–25, 327
research on, 319, 320–21
as traders, 45–46, 65, 247–48, 261, 262
violence against, 223–33
as violent, 244
white people and, 42, 233, 305
black women, enslaved. *See also* apprenticeship (post-slavery); slaves
in 17th century, 70–72
as apprentices, 308–10, 324
and field work, 75–76, 198–201, 203,
207–8, 244–45, 306–10, 312, 324
health, 210–23, 240
as health providers, 212–16, 265, 309
mistreatment of, 226, 230, 237–39, 307,
311–12
as mothers, 220, 240–41, 265, 308–12,
324–25
possessions, 262, 324
punishment of, 227–30, 237–38, 311–12
and reproduction, xxiv, 68, 197, 218–22,
241–42, 323–24
resistance by, xvii, xviii, xxvi–xxvii,
235–40, 311, 322–25
as runaways, 59, 66, 244–51, 322–23
shortage of, 193–94
tasks, 72, 198, 203–5, 206, 212–16
verbal skills, 235–37, 238
as workers, 193, 197, 206–7, 209, 222,
308–9
Blome, Richard, 69, 70
Boa, Sheena, xxv–xxvi
Bob (Esher estate slave), 203
Bogle, Amelia, 308
Bolland, Nigel, xxv
Bollinda (Bodles Pen slave), 212
Booth, Simon, 61
Bosman, William, 43, 48, 51–52, 83
bounties, 60–62
Bowerbank, Lewis, 116
Boyden, Joseph, 226
Boyfield, Mary, 21
Boyle, William, 34
Braffo, Aguaba, 52–53

Brathwaite, Edward Kamau, 41, 133, 186,
321, 326–27
Bravo, Mr (Clarendon planter), 301
breastfeeding, 46, 119, 240–41, 308, 324.
See also weaning
Brereton, Bridget, xxiii, xxix
Brewer, Penelope, 286
bride wealth, 44, 45, 49
Bridges, C.W., 113–14, 178, 230–31
Bridget (Bodles Pen slave), 212
Brodbelt family, 124–25, 126, 160, 166, 172
Brodbelt, Frances, 115, 124, 136, 183
on social life, 103, 104, 126
Broghill, Lord, 20
Brooks, George, 364n99
Brown, Alice, 277
Brown, Ann (free mulatto), 217
Brown, Ann (Unity Valley slave), 217
Brown, Mr (magistrate), 308, 309
Brown, Richard, 253
Brown, Susannah, 277
Buckmaster, Harriet, 238
Burke, Jenny, 278
Burnard, Trevor, xxv–xxvi, xxvii
Burnett, Frances, 76
Burton, Ann, 145
Bush, Barbara, xxv, xxvii
Butler, Kathleen, xxv–xxvi
Buxton, Thomas, 227
Byndloss family, 12

Cadaway, Anne, 19
Cadogan, Elizabeth, 96
Cadou, John Batiste, 226
Caesar (Esher estate slave), 203
Caesar (slave of Sarah Davis), 134
Caillard, Peter, 91
Campbell, John, 293
Campbell, Mary Ann, 140
Campbell, May, 284–85
Candid Reflections (Long), 78
Canning, Lord, 227
Cape Verde Islands, 79, 82
Capitalism and Slavery (Williams), xii
Caribbean, xi–xiii. *See also* specific islands

Caribbean (cont'd)
  immigration policy in, 36–37
  indigenous peoples in, 3, 6
  international rivalries in, 55, 56
  mortality in, 14–15
  settlers from, 19, 22–25, 68
Carleton, Mary ("German Princess"), 39
Carmichael, Mrs, 113
Carmichael, A.C., xxiii
Castañeda, Digna, xxii
Chambers, Bessy, 237
Champnoys, Caroline Anne, 269
Chancery, Courts of, 155–56
charity, 140, 145
Charles (Bog Estate slave), 203
childbirth, 14–15, 117–18, 214–16, 218, 300.
  See also midwives
children, 166, 190. See also education
  elite, 118–19, 120–22, 172, 176
  female, 45–46, 121–25
  of mistresses, 80, 86, 88–89, 174, 176, 272
  mortality of, 14–15, 119–20, 220
  mulatto, 80, 86, 88, 89, 92
  natural, 173, 174, 176, 272, 283–85
  poor, 144, 145–46
  of slaves, 179, 180, 220–21, 257, 308–12,
    324
Chloe (Amity Hall slave), 225
Christianity, 92, 255–56, 286–87, 313. See
  also specific religious groups
Church of England, 178, 286, 289
circumcision, 56–57
citizenship, 94, 97, 283–84, 286, 291
Clare, M. (doctor), 242
Clarendon parish, 14
  land holdings in, 11, 12, 21, 201
  population of, 13, 106, 107
  resistance movement in, 17, 58
  slaves in, 201, 210, 214, 219, 263
Clementina (Port Royal slave), 235
coffee estates, 128–29, 200
Coke, Thomas, 180
Cole, Lawrence, 96
colour, 144, 145, 269–70, 271–74, 316–17,
  321–22

concubinage. See also mistresses
  black/white, 76, 80, 151
  brown/white, 86, 89, 270, 272–73, 281–85
Condall, Frances, 22
Congo (Africa), 52, 79
Congo Molly (freed slave), 66–67
Congo Nancy (Craig Hill slave), 250
Consolidated Slave Act (1792), 197, 220,
  229
convicts, 36–37, 39, 193
Conway, Mrs (lodging keeper), 137–38
cooks, 212–14
Cooper, Thomas, 208, 224, 279
Corker, Deborah, 14–15
Coromantees, 63, 67
cotta, 254–55
Cotton, Major General, 242–43
coverture, 151
Cowper, Margaret (and family), 109–10,
  111–12, 127, 130–31
Cox, Sarah, 173
Craig, Elizabeth, 237
Craig, Robert, 294
Creole Joba (Bodles Pen slave), 212
crime, 39, 140, 223–24, 243–44, 271,
  280
Cromwell, Oliver, 5–6, 20, 21
Crow, Francis, 13, 344n170
Cuba, 249–50
Cubah (rebel leader), 63, 67
Cudjoe, Colonel, 61, 62, 63, 64, 65
Cudjoe (Esher estate slave), 203
Cuffee (slave of Sarah Knaggs), 134
Cuffee (slave of Williams), 62
Cunningham, Rebecca, 141
Curaçao, 55
Cynthia (runaway slave), 250

Dahomeans, 45–46, 47, 50, 52
Dallas, Margaret, 237
Dallas, Robert C., 63
Dalling, John, 158–60
Dalzell, Gibson, 91
Damsel (convicted poisoner), 243
Danish, 80

Daphny (slave of Henry Jackson), 214
Dapper, Olfert, 349n6
Davis, Sarah, 133–34
Deacon, Rebecca, 132
death. *See* mortality
debts, 167, 168–71
deficiency laws, 30–31, 37, 133, 277
Delpratt, Elizabeth (and family), 173, 284
Demetrius, Sarah, 132
de Pass, Rebecca, 132
depopulation (white), 30–31, 32, 36, 75, 96, 185–86. *See also* absenteeism
Devises Act (1761), 95, 276
Dick (slave of Sarah Knaggs), 134
Dido (Bodles Pen slave), 205
Dido (Orchard estate slave), 239, 241
Dido (Port Royal slave), 244
diet, 71, 118, 218, 304
Dillon, J.A., 312
disease, 212, 214, 216, 300–301. *See also* health; mortality
  in 17th century, 14, 18, 23
  in 18th century, 119–20, 217
  in 19th century, 305
  feigned, 239–40, 323
division of labour. See labour
divorce, 49, 155, 255
doctors, 216, 217–18
doctresses. *See* midwives; nurses
Domingo (freed slave), 66
Douglas, James Charles Sholto, 152
Douglas, Mrs (John Jackson's mother-in-law), 169
Dove family, 128
dower entitlement, 153–54
D'Oyley, Edward, 10, 11, 70
drinking, 39, 140, 271
du Casse (governor of Hispaniola), 15–16
Ducke, Edmon and Martha, 17
Duffus, Margaret, 147
Du Fresnay, Ann and Samuel, 96
Duncan, Peter, 180, 264–65
Dundas, Henry, 196
Dunn, Richard, 14
Dutch, 52, 54, 55

Dutton, Geoffrey, xxix
Dwarris family, 161, 164–65
Dwarris, Sarah, 115, 118–19, 127–28, 135–36, 139, 182–83
Dwarris, William, 118, 127–28, 135–36, 161

education. *See also* schools; teachers
  abroad (in England), 92, 123–25, 159–60, 291
  of black people, 301–2, 311
  and citizenship, 94, 291
  of girls, 45–46, 121–25
  missionaries and, 179–81, 264–65, 290–91, 299
  of mulattoes, 92, 290–92, 314–15
  of the poor, 144, 145–46
  slaves and, 179, 180, 181, 264–65
Edwards, Bryan, 130
  on slaves, 216, 226
  on slave sex ratios, 192, 194, 195, 196
  on women, 40, 113, 290
Egan, James, 153–54
Elenor (slave of Isabella King), 247, 271
elite, 30–31. *See also* white women, elite
  in 17th century, 11–12, 17–18
  household furnishings of, 91, 110, 132
  land holdings of, 11–12, 29–30
  and race, 17, 77–78, 87–88
Elkins, John, 248
Elkins, Stanley, 187
Elletson, John (and family), 94–95
Ellis, George (and family), 158, 159
Else (Port Royal slave), 244
Else (slave reprimanded for dancing), 244
Eltis, David, xxiii
emancipation, xxvi. *See also* Abolition Act (1834)
  historiography and, xxvii–xxix
  Jamaica after, 297–317
  missionaries after, 298–303
  movement towards, 227–30
  mulattoes after, 314–17
  rejection of, 184, 298
  results, 312–13
  support for, 181, 189

emigration. *See* immigration

enfranchisement, 87, 89, 96, 149, 273, 363n63

England, 160, 297. *See also* English
army of, 10–11, 18–19
Jamaicans educated in, 92, 123–25, 159–60, 291
Protectorate in, 10–11
reform movement in, 189, 227–30
ties to, 189, 315

English, 26–27, 55, 70, 127. *See also* England
in Africa, 52–53, 79, 81
colonization by, 3–9
vs. Spanish, 57–58

Enguston, Jane, 93

entails, 154, 168

epidemics, 217

Equiano, Olaudah, 46, 50

Essey (Nutt's River slave), 205, 269

estates. *See* plantations

Esther (runaway slave), 247–48

Esther (seamstress/washerwoman), 247

Eve (slave of Henry Shirley), 172

Eyre, Edward John, xxix

Falconbridge, Anna, 182

families
in Africa, 46–48, 49–50, 53
under apprenticeship, 308–10
financial disagreements in, 167–72
as fragmented, 162–64
gender roles in, 252–54
as hierarchy, 49–50, 65
miscegenation patterns in, 282–84
relationships in, 156–66, 167–72, 257
as settlers, 22–23, 24–26
under slavery, xxv, 69–70, 251–57, 259–60, 261–62
of white people, 149–50, 298–99, 300

Fanny (runaway seamstress), 247

Fanny (runaway slave), 249

Fanny (slave reprimanded for dancing), 244

Fanny (St Elizabeth slave), 249

Farley, Elizabeth, 141, 142

Farquharson family, 179

fashion, 262–64, 282–83

Felix (Pleasant Hill slave), 254

Felsted, Ione, 142

fertility (reproductive)
in Africa, 48–50
of slaves, 66, 68, 192, 195, 220–22
women's control over, 241–42

Ffrench, Catherine, 288

Fish, Ann, 146

Fisher, Sarah, 294

Fitzhugh, William, 187

flogging. See whipping

Fogarty, Mary, 146

food, 47, 59, 65, 135. *See also* diet

Foord, Mary, 173

Forbes, Harriet, 171

Fort Augusta, 249

Fortescue, Major-General, 10, 12

Foster, William (and family), 91

Fountain, Captain, 193–94

Frank (Bog Estate slave), 203

Fraser, Jane, 284

free coloureds, 87, 274–81. *See also* mulattoes
economic circumstances, 92–93, 279–80
as farmers, 130, 276–77
occupations, 95–96
and religion, 286–88
sex balance among, 190–91, 274
status, 84–86, 89, 274, 294
women's role among, 293–94

freedom, 272–74, 311. *See also* emancipation; manumission

French, 79

French Becky (runaway slave), 250

French Company of the Indies, 80

Freyre, Gilberto, 83

Friendship (runaway washerwoman), 247

Fuentes family, 7

Fulani, 49

funeral rites, 50, 255, 261

Gallant, Lucy, 137

Gambia, 79–80, 81

Gardner, Nancy Prince, xxvii
Gardner, Sarah, 277
Gaspar, Barry, xxvii
Gautier, Arlene, xxii
gender
    and absenteeism, 185–89
    and division of labour, 74–76, 198–210,
        259
    and family roles, 252–54
    in historiography, xii–xiv, xix, xx, 318
    and status, xv, xvii–xviii
Geoghegan, Mrs (Methodist supporter),
    288
Gibson, John, 298–99
Goderich, Viscount, 225, 230–31, 232
Gold Coast, 52, 79, 81
Golding, Thomas, 90–91
Gonçalvez, Antom, 41
Goodin family, 158
Goodman, Ann, 271
Goodson, Vice-Admiral, 12
Gookin, Daniel, 21
Gordon, Aimey (and family), 284
Gordon, T., 90, 94
Goulbourne, Tabitha, 132
Goveia, Elsa, xviii–xix, 203, 321
governesses, 122, 138
Grace, Leslie, 210–12
Grace (Port Royal slave), 244
Grace (runaway slave), 248
Green, Sarah, 132
Gregory, Lucea (Wyllis), 96
Gregory, Lucretia Favell (Scott), 156–57
Gregory, Matthew (and family), 12, 140,
    156, 157, 158, 159
Gregory, William, 96
Grey, Widow (St Catherine landowner), 17
Grubbin (privateer), 15–16
Guinea, Upper, 79, 81–82
Gurnery, Joseph, 312–13
Guthrie, Janet, 141
Guthrie, Mary, 17
Guy, Colonel, 58

Haiti, 278–79

Hales, Priscilla, 144
Hall, Douglas, 167, 186
Halliburton, Ann, 110, 132
Hamel, the Obeah Man, 292
Hannah (Port Royal slave), 244
Hanover parish, 111, 134, 199, 269
Harding, Mary, 36
Harriet (Port Royal slave), 244
Harriet (runaway slave), 224, 250
Harris, Jane, 94–95, 173
Hausa, 46–47, 49, 52
Hayes, Mrs (midwife), 118
Haynes, Julienne, 143
Hazzard, Robert, 243–44
health, 305. *See also* disease; medical care;
    mortality
    in 17th century, 9, 14–15, 18, 23
    of slaves, 210–23, 240
Heathcote, Gilbert, 30–31
Helyar, Cary (and family), 20, 26, 30, 70,
    86
    workers of, 28, 71, 72, 354n93
Hemming, Samuel (and family), 120, 158,
    159
Henry, Sarah, 250
Herring family, 17
Hettington, Thomas, 243
Heuman, Gad, xxix
Hibbert, Robert, 74
Hickey, William, 112, 137, 281
higglers, 247–48
Higman, Barry W., xxiv, xxv, 200–201, 253,
    268, 293
Hinde, William, 34
historiography, xi–xiii, 318–28
    and emancipation, xxvii–xxix
    gender in, xii–xiv, xix, xx, 318
    of slavery, xxii, xxiv–xxv
Hodge, Matthew (and family), 299,
    300–301
Hodges, Henry, 28
Hogg, John, 34
Holland, Lord, 306–7
Holmes, Margaret, 375n284
Holt, Thomas, xxviii

homes, 110–11, 304
  of slaves, 261–62, 310
Hooker, Mary, 34
Hope, Thomas (and family), 9, 11
hospitals, 141, 142–43, 216–17
House of Correction, 39
How, Alice, 22
Howell, James (and family), 299, 301
Hudson, Elizabeth, 139
Huggins, Elizabeth, 93
Hull, William, 294
humanitarians, 140, 145, 178–81
Humphreys, Colonel, 9
hurricanes, 134, 259
husbands. *See* marriage; men; wives
Huskisson, Lord, 228
Hutchins, Mary Ann, 181
Hutton, Clinton, xxix
Hyde Clarke, George (and family), 157
Hylton, Kitty, 230

Ibo, 45–46, 50
immigration, xxviii–xxix, 20, 24, 29–35,
  303–6
  disincentives for, 14–15
  from England, 26–27, 36–37
  from Germany, 305
  incentives for, 18–29, 31–33
  from New World, 19, 21–25, 34–35, 68
  policies on, 36–38
  from Scotland, 304–5
indentureship, xxviii, 26–28
Industry (Port Royal slave), 323
infant mortality, 117, 214, 300
Ingraham, Reverend (American minister),
  298
Ingrain, Misses (Claremont mulattoes), 302
inheritance, 132, 150, 152, 276. *See also*
  bequests; marriage contracts; primogeniture; wills
  of encumbrances, 168–69
  matrilineal, 49–50
  by mulattoes, 90–92, 94–95, 96, 173–75,
    283–85
  in slave families, 253, 257

Irvine, Susan, 238

Jackey (Port Royal slave), 244
Jackson, Hannah, 144
Jackson, John (and family), 169–71, 199,
  205–6, 214
Jackson, Mr and Mrs (Port Royal custos),
  231–32, 390n78
Jackson, William (general), 84
Jamaica, 21–22, 134, 155. *See also* specific
  towns and parishes; demographics
  (below); government (below); legislation
  (below); vestries
  economy, 13–14, 138
  after emancipation, 297–317
  English values in, 189, 297–303, 316
  entertainments in, 103–4, 112, 264, 278
  equality in, 93–95
  invasions of, 15–16, 24, 35–36
  labour needs, 37, 192–93, 220–21, 306–7
  land ownership in, 29–30
  and reform, 227–30, 233
  security issues, 12, 31
  settlement of, 3–9, 12–14
  and slave trade, 54, 56
  social life, 103–5, 125–26, 281
  social structure, 70–71, 166–67, 188
  under Spanish, 6–8, 57–58, 59, 84
Jamaica: demographics. *See also* depopulation
  in 17th century, 12–13, 19–20, 57, 68–69,
    70–71
  in 18th century, 66, 73, 87, 105–9
  in 19th century, 221–23, 303–4, 306
  of black women, 190–97
  of mulatto women, 268–69
  racial imbalance, 27, 37, 113, 277, 303–4,
    322, 341n101
  sex imbalance, 86–87, 105–9, 186, 190–97,
    306
  of slavery, xxiv, 68–69, 190–97
  of white women, 105–9
  of working class, 70–71
Jamaica: government, 11, 101–2, 105,
  160–62, 197

Council of Jamaica, 31, 37
Council of Protection, 229, 231, 232
Council of State, 9–10, 12, 20, 31–33
Council of Trade and Plantations, 31, 37
House of Assembly, 34–35
Jamaica: legislation
    1674 (slaves as chattels), 70
    1696 (Slave Act), 70, 73
    1711, 1713 (discrimination), 85
    1730 (free blacks/coloureds), 95–96
    1733 (Act 98: mulatto status), 89–90,
        365n104
    1733 (free elections), 96
    1738 (non-whites in military), 88
    1748 (Act 153: free coloureds as witnesses),
        96
    1761 (Devises Act), 95, 276
    1788 (Consolidated Act), 197
    1792 (Consolidated Slave Act), 197, 220,
        229
    1796 (relieving act), 286
    1807 (abolition acts), 197
    1817 (Slave Registration Act), 105, 192,
        197, 220–21, 222
    1826 (Slave Act), 228, 233, 255
    1831 (slave code), 230
    1834 (Abolition Act), 189, 298, 307, 311
    1834 (Jamaica Gaol Act), 312
    1840 (Marriage Act), 316
    Acts of Privilege, 92, 93–95, 96, 283–84,
        286, 291
    deficiency laws, 30–31, 37, 133, 277
James, Eleanor, 231
James, Eliza, 246
James, Judy, 278
James, Margaret, 224
James, Sarah Preston, 279
Jameson, Mary, 146
Jane (slave of Isabella King), 247, 271
Jennerson (free black woman), 91
Jervis, Catherine, 289
Jervis, John, 18
Jews, 7, 139, 344n170, 347n256
Jimenez, Juan, 6
John, Meredith, xxiv

jointures, 153, 154
Jones, Robert, 299
Jones, William, 115, 122, 184
Jordan, Judith, 24
Juba (Moors Estate slave), 212
Judy (Nutt's River slave), 269
Julia (slave of I.P. Levy), 224

Keith, Basil, 101–2, 153
King family, 171–72, 176
King, Isabella, 171, 247, 271
King, Louisa, 115, 150, 157–58, 171, 178
King's House, 101, 136
Kingston, 274, 315
    debtor's jail, 279–80
    Methodists in, 287, 289
    mulattos in, 268–69, 277, 278–79
    poor relief in, 139–40, 141–46, 249, 279
    vestry, 139–40, 141–42, 147
kinship, 49–50, 257. *See also* families
Kiple, Kenneth and Virginia, xxiv
Kitty (apprentice of James Archer), 309
Kitty (midwife), 216
Knaggs, Sarah, 134
Knox, John (surgeon), 193
Kofi (rebel leader), 256
Kongo, 52

labour
    gender division of, 43–45, 47, 74–76,
        198–201, 259
    in Jamaica, 37, 192–93, 220–21, 306–7
lactation. *See* breastfeeding
land grants, 19, 21, 32–33
Lang, John, 392n122
Langslowe, Mr (Methodist missionary),
    290
Lawes, Amy (Archibould), 340n73
Lawes, Nicholas, 31–32, 340n73
Lawrence, John, 284–85
laws. *See* legislation
Laye, Camara, 56–57
Lean (runaway slave), 248–49
Lee, Elizabeth, 142
Lee, William, 226

Leeward Islands, 19, 22, 68, 87, 321–22. *See also* specific islands
Leslie, Charles, xxiii, 76, 77
Leverett, Alice, 19
Levermore, Lucius, 91
Levy, I.P., 224
Lewis, Gregory "Monk," xxiv
Lewis, John, 158
Lewis, Matthew, 156, 208, 210
    on slaves, 216–17, 218, 221–22, 254, 258
    on slave women, 235, 239–40, 242, 267, 398n233
Lewis, William, 152, 157
Ligon, Richard, 27, 69, 72
Littleton, William, 193
Lizzy (Orchard estate slave), 241
lockjaw (tetanus), 214
lodgings, 137–38, 278, 315
London Missionary Society, 298
Long family, 153, 158, 159, 173, 340n73
Long, Catherine (Moore), 158
Long, Edward, xxiii, 63, 101, 156, 176, 209
    on childrearing, 118, 119
    family relationships, 158–59, 160, 161, 162
    as friend, 160, 168–69
    on marriage, 150, 153
    on mulattoes, 281, 291
    on planter life, 103, 110, 111
    on population, 38, 108
    as racist, 77–78, 88
    on servants, 136
    on slaves, 77–78, 222, 253, 254–55
    on slave sex ratios, 74, 192, 194
    on women, 38, 40, 113, 122, 150, 176
Long, Elizabeth Amelia (Hemming), 120, 159
Long, Susanna Charlotte (Ellis), 159
Lost, Stephen, 92, 93
Louisa Marie Theresa (protégée of Louis XIV), 80
Love, Malcolm, 142
Lubola, Juan, 59–60, 70
Lucky (Pleasant Hill slave), 254
Lynch, Mrs Henry, 104, 116, 182, 183
Lynch, Thomas, 24, 29, 30, 54

Lyttleton, Charles, 70, 101

Madam (runaway slave), 249
Madden, Mr (magistrate), 308
Madgett, William, 225
magistrates, 300
Maigari, Malam, 46–47, 48
malaria, 120
"Mammy Luna," 265
Manchester parish, 106, 132–33, 147–48
Mandingo, 54
Manning, Edward, 76, 110
Manning's Free School, 315
manumission, 66–67, 70
    of mistreated slaves, 226, 229
    of mistresses/children, 89, 90, 91, 174, 272–73
    of mulatto slaves, 271–74
Margaret (alias Amey), 248, 323
Margaret (Nutt's River slave), 269
Maria (Port Royal slave), 235
Maria (runaway slave), 249–50
markets, xxv, 260–61
Marlborough, Earl of, 20, 29
Marly, 281, 282, 285
Maroons, 16–17, 32, 59, 62–66, 191, 325. *See also* resistance movements
    Leeward, 62, 63, 64
    settlements of, 65–66, 251, 277–78, 393n140
    wars with, xxvi, 17, 32, 62, 64
    Windward, 59, 60, 63–65
marriage, 42–43, 150–51
    in Africa, 42, 43–45, 46–47, 53, 80, 193–94
    of black people, 65, 254–56, 289, 313
    common-law, 254–55
    among elite, 11–12
    mixed, 80, 96, 184, 315–16
    polygynous, 43–45, 46–48, 65, 193–94, 255
marriage contracts, 152–54, 163–64
Marshall, Woodville, xxvii
Mary Ann (apprentice of James Archer), 309
Mary (Round Hill slave), 235
Mary (slave reprimanded for dancing), 244

Mathurin Mair, Lucille, x
  and gender history, xiii–xiv
  as graduate student, xviii–xix
  on historiography, 318–28
  as researcher, xiv–xv, xvi
Matos Rodríguez, Félix, xxii
McCrash, Dennis, 61
McGeorge, Mrs, 146
McGregor, John, 249–50
McIntosh, William, 194
McKay, Mary, 133
McLean, Bessy, 278
McLeod, Richard, 248, 323
McNeil, Thomas, 208, 304, 305, 306–7, 311, 312
McNeill, Hector, 193, 281–82
measles, 119, 217
medical care, 216–17, 301
"Melissa," 125, 126
men, xxvii, 4, 42, 44, 59. *See also* black men
  as fathers, 80, 86, 89, 283–85
  as husbands, 45, 48, 151
  mulatto, 293
  white, 42, 293
Mendes, 46
menstruation, 46
Methodists, 180, 287–90
Middle Passage, 55
Midgeley, Claire, xxvii
midwives, 118, 136, 203, 205, 212
  as authority figures, 241–42, 324
  for slaves, 214–16, 309
migration. *See* immigration
Miller, Mrs (of Malvern), 179
milliners, 137, 146
Millward, Elizabeth Croder, 108
Mimba (rebel captive), 67
Mimba (slave of Henry Jackson), 214
miscarriages, 241
miscegenation, 79–80, 86. *See also* mulattoes
  in Africa, 79–80, 83–84
  as family pattern, 282–84
  sex imbalance and, 84, 269
missionaries, 266, 280–81

and black people, 255–56, 303, 313
and education, 179–81, 264–65, 290–91, 299, 302–3, 314
after emancipation, 298–303
fund raising by, 288, 299
and mulattoes, 285, 287–88, 289–90, 302–3, 314
opposition to, 289, 298
and planters, 179, 301–2, 311
women as, 298–300
mistresses, 175–76
  bequests to, 90–92, 284–85
  children of, 80, 86, 88–89, 174, 176, 272
  manumission of, 89, 90, 91, 174, 272–73
  mulattoes as, 86, 89, 97, 270, 272–73, 281–85
Modyford, Thomas (and family), 8, 24, 29–30, 70, 86
Mohammed, Patricia, xxviii
Moitt, Bernard, xxii
Molesworth, Governor, 62–63, 355n120
Moll (freed slave woman), 66–67
Molly (convicted poisoner), 243–44
Molly (slave of James Affleck), 174
Monck, George, 11
Montego Bay, 139, 140, 277
Montserrat, 24
Moon, Alice and Robert, 34–35
Moore, Henry (and family), 153, 158–59
Moore Town, 65, 412n71–72
Moravians, 179, 280–81, 303
  and black marriages, 255, 256, 313
  and mulatto women, 285, 290
Moreton, J.B., 253
Morgan, Anna Petronella (Byndloss), 12
Morgan, Edward, 12
Morgan, Henry, 12
Morgan, Johanna Wilhelmina (Archibould), 12
Morgan, Nancy, 184
Morris, Sarah, 276
Morrison, Charlotte, 310
Morrissey, Marietta, xxv
mortality
  of children, 14–15, 119–20, 220

mortality (cont'd)
of infants, 117, 214, 300
of slaves, 68, 192, 195, 219, 222
of white people, 19, 190, 300–301
mosquitoes, 118, 120
motherhood, 48–50, 52, 117–19, 240–41. See
also mothers
mothers, 53, 220–21, 258
slaves as, 220, 240–41, 265, 308–12,
324–25
Moulton family, 158
mourning customs, 255
mulattoes, 79–97, 286–92, 293. See also free
coloureds; mulatto women
in 17th century, 84–88
in Africa, 79–84
attitudes towards, 83, 87–88, 277
bequests to, 88–89, 90–92, 94–95, 96,
173–75, 283–85
and education, 92, 290–92, 314–15
legal status, 87, 88, 89–90, 95, 274–76,
283–84
missionaries and, 285, 287–88, 289–90,
302–3, 314
as property owners, 90–91, 93, 94–95, 96
as slaves, 87, 89, 91, 201, 268–74, 293
social status, 82–83, 188, 257, 283, 292,
314, 322
as traders, 81–82, 278–79, 315
and white culture, 82, 97, 171–76, 273,
283, 285–86, 292–93
as witnesses (in court), 96, 286
mulatto women, 188, 268–94, 314–17, 319.
See also women
attitudes towards, 83, 89, 282–83, 285,
292–93
demographics, 268–69
after emancipation, 314–17
as farmers, 276–77
lifestyle, 278, 281–85
as lodging keepers, 138, 278, 315
as mistresses, 86, 89, 97, 270, 272–73,
281–85
occupations, 205, 278–79, 282
and religion, 287–90

as slave owners, 277, 279, 281–82
as slaves, 269–71, 272–73, 293
as teachers, 290, 314
upward mobility, 281–82, 294
urban, 277–79
Munro, Thomas, 157
Murray, Mary, 271
Murray, William, 309, 310
mustees, 90
mustifinos, 89–90
Mutton, Miss (Methodist supporter), 288

Nancy (slave of John Jackson), 206, 214
Nanny (Maroon leader), xviii, 62, 63–65,
320, 325, 326
Nanny Town, 60, 63–65
Nedham, George, 159
Nelly (runaway baker), 247
Nevil, Mr (early settler), 16
Nevis, 22
New England, 21, 22, 34–35, 87, 155
Nigeria, 51
Nisbett, Robert, 284
Nonconformists, 255, 256, 266, 287–88,
290–91. See also Baptists; Methodists;
Moravians
churches of, 178, 179, 286
Norice, Jane, 280
Normanby, Lady, 184
North America, 86, 87, 155. See also United
States
Nugent, George (governor), 278, 293
Nugent, Maria, xxiii, 108, 316
on birth and children, 118, 119, 120–21,
216
as governor's wife, 102, 104, 183
on Jamaican life, 102, 103, 115, 367n55
on Jamaican women, 122, 125, 128,
282–83
on mosquitoes, 118, 120
and religion, 178–79
and servants/slaves, 136, 181–82
nurses, 5, 203, 214, 315
nursing. See breastfeeding
Nzinga, Mpemba, 52

Oba, 68
obeah, 62–64, 265–66
Oburne, Mary, 15
Oliveira, Jose D', 82
Oliver, Eliza, 238
Olivier, Sydney, xxix
oral tradition, 325–26, 327
Orgill, Thomas, 91

Palmer, Elizabeth (Ellis), 159
Palmer, John, 159
Palmer, Sarah, 36
Parker, Mary, 108
Parry, J.H., 188
Paton, Diana, xxviii
Patoun, John, 90
patriarchy, xxvii, 186–87
Patterson, Orlando, xiii, 186, 321
Patt (mistress of Scudamore Winde), 173
Paul, John, 58
Peddar, Frances, 173, 294
Peddar, James (and family), 173
pensions, 284–85. See also annuities
Peters, Thomas, 173
Peyton, Edward, 140
Philips, Ulrich, 187
Philips, William, 21–22
Philip (slave of McCrash), 61–62
Phillippo, J.M., 313, 314
Phillips, Mary, 139
Phoebe (slave reprimanded for dancing), 244
Pike (Kingston shoemaker), 253–54
pimento production, 129–30, 138
Pindar, Paulina, 19
Pinnock, Mrs (companion to Jim Archer), 163
pirates. See privateers
Pitt, William, 196
plantations, 75–76, 108, 187, 209–10. See also planters; sugar industry
construction, 29–35
economics, 167–69, 209
isolation, 111–12, 177
mulattoes on, 269, 273, 285–86

racial balance on, 111, 133, 188
slave sabotage on, 239–40, 323
small/medium, 18, 29, 30–31, 38, 128–31
planters, 32, 69, 112–14, 172
and apprentices, 306–10
economic concerns, 135–36, 138, 164–72
households, 109–17, 367n55
labour concerns, 306–7, 311
and missionaries, 179, 301–2, 311
relationships among, 158–62
and slave family life, 251–52, 254, 255, 256–57
women as, 21, 131
poisoning, 243–44, 271
polygyny, 43–45, 46–48, 65, 193–94, 255
poor relief, xxiii, 141–42, 143–44, 249, 312
poor houses as, 141, 144–46, 279
population. See Jamaica: demographics
Portland, Duke of, 252
Portland parish, 31–32, 106, 107
Port Maria, 226, 243, 250
Port Morant, 24
Port Royal, 13, 106
Methodists in, 287, 289
slave courts in, 224, 235, 244
women in, 39, 277
Portuguese, 7, 82
in Africa, 41, 79–80, 81, 82, 83
and slave trade, 54, 55
poverty, 128–29, 139, 279–81, 301. See also poor relief
Powell, Rowland, 15
pregnancy
in Africa, 45, 46
among elite women, 117–18
among slaves, 218–19, 222, 255, 308
Presbyterians, 180
Price family, 10, 15, 114, 159
primogeniture, 132, 150, 152, 154, 253
Primrose, Mary, 147
Prince, Mary, xxvi
Princess (runaway slave), 246
Princess (slave of John Jackson), 206
privateers, 8–9, 15–16, 30, 39, 55
in Jamaica, 56, 111

property
  acts of privilege and, 92–93
  of mulattoes, 90–91, 93
  slaves as, 70, 73, 154–55, 209–10
  women as, 44–45
prostitutes, 39, 42–43
provision grounds, 59–60, 224, 259–61, 310, 312, 324
Prudden, Mr (New Layton overseer), 237
Prue (Mamie Gully slave), 212
Pryce, Mr (magistrate), 311
puberty rites, 45–46, 48, 50, 65
punishment, 250, 312. *See also* whipping
  of slave women, 227–30, 237–38, 311–12

Quaca (slave of Sarah Davis), 134
Quaco (freed slave), 66–67
quadroons, 90, 91
Quakers, 24
Quao (rebel leader), 64, 65
queens, 52–53
Quier, John, 119, 217–18

racism, 145, 302
  among elite, 17, 77–78, 88
  and patriarchy, 186–87
  sex and, 83–84, 176–77, 184–85
Racster, Sarah, 288–89
Ramsey, Mary, 19
rape, 184–85, 233
Reddock, Rhoda, xxviii
Registration Act (1817), 105, 192, 197, 220–21, 222
Reid, Ebenezeer, 146, 291, 315
Reid, Elizabeth and George, 11
Reid, James, 199
religion, 24, 287
  black people and, 178, 179, 265–67, 312–13
  mulattoes and, 286–90
  slaves and, 178, 179, 180, 181
  women and, 51–52, 177–81, 266, 287–90, 298–300
Render, Eliza, 25
reproduction, 44, 49–50. *See also* fertility; motherhood; pregnancy

among slaves, xxiv, 68, 197, 218–22, 241–42, 323–24
resistance movements. *See also* Maroons
  black, 7–8, 16–17, 57–67, 84, 184–85
  settlements of, 58–59
  Spanish, 7–8, 84
  traitors to, 61–62, 66–67
Richardson, Elizabeth, 145, 279
Ricketts, Mary (free mulatto), 92
Ricketts, William, 17–18, 221, 256
  and family, 104, 160, 161, 162–63, 167–69, 176
Ridway, John and Mary, 26
rights
  of mulattoes, 84–86, 93–95, 96
  of slave mothers, 240–41, 309–10
  of women, 94, 149–56
rites of passage, 56–57, 326. *See also* puberty rites
Roberts, George, 190–91
Roberts, Libbe, 145, 279
Robertson, Grace Elizabeth, 294
Robertson, William, 146
Robinson, Mrs (milliner), 137
Robinson, Rebecca, 93
Rodney, Walter, xii
Rogers, Elizabeth, 92
Rosanna (slave reprimanded for dancing), 244
Rose family, 115, 160
Royal African Company, 73, 74, 80, 193
rum, 138, 139, 140
runaways
  settlements of, 250–51
  slaves as, 16–17, 28, 133–34
  support for, 245–46, 248–49
  women slaves as, 59, 66, 244–51, 322–23
Russell, Henry, 302
Ryder, Mary, 19

St Andrew parish, 11, 12, 14, 21, 38
St Ann parish, 13, 17, 111, 132, 201, 277
St Catherine parish, 12–13, 14, 21, 209–10
  free black people in, 312–13
  resistance movement in, 17, 58, 250

slaves in, 200, 268–69
St Christopher (St Kitts), 56
St David parish, 13, 106, 108
St Elizabeth parish, 13, 16, 38, 179, 269, 280
St Eustatius, 55
St George parish, 13, 16, 106, 224, 355n120
St Jago de la Vega, 6. *See also* Spanish Town
St James parish, 108, 141, 143
  population of, 13, 106, 108–9, 329–31
  slaves in, 111, 198–99, 269
St John parish, 11, 58, 198
  population of, 13, 14, 26, 70
St Mary parish, 13, 17, 58, 111, 200
St Thomas parish, 16, 106, 133, 141
  settlement of, 22–24, 33–34
  slaves in, 111, 200, 263
Sally (runaway slave), 246
Sandy (Port Royal slave), 244
Sarah (convicted poisoner), 243
Sarah (rebel captive), 67
Saunders, Mr (Windsor Castle overseer), 237–38
Scarlett, William, 233
schools, 144
  free, 290–92
  missionary, 179, 180, 265, 299, 302–3, 314
Schuler, Monica, 244–45
Scots, 304–5
Scott, John (and family), 152, 156–57, 158
Seacole, Mary, 314–17, 319–20
Seagrove, Samuel, 91
seamstresses, 137, 146, 203, 205, 247
Sedgwick, Major, 12
Sedgwicke, Robert, 9, 16, 19, 58
Senegal, 79, 80
Senior, Bernard, 112–13, 114, 128, 185, 253
Serle, Daniel, 12
servants, 113–15
  white, 26–29, 31, 70–71, 75, 136, 347n256
settlement, 12–13. See also settlers
  disincentives for, 19, 30, 31, 32, 33–34
  incentives for, 18–29, 31–33
settlers, 6, 10–11, 19, 21–25, 108
  families as, 22–23, 24–26
  soldiers as, 18–19, 32–33

women as, 4–5, 131, 134, 187–88
sex
  abstention from, 42, 46, 193, 255
  extramarital, 42–43, 184
  and fear, 176–77, 184–85
  interracial, 77, 83, 86, 175–77, 184, 285–86
  and race, 83–84, 176–77, 184–85
sex education, 45
Shand, William, 273
Sharp, "Daddy," 256
Sharp, Mrs (tutor), 141
Shaw, Margaret, 140
Shaw, Mary Ann, 246
Sheridan, Richard, xxiv, 38, 75–76
Sherlock, P.M., 188
Shirley, Henry, 172
shopkeepers, 139. *See also* traders
Shreyer, Godfrey (and family), 76, 96
Sierra Leone, 46, 81
Simmonds, Lorna, xxv
Simpson, Thomas, 233
Slatyer, William, 300
slave acts
  1696, 70, 73
  1792, 197, 220, 229
  1826, 228, 233, 255
  1831, 230
slave courts, 224, 226, 235, 237–39, 243–44, 250
Slave Registration Act (1817), 105, 192, 197, 220–21, 222
slavery, xxiv–xxvi, 229. *See also* slaves; slave trade
  apologists for, 77–78, 181, 182–84, 187, 193–94
  demographics, xxiv, 68–69, 190–97
  gender and, xv
  historiography, xxii, xxiv–xxv
  in urban context, xxv, xxvii, 270–71, 274
  white women and, xvii–xviii, xxiii
slaves, 66, 68–69, 73, 319. *See also* black women, enslaved; mulattoes; runaways
  as artisans, 201–3, 262
  care of, 187, 216–17, 220, 309

slaves (*cont'd*)
  children of, 179, 180, 220–21, 257, 308–12, 324
  as commodity, 131, 205–6
  community life, 237–38, 257–58, 259–60
  cultural life, xxiv–xxv
  diet, 71, 218
  economic activities, 260–61, 262, 263–64
  and education, 179, 180, 181, 264–65
  family life, xxv, 69–70, 251–54, 259–60, 261–62
  fertility, 66, 68, 192, 195, 220–22
  hiring out of, 133, 155, 208–10, 247, 254, 271, 279
  and injustice, 230–32, 237–40, 324–25
  living conditions, 71, 208–9, 261–62, 310
  management of, 25, 133–34, 155, 224–25, 228, 235
  and marriage, 254–56
  mistreatment of, 226–27, 229, 230–32, 237–39, 307, 311–12
  mortality, 68, 192, 195, 219, 222
  mulattoes as, 87, 89, 91, 201, 268–74, 293
  music, 235–37, 244, 395n174
  patriarchal attitudes to, 187
  and pregnancy, 218–19, 222, 255, 308
  as property, 70, 73, 154–55, 209–10
  punishment of, 71, 206–7, 227–30, 237–38, 311–12
  rebellions, 184–85, 242–43
  and religion, 178, 179, 180, 181
  runaway, 16–17, 28, 133–34, 244–51, 322–23
  sex ratios among, 68–69, 73, 74–75, 192–94, 196–97
  sexual harassment of, 177, 206, 285–86
  treatment of, 176–77, 183, 226, 227–30
  as "well off," 181, 182–83, 261–62, 263–64
  as witnesses (in court), 226, 229, 232
slave trade, 41, 54–57, 74
  in 17th century, 29–30, 54–56, 193
  in 18th century, 73–74, 192–95
  campaign against, 181, 189, 192, 194
Sligo, Governor, 308
Sloane, Hans, 39, 69, 71, 72, 77

smallpox, 119
Smart, Colonel, 158
Smith, Annabella, 122, 138
Smith's Free School, 315
Smithy, Mary Ann Able, 180
social status, 10–11, 166–67, 206
  of free coloureds, 84–86, 89, 274, 294
  gender and, xv, xvii–xviii
  of mulattoes, 82–83, 188, 257, 283, 292, 314, 322
Society of West Indian Merchants and Planters, 252
soldiers, 10–11
  black men as, 184–85, 243, 252
  as settlers, 18–19, 32–33
  wives of, 5, 9–10, 19
  women as, 35–36
songs, 235–37, 395n174
Sophia (Mount Pleasant slave), 205
South Sea Company, 73
Spanish
  attacks by, 35–36
  and indigenous peoples, 3, 6
  in Jamaica, 6–8, 57–58, 59, 84
  resistance movement of, 7–8, 84
  and slave trade, 55, 56, 193
Spanish Town, 13, 278, 281, 289. *See also* King's House
Spicer, Thomas, 243
Spruill, J.C., 150
Squires, Georgina and Jemima, 299
status. *See* social status
Steadman, Miss (Clarendon mulatto), 302
Stewart, James, 112, 113, 121, 176–77, 205
Stokes, Luke, 22–23
Style, John, 59
Sue (alias Susanna), 247–48
sugar industry, 130, 138, 206–8. *See also* plantations
  in 17th century, 13, 30, 71
  in 18th century, 75, 108–9
  in 19th century, 222–23
  division of labour in, 198–210
  economics of, 30, 167
  in Lesser Antilles, 6, 22, 55

Surge, William, 233
Suriname, 24–25, 56
Susanna (free mulatto), 280
Susanna (mulatto slave), 270
Susan (slave of Isabella King), 247, 271
Sutcliffe, Mary, 287
Sutton, Elizabeth, 278, 279
Suzanna (Moors Estate slave), 212
Swiney, Samuel, 253
Sylvia (freed slave), 66

Tabby (Brodbelt nurse), 172
Tacky (anti-slavery activist), 256
Taino (Arawak) people, 6
Talbot, Charles, 222
Tate, Mary (Long), 153
Taylor, John, 13, 69–70, 77
Taylor, Simon, 104
Taylor, William, 207–8, 222, 228, 231, 252, 273
teachers, 138, 290, 299, 314
Tello, Catalina, 7
tetanus, 214
Thomas, Dalby, 52–53, 73
Thompson, Eliza, 278
Thompson, Harriett (née King), 115–16
Thompson, Nancy, 250
Thompson, Mrs (née Lloyd), 136
Thomson, James, 301–2
Thomson, Mary, 91
Three-Finger Jack (rebel leader), 256
Titchfield Free School, 315
tobacco industry, 65
Tounes, Elizabeth, 21
traders. *See also* slave trade
  black women as, 45–46, 65, 247–48, 261, 262
  mulattoes as, 81–82, 278–79, 315
  white women as, 139
trades, 34. *See also* artisans
  apprenticeship in, 144, 145–46, 388n68
training. *See* education
Trapham, Thomas, 71
Trelawney, Governor, 59
Trelawney parish, 16, 111, 250–51, 269

Trinidad, 227, 229–30, 396n197
Tucker family (Sierra Leone), 81
Turner, Mary, xxv
tutoresses, 141, 144, 145
Twist, Barbara, 142
Tyndall, William, 364n80

United States, 155, 186, 187. *See also* New England

vaccination, 119, 217
Vassal, Richard, 123
Vaz family (Upper Guinea), 81–82
Venables, Elizabeth and Robert, 4–5, 9
venereal disease, 212
Venn, John, 140, 160
Venus (Port Royal slave), 244
Venus (St George slave), 242
Verdon, Elizabeth, 280
Vere parish, 30, 38, 58, 106, 263–64
vestries, 139–48, 279. *See also* specific jurisdictions; poor relief
Vidal, Polly, 278
Violet (slave of John Jackson), 214

Waddell, Hope, 180, 299
Waldt, Evelina, 145
Walker, Mrs (teacher), 141
Wall, Mrs (hospital matron), 142–43
Wallace, Sarah, 284, 294
washerwomen, 247
Watkins, Mary, 279
Watkis, Robert, 289
Wayle, Dorothy, 25
weaning, 240–41, 256
Weekes, Mary, 15
Welch, Pedro, xxv
Wesleyan Methodists. *See* Methodists
Westmoreland parish, 38, 106, 132, 134, 142
  slaves in, 201, 269, 388n59
wet-nurses, 119
whipping
  as criminal punishment, 223–24
  of women, 228, 230, 237, 311–12
  as work management tool, 224–25, 228

Whistler, Henry, 57
White, Susanna, 294
Whiteley, Henry, 225, 230
white people. *See also* men; white women
  and Africa, 53, 188
  and black people, 32, 42, 233, 305
  as immigrants, 303–6
  in Jamaica, 14, 19–20, 25
  middle-class, 18–29, 127–34, 139, 188
  mortality, 19, 190, 300–301
  poor, 128–29, 140–48
  racism among, 17, 77–78, 88
  as servants, 26–29, 31, 70–71, 75, 136,
    347n256
  sex ratios, 105–9, 306
  working-class, 38–39, 70–71, 135–48
white women, 3–40, 105–9. *See also* white
  women, elite; women
  in 17th century, 3–9
  deference to men's views, 183, 189
  family role, 149–50, 151
  fear of black people, 181–82, 184–85
  as humanitarians, xxvii, 178–81
  as marginal, xxvii, 37–38
  in militia, 35–36
  occupations, 305
  research on, 318–19
  as scarce, 105–9, 186
  as settlers, 4–5, 131, 134, 187–88
  sexual attitudes, 176, 184–85
  and slavery, xvii–xviii, xxiii, 181–82
  social conscience, 177–85
  social role, 35–40, 187–88, 189, 322
  status, 149–56, 305
  unhappiness in Jamaica, 17–18, 176,
    300–301, 317
  vs. mulatto women, 175, 176, 283, 285–86,
    292–93
white women, elite, 117–27, 167, 322
  in 17th century, 9–10, 17–18
  in 18th century, 101–5, 109–10
  amusements of, 126, 166
  as Anglocentric, 126–27, 137
  daily life, 109–10, 113–16, 125–27
  as entrepreneurs, 115–16

image, 38, 40, 116–17
  as litigious, 167, 170–71
  and motherhood, 117–19
  as slave owners, 116, 176–77
widows, 5, 36, 45
Wilberforce, William, 196
Wildman, Harriet, 265
Wildman, James, 231
Wilkinson, Mrs (Methodist), 289
Williams, Cynric, 112, 125, 128–29, 177, 252,
  270
Williams, Eric, xii
Williams, Joanna, 231
Williams, Sally, 248
Williamson, Governor General, 103–4
Williamson, James, 214–16, 293
Willoughby, Priscilla, 11, 21
wills, 152, 153–54, 164, 173–75, 272–73. *See
  also* bequests; inheritance
Wilmot, Swithin, xxvii, xxviii, xxix
Wilson, Cardina, 238
Wilson, John, 16
Wilson, Mr (Good Hope owner), 238
Winde, Scudamore (and family), 159, 173
Windsor, Lord, 24
Witter, Elizabeth Eleanor (Jackson), 169–71
Witter, Thomas, 169
wives, 5, 298–99, 304
  in Africa, 43–44, 46–48
  governors', 102, 104, 105
  of soldiers, 5, 9–10, 19
Wolmer's Free School, 144, 145, 291, 315
women, ix–x, xv–xvi, 15–17. *See also* black
  women; motherhood; mulatto women;
  white women; widows; wives
  aged, 51, 210–12
  in Caribbean history, xiii–xiv, 3
  economic impact, 44–45, 47, 131, 136, 167,
    171
  education of, 45–46, 92, 121–25
  ethnicity and, xv–xvi, xvii–xviii
  and food, 47, 59, 65
  friendships between, 50–51
  as healers, 46, 265, 266
  history, ix–x, xiii–xv, xvi, xix, xx, xxii–xxx